There was something awesome in the thought of the solitary mortal standing by the open window and summoning in from the gloom outside the spirits of the nether world.
Sir Arthur Conan Doyle

INTRODUCTION – 5

1. REVELATIONS – 8

2. "MR. SPLITFOOT, DO AS I DO.." – 27
The Story of the Fox Sisters

3. AND THE DEAD KNOCKED – 46
The Rise of An American Original

4. MEDIUMS IN THE WHITE HOUSE – 80
How Lincoln and the Civil War saved Spiritualism

5. MYSTERIES IN THE SEANCE ROOM – 102
The Oddities that made Spiritualism Endure

6. THE WOMEN BEHIND THE CURTAIN – 148
Sex, Seances and the Supernatural

7. SCIENCE AND THE SUPERNATURAL – 185
The Beginnings of Paranormal Research

8. "GAMBOLS WITH GHOSTS" – 214
The Death Knell of the Spiritualist Movement

9. AMONG THE SPIRITS – 265
Houdini, Conan Doyle and the Battle that Killed Spiritualism

10. THE ORIGINAL "MODERN GHOST HUNTER" – 303
Harry Price and the Search for Haunted Houses

11. PARANORMAL PRELUDE – 323
Prophets, Past Lives and Paranoia

12. THE DEVIL RIDES OUT – 338
The Rise of the Occult in 1960s and 1970s America

13. "AMERICA'S GHOST HUNTERS" – 354
Ghosts and Gullibility in the Amityville Era

14. THINGS THAT GO BUMP IN THE NIGHT – 379
Poltergeists of the 1970s and 1980s

AFTERWORD – 394
The 1990s and the Rise of Paranormal Reality TV

AMERICAN HAUNTINGS

The Rise of the Spirit World
& the Birth of the Modern Ghost Hunter

TROY TAYLOR

© **Copyright 2017 by Troy Taylor & American Hauntings Ink**
All Rights Reserved, including the right to copy or reproduce this book, or portions thereof, in any form, without express permission from the author and publisher.

Original Cover Artwork Designed by
© Copyright 2017 by April Slaughter & Troy Taylor

This Book is Published By:
American Hauntings Ink
Jacksonville, Illinois | 217.791.7859
Visit us on the Internet at http://www.americanhauntingsink.com

First Edition – April 2017
ISBN: 978-1-892523-99-0

Printed in the United States of America

INTRODUCTION

There is no question that history and hauntings go hand in hand. Without the events of the past, there are no hauntings for us to write about, seek out, research, examine, or be mystified by. Ghosts simply cannot exist without history. And neither can the world of paranormal investigation. Without the events of the past and without the stage being set by those who came before, there would be no modern-day ghost hunters. No paranormal television shows would exist. There would be no so-called paranormal "celebrities." The field of psychical research did not begin with the advent of television reality shows in the early 2000s. It began long before that, when the first scientists, skeptics, magicians, and amateurs began trying to discover if what they were seeing, hearing, reading about, and photographing at haunted places and in séance chambers was truly real. They needed to know if the impossible was really possible after all.

But those men and women did not simply wake up one day and decide to look for ghosts. In the middle of the nineteenth century, it seemed that ghosts were everywhere. This explosion of the supernatural upon the popular culture of the country came about because of the Spiritualist movement, which, like jazz, was purely an American invention.

Although the idea that man could communicate with spirits had been around for centuries, modern belief in such things emerged in March 1848, springing to life in the tiny town of Hydesville, New York. The belief became a movement and it came to be called Spiritualism. It galvanized American society for nearly a century, fascinating people from every walk of life. It was founded on the belief that life existed after death and that the spirit could continue to exist outside of the body. Most importantly, Spiritualists maintained that these spirits could – and did – communicate with the living.

The rise of the Spiritualist movement started a revolution, first in America, then in Britain, across Europe, and finally, around the world. The beginnings of the movement remain shrouded in mystery today, however. That mystery, in turn, has led to greater mysteries in regards to the entire movement. Were the followers of Spiritualism really communicating with the dead? Skeptics of the day were convinced that they were not, but the public was not easily discouraged. Seemingly overnight, Spiritualism became wildly popular, eventually turning into a full-blown religious movement. It had scores of believers, its own unique brand of phenomena, and even codes of conduct for everything from spirit communication to séances.

Spiritualists believed that the dead communicated through "mediums" – sensitive men and women who slipped into trances and passed along messages from the other side. Sometimes, during séances (or "sittings"), the dead produced physical phenomena like mysterious lights, unearthly music, levitating objects, disembodied voices, or actual apparitions. Séances took place around a table in a darkened room, or around a curtained-off cabinet, where a medium would sometimes sit. Believers felt that the dark room was essential because it provided less distraction for the audience and the medium. Skeptics, of course, just believed that the dark rooms made it harder to see that a fraud was being perpetrated. Many mediums gained public notoriety during the heyday of the movement, earning fortunes and followers, while others were disgraced when they were exposed as frauds.

Spiritualism took root in the American consciousness during a time of religious fervor in the country. The promises of life after death that the movement offered was its initial draw, but it saw an incredible resurgence after both the Civil War and World War I. Those two wars saw the wholesale slaughter of young men in America and Europe like nothing the world had witnessed before. The Spanish Flu epidemic that followed the Great War saw countless more deaths. But thanks to Spiritualism, lost loved ones were no longer lost at all. They could speak and be spoken to as if they were still alive. Spiritualism filled the huge void that death had made in the lives of the everyday person. They now had something to cling to and a belief that their family members and friends had gone on to a better place.

In time, though, the public's enthusiasm for Spiritualism cooled. By the late 1920s, the era of flying trumpets and whirling tambourines was over. The movement had been largely killed off by the continued attacks by magicians and debunkers, who exposed so many frauds that even those legitimate practitioners began to be shunned. Soon, mediums no longer wanted to expose themselves to scrutiny so they abandoned the physical medium effects of levitating tables and spirit materializations and focused on trance messages from the spirit world. They paved the way for the television psychics of the late twentieth century who also claimed to receive contact from the dead while presenting little evidence of their alleged communications.

From its start in the 1840s, to its peak in the 1920s, to its lingering presence today, Spiritualism's journey through the American consciousness has been a strange one – as has the study of the things that go bump in the night. The rise of the spirit world created the need for supernatural research. The claims of the Spiritualists, about their contact with the dead, created a need for someone to investigate such claims. Psychical investigation began almost as soon as Spiritualism was born.

By the 1850s, science had begun to challenge the hold that religion maintained on society, offering a new version of truth for people to examine. When the public became fascinated with Spiritualism, the scientific establishment rebelled against it. Resentful over the fact that they had finally managed to somewhat dispel the superstitious beliefs of religion, they were angered to see Spiritualism start to be taken seriously by so many people. Scientists and scholars reflexively attacked the Spiritualists. They encouraged the debunking of mediums and spoke out with blatant disregard against anything that even hinted at the supernatural.

But even among the scientists, there was disharmony. A small number of them, always ones who had taken the time to attend a few séances, began to consider the idea that there might be something to the strange phenomenon. They decided to try and apply the laws of science while investigating the reports of strange happenings and this became the start of the paranormal investigation field.

But just as Spiritualism took the country by storm and then fell apart in disarray in the 1920s and 1930s, the field of paranormal investigation also began to change. Without mediums to investigate, many of them lost interest in the supernatural. Some turned their attentions to the burgeoning field of psychic phenomena, testing subjects for Extra-Sensory Perception (ESP) and investigating cases of psychokinesis and poltergeists, while others left the field entirely. The early wave of investigators retired, altered their interests, or passed away.

In this period after the decline of Spiritualism, the first wave of modern ghost hunters began to gain public attention. Men like Harry Price captured the attention of millions with his stories of haunted houses like Borley Rectory. He was followed by men like Elliott O'Donnell, Peter Underwood, Guy Lyon Playfair, and others. In America, the middle part of the twentieth century introduced readers – and soon, television audiences – to investigators and ghost chasers like Hans Holzer, William Roll, and Ed and Lorraine Warren. Some of them became famously linked to towns like Enfield, while connections to places like Amityville became infamous.

But this is all a part of our history. And sadly, it's a history that far too few members of the paranormal community today actually know. We now see this history being re-written with books that are compiled from nothing more than internet websites, with televisions shows that are presented as authentic depictions of paranormal research, and in feature films that are "based on true stories" but barely resemble anything close to the truth.

Far too much of our paranormal history has been forgotten, embellished, or simply fabricated and without our true history, what do we have? Hauntings cannot exist without the history that created them and I believe that the same can be said for the legitimacy of the paranormal field. What are we today without the history that created us? If we don't know how it all started, what it all means, and what events shaped the face of the field today, then how can we expect anyone to take us seriously in our beliefs?

With this book, my goal is to take the reader back to the beginning, to the "gaslight era" of yesterday so that we can explore the people and events that created the paranormal research field that exists today. Along with this, we'll see how the paranormal popular culture of past decades has had a marked effect on the history of America itself. As we go, I think you will find that the days of Spiritualism were not as dusty and antiquated as you might initially believe. That history was both alive and vibrant and had a lasting effect on American history, as well as on the paranormal field of the present day. Our history is filled with compelling characters, eccentric investigators, unexplained events, amazing happenings, colorful personalities, menacing magicians, and more outright frauds than you can count on one hand.

But this is our story. It's one that is uniquely American – even if it does sometimes stray from our shores – and its one that everyone who claims to be a paranormal researcher or ghost enthusiast needs to know. A look at our history will illuminate the mysteries of today in ways that you might never imagine.

Troy Taylor
Winter 2016-2017

1. REVELATIONS

Historians are often fond of remarking that America, throughout its relatively short history, has been a nation of extremes. And it goes without saying that the rise of the Spiritualist movement was not America's first flirtation with the supernatural. Ghost stories have been a part of the nation's fabric since the first settlers arrived on our shores. In the latter years of the seventeenth century, the witch hunt fervor swept the colonies, leading to the tragic events that occurred at Salem. The madness that arose there drained America of its lust for the supernatural for many years to come. There was no organized interest in the occult and while many people still quietly practiced divination and folk magic, any serious scientific interest in alchemy simply disappeared.

As time marched into the latter years of the eighteenth century, Americans were preoccupied with a war for independence from Britain and yet tales of ghosts and hauntings took root in the popular culture. In the early 1800s, the shocking story of the Bell Witch in Tennessee spread throughout the young nation, growing and spreading largely thanks to the involvement of Andrew Jackson, who became president of the United States.

But if there was anything that directly led to the rise of Spiritualism in the country, it was the public's fascination with "mesmerism" and "hypnotic trances" and the religious excitement that swept the nation like wildfire in the 1820s and 1830s. Spiritualism would, in fact, be born in an area of the country that was inundated with religious sects, groups, and cults. It is unlikely that this was a coincidence.

Mesmerism planted the seed of things to come. It was named for the man who developed it, Franz Anton Mesmer, who was born in Germany in 1734 and later earned a medical degree from the University of Vienna. He theorized that a magnetic fluid surrounds, or links, all things and beings on earth and in the heavens and that the "universal fluid" in the human body could be influenced to treat illnesses. Mesmer called his new method "animal magnetism" and he began to attract a huge following in Paris. In 1773, he produced his first cure when he applied "magnetic plates to a patient's limbs" but in 1778, he purportedly cured a blind girl, which won him even greater fame. More claims of healings followed his development of a *baquet*, a large circular tub filled with water that contained "magnetic" substances. Iron rods with magical properties from the water were applied to the patient's body to affect a cure.

There was sufficient controversy around these methods that an official French scientific commission, led by Benjamin Franklin, was asked to investigate Mesmer's claims. According to the group, they could find no evidence of this mysterious physical force, or "magnetic fluid." Franklin chalked up the successful healings to the imagination of the patients. As a result, public interest declined and Mesmer was branded as a fraud.

But in 1823, a French doctor, Alexander Bertrand, became curious about Mesmer's work and a renewed interest in "animal magnetism" emerged in Europe.

During the experiments that followed, subjects were placed in hypnotic trances, which became known as being "mesmerized." Anything that occurred during them was believed to be caused by the power of suggestion. Benjamin Franklin had not been too far off the mark – patients had been healed because they *believed* they could be. Mesmerism was literally affecting the human mind and imagination. Traditional science and medicine rejected mesmerism as a cure for anything, but the few who delved into it made another discovery – a very unusual one. It seemed that many test subjects, while in a trance, demonstrated psychic abilities that they did not ordinarily have, such as telepathy, seeing objects when their eyes were closed, clairvoyant abilities, speaking in voices not their own, and even precognition of future events. Skeptics and most doctors rejected these new claims, but they got enough attention that another scientific commission was formed in 1836. It ended with a recommendation that mesmerism needed further study.

Mesmerism arrived in America at a perfect time. During the first half of the nineteenth century, Americans were seeking and exploring new religious and spiritual ideas. Demonstrations of mesmerism became popular with the public in the 1830s and 1840s. There were as many as 30 different mesmerists on the lecture circuit in New England at one time and in Boston alone, at least 200 men who were practicing the trade.

In one widely reported experiment of the time, a blind girl was able to "psychically discern" the contents of sealed envelopes while she was in a trance. Skeptics blasted the demonstration as a fraud. Even if the effects of mesmerism were genuine, one of their valid criticisms asked, what caused enhanced psychical abilities to occur while she was in her trance?

Nathaniel Hawthorne, one of the most noted writers of the time, was fascinated with mesmerism. However, in his 1851 book, *The House of Seven Gables*, a mesmerist fails to find a missing paper. He employs his ability to control a young woman until he causes her to die. Edgar Allan Poe also used mesmerism in the middle 1840s in one of his short stories, "Mesmeric Revelation," in which a character wants to live forever. The story caused a storm of controversy, for if mesmerism could accomplish immortality, it was equal to blasphemy. Although Poe, after seeing a demonstration of mesmerism, wrote the story as fiction, there were many that worried such a possibility might occur. In 1837, Ralph Waldo Emerson had written that he feared someone – even himself – might be mesmerized against his will.

As with most aspects of the unexplained, mesmerism lured in new audiences and provoked their curiosity, but it also frightened them at the same time. Some, of course, called it the work of the Devil. But to their credit, mesmerists quickly learned to answer their critics and detractors and corrected the misconceptions that surrounded their methods.

The mesmeric "trance state" was embraced by the Spiritualists at the close of the 1840s and became an important part of the movement's growth. Although Mesmer had never shown any interest in the use of his technique for paranormal purposes, mediums claimed that when they were in the trance state, they could communicate with the spirits of the departed. At Spiritualist séances throughout the nineteenth century, it became customary for participants to join hands while the medium entered a trance and then brought forth messages from the spirit world. One of the first to be known as a trance medium was Mrs. W.B. Hayden. In 1852, the Boston woman utilized metal disks to induce a trance state that allowed her to provide highly accurate information for her audiences about their deceased loved ones.

Ultimately, what was first called animal magnetism, then mesmerism, evolved into what we today call hypnotism. But while the mesmeric movement was folded into Spiritualism, hypnosis eventually became an accepted "medical technique." It's a far cry now from the time when it was labeled as part of the "occult," and the medical and scientific communities were shunning mesmerists.

Altered states of consciousness – like trances – have played an important role in the paranormal. The rapid growth of Spiritualism in the nineteenth century owed a great debt to mesmerism. The trance state that mediums used to contact the dead was a form of self-induced hypnosis and it was said to greatly enhance the abilities that the medium already possessed.

THE BURNED-OVER DISTRICT

There were many wide-ranging social changes that came to America in the first half of the nineteenth century and the supernatural played a significant role in how Americans thought, and in what they believed. Long-established Christian denominations now faced the threat of new and emerging religious sects and utopian social movements as Americans looked for alternative ways to express their spirituality.

There was also a steady stream of immigrants arriving on American shores. The land, with its wide-open spaces, offered unprecedented freedom, opportunity and expansion. These immigrants brought with them their own religious and cultural beliefs. In addition, many people were finally starting to move westward from the cities and towns that crowded America's Atlantic coastline. They began seeking land and wilderness, like the frontiers of western New York, Ohio, and beyond. By 1800, the nation's population had increased to five million people – one million more than in 1790. In 1803, the Louisiana Purchase added more than 830,000 square miles to the country.

The mesmerists were also out and about with their lectures in the 1830s and 1840s and were immensely popular with the public, if less so with the scientists. They were the period's version of a "self-help" movement, which in those days meant creating a completely fresh and new perspective on life. The mesmerists claimed that they could restore a deeper sense of one's balance and an understanding between people and the unseen spirit world. Mesmerism, in its efforts to restore "health and virtue," was not unlike the religious revival sweeping America at the same time.

Christianity had long taught that the way to betterment was through God. America's religious teachings had always raised mistrust about the extent to which people could make personal improvements unless they did so through the intervention of the Holy Spirit. The revivalists offered the opportunity to be "born again" through fundamentalist Christianity, maintaining that people could "take responsibility" for seeking their own deliverance from sin and damnation. This is a common religious teaching today, but at the time, it was groundbreaking. It differed completely from the Puritan and Calvinist beliefs of an earlier era, but its focus was narrow and anything that strayed from the fundamentalist belief system, like the occult or the supernatural, was considered the work of the Devil.

In 1825, the Erie Canal opened in Western New York and provided a direct east-west water route across the state from Albany to Buffalo. This new method of transportation meant improved services, more commerce, and growing cities and towns. One of the thriving communities was Rochester, New York, which would become known, thanks to its mills, as the "Flour City." It would also be the center of a region that birthed great social movements, including abolitionism, women's suffrage, scores of religious sects, and Spiritualism.

As the people moved west to build the new towns, the religious men and women followed. Traveling preachers found fertile territory in which to convert many to evangelical Christianity in the newly-settled communities. There were ministers who preached fire and brimstone, hell and damnation, and the end of days. The era became known as the country's "Second Great Religious Awakening." Eventually, so many fiery preachers flocked to Western New York that it seemed there was no one left to convert. It became known as the Burned-Over District.

What attracted the religious, the eccentric, and the strange to this region? Was it merely happenstance, or was there a deeper reason for the bizarre pull that it had on so many? Before the American Revolution, the Burned-Over District was home to the Iroquois nation, who were pushed out by the American government, partly in retaliation for the tribe's alliance with the British during the war, and partly just to make room for the settlers and land speculators that greedily rushed into the region. The Iroquois left behind thick forests, open land, vast lakes – and plenty of mystery.

The itinerant ministers crossed and re-crossed the newly settled region, traveling along hills and valleys and spreading the word of God. The preachers and their tent revival meetings ignited a fervent passion among the simple farmers and tradesmen. For days after they departed, without the prompting of the revivalists, men and women would speak in tongues or fall to the ground in religious ecstasy. Many reported visitations from angels and spirits.

Legends of the area claimed that it had once been home to a mysterious tribe – one even older than the oldest Native Americans, perhaps even one of the lost tribes of Israel. The stories said that these ancient beings were wiped out in a great battle with the Indian tribes. And they went on to claim that their spirits, posing as mysterious messengers from the past, still walked the land of the Burned-Over District.

Soon, even stranger tales would be told.

THE SHAKERS

The story of the Shakers began in England with a young woman named Ann Lee. She lived in the industrial town of Manchester and spoke of magical visions and prophecies. She belonged to a radical religious sect that would come to be known as

Mother Ann Lee

the Shaking Quakers, or the Shakers, and for her beliefs, she was laughed at, beaten, and jailed on charges of sorcery and public disruption. Local authorities had no idea what to make of the otherworldly possession that seemed to grip her and the other Shakers when they quivered and shook in their spirit trances. Ann was not determined not to become another victim of persecution and she fled from England.

In 1774, the woman now known as Mother Ann landed in New York with eight followers. They included her unfaithful husband, with whom she had suffered through the births and deaths of four children.

The group, which grew to include twelve people, minus Ann's husband, toiled at menial labor until 1776, when they had managed to save enough to form a small colony in the marshy fields of Niskayuna, near Albany in New York's Hudson Valley. They anointed the place "Wisdom's Valley." It was a brutal 200 acres of swampland that was punished by cold winds in the winter and transformed into a muddy, mosquito-infested field in the summer. The neighbors were no friendlier than the landscape. Rumors claimed that Mother Ann's flocks – all sworn pacifists – were British sympathizers or spies. Ann was briefly jailed in Albany on charges of sedition. She was released, but treated horribly. During a missionary trip to Massachusetts, a band of thirty men seized Ann and stripped her naked, claiming that they were checking to see if she was a British spy in women's clothing. She was accused of both witchcraft and heresy and yet, the odd little sect – celibate and steeped in a life of poverty and hard labor – began to grow.

Soon after a brutal upstate New York winter in 1780, two men from across the Hudson River in the farm community of New Lebanon took advantage of the spring thaw to visit the Shaker colony. The men were disappointed followers of one of the many Baptist revivals that had been sweeping the region and they wanted to meet the woman whom followers called Christ returned in female form. When they found Mother Ann and her colony in the wilderness, they could scarcely believe they had survived the winter. They were granted an audience with Ann and asked about her mystical teachings and the rumors of the sect's practices, in which they spoke of prophecies, saw visions of the dead, and danced, jumped, and shouted while possessed by the Holy Spirit. "We are the people who turn the world upside down," she told them.

The men returned to New Lebanon to tell of the people in the woods and soon, more curiosity-seekers began arrive at "Wisdom's Valley." Strange natural events brought even more newcomers to Mother Ann's doorstep. On May 19, 1780, many parts of New England experienced "The Dark Day" – a period when the daytime skies were mysteriously blackened. The cause may have been a rash of local fires to clear fields, but the effect was panic. Scores of people were convinced that it signaled the end of days. Mother Ann saw many new converts flock to her community. She had predicted it all and to the Shakers, the dark days were expected. Soon, New Lebanon itself grew into a much bigger colony and was eventually known for its immaculate whitewashed buildings, tidy yards, and brick meetinghouses. Each was filled with the simple, clean lines of furniture for which the Shakers became famous. It was as if the purity to which they aspired to was given life in the objects they created with their hands.

Mother Ann died in 1784, but her influence extended further after her death than it ever did in life. The late 1830s saw the dawn of an inspired and influential period of Shaker activity that became known as "Mother Ann's Work." Shakers believed that their departed leader appeared as an otherworldly spirit guide, directing a wide range of supernatural activities and teachings. Shaker villages – which had now spread as far away as the wilds of Kentucky – recorded visits from the ghosts of historical figures and the spirits of vanquished Indian tribes. Mother Ann's followers claimed to receive ghostly visions and songs, which they turned into beautiful paintings and haunting songs that still survive today. They spoke in mysterious tongues, thrashing and rolling about on the floors during meetings that lasted all night. They were, it was believed, possessed by the spirits of those who passed away long before.

In an America that had not yet experienced the heyday of Spiritualism, which would offer séances, table tilting, and conversing with the dead, the Shakers foretold that beings from the other side would soon "visit every city and hamlet, every palace and cottage in the land."

THE MILLERITES

The Burned-Over District attracted every different kind of sect, order, and outright cult imaginable, giving birth to alternative religions that continue today. One of those sects was called the Millerites, which would later become the Seventh-Day Adventists. This group of believers, which numbered in the thousands by the 1840s, followed the utopian ideas of a Freemason and Baptist clergyman named William Miller.

Born in Pittsfield, Massachusetts, Miller grew up estranged from his Baptist upbringing, largely indifferent to religion. After serving in the army during the War of 1812, though, he began to embrace a view that was common among returning soldiers – that his survival had been divinely ordained. The man who had largely ignored religion came home with a deep interest in questions of faith and immortality.

Convinced that the Bible was a literal record of truth, Miller undertook an obsessive study of every word, line, and letter to determine the exact date of Christ's return – a date that he believed would usher in a millennium of peace. Although only moderately

"Mad" William Miller

educated, Miller spent the next 14 years poring over the scriptures, organizing and cross-referencing all that he found, to build an orderly blueprint of what he believed was God's plan. After all his grueling efforts, his research pointed to the end falling somewhere between March 21, 1843 and March, 21, 1844. But he wasn't finished. Wanting to narrow the date even further, he went back to work and finally decided on October 22, 1844. In the end, he based his prediction on a single line in the book of Daniel: "And he said unto me, in two thousand and three hundred days; then shall the sanctuary be cleansed." By counting "days" as years, be calculated the second coming of Christ.

By the early 1830s, Miller had started to gain a serious audience, first as one of the Burned-Over District's wandering religious speakers and later as a Baptist minister. As his portentous date neared, hundreds and then thousands of his followers gathered at tent revival meetings across Central New York. They filled, and often overflowed, the largest tent in the country, one that could seat as many as 3,000 people. Once, near Rochester, a strong wind snapped 15 of its chains and several inch-thick ropes, violently ripping the tent into the air. Amazingly, no one was hurt – which just deepened the belief in the region that Miller was somehow blessed by God.

When a financial depression hit the Burned-Over District in the late 1830s and early 1840s, it served to only heighten the need for deliverance. Familiar institutions were slipping away and the people were ready to hold onto anything that came along that promised a way out. Miller and his radical beliefs were there to offer a lifeline to all who wanted to take it.

A popular myth claims that as 1844 approached, the man the press called "Mad Miller" and his followers gave away all their possessions, donned white "ascension robes," and waited on hilltops for Christ to return. Stories circulated that the Millerites ran amok, engaging in "free love" and throwing all their money into the wind, anticipating a world without wants or demands. However, there is no truth to these tales and, in fact, the stories misunderstand the unusual blend of magical beliefs and practical habits that were part of the lives of the people of the Burned-Over District.

Miller's followers never sold their belongings, waited in robes on hilltops, or – except in a few rare cases – abandoned their responsibilities as they waited for Christ's return. What few such episodes did occur were exaggerated by neighbors who mocked, and in some cases physically attacked, the Millerites as they gathered in homes and meeting halls. Most of them toiled away at their daily lives right up to Miller's end-time, working at their jobs, maintaining their farms, and attending school. While followers believed in – and were desperate for – progress and perfection, they never abandoned their worldly lives.

This was the way of the Burned-Over District: the ability to believe so deeply in the otherworld that it could be felt as an actual presence but also to possess the soundness of mind to keep their hands hard at work as their hearts searched for the divine. Soon, such a mind-set would sweep through the rest of New York and then across America.

THE PUBLICK UNIVERSAL FRIEND

One of the common threads among the dreamers and cultists who flourished in the Burned-Over District was the desire to split apart the already existing orthodoxies of standard religion and remake Christianity into a new source of magic and mystery. One woman in particular, largely forgotten today, created a new idea in the minds of her followers about what a divine messenger could be. She became the first American women to found a spiritual order. Unlike Mother Ann, who had proclaimed herself the female return of Christ, she was a channel who was possessed by the Divine Spirit. Her name was Jemima Wilkinson.

Jemima Wilkinson

Born in 1752 to a moderately prosperous Quaker family in Rhode Island, Jemima lost her mother at 12 and was raised by her older sisters, riding horses, gardening, and learning the tenets of Quaker theology. She grew into a young woman of "personal beauty" who "took pleasure in adding to her good appearance the graceful drapery of elegant apparel." Later in her life, admirers commented on her fresh complexion and gently tanned skin, her chestnut-brown hair, and flashing black eyes. The attractive woman was a striking contrast to Mother Ann Lee, who was later described as a dark, straight-haired woman with an unusually large forehead, dull eyes, and thick, masculine lips. The description accurately captures the world-weariness of Ann's life, far different than that of Jemima Wilkinson, who was raised amidst the comforts of a successful New England farm.

By age 16, Jemima had been educated in the subjects expected of a girl from a modest estate – poetry, current events, and light literature. But in in a short time, she became immersed in the religious revival of the era, and her life took a dramatic turn. Jemima fell in with a group of revivalist Baptists and began to comb through the Bible with strange intensity. She often locked herself in her room, meditating for hours. Within a few years of her religious rebirth, she became entangled in something else that was sweeping through the region: typhus fever.

On October 4, 1776, Jemima stumbled to her bed with a high temperature. Her skin clammy, wet, and burning from within, she slipped in and out of delirium, returning to consciousness to describe dreams of being in heaven and speaking with the dead. Her health worsened and she slipped into a coma. Her breathing grew faint and her pulse slowed. The end seemed near. But after 36 hours near death, she suddenly got out of bed with a renewed energy. Jemima had "passed to the angel world," she told her family. She was now "reanimated with the spirit," and destined to "deliver the oracles of God." She was a new entity, she told her family and friends, and was no longer Jemima Wilkinson. She would now only respond to the name "Publick Universal Friend."

On the Sunday after her seemingly miraculous recovery, still frail and washed-out from her illness, the Publick Universal Friend went to the local church that had become the center of the area's Baptist revival. The congregation was shocked by the reappearance of the young woman that nearly all assumed was dead. After the service, their shock was even greater after she walked out to a shady tree in the churchyard and began preaching. It was probably the first time that any of them had seen a woman deliver a sermon in public. Her message – repentance from sin, humility, and the Golden Rule – was little more than warmed-over Quakerism, but it electrified the crowd. They marveled at the confidence and eloquence of the girl returned from the dead, who now claimed to be a voice for the supernatural.

The Friend soon began traveling all over New England and down to Philadelphia, not exactly seeking converts to a religion but followers of as a direct line from God. While in Philadelphia, she came under the influence of at least one admirer with ties to a mystic commune at Ephrata in Lancaster County. The commune had been founded in 1732 by Johann Conrad Beissel, who had links to divine mystics from Germany. Following the lead of the commune members, the Friend began to reject the formality of church services, liturgy, confessions of faith, and vows. She also changed the day of the Sabbath to Saturday. Also like the German mystics, she encouraged – but stopped short of demanding – celibacy among her followers. If anything, the Friend's appeal was that she never required any kind of strict doctrine. She relied instead on the teachings of the scriptures and a simple do-unto-others ethic. Her teachings – in contrast to her extraordinary claims about herself – seemed downright ordinary, relying heavily on punctuality and being a good neighbor.

Unlike the intense devotees that had flocked around Mother Ann, the Friend attracted a circle made up of landowners and merchants. The Shakers, who had frequently run afoul of the authorities, were largely made up of kitchen maids, hired hands, and hard-luck farmers, and had seen the inside of a jail on several occasions. Thanks to the status of her followers, the Universal Friend moved freely about the region, even during the Revolutionary War, preaching to both American and British troops. Even when the Friend did end up in court after the war, the results were laughable. In a dispute with an angry former follower, the Friend was forced before the Central New York circuit court on charges of blasphemy, only to hear the presiding judge state that blasphemy was not an indictable offense in the new nation. Unbelievably, Judge Morgan Lewis, who later served as governor of the state, even invited the Friend to preach before the court and applauded her for her "good counsel." It was certainly not the kind of reception that Mother Ann could have expected under those circumstances.

Times were already beginning to change.

Influenced by the success of the Germans at Ephrata, the Friend's followers began to discuss creating a community of their own. By late 1788, a cluster of devotees journeyed to Central New York to break ground for a settlement where the Universal Friend could reside. They became some of the earliest white settlers in the area. Their community of Jerusalem eventually grew near Crooked Lake – now called Keuka Lake

– and continues to exist today. Many of the descendants of the Friend's followers still live in the town.

As time passed, many Central New Yorkers began to have conflicting opinions about their spirit-possessed pioneer, who was a theatrical presence in her trademark cape and wide-brimmed hat. Most of the ill feelings came from rumors that depicted the Friend as, at best, a shrewd operator, and at the worst, a con artist of massive proportions. A popular story told about the Friend leading her followers to the lakeshore one day, where she preached to them about the powers of faith. At the conclusion of the story, she proclaimed that she was going to walk on water. She asked her followers if they had faith that she could do it and they replied that they did. "Then if you have faith," the Universal Friend replied, "there is no need for any vulgar spectacle." With that, she climbed into her carriage and drove away.

There was also the shady business of her death, or so the stories went. Her detractors claimed that the Friend said she was immortal, so when she died in 1819, her minions snuck her body out of her basement in the night and buried her in a secret, unmarked grave. In truth, though, Jemima Wilkinson's body was interred with several others in a traditional burial vault on her property. Several years later, her remains were removed, in Quaker fashion, to an unmarked plot.

Legal battles over the township land began even before the Friend's death, but for the most part, her followers and their families – like the Millerites -- were able to keep a steady balance between their fantastical beliefs and their successful public lives. Following their teacher's death, the merchants and tradesmen that had believed in her, remained to populate many of the region's liberal and experimental religious communities. The Friend's ministry, which was both supernatural and down-to-earth, left a lasting impression on the Burned-Over District, and on the most prominent movements that it would give birth to in the years to come.

THE MORMONS

Near the town of Palmyra – about 40 miles north of the Universal Friend's community – was the home of a young man who would become one of the most influential people to spring forth from the Burned-Over District. Raised on the folklore of the region, he used his cleverness and claims of extraordinary visions to establish one of the largest religious groups in the modern world – the Mormons.

As a teenage boy in the 1820s, Joseph Smith of Palmyra was locally-known as a clairvoyant who could track down hidden treasure using a "seer stone" – a smooth, rock, that might be opaque or marked with magic symbols, He would place the stone in his hat and gaze into it so that he could gain the power of second sight. Treasure hunters who lived in the area valued his scrying talents. In the Western and Central New York region of the early nineteenth century, there were many who believed that ancient artifacts were hidden away in Indian mounds or in secret chambers under the local hills and hollows. As mentioned earlier, the legends of the Burned-Over District told of buried ruins that belonged to a civilization older than the Indians.

Joseph Smith

The Smith household was immersed in magic and myth. The family owned magical charms, dowsing rods, amulets, a ceremonial dagger inscribed with astrological symbols, parchments marked with occults signs and cryptograms that were popular in early nineteenth century American lore. In an 1845 memoir, the family matriarch, Lucy Mack Smith, recalled the Smiths' interest in the "faculty of Abrac" – a Gnostic term for God that also served as a magical incantation. It forms the root of a magic word that is known to every child: *abracadabra*.

Joseph Smith was enthralled with the powers of the planet Jupiter, which was prominent in his astrological birth chart. Smith's first wife, Emma, reported that Smith carried an amulet that was composed of a dove and an olive branch, plus the astrological sign of Jupiter until the day he died.

Smith's occult interests were simply a part of everyday life in Central New York. Later in life, he would suggest the existence of a male-female God, an idea that he likely lifted from the teachings of Mother Ann Lee or the Universal Friend. He was also fascinated with the temple rites and symbols of Freemasonry, a movement of tremendous influence – and controversy – in the Burned-Over District.

The rebellious and spiritually adventuresome Smith began reporting divine visitations in the 1820s, although these claims were not that much different from other such reports in the region. What made Smith's claims different was that they culminated in an angel named Moroni directing him to some golden plates that were buried in the Hill Cumorah, near his home. It was the same place where local legends held that a great civilization – some believed it to be the lost tribe of Israel – made its last stand against the marauding Indians. This story would become an important part of Smith's later theology.

Like Smith, many men of the time took seriously the existence of a highly-developed civilization in the area that pre-dated the Native Americans. Those who studied the history of the Iroquois found esoteric fraternities among them, which some considered a form of "ancient Freemasonry." These speculations were heightened when Seneca leader Red Jacket and other New York-area Indians were seen wearing Freemason-style medals in the shape of the square and compass of the order.

All the area myths – from the lost civilization, the use of peep stones, and the lure of ancient treasure – seeped into Smith's expanding worldview. They intertwined into the narrative found on the golden plates that Smith discovered at Cumorah, which had been conveniently been written in "reformed Egyptian hieroglyphics." Naturally, no one could read them but Smith and he had to do by using a pair of ancient seer stones that were the equivalent of magic spectacles. In 1830, they revealed that the words on the tablets were the Book of Mormon, which traced a vast alternate history, involving a tribe of Israel fleeing from the Holy Land for the American continent. They were later visited directly by Christ and then defeated at "a great and tremendous battle at Cumorah... until they were all destroyed." The scale and scope of the Book of Mormon, no matter what one thought of its dubious origins, was seen by his followers as evidence of the truth of local folklore, rather than Smith's obvious pilfering of it.

Those followers were few in number at first, though. Many saw him as nothing more than a former "peep stoner" peddling himself as a prophet. Like Israel's mythical lost tribe, Smith and his followers would have to journey west to attain their destiny.

But Smith's connections with the Burned-Over District were not quite over. The ideas and loyalties that he developed in Central New York soon had profound consequences over the lives of Smith and the small band that followed him to his eventual doom.

There was no question that Smith was fascinated with Freemasonry and many of the rituals and rites practiced by the order eventually seeped into the ceremonies – in various ways – that became part of the inner doings of the Mormon church. Freemasonry has strong roots in American history and it was especially prevalent in the Burned-Over District. Early American Freemasons professed a religious tolerance and in so doing, they may have been influenced by the so-called Rosicrucian manuscripts that aroused the imagination of the radical Protestant reformers. Beginning in 1614, Europe had marveled over cryptic manuscripts that were written by the Rosicrucians, an "invisible college" of adepts who extolled the virtues of mysticism and higher learning, while also prophesying the dawn of a new era, education, and enlightenment. No one knows if a secret order of Rosicrucians really existed, or if the manuscripts were produced by a group of mystics, laced with symbols and parables, that were meant to give expression to the principle of ecumenism, which was a desire to promote unity among all of the world's Christian churches, Protestant, Catholic, and alternative alike. It was an unthinkable idea for that era, but one that would find its way into American Freemasonry, starting in the eighteenth century.

Freemasonry drew upon arcane codes for personal and ethical development. As members rose through the fraternity's ranks, their achievements were noted on ceremonial aprons as rising suns, glowing eyeballs, pentagrams, and pyramids. This practice informed one of the greatest symbols of Freemasonry: the all-seeing eye and the unfinished pyramid of the Great Seal of the United States, which any reader can find on the back of a $1 bill. The seal was designed (appropriately) on July 4, 1776, under the direction of Freemasons Benjamin Franklin, Thomas Jefferson, and John Adams. The Latin maxim that surrounds it can be translated, "God Smiles on Our New Order of the Ages." It is Masonic philosophy to the core in that the pyramid, a symbol of worldly achievement, is incomplete without the blessings of providence. The Great Seal did not actually appear on the back of the bill until 1935, when it was directed to be placed there by President Franklin D. Roosevelt and Vice-President Henry A. Wallace. Both men were Freemasons.

But Freemasonry did not last as long as it should have in the murky mysticism of the Burned-Over District. It ran into trouble, thanks to a scandal that nearly threatened its existence in America. It began in the 1820s, sparked by an incident that occurred not far from the home of Joseph Smith and it would affect not only his life, but his death, as well.

In 1826, William Morgan was a disgruntled Freemason living in Batavia, New York. He was threatening to expose all the order's secret rites in a manuscript that he was preparing to publish. When word spread of his plans, Morgan began to suffer from a variety of misfortunes, ranging from his arrest on false charges to the attempted arson of the print shop that planned to release his book. He was eventually kidnapped and never seen again. He was possibly murdered at the hands of Freemason zealots – or at least that's what many residents of the Burned-Over District believed.

The presumed homicide and the failed investigation that followed raised suspicions about the influence that the Freemasons had over the law and courts. The incident began a wave of anti-Masonic feeling, first in the Burned-Over District and soon throughout the country, spread by a general mood of discontent over corruption in high places. In time, 52 anti-Masonic newspapers started in America, and dozens of anti-Masonic politicians were sent to state legislatures. Things soon calmed, but Freemasonry would never again command the same level of respect in American life.

But the order's influence still managed to spread in some unexpected ways.

William Morgan, the disgruntled former Freemason who vanished, left behind an attractive widow named Lucinda. She eventually remarried a man named George Harris, with whom she traveled west as part of a new religious order: Mormonism. But Lucinda was no ordinary convert to Joseph Smith's new faith. Around 1836, the blond, blue-eyed young woman, though since remarried, became one of many "spiritual wives" of the prophet Joseph Smith. Smith had lived about 50 miles east of the Morgans in Palmyra, but it is unlikely that he met Lucinda until the Mormons began moving west. As a younger man, Smith had been swept up in the region's wave of anti-Masonry, but an older Smith became secretly fascinated with the society that had allegedly widowed his new bride.

The Mormons wandered through Ohio and on to Illinois, searching for a new home, Smith found a safe place in the community of Nauvoo, where he founded a Masonic lodge. Smith believed that the priestly rites of Freemasonry represented a degraded version of the lost rituals of Hebrew priests and since Mormon lore dated back to the Lost Tribe of Israel, it was natural for the Mormons to embrace them. Such rites, he believed, were the link to the ancient temple of the Hebrews. He was determined to take that link, mix it with the divine revelations of his own, and restore the old ceremonies.

In the early 1840s, Smith introduced the Masonic symbols of the rising sun, the square and compass, and the beehive into Mormonism. He created his own versions of Freemasonic rites – which included ritually bathing neophytes, clothing them in temple garments, and giving them new spiritual names and instruction in secret handgrips and passwords – and conducted initiation ceremonies in a makeshift temple over a store he owned in Nauvoo. Smith also studied Hebrew and possibly elements of the Kabbalah -- the ancient Jewish tradition of mystical interpretation of the Bible – with a Jewish scholar and Mormon convert named Alexander Neibaur. It was a period of wild innovation within the burgeoning religious movement, but it quickly came to an end.

In 1844, Smith turned himself over to authorities at Carthage, Illinois, where he was placed in jail to await charges against him for destroying a Mormon opposition newspaper. Smith had directed the burning of the critical newspaper's office and though his act was indefensible, the charges merely served as an excuse for the state's government to finally get its hands on the troublesome religious leader – who had a militia that rivaled the size of the state's own at the time. Local residents had become increasingly suspicious of the Mormon settlers and politicians feared the number of votes that Smith could command.

While the prophet and his brother waited on the second floor of the jail, they found themselves without the protection that the state's governor had promised. The days turned tense as armed men began arriving in town. During the early evening of June 27, a mob – which included Illinois militia with soot-disguised faces who were supposed to be guarding Smith – stormed the jail. Before jumping from a window in a vain attempt at escape, Smith was reported by witnesses to have issued the Masonic distress signal, lifting his arms in the symbol of the square. He shouted, "Oh Lord, my God, is there no help for the widow's son?" just before he was shot. It was a code used by Freemasons looking for help – but it didn't save Smith.

He was shot several times and fell to the ground, dead where he lay. On his body was an old protective amulet with the astrological symbol of Jupiter. Even the old ways couldn't save him. At just 38-years-old, he was the most famous son of the Burned-Over District – killed because of the faith he had created, quite literally, from the soil of his New York home.

THE UTOPIANS

The people of the Burned-Over District believed in the power of ideas – whether political or spiritual – as the catalyst for the redemption of the soul. Rare was the person who was part of one of the region's mystical sects that did not also have a part in a social sect, as well. For many, the two worlds naturally blended.

The area hosted some of America's earliest utopian religious communities, including the nation's longest-running and most economically successful commune at Oneida, New York. The Oneidans thrived from the manufacturing of animal traps, cutlery, and other high-quality goods, while experimenting with biblical communism, attempts at human perfectionism, and sexual liberation. It was at the Oneida commune where the term "free love" was actually coined.

From about 1848 to 1880, the commune was under the leadership John Humphrey Noyes, who had been expelled from the Yale School of Divinity after he made the claim that all religions were flawed. He believed that if God did indeed give mankind free will, then everything that a person chose to do, in his reasoning, was divine. Noyes's path to God was achieved by striving toward "perfectionism" in both body and mind. He wanted to emulate the example of the first-century Christians, who in the face of persecution, often survived in self-sustaining, tight-knit communities where everything was shared. Inspired, Noyes decided to form a similar utopian society. Noyes's troubles really began because of his broad definition of Christian love, which to him naturally included sex – and a lot of it. After his arrest for adultery in 1847, he and his followers fled Vermont and started a commune for like-minded "perfectionists" at Oneida.

John Humphrey Noyes

The experimental community was a profitable one. Members worked diligently at farming or in manufacturing and all worked without a salary. Noyes built a giant dormitory called "Mansion House," where more than 50 followers lived in "complex marriage" arrangements. Noyes considered sex with varying partners an antidote to selfishness. Sharing your husband or wife was one of the noblest demonstrations of Christian love. Accordingly, he encouraged his followers to engage in sex as often as possible. Not surprisingly, branches of his commune were establishing from Brooklyn to Ontario.

There was only one rule to sex at Oneida – have as much of it as you wanted, but a man always had to pull out prior to climax. This withdrawal method of birth control was part of Noyes's bigger plan, which was an attempt to engineer the perfect human being. He only selected those considered the most flawless and attractive to produce children. Noyes subsequently fathered nine of his own.

In 1879, a warrant was issued for Noyes's arrest for statutory rape. He fled Oneida for Canada and never returned. He soon sent the various communes instructions to abandon "complex marriage" and accept traditional nuptial arrangements. He eventually gave ownership to the wide array of businesses to all the commune members in the form of stocks. In the early 1900s, one of his sons turned the original communal enterprise into Oneida Unlimited, which remains today one of the largest manufacturers of quality forks, knives, and spoons in the world. Interestingly, their "official" company history marks their founding date as 1880 – when John Noyes fled New York.

The Oneida commune may have been one of the only sects to survive into the twentieth century, but it was not alone in the Burned-Over District. By the middle nineteenth century, there were at least 20 villages or active societies that were operating as utopian communities. Most were short-lived.

The Burned-Over District continued to attract the unusual and the bizarre. A wide range of reformist, civic, and spiritual movements shared members and blended together in the region. Suffragists, abolitionists, and temperance marchers each had deep footholds in the area. As people and ideas crossed the land on their way to the west, they left behind new ideas where strict beliefs in God were replaced by Transcendentalism, Unitarianism and Universalism, and other liberal ways of seeking spirituality. Freemasons and anti-Masonic activists clashed and, eventually, the Burned-Over District gave birth to one of the strangest and most influential of America's movements: Spiritualism.

Spiritualism shared a common trait with the utopian movements that dotted the region. Spiritualists harbored the Yankee attitude that religion rested not just on faith, but on proof. Like William Miller spending years poring over scriptures to pinpoint the date of Christ's return, Spiritualists found tantalizing "facts" to back up their belief in the reality of the afterlife: spirit raps, tilting tables, and messages through mediums. The utopians maintained that they, too, were simply following a process of logic -- in their case, the cause-and-effect of better styles of living creating better men and women. In the Burned-Over District, mystics and radicals had a shared stake in the prophecy of progress. They believed that spiritual and social forces, if they were properly used, could remake a person, inside and out.

And they were soon to have a prophet enter their midst who would herald the dawning of the Spiritualist movement and unify the reform and religious movements of the region. At the same time that Miller was foretelling the return of Christ and Joseph Smith was spreading his new gospel, a 17-year-old, half-educated cobbler's apprentice was experiencing cosmic visions of his own. His name was Andrew Jackson Davis and his influence did more than any others to shape the occult traditions of a growing nation – and to usher in the age of ghosts and spirits.

THE "POUGHKEEPSIE SEER"

Andrew Jackson Davis was born in 1826 to an upstate New York family. The child was named "Andrew Jackson" by a drunken uncle who wept with sentiment over the future president and hero of the Battle of New Orleans. Davis's home life was dreary. His mother toiled away at never-ending housework and his father was a cobbler and drinker who barely kept his family fed and clothed. Andrew, his older sister, and their parents were forced to pick up odd jobs and work the harvest on local farms to survive. With little money and a lot of work to do, there was little time for education. Davis's mother – a kind and honest woman who suffered from poor health – often told of prophetic dreams and visions. Davis's young mind was heavily influenced by her accounts, as well as by local lore of spooks and witchcraft and neighbor's stories of strange signs and omens.

But Davis was not a superstitious country boy. He thought little of the fire-and-brimstone sermons of the ministers who plied the Burned-Over District in search of converts. He took careful notice of the outwardly pious men who neglected their debts at the store where he worked. His neighbors often cowered in fear before the well-rehearsed preachers who accosted them on country roads and commanded them to repent or burn in hell. But Davis argued back. He was not afraid to meet God, he told them. Davis would later say that an inner voice spoke calmly to him and assured him that all would be well in his life.

In 1839, the Davis family moved to the growing town of Poughkeepsie and Davis's parents were able to enroll him in an inexpensive Quaker school – inexpensive because there were

Andrew Jackson Davis

no teachers. Founder Joseph Lancaster was experimenting with the idea of having the children teach each other. Soon, Davis was in charge of the class. At age 16, he was apprenticed to a local shoemaker, presumably set to follow in his father's career path. The boy's employer treated him kindly and honestly, though he once wrote in a letter that Davis barely had a knowledge of "basic reading, writing, and the rudiments of arithmetic." If he never turned to drink, like his father, Davis had the promise of a stable, rather ordinary future to look forward to.

But an ordinary life was the last thing in store for the polite young man.

News of a strange practice had started to spread throughout the region, one by which men could be induced into a half-conscious condition called a "trance." The practice of mesmerism had spread to America from France, setting the stage for events that would lead to a wildly unexpected turn in Andrew Jackson Davis's life.

In the same year that Davis began his apprenticeship as a cobbler, he attended a series of lectures about mesmerism by Dr. J. Stanley Grimes. After watching the demonstrations, he volunteered to be a subject but was unable to go into a trance. He had become intrigued with the subject, though, and later tried again with help from a local tailor who shared his fascination with the subject. Davis soon found that he was actually an easy subject – someone who could enter a trance quickly and deeply. At first, he was terrified by the loss of bodily control, but soon he grew used to the warm, shimmering sensation that accompanied the trance. He felt plunged into inner darkness and experienced a sense of weightlessness. He felt his body glowed with lightness and caused a mental acuteness like nothing he had ever experienced before.

Davis believed that he was in touch with higher realms while in a trance and poised to receive some great message. He was not the only one to experience this. During this time of great religious fervor and spiritual awakening, mesmerism gained new followers. It seemed that mesmerism could fit comfortably within any of the new belief systems that were emerging, yet it was never associated with any particular religious denomination. Mesmerists believed they could bridge the traditional divide between science and religion. Mystical illumination and ecstatic revelations were no longer dismissed as fanciful irrationalities. Mesmerism found itself welcome by many of the new sects because it provided a scientific underpinning for spiritual beliefs. For those who were scientifically inclined, mesmerism was evidence that the abilities of the mind could go beyond the limits of the brain.

In the winter of 1844, Davis found that after an especially deep mesmeric session, he was unable to return to ordinary consciousness. He stumbled back to the room where he was staying, dropped into bed, and immediately fell asleep. Later, he awoke to a voice outside that sounded like that of his deceased mother. He ran outside and had a vision of a flock of unruly sheep being led by an overwhelmed shepherd. The shepherd seemed to need his help, he recalled. At this point, Davis said that embarked on a psychical "flight through space" – traveling in either mind of body (possibly both since he vanished until the next day) over the winter terrain of New York.

While on his journey, he claimed that he received spirit visitations from the ancient Greek physician Galen and the Swedish mystic, Emanuel Swedenborg, who told him, "By thee, a new light will appear."

The experience changed his life and he returned home the next day, shaken, but with a sense of mission. He no longer desired to be a cobbler's apprentice or do mesmeric stage tricks. Instead, he began delivering lectures on religion and metaphysical topics while in a trance state. His ideas, he claimed, came from higher regions that he visited during his trances. Davis was determined to dictate an entire trance in this way and it would be the method of sending out the "new light" that Swedenborg told him to deliver to humanity.

In 1845, Davis decided to leave Poughkeepsie. Accompanied by two new collaborators – a doctor of "botanic remedies" and a Universalist minister – he moved to Manhattan. While living in a series of low-rent apartments, he entered a trance day after day for months, dictating what would become a massive, 800-page book. He told of visions of other planets, heaven, angels, afterlife realms, and the mechanics of the spirit world.

Davis began to attract a group of followers. His trance sittings were open to the public and scores of people crowded into his rooms to witness his trances. One of them was a journalist named Edgar Allan Poe, who became fascinated with mesmerism. He used it in several of his stories, including "The Facts in the Case of M. Valdemar," a tale that he wrote that same year. Poe's story is about the sickly Valdemar, who agrees to be suspended in a mesmeric trance at the moment of his death. For seven months, the mesmerist keeps Valdemar's consciousness separated from the man's physical form, suspending in a state of half-life. The body can only move the "swollen and blackened tongue" in its open mouth, from which comes a horrifying voice that begs the mesmerist to set him free. When Valdemar is finally released from the trance, the body suddenly rots away, dissolving into a stinking ooze.

It became one of Poe's most widely-read tales. It was never explicitly billed as fiction and was written like a medical case study, causing it to be initially taken as literal reportage by some in America and Britain. The *Sunday Times* in London reprinted it without comment in January 1846 under the banner *Mesmerism in America: Astounding and Horrifying Narrative*. Whatever the author's intent, the story served to popularize and lend credibility to the mysterious method.

Davis finished his book and it was published in the summer of 1847. The weighty tome had an equally weighty title of *The Principles of Nature, Her Divine Revelations and a Voice to Mankind.* The book became an instant sensation and sold the first 900 copies in a single week. Although dense, ponderous, and repetitive, the book attempted great heights, even setting forth its own creation story that described the making of a great universe and all its spiritual dimensions. In his trances, he told of making journeys to other planets and provided details of the afterlife and the workings of the "eternal mind."

To some critics, the book was an obvious pilfering of Swedenborg's ideas, noting that passages about the planets and discourses on extraterrestrial beings as direct echoes of the Swedish mystic, who had written his own massive treatises on the same subjects before his death in 1722. Swedenborg's translated books were first widely circulated in America in 1845, about the same time that Davis embarked on his trance dictations. But Davis had an answer for the critics – he acknowledged his "debt" to Swedenborg, claiming that he was a spiritual student to the master because

Swedenborg was his spirit guide. It was no surprise that his work so closely followed the same path. He had read very little in his young life, Davis said, certainly not the formidable works of Swedenborg.

Some influential observers didn't know what to think. Davis was fortunate to receive support from a highly-regarded professor of Hebrew at New York University named George Bush. The professor called his book a "work of profound and elaborate discussion of the philosophy of the universe."

The Church of New Jerusalem, the religious order that was founded in North America on the principles of Swedenborg, kept its distance from the controversial seer. At that time, the Church was attempting to find acceptance and respect. The last thing it needed was to embrace a mystic who was claiming to be a protégé of it ghostly founder and quite possibly lifting ideas from the theologian's writings.

The controversy that surrounded Davis served to make the public more curious about him. He would never again dictate a book while in a trance state, but the former cobbler's apprentice would start writing his own cosmic treatises. He wrote as many as 30 of them by the time he died in 1910. They continued to be based on his psychic visions, which he obtained by going into trances on his own. He no longer needed a mesmerist to reach a trance state. To his growing body of readers, Davis's writings were considered a divine revelation. He wrote reassuringly of heaven – or the Summer Land, as he called it – which sounded a lot like an idyllic version of the Burned-Over District, with rivers, streams, mountains, and a landscape that was forever green. The beliefs and reformist ideals of the region formed the model for Davis's utopian afterlife. Summer Land included people of all races and creeds, where all were equal and free and offered a universal faith that was based on reason.

In the philosophy of Andrew Jackson Davis, the various ideas of the Burned-Over District were becoming joined. The concept of entering a trance state to reach the afterworld was appealing to the public imagination and the notion of higher dimensions being open to everyday Americans made things seem even more enticing. Davis had set the stage for events that were still to come but he would soon find his accomplishments overwhelmed by the startling proclamations that were about to come from the other side.

2. "MR. SPLITFOOT, DO AS I DO..."
THE STORY OF THE FOX SISTERS

According to reports, the winter of 1847-1848 was one of the worst in memory in the Burner-Over District of New York. Bitter wind, frigid temperatures, and blinding snow battered the region. On December 11, 1847, two weeks before Christmas, John and Margaret Fox and two of their daughters moved into a small wooden-frame house in the village of Hydesville, which was really just a group of homes, several small stores and mills, and typical of other small farm communities scattered across the countryside.

Legends say that the house was haunted before the Fox family came to live there. Those in the neighborhood often referred to it as "the spook house." Between 1843 and 1844, a couple named Bell occupied the cottage. In the last few months of their occupancy, a young local woman named Lucretia Pulver handled the household chores. She acted as a maid and carried out the cleaning and cooking duties for the Bells.

The story that Lucretia would later tell stated that a peddler came to the door of the house one day with a case of merchandise. The friendly young man offered goods for sale like pots, pans, cutlery, and other items for the kitchen. He stayed with the family for several days and it has been suggested that perhaps he enjoyed a closer than was proper relationship with Mrs. Bell. With no explanation, Lucretia was told that her services would no longer be required by the Bells. Saddened, but understanding, the young woman gathered her things, pausing only long enough to purchase a small kitchen knife from the peddler. He offered to deliver the knife to her father's farm, but it never arrived.

Barely a week later, Lucretia was surprised to find that Mrs. Bell was again requesting her services. Thankful to have her job back, she reported for duty the next morning. The peddler who had been staying with the family had departed but she found that many of the items that he had been selling were now in the Bell home. Lucretia assumed that the items had been purchased from the peddler before he left and thought no more about it. Nothing seemed out of the ordinary about the house, but that was soon to change.

Soon after returning to work, Lucretia noticed some particularly strange things were occurring. She heard unaccountable knocking and tapping sounds in the walls and, on several occasions, heard footsteps walking about the house and descending the stairs to the cellar. The house was empty at the time. Lucretia began to feel uneasy when left in the house alone. She would often send for her brother, or a friend, to come and stay with her and usually, the strange sounds would cease. However, on one occasion, they continued for hours and scared Lucretia's brother so badly that he left the house and refused to return. One afternoon, while in the cellar, Lucretia stumbled over a pile of freshly turned dirt. Her employers told her that the dirt had been used to cover "rat holes." The young woman's employment with the Bell family ended a short time later when they moved out of the house and settled in another part of the state.

Lucretia never expected to enter that cottage again but soon, odd happenings would draw her back to its doorstep.

After the Bells moved out of the cottage, the Weekman family, along with a relative, Mrs. Lafe, moved in. They did not remain in the house for long. One day, Mrs. Lafe entered the kitchen and was confronted by a man wearing a long, black frock coat. When she screamed in terror, he disappeared. The residents of the house reported hearing rapping sounds on the walls and heavy footsteps on the floors. They occurred during the daylight hours, but usually they were heard at night, disrupting the household as they tried to sleep. Eventually, the odd sounds proved too much for them to bear and they abandoned the cottage.

Then, in late 1847, the Fox family moved into the house. John Fox and his wife, Margaret, were both past 50. The two girls, Margaretta (known as Maggie), 10, and Catherine (called Kate), 7, were both pretty girls with dark hair and eyes. They also had older children who were married and lived on their own. A son, David, lived nearby with his family, as did a sister, Maria. One daughter, Elizabeth, lived in Canada with her husband. Leah, the oldest of the Fox siblings, was a piano teacher and lived in Rochester, which was about 30 miles away. She was about 20 years older than her two younger sisters. She did, however, have an adolescent daughter, Lizzie, who spent as much time in Hydesville with her young aunts, Kate and Maggie, as she did at home.

The Foxes were a close-knit family, but had been through their share of troubles in the past. John and Margaret were married in 1812 and had four children in relatively quick succession, starting with Leah in 1813. By the 1820s, they had moved to Western New York with relatives from both sides of their respective families. Their decision, like that of thousands of other Americans at the time, was undoubtedly inspired by the abundance of land in the region and the promise of the Erie Canal, which opened in 1825.

Not long after moving to the area, though, John and Margaret separated. John had become acquainted with what was called the "sporting life," spending his time and money on liquor, gambling, cards, and horse races. Margaret survived on her own thanks to money that had been left to her from her grandfather's will. He had loathed John Fox and stated that Margaret's share of his estate was to be held in trust for her until she was lawfully separated from John. It was an unusual provision for the time – and was likely unenforceable by law since husbands controlled their wives' money – but it literally saved her life. She moved in with an unmarried sister, Catherine Smith, in Rochester, where she raised the children alone.

Around 1827, Leah, 14, married a man named Bowman Fish. Their time together was brief and ended without regret. Fish left town and was never seen again. They never divorced, but this was not uncommon at a time when many legal marriages were considered legitimate if a couple viewed themselves as married by mutual consent. They had one daughter, Lizzie, who was born around 1830. Leah would also refer to her nieces and nephews as her own, as taking charge of other people's children would become one of her lifelong habits.

In the early 1830s, John Fox had a change of heart. He transformed himself from a drinker and gambler to a sober, serious man. Thanks to the Methodist revivals of the Burned-Over District, Fox found salvation. He returned to his wife and children a devout and introverted man. The now middle-aged couple uprooted their lives to Canada, where Kate and Maggie were born. The two girls were raised in Consecon, a tiny village in Prince Edward County, Ontario, where John owned a farm.

No one knows what brought the family back to New York, but in the 1840s, they moved to Rochester, leaving Elizabeth behind in Canada with her new husband. They found themselves in Hydesville near the end of the decade. Their stay in town was meant to be a temporary one. John had purchased some land nearby and while a home was being built, he rented a cottage in town where they could live. Their stay would turn out to be very eventful.

While not large, the cottage was serviceable, with a good number of windows and two stoves. The front door opened directly into the south-facing parlor. The kitchen was set back, on the northwest side, and had its own door to the yard. On the east side, a pantry – sometimes used as a second bedroom – connected to the kitchen, and the main bedroom adjoined the parlor. An enclosed staircase between the pantry and the main bedroom led up to a large attic, and another staircase led down to the cellar. The house was located on the busy corner of Hydesville and Parker Roads, which would make it easy to find for the scores of people who came to see if the stories they heard about the strange activities taking place there were true.

The cottage was an unlikely place for the birth of an enormous national movement that would attract millions of people and dramatically change the way that Americans would come to view life and death. But it was in that small house, in that small town, where Spiritualism began on a cold March night in 1848.

America would never be the same again.

THE "MYSTERIOUS RAPPINGS" BEGIN

The first three months that the Foxes lived in their rented home, life was fairly normal. It wasn't long, though, before friends and neighbors began sharing stories of the house's "spooky" reputation for "mysterious rapping noises." The family tried to ignore the tales because they were already experiencing the strange happenings for themselves. The noises became worse toward the end of the winter. The banging and rattling sounds pounded loudly each night, disturbing them all from their sleep.

At first, John Fox thought nothing of the sounds that his wife and children reported and were so frightened by. He assumed that they were merely the sounds of an unfamiliar dwelling, amplified by active imaginations. Soon, however, the reports took another turn. Kate woke up screaming one night, saying that a cold hand had touched her on the face. Maggie swore that rough, invisible hands had pulled the blankets from her bed. Even Mrs. Fox swore that she had heard disembodied footsteps walking through the house and then going down the wooden steps into the dank cellar.

John, not a superstitious man, was perplexed. He tried walking about the house, searching for squeaks and knocks in the floorboards and along the walls. He tested the windows and doors to see if vibrations in the frames might account for the sounds. He could find no explanation for the weird noises and Mrs. Fox admitted that she was upset by the inexplicable sounds and the mysterious footsteps. She concluded that some "unhappy restless spirit" was haunting the place.

On the evening of March 31, John began his almost nightly ritual of investigating the house for the source of the sounds. The tapping had begun with the setting of the sun and although he thoroughly searched the cottage, he was no closer to finding the source of the sounds. Then, Kate began to realize that whenever her father knocked on a wall or doorframe, the same number of inexplicable knocks would come in reply.

It was as if someone, or something, was trying to communicate with them.

Finding her nerve, Kate spoke up, addressing the unseen presence by the nickname that she and her sister had given it. "Here, Mr. Splitfoot," she called out, "Do as I do!"

She clapped her hands together two times and seconds later, two knocks came in reply, seemingly from inside of the wall. She followed this display by rapping on the table and the precise number of knocks came again from the presence. The activity caught the attention of the rest of the family and they entered the room with Kate and her father. Margaret Fox tried asking aloud questions of fact, such as the ages of her daughters. To her surprise, each reply was eerily accurate.

Unsure of what to do, John summoned several neighbors to the house to observe the phenomenon. The first was Mrs. Mary Redfield, who was blunt and dismissive about the presence of a spirit and assumed the girls were playing a prank. She quickly changed her mind. After questioning the spirit and receiving correct answer to her inquiries, she became frightened and left the house.

One neighbor, William Duesler, decided to try and communicate with the source of the sounds in a more scientific manner. He asked repeated questions and created a form of alphabet using a series of knocks. He also determined the number of knocks that could be interpreted as "yes" and "no." In such a manner, he divined the subject of the disturbances. The secret of the haunting came out, not in private, but before an assembled group of witnesses. The presence in the house claimed that it was the spirit of a peddler who had been murdered and robbed years before.

As it happened, one of the neighbors who came to the house was the former maid, Lucretia Pulver. She came forward with her story of the peddler who had vanished from the house and the dirt that she discovered had been unearthed in the cellar. John Fox and William Duesler went to the area that Lucretia described and began to dig. It took them more than an hour, but they managed to unearth a small piece of human skull with strands of hair still clinging to it. They also found a few scraps of clothing, as well. It was enough for a local doctor to determine that someone had been buried there and that charcoal and quicklime had been used to hasten the body's decay. The Foxes and their neighbors became convinced that the presence in the house truly was that of the murdered peddler.

Soon, news of the spirit rappings attracted so much attention that a great many visitors began showing up at the Fox home, many of them demanding entry, numbering up to 500 people in a single day. Mr. Fox complained: "It caused a great deal of trouble and anxiety. I am not a believer in haunted houses or supernatural appearances." But John could not account for the noises, or for the other manifestations that began to occur. Door slammed, beds shook, footsteps paced back and forth and down the stairs to the cellar, and the rapping sounds continued to be heard. By early April, the sounds were heard both day and night.

The startling stories about the Fox house quickly spread throughout the Burned-Over District and beyond. The events attracted curiosity from both believers and skeptics. This was no mere ghost story. This was a situation in which it seemed that the Fox sisters and an alleged unseen entity had established a communication network that was unlike anything people had heard about before. The story touched a nerve among a population that was eager to look beyond the limits of ordinary life and ponder the mystery of what came next.

The local newspaper, the *Western Argus*, quickly reported the story and it wasn't long before an enterprising writer named E.E. Lewis, published a pamphlet called *Report of the Mysterious Noises*. Another local writer published a booklet about the Weekman family's "unpleasant experiences" in the house. Mrs. Fox contributed her own written statement about the events: "I am not a believer in haunted houses or supernatural appearances. I am very sorry there has been so much excitement about it. It has been a great deal of trouble to us. I cannot account for the noises; all I know is that they have been heard repeatedly as I have stated."

With the ability to receive a response from the spirit inhabiting their house, the young Fox sisters had tapped into the public's enthusiasm for the supernatural. Within a matter of months, what began in Hydesville spread to surrounding communities, and from there, via newspapers, to the large cities. There was no way to explain why this one particular event so vividly captured the imagination of the public. It was as if people suddenly found confirmation of the spirit world's ability to communicate with the physical world.

AMERICA'S FIRST MEDIUMS

As the public became more and more fascinated by the rappings at the Hydesville house, it was decided that Kate and Maggie should be sent to stay with their older sister, Leah, in Rochester. This may have had the opposite effect to that intended by the girls' parents, for the rapping sounds followed them to Rochester. In this much larger town, the Fox sisters attracted even more attention. Kate was soon sent to Auburn to stay with her brother in hopes that she would be free from the harassment of the knockings, but Maggie became the center of a devoted "spirit circle," which allowed participants to come together to receive spirit communications. The circle worked out a more

Kate and Maggie Fox in 1852

manageable code to communicate with the spirits: one rap indicated "no," two raps that the spirit was unable to answer a question, and three raps meant "yes."

As many enthusiastic residents of Rochester made it a nightly occurrence to gather at Leah's home to witness the wonderful revelations that Maggie produced from the spirit world, Leah began doing the math and realized that she was sitting on a fortune. Leah began telling her friends that she had suddenly become aware of the financial responsibilities that she faced because of Maggie's talents. "All of Western New York," she said, "was excited by the reports and doctrines of Spiritualism."

About that, Leah was correct. The Burned-Over District, long home to every kind of religious sect and social movement imaginable, was ablaze with news of the spirits. It had only been a few years since Samuel Morse had first successfully demonstrated the miracle of the telegraph. If electricity could provide instant communication between distant places, why then wasn't contact possible between the living and the dead? Perhaps the marvel of electricity played some role in spirit contact, some suggested, and the term "rapping telegraph" began to be heard.

But Leah's motivations had little to do with furthering the cause of Spiritualism, or even merely with paying the bills that she would face by taking Maggie in to live with her. She had been living in near poverty for years. With no husband to support her, she had been teaching piano. However, some of her students had left her due to the sensational publicity surrounding Maggie's strange talents. Leah now realized that she had a way out of her dire circumstances.

Rochester was sharply divided about the reality of what was taking place in Leah's home. While Maggie had many supporters, there were some, especially Christian fundamentalists, who denounced the girl for "heresy" and "blasphemy." Leah cleverly arranged a public lecture and demonstration so that everyone could see for themselves. The event was held at Corinthian Hall, the city's largest auditorium, and the admission was the steep price of one dollar per person. The audience was made up of a wide range of people, from the simply curious to those who believed they were witnesses to a spiritual revolution in the making, and they filled the hall to capacity. With a sold-out crowd of more than 400, Leah profited handsomely, while Maggie's career as a medium was launched.

Of those who attended the demonstration that night, many were certain they had witnessed genuine spirit communication, while others were just as sure they had witnessed a fraud. If the skeptics of the city expected to witness a public exposure of fraud in return for their dollar, they were sorely disappointed because no one could explain what caused the rappings. A committee of leading citizens reported itself completely unable to give a natural explanation for the rappings, which each of them had heard. Disappointed, the debunkers formed a second committee, which would announce a solution at a later date – and when that date came, they also declared that they had been unable to detect any trickery. A doctor had even listened to Maggie with a stethoscope to rule out ventriloquism, all to no effect.

More public demonstrations followed. Public opinion in Rochester soon became heated. A third committee was formed and one of its members swore publicly that if he could not discover how the raps were made, he would throw himself over Genesee Falls. Hopefully, this man's friends were able to dissuade him from such a course of action because the third committee had no more luck than the previous two. Though some of its members were privately certain that spirits did not cause the raps, the third committee, like the others, was forced to admit that it couldn't tell how the sounds were being accomplished.

At the last demonstration at Corinthian Hall, the audience became so frustrated that a disturbance broke out. Amid angry shouts and threats, a squad of police arrived to break up the meeting and was forced to escort Maggie and Leah home to protect them from the indignant mob. Even though most the spectators on this particular night proved they had little use for the spirit world, this meeting in Rochester was only the first ripple in a flood that soon spread far beyond the city.

Kate soon rejoined her sister and the two girls quickly became the talk of Rochester and were also receiving publicity from throughout the state. While Kate had lived in Auburn, she had not been idle. She had also conducted séances there and had her own believers flocking to join her spirit circle. It wasn't long before news of their demonstrations was being reported in other large cities, and the girls were becoming nationally known, which was unusual in an era when such celebrity was rare. A few months later, with their popularity still surging, they began traveling around the country, appearing in a variety of venues. The publicity around them was intense. Some newspapers and public venues hailed them as frauds and others as sensations. Regardless, people flocked to see them in massive numbers, all of them gladly paying for the privilege. They toured the country, becoming hugely popular and their séances became more elaborate, with objects moving about, spirits appearing, and tables levitating. They also gave private demonstrations for those customers who could afford them.

The Age of Spiritualism had begun and was already generating money. Skeptics, to their dismay, were powerless to curb the enthusiasm of hundreds of thousands of people who sought contact with the spirit world. There was a sudden demand for mediums, and although the Fox sisters were there first, they soon had competition that would force them to fight for a place in an increasingly crowded market. Other mediums were soon breaking into the scene for their share of the limelight.

When the girls had first appeared on the scene, they were lauded by believers, who saw their gifts as blessings from the spirit world. Of course, not everyone felt that way. They were also slammed by skeptics and detractors –who actually did the sisters the greatest favor. Since the girls could not easily be exposed as frauds, most people concluded that they must be genuine. It also didn't hurt that Maggie and Kate were both young and attractive. The sisters were embraced by such celebrities as P.T. Barnum, William Cullen Bryant, Harriet Beecher Stowe, and newspaper editor Horace Greeley, who provided quarters for the girls at his home.

Greeley and his wife had lost four of their five children and when he met the girls, he was still grieving over the recent death of his son. The possibility that the dead might be still accessible to the living was of great interest to him. After he witnessed the "rapping phenomena" several times, under what he described as "test conditions," he pronounced himself perplexed by what he saw. He wasted no time in writing an editorial in the *New York Tribune* titled "The Mysterious Rappings." Greeley said that he believed the raps were genuine, if inexplicable, but initially had doubts that spirits were responsible. He later changed his mind and there is no question that Greeley's support for the Fox sisters did a great deal to boost their fame and credibility, as well as that of the entire Spiritualist movement.

P.T. Barnum, that sensational showman, read and enjoyed news accounts of the Fox Sisters' powers and he offered to feature them at his American Museum. The building was a marble showcase on Lower Broadway in New York City, decorated with blazing flags and packed with more than 600,000 living and dead curiosities ---- from stuffed animals to fortune-tellers, to three-legged men and bearded ladies.

The pretty Fox Sisters became quite an attraction. They were shy, barely educated, and simply dressed in neat dark frocks with white collars, but quickly attracted a crowd. Barnum was sure that guests would sit down with the girls who talked to the dead and he was right. Regular admission to the American Museum was 25-cents but to converse with ghosts, people might pay as much as a dollar --- or perhaps even more.

One of those who came to see Maggie Fox was famed novelist James Fenimore Cooper, the author of *The Last of the Mohicans* and other classic American novels. He had heard all the fuss about the girls and wanted to see them for himself. He also had questions that he wanted to ask:

"Is the person that I inquire about a relative?" he asked.
Three knocks came in reply, meaning yes.
"A near relative?"

Yes.
"A man?"
One knock sounded from the table, meaning the answer was no.
"A woman?"
Yes.
"A daughter? A mother? A wife?"
No.
"A sister?"
Yes.

Cooper paused before he asked another question. He was becoming unnerved by the strange replies and by the correctness of the ethereal responses. Finally, he spoke again and asked how long ago his sister had died. There were 50 raps in response, one for each year.

"Had she died of an illness?"
No.
"An accident?"
Yes.
"Was she killed by lightning? Was she shot? Did she fall from a carriage? Was she lost at sea?"
A single knock followed each question.
"Was she thrown by a horse?"
The three knocks --- meaning yes --- rapped hard on the table. There was no question as to the solidity of the reply.

When he left the museum, Cooper told his companions that every answer that Maggie had given to him had been correct. He had been thinking about his sister who, 50 years ago that month, had been killed when a spooked horse threw her. Cooper decided not to return to see the girls again. He was unnerved and not afraid to admit it. He later stated that it would be cowardice to deny the sensations of spirits knocking at the door.

THE FIRST SEANCES IN THE WHITE HOUSE

As time passed and the girls received more national attention and press coverage, the controversy about their séances intensified. Were the raps evidence of communication with the dead? Or was it all a clever hoax that had been perpetrated on the gullible public? Every time a skeptic failed to expose the Fox sisters, their credibility was enhanced. But they would not corner the supernatural market for long. Soon, thousands across the country were claiming to be mediums, hailing from every town and city. Regardless, the Fox sisters became so famous that their reputations brought them all the way to the White House.

Jane Pierce and her beloved son, Benjamin

On January 6, 1853, only two months before Franklin Pierce was to be inaugurated as America's fourteenth president, tragedy struck he and his wife, Jane. The Pierces were traveling by train with their only child, Benjamin, 11, and the car they were traveling in became uncoupled and derailed. The train tumbled, split apart and crashed down a rocky ledge. President-elect and Mrs. Pierce suffered only minor injuries. There was only one death in the crash – young Benjamin Pierce, whose head was struck by a large rock, crushing his skull while his parents helplessly watched.

For the frail Jane Pierce, witnessing her son's horrible death was so traumatic that she never recovered emotionally. She was inconsolable for weeks and so paralyzed by grief that she was unable to attend her husband's inauguration in March 1853. Benjamin's death cast a pall over their life and over the presidency. Jane became one of the most tragic figures to ever occupy the White House. Those who knew the pretty young woman scarcely recognized the pallid, sad shadow that she became. Her life had effectively ended on the day of the railroad accident.

She remained in solitude in the White House family quarters, where she wrote lengthy letters to her dead son, whom she never stopped mourning. Servants said that they would hear her call to Benjamin, while at other times she was heard playing with her three departed children – Benjamin, a first-born son who died as an infant and a second son who died at age four.

To skeptics, Jane's behavior was evidence that she was unbalanced, but who can say with certainty that she did not actually make contact with her deceased boys? Millions of bereaved parents have reported similar experiences over the centuries. But if Jane was unbalanced, her religious beliefs could easily be blamed. She had been raised in a strict family, awash in Calvinist beliefs. Not surprisingly, she arrived at the erroneous assumption that Benjamin's fate was divine punishment for her husband's political ambitions. Franklin Pierce, himself pierced with guilt, also concluded that his son's death was God's judgment against him.

Jane Pierce ached for contact with her son's spirit and was now familiar with the Fox sisters, who were receiving national publicity as Spiritualism swept the nation. The two young mediums were invited to a séance at the White House, where they would attempt to receive spirit raps from Benjamin in the next world. Exactly what occurring during this séance is unknown, for no records exist to say what messages were given to Mrs. Pierce. The sisters never revealed any details about their White House experience, but rumors circulated that it was successful.

FAME, GLORY, AND THE FALL FROM GRACE

Even though most major American newspapers branded Spiritualism a fraud and a swindle, the criticism was largely ignored by people enthusiastically seeking out mediums to contact the spirit world. Skeptics continually ranted against Spiritualism, but a huge number of Americans weren't listening. What they preferred to hear was a message from parents, aunts, uncles, cousins and children in the next world.

Notwithstanding the genuine problem of fraud and trickery in the Spiritualist movement – and there was plenty – people were anxious for a sign from a departed loved one or some message from beyond the veil. A significant change in the American attitude about death was taking place, for Spiritualism was encouraging a new outlook about the possibility of the afterlife.

Spiritualism was also polarizing public opinion. There were millions of adherents and believers who had little or no doubt that the Fox sisters were in contact with the other side. On the other hand, many were quick to debunk even the possibility of communication between the living and the dead. Traditional members of the clergy promptly denounced Spiritualism as a manifestation of evil. It was surely, they thought, the work of the Devil. Even the Fox sisters, upon hearing the first raps, dubbed the presence in the house "Mr. Splitfoot," a religious allusion to the Devil's cloven hooves. The rappings, from a Methodist perspective, must be evil. Conversely, others interpreted the spirit raps heard at séances as evidence of God. The bottom line was that Spiritualism could be viewed in different ways: to some it was a "devil's tool," to others it was the herald of the new age, while for many there was great uncertainty about the source and meaning of spirit raps.

There was a sufficient number of the curious at the beginning of the Spiritualist craze determined to find an answer – no matter what. Not everyone was convinced by the sisters as Greeley, Cooper, and the Pierces had been. The Fox sisters were routinely exposed by skeptics as fakes and it was claimed they produced their phenomena in a variety of ways ranging from toe, knee, and ankle cracking to ventriloquism, to assorted mechanical devices. Despite these accusations, though, no trickery was ever discovered. A number of committees and forums were created to test the powers of the sisters.

Most involved posing questions to the spirits and while the replies were often inconsistent, they were accurate enough to make an impression. One test involved the girls being bound tightly about the ankles so that they could not move their feet. Even trussed up, they still managed to produce eerie rapping sounds. A committee of women also checked the girl's undergarments to ensure that nothing was hidden there to produce the sounds. They found nothing and despite the hostility shown to the sisters by the committees, the members were forced to admit that they were unable to detect fraud.

Even so, some of the accounts of the sister's methods and activities are troubling. Leah was often accused of trying to glean personal information from the sitters at the séances that would help the "spirits" to give out correct answers. They also excelled at calling on the spirits of the famous dead. The results of this were not always impressive. When one sitter noted that Benjamin Franklin's spirit seemed to be surprisingly lacking in good grammar, Maggie Fox stomped away from the séance table with only the reply of, "You know I never understood grammar!" As dubious as the séances may have been, though, thousands were convinced that the girls were genuine and business boomed.

In March 1850, yet another committee was formed to investigate the sisters. It was far from the first such committee to be formed, but it was the first to offer a solid opinion about how the girls were "creating" the rapping phenomena. The members of the committee, all professors of medicine, took their task very seriously. In addition to conducting the usual examinations, the three of them sat on the floor in a soundproof room for an hour while firmly holding onto Maggie's legs. It was a rather undignified way for three gentlemen to pass the time with a young and unmarried girl in those days, but they tackled the task with great fervor. According to their report, they were rewarded for effort. It was noted that the spirits only chose to make themselves heard when one of the investigators was forced to relax his hands a little bit from fatigue. The committee stated that, in the opinion of the investigators, Maggie's knee joints made the spirit rappings. It was suggested that she had the ability to snap these joints in much the same way that some people can crack their knuckles. She accomplished this, the investigators believed, without any visible motion, however.

Shortly after the committee report became public, the Fox sisters (especially Leah) issued immediate denials. She asserted that there had been few rappings during the investigation because the "friendly spirits had retired when they witnessed the harsh proceedings of the persecutors." Leah's defensiveness was understandable, since she stood to lose her share of what had become a thriving business, but what was more remarkable was the way that many prominent people sprang to Maggie's defense. The accusations were untrue, they insisted, simply because they could not be true! Everyone knew that spirits existed, so why in the world would Maggie use her knee joints to imitate their rappings?

One of the members of the controversial committee had been Dr. Charles Alfred Lee. He became so disturbed by the fact that the committee's findings were being ignored, and the Fox sisters more in demand than ever, that he decided to do something about it. Lee conducted a search among his friends and patients until he found a man who had the ability to produce joint noises that were even louder, and harder to detect, than those he believed Maggie could make. Then, under the sponsorship of the

University of Buffalo, he set out to put an end to the nonsense of spirit rappings once and for all. Accompanied by the man with noisy joints, Lee went on a lecture tour of upper New York State, stopping to give demonstrations and to show how the Fox Sisters were frauds. Unfortunately for Lee, he fell into the trap that has ensnared so many other debunkers over the years ---- just because he could duplicate what was being done by the Spiritualists did not mean the original phenomena was not occurring.

Dr. Lee soon came to the realization that his lectures were having the opposite effect from what he had intended. Instead of being warned away from the tricks of false mediums, many of those in Lee's audience became converted to Spiritualism instead. The Fox sisters had apparently aroused a determination to believe that simply could not be undermined.

In 1853, the sisters demonstrated what was described as "their most powerful early manifestations." It consisted of a table levitating with a well-known politician, Governor George Talmadge, seated on top of it. Talmadge also claimed that he'd received a message through spirit writing from the ghost of another notable political figure, John C. Calhoun.

In 1854, it appeared that the Fox sisters' popularity was beginning to wane. For one thing, the public wanted more exciting spirit demonstrations than mere rappings and the girls were facing competition from many other mediums, even as the skeptics continued their attacks on them. In 1857, the *Boston Courier* arranged for a committee of four Harvard professors to examine several mediums. Among those who accepted the invitation were Kate and Leah Fox. The group of skeptical academics was difficult to please. The committee promised to issue a report of its findings and conclusions, but it never did.

Later in their lives, Kate and Maggie fell on hard times. They had suffered through years of séances, public appearances, tours, tests, and scrutiny, much of it antagonistic. Those who knew the sisters felt they had been physically and emotionally drained by their grueling schedule. They simply were not sophisticated enough to understand when they were young that they were being exploited by their older sister, their promoters, and their desperate audiences. Nor did they fully comprehend the depth and hostility of the religious and scientific controversy that surrounded Spiritualism. They were the first to venture professionally into the new movement, and each paid the price for it.

Maggie abandoned mediumship for love. In Philadelphia, she met and fell in love with famed Arctic explorer Elisha Kent Kane, the dashing son of an aristocratic family, who did not deem Maggie worthy of marrying into their line. They did exchange vows and rings in the company of friends but were never legally wed. Unfortunately, the affair ended in tragedy when Kane died in 1857. Maggie was left broken-hearted and almost penniless. She had abandoned being a medium but now had to take it up again. She began drinking and her health and her mental state began to decline.

Leah, who in addition to taking advantage of her younger sisters also began practicing as a medium, married for a third time in 1858 to Daniel Underhill, a successful insurance man. Leah, like Maggie, withdrew from Spiritualism for a time.

Kate, however, continued her career. In 1861, she went to work as a medium for wealthy New York banker Charles Livermore. His wife, Estelle, had died the previous year. Over the next five years, Kate provided the banker with close to 400 séances in his home. There were many witnesses to the sittings and written documentation was kept. Eventually, at the 43rd sitting, the spirit of Estelle Livermore "materialized" and was seen surrounded by what was described as a "psychic light." The spirit communicated to Kate via rappings and automatic writing. According to accounts, Estelle and another spirit, calling himself Benjamin Franklin, wrote on cards before Livermore. While Estelle was writing, Kate's hands were held tight. Witnesses claimed that the script on the card was the perfect reproduction of Estelle's earthly handwriting.

Finally, during the 338th séance, Estelle made it known that she would no longer materialize. True to this communication, Livermore never saw his late wife's spirit again. But because he was grateful to Kate for the comfort that she had brought him in his grief, he paid for her journey to England in 1871 so that she could continue her work as a medium.

In England, her career thrived and she often gave sittings for well-known figures of the day. Kate also made herself available for testing by British scientists like Sir William Crookes, one of the greatest physicists of his time and one of the first advocates for serious inquiry into the paranormal. She also shared several séances with the famed mediums of the era, Daniel Dunglas Home and Agnes Guppy-Volckman.

She remained in England and the following year, married Henry Jencken, a barrister, with whom she had two sons. The first, Ferdinand, was born in 1873 and was reportedly a medium by the time he was three years old. It was said that spirits took over his body and caused an "unearthly glow" to emanate from his eyes. Her reputation as a medium earned Kate a visit to Russia in 1883, where she demonstrated her gifts for the czar.

There was a lesson to be learned by Kate's rise to stardom in Europe and by her earlier employment by men like Charles Livermore. It was a lesson that was overlooked by many scientists, clergy, intellectuals, and rational thinkers in their zeal to debunk and expose Spiritualism as a fraud. The fact was that millions of people, just like Livermore and Jane Pierce, regardless of their social or economic status, were seeking a way to cope with death and the grief that followed. Spiritualism, for all its flaws, fakes, and frauds, offered a connection between this world and the afterlife. The spirit world offered hope that death was not the end and that we would be reunited with our loved ones in the next world. Many scientists, skeptics, and rationalists never quite grasped the value of Spiritualism and the need that it fulfilled for so many people. Nor could they understand that their cold logic failed to offer anything that could ease the fear and mystery of death.

Like it or not, Spiritualism in the nineteenth century produced a critical shift in the way that Americans thought about life and death. Promising mediums had emerged and many of those who investigated them, including some of the most learned men in the country, concluded that there was evidence to make a case for communication with discarnate spirits.

For both the dying and the bereaved, Spiritualism offered something more tangible than unyielding and often impersonal religious dogma, which is why it attracted people from everyone church denomination across America. Although fundamentalist clergy strongly disapproved of it, many people found that the message and hope of Spiritualism was very similar to Christian teachings. In many places in the New Testament, the Bible spoke of eternal life, the same belief that the Spiritualists espoused about the afterlife. However, traditional Christianity would continue to preach against Spiritualists, reminding the faithful that the Old Testament condemned any association with mediums, fortune-tellers, necromancers, and the like.

Americans in the nineteenth century had a much closer contact with death than recent and present-day generations. More people died at home, and were typically laid out in the parlor, which is why the term "funeral parlor" was used when ceremonies surrounding death were moved out of the home. The parlors once found in homes began to be called the "living room" to erase the memory of what the rooms were once used for. Life expectancy in the nineteenth century was much shorter than it is today. Infections, epidemics, and unsophisticated medical treatments claimed many lives. Families had large numbers of children because high infant mortality rates, accidents, and childhood diseases claimed the lives of so many infants and toddlers.

When the Fox sisters were growing up, death was not an unusual topic, even in public schools. Schoolbooks, songs, and poems featured accounts of dying children and by today's standards, seem morbid and inappropriate for young children to read in class. But death was ever-present in the nineteenth century and making sure children were prepared for it, even at an early age, was both practical and responsible on the part of parents, schools, and churches. When the Civil War came along, Americans saw wholesale slaughter in numbers that could never have been imagined before. With all this death, it was no surprise that Spiritualism was instantly popular when it arrived on the scene. It added a measure of comfort and acceptance of death and offered hope of what awaited us when we left our physical body.

In 1876, Maggie Fox visited England for a time and then returned home to the United States. She was still a medium, albeit a reluctant one, forced to continue practicing because of her dire economic situation. Those who knew her recalled that she lived in poverty during her last years.

Then, the lives of the Fox sisters took another unhappy turn. While the reasons remain unclear, the three of them became embroiled in quarrels and disputes with one another that were apparently instigated by Maggie. Their later years were mired in public controversy and personal difficulties, not the least of which was alcohol and a lack of funds. Only Leah had ever prospered from the talents of her younger sisters.

Still, the Fox sisters remained known in the Spiritualist community. In 1884, Maggie appeared before the Seybert Commission in Philadelphia. The commission was founded by a local Spiritualist named Henry Seybert, who donated $60,000 to the University of Pennsylvania for an investigation of Spiritualism. Among the psychic phenomenon that the commission studied were slate writing, spirit materialization, spirit photography, spirit rapping, telekinesis, and "direct voice" phenomena.

When Maggie demonstrated the rapping noises that she and her sisters were famous for, she did so while standing on "four glass tumblers." Commission members, however, were unable to arrive at any definitive conclusions about the nature of the rappings. One member, Horace Howard Furness, stated that he believed the rappings were being created outside of her body and yet, overall, suggested that they might not be supernatural. The noises could have been made by voluntary muscular action, the commission said.

The Seybert Commission's findings were largely negative about Spiritualism. The results outraged the community and some of their frustration might have been legitimate. For one thing, out of the 11 members of the commission, there was only one Spiritualist among them, Thomas Hazard, a close friend of Henry Seybert. Hazard had been picked by Seybert to determine the best means of testing mediums, but his ideas were largely ignored. He lodged a formal protest about the techniques that the commission members used to investigate Spiritualism, but no one listened.

In May 1887, the Seybert Commission issued a preliminary report about the tests that was substantially unfavorable about the entire subject of Spiritualist phenomena. The findings of the commission, legitimate or not, were damaging to Spiritualism, especially in the eyes of many other scientists. Several years later, a commentary written by Frank Podmore acknowledged that the intentions of Mr. Seybert were never fairly carried out. This was typical of how psychical phenomena was often treated by the orthodox scientific community. Medical doctors were among the most hostile to Spiritualism, apparently fearing competition from mediums, some of whom employed spirit contact or clairvoyance to diagnose and treat illnesses. It was all "humbug," said the scientists, skeptics, and debunkers of the nineteenth century – an opinion still shared by most in those categories today.

By 1885, Spiritualism was on the decline and investigations of fraud began to increase. This year brought further tragedy to the Fox sisters. Maggie performed before a commission in New York to prove her skills -- a test that she failed miserably -- and Kate suffered the death of her husband from a stroke. She returned to New York and here, in early 1888, she was arrested for drunkenness and idleness and welfare workers took custody of her sons. Maggie, in a moment of kindness for a sister with whom she had been feuding, was unable to get the boys herself but she did manage to get them into the custody of an uncle in England.

In 1888, Spiritualism was dealt a savage blow that sent it reeling. On October 21, Maggie took part in a lecture and demonstration that has become an infamous event in the history of the Spiritualist movement. On this night, at the New York Academy of Music, she denounced Spiritualism as a complete and total sham. The years of alcohol abuse, loneliness, and grief had taken their toll on her and she weighed the idea of committing suicide before finally choosing confession instead. She walked out on stage to announce that she and Kate had created the strange rappings heard in their Hydesville home by simply cracking their toes. She also stated that Leah had forced them into performing as mediums for the public. She reportedly told the audience: "I have seen so much miserable deception. That is why I am willing to state that Spiritualism is a fraud of the worst description... It is the greatest sorrow of my life. I began the deception when I was too young to know right from wrong."

In their coverage of the shocking events, the *New York Herald* described the audience's reaction to Maggie's public confession:

> *There was dead silence; everybody in the hall knew they were looking upon the woman who is principally responsible for Spiritualism. She stood upon a little pine table*

with nothing on her feet but stockings. As she remained motionless, loud distinct rappings were heard, now in the flies, now behind the scenes, now in the gallery.

It was believed that while Maggie was causing the raps, it was the acoustical properties of the room that was giving the audience the illusion that the sounds were coming from different directions.

While the critics laughed, and cried, "I told you so," devoted Spiritualists denounced Maggie's confession as the ravings of a sad and tired drunk. Kate, who did not speak at the public appearance, later stated that she did not agree with her sister and she continued to perform as a medium. It was also publicly argued by various individuals and groups that Maggie had been forced into a false confession by churches or had been bribed by the newspapers. It was also pointed out, a little more reasonably, that the existence of one fraudulent medium did not prove that all others were not genuine. Some even claimed that Maggie did not know her own powers and was a true medium, despite what she may have thought about herself.

There was also an alternate theory that later emerged to explain the confession. After Maggie had stepped into help Kate with her children, the two sisters mended fences and began battling with Leah. Tensions were high and the younger sisters blamed Leah for their problems – and there were plenty of problems. Maggie and Kate were nearly penniless alcoholics and resented Leah for good reason. Married three times, Leah had profited nicely from a career that she had built at the expense of her sisters. It had been Leah who had accused Kate of being an unfit mother and had her children taken away. The result of all this anger was an alleged plan between Maggie and Kate to ruin Leah – a plan that became even darker when Kate, possibly to ruin Leah's reputation, decided to join Maggie and support her confession by making one of her own. However, she never had the chance to make the confession public.

The convoluted story soon became stranger. In early 1889, Maggie recanted her confession. She explained that the financial pressures she faced were responsible for her temporary disavowal of Spiritualism. She also implied that influence from certain groups who were hostile to the subject, likely churches, forced her into the erroneous confession. The obvious implication was that Maggie and Kate would be paid to say that the spirit rappings were a hoax. Now, in her retraction, she said the opposite. Some historians have suggested that the sisters had been promised a sum of money to renounce Spiritualism but when they were never paid, they were forced to return to being mediums to eke out a meager living. We may never know for sure.

The confession and the retraction did nothing for Maggie's career. The public was angry, indignant, and confused. But both Maggie and Kate were plagued by poverty, alcoholism, loneliness and a variety of serious physical and emotional problems, so the turmoil that surrounded them probably didn't matter as much as it once might have. The publisher Isaac Funk, who knew the sisters, remarked at the time about Maggie, "For five dollars she would have denied her mother, and would have sworn to anything."

For debunkers, the confession had been the news they had been waiting for. They were elated that Maggie claimed the rappings were her own creation and not the work of the supernatural. Her hardships, alcoholism, and mental illness meant nothing to them.

In the end, the confession really didn't mean much either. It should have been a crippling blow to the credibility of Spiritualism, but it came too late to destroy a movement that had captivated the country for four decades. Spiritualism was not dead, much to the frustration of its enemies. The Spiritualists simply rallied their forces and offered explanations for Maggie's behavior, ranging from alcohol to bribes.

The controversy did come near the end of Kate and Maggie's struggling careers. Leah, on the other hand, lived well until the end of her life. She was the first of the sisters to die, in 1890. Neither Maggie nor Kate attended her funeral. The other Fox sisters both died tragically, having been largely abandoned by those whose fortunes they had created with the birth of the Spiritualist movement. Kate drank herself to death in July 1892 at the age of only 56. Her body was discovered by one of her sons.

Maggie died in March 1893, at age 59. She spent her final days bedridden in a friend's tenement apartment in Brooklyn. She was attended by a female physician named Dr. Mellen. The doctor was not a Spiritualist, which makes her observations about Maggie's last minutes all the more curious. Dr. Mellen said that during Maggie's last hours of life, there was a series of loud raps in the room. The tiny apartment contained no hiding places, not even a closet. In addition, Maggie was nearly paralyzed; she could move neither her arms nor legs. When the doctor asked about the noises, Maggie replied in a quiet, labored voice, "It was my friends watching over me." A few minutes later, she died.

THE BIRTH OF THE MOVEMENT

The story of the Fox sisters is a tale that must be told to explain the rise of a belief system that captured the attention of a nation. In 1904, more than a decade after Kate and Maggie had died, workmen who were digging in the cellar of the home their father once rented in Hydesville discovered the skeleton of a man and a tin box that contained trinkets like those once sold by traveling peddlers. Were these the remains of the murder victim who communicated with Kate and Maggie on that night in March 1848? Spiritualists considered the discovery to be evidence that the sisters had been authentic mediums. Skeptics, of course, charged that the bones and the trunk had been planted by Spiritualists looking to perpetrate a hoax.

To this day, opinions still vary as to the veracity of the Fox sisters' rappings.

But the significance of the Fox sisters' story goes far beyond whether or not the women were genuine mediums. The importance of their story is the fact that Spiritualism became a massive movement in American history and attracted millions of believers, from common homes to the White House. It happened because of those two young girls, who either communicated with a spirit or managed to scare their parents with rappings noises one cold night.

If they were frauds, no one has explained how they so successfully perpetrated a hoax for so many years. Could the rappings have been carried out by trickery? Of course, that was a possibility. But many questions remain unanswered so no one can say with any certainty what actually occurred in those theaters, opera houses, meeting halls, and private residences where they performed. Perhaps the sisters really did contact the spirits. Or perhaps they manifested psychic abilities, like psychokinesis, that allowed them to make sounds and move objects, meaning the rappings had nothing to do with spirits at all.

In the end, it may not matter. From a historical perspective, one has to be amazed that two young girls from a tiny farm community caused a stir that captured the attention of millions of Americans for more than half a century. Spiritualism became a significant force that spurred science, psychology, and theology to think in new ways. While it challenged long-held beliefs, it motivated millions to question the very nature of life and death. It also proved to be a very important solution to grief, especially after the Civil War. The movement that the sisters began grew to be much larger than just two women. Their confessions and recantations came too late to stop Spiritualism and the surge of interest that it created in the supernatural that continues to this day. The bottom line was that Spiritualism represented great change – which was a threat to many, but offered great promise to others.

The story of the Fox sisters was merely the beginning of the Spiritualist movement. There were still many stories to tell.

3. AND THE DEAD KNOCKED

THE RISE OF THE AMERICAN ORIGINAL

America has always been, as mentioned previously, a nation of extremes. It's a place of strong passions and great enthusiasm, both good and bad. Those passions have ranged from the vicious hysteria of the lynch mob to the ecstasies of the religious revival meeting and covered everything in between. Nowhere is this great passion as evident as it is in the history of Spiritualism. The movement swept across the country, even in those days before radio, television, and mass communication. People became obsessed with the idea that the living could communicate with the dead – and receive a reply – and even the most conservative, uneducated, and average people in the country became part of the new movement.

However, it did not spread without opposition. Most of the attacks against Spiritualism in the early days came from the fundamentalist Christians. Conservative religious groups held the opinion that communion with the spirits was possible, but it was evil and dangerous to the welfare of one's soul. Many church leaders saw Spiritualism as a grievous threat to organized religion, but interestingly, Spiritualism was never meant to turn into a faith or a religious movement. It was little more than a popular pastime at first and the idea of communicating with the spirits was an amusing way to spend a long winter evening. There were several factors that worked independently to cause Spiritualism to be inflated in importance and to be accepted as an actual religious faith. A major one was the rise of the Apostolic movement in America, which also got its start in New York. Based around speaking in tongues (glossolalia) and literal possession by the Holy Spirit, the Pentecostal faith (and its many offshoots) is still a major religious movement today. As documented in the first chapter of the book, it was a time of many new religious movements in the country and although many ministers condemned Spiritualism as the "work of the Devil," it was not difficult for religious fervor and spirit communication to blend together in the hearts and minds of people who were seeking enlightenment.

Scientific realists had their own beliefs. They believed that spirit communication was impossible and that all Spiritualists must be frauds or candidates for the asylum. A great many ordinary Americans espoused this point of view, as well. Many of them were doggedly determined to defeat the pro-Spiritualism forces and these opponents of Spiritualism were often as energetic as its advocates were. In addition to scathing denunciations in the press, books were published, public prayer meetings were held, and lecture tours were organized so that the opponents could express their views. Lecture tours were popular forms of entertainment in those days and speakers on controversial subjects often attracted large audiences.

The opposition to the movement caused damage to its credibility before the Civil War. In fact, Spiritualism saw a period of steady decline between 1856 and 1860. Over the next few years, the country had too much on its mind with the horrors of war to pay much more than a passing thought to Spiritualism. In the post-war period, though, it would be the death and destruction of the fighting that made the movement stronger than ever. Thanks to the huge number of bereaved wives, parents, and loved ones, Spiritualism offered the hope of direct communication with those who had died. Soon, an even greater number of people from all economic levels began flocking to mediums and séances around the country.

After the war, Spiritualism finally began to leave America and spread around the world. Introduced into England as early as 1852 by the American medium Mrs. W.B. Hayden, it had quickly spread throughout the British Isles and continental Europe. The supernatural had, of course, been popular in those areas for some time, but it was Mrs. Hayden's contributions that made believers in the spirit world start to consider active communication with the other side.

As an introduction to Spiritualism, Mrs. Hayden was a good deal less exciting than the Fox Sisters. She was the wife of a Boston newspaper editor and her mediumship consisted of a limited sort of rapping that was not as fluent or complex as the Fox Sisters, or of other mediums of the time. She made her historic trip to England in the company of a man named Stone, of whom little is known except that he called himself a lecturer on "electro-biology," a technique of hypnotism that used metal disks. Mrs. Hayden soon began to draw bigger crowds than her mentor and customers flocked to her sittings, paying a half-guinea each.

The British Press was quick to ridicule Mrs. Hayden's powers. It claimed that her control spirit could not even spell out messages alphabetically unless she herself could see the alphabet as each letter was indicated. If true, this fact should have aroused suspicion in even the most gullible, since more accomplished spirits of the time seemed quite independent of the medium in their ability to "see" the letters. Despite this, sitters claimed to have received information about their departed friends and relatives that could not have been known by Mrs. Hayden under ordinary circumstances. A number of influential people became supporters of the medium.

In the earliest days of British Spiritualism, two tendencies had already appeared that were going to set the British movement apart from its more flamboyant American counterpart. The first would be the tendency toward organizations to form in Britain, rather than independent mediums operating strictly on their own, as they did in America. Several Spiritualist churches, newspapers, and associations would form in America but the British equivalents became more numerous, more stable, and more widely patronized.

A second British trend became more important for the development of the movement as a whole. Scientific research, before the turn of the century, was much farther advanced in Europe than it was in America, although that situation did improve dramatically after the Civil War. However, it would be many years before the Spiritualist hypotheses and happenings would be given as thorough testing in America as they were to receive at the hands of British scientists. The period of the great mediums -- and the equally great men of science who investigated them -- was soon to come.

But Spiritualism's greatest impact in those days was in America. The movement spread quickly across the country until there was an estimated two million Spiritualists in the early 1850s, with the movement showing no signs of slowing down. It was easy to find people from every level of the social ladder who believed in contact with the spirits, from the lowliest tenement homes to the very steps of the White House.

It was time of prominence for some of America's greatest literary figures. As Spiritualism was now doing, all of them had a great effect on the popular culture of the country. And almost all of them expressed curiosity – or disdain – for the growing Spiritualist craze, but they did not reject supernatural or psychic events.

Ralph Waldo Emerson was a transcendentalist who believed in the afterlife. Henry Wadsworth Longfellow shared his views. Henry David Thoreau, also a transcendentalist, expressed interest in reincarnation. William Cullen Bryant took part in séances and so did Nathaniel Hawthorne, who then rejected Spiritualism, but created a Spiritualist character for his 1852 novel, *The Blithedale Romance*. Throughout his life, he acknowledged that he had witnessed apparitions. In one incident, Hawthorne, who often went to the Boston Athenaeum, a research library in the city, always noticed an elderly minister there reading. One evening, as usual, Hawthorne saw the same gentleman in his usual chair. He was stunned to learn that the man had already died before he saw him. Hawthorne concluded that he had seen the man's ghost, which continued to appear for several more weeks.

Herman Melville, author of the 1851 book *Moby Dick*, was a believer in the afterlife. Walt Whitman understood phrenology (an occult "science" based on the measurements of the skull) well enough to allude to it in his poetry. It was in 1851 that James Fenimore Cooper, supporter of the Fox sisters, died. Later in the century, Henry James included Spiritualists in his books and the creator of Sherlock Holmes, Sir Arthur Conan Doyle, became one of the greatest proponents of Spiritualism in history.

The popular English poet Elizabeth Barrett Browning, drawn to Spiritualism, joined in séances conducted by the famed medium Daniel Dunglas Home. However, her husband, Robert Browning despised Home and publicly mocked Spiritualism as a fraud, hoping in some small way to injure the reputation of the medium. Novelist William Thackeray, whose works included *Vanity Fair*, attended séances given by the Fox sisters and D.D. Home, but admitted his reaction to Spiritualism was "mixed" at best.

In 1852, the best-selling author Harriet Beecher Stowe published one of the most influential books of all time, *Uncle Tom's Cabin*. It was responsible for changing public opinion in the northern states against slavery. Stowe was seriously interested in the new Spiritualist movement and attended séances, as did noted abolitionist and newspaper publisher William Lloyd Garrison, whose interests also included mesmerism and phrenology.

Poet Emily Dickinson mentioned the spirit world in her writings and author Louisa May Alcott discovered that supernatural events did not occur only at séances. Alcott, who later wrote the classic novel *Little Women* was only 25-years-old in 1858 and lived at her family's home in Concord, Massachusetts. Despite the great interest in Spiritualism, she remained uninvolved. But she found out that one did not need to be a Spiritualist to have an experience with ghosts. At the time, her younger sister, Beth, was desperately ill with scarlet fever and her condition was growing worse. Louisa and her mother remained at Beth's bed side as her health declined. They knew that Beth was dying. Louisa wrote the following in her diary on March 14, 1858:

My dear Beth died at three this morning, after two years of patient pain. Saturday, she slept, and at midnight became unconscious, quietly breathing her life away until three; then with one last look of the beautiful eyes, she was gone.

A curious thing happened, and I will tell it here, for Dr. G said it was fact. A few moments after the last breath came, as Mother and I sat silently watching the shadow fall on the dear little face, I saw a light mist rise from the body and float up and vanish in the air. Mother's eyes followed mine, and when I said, "What did you see?" she described the same mist. Dr. G said it was the life departing visibly.

Did Louisa and her mother see Beth's spirit as it left her body? It seemed so. What is equally amazing about this excerpt from her diary is the doctor's reply to her about what she had seen – that he had witnessed this phenomenon on other occasions. The Alcotts' experience also suggested that what they had witnessed was more than a belief; it was a genuine paranormal event.

In America and Europe, scientists were experimenting at that time with the fascinating energies of electricity and the workings of electromagnetism. The telegraph had already changed the nature of communication and no one had any idea what marvels were yet to be discovered. Science and religion were not yet at serious odds, but that would happen later in the nineteenth century.

One of the pioneers of photography, the Frenchman Louis Daguerre, died in 1851. He would not live to see the controversy in the decades ahead about whether photography could capture the images of spirits, as it had physical objects, places, and people.

It was around this time, in 1852, that the terms *Spiritualism* and *Spiritualist* came into popular use. Before that, no one was sure what to call the strange and inexplicable ghostly events. Suddenly, the Fox sisters were not the only mediums of note, although they were still the best known in those days. Mediums, séances, and spirit circles could be found in most communities, large and small, throughout the country. New York City reported hundreds of known mediums and no less than 40,000 serious believers in "spirit rapping." Even a small town like Auburn, New York, not far from where the Fox sisters grew up, had dozens of mediums by the 1850s. Across the country, especially in the Northeast and New England, the number of mediums exploded. Philadelphia claimed 50 to 60 private spirit circles and a large number of mediums. In Ohio, there were over 200 spirit circles reported. In 1854, Illinois Senator James Shields presented the U.S. Congress with a petition containing 15,000 signatures, calling on the federal government "to investigate communications from the dead." U.S. Senator N.P. Tallmadge and Ohio Congressman Joshua Giddings were among the politicians who practiced Spiritualism.

Whether the spirit communications of the Fox sister had been fake or genuine didn't seem to matter. They had made an impact that had changed the country. By 1855, the New England Spiritualist Association estimated some two million believers across America.

As the popularity of the movement continued to spread, there were many publications, both supportive of and opposed to Spiritualism, being printed across the country. By 1851, New Yorkers had a new daily newspaper to read – the *New York Times*. It immediately took a strong anti-Spiritualism stance, but if Spiritualism caught your fancy, there were dozens of publications devoted to the movement that were readily available in towns and cities across the country.

The *New York Tribune*, whose publisher Horace Greeley welcomed the Fox sisters into his home, was always the city's "radical newspaper." It was supportive of the rise of the movement and Greeley and his wife became converts after the death of their son in 1849.

In Washington D.C., a newspaper called the *National Intelligencer* was so opposed to Spiritualism that in April 1853, it branded the movement a "pestilence" and stated that it was a product of "delusions." It accused Spiritualism of "distracting the minds of the nervous, feeble-witted and the timid into actual insanity." The editors went on to demand laws to prohibit séances.

The popular magazine *Harper's Weekly* also strongly objected to Spiritualism, suggesting that spirit circles, like "gambling dens and other places of ill-fame," should be closed.

But the several million Americans who were adherents to Spiritualism had no lack of their own publications to choose from as an antidote to the skeptical press and to magazines put out by the Catholic Church and the fundamentalist Christians. These groups had an antipathy against Spiritualism based on religious grounds – and because of the threat they believed the new movement posed for organized religion.

For Spiritualists, there were literally, starting in the 1850s and through the 1890s, hundreds of magazines, pamphlets, and newspapers devoted to the movement that came and went. Among the most successful were *Messenger of Light*, *Banner of Light*, *The Spirit World*, *Spiritual Philosopher* and, perhaps best known, the long-running *Spiritual Telegraph*, which started publication in 1852. There were also many books published on the subject throughout the second half of the nineteenth century. By the early 1870s, annual sales of books about Spiritualism totaled over 50,000 copies; and another 50,000 pamphlets devoted to the subject were also sold each year.

KNOCKINGS IN STRATFORD

The Spiritualist movement was just getting started when a shocking story appeared that couldn't be ignored by any newspaper, no matter what the editors believed about Spiritualism. It swept the country and captured the imagination of Americans in 1850. It was the story of a poltergeist that was wreaking havoc in the home of a minister in Stratford, Connecticut, and it was a story like nothing that had been heard before.

And there's been nothing like it since.

In 1848, the Reverend Eliakim Phelps, his wife, and four children moved from Massachusetts to a house that he had purchased on Elm Street in Stratford. Phelps was a Presbyterian minister and "mesmeric healer." He had been born in Belchertown, Massachusetts, to an old and respected New England family and was a graduate of the Union and Andover Seminaries. Before coming to Stratford, he had led two congregations in Geneva and in Huntington, New York. He was widowed in his middle-fifties, but his children were all grown and had moved from home by then. He was well-known in religious circles and appeared to be a model clergyman of the time. His only eccentricity seemed to be his beliefs in clairvoyance and his attempts to treat illnesses through mesmerism, which was not altogether uncommon in that era.

The Phelps home in Stratford

At age 59, Phelps decided to get married again. His new bride, a widow, was many years younger than he was and they decided to move to Stratford. The home was enlivened by the presence of children from his wife's previous marriage. Despite what seemed to be a blissful life, some accounts state that the family was not entirely happy. Apparently, Mrs. Phelps did not care for Stratford and did not like her neighbors. She was constantly tired and upset and it was said that her daughter, Anna, suffered from a nervous disposition.

On March 4, 1850, an acquaintance of Reverend Phelps' from New York came to visit the family. After dinner that evening, he suggested that they attempt to contact the spirits by means of knocks and rappings. Spiritualism had quickly become the most popular fad in the country and the Fox sisters were America's newest celebrities.

Thousands of people all over the country were busy trying to contact the spirit world and the Phelps family was no exception. No one present that night was taking anything too seriously. They heard a few tentative rappings, but little else.

But soon, Reverend Phelps would get the surprise of his life.

On Sunday, March 10, the entire Phelps clan returned from church services to find the doors of their house standing wide open. The doors had been locked when they left. Their maid was away so Phelps had been sure to secure the house when they left. He had even locked the interior doors and the only keys were in his pocket. And yet, somehow, all the doors had been flung open.

Dr. Phelps cautiously entered the house, unsure of what he might find. What he discovered was chaos. Someone had ransacked the place, knocking over furniture, smashing dishes, and scattering books, papers and clothing. Tables and chairs had been overturned and the closets rifled. The house appeared to have been attacked by vandals, but they had not been robbed. Phelps found that his gold watch, the family silver, and his loose cash were in plain sight, but had been left alone.

Phelps summoned his family and they went upstairs to inspect the bedrooms. They found no burglars hidden away but discovered something even more unnerving. In one of the bedrooms, someone had spread a sheet over the bed and had placed one of Mrs. Phelps' nightgowns on top of it. Stockings had then been placed at the bottom of it to suggest feet and the arms of the gown had been folded over the chest as though crossed in preparation for a funeral. What sort of message had the intruders been trying to send?

The family attempted to restore some order to the house before returning to the church for the afternoon services. When the clock struck noon, Mrs. Phelps and the children departed, but Dr. Phelps remained at the house, hoping to catch the burglars if they returned. He hid in his study, armed with a pistol, and waited in silence. A few hours passed and he heard no sounds but the house creaking in the wind. No doors opened or closed, no footsteps fell in the rooms or the corridors.

Eventually, he left his hiding place and wandered about the lower floor. He opened the door to the dining room and made another shocking discovery. A seemingly mad sculptor had created 11 human figures, formed out of clothing and other items. The figures were all arranged to represent a mysterious religious ceremony – standing and kneeling before a small central figure in the middle of the room. Several of them held Bibles, while others bowed so low that their foreheads nearly brushed the floor. The incredibly life-like effigies had been fashioned from rags, muffs, dresses, coats, and other materials from around the house. The dummies had somehow been created and positioned during the short time that Mrs. Phelps and the children had been away from the house -- and while Dr. Phelps had been so vigilantly standing guard. How could it have been done? And more importantly, what did it mean?

On that afternoon, the strange happenings seemed to be the work of a neighborhood prankster, but Phelps would soon change his mind about that. Initially, in all of the excitement, he forgot about the séance of March 4. Soon, he wondered if whatever was inhabiting his house had come there because it had been invited.

Convinced at that moment that earthly visitors had gotten into the house, the family was on alert. Rooms were watched and doors and windows were kept locked, but in spite of this, the invisible model-maker continued his work. During the first weeks of the haunting, 30 new creations, made from clothing and sheets, appeared in the house. They were just as eerie as the original set had been. In the *New Haven Journal*, the figures were described as, "...most beautiful and grotesque. The clothing of which they were constructed was somehow gathered from all parts of the house, in spite of the strict watch that was kept... Some of them were so life-like that, a small child being shown in the room, thought his mother was kneeling in prayer..." The editor of the newspaper was convinced that a supernatural agent was at work.

Reverend Phelps began making attempts to contact what was thought to be a spirit in the house. The attempts were successful in that he began to receive blasphemous replies to his questions, after which he cut off all communication. There are no details about the messages, but we know that they were so outrageous that Phelps not only stopped all communication, but forbid his family to engage in any dialogue with the foul-mouthed ghost. The spirit was not so easily stymied, however. Messages appeared scrawled on walls, written on scraps of paper, and in letters that were mysteriously dropped from the ceiling. The ghost revealed a crude sense of humor since many of the messages were nasty notes about Dr. Phelps' fellow clergymen.

The mansion became a madhouse. Objects moved about the house. An umbrella jumped into the air and traveled nearly 25 feet. Forks, spoons, knives, books, pens, and assorted small objects launched from places where no one had been standing. Pillows, sheets, and blankets were pulled from beds and fluttered into the air. This continued all day long and finally, by evening, the activity seemed to be exhausted and the house fell silent. When H.B. Taylor, an investigator of the supernatural, visited the house, he was treated to several unusual sights: "In my presence, the elder boy was carried across the room by invisible hands and gently deposited on the floor. A supper table was raised and tipped over when the room was completely empty of people."

During the chaos, Mrs. Phelps pleaded with her husband to call someone for help. Phelps contacted Reverend John Mitchell, a friend and a retired minister. Mitchell listened to the story and quickly suggested the most obvious solution -- that the maid or the older children were playing tricks. He took the suspects away from the house and sequestered them nearby, but the activity continued. He still suspected some natural explanation, though, until he saw some of the objects move for himself. He soon became convinced that the events were unexplainable.

On March 14, a potato literally dropped from nowhere and landed on the breakfast table. Throughout the rest of the day, the Phelps family, along with Reverend Mitchell, witnessed 46 objects appear and drop out of the air in the locked parlor. Most of the items were articles of clothing that had been somehow transported from the upstairs closets.

In the weeks that followed, the family, along with friends, observers, would-be investigators, and curiosity-seekers witnessed objects appearing and flying through the air. Most of these items moved at abnormally slow speeds and they would touch down on the floor as if carefully placed there. Phelps and others also claimed to see the objects change course while in flight. There were many accusations of trickery made against the Phelps family but with each, Dr. Phelps invited the skeptics to see the house for themselves. He was hospitable to reporters, investigators, and even mere curiosity-seekers, and he permitted them to come to the house and to stay as long as they liked. Many of them would witness the disturbances first-hand – and would go away scratching their heads in puzzlement.

Finally, after reading accounts of the haunting in newspapers, Austin Phelps, the minister's son from his first marriage, journeyed to Stratford to try and help his father get to the bottom of the matter. His uncle, Abner Phelps, a well-known Boston doctor and Massachusetts legislator, accompanied him. Austin himself was a professor at Andover Theological Seminary. Neither of the men was pleased with the family's growing notoriety and neither of them had approved of Dr. Phelps' marriage to his young wife either. They were sure that they would discover a trickster among the family members.

During their first night, they heard a loud pounding noise that they surmised was coming from the knocker on the front door. They took turns pulling it open and guarding the door, but each time they expected to pounce on the prankster, they found the doorstep to be deserted. Finally, they stood on both sides of the door, Austin on the outside and his uncle inside. The loud knocking continued, but the source was a mystery. The men were also disturbed by rapping noises upstairs. On the second night, they determined the noise was coming from the room that belonged to Anna, the daughter with the nervous condition. The hammering seemed to be coming from the inside panel of the door. They burst into the room, thinking to catch her in the act, but she nowhere near the door when they entered. Austin later wrote: "The young lady was in bed, covered up and out of reach of the door. We examined the panel and found dents where it had been struck." The two men would depart from the house believing that whatever phenomenon was being experienced there, it was genuine.

Anna, age 16, was a particular target of the haunting. At one point, she suffered the terror of having a pillow pressed over her face while she slept, and was nearly strangled by tape wrapped around her throat by unseen hands. The ghost seemed to have an unusual dislike for her. Anna was often slapped by unseen hands. Those present sometimes only saw the girl shake or jerk her head, but reported hearing the sound of a slap. They often saw red marks and welts appear on her skin. When a reporter for the *New York Sun* came to Stratford, he sat alone in a room with Mrs. Phelps and the girl, who suddenly cried out, "I am pinched!" When she rolled up her sleeve, she revealed a bright red finger mark, apparently fresh, on her arm.

Mrs. Phelps's older son, Henry, 11, was tortured even worse. He was beaten, pinched, struck, and occasionally rendered unconscious. Once, in the presence of Dr. Phelps, he was hit with a flurry of small stones. A newspaper reporter claimed that he once saw the boy carried from this bed by an invisible force and dumped on the floor. In front of several witnesses, he was once lifted into the air so high that his hair brushed the ceiling of the room. Henry was even abducted! One day, he vanished and was found outside, tied up and suspended from a tree. He had no idea how he had gotten there. The young boy was also burned, thrown into a cistern of water, and had his clothing torn apart in front of visiting clergymen. He went missing again one afternoon and he was later discovered shoved onto a closet shelf with a rope around his neck.

Mr. Beach, the reporter from the *New York Sun*, witnessed an eerie happening in the boy's bedroom one evening in April. Henry was sitting on his bed when, in view of many witnesses, a metal matchbox fell from the mantelpiece, striking the floor with a loud clatter. "The box, untouched by any visible hand, slid toward the bed and disappeared under it." Henry jumped up, crying that he was burning, and Beach, hurrying to the rescue, found a flaming piece of paper under the bed.

Reverend Mitchell convinced Phelps that, despite his moral repugnance, he needed to try and resume communications with the ghost. Those communications became more than mere knocks and raps. On one occasion, Dr. Phelps was in his study alone, writing at his desk. He turned away for a moment and when he turned back he found that his sheet of paper, which had been blank, was now covered with strange-looking writing. The ink on the paper was still wet. In the days that followed, other family members and friends would experience the same thing and would find papers with writing on them. The letters sometimes appeared from thin air, floating down over the dinner table or appearing in a sealed box. None of the messages were very revealing and unfortunately, they were all disposed of because Dr. Phelps felt they were missives from an evil source.

Desperate for information that the spirits had been unwilling to provide, Dr. Phelps reluctantly agreed to perform another séance in the house. This time, communication was easily resolved and the spirit claimed to be a soul in hell, enduring torment for the sins he had committed in life. Dr. Phelps asked the spirit what he could do to help and, using the knocking code, the ghost asked that Phelps bring him a piece of pumpkin pie. Thinking that he had been misunderstood, he asked again and this time the spirit asked for a glass of gin. Finally, Phelps asked why the spirit was causing such a disturbance in the house and the spirit replied: "For fun."

Then, the spirit further detailed its history, claiming to be a law clerk who had done some financial work for Mrs. Phelps. He confessed that he had committed fraud and had been sent to hell when he died. He did not explain why he was haunting the Phelps home, though. Eerily, Dr. Phelps later made a visit to the Philadelphia law firm where the spirit claimed to have been employed and he examined the papers in question. It turned out that a fraud had been committed and that it had been serious enough to warrant the man's prosecution, had he lived until his arrest and trial.

Later, though, Phelps would change his position about the identity of the ghost and would feel that he had been tricked using the fraudulent papers. It is unknown what made him change from his original position. He simply stated that: "I am convinced that the communications are wholly worthless, in that they are frequently false, contradictory and nonsensical."

The haunting continued, becoming both a physical and psychological attack on the entire family. The night-time hours were filled with rapping, knockings, voices, screams, and bizarre sounds. The daylight hours saw objects sailing about through the rooms. Silverware bent and twisted, windows broke, papers scattered, and tables and chairs danced across the floor as if they had come to life.

And, perhaps spookiest of all, the strange effigies continued to appear.

It was reported in the *New Haven Journal*, "In a short space of time so many figures were constructed that it would not have been possible for a half a dozen women, working steadily for several hours, to have completed their design, and arrange the picturesque tableau. Yet these things happened in short space of time, with the whole house on the watch. In all, about thirty figures were constructed during this period."

As news of the strange events spread, the Phelps home received a visit from Andrew Jackson Davis, the famed "Poughkeepsie Seer." Davis arrived in Stratford with a fanfare of publicity and his presence brought even more attention to the Phelps haunting. He spoke learnedly of "vital radiations," felt powerful emanations when he touched the Phelps children, and trembled when he received magnetic charges. Dr. Phelps, himself interested in mesmerism, likely watched all of this with interest. He permitted Davis to look through the house, inspecting rooms, and examining spots where activity had occurred, but refrained from telling him too much.

Davis was fascinated with magnetism and electricity and undoubtedly his opinions about the case were influenced by a brand new occult oddity known as the "Electric Girls." They were not, as one might suppose, shocking young females, but women of all ages in whose presence strange forces seemed to occur. They were rather like physical mediums, although the phenomena that surrounded them resembled the work of poltergeists. The most famous "Electric Girl" of the era was Angelique Cottin, the daughter of a French farmer. When Angelique was near a compass, the magnetic needle lost all sense of direction, various metal objects were both attracted and repulsed by her, and heavy iron castings shifted when she was near them. A few years before the Phelps case, some Electric Girls made their American debut and Andrew Jackson Davis was quick to observe a connection between them and poltergeist activity. With this in mind, Davis examined the Phelps family, concentrating especially on Anna and Henry. He pronounced both "electric" and noted that Henry, whose "organism released vital radiations," was likely unconsciously causing the spirit happenings. The children were given to sudden changes of radiation, he claimed, rather like an alternating current. This caused objects to either become attracted or repelled by them, depending on the magnetic energy in the house. Because of this, chaos had ensued in the Phelps home.

However, Davis did not declare that everything happening in the house was caused by electromagnetic energy. There were also spirits staging a performance in the Phelps home – he himself saw five of them.

Davis' conclusions about the haunting evoked a clamor from traditional Spiritualists across the country, who insisted that the place was infested with ghosts and all that twaddle about electricity was not only blasphemous, but unscientific.

Meanwhile, the Phelps family had gone through just about all they could take.

After months of madness in the house, Phelps sent his wife and stepchildren to Philadelphia for a much-needed rest. The manifestations stopped at once. Dr. Phelps remained alone in the house for five weeks and observed nothing unusual. Nor did the haunting resume when the family returned to Stratford the following spring.

Phelps, in a long interview with Harvard's Charles W. Eliot, gave a complete summary of the case from his point of view. He suffered through the haunting with most of his humor intact, although he made many mentions about its financial cost with so many things being destroyed, windows broken, and servants who refused to return to work.

Were spirits at work? Phelps replied, "I have never seen a spirit; I do not know what a spirit could do if it would, or what it would do if it could! The facts... render the idea of tricks or design and deception wholly inadmissible... They were not produced by human agency and were absolutely inexplicable. Fifty-six articles were picked up at one time which had been thrown at someone's head... Heavy marble-topped tables would rise on two legs and crash to the floor with no one within six feet of them..."

Dr. Phelps staunchly defended his step-children, citing many incidents in which they could not have been the perpetrators. The Phelps children were fortunate to have a loyal stepfather. Other youngsters, in years to come, suspected of faking occult phenomena have fared badly – bound, gagged, chained, and locked in closets to prevent mischief.

Could the two older children have committed fraud in the Phelps case? It seems impossible that they could have been the sole participants, assuming, of course, that fraud existed. There was no haziness about this case, no lack of relevant reporting. At Stratford, every incident was carefully detailed. Accounts published in the *New Haven Journal* and *Courier* are very precise and further, the *Journal's* reporter was a witness to some of the remarkable happenings. The *New York Sun* also had a man at the house.

Another reputable corroborating witness was Reverend John Mitchell, a frequent caller and investigator at the house. He testified to the hurling of objects, declared that he heard unearthly shrieks, and was emphatic about the fact that no member of the household could have tricked him. There were also neighbors and members of Dr. Phelps's congregation who were present during various unexplained happenings.

Numerous theories were put forth (and continue to be today) as to just what was going on in the Phelps house. Many believed that the house had been invaded by spirits, bound and determined to wreak havoc with the family. But why? Locals stated that the haunting was caused by the ghost of a Goody Bassett, who was hanged near the house for witchcraft in 1651. However, there was no evidence to support this piece of fanciful lore.

The Phelps poltergeist has been studied by many investigators, including Sir Arthur Conan Doyle, Frank Podmore, Hereward Carrington, and others, but none of them have ever been able to shed much light on this curious affair.

A hoax seems even more difficult to believe than the idea that it was a supernatural event. If it was an elaborate hoax, then we must assume that Reverend Phelps was the chief mischief-maker. The single incident of the strange writing that appeared when he was alone is enough to establish his participation. But if he was a trickster, then his two oldest children had to have been accomplices. Mrs. Phelps at first appears to be the one member of the household who could be acquitted of complicity. Nothing seems to have happened when she was alone. But it would require astounding gullibility to go through the many months of the violent haunting and not detect a hoax. Mrs. Phelps was an educated woman, active in church affairs, so it is hard to believe that she could have been fooled so often and for so long. This means that four members of the family – one of whom was a respected clergyman – had to have been in on the fraud. Based on the testimony of everyone else involved, this seems very unlikely.

The events in Stratford are astonishing, no matter what view one takes and questions raised by the haunting lead to fascinating speculations. Would respectable Dr. Phelps risk disgrace by initiating a preposterous deception? Would he trust two teenagers as his accomplices? If the stepchildren originated the haunting, did the reverend perpetuate it to prevent their exposure after the matter became public? Was everyone involved in the affair simply gripped my mass hysteria, mistakenly reporting the things they saw? Were four clergymen, a professor, three reporters, and a battalion of witnesses all mad, deceived, or lying?

Or was the Stratford case exactly what it seemed to be? Was it a significant paranormal experience of the nineteenth century that captured America's attention at a time when the Spiritualist movement was emerging as the most fantastic phenomenon in our country's history?

There were more – even more fantastical – communications with the spirit world that where still to come and they would take America by storm.

AROUND THE SEANCE TABLE

The séance grips the imagination, lays hold of emotions, causes blood to tingle and hair to rise... all these combine to play upon our sensibilities creating an effect which no utterance of prophecy, no reading of minds, stars, crystal balls or tea leaves, can produce.
Robert Somerlott

Whether a believer in the movement or a skeptic of anything that reeked of spirits, the debate over Spiritualism was a boisterous one. There were even multiple debates taking place on both sides of the table. Within the movement, there was a debate about whether Spiritualism should be defined as a religion, as many believers considered it. Some called it a "scientific religion;" others thought of it as a "quasi-religious" movement. But there were practical reasons for Spiritualists to want their beliefs under an umbrella of religion. Several states were passing laws against "fortune-tellers and conjurers," as a way to limit the rights of Spiritualists. If they could claim protection as a religious denomination, they would have a weapon to use against hostile government authorities that were trying to legislate the movement out of existence.

The growth of Spiritualism had not gone unnoticed by those that opposed it. In Alabama, for example, a law was passed to impose a $500 fine on anyone who gave a public display of mediumship. Other states followed their lead, limiting or banning displays by mediums. Fortunately for Henry Gordon, New York City did not take such a harsh stand when he allegedly became the first American medium to perform levitation, lifting himself off the ground in full view of an audience in 1852.

But despite the critics and the skeptics, it was astonishing to see the speed with which interest in Spiritualism spread across America. Much to the surprise of the critics, it was not just the so-called superstitious and uneducated who were drawn to the movement. Increasingly, many educated, wealthy, and prominent people could be found at séances. When the first large scale Spiritualist society was founded in 1854, its organizers included a former U.S. senator, four judges, two military officers, and several successful businessmen.

Even since that time, there has never been another cultural phenomenon that affected so many people or stimulated as much interest as Spiritualism did in the decade before the Civil War or, for that matter, in the subsequent decades that followed it. Yet, nearly even recent traditional history book or biography about this period either chooses to ignore Spiritualism entirely, or makes a short reference to it, dismissing it as a short-lived fad. To the contrary, in its time, Spiritualism became so popular that even many non-believers felt that it might become "the religion of America." But Spiritualism never assumed the rigid structure of ordinary church denominations. It was accessible to everyone and while that openness appealed to many, ironically, the lack of organization may have been the movement's greatest weakness.

It quickly became apparent that the movement was riddled with trickery and fraud. Still, people of all kinds sought out mediums and séances for the hope of communication with the next world – much to the shock of those who despised the movement. They could not believe that people could be so gullible. Believe in it or not, though, the country was experiencing unprecedented growth and mobility, and Spiritualism appeared to reflect the changes that America was going through. It was an age of religious and social agitation and excitement, coupled with new marvels in science and technology.

In 1859, barely a decade after the Fox sisters became public figures, Charles Darwin published his controversial book *Origin of Species*. The impact of his theory of evolution was stunning. Some said that by accepting Darwin's theory, it meant that you were replacing a God in whose image man was created with the anatomical results of natural selection and an ape for an ancestor. In this heady mixture, Spiritualism threatened to redefine man's very nature, abilities, and purpose. For if people did possess "other abilities," then the current concept of mankind, religion, and perhaps even God, would have to be changed, or at least re-examined. Spiritualism became a starting point for a great many people in search of answers to some of the great mysteries of life and death.

For the bereaved, Spiritualism was a godsend. The early and middle nineteenth century was a time of short life expectancy and high child mortality rates. Two out of every ten babies did not live to see their first birthday. It was not unusual for mothers to die during childbirth. Simply living to adulthood was a great achievement and even then, a great many people did not live beyond their forties. Medical treatment was limited, painful, and often deadly. There were no therapists to help the grieving deal with death. Whether they knew it or not, mediums were suddenly placed in the role of grief counselors. Spirit contact meant comfort, no matter what the church, the press, and the scientists said about it. Attending séances became more than mere entertainment. For many, it became a necessity of life.

Séances were usually held in the home of the medium or in the home of one of the sitters. To begin, the lights were normally turned down very low or extinguished altogether. The reason for this, Spiritualists believed, was that spirit forms were more easily seen in the darkness. Often they manifested as luminous apparitions or would cause things to move about in ways that would only be done if it could remain unseen. Debunkers and skeptics, of course, offered other reasons for this -- that darkened conditions would hide the deceptive practice of fraud.

The sitters were normally divided equally by gender and those who were skeptical were generally excluded. A circular arrangement of chairs worked best, normally around

Newspaper illustration of a home séance of the 1850s

a large table. Their hands were placed flat on the table, sometimes clasped together or merely with their fingers touching.

There were several unwritten rules for séances. Usually, no more than two or three séances were held in a week and they were to last for no more than two hours unless the spirits asked for an extension. Sitters were not allowed to touch the mediums or any of the manifested spirits, unless the spirits touched them first. This could cause the medium to snap out of her trance and a sudden return to consciousness caused by interfering with the medium could cause illness, insanity, or even death.

The phenomena reported at the séances varied greatly. Sitters often recognized the "arrival" of the spirits by a rush of cold air in the room, followed by rapping and tapping, knocking and perhaps strange lights, sounds, and voices. The phenomena would often intensify as the evening progressed. Simple noises and lights were often followed by elaborate messages from the beyond, usually coming directly through the medium.

In the most dramatic cases, some mediums, who claimed to be adept at spirit summoning, could cause ghosts to appear amid the sitters. In some of the most famous cases, like that of medium Florence Cook, spirits materialized who could touch, shake hands, and even embrace the sitters.

Another vital ingredient for a successful séance was appropriate music. Most sittings opened with hymns or prayers and on many reported occasions, the spirits chimed in with ghostly music and the creation of melodies through instruments like trumpets, horns, and tambourines.

The furnishings of the séance room were normally simple and made of wood. Small tables were often needed for tilting and tapping by the spirits and sitters were normally provided with basic wooden chairs.

Many physical mediums also made use of what were called "spirit cabinets," an enclosure where the medium could be segregated while entering the trance state. Many of the cabinets were actual wood enclosures, like what a telephone booth would look like in the future. The booths were usually closed with a curtain, although shutters or wooden doors were also used. Many spirit cabinets were simply a corner of a room, where a curtain was hung, blocking the view of the medium. The cabinets became the physical medium's work space and its purpose was to "attract and conserve spiritual forces." Paranormal researcher Hereward Carrington referred to a spirit cabinet as a "spiritual storage battery."

An early 1900s photograph of a typical séance room. In most instances, the "spirit cabinet" used for the séance was a curtained-off corner of the room where the medium could be sequestered.

Although spirit cabinets later became the standard for mediums, they were first introduced into the American Spiritualist movement by the Davenport Brothers in the middle 1850s. None of the earlier mediums in the movement, including the Fox sisters, ever used such a device. The idea behind the cabinet was to be able to section off the medium from the sitters so that they would be out of direct view when producing strange phenomena. This would prove to be both popular and astounding to audiences as the mediums were generally bound hand and foot in the cabinet while seemingly impossible phenomena manifested around them.

For fraudulent mediums, the spirit cabinet was a great gift. With only a limited amount of skill as an "escape artist," the medium could now amaze their sitters while hidden away behind curtains and wooden doors. Ropes could be easily shed and then an assortment of "spirit phenomena" could be produced. In most cases, the sitters would be invited to inspect the cabinet ahead of time so that they would be satisfied that no secret entrances or trap doors were present.

The medium would then enter the cabinet and be seated in a single chair, where he or she would be tied up to prevent fraud. Of course, the ropes were easily slipped and soon, the phenomena would begin. There were several ways for the mediums to collect their materials for the hoax. Often, "spirit forms" would appear, which were usually made of soft cloth or chiffon, which was very compressible. It could be easily secreted in the clothing and when unwrapped (or draped over the medium for a full materialization) would appear "ghostly" in the dim light. If the medium allowed himself or herself to be searched prior to the séance, the materials could also be smuggled in by the "cabinet attendant," who acted as the medium's bodyguard. Spiritualists said that this person was present to protect malicious intruders from touching the medium's ectoplasm (which could cause injury or death) but, in reality, they accomplices in the fraud.

The medium would be dressed completely in black and when they emerged from the cabinet with the "ghostly" cloth, it would appear to be moving on its own. The ball of material would be slowly unwound and in the near total darkness, would be eerily convincing. The medium could also drape his body in the material and then, while standing in front of the cabinet and moving the black curtains back and forth, he could create the illusion that the spirit form was moving sideways and up and down. Combined with music and chilling dramatics, it is no wonder that so many were convinced of the reality of the spirit cabinet séances.

The rise in the popularity of Spiritualism made it imperative that physical mediums put on quite a show at their séances. Objects flew about, music played, and spirits materialized, always to the delight of the participants. Another phenomenon was a physical manifestation called an "apport." An apport was any object that a medium could make appear. It might be a piece of jewelry, vase, flowers, fruit, or even a small pet. One favorite apport was a dove. At one spirit circle in Boston, no less than 11 people confirmed that a white dove inexplicably appeared in a closed room.

For believers, it was all wondrous work attributable to the spirit world. To skeptics, séances were nothing more than the product of trickery and deception, just like that employed by stage magicians, not the spirits of the dead. As séances participants and witnesses grew more sophisticated, many of the tricks used by fraudulent mediums were exposed as hoaxes. As physical mediums were forced to perform bigger stunts, more of them turned to trickery.

But not all of them were exposed as charlatans. There were always those whose demonstrations of psychic abilities were uncanny, beyond the explanations of the most hardened debunkers.

Mysterious photograph of well-known medium Agnes Guppy-Volckman (standing, on right)

One British medium who made a name for himself was William Stainton Moses, a Spiritualist and ordained minister. He was somehow able to make a bell move and ring by itself as it flew around the séance table in front of startled witnesses.

Another who baffled the skeptics was Agnes Guppy-Volckman, who also hailed from England but was well-known to American Spiritualists. At her séances, music would play and apports such as fruit or flowers would fall onto the table. Other times, a dog, cat, or butterflies would materialize. At one séance, a storm of small white feathers mysteriously showered down on the sitters. Debunkers made earnest efforts to determine how Agnes produced these phenomena, but to no avail. In 1869, when she was studied by an investigative committee, one member noticed that the bottom, or ends, of flower apports looked like they had been burned. When asked about it, Agnes replied that electricity from the spirit world was to blame. The oddities that surrounded her were made even more astounding by the fact that they all took place in brightly-lit rooms – never in a darkened séance chamber.

But there were far too many other mediums who failed spectacularly when it came to impressing their audiences. As physical effects and mysteriously appearing apports became seen as proof that the spirit world was at work, mediums felt the pressure to make sure that they happened. This, of course, brought about relentless accusations of fraud. When a great number of mediums were tested under more or less controlled conditions, the deceptions they attempted were easily exposed. So many deceptive mediums were uncovered that the credibility of all of them was called into question. By the end of the nineteenth century, far fewer mediums were manifesting apports and eventually, they stopped almost completely.

Perhaps more important to the question of apports was not so much how, but why? The demonstrations by physical mediums were raising important concerns about how much these demonstrations truly elevated spirituality. The majority of people who attended séances did so in order to witness contact with the other side. But was a person's spiritual growth really aided by trumpets floating in the air, bells ringing, and birds appearing out of nowhere? Were the critics correct: was it just good theater? Was there anything to be learned by such stunts? Even if psychic powers were genuine, what inspired lessons could be learned from flying tambourines?

Even some of the most ardent Spiritualists of the day grew critical of the emphasis on showmanship. One of those was Andrew Jackson Davis, the respected medium and trance reader. He eventually became so disenchanted with physical mediums that he broke ranks with those who stubbornly defended them.

Critics complained that if the spirit world had any real wisdom to impart, very little of it was being communicated at the séances that were being reported on in the newspapers. In addition, some claimed, if the discarnate communication was genuine, then how were men who never had schooling beyond third grade suddenly in possession of the "wisdom of the ages" now that they were on the other side? Time and time again, throughout the history of Spiritualism, debunkers found fault with messages from departed loved ones that seemed rather trivial and mundane. Even when the message contained information known only to the recipient, it was rarely profound or revelatory. Spirit messages were more like letters or telegrams; often they were simply greetings or assurances to loved ones left behind.

In the early years of Spiritualism, some mediums offered communications from famous historical figures that were now supposedly imparting great wisdom. One of the most popular spirits to contact was Benjamin Franklin. Hundreds of mediums claimed that they contacted him, but the messages were always generalizations or things already known. Isaac Post, who with his wife, Amy, befriended the Fox sisters, published a book in 1852 that allegedly contained spirit messages from George Washington and Thomas Jefferson. Not surprisingly, the book didn't reveal anything new. The public soon tired of this and the mediums correctly guessed that continuing along this line was going to put their reputations into question. Besides, more people preferred to hear from departed loved ones at the séance table, rather than famous men that they never knew.

TIPPING, TAPPING AND TABLE RAPPING

In the 1850s, it was not unusual to be invited to someone's house for tea and "table tipping," one of the most popular home circle entertainments of the day. Those who participated in this type of séance were asked to place their hands on a small table and then wait until the table moved, turned, or tilted of its own volition. Not unlike spirit rapping, messages were tilted in code that corresponded to the alphabet. Séance participants would often communicate directly to the table by asking questions that it answered through turns and tips.

Although the process of table tipping dated back to the days on ancient Rome, it became enormously popular in America during the early days of Spiritualism. Spiritualists explained that table tipping worked as a result of a form of psychic energy that emitted from each and every object in the world. Mediums were supposed to be especially sensitive to this energy.

But table tipping was just as controversial as any other alleged psychic power. In churches, ministers railed against it as demonic and many physicians warned of the danger to one's sanity from participating in supernatural activities.

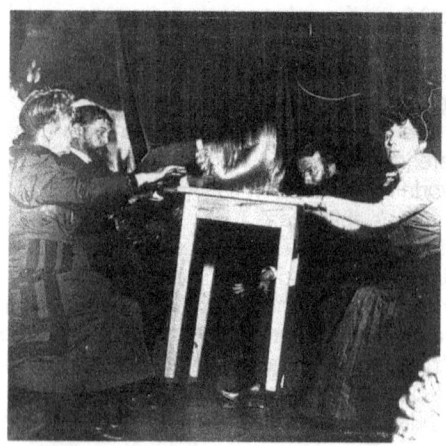

In 1853, famed British scientist Michael Faraday rejected Spiritualist explanations and announced his tests had produced the theory that table tipping had nothing to do with ghosts. The table moved thanks to the séance participants and their own "unconscious muscular action." While many scientists agreed with Faraday, table tipping had its defenders who insisted that the movements were generated by spirit forces or some kind of psychic energy.

There was also a phenomenon known as "automatic writing," a type of mediumship that became very popular in the nineteenth century. As interest in

Spiritualism grew and more people became involved in it, the tiresome and time-consuming method of knocking and rapping fell out of fashion and mediums began to produce messages through automatic writing. This was essentially writing that was done in an altered state of consciousness and was attributed to spirits of the dead. It was believed by some that the spirits literally manipulated the writing utensil in the hands of the medium to communicate, as the writer was 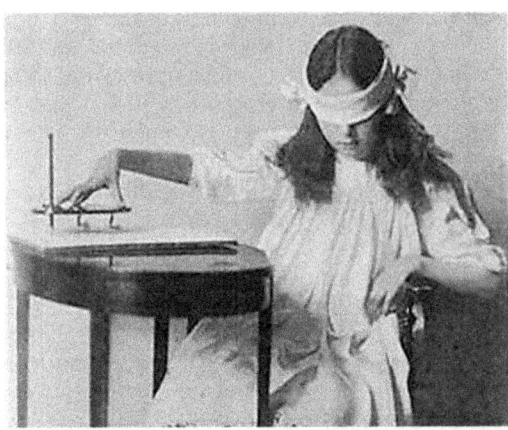 often unaware of what was being written and would often scrawl out text in handwriting that was markedly different than her own. Others believed that perhaps the spirits communicated by forming messages in the mind of the medium, which were reproduced on the page.

Through automatic writing, mediums claimed to produce messages from famous persons of history, deceased authors, and even classical music composers. In the 1850s, John Worth Edmonds, a judge on the New York Supreme Court, became interested in Spiritualism after the death of his wife. After a séance with the Fox sisters, he became intrigued with the movement and publicly acknowledged his support of it, despite the potential damage to his legal career. He became most interested in spirit communications and began encouraging a medium friend, Dr. George T. Baxter, to try and contact famous and literary figures that had passed over. In no time, Edmonds and his small circle of Spiritualists were receiving discourses from Francis Bacon and Emanuel Swedenborg, or as the Swedish seer insisted on spelling his name when communicating with the judge -- "Sweedonborg."

The material produced by these sessions sounded nothing like the earthly work done by either man and were described as pompous, artificial, slightly condescending in tone, and often sounded as though the entire personality of the author had been eliminated. As William James stated: "One curious thing about trance utterances is their generic similarity in different individuals ... It seems exactly as if one author composed more than half of the trance utterances, no matter by whom they are uttered."

Other forms of automatic writing went beyond mere messages and included drawings, paintings, and even musical pieces that were allegedly inspired by the dead. In some cases, mediums or individuals with little or no artistic training would suddenly feel compelled to paint or draw in distinctive, professional styles. They felt taken over by a spirit, as if another hand was guiding their own.

If séance participants wanted physical manifestations of spirit contact, there was also what was called "slate writing." It became another favorite form of psychical phenomena. The technique consisted of the medium and the attendee seated opposite each other at a table small enough that each could hold a corner or edge of a chalkboard slate, like those used in schools at the time. The slate was then pressed tightly against the underside of the table. Between the slate and the table, a small piece of chalk had been placed so that it could be used by the spirit writer. If a scratching noise was heard a short time later, it presumably meant that the spirit was writing something on the slate. When the process was completed, raps were heard, the slate was turned over and read and there would be a message on it – supposedly written by the spirits.

Although slate writing was often criticized, it remained popular throughout the nineteenth century. There is no question that it was susceptible to fraud, which was proven by scores of magicians in the early 1900s. Even so, there were an estimated 2,000 "writing mediums" all over America who claimed they wrote down, under spirit control, messages communicated to them from the other side.

One American medium named Henry Slade became particularly known for his slate-writing abilities. After working as a medium in the United States for 15 years, he went to perform in St. Petersburg, Russia. Among those who observed him was Helena Petrovna Blavatsky, the founder of the mystical Theosophical Society in 1875. She was impressed with Slade and called him a genius. She described his technique of using "double slates, sometimes tied and sealed together, while they either lay upon the table in full view of all…or held in a …hand, without the medium touching it."

Then, at the peak of his popularity, Slade became embroiled in allegations of fraud when debunkers found a previously written message on what was supposed to be a blank slate. In London, he faced criminal charges after a similar deception was discovered. He was found guilty, but the verdict was overturned on a technicality, and he wasted no time in getting out of England.

In 1885, Slade was tested by the Seybert Commission in Philadelphia and they declared him a fraud. The accusations of trickery claimed that Slade prepared writing on the slates in advance. Each was sketched with a generalized message that offered no evidence that they were produced by spirit phenomena. By the early part of the twentieth century, slate writing was thoroughly discredited and was rarely seen again.

Another form of spirit communication became a lasting favorite. In 1853, a French Spiritualist named Planchette invented a heart-shaped device made from wood with three small wheels on the bottom of it. The point of the heart held a small, downward-facing pencil. The idea was for the medium to place his or her hand on the planchette and then the pencil would write out messages from the spirit that was controlling the medium. When the planchette became available in America in 1868, thousands were sold. It was the forerunner of the immensely popular Ouija board. To what extent the messages obtained are from spirits or from unconscious activity by the person holding the planchette is still debated today.

Direct voice phenomena, like automatic writing, was supposedly produced by the spirits without the intervention of the medium. One favorite test of the debunkers was to have a medium fill her mouth with water while the discarnate entity spoke at the same time. Assuming there were no confederates creating a second voice, this was one way of determining whether or not the medium was engaged in trickery. In some documented cases, two distinct voices were heard, one presumed to come from the medium and one from the spirit. Several mediums confounded skeptics with "direct voice" phenomena, particularly in the days before recordings.

IT CAME FROM THE OTHER WORLD

One of the strangest of all the manifestations produced by physical mediums was "ectoplasm," an odd and elusive substance that was described in ways that made it sound pretty repulsive. It was a seemingly life-like substance, described as both solid and vaporous, that allegedly exuded from the body of spirit mediums. It was said to transform into shapes, rods, hands, limbs, faces, and even the entire bodies of spirits. Ectoplasm often appeared to be milky white in color and smelled like ozone, according to most reports. Coined by a French scientist named Charles Richet in 1894, the term ectoplasm came from the Greek words of "ekto" and "plasma," meaning "exteriorized substance." There were countless witnesses to the peculiar substance emanating from mediums during séances, but no one was certain about what its function truly was. According to one Spiritualist theory, it may have been the physical manifestation of some kind of essential energy that was then fully absorbed back into the medium's body.

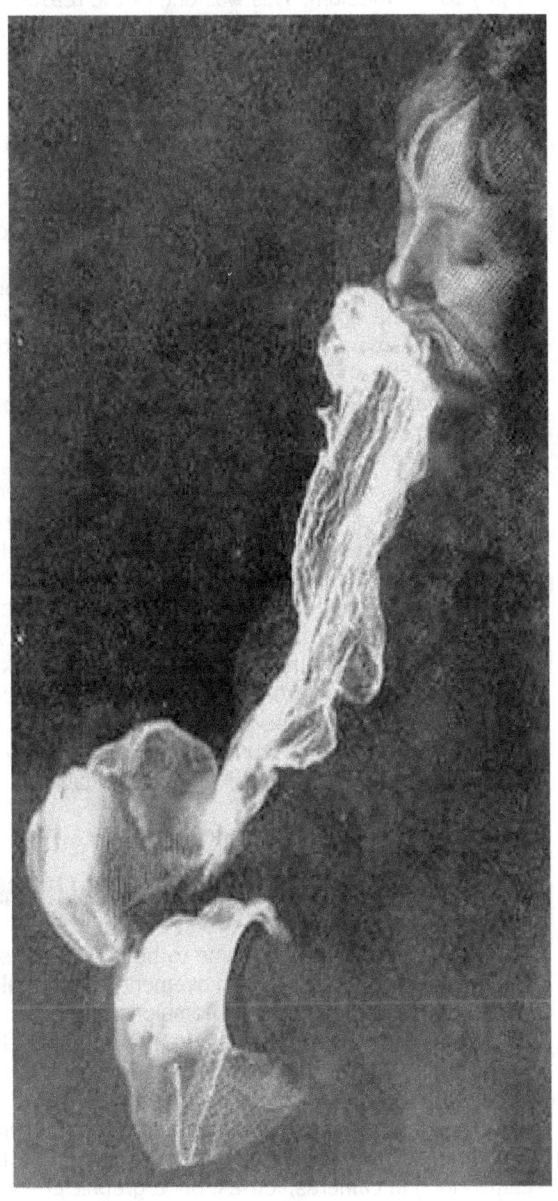

The emanations were warm to the touch and often were reported as thick, clotted, mucus-like substances. They could be rubbery and dough-like and emerged from a body orifice, such as the mouth, ears, or nose, but could also come from the eyes, navel, nipples, and even the vagina. Ectoplasm was also reported to disappear when exposed to light and would snap back violently. Touching the ectoplasm, or exposing it to light, was said to be able to cause injury to the medium. This was one of the reasons that mediums insisted that séances should take place in near darkness and that sitters should not approach the mediums or the emanations that formed.

Critics, of course, had their own explanations for the darkness and the avoidance of exposing ectoplasm to investigation: fraud. Analysis that had been carried out on samples of the substance yielded few clues. Most critics claimed that it was chewed paper, gauze, or fabric, which had likely been regurgitated. One investigator stated that the ectoplasm that he studied was nothing more than "butter muslin." He added: "I did see some produced in a séance once. It smelt appallingly of body odor, which wasn't surprising, considering where it was kept."

Investigator and magician Harry Houdini found most of the ectoplasm that he collected to be obvious trickery. He had seen mediums who used rubber bladders to blow ectoplasm from their mouths and had found others using cotton rubbed with goose grease and still others using strips of cloth that had been fashioned into odd shapes and veils. It was also easy, as Houdini knew from his own act, for the mediums to swallow all sorts of substances and then regurgitate them at will. Houdini had done the same trick with keys and needle and thread.

Most investigators concluded that séance attendees were so amazed by ectoplasm due to the power of suggestion. Strange and bizarre substances that appeared during a sitting would seem incredibly dramatic in a dimly lit séance chamber and once the lights came up, the ghostly emanations would have vanished. Who wouldn't be amazed?

Believers were absolutely convinced of the reality of the stuff and skeptics dismissed it all as humbug. Who was right and who was wrong? Hard to say, but Houdini once wrote: "Nothing has crossed my path to make me think that the Great Almighty will allow emanations from the human body of such horrible, revolting, vicious shapes, which like 'genie from the bronze bottle' ring bells, move handkerchiefs, wobble tables and do other flapdoodle stunts." The fad eventually faded away – but not without some notable exceptions, which will be featured later.

FACES OF THE DEAD
PHOTOGRAPHY AND THE SPIRITUALIST MOVEMENT

The practice of what came to be known as "spirit photography" was born during the heyday of the Spiritualist movement, which makes it nearly as old as the science of photography itself. The first anomalous photographs ever taken were assumed to be caused by unknown variables in the strange chemicals and new apparatus that photographers were then just learning to use. At the dawn of photography, it was nearly impossible to take photographs of people. With the exposure times of a half hour or more needed to impress an image on the paper films and coated plates of the day, it was impractical to expect anyone to sit still for so long. It was not until improvements came along in cameras, lenses, photographic chemicals, and developing processes that

Two "spirit photographs" producer by Boston engraver and photographer William Mumler in the 1860s. Each was accepted as genuine by the sitters, but Mumler would go on to earn a rather questionable reputation as a fraud.

exposure times were reduced to a matter of seconds instead of dozens of minutes. By this time, people were flocking to the portrait studios to have their images immortalized in time.

Interest in the Spiritualist movement had been on the rise since the announcements of spirit rappings at the home of the Fox family of New York in 1848. Of course, no photographs were taken of the Fox sister's séances at the Fox home or at Leah's home in Rochester, because indoor photography was impossible for years afterward. But the days of spirit photography were coming.

In those days, the photographer had to first prepare a plate by coating it with collodion, bathing it in silver nitrate, and then taking the photo while the plate was still wet. Each new exposure was an exciting event, but imagine how excited W. Campbell of Jersey City must have been when he achieved what is considered to be the first "spirit photograph." At the American Photographic Society meeting of 1860, he displayed a test photograph that he had taken of an empty chair. There had been no one else in the studio at the time, but when the plate was developed, it showed the image of a small boy seated in the chair. Campbell was never able to produce any other photographs of this sort and, thanks to this, it would not be until the following year that the real history of spirit photography began.

On October 5, 1861, in a photographic studio at 258 Washington Street in Boston, an engraver and amateur photographer named William Mumler was developing some experimental self-portraits that he had taken and was startled to find that the image of a ghostly young woman appeared in one of the photos with him. He was said to have recognized the young woman as a cousin who had passed away 12 years before. He later recalled that while posing for the portrait, he had experienced a trembling sensation in his right arm that left him particularly exhausted. The photograph attracted great attention and it was examined by not only Spiritualists but by some of the leading photographers of the day. They all came to accept the fact that, as Mumler stated: "This photograph was taken by myself, of myself, and there was not a living soul in the room besides myself." Mumler was soon overwhelmed by public demand for his photographs and he gave up his regular job as an engraver to devote himself entirely to spirit photography.

William Black, a leading Boston photographer and the inventor of the acid nitrate bath for photographic plates, was one of the professionals who investigated Mumler and his methods. After sitting for Mumler in his studio, Black examined his camera, plate, and bath and kept his eye on the plate from the moment its preparations began until it was locked into the camera. After his portrait was taken, Black removed it from the camera and took it into the darkroom himself, where, as it developed, he was stunned to see the image of a man, leaning over his shoulder. Black was convinced that Mumler was the genuine article and could somehow entice the spirits to appear on film.

Others were, of course, not so sure.

Mumler had never been interested in the spirits or Spiritualism prior to his first alleged spirit photograph and his steep charge of $5 per photograph began to arouse suspicions that he was just in it for the money. He became the object of great controversy and eventually moved to New York, where he then began charging $10 for photographs. His critics howled once more. Mumler had many supporters, though. One of them was U.S. Court of Appeals Judge John Edmonds, who had originally come to Mumler's studio with intentions to expose him as a fraud, but left convinced that he could actually conjure up genuine psychic photos.

In 1863, Dr. Child of Philadelphia reported that Mumler was willing to allow him to thoroughly investigate the methods of his spirit photos and, as he said, find a rational explanation for the mystery. He permitted Child to watch all his operations in and out of the darkroom, and allowed him to examine his apparatus. Dr. Child displayed the pictures made at the time, while he and several friends watched the entire process, from the plate cleaning to the fixing. He took the precaution to mark each plate with a diamond before it was used and yet on each one of them was a spirit image. Child had failed completely to discover any human agent that was responsible for the formation of the spirit picture. Each of them differed considerably from one another and Child could not come up with a way to duplicate them.

However, the "extras," as they came to be called, in Mumler's photographs did not amaze everyone. After much controversy, pressure from city officials led to him being arrested and charged with fraud. But the testimony of several leading New York residents, including famed Broadway producer Jeremiah Gurney, who affirmed that as a professional photographer he had never seen anything like the images that were produced, led to Mumler being exonerated and his case dismissed.

Later, however, it turned out that the courts may have been a little too hasty when they dropped the charges against William Mumler.

According to an article in *Scientific American* magazine in 1902, Mumler may have been cleverer than anyone ever gave him credit for --- and a much bigger fraud. Experiments in duplicating spirit photos that were done long after Mumler was producing his controversial images discovered a simple way of creating spectral images that would have passed inspection by those who examined Mumler's plates and apparatus at the time. This method involved making a very thin positive image on glass that was the same size as the plate that was to be used in producing the spirit photo. The glass was then placed in the holder where the plate would later be placed, as well. With the glass in position, the plate could be inserted under the watchful eye of the examiner and the photograph produced. With the weak positive superimposed, the ghostly image would appear, along with the sitter, on the negative plate. In this way, the plates would never be tampered with and in examinations like those conducted by Dr. Child, his mark would appear on the plate that was used and he would never assume that anything out of the ordinary was taking place.

Could this have been Mumler's secret? If we assume that fraud may have been involved with the creation of his photos, then yes, it could have been. But what about those photos that contained the images of loved ones that Mumler knew nothing about? Could his research have been so thorough that he delved into the private lives --- and photographs --- of those who made appointments so far in advance that he could obtain photos of dead relatives that would then appear in his spirit photographs? And what of those who came to him without an appointment and yet their loved ones still managed to appear on film? Was it wishful thinking that the extras appeared to be so familiar? Perhaps --- or perhaps not.

Other photographers, both amateur and professional, soon began to appear, eager to capitalize on the success of William Mumler. In America and Britain, new studios began to open and the photographers also began to call themselves "mediums," claiming the ability to make dead appear in photographs was just as relevant as those who contacted the spirits at séances. Spirit Photography became wildly popular and literally thousands of dollars were made from those who came to have their portraits taken. One photographer, William Hope, claimed to take more than 2,500 spirit photographs during a period of about two decades.

William Hope was one of the premiere spirit photographers of the era and was considered by believers and supporters to be a true master of the art of producing spirits on ordinary photographic plates. Critics believed him to be a clever fraud and while he weathered many accusations, he was never caught tricking anyone – but largely because of the controversy that surrounded the attempts to expose him.

Hope was born in Crewe, England in 1863 and as a young man, went to work as a carpenter. His talent for capturing the spirits in photographs allegedly came about around 1905 when he and a friend were taking turns photographing one another. In a photo that was taken by Hope, there was an extra that appeared in it and, as it turned out, the extra in question was the deceased sister of the photograph's subject.

Not long after this incident, a group of six people organized a Spiritualist hall in Crewe for creating spirit photographs. The group became renowned as the "Crewe Circle" with William Hope as its leader. During their early efforts, the circle destroyed all the negatives of the photos they took for fear of being suspected of witchcraft. However, when Archbishop Thomas Colley, a lifelong enthusiast of both the supernatural and Spiritualism, joined the circle, they began to make their work public.

Ironically, Hope's first brush with exposure as a fraud came when Archbishop Colley arranged his first sitting. Reports say that Hope doctored the photograph with the wrong spirit extra, substituting another elderly woman for Colley's mother. When Hope tried to confess his fraud to Colley, the other man dismissed his confession

One of William Hope's numerous "spirit photographs." The hundreds that he produced were all of similar quality.

as "nonsense"--- he would recognize his mother when he saw her and the extra in the photo was certainly his mother, he stated. To prove his case, he even put a notice in the local newspaper and asked that all of those who remembered his mother should call at the rectory. No fewer than 18 people selected Hope's mistake from among several others and said that it definitely showed the ghost of the late Mrs. Colley. The fast was that it wasn't her, but it became impossible to find anyone to admit it.

In February 1922, Hope was nearly exposed again but this time, the attempt almost backfired on the accuser and there remain some questions about the incident to this day. By this time, Hope had moved to London and had established himself as a professional medium. The Society for Psychical Research (SPR) decided to investigate Hope's claims and sent a new member, Harry Price, to look into them. The young Price had a good working knowledge of conjuring and would later make a name for himself as one of Britain's leading ghost hunters. During the investigation, Price claimed to detect evidence of trickery by Hope but questions immediately arose as to whether it was Price, and not Hope, who had tampered with the photographic plates.

Price told a different story of the incident and blamed his problems with the Spiritualist community for the controversy. Even though he had recently joined the SPR, Price had already exposed several fraudulent mediums, earning him the dislike of much of the community. During the sitting, which was organized with hymn singing and prayers like a standard séance, Hope and Price went into the adjoining dark room. Price examined the photographic slide that Hope planned to use and he secretly impressed 12 small punctures into it with a needle. He then was asked to open a packet of plates that he had brought with them. These plates had come from the Imperial Dry Plate Co. and had been imprinted (at Prices' suggestion) with their trademark in the corner. The trademark would then appear on the negative of whatever picture was developed. Price loaded two plates into the slide and then Hope asked for the slide.

As he took it from Price's hand, Harry watched Hope's movements very carefully, which was hard to do in the dull, red darkness of the room. Very quickly, in one smooth movement, Hope placed the dark slide into the left breast pocket of his coat and then, apparently, pulled it back out again. Price knew that the slide had been changed but sat down for the photograph to be taken anyway. When it was over, he refused to sign the plates, as Hope wanted him to, and as he examined the slide, he discovered that his 12 needle marks had "mysteriously" vanished. It was clearly not the same slide that he had given to Hope to use. He did not accuse Hope of a swindle on the spot, fearing that his evidence of deception would be destroyed, but took away two photographs that had been taken of Price, one of which contained a beautiful female "extra," but neither plate bore the Imperial Dry Plate trademark. Hope had managed to switch the plates, as well. Price knew they were not the same type of plates that he had given to Hope to use, as they were a different thickness, weight, and color and were "fast" plates, while the ones that Hope gave back to him were "slow" ones.

In the May issue of the *Journal of the London SPR*, Price published a report about the incident under the title "Cold Light on Spiritualistic Phenomena" and it was later reprinted as a separate booklet. Immediately, he was attacked from the Spiritualist camp. Price and his methods were denounced and he was accused of switching the plates himself in a plot to discredit the medium. Many prominent Spiritualists, including scientists who were sympathetic to the cause, criticized Price. Spiritualism's spokesperson in England, Sir Arthur Conan Doyle, featured Hope in his book *The Case for Spirit Photography* and harshly spoke against Harry Price. Sir Oliver Lodge, though, who was a proponent of Spiritualism, believed that Hope was a fraud and wrote to Price: "I don't see how your proofs of Hope's duplicity could be more complete."

More than 11 years after this incident, the widow of a man who worked for Hope admitted in an article that after Price's séance, her husband went through Hope's luggage and "found in a suitcase a flash lamp with a bulb attachment, some cut-out photographic heads and some hairs." Unfortunately, these devastating facts were suppressed in 1922 and Price would later comment that if not for this suppression, his entire relationship with Conan Doyle could have been preserved. "This vital information would have ended my controversy with Sir Arthur," he said. "Incidentally, it would have ended Hope too!"

Oddly, not all the sittings that Hope arranged had such questionable outcomes. Throughout his career, Hope gained support from many important figures and was featured prominently in a book about survival after death by Reverend Charles Tweedale, who owned a haunted house in the town of Otley in Yorkshire. In his writings, Tweedale, gave many accounts of Hope's prowess as a spirit photographer, stating that there was no fraud evident in most Hope's cases in which people called upon him unannounced, even with secret identities, and obtained clearly recognizable spirit images. One case was that of Mrs. Hortense Leverson, who came to Hope and was given a psychic photograph of her recently deceased husband, Major Leverson, who had been on the staff of the War Office. She was absolutely convinced that the photograph was legitimate. She, along with dozens (perhaps hundreds) of others, believed that Hope was genuine.

William Hope died on March 7, 1933, leaving many mysteries behind. Was he genuine – or was he merely a fraud? No one can say for sure and like so many of the other enigmas connected to the practice of spirit photography, this one also remains unsolved.

In many cases, the answers are not as mysterious. Typically, in spirit photographs, ghostly faces appeared, floating above and behind the living subjects. In others, fully-formed spirits would appear, usually draped in white sheets. Unfortunately, the methods of producing such images were simple. The fraudulent photographers became adept at doctoring their work, superimposing images on plates with living sitters, adding ghostly apparitions, and double exposures. The appearance of the fully-formed apparition was even easier. Many cameras demanded that the subject of the photo remain absolutely still, sometimes for periods of up to one minute, all the while, the shutter of the camera remains open. During this time, it was very simple for the photographer's assistant to quietly appear behind the sitter, dressed in appropriate "spirit attire." The assistant remained in place for a few moments and then ducked back out of the photo again. On the finished plate, it seemed a transparent "figure" had made an appearance. This could be done with cameras that required even an exposure time of a few seconds with an assistant appearing for only a second or two from behind a curtain.

This type of "trick photo" was first mentioned in photography journals in 1856. Ten years later, Sir David Brewster recalled the technique when he saw some of the early spirit photos that were produced. He remembered another photo that he had seen of a young boy who had been sitting on a step near a doorway and who had apparently gotten up and left about halfway through the exposure. The result was that the seated image was transparent in the finished photo. Brewster wrote: "The value and application of this fact did not at first present itself to me, but after I had contrived the lenticular stereoscope I saw that such transparent pictures might be used for the various purposes of entertainment." Ghost and spirit photographs and stereographs were sold commercially in America through the 1860s and 1870s, but were nothing more than a parlor novelty and were never meant to be taken as genuine spirit photographs.

Other methods of obtaining fraudulent photographs were used, as well. Prepared plates and cut films were often switched and substituted by sleight of hand tricks, replacing those provided by the investigator. And while this might have fooled a credulous member of the public, sleight of hand maneuvers and instances of assistants prancing through photos draped in sheets did not convince hardened and skeptical investigators that the work of the spirit photographers was credible or genuine. However, in case after case, investigators walked away stumped as to how the bizarre images managed to appear on film. For every fraud who was exposed, there was at least one other photographer who was never caught cheating. More than a century later, many incidents with spirit photographs are as baffling now as they were then.

Unfortunately, that wasn't usually the case, though. Around the same time that William Mumler was going on trial for fraud in New York, a popular spirit photographer named Frederick Hudson emerged on the scene in London. Mrs. Samuel Guppy, a well-known medium of the day, brought him to the public's attention.

One of Frederick Hudson's entertaining -- although obviously fake -- spirit photographs.

A famous professional photographer named John Beattie eventually investigated Hudson in 1873. He carried out a series of experiments that were later published in the *British Journal of Photography*. At that time, Hudson was charging a steep fee for his photos, but only with the understanding that he could not be blamed if nothing unusual appeared, which often happened.

In his article, Beattie described how, with a friend, he had examined the glass room in Hudson's garden where the experiments were to take place, the operating and developing room with its yellow light and porcelain baths, the 10 x 8-inch camera with its 6-inch lens, and all the machinery involved. He also maintained that he had marked the photographic plate to be used and watched it being coated and prepared.

For the first photograph that Hudson took, using an exposure of about one minute, Beattie sat as the subject in profile to the background and Hudson's daughter (acting as the medium) stood next to him. No extra appeared in the photo. For the next experiment, Beattie wrote: "All was the same except that the medium sat behind the background. On the picture being developed, a sitting figure beside myself came out in front of me and between the background and myself. I am sitting in profile in the picture -- the figure is in a three-quarter position -- in front of me, but altogether between me and the background. The figure is draped in black, with a white colored plaid over the head, and is like both a brother and a nephew of mine. This last point I do not press because the face is like that of a dead person and under lighted."

Beattie continued: "In my last trial -- all, if possible, more strictly attended to then before, and in the same place relative to me -- there came out a standing female figure, clothed in black skirt, and having a white-colored, thin linen drapery something like a shawl pattern, upon her shoulders, over which a mass of black hair loosely hung. The figure is in front of me and, as it were, partially between me and the camera."

Beattie had initially assumed that Hudson was in some way faking the photographs but was no longer convinced of this. He was sure that the figures were not double exposures, had not been projected in some way, and were not the result of mirrors or even the result of images that had been manipulated onto the plates during the developing process.

What he did not take into consideration, though, was that the images could have been on the plates all along -- that the photographer had switched Beattie's plates for "trick plates." This seems to have been the standard operating procedure for many of the so-called spirit photographers of the day, as was described in the *Scientific American* article referenced earlier. Many spirit photographers, including a Mr. Parkes, who produced many psychic images, even allowed themselves to be observed while working on the plates. Parkes, for instance, had an aperture cut into the wall of his darkroom so that investigators could see inside while he went through the developing process. The problem was that the investigators had no idea just what plates he was actually developing.

In 1874, a French photographer named E. Buguet opened a studio and began a career capturing the spirits on film. Most of his photographs were of famous people, most of who claimed to recognize deceased loved ones and family members as extras. This did not stop him from being arrested for fraud and tried by the French government. He admitted deception but even then, there were many who refused to accept his confession as genuine, claiming that he had been paid off by the church to plead guilty. In his confession, he stated that his photographs were created by double exposure. He would dress up his assistants to play the part of a ghost, or would dress up a doll in sheet. This figure, along with a stock of heads, was seized by the police when they raided his studio. Buguet was fined and sentenced to a year in prison. Even after this, his supporters continued to insist his photographs were real. Reverend Stainton Moses, the famous medium, was convinced that at least some of Buguet's spirit photographs were authentic. He said that the prosecution of the case was tainted by religious officials, that the judge was biased, and that Buguet must have been bribed or terrorized to confess.

The 1870s saw the first general acceptance that there might be something credible to at least some aspects of spirit photography. Several references to it appeared in issues of the *British Journal of Photography* and in other periodicals of the time. In the 1890's, J. Traille Taylor, the editor of the Journal, reviewed the history of spirit photography and detailed the methods by which fraudulent photos were sometimes produced. He approached the phenomenon as a true skeptic, not immediately disbelieving it, but studying it in a scientific manner. He used a stereoscopic camera and noted that the psychically produced images did not appear to be in three dimensions. He used his own camera and he and his assistants did all the developing and photographing themselves. Strangely, they were still able to produce mysterious results.

In 1891, the practice of spirit photography gained more credibility when Alfred Russell Wallace, the co-developer of the theory of evolution, stated that he believed spirit photography should be studied scientifically. He later wrote about his own investigations and included a statement that he believed the possibility of it was real. He did not feel that just because some of the photos that had been documented were obviously fraudulent, that all of them could be dismissed as hoaxes.

Despite such notable interest in the field, little was heard of spirit photography (outside of Spiritualist circles) for many years. In 1911, spirit photography entered the mainstream with the publication of the book *Photographing the Invisible* by James Coates. It covered dozens of cases of spirit photographs in detail and it was later revised and expanded in 1921. It remains one of the most comprehensive books on the subject written during this period and it managed to bring spirit photography into the mainstream for the first time.

Following the publication of the book, several noteworthy articles appeared on spirit photography, including one by James Hyslop, a Columbia University professor. He wrote an introduction to a series of experiments carried out by Charles Cook of two American spirit photographers, Edward Wyllie of Los Angeles and Alex Martin of Denver. Cook did extensive work with the two men in 1916, providing them with his own plates and having them developed by a commercial studio. In this way, he eliminated any opportunity that the two men might have had to doctor the images. Cook concluded that the photographs submitted were genuine but in these cases thought the name "psychic photography" better matched the phenomenon. He believed that the two men produced the images through some psychical means, rather than by actually photographing ghosts.

In addition to the photos created by Wyllie and Martin, there were a number of spirit photographs that appeared in those days for which critics could find no plausible explanation. Despite the failure to debunk many of these photographs, the reality of them was not accepted by the scientists of the day. As it is today, many them simply refused to examine the data and assumed that fraud was more than adequate to explain the findings. One of the few exceptions was Sir William Crookes, the distinguished chemist and physicist. For 30 years, he was a member of the Royal Society and was known for his discovery of thallium, his studies of photography, and other scientific work. At the invitation of several skeptical members of the Royal Society, he agreed to take on a six-month study of psychic phenomenon. Instead of just six months, though, his work continued for years and he came to the conclusion that much of what he studied (including psychic photographs) was genuine. He presented his findings in both book and article form but soon became discouraged when he failed to convince most of his scientific colleagues of the reality of what he was doing. He endured ridicule and disdain, but never wavered from his beliefs. More than 25 years later, he would maintain that spirit photography could, and did, exist.

As time passed and photographic techniques and equipment became more advanced, researchers began to discover that some of the photographs being taken in allegedly haunted locations could not be explained away as film flaws and tricks of light. Gone were the days of phony photos that were taken by so-called spirit mediums in studios. They had been replaced by often accidental photos that defied all logic.

The famous Brown Lady of Raynham Hall photograph, taken in 1936

One of the most convincing photographs was the famous image of the "Brown Lady" of Raynham Hall in Norfolk, England. The photo was taken by Captain Provand, a professional photographer, who was taking snapshots of the house for Britain's *Country Life* magazine in September 1936. His assistant, Indre Shira, actually saw the apparition coming down the staircase and directed Provand to take the photo, even though the other man saw nothing at the time. Experts have examined the resulting image many times, although no explanation for it has ever been given.

So, what are we to make of the reality of spirit photographs?

The emergence of modern science in the first half of the 1800s had helped to dispel the superstitions of the past but scientists were unable to connect the mysterious evidence obtained by spirit photography to the progress they were making in other fields. Because of this, most of the investigation and research into the field was carried out by Spiritualists, who believed that far too many of the photographs were genuine, thus validating their often unpopular beliefs. The debunkers of today simply point to the usually ridiculous images that were produced as proof that the entire field was corrupt. But was it really?

There are still many who believe that the ability to photograph the unseen is no more improbable than the discovery of latent images was back in the early 1800s. Attitudes toward aspects of the supernatural continue to undergo radical changes and move slowly toward acceptance, even though these types of photos still involve an infringement on scientific assumptions and rules. Despite this, evidence of a common ground between psychic phenomena and physics continues to grow and the times grows ever closer when perhaps the two will come together and explain just how spirit photographs are produced.

Spirit photography, like séances, table tipping, and ectoplasm were all part of a movement that came into its own in the 1850s and as time passed, many hoped this bizarre bit of American nonsense would simply fade away. Just as it is today, fads quickly came and went in the nineteenth century, too. Americans soon grew bored with the same demonstrations of the same psychic phenomena. This was the reason that mediums found it necessary to progress from spirit rapping to the more elaborate séances that included automatic writing, trance speaking, levitations, and spirit manifestations in the first place.

By the early 1860s, Spiritualism was starting to lose some of its appeal and seemed to be – as many hoped – finally disappearing for good. But national politics and war would soon intervene and would bring a renewed and even greater interest in the Spiritualist movement.

4. MEDIUMS IN THE WHITE HOUSE
HOW ABRAHAM LINCOLN AND THE CIVIL WAR SAVED SPIRITUALISM

Spiritualism was born among the religious and reform movements of the Burnt-Over District and from the start, many of its adherents had aligned themselves with another cause embedded in the region – the abolitionist movement. By the 1850s, the nation was moving in an incredibly divisive and treacherous direction over the institution of slavery. Slavery in America was a way of life that no one could truly defend and yet the Southern economy had been built upon the backs of its slaves. While the North became more industrialized, the South remained stagnant, entrenched in their farms and plantations. Throughout the first half of the nineteenth century, abolitionists in the North had become increasingly influential. In 1831, William Lloyd Garrison began publishing *The Liberator,* a radical abolitionist newspaper, in Boston. Garrison, in addition to his interest in Spiritualism, was unequaled in his passion against the horrors of slavery.

Then there was the amazing impact of "serious Spiritualist" Harriet Beecher Stowe's novel *Uncle Tom's Cabin*. It sold more than 300,000 copies in 1852, the year it was published, while another million and a half unauthorized copies were also in print. Its portrayal of the evils of slavery was so emotionally effective that it touched the hearts – and enraged the passions-- of millions of people in the North. The book had more power than Stowe, or any of the abolitionists, could have imagined. Some years after the Civil War began, President Abraham Lincoln met Mrs. Stowe for the first time. He smiled kindly as he shook her hand and then sighed softly, "So, you're the little lady who started this war."

In October 1859, a militant abolitionist named John Brown and a band of followers staged a failed raid on the federal arsenal at Harper's Ferry, Virginia. Their plan was to arm the slaves of the South and start a bloody insurgency. But Brown's plan failed and he was hanged in December. In the North, he became a martyr to the abolitionist cause.

On the gallows, Brown prophesized that slavery would only be eradicated by bloodshed. Sadly, his prediction was proven correct within a few years.

Several Spiritualist mediums also reported that they had experienced ominous visions of a terrible war ahead. Increasingly, there was talk of secession in the South. Southerners insisted that they needed slavery for their economy to survive. In the North, the abolitionists were equally committed to ending the "evil institution." It appeared that no compromise could be reached and there were grave doubts that the Union could be preserved. The nation was in danger of coming apart.

In November 1860, Abraham Lincoln was elected as the sixteenth president of the United States. The victory did not sit well in the south, even though he had pledged not to intervene in states where slavery already existed. But there was such anger at Lincoln – and at a Union that was meddling in the rights of the individual states – that South Carolina took the step that all had feared. In the autumn of 1860, it became the first state to secede from the United States. Other Southern states quickly followed. By February 1861, the Confederate States of America formed and Jefferson Davis was named as its president. In April 1861, the Confederate artillery fired on Fort Sumter, a federal fortress in Charleston harbor. The Civil War had finally begun.

Abraham Lincoln – the American President with the deepest connection to the spirit world

Although it has been largely ignored by traditional historians and biographers, there is no other president in our history that is more closely connected to the supernatural than Abraham Lincoln. Poet Walt Whitman, who witnessed the horrors of war first-hand, once wrote to describe Lincoln, "More than any other man in history, the foundation of his character was mystic." It cannot be disputed – no matter how many have tried – that Spiritualism, precognitive dreams, visions, premonitions, and clairvoyance all played important roles in Lincoln's life – even when it came to managing the country during the years of the Civil War.

Lincoln was born on February 12, 1809, in a small log cabin in Hardin County, Kentucky, where his father, Thomas, worked as a farmer and carpenter. When he was seven years old, the family moved to Indiana. By then, Abraham was old enough to start taking on family chores. One chore in particular, milling corn into meal, may have been responsible for an event that suddenly led to Lincoln's psychic abilities when he was a boy. Hurrying to finish his work one evening at a mill about two miles from his house, Lincoln snapped the whip on the horse that was turning the grindstone. The horse kicked backwards and knocked the boy to the ground. He lay unconscious and bleeding for an unknown amount of time before the mill owner discovered him and summoned his father. Thomas rushed the boy home, but there was little hope that he would survive the accident.

Abraham remained still and silent for hours. Several times, his family feared that he had died. Then suddenly, he seemed to recover. If there were any lingering after effects or damage, they were never reported. Some believe that the blow initiated the psychic abilities that Lincoln would manifest throughout his life. Some believe that trauma to the head can cause a rerouting of the neurological impulses to the brain, perhaps even awakening dormant areas of the brain where psychic abilities manifest themselves. Emotional issues sometimes accompany such accidents and some believe it might also explain the melancholia that Lincoln suffered from as well.

A year after the accident, Abraham was at his mother's bedside when she died of "milk sickness." His father remarried a kind widow named Sarah Bush Johnston, who had three young children of her own. For Abraham, she became a treasured friend, in whom he found lifelong love, support, and encouragement. The affection was mutual and Sarah encouraged him to read and find a profession that would make him happy. Abraham became a voracious reader and when his family moved to Illinois, he accompanied them and made a name for himself splitting rails and hiring out to neighboring farms. By the time he was 16, he stood over six feet tall and was known for his incredible strength. But he had no desire to be a farmer, which caused Abraham and his father to grow apart.

In 1831, he left home for good, traveling first to New Orleans on a Mississippi River flatboat. For the first time in his life, Lincoln witnessed large number of slaves in chains, working on the docks and being ill-treated. The sight profoundly disturbed him and it remained with him for the rest of his life.

After traveling back north, Lincoln settled in the small Illinois village of New Salem. He lived there for six years as a postmaster and as a clerk at the general store. After serving in the short-lived Back Hawk War, he returned to New Salem, took over ownership of the store and worked as a surveyor. By now, his lifelong belief in predestination was firmly set. He believed that fate guided each man's path and what happened was meant to be. Although raised by Baptist parents, Lincoln was never comfortable with traditional belief. He gravitated toward the free-thinking philosophers who gathered at his store, where they debated the likelihood of miracles and the reality of free will versus destiny. Lincoln's friends stated that he would often become so quiet that he seemed to be in a trance, which seems likely given his later examples of precognition and his belief in signs and portents.

Lincoln ran for a seat in the Illinois State Legislature, studied law, and was soon admitted to the Illinois Bar. His prospects were on the rise. However, after a tragic love affair with a young woman that ended with her death from typhoid in 1835, he fell into a deep depression. His law partner, William Herndon, would later state that her death "exerted a mystic, guiding influence throughout [Lincoln's] life."

Two years later, Lincoln's place in Illinois politics began to rise. In 1837, he moved to the state capital of Springfield to practice law. There he met and courted the pretty and socially prominent Mary Todd. She was the high-spirited daughter of one of the city's most successful bankers and merchants. Lincoln, on the other hand, was a rough-hewn backwoodsman-turned-lawyer and a gangly, awkward-looking giant. But he was a gentle, courteous, impeccably honest man with a penchant for humorous stories and laughter. As a young attorney, he quickly caught the eye of the most powerful politicians in the state and won the heart of Mary Todd.

Lincoln's relationship with Mary flourished and they soon found themselves on the invitation list for the best parties in the city. Under the surface, though, Mary was moody and hot-tempered, which may have led to the couple's brief separation. In 1842, however, Lincoln overcame his fear of marriage and the two were wed. A year later, their first son, Robert, was born.

Arguments, long absences when Lincoln was on the law circuit, and Mary's explosive temper frequently caused problems in the marriage. Today, Mary would likely be diagnosed and treated for bipolar disorder, but in the nineteenth century, such ailments were unknown. Her wild fluctuations in mood were attributed to her temperament. It was just the way that she was and her friends and family accepted it as her eccentricity. Many believe that Mary may have also been endowed with psychic gifts. However, she was emotionally needy, required constant attention and could not tolerate being ignored, especially by her husband. But he also had to deal with his own melancholy and their depressive personalities seemed to feed off one another. Lincoln was dealing with not only a troubled marriage, but a growing family and his law and political careers at the same time. Unhappy or not, the Lincolns remained devoted to one another and no one would have ever suggested that they were not deeply in love.

In 1846, the Lincolns' second son, Edward, was born. His birth drew the couple closer, but his death shattered their happiness in 1850 when he succumbed to tuberculosis. Their third son, William, was born later that year in December. A fourth son, Thomas, nicknamed Tad, was born in 1853.

As Lincoln became more important in Illinois politics, he served one term in Congress. Meanwhile, the country was sliding toward a constitutional crisis over the issues of state's rights and the demand to abolish slavery. In 1850, the Fugitive Slave Act made it possible for vigilante groups to seize free blacks as runaway slaves with no legal ramifications. Then, in 1854, the Kansas-Nebraska Act was passed. These were laws meant to preserve the Union by not interfering with slavery where it already existed, but preventing it from expansion. Many in the North who wanted slavery abolished everywhere in the country were enraged, and that led to the creation of the Republican Party. Its compromise platform was that slavery would not be allowed in new states and territories. The nation was bitterly divided.

Lincoln was considered a moderate in the presidential election of 1860. He had carved out a position that he hoped would appeal to both the North and the South. With radical tensions running high, he carefully tried to walk the fragile middle ground. In November, Lincoln was elected president. But while Lincoln had won the day, he had fared poorly in the popular vote. He had soundly defeated the other candidates in the Electoral College, but had won just 40 percent of the vote among the people. He had become a minority president with no support at all in the southern states.

And it was obvious to everyone that America was coming apart.

On the night of the election, Lincoln returned home in the early morning hours. He went into his bedroom for some much-needed rest and collapsed onto a couch. Nearby was a large bureau with a mirror on it and Lincoln stared for a moment at his reflection in the glass. His face appeared angular, thin, and tired. Several of his friends suggested that he grow a beard, which would hide the narrowness of his face and give him a more "presidential" appearance. Lincoln pondered this for a moment and then experienced what many would term a "vision" --- an odd, mystical glimpse that Lincoln would come to believe had prophetic meaning.

In the mirror glass, he saw that his face had two separate, yet distinct, images. The tip of one nose was about three inches away from the tip of the other one. The vision vanished but appeared again a few moments later. It was clearer this time and Lincoln realized that one of the faces was much paler than the other, almost with the coloring of death. The vision disappeared again and Lincoln initially dismissed the whole thing to his lack of sleep.

The next morning, he told Mary of the strange vision and attempted to conjure it up again in the days that followed. The faces always returned to him and while Mary never saw them, she believed her husband when he said that he did. She also believed she knew the significance of the vision. The healthy face was her husband's "real" face and indicated that he would serve his first term as president. The pale, ghostly image of the second face, however, was a sign that he would be elected to a second term --- but would not live to see its conclusion.

At first, Lincoln refused to accept the incident as anything other than an imperfection in the glass, but later, the vision would come back to haunt him during the turbulent days of war. It was not Lincoln's only brush with prophecy either. One day, shortly before the election, he spoke to some friends as they were discussing the possibilities of Civil War. "Gentlemen," he said to them, "you may be surprised and think it strange, but when the doctor here was describing a war, I distinctly saw myself, in second sight, bearing an important part in that strife."

Throughout his career, especially in his leadership during the war, Lincoln remained a fatalist, seeing himself as destiny's tool rather than someone who shaped destiny. He did not deny his psychic inclinations, even though he did not publicly embrace them. From almost the time he was elected, there were threats to kidnap and murder him, but Lincoln, believing that his life was in the hands of fate, allowed few safeguards to be taken. This was a habit that would be infuriating to his close friends and bodyguards during the war. It became hard to count the number of times that they resigned in frustration, only to return to try and keep Lincoln alive the following day.

Shortly after the inauguration, the *Cleveland Plain Dealer* published an article based on comments from Spiritualist medium J.B. Conklin, who asserted that Lincoln was a "sympathizer with Spiritualism," because Conklin claimed that he had seen Lincoln anonymously attending several of his séances. The newspaper's assertion that Lincoln was a Spiritualist gained further credence from a report in the *Spiritualist Scientist* newspaper that the medium Conklin was "a guest at the Presidential mansion." If the newspaper expected a denial from Lincoln, they were likely surprised, for when he was shown the story, he answered, "The only falsehood in the statement is that the half of it has been told. The article does not begin to tell the wonderful things I have witnessed." It was one of the few times that Lincoln publicly stated his belief in Spiritualism, although he never denied it.

The war took a terrible toll on President Lincoln but there is no doubt that the most crippling blow that he suffered in the White House was the death of his son, Willie, in 1862. Lincoln and Mary grieved deeply over Willie's death. Lincoln was sick at heart over Willie's death and it was probably the most intense personal crisis in his life. Some historians have called it the greatest blow he ever suffered. Even Confederate President Jefferson Davis sent a letter to Washington to express his condolences over the boy's death.

Death came for Willie on the afternoon of February 20, 1862. Lincoln covered his face and wept in the same manner that he had for his mother many years before. He looked at Willie for a long time, refusing to leave his bed side.

Mary collapsed in convulsions of sobbing and her closest confidante, her black seamstress Lizzie Keckley, led her away to comfort her. The talented Mrs. Keckley, a former slave who previously worked for Mrs. Jefferson Davis, had become an almost constant companion of Mrs. Lincoln after completing her ball gown for the inauguration. She was one of the few people who possessed the patience and strength needed to deal with the high-strung First Lady. Mary trusted her implicitly, confided in her, and called the woman her best living friend. Keckley listened to Mary, sympathized with her and advised her as best she could. She would soon influence Mary greatly when it came to her beliefs in Spiritualism.

Willie Lincoln, whose death so deeply grieved Abraham and Mary Lincoln that they turned to Spiritualism to contact him again.

Mary was destroyed by Willie's death, and was never the same. She never again set foot in the room where Willie died, or in the East Room, where his body was embalmed. Nor could she summon the strength to attend her son's funeral. As the president gazed down at the face of his dead son, overwhelmed with emotion, he stated, "He was too good for this earth, but then we loved him so."

It was a tragic time in the White House. Most of official Washington attended the funeral. Lincoln stood frozen next to Willie's coffin with Robert standing stiffly at his side. Members of Lincoln's cabinet wept openly. General George McClellan was so moved by the President's suffering that he later sent Lincoln a compassionate note expressing his sorrow and thanking him for standing by him during failure after failure on the military front. When the service was concluded, the pallbearers and a group of children from Willie's Sunday school class carried the coffin outside and to the waiting hearse.

Willie was placed in a tomb at Oak Hill Cemetery in Georgetown but Lincoln wasn't able to leave his son unattended there for long. Word spread that Lincoln returned to the tomb on two occasions and had Willie's coffin opened. The undertaker had embalmed Willie so perfectly that he appeared to be merely asleep. The President claimed each time that he opened the casket that he wanted to look upon his boy's face just one last time.

After the funeral, Lincoln tried to go on about his work, but his spirit had been crushed by Willie's death. One week after the funeral, he closed himself up in his office all day and wept. He tried to move on, placing small items and drawings given to him by Willie on his desk, hoping to capture the boy's essence. His friends stated that Lincoln would often watch the door while he worked, as if expecting the boy to run through it and give his father a hug, as he often did in life.

Lincoln began to speak of how Willie's spirit remained with him and how his presence was often felt in his home and office. Some mediums theorized that Lincoln's obsession with the boy's death may have caused Willie's spirit to linger behind, refusing, for his father's sake, to pass on to the other side.

The loss of Willie was more than Mary Lincoln could bear. She plunged into a deep depression and Spiritualism became the only thing that gave her comfort.

Lincoln may not have publicly acknowledged his belief in Spiritualism, but after Willie's death, Mary embraced them openly. This is not surprising with the atmosphere that existed in the White House at that time. The President managed to escape from his despair with work, even though his moments with Mary and Tad tended to bring back his pain again. Mary was deeply affected by Willie's death. Always high-strung and emotional in the best of times, she suffered what was likely a nervous breakdown and she shut herself in her room for three months. She took to her bed, broke into fits of weeping and begged Willie to come back to her. Lizzie Keckley would later recall how tender President Lincoln was with his anguished wife but he worried about her as well, fearful that she would lapse into insanity. She often fought with him, though, when he seemed to pay too much attention to matters of war and not enough to their shared sorrow. Lincoln was torn between the bloody fighting between the North and South and the war at home with his troubled wife.

As time wore on, Mary remained unstable. Her mood swings, headaches and explosive temper were worse than ever. Perhaps the only thing that really provided Mary with any comfort at all was her embrace of Spiritualism. By the summer of 1862, Mary was meeting with many different Spiritualist mediums and invited a number of them to the White House, as each claimed to be able to "lift the thin veil" and allow Mary to communicate with Willie.

Through Lizzie Keckley, Mary made the acquaintance of a Miss Bonpoint, a journalist who was writing about Spiritualism in the papers. It was she who introduced Mary to Mrs. Cranston Laurie, a medium who practiced from her home in Georgetown. Mrs. Laurie was the first medium to try and communicate with the spirit of Willie Lincoln in the White House. Between 1862 and 1865, the black presidential carriage was often seen outside of the Lauries' brownstone.

Later in 1862, Mary met the woman who became her closest Spiritualist companion, Nettie Colburn Maynard. Mrs. Laurie had arranged the meeting and soon after, Nettie, who never charged for her services, offered to help Mrs. Lincoln make contact with her son. Nettie's first sitting for Mary took place in the Laurie home, where, for an hour, she demonstrated her abilities. The First Lady was so impressed that she insisted that Nettie not leave Washington – she had things to tell President Lincoln that he needed to hear. Mary arranged for Nettie to work in the Agriculture Department and her a new salary-paying job, she was able to accommodate the growing number of people in Washington who sought out her mediumistic gifts – including Abraham Lincoln.

Many are familiar with a tale told about a séance attended by Nettie Maynard in 1863 where a grand piano levitated. A medium was playing the instrument when it began to rise off the floor. Lincoln and Colonel Simon Kase were both present and it is said that both men climbed onto the piano, only to have it jump and shake so hard that they climbed down. It is recorded that Lincoln would later refer to the levitation as proof of an "invisible power."

Rumors spread that Lincoln consulted with mediums and clairvoyants to obtain information about future events in the war. He found that sometimes they gave him information about matters as mundane as Confederate troop movements --- information that sometimes matched his own precognitive visions. There is much written about Lincoln and the Washington Spiritualists of the day in the accounts and diaries written by friends and acquaintances. One such acquaintance would even claim that Lincoln's plans for the Emancipation Proclamation, which freed the southern slaves, came to him from the spirit of Daniel Webster and other abolitionists of the spirit world.

A statement from Jack Laurie, the son of Mr. and Mrs. Laurie, established that both Lincolns were present at the Laurie home for séances. He wrote:

I have on several occasions seen Mr. Lincoln at a circle at my father's house... take notes of what was said by mediums. At one circle... a heavy table was... raised and caused to dance about the room... Mr. Lincoln laughed heartily and said to my father, "Never mind, Cranston, if they break the table, I will give you a new one." On one occasion, my father asked Mr. Lincoln, if he believed the phenomena was caused by spirits, and Mr. Lincoln replied, that he did so believe. This was on a Sunday evening late in 1862. I fix the time by the fact that I was injured that same evening by a runaway horse. In 1862, I was fifteen years of age...

J.C. Laurie

Another observer, Mrs. Elvira M. Debuy, also participated in séances with the President. She wrote, "I have always known from my husband and others that Mr. Lincoln attended circles and séances and was greatly interested in Spiritualism. My husband was a visitor to séances where Mr. Lincoln was present, and he told me of many interesting occurrences. In the winter of 1862-1863, I attended a séance at Mrs. Lauries' in Georgetown, where Mrs. Lincoln was present. She was accompanied by Mr. Newton, Commissioner of Agriculture. At the séance, remarkable statements were made, which surprised Mrs. Lincoln to such a degree that she asked that a séance might be given to Mr. Lincoln."

Most of the information about Lincoln and his interest in Spiritualism came from Nettie Colburn Maynard, who published a manuscript on the subject in 1891. In the 1850s, a teenaged Nettie became aware of her mediumistic abilities when she discovered that she could induce spirit rappings from the other side. Her ability manifested itself during the 1856 James Buchanan and John C. Fremont presidential election, in which Nettie's father, a staunch Fremont supporter, found out how accurate his daughter's talents could be. Too young and inexperienced to comprehend the political differences between the two candidates, she was nevertheless "seized by a power that I could not control" on the day before the election. Grabbing a piece of paper, Nettie scrawled the word "Buchanan" on it and as she did "loud raps came upon the table." Her startled father asked if this meant that Buchanan would win the election. Nettie said that it did and the next day, her prediction proved to be accurate. Her father became convinced that she could help others with her talents.

With her father's approval and support, Nettie went on to become a "spirit lecturer," mainly in New England towns and villages. When the Civil War began in April 1861, despite northern boasts of a quick victory, she predicted otherwise. "Our spirit friends," she said, "reply ... it would continue four years and require five practically to end it."

Nettie moved to Washington during the years of the war and took up residence in the home of a friend, Mrs. Anna Crosby, whose father had been Robert Mills, the architect who had designed the Capitol building. While living in the Crosby home, Nettie met many prominent people, including General Simon Cameron and Joshua Speed, one of Lincoln's closest friends. She gave private and public séances for many of them, and through Spiritualist circles, became acquainted with Mary Lincoln.

According to Nettie, she first met President Lincoln on February 5, 1863, during a séance in Georgetown that he was not scheduled to attend. The medium would later claim that her "spirit guide" told her that Lincoln would be in attendance. The host of the party declared that this was unlikely to happen, as Lincoln rarely attended séances away from the White House. To his surprise, though, the President did come and the host exclaimed upon seeing him that he had been expected. Lincoln was reportedly shocked and stated that he had not been planning to come, but only accompanied Mary that night on a whim.

During the séance, Lincoln was allegedly contacted by an "old Dr. Bramford," who is said to have given him information about the state of the war. Nettie later quoted the spirit as saying, "a very precarious state of things existed at the front, where General Hooker had just taken command. The army was totally demoralized; regiments stacking arms, refusing to obey orders and do duty; threatening a general retreat; declaring their purpose to return to Washington." She wrote that the vivid picture of this terrible state of affairs seemed to surprise everyone but Lincoln, who spoke up to the spirit. "You seem to understand the situation," he said. "Can you point out the remedy?"

Dr. Bramford replied that he had one, but only if Lincoln had the courage to use it. The President smiled and challenged the eerie voice that was coming to him from the darkness. According to the spirit, the remedy for success lay with Lincoln himself. He spoke: "Go in person to the front; taking with you your wife and children; leaving behind your official dignity, and all manner of display. Resist the importunities of officials to accompany you and take only such attendants as may be absolutely necessary; avoid the high-grade officers, and seek the tents of the private soldiers. Inquire into their grievances; show yourself to be what you are -- 'The Father of Your People.' Make them feel you are interested in their sufferings, and that you are not unmindful of the many trials which beset them in their march through the dismal swamps, whereby both their courage and numbers have been depleted."

Lincoln is said to have replied that if this would do the soldiers good, that such a thing was easily done. The mysterious voice explained that it would do all that was required to unite the soldiers again. In April, Lincoln paid the Army of the Potomac a lengthy visit, arriving at Aquia Creek and traveling by train to Falmouth where Hooker's men were camped. From there, Lincoln could see with a spy glass across the Rappahannock to Fredericksburg, where Robert E. Lee's Army of Virginia waited, less than a half mile away. A short time later, the overconfident Hooker led the Union to one of the costliest defeats of the war at Chancellorsville. Amid this disaster, though, his men followed him bravely into battle. Some say their courage had been restored by the visit from President Lincoln.

Nettie Maynard later recalled that after the advice given by Dr. Bramford, the spirit and the President continued to speak about the state of affairs in regards to the war. The spirit also told him that "he would be re-nominated and re-elected to the Presidency." This was more unusual than most modern readers might believe. At that point in American history, no President had ever been elected to a second term. Lincoln was not shocked by the news. He smiled sadly, however, and said, "It is hardly an honor to be coveted, save one could find it his duty to accept it."

It was during this very séance that the famous incident with the levitating piano took place. The medium said to have performed this wonder was Mrs. Belle Miller, a prominent Washington Spiritualist. Mrs. Miller was playing the piano and under her influence, it "rose and fell," keeping time to her touch in a regular manner. One of those present suggested that, as an added test of the invisible power causing the instrument to move, Belle should place her hand on the piano and stand at an arm's length from it. This would show that she was in no way connected to it except as an agent of the mysterious power. President Lincoln then placed his hand underneath the piano, at the end that was closest to Mrs. Miller, who placed her hand upon his to demonstrate that neither strength nor pressure was being used. In this position, the piano rose and fell several times, seemingly at their bidding. Lincoln even changed places to stand on the other side of the piano, but the same thing continued to happen.

The President was reported to have grinned at the display and said that he believed he could hold the instrument to the floor. He climbed up onto it, sitting with his long legs dangling over the side, as did a Mr. Somes, Colonel Simon Kase and a

Federal Army officer. The piano, ignoring the enormous weight now upon it, continued to wobble up and down until the sitters were obliged to "vacate the premises."

The audience was, by this time, satisfied to the fact that no mechanical means had been used to move the instrument and Lincoln himself declared that he was sure the motion was caused by some "invisible power."

Mr. Somes spoke up, "Mr. President, when I have related to my acquaintances that which I have experienced tonight, they will say, with a knowing look and a wise demeanor, 'you were psychologized and as a matter of fact, you did not see what you, in reality, did see.'"

Lincoln quietly replied: "You should bring that person here and when the piano seems to rise, have him slip his foot under the leg and be convinced by the weight of the evidence resting upon his understanding."

His sly comment brought a wave of laughter to the room but when the chuckles died down, the President wearily sank into an armchair, "the old, tired, anxious look returning to his face."

Nettie Maynard held many séances with the Lincolns during the latter days of February and early March 1863. The séances all took place by appointment and after the close of each session, Mary made another appointment to come at a certain hour of another day, usually around the time that the President took his lunch in the afternoon.

On one occasion, Nettie was summoned to a séance by Mr. Somes, who told her that the meeting was of such a private nature that he was not at liberty to say more. Somes picked her up in a carriage that evening and informed her that her destination was the White House. He explained that while at the War Department that afternoon, he had met President Lincoln coming from Secretary Stanton's office. Somes spoke to him briefly and Lincoln asked him if he knew if Nettie was in the city and if so, would it be possible for her to visit the White House that night. When Somes told him that Nettie was indeed in Washington, Lincoln asked that she come that evening, but that the matter should be kept confidential.

By the time that Somes had finished explaining what had occurred, the carriage had arrived at the White House. A waiting servant ushered them inside and they were hurried up to the President's office, where Lincoln and two other men were waiting. The President sent the servant out of the room and a few moments later, Mary entered the chamber. Lincoln told Nettie that he wished for her to give the visitors an opportunity to witness something of her "rare gift" and he added that "you need not be afraid, as these friends have seen something of this before."

Nettie described the men as being military officers, although their coats had been buttoned to conceal any insignia or mark of rank. One of the men was tall and heavily built, with auburn hair and dark eyes. He had thick side whiskers and carried himself like a soldier. The other man was of average height and she had the impression that he was of a lesser rank than his companion. He had light brown hair and blue eyes and was quick in manner but deferential towards his companion.

The group sat quietly for a few moments and then Nettie entered a trance. One hour later, she became conscious of her surroundings and was standing at a table upon which was a large map of the Southern states. She held a lead pencil in her hand and

Lincoln and the two men were standing close to her, bending over the map. The younger man was looking curiously and intently at her.

"It is astonishing," Mr. Lincoln was saying to the larger of the soldiers, "how every line she has drawn conforms to the plan agreed upon."

"Yes," answered the other man. "It is astonishing."

Looking up, both men saw that she was awake and they instantly stepped back. Lincoln took the pencil from Nettie's hand and eased her into a nearby chair. Mary soon appeared at her side to offer some comfort.

"Was everything satisfactory?" Somes asked the assembled men.

"Perfectly," Lincoln replied. "Miss Nettie does not seem to require eyes to do anything."

Shortly after, the conversation turned to more mundane matters and after a brief time, the military men took their leave and then it came the President's time to depart. He carefully shook Nettie's small hand and said to her in a low voice: "It is best not to mention this meeting at the present."

This was the last time that the private séance was ever mentioned and Nettie never learned the identity of the two men who were with President Lincoln that night --- or just what the spirits may have revealed with the map of the Confederacy.

According to accounts, Nettie Maynard's contact with the next world was said to have brought relief to Lincoln on more than one occasion. She was at the White House to visit Mrs. Lincoln in May 1863, around the time that the battle of Chancellorsville was being fought. Nettie was brought into Mary's bedroom and found the First Lady wearing only her dressing gown. Her hair was loose and she was pacing back and forth in a distracted manner. Mary cried, "Such dreadful news; they are fighting at the front; such terrible slaughter; and all our generals are killed and our army is in full retreat; such is the latest news. Oh, I am glad you have come. Will you sit down a few moments and see if you can get anything from the beyond?"

As no news of the battle had yet reached the public, Nettie was surprised by what she heard. She put her things aside and sat down with Mary to let her spirit guide take control of her. In a few moments, she assured Mary that her fears were groundless. A great battle was being fought but the Union forces were holding their own and while many thousands had been killed, none of the generals, as she had been informed, were slain or injured. She would, Nettie assured her, receive better news by nightfall.

This calmed Mary somewhat but when President Lincoln entered the room a short time later, it was obvious that he was still anxiously worrying about what was occurring at the front lines. He greeted Nettie with little enthusiasm but Mary insisted that he listen to what the medium had to say. Lincoln listened attentively to what had been passed on from Nettie's spirit guide, recounting the true conditions at the front and assuring him of the good news that he would receive before nightfall. The battle would be costly, the spirits said, but not disastrous, and though not decisive in any way, it would not be a loss to the Union cause. Lincoln brightened visibly under the assurances that he was given and he later learned that Nettie's information had been correct. Chancellorsville resulted in the lives of many men lost and effectively ended the career of General Joseph Hooker but no real ground was lost by the Union. Hooker had marched into a Confederate-controlled area and his outnumbered army was sent into retreat but regrouped to fight another day.

Perhaps the most notorious White House séance attendee, who also had an encounter with Nettie Maynard, was General Daniel Sickles. The colorful and controversial politician and Civil War officer spent nearly three months in Washington in the summer of 1862 and became well acquainted with the Lincolns. Sickle was an unusual man and as an antebellum New York politician, was involved in several public scandals, most notably the killing of his wife's lover, Philip Barton Key, son of Francis Scott Key. Sickles was acquitted with the first use of temporary insanity as a legal defense in American history. He became one of the most prominent political generals of the Civil War and at the battle of Gettysburg, he insubordinately moved his troops to a position in which it was virtually destroyed. His combat career ended at Gettysburg when he lost a leg to cannon fire.

General Daniel Sickles had a deep interest in Spiritualism and attended a number of séances at the White House with the Lincolns.

Sickles was interested in Spiritualism before the war. In fact, on the night that he learned that his wife was cheating on him with the handsome widower Phillip Barton Key (February 24, 1859), Mr. and Mrs. Sickles had given a dinner party at their Washington home that was enlivened by the presence of the Scottish wife of *New York Herald* editor James Gordon Bennett, an ardent Spiritualist. Mrs. Bennett had attended many séances in Washington and spoke openly of them.

A few years later, during the summer after Willie Lincoln's death, Sickles often joined Mary at séances in the city. He returned to Washington after losing his leg at Gettysburg and continued the regular visitations. In fact, in early 1864, Sickles concocted a ruse to test the mediumistic powers of Mary's young medium, Nettie Maynard. Mary agreed to go along with the ruse, perhaps to teach a lesson to the arrogant general.

Nettie had recently returned to Washington after a brief absence and was living at the home of Mr. and Mrs. Somes. Nettie soon called at the White House, to pay her respects to the President and the First Lady, and was warmly received. Lincoln expressed the hope that she had come to Washington to spend the rest of the winter.

A few days later, Nettie and the Mr. and Mrs. Somes were invited back to meet a friend – Daniel Sickles in a disguise. Mrs. Lincoln, in her invitation to Nettie, mentioned her desire to see if Nettie's spirit guide would be able to tell who the friend was. They were welcomed at the White House that evening by the First Lady, who introduced them to a distinguished, soldierly gentleman, who was wrapped in a long cloak, completely concealing his person. Mrs. Lincoln did not call him by name, apologizing for not doing so, and explaining that she wanted to see if her spirit friends could recognize him. She promised to present him afterward. Mr. Somes recognized Sickles immediately, but gave no hint of the general's identity.

President Lincoln had a late-night Cabinet meeting and after joining the group, asked that the proceedings be brief. The room fell silent and Nettie entered into a trance. The spirits that spoke through her turned all their attentions toward Lincoln. Their remarks related to the condition of free black people in Washington, declaring that their condition was deplorable – half fed and half clothed – and that the manner of their existence should be an embarrassment to the country. The spirits called on Lincoln to form a special committee to investigate the condition of these people, and to organize a bureau to control and regulate the affairs of the freedmen. (The bureau was eventually formed in March 1865.)

It was only after this communication that the spirit, through Nettie, turned to Sickles and referred to him as "General" and praised him for the "noble sacrifice" of his leg at Gettysburg. A few moments later, another presence took control of Nettie – her usual spirit guide, an Indian maiden – and she turned to Sickles and addressed him as "Crooked Knife," her Native American name for him, which was close enough to "Sickles" that everyone present was satisfied.

After Lincoln hurried off to his meeting and Nettie awoke, Mary made the promised presentation of General Sickles, who put aside the cloak, revealing his uniform and concealed crutch. Sickles had no choice but to confess that he was impressed with Mary's young medium.

As time passed and the war dragged on, Lincoln came to believe that a portent of doom hung over his head. The constant threats of death and violence that he received kept his personal bodyguards on edge at all times. It is also believed that some of his Spiritualist friends felt the end was near.

During the winter of 1864 and 1865, though, the war was nearing its end. In February 1865, Washington was filled with people who had come to witness the second inauguration of President Lincoln and Nettie Maynard received a dispatch from home, informing her that her father had taken ill. She was asked to come home at once. She had an appointment to meet with the First Lady the following week and Nettie went to cancel it in person. When she arrived at the White House, she was told that Mary was out, so Nettie proceeded upstairs to have a word with the President instead.

It was the early part of the afternoon, and with it being the last days of the expiring Congress, the President's waiting room was filled with senators and congressmen, all anxious to speak with Lincoln. Nettie noted the prominent men who had been waiting for hours and doubted that she would be able to get time to speak to the President. Edward, Lincoln's usher, was walking back and forth and collecting calling cards to take into the President and Nettie called him over. She explained that she needed only a moment with Lincoln and asked for any opportunity to tell him why she would have to cancel her appointment the following week.

Half an hour went by and Edward appeared and asked Nettie to follow him. Several of the senators that Nettie knew personally laughed to her and asked with a smile that she put in a good word for them. She was soon in the presence of the President. He stood at his desk, looking over some papers but laid them down and greeted her with a genial smile. In as few words as possible, knowing how precious his time was, she informed him of her unusual call and told him that she had been summoned out of town because her father was seriously ill. Lincoln looked at her with a curious smile. "But cannot our friends from the upper country tell you whether his illness is likely to prove fatal or not?"

Nettie replied that she had already consulted with her "friends" and that they had assured her that his treatment was wrong and that her presence was needed to affect a cure.

Lincoln laughed and turned to his secretary. "I didn't catch her, did I?" he teased Nettie and then seriously added that he was sorry that she would be away during the inauguration.

"I would enjoy it," she assured him, "but the crowd will be so great that we will not be able to see you, Mr. Lincoln, even if I remain."

"You could not help it," he answered, drawing his lean figure to its full height and glancing at her in an amused way. "I will be the tallest man there."

"That is true, in every sense of the word."

Lincoln nodded pleasantly at the compliment and then asked Nettie what her "friends" predicted for his future.

"What they predicted for you, Mr. Lincoln, has come to pass and you are to be inaugurated for the second time." He nodded his head and she continued. "But they also reaffirm that the shadow they have spoken of still hangs over you."

Lincoln shook his head impatiently. "Yes, I know," he said quickly. "I have letters from all over the country from your kind of people --- mediums, I mean --- warning me against some dreadful plot against my life. But I don't think the knife is made, or the bullet run, that will reach it. Besides, nobody wants to harm me."

A feeling of sadness overwhelmed Nettie. It was a feeling that she could not account for and one that she could not conceal. She spoke to the President boldly: "Therein lies your danger, Mr. President --- your overconfidence in your fellow men."

The old melancholy look that Nettie had grown so used to in her time of friendship with the President and his wife descended over his face. His voice was quiet and subdued. "Well, Miss Nettie," he said, "I shall live until my work is done and no earthly power can prevent it. And then it doesn't matter so that I am ready and that I ever mean to be."

Then, brightening a little, he extended his hand to her. "Well, I suppose that I must bid you goodbye but we shall hope to see you back again next fall."

"I shall certainly come," Nettie told him, "if you are still here."

With another cordial shake of the President's hand, Nettie passed out of Lincoln's presence for the last time. "Never again," she later wrote, "would we meet his welcome smile."

As the war dragged on, threats of death and murder seemed to multiply. Lincoln's bodyguards, as well as the soldiers assigned to his protection, were constantly thwarted from their duty by Lincoln himself. He often slipped out of the White House at night for solitary strolls and refused to take precautions that were necessary to keep him protected. Many felt that it was only a matter of time before the assassin's bullet caught up with the President.

One of Lincoln's old friends from Illinois was a lawyer with whom he had ridden the legal circuit named Ward Hill Lamon. Lincoln had appointed him to a security position in the White House and Lamon worried constantly over Lincoln's seeming indifference to threats and warnings of death. Lamon resigned his position numerous times because his friend did not take the danger seriously. Lincoln always convinced him to stay on, promising to be more careful ---- then vanished out of the White House at night, or attended the theater without protection.

Lamon became obsessed with watching over Lincoln and many believe that the president would not have been killed at Ford's Theater had Lamon been on duty that night. As it turned out, the security chief was in Richmond, Virginia, on an errand for the president, when disaster struck. He never forgave himself for what happened --- especially since he believed that he had a forewarning of the event, from Lincoln himself.

Years later, Lamon would remember that Lincoln had always been haunted by the strange vision that he experienced in the mirror in 1860. Several years after that, the president told Lamon and Mary about an eerie dream of death that he had just shortly before his assassination.

About ten days ago, I retired late. I soon began to dream. There seemed to be a death-like stillness about me. Then I heard subdued sobs, as if a number of people were weeping. I thought I left my bed and wandered downstairs. There the silence was broken by the same pitiful sobbing, but the mourners were invisible. I went from room to room; no living person was in sight, but the same mournful sounds of distress met me as I passed along.

It was light in all the rooms; every object was familiar to me, but where were all the people who were grieving as if their hearts would break? I was puzzled and alarmed. What could be the meaning of all this? Determined to find the cause of a state of things so mysterious and so shocking, I kept on until I arrived at the East Room, which I entered. Before me was a catafalque, on which rested a corpse wrapped in funeral vestments. Around it were stationed soldiers who were acting as guards; and there was a throng of people, some gazing mournfully upon the corpse, whose face was covered, others weeping pitifully.

"Who is dead in the White House?" I demanded of one of the soldiers.

"The President." was his answer, "He was killed by an assassin."

Then came a loud burst of grief from the crowd, which awoke me from my dream. I slept no more that night; and although it was only a dream, I have been strangely annoyed by it ever since.

Lincoln was murdered just a few days later and his body was displayed in the East Room of the White House. Mary recalled her husband's dream quite vividly in the days that followed. It was said that her first coherent word after the assassination was a muttered statement about his dream being prophetic.

On Good Friday, April 14, 1865, the Lincolns left the White House to attend a play at Ford's Theater in Washington. The Lincolns arrived at the theater and entered their reserved box, which had been adorned with drapes and American flags. The orchestra struck up the strains of "Hail to the Chief" and the crowd cheered wildly. On stage, the actors ceased their dialogue in deference to Lincoln. The play was a production called "Our American Cousin" presented by actress Laura Keene. It was a comedy, the sort of show that Lincoln liked best.

The Lincoln's were accompanied that night by a young couple, Major Henry Rathbone and his fiancée, Clara Harris. Lincoln slumped into a rocking chair that had been provided by the management to fit his long body and Mary was seated beside him, with Rathbone and Clara Harris to their right. On stage, Harry Hawk, the male lead, ad-libbed a line: "This reminds me of a story, as Mr. Lincoln would say..." The audience roared and clapped and Lincoln smiled, whispering something to Mary. Behind him, the box door was closed but not locked and in all the excitement over the President's arrival, no one noticed the small peep hole that had been dug out of it.

As the play progressed, guard John Parker left his post in the hallway outside of the box and either went down into the gallery to watch the play or left to have a drink. Those who believe there was a government conspiracy to kill Lincoln often point to Parker as proof of it. He was Lincoln's only bodyguard that night and he had gone ahead to Ford's Theater that evening rather than accompany the President to the venue. Parker was a patrolman on the Washington City police force and had a reputation as a lazy drunk with an appalling history of insubordination and insufficiency. He was totally unsuitable to guard the President and it is believed that if Ward Hill Lamon had been aware of the posting, he would have never allowed himself to be removed from the detail that night.

On stage, the players hammed it up in silly and melodramatic scenes and laughter rolled through the audience. As the Lincolns watched the play, actor and Confederate sympathizer John Wilkes Booth approached the president's box. He showed a card to an attendant and gained access to the outer door, which was unattended. As he slipped into the box, Booth jammed the door closed behind him. The laughter of the crowd concealed any noise that he might have made.

While the play was going on, the Lincoln party chatted and talk turned to the Holy Land. The President made a comment about wanting to visit Jerusalem someday and as he leaned forward, he noticed General Ambrose Burnside in the audience below the box. At that moment, Booth stepped forward. Major Rathbone caught the movement out of the corner of his eye and bolted from his seat to confront the intruder. Before he could act, though, Booth raised a small pistol and fired it into the back of President Lincoln's head.

Rathbone seized the actor but Booth slashed him with a knife. Lincoln fell forward, striking his head on the rail of the box and slumping over. Mary took hold of him, believing him to have simply fallen. Booth pushed past the Lincolns and jumped from the edge of the box towards the stage below. His boot snagged on the bunting across the front of the box and he landed badly, fracturing his leg. As he struggled to his feet, he cried out "Sic Semper Tyrannis!" (Thus it shall ever be for tyrants) and he stumbled out of the theater using the back stage door.

Major Rathbone shouted at the stunned audience, "Stop that man! Stop that man!"

"Won't somebody stop that man," Clara Harris pleaded. "The President is shot!"

Her final scream snapped the audience out of its stunned stupor. Soon, voices began to take up the call of "Booth!" Many of them had recognized the famous actor as he landed on the stage. Despite this, however, he managed to escape from the crowded auditorium. The rooms was filled with screams, groans, and the crashing of seats ---- but above it all, was Mary Lincoln's shrill and terror-filled scream for her husband.

By now, the theater was in chaos. People were shoving into the aisles and rushing for the exits, with Laura Keene yelling at them from the stage: "For God's sake, have presence of mind and keep your places, and all will be well."

In the theater's audience was a young doctor named Charles Leale, who rushed upstairs to Lincoln's aid. He fought his way into the President's box, where a weeping Clara Harris tried to console Mary, who was holding Lincoln in the rocker and weeping hysterically. Leale placed the President on the floor and removed the blood clot from the wound to relieve the pressure on the brain. The bullet had struck him just behind the left ear, had traveled through the brain, and lodged behind his right eye. Even this young doctor could see that the wound was a fatal one --- the President was nearly dead. Lincoln's heart was beating faintly so Leale reached into his mouth, opened his throat, and applied artificial respiration in a desperate attempt to save him. A few moments later, Leale was joined by Dr. Charles Sabin Taft and the two men continued their efforts. They raised and lowered the President's arms, while Leale massaged his chest, and then he forced his own breath into Lincoln's lungs again and again. Lincoln somehow began to breathe on his own, his heart beating with an irregular flutter. Lincoln was in a dire condition --- but he was still alive.

The two doctors, with help from bystanders, managed to get the President out of Ford's Theater. Soldiers cleared a path through the crowd outside, where people rushed madly back and forth and milled about in confusion. A man named Henry Safford, who worked as a clerk at the War Department, beckoned to the doctors and they carried the President across the street into the Petersen house. Lincoln's unconscious form was laid in a small bedroom at the back of the house. His lanky frame was too long for the bed and they were forced to lay him down at an angle. Clara Harris and Major Rathbone, with his untreated arm bleeding profusely, brought Mary to the house. When she saw Lincoln in the back room, Mary ran to him, fell to her knees and called him intimate names while she sobbed and begged him not to die. She remained there, weeping, until doctors finally led to the front parlor, where she collapsed in grief.

Help was summoned as Lincoln's aides and security men attempted to try and calm the frenzy around them. Meanwhile, the Surgeon General, Joseph K. Barnes, and Lincoln's own doctor, Robert Stone King, set to work on the President. They soon realized that it was no use --- there was nothing that could be done for him.

By now, word had spread through Washington and a procession of government officials came running to the house, crowding into the room where Lincoln lay with a cluster of doctors at his side. Robert Lincoln arrived with John Hay, barely hearing the words of the doctor who told them at the doorway to the room that there was nothing that could be done for the President. When Robert saw his father lying diagonally across the bed, his brain destroyed and his eye swollen and broken with blood, the usually calm and collected young man broke down in despair and disbelief. Finally, in shock himself, he went into the front parlor to try and comfort his mother. Mary had been sedated by one of the doctors. She hardly knew he was there.

As Robert left the room, Senator Charles Sumner entered, his face twisted in anguish. The senator took Lincoln's hand and spoke to him but a doctor assured him that Lincoln was beyond hearing, that he was dead. "No, he isn't dead," Sumner protested in anger. "Look at his face, he is breathing." The other physicians assured him that Lincoln would never regain consciousness and, at that, Sumner clasped Lincoln's hand tightly, bowed his head close to the pillow and began to weep.

With the President near death and the government at a standstill, Secretary of War Stanton took over. Close to breaking down himself, tears burning in his eyes, Stanton set up headquarters in the back parlor. A Federal judge, along with two other men, helped him to take testimony from the witnesses at the theater. All of them identified the assassin as John Wilkes Booth, the actor and Confederate sympathizer. At once, Stanton placed the city under martial law and ordered search parties to track down Booth and all other suspects.

As Stanton came and went, issuing orders, calling for Vice President Andrew Johnson and mobilizing troops and police officers, Mary lay on the sofa in the front parlor, wavering back and forth between eerie quiet and fits of weeping. When she recalled Lincoln's dreams of mournful voices in the White House, she cried miserably that his dream had come true. She begged God to take her with him, or to trade her life for her husband's. Outside the windows of the Petersen house, a crowd gathered in the foggy night, keeping a constant vigil and asking the officials who came and went if there was any word ---- or any hope.

The gloomy watch continued throughout the night. The hours slowly passed and the doctors released press bulletins about the president's condition that were sent out over telegraph lines every half hour. By dawn, the President's condition had worsened and as the first gray light began to appear at the windows, a heavy rain began to fall, as if the heavens were weeping. Sumner was still holding Lincoln's hand when Mary came to see him one last time. She kissed his face and whispered to him, "Love, live but one moment to speak to me once," but then she looked at his shattered face and realized, perhaps for the first time, that he was beyond hope. She wailed as she was led away.

With the end now close, Lincoln's friends and colleagues gathered at his bedside. Stanton and Robert Lincoln came in from the front room and Robert, giving away to his agony, put his head on Sumner's shoulder. At that, many of the others present also began to cry. Finally, Lincoln took one great breath, his face relaxed and then he faded into oblivion.

The Surgeon General carefully crossed the lifeless hands of Abraham Lincoln at twenty-two minutes after seven on the morning of April 15, 1865.

Edwin Stanton stood by the bedside of the slain president. He raised his head and with tears streaming down his face, uttered the most unforgettable words that a man not known for his poetic soul could ever manage... "Now, he belongs to the ages."

Just as he had seen in his premonition, Lincoln's casket was placed on display on a platform in the East Room of the White House, watched over by soldiers. Then after lying in state for crowds of mourners, a special train took his body home for burial in Springfield, Illinois. Along the route of the sorrowful journey, the train made its way through towns and cities where millions turned out to pay their last respects to the fallen president. The nation had been plunged into a deep and unprecedented grief.

While the nation mourned, the authorities pursued John Wilkes Booth and his conspirators. Booth, trapped in a Virginia barn, was shot to death 11 days after the assassination. His confederates were captured and ultimately tried and convicted. Some were imprisoned and the others went to the gallows.

Mary Lincoln went on to become one of the most misunderstood and maligned figures in American history. Most of the later biographies of her life, if they refer to her interest in Spiritualism at all, regard it as a reflection of her emotional problems or eccentricity. At the same time, her husband's interest in one of the greatest American cultural movements of all time is ignored almost entirely.

But Mary's many problems – and the fascination with Spiritualism that she shared with millions of others -- deserves more sympathy than has been given. Like Jane Pierce, the wife of her husband's predecessor in office, Mrs. Lincoln experienced the untimely deaths of two of her children, Eddie and Willie. By the end of the Civil War, notwithstanding whatever mental issues she may have suffered from, she was also a bereaved mother and a disconsolate widow. While still aching from the loss of Willie, Mary suffered another staggering loss when her husband was assassinated. Still, her faith in her ability to contact the spirit world remained intact and she continued to practice Spiritualism throughout the rest of her life.

Just as she had been desperate to hear from Willie at séances, she also ached for a message from her departed husband, which was a sign to skeptics that she had been "unhinged." In fact, people believed that Mary had lost her mind when, in reality, she had retreated into the only refuge that she knew that ease her loneliness and grief – Spiritualism. Like so many millions of others who had lost loved ones during the war, Mary embraced Spiritualism to cope with her pain. Before the war, the movement had started to fade in popularity, but after the devastation felt by untold wives, mothers, children. and loved ones, the hope of communication with the dead was greater than it had been before.

For Mary Lincoln, her grief was exacerbated by the result of another personal tragedy in 1871 when Tad, who had been his mother's only constant companion since his father had been killed, fell ill with tuberculosis and died at age 18. Mary bitterly wrote, "Ill luck presided over my birth and has been a faithful attendant ever since."

Mary found some sanctuary in her beliefs, residing in a "Spiritualist commune" for a time, so that she could develop her ability to see spirit faces and to attempt contact with her late husband. Mary later traveled to Boston, where, using an alias and a heavy veil to avoid being recognized, she attended a séance and reported contact with Lincoln's spirit and said she felt his hands on her shoulders. She also visited a Spiritualist photographer, who claimed that he could capture the images of the spirits on film.

Mrs. Lincoln yearned for her husband to manifest in one of these photographs and so, under the assumed name "Mrs. Tundall," she visited William Mumler, the best-known spirit photographer of the time. Wearing her widow's black, Mary sat, her hands folded, her round face older, more tired and heavier than only a few years before, while Mumler

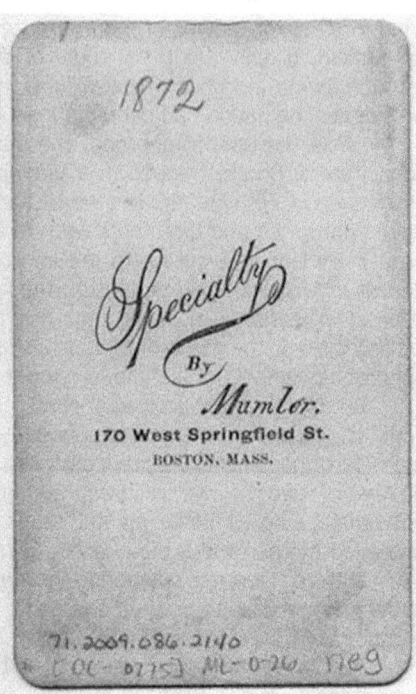

placed photo plates into his camera and asked her to stay motionless so that he could expose the picture he was taking of her.

When the plate was developed, Mrs. Lincoln was not disappointed because behind her she could make out the hazy, nearly transparent image of Abraham Lincoln with his hand on her shoulder. He was bathed in a cloudlike fog and his body appeared as a white form. Many suspected an obvious double exposure, although Mumler had many supporters who vouched for his honesty. Mrs. Lincoln was certain that Mumler did not recognize her – and that the photograph was genuine. The spirit photograph of Mary Lincoln, with her late husband looming behind her, became Mumler's most famous image. Was it genuine? There is no clear answer to that question – but it should be noted that Mumler was later arrested and charged with fraud for some of the other photographs that he produced.

Mary Lincoln's last years were spent in misery and depression. She died in Springfield, Illinois on July 16, 1882. When she was laid to rest, she was buried wearing her wedding ring, which was inscribed with the words *Love is Eternal*.

At the end of the Civil War, interest in Spiritualism increased again among the bereaved who had lost loved ones in the fighting and yearned to speak with them again. Nearly every family in the nation, North and South, had been touched by the unwelcome presence of death and was paralyzed with grief. The scale of the carnage was almost unimaginable – the war had left more than 600,000 men and boys dead, and nearly another million wounded.

As a result, many turned to Spiritualist mediums in hope of hearing from their departed husbands, sons, brothers, and friends. Physical mediums entered the spotlight in a way that they had never done before, and mental, or speaking mediums, began to pass along scores of messages from the spirits.

The Golden Age of Spiritualism had arrived.

5. MYSTERIES IN THE SEANCE ROOM
THE ODDITIES THAT MADE SPIRITUALISM ENDURE

By the end of the war, interest in Spiritualism had reached a new level of excitement among Americans who had lost loved ones it the fighting and yearned to hear from them again. By that time, "rappings" were a thing of the past. They had been replaced by automatic writing and trance speaking and physical mediums were stunning their séance audiences with baffling and theatrical presentations – all as proof of visitations from the other side. People were so excited about the proliferation of messages from the dead that grand parties were held to celebrate the soul's survival in the next world.

There were many factors that continued to the rise of the Spiritualist movement in what became known as the Gilded Age in American history, but the roots of that popularity dated back in some cases to the decade before the Civil War. It was at that time that a sensation arose in the form of two brothers, who would go on to mystify audiences on several continents.

The brothers created a sensation that lasted for decades and introduced the "spirit cabinet" to séance attendees. It soon became a common accoutrement for mediums across the nation. The cabinets, or enclosures, hid the mediums from prying eyes while they produced their strange phenomena. The cabinets would prove to be wildly popular and would baffle audiences because the mediums locked inside were usually bound hand and foot at the impossible supernatural happenings whirled and manifested about them.

The introduction of spirit cabinets would permanently change the face of Spiritualism and mediums across American had William and Ira Davenport to thank for this wondrous innovation.

THE MYSTERY OF THE DAVENPORT BROTHERS

The Fox sisters were still drawing crowds all over the country when the Davenport brothers, who would become the two most widely-known mediums in America for a time, made their first public appearance.

Ira Davenport was born in 1839, and his brother, William, came along two years later in 1841. Their father, a Buffalo, New York policeman, was intrigued by the stories of the spirit rappings in Hydesville, so the family decided to try their own sittings at home. Immediately, they got chilling results and Ira would later tell friends that his younger sister, Elizabeth, actually levitated about the room. As no one other than the boys' father, who later marketed them shamelessly on stage, ever reported Elizabeth's gravity-defying stunts, it's hard to take the story too seriously. Regardless, private exhibitions began taking place in the Davenport home, drawing neighborhood crowds.

After a month or so, the family got in touch with what would become the Davenport's spirit guide, a phantom named John King (who would go on to become the busiest spirit guide in the Spiritualist movement). King allegedly told the family to begin renting a hall and giving public performances of the Davenport brothers' reputed powers. The boys were only 16 and 14 when they went on stage for the first time in 1855.

The famous Davenport brothers, Ira and William

The initial performances contained the now standard manifestations offered by the Fox sisters and others in the growing Spiritualist movement, like table tipping and mystery rapping. But soon, the Davenport brothers began to introduce other phenomena into the act, like musical instruments that floated in the air, playing under their own power, and spirit hands that touched and pulled at sitters and audience members.

Among those who experienced the Davenport séances in the early days was Stephen Albro, editor of the Spiritualist weekly, *Age of Progress*. Albro had already attended one of their séances and had, as he delicately put it, "detected impositions." On his second visit, however, Albro was convinced that the manifestations he witnessed were genuine. Being wary this time, he carefully inspected the room, saw to it that the two doors were locked, and that the table had nothing hidden beneath it. When the room was darkened, there was still enough light for him to read an advertisement on the wall that was 10 feet from where he sat.

The séance had barely begun when loud raps were heard from the underside of the table, where a few musical instruments had been placed. A large black arm somehow rose from under the table, picked up the trumpet, and held it in the air. Then it suddenly flung itself across the room and knocked Abro's hat off a nearby chair. Hands of other sizes appeared from beneath the table. One, Albro reported, was a child's hand and others belonged to adults. Albro thrust his own hand under the table, checking for an accomplice, and felt a cold finger grab his thumb. Another hand then seized his wrist. The spirits claimed that this hand belonged to his dead father. An umbrella was placed underneath the table. It was immediately opened, raised up, and held over the head of one of the Davenport brothers, moved up and down, and twirled around. Albro claimed that the umbrella was held by the disembodied hand of a woman.

At the end of his report, he repeated that he was positive that the phenomenon was genuine and there were no confederates in the room that were engaged in fraud.

Judging by later descriptions of Davenport exhibitions, the séance that Albro witnessed was a moderate performance. Toward the end of 1855, the brothers were in New York City with a more spectacular repertoire of manifestations. Among them was one that they exhibited in public for the next 25 years and became a signature part of their shows. It consisted of them freeing themselves from ropes which volunteers from the audience had bound them in full view of everyone. The process often required an hour or more, but the boys seldom took more than two minutes to get free, untying every knot – with help from the spirits, of course.

During their first appearance in New York, they rented a small assembly room on the Bowery. A group of 17 members of the press were invited to a private séance. The newspapermen kept the boys under close surveillance and after witnessing the usual manifestations, tied the boys to chairs with ropes and then bound their hands tightly with handkerchiefs. The lights were turned off and, according to a writer from the *Sunday Dispatch*, "Instantly, the manifestations commenced, more animatedly than ever. The tambourine was beaten vigorously, the bell clattered, and the string instruments, which appeared to fly about the room, twanged. It was a perfect confusion of discordant sounds, to say the least." When the gas was lighted, the brothers' bonds were found to be intact. Before they left, the reporters all signed a paper describing what they had seen and stated that they were unable to detect any trickery.

After spending a few weeks in New York City, the Davenports returned to Buffalo, where they began working on improvements to their exhibitions. At the suggestion of an audience member during a performance, a cabinet – sort of a portable closet – was assembled on stage. The cabinet allowed the brothers to perform in lighted rooms, but away from the prying eyes of the audience. Part of the act was to look for volunteers from the audience who would tie the brothers up inside of the cabinet. Overeager skeptics often tied the Davenports with elaborate and painful knots that sometimes drew blood. Despite this, once the cabinet doors were closed, wondrous spirit music filled the air from inside and disembodied hands would appear through apertures that had been left open on the exterior walls. The cabinet became an essential prop for their séances and traveled everywhere with them on tour.

Taking Spiritualism several steps past the mere spirit rappings of the Fox sisters and their imitators, the Davenports became a sensation. Spiritualists hailed their exhibitions as genuine proof of spirit phenomena, while critics claimed that were simply stage magicians – good ones, but magicians, nonetheless. Interestingly, neither brother ever claimed to be a medium. They left that up to the audience to decide. They did. However, bill their show as a séance and most Spiritualists believed what occurred during them to be manifestations by the spirits.

The Davenport brothers inside of the spirit cabinet that changed paranormal popular culture. The brothers never claimed to be mediums — they allowed the audience to decide for themselves.

Several universities tested the brothers, trying to determine if they were skillful conjurers, or actually possessed supernatural abilities. In 1857, they were contacted by Harvard University and asked to submit to testing. They agreed to be handcuffed, bound, and held by a dozen men but each time they agreed to any kind of restraint, the Harvard professors dismissed it, believing the Davenports knew how to escape from it. Finally, the professors bought 500 feet of new rope, built their own cabinet, and tied the young men up with complicated and elaborate knots. Each of the knots was also secured with delicate linen thread, which insured that they could not be undone without leaving some sign of it. As the séance was ready to begin, one of the Harvard men, Professor Benjamin Pierce, climbed into the cabinet with the Davenports.

As the session began, a spirit hand appeared from a hole in the side of the cabinet and began to rattle the instruments that had been placed inside with the three men. At one point, Professor Pierce felt the hand graze through his hair and he immediately reached out for the Davenport brothers, only to find them still securely bound in their chairs. The séance continued and when it ended, the doors were flung open. The spirit hands had apparently released the Davenports from their bindings and all the ropes were now found twisted around the neck of the professor. Pierce might have been stunned by what happened, but his colleagues refused to believe it. Harvard University filed no official report about the séance.

But not all university professors were so hesitant. Dr. S.L. Loomis, of the department of chemistry at the Medical College of Georgetown University in Washington, attended a performance by the Davenport brothers in 1864. He was one of three audience members selected to watch the séance on the stage. Loomis made it clear in his report that he didn't have the slightest belief in Spiritualism and that he was familiar with the methods of sleight-of-hand performers.

He was soon startled by what he what he witnessed that night.

Dr. Loomis was the most competent investigator that skeptics could have hoped for. He was a graduate of Wesleyan University, studied medicine, and served as an astronomer for the United States Coastal Survey from 1857 to 1860. For the next seven years, he taught at Georgetown and was later a professor in the medical department at Howard University. He was a member of various scientific organizations, president of the Washington Scientific Association, and the author of several books on mathematics.

At the start of the séance, Loomis inspected the spirit cabinet. It resembled a large packing case, constructed of wood, and measuring seven feet high, six feet long, and two feet deep. It rested on three wooden sawhorses, with nothing else between the cabinet and the floor. The cabinet had no hidden trap doors. The front side was enclosed by three doors running from the top of the cabinet to its base. When opened, the entire inside was revealed to the audience.

The brothers sat at opposite ends of the cabinet on a plain wooden bench. The center space between them on the bench was filled with musical instruments or, occasionally, a brave member of the audience was permitted to sit there. A diamond-shaped aperture had been cut near the top of the center door so that "spirit hands" could emerge. Professor Loomis was convinced that nothing was hidden inside.

After the inspection of the cabinet, Loomis and two other men were asked to tie up the Davenports. Loomis watched as the other men performed the task. One of them was a sea captain and was used to tying intricate knots. Loomis noted that he bound one of the boy's hands so tightly that they became "puffed with blood and quite cool." His arms and body were trussed and he was placed on the cabinet bench, where his legs were tied up, and ropes attached to his wrists were run through holes in the bench and secured underneath. The other Davenport was bound by the third member of the committee and was seated at the opposite end of the cabinet, facing his brother. Loomis was satisfied that it was physically impossible for the boys to free themselves and there was nothing in the cabinet but the boys and the ropes that bound them.

The doors of the cabinet were closed and the gaslight was lowered, leaving the hall in a gloomy state. Ten seconds passed. Suddenly, two hands emerged from the aperture at the top of the center door. They were fully visible to the committee and the audience. A minute after this apparition appeared, the doors opened, apparently under their own power, and the boy who had been bound so securely by the sea captain walked out of the cabinet, leaving the ropes behind him on the floor, every knot untied. The other Davenport was still bound, and a close inspection by Professor Loomis showed that the knots were still intact. The doors were closed again and, in less than a minute, the boy climbed out of the cabinet unfettered.

Of course, such a stunt would become famous among magicians on the sideshow and vaudeville circuit, but what followed immediately after was never duplicated by any escape artist. The brothers, free from their bonds, now returned to their seats in the cabinet. A pile of rope was placed between them and the doors were closed. Less than two minutes passed by the professor's watch before the doors swung open and the two Davenports were found tied up as securely as before. Every one of the knots, Loomis stated, was beyond the reach of their hands.

While the brothers were sitting bound and motionless in the cabinet, one of the committee members closed two of the doors and was about to close the third when two hands emerged from the opening. They were clearly visible to everyone because the gas light had not yet been turned down again. As if to prove that they were not theatrical props, one of the hands struck the committee member on the right shoulder with enough strength that he was turned partly around. Loomis immediately flung open the other two doors and found both Davenports sitting tied and motionless on the bench. He examined their ropes and found them intact.

The doors were closed once more and this time, within a few seconds, a violin that had been sitting in the center of the bench began to play. It was followed by sounds from the bell, guitar, and tambourine. At one point, a spectral arm emerged from the aperture in the center door and madly rang the bell. All the instruments continued to play wildly until a force from inside of the cabinet threw open all three doors and the instruments tumbled out onto the stage.

Until now, Loomis had been a spectator to the weird events, but at this point, he was invited to enter the cabinet and sit between the Davenports. Seated on the center bench, he extended his arms and took hold of a leg of each of the brothers. He would know if either of them moved. A violin was placed in his lap, and the other instruments were placed at his feet. The doors were closed and, according to the professor's first-hand account, the strange happenings began.

Within seconds, knocking sounds began. He felt fingers passed over his head and face. A hand unfastened his cravat and took it off his neck. He was told to request that the musical instruments begin to play and instantly, the violin raised from his lap, brushed past his face, and began to play. It raised up to within inches of the top of the cabinet and continued to play on its own. The tambourine came up in front of him, gently tapped his cheeks and the top of his head, and then flew over and struck one of the Davenports. At his feet, the trumpet slid across the floor of the box, slid up one wall, and hovered in the air with the violin. The horn began to blow. The tambourine now flew over and landed on top of the professor's head. At the same time, he said that hands were touching his face, hair, head, and sides.

During all of this, Loomis swore, the Davenport brothers never moved. It would have been impossible, he later wrote, for them to move their hands from behind their backs without him noticing it. Even if they had been free, their four hands would not have been sufficient to play all the instruments and still manage to touch Loomis's face and body. They also could not have untied themselves and then readjusted the ropes

Newspaper illustration from a Davenport brothers' seance

before the cabinet doors were opened. Loomis would have detected their movement – he was convinced of that fact.

Loomis stepped out of the cabinet after the doors flew open, and they closed again behind him. In less than a minute, they opened again and the Davenports emerged, leaving the ropes, with every knot untied, behind them.

Loomis went on to write a 10-page report about the séance, repeating several times that while he was not a believer in Spiritualism, he had written the account of what he had witnessed "as correctly as he was capable and precisely as he would describe any other phenomenon." Moreover, he was convinced that the bizarre events were produced by a power with which he was unacquainted and that no trickery took place. He concluded: "As far as I could perceive, the phenomena was real and must be accounted for through the agency of a new force."

No matter whether the Davenport brothers referred to themselves as spirit mediums or not, those who came to their exhibitions were convinced they were genuine. Some newspaper accounts even gave them credit for producing miracles. In one news account of a séance, it was written:

The musical instruments, bells, etc., were placed on the table; the Davenport Brothers were then manacled, hands and feet, and securely bound to the chairs by ropes. A chain of communication (though not a circular one) was formed, and the instant the lights were extinguished the musical instruments appeared to be carried about the

Illustration from a Davenport brothers' seance

room. The current of air, which they occasioned in their rapid transit was felt upon the faces of all present.

The bells were loudly rung; the trumpets made knocks upon the floor, and the tambourine appeared running around the room, jingling with all its might. At the same time, sparks were observed as if passing from south to west. Several persons exclaimed that they were touched by the instruments, which on occasion became so demonstrative that one gentleman received a knock on the nasal organ which broke the skin and caused a few drops of blood to flow.

There was no question that the brothers were a sensation and were largely responsible for the demand that was created for mediums to do more than simply cause the spirits to knock on tables and walls.

In the summer of 1864, the Davenports went international and traveled to England in the company of a famous Southern minister and speaker, Reverend Jesse Babcock Ferguson. He made an unusual addition to their entourage, but after witnessing one of their exhibitions, he was so impressed that he came to every show for the next 11 days. He had never seen anything like the two young men, even though he had been interested in mesmerism and Spiritualism since the 1840s. He had attended scores of séances and his wife was an accomplished writing medium. When he joined up with the Davenports, he did not come to them as a naïve man who was gullible enough to believe anything. He was convinced in the reality of spirit communications and he was also convinced that the Davenports were the real thing.

After joining with the brothers, Ferguson occasionally acted as their advance booking agent, traveling ahead of them and with them for several months in Canada and New England. The Civil War was still raging at the time and Ferguson's sympathies for the Union had made him unwelcome in the southern states. In the late spring, the group returned to New York and then after a brief stay, sailed to England. They took with them an adjutant medium named D.H. Fay, who was several years older than the brothers and was also known for his physical manifestations.

Almost as soon as they arrived in England, they were immediately contacted by prominent writers and members of aristocracy with requests to conduct séances in private homes. The Davenports, flattered by attention that was unlike anything in America, readily agreed. Several of the exhibitions were reported in the newspapers by people like Sir Edwin Arnold and Sir Richard Burton, who had witnessed more than his share of strangeness during his travels in the Far East, a mysterious and exotic region in the 1860s.

The first to engage the Davenports for a private exhibition was Dion Boucicault, a well-known actor and author of the day. He hosted an exhibition in his home on September 28, 1864. Also in attendance were 24 guests of various professions – lawyers, diplomats, journalists and others. They included Sir Richard Burton; Sir Charles Nicholson, the chancellor of the University of Sydney; Robert Chambers; novelist Charles Reade; and others.

Boucicault obtained plenty of rope, as well as six guitars and two tambourines. The various guests were asked to make a critical examination of all the proceedings and when the Davenports arrived, they were carefully searched.

Both Ira and William were bound hand and foot, with the additional precaution of securing the knots with sealing wax. They could not be broken without leaving evidence of it behind. While the doors of the cabinet were still open, Boucicault later wrote, with the Davenports inside and Lord Bury, who had helped tie them up, was bending forward and looking into the cabinet, "A detached hand was clearly observed to descend upon him and he started back, remarking that a hand had struck him. Again, in the full light of the gas chandelier and during an interval in the séance, the doors of the cabinet being open and while the ligatures of the Brothers Davenport were being examined, a very white, thin, female hand and wrist quivered for several seconds in the air above. The appearance drew a general exclamation from all the party."

One of the guests, Sir Charles Wyke, then entered the cabinet and sat between the two brothers. Like Professor Loomis, he put his hands in contact with the brothers' legs. The doors were then closed, followed by a cacophony of strange sounds and the appearance of several spectral-looking hands at the opening in the center door. When Sir Charles emerged, he reported that while his hands were on the brothers' legs, hands touched his face, pulled his hair, and the musical instruments slithered over his body and over his head. Another guest, Captain Inglefield, the famed arctic explorer, also asserted that when the hands appeared, he touched and held them and that they were apparently human but "passed away from his grasp."

After the brothers had completed the first part of the séance by stepping out of the cabinet free of their restraints, one of the brothers and Mr. Fay seated themselves in two chairs outside of the cabinet. Ropes were tossed on the floor at their feet and the lights were extinguished. Boucicault said that within two minutes, they were tied hand and foot, their hands behind their backs, bound tightly to their chairs, and their chairs bound to a nearby table. While this was happening, a guitar rose from the table and floated over the heads of the seated guests, sometimes brushing the hair of some of the men. A glowing light appeared and moved from side to side above the audience, landing on the hands, laps, and shoulders of several of them. Bells whisked here and there and the violin strummed with a nameless tune. Two tambourines rolled back and forth on the floor, shaking violently. One of the guests, Mr. Rideout, grabbed a tambourine as it rolled near his foot and it was immediately jerked out of his hand.

At the end of the séance, all 24 of the witnesses were unanimous in the opinion that "the phenomena which had taken place in their presence were not the product of legerdemain." Boucicault concluded his own report about the night with a paragraph that stated that he was not a Spiritualist and had no reason, before that evening, to feel one way or another about the supernatural.

Sir Richard Burton attended four separate séances with the Davenports, all in private houses, including one in his own home. He too reported seeing and hearing the flying musical instruments above his head, seeing and feeling the spirit hands. He added, "A dry, hot, and rough hand, on one occasion, felt my hand, fell on my face, and then pulled my mustaches, and finally thrust between my lips a cigar, taken from the mantelpiece. My legs have also been twitched and my head patted."

Sir Edwin Arnold, editor of the *Daily Telegraph*, published a long account of a Davenport séance and he also testified to seeing the flight of the musical instruments, among other things. Although after all of it, the ropes that bound the Davenports remained intact.

The many eerie accounts of the Davenports' séances raise many questions – not only about that night, but also about many others. Could mere stage magic have produced the effects that were written about by Boucicault, Burton, and the others? Simply having the skill to slip out of ropes would not explain all the things that were credited to the Davenports. Even if their hands were somehow freed, how did they cause objects to fly about the room or create spectral hands that touched audience members who were a dozen or more feet away?

The effects appeared to be wondrous, but were they really? There were those who didn't believe that the Davenports' exhibitions were anything other than a clever stage show and soon, things in England would take an ugly turn.

In October 1864, the brothers began offering public séances at the Queen's Concert Rooms in Hanover Square. Committees were appointed from the audience each night and every effort was made to try and discover how the effects were being accomplished, but to no avail. They continued these performances, interspersed with private ones, until the close of the year. The Davenport brothers were introducing the British to a taste of American Spiritualism and audiences were finding it to be like nothing they had experienced before.

Early in 1865, they toured the English provinces and while most shows were well received, they did suffer violence at the hands of mobs in Liverpool, Huddersfield, and Leeds. At Liverpool, in February, two members of the audience tied their hands so tightly that the brothers claimed their circulation was cut off. An angry Reverend Ferguson cut the ropes, freed them, and then canceled the show. A mob ended up rushing the platform and smashing the spirit cabinet. The same type of events occurred in Huddersfield and Leeds and led to more shows being canceled.

Then, in March 1865, the Davenports played at the Cheltenham Town Hall and encountered John Nevil Maskelyne, one of Britain's most popular stage performers. He was the only investigator to ever accuse the Davenports of fraud – and claimed to be able to prove it.

On March 7, 1865, Maskelyne attended the brothers' séance. Although it was the middle of the afternoon, heavy curtains were fastened over the windows to darken the hall. Lamps were used to illuminate the stage where trestles had been erected to support the brothers' three-doored wooden cabinet. The doors were standing open when Maskelyne entered the hall. Plank seats were nailed down the middle and a guitar, violin and bow, two hand bells, tambourine, and a trumpet had been placed inside.

A lecturer introduced the Davenport brothers and then called for volunteers. Maskelyne and several other men rushed to the front of the theater to inspect the paraphernalia. The committee members lashed the medium's wrists behind their backs and tied their ankles as they sat facing each other in the cabinet. Then, the lecturer closed the doors and signaled for the lamps to be put out.

Almost immediately, bells rang and flew out onto the floor of the stage. Pale, ghostly hands waved through the apertures in the center of the cabinet. A tambourine jangled, a guitar strummed and a violin played eerie music. Yet, when the lamps were lighted and the doors opened, the brothers sat tightly bound, exactly as they had been when the séance had started.

Purely by chance – or so he claimed – a stray bit of sunlight from a poorly draped window had flashed briefly on the stage during the performance and illuminated the trickery of the two mediums. From his vantage point on the side of the stage, Maskelyne claimed that he had seen through a crack in the cabinet door and saw Ira Davenport vigorously ringing a bell. If one brother could free himself, he realized, then the other one could do the same. Maskelyne told several people what he had seen, but a clergyman who had been watching from the same spot on the stage scoffed at his claims. He had seen nothing like what the magician described and suggested that Maskelyne had guessed at how the Davenports might perpetrate fraud, but had no actual evidence of it.

The clergyman might have been correct, but Maskelyne did spend the next three months attempting to recreate the exhibitions of the Davenport brothers. He persuaded a friend to help him build a cabinet so that they could work together and duplicate what the Davenports were doing on stage. Once they learned the technique of slipping out of, and back into, tightly knotted ropes, producing "spirit music" was a simple task. One June 19, Maskelyne appeared at Jessop's Gardens. Trick by trick – and he stressed they were tricks – he and his friend created their own séance. Five days later, the *Birmingham Gazette* offered an account of the performance and stated that Maskelyne had shown that spirits were not necessary for a "spirited" séance.

But his exhibition had little impact. The country was already divided on whether or not the Davenports were genuine and the description of Maskelyne's performance falls far short of the kind of phenomena that was reported at the Davenport's exhibitions. Also, by then, the Davenports had already moved on to France, Germany, and Russia, where they were being wined and dined by royalty.

The violence that had marred the Davenports' exhibitions led to them canceling the rest of their engagements in England. They traveled to Paris after receiving a summons to appear at the Palace of St. Cloud, where the Emperor and Empress witnessed a séance with about 40 members of their court. While in Paris, they performed a séance for Pierre Etienne Chocat, the successor to the famous magician, Robert Houdin. He wrote about the séance in the newspaper the following day: "The phenomena surpassed my expectations, and the experiments are full of interest for me. I consider it my duty to add that they are inexplicable."

After a brief return to London, the Davenports went to Ireland in early 1866. In Dublin, they provided séances for many influential audience members, including the editor of the *Irish Times* and the Reverend Tisdal, who publicly proclaimed his belief in the manifestations.

In April 1866, the Davenports went to Germany, with stops in Hamburg and Berlin. They only performed privately in Germany, never renting out theater space, as they had done in the past. The brothers remained in Berlin for a month and were visited by members of the royal family while they were there. After Germany, they went to Belgium, and then went on to Russia. They arrived on December 27, 1866, and on January 7, 1867, gave their first public exhibition with over 1,000 people in attendance. The followed this event with a séance at the residence of the French ambassador for about 50 people, including officers of the Imperial Court. The men were so impressed that word spread quickly to the Czar, who arranged for the Davenports to visit him at the Winter Palace. The brothers performed for the Imperial family on January 9 and, by all accounts, were well received.

After Russia, the Davenports visited Poland and Sweden and then returned to England. On April 11, 1868, they returned to the home of Dion Boucicault and received another enthusiastic response from those who witnessed the exhibition. Writers and newspaper reporters heaped praise on the two young men and by all accounts from the press, it's no wonder that those who actually saw them perform were both impressed and amazed by what they accomplished.

The Davenports never once made the claim that they were true spirit mediums, but they were certainly peculiar. Even during a time of less sophisticated investigation, they were never once caught cheating. John Maskelyne was the only person who was ever able to duplicate their feats, and even then, his tricks paled in comparison.

Were they mediums, or were they something else?

They never claimed that the spirits were responsible for their manifestations. Moreover, they never dealt in spirit communications. Throughout their career, they exhibited the manifestations as itinerant vaudeville performers and left the audience to decide whether spirits or human beings were responsible for what happened on stage. Other mediums, usually because of petty jealousies, were inclined to suspect them, for the brothers almost never failed to give an exhibition when even the most gifted mediums never knew if a séance was going to be successful.

One of the few times that the Davenports failed – or partially failed – occurred during an investigation under the auspices of the *Boston Courier*. Three Harvard professors offered their services as investigators, along with a doctor from Cambridge, and George Lunt, one of the editors of the *Courier*. It's clear from Lunt's report of the proceedings that the investigators were more intent on exposing mediums as frauds, and Spiritualism as a popular delusion, than on making a careful and dispassionate inquiry into the paranormal.

The Spiritualists themselves had selected the rooms, made the arrangements, and gathered a number of well-known mediums, Kate Fox and the Davenports among them. As might be expected, and as Lunt made clear in his report, the investigation was carried on in an atmosphere of hostile suspicion. Lunt and one of the professors refused to even sit at the table with Kate Fox. They remained seated apart on a sofa, occasionally offering sarcastic remarks at her efforts to produce spirit raps.

Under these conditions, even an ordinary person would have found it difficult – if not impossible – to operate in any mental capacity, but for mediums, who were notoriously sensitive to the attitude of the sitter, especially if it is one of ridicule and contempt, the result usually is a complete paralysis of the psychic faculties. It is therefore remarkable that Kate, under the belligerent scrutiny of these academics, managed to produce a number of audible raps. However, since no spirit messages were forthcoming, the raps were dismissed as "artificially produced," but never explained.

The Davenports also put on a mediocre performance. The investigators bound them with great care with stout cords, some of which were run through holes in the cabinet and knotted on the outside. After the doors were closed, and with one professor seated in the cabinet between the two brothers, the usual musical performance failed to develop. Left together in the cabinet, only one brother was liberated from his bonds, and only partially, for his legs and waist remained tied.

The three-day investigation left the Spiritualist community crestfallen and the Harvard professors triumphant. They had proved to their own satisfaction that Spiritualism was a "delusion" and immediately issued a statement declaring that they deemed it "their solemn duty to warn the community against this contaminating influence, which surely tends to lessen the truth of man and the purity of women." It was also announced that a full report would be forthcoming, but the only report was made by Lunt in 1859, two years after the investigation took place.

If the Davenports used trickery to produce their manifestations, it is difficult to explain why their methods were never detected and how they managed to delude so many alert and intelligent investigators who not only inspected all the trappings of their exhibition – from cabinet to clothing and ties – but watched the manifestations at close range in private rooms. It is possible that the brothers learned how to release themselves from ropes, but this doesn't explain how they could have done so in the miraculously brief time their exhibition required.

Witnesses invariably reported that the moment the cabinet doors closed on the two young men, bound hand and foot, arms and hands immediately emerged from the small window in the center door and musical instruments played. If they had released themselves from their ropes, it would have taken more time than mere seconds and, in addition, the ropes would have been discovered with every knot untied.

Frequently, members of the audience, after securely binding the brothers in the cabinet, would fill their hands with flour or birdshot, but even after they had been released from their ropes and other manifestations had occurred, they would still be found holding the flour or shot in their fists, and no trace of it would be discovered on their clothes or on the floor of the cabinet.

So, what was the explanation? Well, that's when things get weird.

One explanation was offered by an English investigator, Benjamin Coleman, who expounded the theory that the manifestations were produced by the by the brothers' doubles – astral projections of their actual bodies. Coleman wrote: "After close observation and calm reflection upon the whole range of the Davenport manifestations, I am inclined to believe that the rope tying and untying, the handling and carrying about of the musical instruments, etc., are partly effected by their 'doubles,' and it may be that these are in part assisted by other spirits." On several occasions, Coleman stated, the figure of Ira Davenport, who had been left tightly bound in the cabinet, was seen outside of it when a match was suddenly lighted. He cited the statement of two witnesses who swore they saw the figure of the medium moving a few feet from them, but they also admitted that he was found tied up in the cabinet a few moments later. Another witness, who was present at the same séance, held in a private home in England, also saw the same figure, although he could not definitively identify it as Ira.

In a biography that he wrote about the Davenports, P.B. Randolph stated that their father had once interrupted an exhibition by declaring in a loud voice that he had seen Ira "standing near the table, playing on one of the tambourines when the light was sprung and that he saw him glide back to his seat." Randolph added that several others saw Ira's double, but at the same moment also saw him tied to a chair, and that the double or phantom had glided toward the figure of the seated Ira and vanished when it came within six feet of him.

Another report – more impressive and even eerier – was written by Professor James Jay Mapes, a well-known agriculturalist who entertained the Davenports at his farm near Newark, New Jersey, when they were on their way to New York City for their first exhibition. The professor claimed that during the séance in his home, when both brothers had been tied up and bound to chairs, a figure approached him, which he carefully felt and examined "from head to foot at my leisure" and was convinced that it was young Ira. He could not restrain the figure, which "slipped through my hands, or melted away with apparently utmost ease." Mapes admitted that the hands he felt were much larger than Ira's and that the texture of the clothing was unlike his or, as he carefully ascertained, unlike that of anyone in the room.

Ghosts? Doppelgangers? Psychic projections? Or was the answer to the Davenport mystery much simpler than that?

Harry Kellar, who went on to become one of America's most famous magicians, claimed to have been employed by the Davenports for a time when he was a young man and by observing them, learned to do tricks that eventually surpassed what he believed were the brothers' rope-tying and escapes. He stated that the Davenports had an uncanny – albeit natural – ability to extricate themselves from complex knots and ties and then return to their bonds in record time. He said that the most important part of the procedure took place during the initial binding, when they managed to obtain plenty of slack in the ropes by twisting, flexing, and contorting their limbs. Once they relaxed, the ropes could be easily slipped out of. Of course, while this explained how the Davenports may have released themselves from their ropes, it did not explain the mere seconds it took for manifestations to begin, how no one sitting in the cabinet with them detected their movements, or how musical instruments flew around above the heads of audience members.

Harry Houdini, another famous escape artist who spent many years debunking frauds in the Spiritualist community, also believed that he discovered how the Davenports produced their manifestations. Shortly before Ira Davenport died, Houdini met and interviewed him and claimed they became intimate friends. Davenport told Houdini that they never intended to become known as mediums. However, their act came along during the early heyday of the Spiritualist movement and, rather than turn down money and appearances, they allowed the public to think whatever they wanted to about them. Houdini alleged that Ira showed him some of his best escapes and admitted that they were never caught faking their manifestations because of the elaborate preparations that were taken during their exhibitions, which included hiring as many as 10 accomplices to keep debunkers from sneaking onto the stage and surprising them and setting traps in the aisles of theaters. Houdini offered no proof of his allegation that the brothers were professional magicians and still falls short of explaining all the manifestations that they produced. There is also no mention of accomplices and booby-traps in the accounts of the Davenports' exhibitions in private homes.

So, perhaps the mystery as not as easy to solve as many would like us to believe.

After their travels in Europe in the 1860s, the Davenports continued to travel and perform, but their career came to an end in 1877 when William died suddenly during a trip to Australia. In honor of his brother, Ira ordered a magnificent memorial for him on which was carved a representation of their ropes, cabinet, and other séance props. The cemetery authorities in Sydney, where William was buried, refused to allow the monument on hallowed ground, but did allow its placement outside of the walls.

Ira Davenport died at age 70 in 1911. During his life, he never publicly addressed the controversy over the reality of the spirit manifestations that surrounded himself and his brother. He felt that every audience member should form his or her own opinion about the source of the phenomena.

In the end, the mystery of the Davenport brothers remains unsolved. Mediums or magicians? No one can say absolutely, despite many disagreements on both sides of the subject. For a final word on the question, I will leave you with the writings of Sir Richard Burton:

I have spent a great part of my life in Oriental lands, and I have seen many magicians... But they do not even attempt what the Messrs. Davenport succeed in doing: for instance, the beautiful management of musical instruments. Finally, I have read and listened to every explanation of the Davenport "tricks" hitherto placed before the English public and, believe me, if anything would make me take that tremendous jump "from matter to spirit" it is the utter and complete unreason of the reasons by which the "manifestations" are explained.

THE KOONS FAMILY "SPIRIT ROOM"
A HIDDEN HISTORY FROM SPIRITUALISM IN AMERICA

During the early years of Spiritualism in America, interest in the spirit world usually began in "home circles." Family members, intrigued by stories of rappings in New York and elsewhere, would gather around the dining room table and try to discover if they, too, could receive communications from the other side. And often they did -- they might hear a soft tap, followed by louder ones and soon deafening noises that could be heard all over the house. Questions would be asked, codes devised, and soon information would be flowing from the other side. In many cases, especially with socially prominent families, such manifestations would be kept private, to save themselves from ridicule.

However, in other cases, when social standing was not a concern, spirit contacts would be widely publicized and neighbors would be called in for free performances. This sometimes led to members of the home circle becoming professional mediums, as if had with the Fox Sisters. Another family, about which much less is known, was the Koons family of Athens County, Ohio. Though they did not gain much material profit from their venture, the Spirit Room in Athens County became, for a short time in the 1850s, a Spiritualist destination that attracted hundreds of believers from all over the country.

Guests to the Koons farm were lucky to be rewarded with the kinds of manifestations that became so widely reported because getting to Athens County in that era was a remarkable ordeal. Although still somewhat remote today, it was a virtual wilderness in the 1850s. The county was a rough, wooded, hilly area not far from the Virginia (now West Virginia) state line. To reach it, one had to travel by stagecoach from Columbus over rutted and often washed-out roads. Then, to reach the Koons' farm, visitors still had to walk another two miles along a wooded trail. Once they arrived to face the manifestations that became famous at the farm, travelers never regretted their journey.

Johnathan Koons was a complex man. He was a rough man, who had carved a farm for himself, his wife, Abigail, and nine children, out of the soil and stone of Mt. Nebo, a hill that towers over the present-day town of Athens. But he was also a freethinker and reader, self-educated, and well-versed in the politics, news, and philosophies of the day. Early in 1852, Koons had come across newspaper descriptions of spirit rappings and had decided to make his own investigation of the growing phenomenon. He attended several séances throughout Ohio and allegedly learned from the spirits that he was a gifted medium. When he returned home, he also discovered that Abigail and his oldest son, Nahum, were also endowed with psychic abilities.

After holding several séances of their own, the Koons family was ordered by the spirits to build what was dubbed their "Spirit Room." They were given the exact specifications on how to build it, the size, the furnishings and the equipment to use. The Koonses immediately went to work, and following the spirit's instructions, constructed a log cabin that was 12 x 14 feet, had three shuttered windows, a single door, and a seven-foot-high ceiling. The room was then furnished with benches that would seat about 20 people. The spirits also requested that they equip the Spirit Room with a number of musical instruments: a tenor drum, a bass drum, two fiddles, a guitar, an accordion, a trumpet, a tin horn, a tea bell, a triangle and a tambourine. Koons was not a wealthy man and could not afford all the instruments (plus, he had trouble finding them in this remote part of Ohio) but managed to order some and borrow the rest from neighbors. After another séance, the spirits then demanded two tables, a rack for the musical instruments, and wire with which to suspend a few small bells and some images of doves that were cut from sheets of copper.

After faithfully following these instructions, the Koonses began giving public séances. Jonathan, Abigail, and Nahum acted as mediums and in the darkened cabin, the spirits began giving lengthy communications on various spiritual subjects, as well as concerts on the musical instruments. Neighbors from all over the region began descending on Mt. Nebo and the Spirit Room, attracted by not only the rumors about what was taking place there but also because the racket made by the spirits could be heard for over a mile in any direction.

As word of the strange happenings spread, it was not long before visitors from other parts of the country began arriving at the farm. Charles Partridge, a well-known New York publisher, later wrote that he found at least 50 people gathered for the first performance that he attended. Many of them were from various parts of Ohio, but there were representatives from other states, too. Koons, on the advice of the spirits, gave preference to those coming from far away. There were no admissions or other charges to attend the séances but those who stayed the night at the Koons' home usually contributed some offering. Throughout this, Koons was still working and maintaining his family's farm. He was at times so exhausted that he fell asleep during the séances. There is little reason to believe that the Spirit Room was ever a money-making project.

And while it may not have made money, it certainly attracted attention. Published accounts soon began to appear in journals and Spiritualist newspapers and from these reports, it becomes quickly obvious that the séances were not for spectators with fragile nerves. The exhibition was often loud and the spirit's performances on the musical instruments were usually ear-shattering experiences. All the reports (whether we choose to believe them or not) agree that in the total darkness of the crowded room, it would have been impossible for the Koonses themselves to provide the deafening and boisterous entertainment.

The program usually followed a set routine. After the audience was seated, the lights were turned out and the door and windows closed. The start of the séance was usually announced by the banging of the bass drum, which one witness compared to the firing of a cannon in the close quarters. Then Koons, who sat at a table with his wife and son beside him, would start to play a lively tune on his fiddle. In moments, all other instruments would join in, keeping perfect time, although played by unseen hands. What is more astounding, the reports all stated, was that the instruments did not remain stationary but would circle the room, playing wildly as they danced above the heads of the spectators.

Dr. G. Swan of Cincinnati, who attended a séance, later wrote: "One moment I would feel it on my head or brushing my hair and the next moment, it would be on the other side of the room." The triangle was also carried about the room and played in the same manner. Another witness, John Gage of Illinois, reported that the triangle dashed about over the heads of the visitors and was "occasionally thrust almost in my face, so that I was afraid that it would hit me." On one of its flights, the triangle dropped into his wife's lap and then smacked him up side of the head. Both agreed that it weighed close to 20 pounds.

According to another witness, the floating instruments would play in unison and were so loud that it made the "whole house roar so as to almost deafen us." No one seemed to recognize any of the tunes that the instruments played, but they were melodies of some sort and not just noise. Charles Partridge stated that the instruments would start together and then stop abruptly, "as if by some signal." Songs that were sung in what seemed to be "something like human voices" often accompanied the music. John Gage described them as "unearthly." The words, all the witnesses agreed, were apparently not in English.

Throughout all of this, though, the "master of ceremonies" was not Jonathan Koons, but rather a spectral voice that came through the tin horn. He called himself John King and he proclaimed that he was the leader of the spirits present, which numbered 165 in all. He was said to be the spirit form of the Welsh buccaneer Henry Morgan, who died in 1688. King, and his daughter Katie (who became most famous when later attached to medium Florence Cook) became popular fixtures at the Koons' séances and later, with other famous mediums, as well.

The musical part of the evening was usually followed by the appearance of spirit hands that were either luminous themselves or illuminated by "phosphorized" sheets of paper that were prepared by the Koonses and used to make objects glow. Visible to a little above the wrist, the hands felt like real flesh and according to witnesses were sometimes either hot or cold. Dr. Swan, who requested that a hand be placed in his own, reported, "It felt precisely like the hands of the subjects that I have handled in the dissecting room." Partridge, who also held out a hand and asked the spirits to take hold of it, said that it gave a distinctive grasp when it touched his hand but added, "It did not feel like the hand of a living person."

These phantom hands also played a part in the last feat of the evening, when the luminous appendages would write messages on pieces of paper. All those who described their visit to the Spirit Room saw the hands write out messages at incredible speeds. Many of the witnesses watched the hands from a short distance but one fascinated spectator pressed so close to watch that the hand playfully poked his nose with the end of a pencil. Six witnesses from four different states testified that they watched the armless hand write with a pencil. It wrote very slowly and so one witness asked it to write faster. At this request, the pencil began scrawling so rapidly across the paper that "we could hardly see it go." In five minutes, it had filled the page, which it passed to one of the witnesses, a Mr. Pierce of Philadelphia, who was then given an opportunity to examine the mysterious hand. He reported that it was human in all respects, even to the fingernails, but was slightly cooler than his own. Pierce then took another sheet of paper and the spirit's pencil and began tracing an outline of the hand on the paper as far as the wrist but "found nothing any further than that point." The appendage then shook hands with him and immediately vanished.

Reports of these wonders traveled out across America and hundreds came to Mt. Nebo, claiming that it was a place of spiritual significance and a sacred site to the Shawnee Indians. Some sources claimed that a "psychical society" christened Mt. Nebo as "one of the most haunted spots in the world."

As for the Koonses, their Spirit Room continued to operate and attract visitors until the end of 1858. By this time, they were competing with another Spirit Room that had been started by the Tippie family, who lived three miles across the valley from them. It was never as popular, but it managed to draw some of the visitors who came searching for the spirits of Mt. Nebo. The Tippies, who had 10 children, also boasted musical performances by the spirits, but visitors were reportedly disappointed that no spectral hands appeared.

Both families later moved out of the area. The Tippies went to Colorado and the Koons family moved to Illinois. After this, Jonathan Koons announced that spirit John King had departed and his tin horn was now silent. Koons contributed letters to the *Spiritual Telegraph*, a periodical of the movement, for a time and then lapsed into silence himself. Eventually, he and his family disappeared from the annals of Spiritualism altogether.

What really happened at the Koons' Spirit Room in Athens County?

Could such wonders have really occurred? It is human nature for us to seek an explanation but in this case, does one exist? It is almost automatic for us to say that the whole thing must have been a hoax --- but then how do we explain the independent accounts of strange happenings? Even if all the reports were made by avowed Spiritualists who visited the Spirit Room only to confirm their beliefs, the general agreement of the separate accounts seems to offer evidence pointing toward the fact that the Koons' were not putting on a fraudulent performance. What could they have had to gain from it? Only notoriety, for it was not money, as they did not charge for their séances. And if it was fame they were seeking, then why vanish without a trace after only six years as mediums? And what happened to them after they left Athens County?

The Koonses gave up their medium performances when they moved to Illinois. In an obituary for Nahum Koons, I learned that he died in 1921 at the age of 84 in Franklin County, Illinois. He and his family had accompanied his father and mother to Franklin County, where they lived for about 10 years before moving to Perry County, Illinois. After then living in Missouri for a few years, he returned to work his father's farm in Illinois. He also lived in Oklahoma and Arkansas for a time, after the death of his wife in 1899. He remained a Spiritualist throughout his life, which was described by those who knew him as "exemplary." He passed away in his sleep on October 26 -- leaving no clue as to why he had abandoned what was apparently an amazing career as a medium.

Students of Spiritualist history are sure to recognize through that the Koonses were groundbreakers as far as manifestations go. Many of the happenings at their séances were also reported at later séances, under the control of entirely unrelated mediums. The mobile musical instruments were part of the attractions offered by the Davenport brothers and the spectral hands were seen at many séances, including those of D.D. Home. The hands that materialized during his sittings resembled in every respect the hands that were seen and felt in the Spirit Room. In some cases, with other mediums, these manifestations were exposed as being fraudulent, but not in all cases. And for the most part, in the ones that were fraudulent, the methods used to make the instruments fly and the hands appear were beyond the means and the skill of the Koons family.

The case of the Koons' "Spirit Room" -- like many other aspects of Spiritualism -- remains unsolved.

THE MAN WHO COULD FLY
THE ENIGMA OF DANIEL DUNGLAS HOME

For the most part, the nineteenth century did not offer the kind of celebrity status that we are so familiar with today. With only newspapers, periodicals, pamphlets, and word of mouth, news spread slower and it was more difficult for actors, musicians, and even spirit mediums to attract a cult following. There was, however, one exception to this rule and his name was Daniel Dunglas Home (pronounced "Hume") and he became the most famous and enigmatic physical medium of the era. In his day, no one was better-known or more successful, and Home used his purported paranormal powers to mingle with the rich, the royal, and the famous. Even to this day, he stands unique among the scores of Spiritualists that thrived in the nineteenth century – because many of the feats that he allegedly performed have yet to be duplicated by anyone.

Home was born in Edinburgh, Scotland on March 20, 1833, the son of William Home, who was himself the illegitimate son of Alexander, the tenth Earl of Home. It is not clear why Home was adopted by his mother's sister, Mary Cook, when he was still a young child, but it is known that he immigrated with her and her husband to America when he was nine. Legend has it that Home was sent away because of his psychic talents, inherited from his mother, that were already beginning to manifest when he was an infant. Family members reported that his cradle would rock by itself, as though moved by an unseen hand, and at age four, Home accurately foretold the death of a cousin. He was a sickly and strange child and believed by his family to have remarkable powers. Home went to live with his aunt in Connecticut. His health continued to decline and he was diagnosed with tuberculosis. Unable to exert himself as most boys could, he spent most of his time walking in the woods and reading his Bible. He later became a very talented pianist – and he also came to believe that the spirits of the dead constantly surrounded him.

The first paranormal experience that he could recall occurred when he was about 13. Home had become friendly with a 15-year-old boy named Edwin, and together they often hiked the woods and spent long hours talking. The two boys made a pact that whoever died first would appear to the other. Edwin moved with his family to Troy, New York, and he died there a few years later. One evening, Home saw a "vision" of his

Daniel Dunglas Home

friend's face, bathed in light, at about the same time that Edwin died. This occurred in 1846 and they were many miles apart, so there was no way that Home could have immediately known about his friend's death, other than psychically, that is. Several days later, Daniel received a letter about his friend's passing.

As Home grew older, he had other strange experiences. His mother and father followed their son to America and were not living far from his aunt and uncle in Greeneville, Connecticut. This odd arrangement did not prevent Home from seeing his parents, for his mother reportedly told Daniel of a dream that foretold her own death. Three months later, the prediction was fulfilled to the day and the moment of her death was announced to her son in a similar dream.

Shortly after Home turned 15, the Fox sisters created a sensation with their table-rapping and Spiritualism was first embraced by the public. Not long after, Home's own paranormal talents began to increase. He was living with his aunt at the time and she grew to believe that the eerie events that took place around the boy were the work of the devil. She went to the length of calling in three ministers of different denominations to pray over her nephew but it did little good. Instead of discouraging the strange sounds, the prayers seemed to bring them on. Angry and frightened, Home's aunt threw him out of the house and left the imaginative and delicate young man to make his own way in the world.

For most of the rest of his life, Home had no place of his own to live. Staying in various households as a guest, he traveled about, holding séances for those who were interested. His séances, however, were different than most others because he always held them in brightly lit, rather than darkened, rooms. Home had attended many other séances in the past and regarded most mediums as frauds. He decided to do the opposite of what was being done elsewhere, showing the public that he had nothing to hide. Much has been made of the fact that Home never accepted direct payment for his mediumistic abilities. Most psychic investigators believed that any medium who accepted money for their services had a blatant motive for fraud. So, Spiritualists have long-maintained, Home must have been genuine. However, there are other kinds of "payments." Throughout his life, Home was taken care of by "kind friends," who likely would have never heard of him had it not been for his abilities. He ate at the tables of the rich and entertained with the noble, the brilliant, and the powerful. In short, he did very well for a poor young man who happened to be the illegitimate grandson of an earl.

During the séances that Home began to perform, he displayed a wide array of psychic abilities, including rappings, ghostly hands that ended at the wrist and which reportedly shook hands with audience members, moved tables, chairs and other objects, played spectral music, spelled out messages from the dead using lettered cards, and amazingly seemed to be able to shrink his body in size. While he was doing these things, he would ask the sitters to hold his hands and feet to prove that he was not somehow manipulating the objects with secret devices or wires. He claimed that friendly spirits, over which he had no control, made all his feats possible. Once he became known, by his own admission, he never again knew privacy or peace. He was constantly in demand by thousands for his psychic abilities.

In 1852, when he was only 19, Home paid a visit to one of the early and best-known young mediums, Henry Gordon, who lived in Springfield, Massachusetts. Home always maintained that he'd simply attended one of Gordon's séances, but in later years, critics claimed otherwise, saying that Home spent considerable time with Gordon and learned a lot from him – including the art of levitation. By then, Gordon had already demonstrated his ability to rise off the ground and seemingly float on air. Had Gordon – not the spirits – taught Home what he knew? It was one of many accusations made toward him that no one could answer with certainty.

Other physical mediums of the era attempted to create similar effects and materializations, but none of them could demonstrate such things with the skill of D.D. Home. A Home séance, at the very least, was marvelous, entertaining, and intriguing theater. If it gave evidence of the spirit world or some supernatural ability, that made it all the more extraordinary. Therein lay the controversy that surrounded the charming, tall, slender, and handsome young man with the brownish-auburn hair, full mustache, and penetrating blue eyes – was he performing his feats by supernatural skill or employing a magician's skill and using his good looks and charm as a distraction? The first scientist to study Home was the respected New York theology professor George Bush. Noted individuals also observed him, including the famed poet and journalist William Cullen Bryant. Some were so impressed by what they witnessed that Home was credited as the sole reason why many were converted to Spiritualism, including several scientists and Judge John Worth Edmonds.

Home was so confident of his abilities that he encouraged séance participants to stop him at any time to search for any concealed devices, the kind which were used by stage magicians. But no one ever discovered him engaged in trickery. Many were stumped when they were sure that they had determined how his psychic effects were created, only to be proven wrong. Home astounded audiences in the same way that the Davenport brothers would, except in his case, he had no need for darkened rooms and spirit cabinets.

Tables lifted off the ground, spirit hands appeared and then vanished, and musical instruments played on their own. Yet, of the many Home demonstrations, the one that still provokes the most wonder – and the most debate – was his ability to fly. Was it paranormal phenomenon or a clever illusion? Historically, levitations have been associated with the most holy of various faiths: Catholic saints, Hindu fakirs, and a few mystics. Otherwise, levitating was the domain of the theatrical magician, who created an illusion for the entertainment of his audience.

Home initially demonstrated his power to float in the air in August 1852 at the home of a Connecticut industrialist named Ward Cheney. At the séance, music was heard playing, although no instruments were present. Remember, this was at a time long before recording devices. How Home achieved the effect – whether by trickery or by supernatural means – is still argued today. But that was not his most amazing feat of the evening. To put it bluntly, Home managed to fly.

Present that night at the séance was a reporter for the *Hartford Times*, F.L. Burr, whose assignment it was to find something incriminating against Spiritualism in general and especially about Home, who had debunkers in an uproar with his excellent reputation. However, instead of writing an expose of the evening, Burr instead wrote:

Suddenly, without any expectation of the part of the company, Home was taken up into the air. I had hold of his hand at the time and I felt his feet - they were lifted a foot from the floor. He palpitated from head to foot with the contending emotions of joy and fear which choked his utterances. Again and again, he was taken from the floor, and the third time he was taken to the ceiling of the apartment, with which his hands and feet came into gentle contact. I felt the distance from the soles of his boots to the floor, and it was nearly three feet.

But how was this accomplished? Home claimed not to know himself. He stated that an "unseen power" simply came over him and lifted him into the air. Needless to say, most readers who came upon this article (and it was re-printed many times) were skeptical, as are most who come across it today. Full-body levitation is, and always has been, considered impossible. Throughout history, only a few people had ever been alleged to be able to lift themselves from the ground in such a manner. But in nineteenth century America, only one man – D.D. Home – could levitate without the aid of mirrors, ropes or even a safety net.

No medium during the era would come close to Home for the frequency of levitations or the number of witnesses to them. Home's supporters, of course, claimed his abilities were entirely supernatural and evidence of his psychic abilities. He could not only levitate himself, but he also sometimes caused séance participants to rise and float around the room. At one sitting, a woman felt her hand being inexplicably raised and nothing that she did would bring her arm back down again. Suddenly – in front of stunned witnesses – she was lifted from her seat, dangled in the air for a few moments and then was mysteriously placed back in her chair.

In the spring of 1855, Home traveled to England. In a biography that was later written by his second wife, it was asserted that he needed a rest because of poor health brought on by his numerous séances and was advised to visit England for a change of climate. He arrived in April, looking pale and feeling physically ill and depressed, but he settled in London, where his reputation as a famed medium preceded him. Why with his tuberculosis and bad cough, he'd chosen London with its terrible air quality from fog and smokestacks is unknown, but as he had in America, Home lived with those who invited him to be their guest. In return for their hospitality, he was always willing to give séances and soon found himself in the middle of a raging journalistic dispute over the merits of Spiritualism. Among those who first testified to the authenticity of Home's séances were Lord Brougham, Sir David Brewster, Sir Edward Bulwer-Lytton, and T.A. Trollope (father of novelist Anthony Trollope). Unfortunately, Brewster withdrew his support for Home when it appeared in newspapers. Brewster felt that he had his reputation as a scientist to consider. He was known for his research into the polarization of light and for the invention of the kaleidoscope, and was motivated to withdraw his support by fear of ridicule. He hurriedly wrote to the *London Daily Advertiser* and adamantly insisted that he did not believe in Spiritualism and that any demonstration by a medium claiming contact with the spirit world was a charlatan or imposter.

A contemporary illustration showing Home's alleged ability to levitate

The abrupt change in Brewster's position may have been spurred by his fear of pressure from his scientific peers, who disdained Spiritualism, but he could not avoid the controversy that followed. Edward William Cox, an attorney, psychical investigator, and supporter of Home, had carefully studied Home and was very familiar with the tricks employed by fake mediums. Cox, who attended the same séance as Brewster, wrote to the newspaper and took strong issue with Brewster's public criticisms of Home's abilities. He chided Brewster for acknowledging Home's psychic gifts in private and then denouncing them in the press. Others present at the same séance also pointed out that at the time of Home's demonstrations, Brewster did not express any doubt about their genuineness. In another letter to the press, Brewster answered that he had not been permitted to search beneath the table where Home sat for any evidence of trickery. T.A. Trollope also publicly took issue with Brewster, as did Benjamin Coleman and Lord Brougham. Home himself was also openly critical of Brewster's change of mind, leading the scientist threatening to sue the medium for libel, although he never did.

The last word in the debate did not come until 1869, a year after Brewster had died, when his daughter published his papers. In Brewster's documents and letters were his own writings about the Home experience and they left no doubt about his positive reaction the first time he witnessed the medium's abilities. In his account, he noted, "We could give no explanation of them and could not conjecture how they could be produced by any kind of mechanism."

Posthumously, Brewster's reputation may have suffered a blow because of the Home controversy, but it serves as a good example of the passion that was felt about a movement that had captured the attention of America and the entire world.

The séances that took place during Home's initial time London made it obvious that he was the sort of person to inspire strong feelings, whether favorable or unfavorable, in those who met him. His supporters loved him and far outnumbered those who did not, and it should be noted that he was a generous, affectionate, and volatile young man with good manners and an inclination toward vanity. He was certainly attractive to women, although most observers agreed that he was not conventionally handsome by the standards of the time. He was instead referred to as looking "poetic," an effect that was enhanced by his poor health. He was also an accomplished parlor pianist and had a definite talent for dramatic recitations, which were then almost as popular in genteel society as Spiritualism was. With such wonderful descriptions of him, it seems hard to believe that he ever managed to make a single enemy.

But he did. And that enemy not only hated him with a passion, but was in a position to do Home great harm when it came to his place in fashionable society.

The poet Robert Browning and his wife, Elizabeth Barrett Browning, had been among the earliest visitors to the spirit circle that gathered around Home in 1855. At first, the poets seemed as impressed with Home as any of his new British acquaintances. At one séance, a garland of flowers was brought by a "spirit hand" and placed on Mrs. Browning's head, a gesture of favor, Home explained, from the beyond.

There seems to be little doubt that Mrs. Browning, who was much more accepting of Spiritualism than her husband, enjoyed herself very much at the séance. She wrote about the evening in a letter to her sister: "We were touched by the invisible, heard the music and raps, saw the table moved and had sight of the hands... Robert and I did not touch the hands. Mr. Lytton and Sir Edward both did. The feel was warm and human --- rather warmer in fact than a common man's hand. The music was beautiful."

However, only a day or so after this séance, Robert Browning threatened to throw Home out of his house when the medium came to pay a social call. Neither at that time, nor later, did Browning make a specific accusation of fraud or any other wrongdoing against Home. In fact, the matter would have ended there if Browning had not shortly afterward written a satirical poem entitled "Mr. Sludge, The Medium." Since Browning's aversion to Home quickly became well-known in literary circles (although not the reason for his aversion) it was widely assumed that the poem had been written about Home. Using his flair for dramatic monologue, Browning used the poem to present "Mr. Sludge" as a truly despicable character. He was not only a fraudulent medium but also a liar, false friend, leech, drunk, and a braggart.

The poem probably would have done considerable damage to Home's reputation if it had not been overly long (about 2,000 lines) and occasionally so murky and repetitive that it was almost unreadable. It was definitely not one of Browning's better pieces and was so choked with outrage that it was almost incoherent. Browning's indignation seems a bit out of proportion to the subject, since Home was one of the many mediums on whom the poet might have vented his rage and at the time, was not even one of the most famous mediums in the movement. Some believe that Browning's real anger toward Home was not about his authenticity as a medium, but rather about this attractiveness to women. The special attention paid to Elizabeth Browning by "the spirits" may have enraged Browning and in a jealous fit, he lashed out in the only way that he knew. Fearing that he would look like a jealous fool if he accused Home of flirting with his wife, he instead attacked the medium in a way that he hoped would hurt him the most. Three years later, Browning was still complaining. When author Nathaniel Hawthorne, no fan of Spiritualism, visited Browning in London, Hawthorne asked him to stop talking about Home. Even if he agreed, Hawthorne was tired of listening to his tirades.

The poem did not help Home's reputation at the time, but the poorly-written piece is barely remembered today. Home's career as a medium survived Browning – and "Mr. Sludge" – as he still holds an almost legendary status in the history of the paranormal today.

Browning was not Home's only literary foe, just his most vocal one. Another who took a dislike to Home was famed author Charles Dickens. Although he'd written one of the most popular ghost stories of all time, *A Christmas Carol*, Dickens branded Home an "imposter," and he flatly refused to attend any of his séances, an attitude that irritated Elizabeth Browning. She said, "Dickens is so fond of ghost stories, so long as they are impossible."

Home did not stay in London for long. In the early fall months of 1855, he went to Italy to visit Mr. and Mrs. T.A. Trollope. It became one of the most trying periods of his life. Browning's attack on his reputation in London was followed by an attempt on his life in Florence. A group of superstitious peasants heard that Home was able to converse with the dead and came to the conclusion that he was some sort of witch. One rumor that swirled about was that he was in the habit of feeding the Holy Sacrament to toads in order to raise up evil spirits. Late one night, Home was ambushed in the street by a man with a knife. Fortunately, the medium was only slightly injured. His attacker was never captured.

Perhaps even more upsetting was a message from the spirits that Home received at about this same time – his powers were going to abandon him for one year. It was a prediction that he claimed to receive psychically, but it may have been brought on by his poor health. In any event, Home remained in seclusion for the next year. He held no séances, heard no voices, and produced no spectral manifestations. He plunged into a depression that lasted until the day that his powers returned to him. While he waited for his abilities to return, Home converted to Catholicism and even toyed with the idea of joining a monastery. He was warmly received by Pope Pius IX, but had a change of heart and left Rome.

Why his abilities stopped for a time is unclear, but they returned while he was in Paris in February 1857. As soon as the news spread, the medium was immediately summoned to give a demonstration for Napoleon III and the Empress Eugenie, who had heard much of the magnificent medium. No official records were made of the sitting but the royal couple seemed to be highly satisfied. The Empress was said at one point to have been convinced she held the hand of her dead father in hers, declaring that she would know it anywhere because of a scar on one of the fingers.

After the séances in France, Home returned briefly to America, but soon departed again for Europe. His reputation as a medium was now known across the globe and in the following year, he visited Russia to display his powers for Czar Alexander II. While there, he married the daughter of a Russian nobleman, Alexandrina De Kroll, whom he had met in Rome. One of the witnesses at Home's wedding was noted author Alexandre Dumas, who wrote *The Three Musketeers*, *The Man in the Iron Mask* and many other famed works. Several of Dumas' stories about spirit phenomena were inspired by Home's psychic powers, although Dumas had no personal interest in Spiritualism.

Despite his refusal to accept money for his séances, Home must have been doing well financially during this period. He not only had access to his wife's substantial fortune but also received many gifts from the Russian court. One of these was a valuable ring, presented by Czar Alexander on the occasion of Home's marriage, and another was a valuable sapphire, set in diamonds, which was given at the birth of his son, Gregoire, a year later. Home's wife passed away in 1862, but Czar Alexander remained a lifelong friend. Home's second wife would later recall other gifts from the Russian court at the time of her marriage to the medium years later.

Home remained away from the United States between 1859 and 1862. He divided his time between England and the European continent, presenting séances for the rich and prominent. One of those who joined Home's circle of admirers was the poet Alexis Tolstoy. After describing the manifestations that he had seen in a letter to his wife, Tolstoy concluded: "What would have, above all, convinced me, were I a skeptic, are the hands I have felt, which were placed in mine and melted when I tried to retain them. A cold wind passed around the circle very distinctly, and perfumes were wafted to us."

A more important addition to Home's circle, from a scientific standpoint, was Robert W. Chambers, a prominent publisher, writer of popular novels and later, the classic horror story *The King in Yellow*. Chambers had once been one of Spiritualism's greatest opponents, but he changed his mind after a séance with Home. Although Chamber's change of heart remained anonymous for the sake of his public reputation, his change of heart was well known in Spiritualist circles and it contributed greatly to Home's prestige.

Home was in France in 1862 when he predicted that Abraham Lincoln would be killed by an assassin. Later that same year, his wife, Alexandrina died and he found himself in financial trouble. Her family contested his rights to any inheritance and it would take another decade for the case to be resolved in his favor. His first book, *Incidents in My Life*, had done well, and had entered a second edition, but this was not enough to support the way of life to which he had become accustomed. Meanwhile, he was no longer welcome in Italy because of the allegation that he was a "sorcerer." In 1864, the Italian government ordered Home to leave Rome. He protested and was allowed to remain to study sculpture, if he would not engage in any Spiritualist activities or séances. It was a short-lived agreement since he seemed to have no control over the spontaneous paranormal manifestations and he departed Rome for good.

He returned to America for a time and gave a series of successful "dramatic readings;" he seemed to be unable or unwilling to remain in one place for very long. He went back to London in 1866. He resumed his sittings and among the noted figures who discovered him around this time was William Makepeace Thackery, author of *Vanity Fair*, who had seen Home perform in America and England. Thackery was brutally criticized for his interests in Spiritualism, especially after a popular periodical that he edited, *Cornhill Magazine*, published an article that was favorable toward Home. Actually, Thackery was not a Spiritualist. He'd simply commissioned a writer to describe what he had witnessed during one of Home's séances.

Home had many commitments to meet and was in great demand by royalty in Germany and Holland, but his health was not up to the rigors of his busy schedule. Fortunately, a number of his friends came together to form an organization called the Spiritual Atheneum and they offered Home the position of "residential secretary." It provided him with an income and did not require him to do much work. He also continued to offer private readings, but did not accept payment for them.

Between 1867 and 1869, Home became part of several séances that have intrigued psychical researchers, skeptics, and believers in America and Europe ever since. His frequent levitations expended a great deal of his energy, especially considering his frail health, and yet he continued them. One demonstration in particular has been studied, debated, and analyzed since it occurred in December 1868 – the Ashley Place Levitation. It has been called the "most famous case in the history of levitation" and still stands as one of the landmarks in the history of Spiritualism.

At Ashley Place, Home was in the company of two young men who were well-known to London society: Lord Lindsay and Lord Adare, the latter a close friend of Homes' and the owner of Ashley Place. Also present was Adare's cousin, Captain Charles Wynne. These three irreproachable witnesses reportedly watched as Home went into a trance, floated out the window of the third floor, and came in through the window of another room.

Each of the three witnesses later reported in detail what they saw that night. But what did they see? Skeptics contend the event was a mass hallucination or was somehow accomplished through trickery. They base this on the fact that there are slight discrepancies in the accounts of Adare and Lindsay, mostly concerning the size of the windows that Home floated out of, how high they were off the ground, and whether or not the night outside was dark or moonlit. The debunkers ignore the statement of Captain Wynne, which was simple and straightforward. He wrote, "The fact of Mr. Home having gone out one window and in at another I can swear to. Anyone who knows me would not for a moment say I was a victim of a hallucination or any other humbug of the kind."

What might explain Home's levitations? The longest-held belief is that they were accomplished by some supernatural power. Some scientists have experimented with levitation, describing their explorations into what is known as "electro-gravity" or "anti-gravity effects." Parapsychologists have suggested levitation may be the result of psychokinetic or telekinetic energy. Yet another theory offered is that levitation can be induced by "hypnotic suggestion." Eastern mystics who have demonstrated levitation for centuries have been credited with having a "special breathing technique" that makes it possible. Still other levitation theories range from "possession" to being in a "state of exaltation" with God.

Just as there have been numerous theories to explain Home's seeming ability to levitate, there have been just as many efforts to demystify it, too. How he was able to apparently suspend himself in mid-air has been an ongoing source of debate and controversy. There are no less than 100 separate incidents of levitation attributed to Home, yet no single theory to explain how he was able to do this in front of large and small groups of bewildered witnesses.

Home's abilities attracted attention everywhere he went and the press never failed to report about him, both in America and abroad. Some of the explanations offered for his strange abilities were nothing short of bizarre. For instance, in regards to the Ashley Place levitation, it was suggested he had done it by rigging up harnesses and pulleys outside of the house. However, it should be noted that it was the first time that Home had visited the house and any opportunity that he had to rig up elaborate machinery or engage the services of an accomplice to do so was nonexistent. There is no evidence to say that he ever resorted to such tricks. In addition, he was not exactly a robust character, thanks to his tubercular condition. It would have been impossible for him to go fumbling about on ropes and pulleys – that would have been rigged by who? -- outside of the window of Lord Adare's mansion on a cold December night.

After his death, dozens of explanations were given as to how Home accomplished this feat through trickery, but not even one of these theories was ever proven. In addition, the most prominent stage magicians in the world all claimed they could duplicate his stunts on stage but, for some reason, they never did. Perhaps one of the important notes on this occurrence appears in a diary entry for May 6, 1920 --- a diary that belonged to famed magician Harry Houdini. In the entry, Houdini wrote that he had "offered to do the D.D. Home levitation stunt at the same place that Home did it in 1868." Apparently, however, Houdini's assistant became frightened of the danger involved and refused to take part, bringing the project to an end. One has to wonder what might have happened if Houdini's assistant had been made of sterner stuff. Would Houdini have duplicated the event? And if so, what would it have proved? Houdini was admittedly using an assistant to accomplish the feat but, who had assisted Home?

During his career, Home was never caught cheating, but this didn't stop skeptics from wildly speculating about how he accomplished his strange feats. One suggested that he used a small "trained monkey" that shook hands and performed other acts during séances to fool the participants. There was also a theory that the medium slept with a number of cats in his bed so that he could absorb their electricity and use it to perform his demonstrations. There were rumors that witnesses were hypnotized. Some speculated that those who participated in his séances were chloroformed. Others maintained that Home somehow created illusions with a device of the era known as a "magic lantern," an early version of a slide projector. And of course, there was the old standby that Home's feats and readings were made possible by the use of confederates – some helped with trick illusions, while others secretly gathered information about séance participants. There was no end to people's imaginative assertions where Home's psychic gifts were concerned.

It raised a problem for the paranormal that still exists today. When skeptics attack a psychic ability or paranormal experience, but cannot find evidence of fraud of deception, often their explanation is stranger or more far-fetched than any psychic power could be. Thus, in Home's era, it made more sense to some that a "trained monkey" assisted him than accept the possibility that a telekinetic power was moving an object, a table, or even a person.

As has been noted time and time again, Spiritualism in the nineteenth century was marked by many incidents of fraud and deception. But Home stood apart from other mediums in that regard. Yet when friends tried to arrange for him to meet the respected scientist Michael Faraday so that Home's abilities could be examined, Faraday proved to be less than open-minded. His answer for how tables and other objects moved by themselves was based on his theory of "involuntary muscle action" on the part of Home or the séance participants. Faraday deemed Spiritualism to be absurd and beyond reason and he would not agree to see Home unless the medium publicly disclaimed the phenomena as Faraday had done. Needless to say, no séance was ever arranged for the two of them.

Home's life took another turn when he met a prosperous, elderly widow named Jane Lyon. Oddly, she offered to adopt him, even though he was an adult. She apparently liked him so much that she offered him permanent financial security if she could legally take him as her own and if Home would agree to take her name. Home agreed and became Mr. Home-Lyon. As she promised, Mrs. Lyon deposited £60,000 in his bank account and also prepared a will that would maintain his wealth. But this was not the end of the story.

A short time later, Mrs. Lyon abruptly changed her mind about the situation and brought a lawsuit against Home to regain her money. So, why had she originally offered him access to her fortune? Lyon claimed that she had been under the influence of her dead husband's spirit, who communicated with her through none other than Daniel Home. Critics immediately seized on this and charged that Home had "taken advantage of a wealthy widow." But supporters maintained that Home was the actual victim of a manipulative and unbalanced woman who wanted him to bring her into his inner circle of upper crust admirers. And they were right. Lyon later turned her attention to another medium and duplicated the original scheme.

In the midst of the lawsuit, another attempt was made on Home's life. He was attacked on the street by a man with a knife. Home was able to fight off his attacker, but was stabbed in the hand during the struggle. The assault made another good story for the newspapers. The *New York World* reported that Home had been killed, while other newspapers created their own wild stories, including one that claimed Mrs. Lyon had an artificial hand that Home said he could bring back to life.

Over a two-year period, Home reportedly held around 80 séances and in 1869, the London Dialectical Society arranged for a committee to study Spiritualism. The group's members included several hard-nosed skeptics, one an outspoken atheist. When Home was tested at four separate séances, the results were less than what was expected. There was some evidence of spirit raps and some table tipping, but little else.

It was said that Home's energy was at a low point, thanks to his continuing struggle with tuberculosis, and he was simply too weak to summon the power that he possessed. The committee's conclusion was that little had occurred, but the group acknowledged that Home had been open and willing to be studied through the entire process.

In 1871, Home married again. His new wife, Julie de Gloumeline, like his first wife, was a wealthy, attractive, upper class Russian woman. They'd met in St. Petersburg, Russia, where he was conducting séances. Even though she later wrote a biography of her husband called *D.D. Home, His Life and Mission*, she may have been concerned about her standing in fashionable society and after they were married, discouraged him from offering public séances.

Sir William Crookes, one of the first established scientists to publicly pursue the research of paranormal phenomena.

For this reason, the timing could not have been better when Home began a series of tests that same year with Sir William Crookes, a scientist interested in Spiritualism. Crookes was one of the most eminent physicists of the time, the discoverer of the element thallium, inventor of the radiometer, and was at various times the president of the Chemical Society, the Institution of Electrical Engineers, and the Royal Society. His reputation was such that when he made the announcement that he planned to investigate psychic powers, like it or not, other scientists were forced to listen. He apparently first became curious about Spiritualism following the death of his brother in 1867. He had witnessed a few other mediums before he began his tests with Home.

When Crookes made his intentions public, and it was reported in the press that one of the greatest scientists of the era would investigate "Spiritualistic phenomena," skeptics and debunkers were thrilled since Crookes had announced in the past that he hoped to "drive the worthless residuum of Spiritualism hence to the unknown limbo of magic and necromancy." As it turned out, though, the rationalists, realists, and debunkers could not have been more disappointed. Crookes would surprise them.

Crookes invited members of the Royal Society to take part in his testing, but they declined. However, he brought four others with him to act as witnesses during his examination of Home. Crookes conducted many tests using the best instruments available in the nineteenth century. In a long series of experiments using weights, balances, and other devices to register changes in the weight of objects under the medium's hand, Crookes became convinced that he was in the presence of a real physical force that was previously unknown but just as real and measurable as electricity or gravity. To determine if Home could somehow manipulate electro-magnetic energy, Crookes wrapped an accordion in copper wire and then placed it in a metal cage. He ran an electrical current through the wire, which he believed would block any magnetic energy coming from Home. The medium was still able to make the accordion play, leading Crookes to believe that he possessed an independent psychic force. He published a report that stated this and it stirred up tremendous controversy and led to horrific criticism of the esteemed scientist. His previous work in the scientific field was all but forgotten and his colleagues railed against him as an eccentric fool.

Crookes' conclusions were criticized on many fronts, both at the time and years later. Few dared to accuse the great man of fraud but several felt there was fraud in the construction of his testing apparatus. Even the critics admitted, though, that Crookes had been more than willing to make changes in the equipment to increase its sensitivity and make it harder for Home to interfere with it. This seemed to dismiss the problems with the equipment. A second wave of opinion fell back on the standard "it must have been a hallucination," accusing not only Crookes of being hypnotized by the medium, then recording false data, but also claimed that Home somehow caused the equipment to hallucinate as well. Finally, there is the always popular solution that none of Crookes' experiments mattered anyway. Critics continue to claim that Crookes violated one of the scientific world's most inflexible requirements. To be valid, an experiment must be repeatable --- when the conditions are the same, they must produce identical results.

Instead, Crookes said: "The experiments have been very numerous, but owing to our imperfect knowledge of the conditions which favor or oppose the manifestations of this force, to the apparently capricious manner in which it is exerted, and to the fact that Mr. Home himself is subject to unaccountable ebbs and flows of the force, it has but seldom happened that a result obtained on one occasion could be subsequently confirmed and tested with apparatus specially contrived for the purpose." This meant simply that Home was able to dictate the experimental conditions, such as the degree of lighting used and the relative positions of where the experimenters stood during the sessions. Whenever the setup was not to his liking Home could conceivably declare that the spirits were absent or weak.

Of course, he never did this but the debunkers declared that he *could* have, which, in their opinion, nullified the results.

Whether or not most of Crookes' scientific colleagues were intrigued by his experiments, many former skeptics were convinced of the reality of Home's phenomena. The report may have damaged Crookes' credibility with other scientists but it was tremendously influential to the public and started the scientist on a second career that was only a little less important than his previous work and certainly much more colorful than his role as an establishment scientist.

After the months of testing with Crookes, Home wrote a sequel to his 1863 biography, *Incidents in My Life*. Later, he wrote another book, *Lights and Shadows of Spiritualism*, in which he revealed some of the tricks that fraudulent mediums employed. About the only medium that he was on friendly terms with was one of the Fox Sisters – Kate. They met in 1872 while Kate was in London and the two performed a séance together. Home's book about mediumistic fraud was likely inspired by the deep resentment that most mediums of the era had toward him. He was not only a harsh critic of their deceptive practices, but also ridiculed them for being forced to hold séances in darkened rooms. He did not trust most mediums unless he had witnessed them personally and what he didn't see, he didn't believe. Angry mediums protested that he did not understand the way they worked. Others were, no doubt, jealous of him. From his writings, it becomes apparent that the he thought only one medium was entirely genuine – himself. However, when Home was asked about Kate Fox and the allegations that she'd created the spirit raps by cracking the joints of her toes, he just laughed, as if the proposition was too ludicrous to answer. Sir William Crookes also maintained that it was not possible for cracking toes to create the loud spirit raps that had been produced by the Fox sisters.

By 1876, Home's health had become noticeably worse, forcing him into retirement. Thanks to his marriage, money was no longer a concern. By then, he had little contact with his former circle of friends. His long struggle with tuberculosis had debilitated him, yet he made it clear that he had no fear of death. He lived quietly for another 10 years, cared for by his wife, and died quietly in Paris on June 21, 1886 at the age of only 53. Because he always believed that his work should be taken in context with Christianity, the epitaph on his gravestone is not surprising. It was taken from St. Paul in I Corinthians and reads: "To another discerning of spirits."

Home's death did not end the curiosity and controversy that encompassed him in life. Although he was never publicly detected committing any fraud or deception, no one could say with certainty how he produced some of the amazing manifestations that have been credited to him. Years after his death, debunkers were convinced in hindsight that somehow Home had employed deception – and yet they could not point to any proof of it.

Could the man who was called "the greatest physical medium of the nineteenth century" have engaged in trickery and deception? Of course he could have. But, for example, when debunkers who were not present to see his levitations dismiss them as "illusions," they are essentially taking issue not with Home, but with the many witnesses who were there and insisted they knew what they saw. There is also the unanswered question about how certain feats, such as floating through the air horizontally, could have been so readily achieved. How was furniture able to move, seemingly on its own? Since Home conducted séances in well-lighted rooms, couldn't someone who was there have detected fraud?

Virtually every other nineteenth-century medium, at one point in their career, was accused of some deception – skeptics will assure you of that. Many of the debunkers of the time attended séances for the sole purpose of detecting fraud. Why then were neither skeptics nor scientists able to detect trickery on Home's part? And what can be thought of the scientists who refused to even observe Home and other mediums? Perhaps they feared ridicule, or worse – they feared the inability to explain away what they saw by the laws of science. At that time – just as it is now -- admitting that psychic phenomena might be genuine would have meant redefining science, religion, and the very nature of life and death. It was far easier to simply discredit a medium than to try and re-write long-held scientific and theological ideas.

Home left many unanswered questions in his wake. Was he truly in contact with the spirit world? Might what seemed to be abilities that came from the spirits have been manifestations of a form of telekinetic energy, the kind often reported in poltergeist cases? Theories and speculation will always continue, boiling down to two possibilities:

Daniel Dunglas Home was a unique and remarkable individual who actually possessed the powers that have been attributed to him; or he was one of the most clever and cunning frauds in history.

It's likely that we will never discover which possibility is the truth.

PEOPLE FROM OTHER WORLDS
THE BIZARRE MYSTERY OF THE EDDY BROTHERS

The stories were everywhere in 1874. They were not only in the Spiritualist periodicals of the time; stories even appeared in the popular press. They all reported the same thing – some very strange happenings were taking place on a small farm outside Chittenden, Vermont. The farm belonged to two middle-aged, illiterate brothers, William and Horatio Eddy, and their sister, Mary. The Eddy clan lived in an unkempt, two-story house that was infested with supernatural beings in such numbers that nothing like it had been reported before, or since. People were coming from all over the country and from around the world to witness the manifestations for themselves. Spiritualists had started to call Chittenden the "Spirit Capital of the Universe."

The stories were greeted with skepticism in most circles. One of the skeptics was a successful New York attorney named Henry Steel Olcott. Prior to learning of the Eddy brothers, Olcott had no interest in the thriving Spiritualist movement. However, one day as he was returning to his office after lunch, he picked up a copy of the Spiritualist newspaper, *Banner of Light*. In its pages, he read a graphic account of the events that were allegedly occurring in Vermont. It's unlikely that Olcott had any idea how a simple newspaper article was going to change his life.

With no interest in Spiritualism, mysticism, or anything to do with the supernatural, we'll never know what prompted him to pick up a copy of *Banner of Light* that day. In addition to being a respected attorney and agriculturalist, he had also been an investigator for the U.S. Army during the Civil War. But within two years after his encounter with the Eddy brothers, he would divorce his religiously conservative wife, estrange himself from his sons, and become one of the founders of an occult society that remains prominent in the world today.

And all because of ghosts.

The story of the Eddy brothers is also the story of the man who first investigated their manifestations, wrote the only full-length book about that them exists, and carved out a place for himself in the history of the paranormal. Without Henry Steel Olcott, one of the greatest mysteries of Spiritualism would have been forgotten more than a century ago.

Olcott was born in New Jersey in 1832. His parents were middle-class Presbyterians and his upbringing was largely uneventful. Henry was smarter than most of his peers and by age 15, he was enrolled at New York University, studying agricultural science. His businessman father went broke during his first year and he was forced to drop out. On his own, he traveled to Ohio to live with relatives and try his hand at farming. But the farmlands of Ohio were not enough to satisfy his ambitions. Within a

Henry Steel Olcott

few years, he returned home to work at an agricultural school in Newark. After a relative left him an inheritance, he used the money to open a research farm near Mount Vernon, New York. The young agriculturalist developed expertise in a strain of Chinese sugarcane that seemed promisingly adaptable to the climate of the northern states. As the threat of war had started to loom across America, northerners were growing anxious about their dependence on the southern sugar crop. Not yet 25, Olcott wrote a widely-read pamphlet on the benefits of his imported cane, called "sorgho," which Americans still consume as a sweetener today. In a short time, Olcott went from being a failed college student and Ohio farm boy to an expert in scientific agriculture with his advice being sought by state legislatures and foreign governments. He received international recognition for his research farm and started a school for agriculture students. He published three other scientific works and became the farm editor for Horace Greeley's *New York Tribune*.

When the Civil War began, Olcott gained a new reputation. Originally commissioned as a signals officer, the young man displayed a talent for research, numbers, and money trails. He was appointed as a special investigator in charge of a team of auditors and detectives to investigate fraud and corruption among military contractors. A promotion to the rank of colonel added weight to his investigations. After exposing a racket of fake provision sales, Olcott saved the Union army so much money that Secretary of War Edwin M. Stanton wrote that his efforts were "as important to the government as the winning of a battle." When President Lincoln was assassinated in 1865, Olcott volunteered his services. Stanton telegraphed him in New York to "come to Washington at once, and bring your force of detectives with you." During the days that followed, while John Wilkes Booth remained a fugitive, Olcott and his investigators made the first arrests of suspected co-conspirators.

Rich in government contracts after the war, Olcott studied for the bar and opened a legal practice in New York City. Settling down with a family, he settled into a life of Sunday suppers, gentlemen's clubs, legal work, and perhaps a future run for local office.

But his life changed again after his accidental encounter with the story of the Eddy brothers.

After returning to his office, Olcott read the story and, although skeptical, he knew that if the stories were true, "this was the most important fact in modern physical science," he later wrote. Within days, Colonel Olcott had managed to gain a correspondent's position for the *New York Daily Graphic* and was on his way to Vermont, accompanied by a newspaper artist named Alfred Kappes. Together, they planned to investigate whatever was happening at the Eddy farm and if the stories were a hoax, the charlatans would be exposed in the pages of the newspaper.

The adventure would mark the final turning point in the life of Henry Olcott.

Olcott and Kappes traveled to the western edge of the Green Mountains of Vermont and the isolated town of Chittenden. Named for Vermont's first governor, Thomas Chittenden, its received the first charter granted by the Vermont General Assembly in 1780. Among the town's first settlers was Nathaniel Ladd, who owned a farm on the south side of the community. He was the first town clerk and first tavern owner. As the town grew, Ladd's property was divided and in 1846, his tavern became the home of a newly arrived family in town, the Eddys. The family lived at the tavern for a short time before purchasing a poor, 100-acre farm, where they kept sheep, cows, horses, and hogs. After the death of their parents, the four unmarried Eddy children inherited the family's farm and many debts.

The Eddy brothers home in Vermont, although this photograph is from the 1920s

It was on this farm where Colonel Olcott found them living when he arrived in Chittenden. The trip to Vermont had been uneventful, but Olcott's first meeting with the Eddy brothers was anything but ordinary. The two distant and unfriendly farmers were rough-hewn characters with dark hair and eyes, and New England accents so thick the New York attorney and writer could scarcely understand them.

Olcott would later compile a history of the Eddys that claimed the brothers were descended from a long line of psychics. How much was truth and how much of their history was apocryphal is anyone's guess, but the Eddys stated that a distant relative named Mary Bradbury had been one of the women accused of witchcraft in Salem, Massachusetts in 1692. She had escaped from the village with the help of friends. The Eddys' grandmother had been blessed with the gift of "second sight" and often went into trances, speaking to entities that no one else could see. Their mother, Julia, had been known for frightening her neighbors with predictions and visions, although her husband, Zephaniah, condemned her powers as the work of the Devil. Julia quickly learned to hide her gifts from the cruel, abusive, and narrow-minded man.

But the manifestations refused to be hidden once the couple started having children. Strange rappings began to be heard around the house, disembodied voices echoed in empty rooms, and occasionally, the children even vanished from their cribs. They were likely to be discovered anywhere in the house and even outside. As William and Horatio got older, their strange powers strengthened. On many occasions, Zephaniah would see the boys playing with unfamiliar children who would vanish whenever he approached. When these "visitors" vanished, he would take his boys to the barn and beat them with a rawhide whip as punishment. The strange children returned again and again, though, earning the young Eddy brothers countless beatings. Eventually, they would grow to both fear and hate their father.

Manifestations became so bad that the boys could not attend school. Their early attempts were marked by inexplicable happenings and disturbances -- invisible hands threw books, levitated desks, and caused objects like rulers, inkwells, and slates to fly about the room.

Zephaniah tried everything he could to stop the disturbances, although this mostly consisted of him beating and abusing the boys. But the beatings did not stop the eerie happenings. When he realized this, he grew furious. Each time the boys fell into a trance, he would berate and verbally abuse them. He would try to rouse them by pinching and slapping them until they were bruised and battered. Once, on the advice of a sympathetic Christian friend, he doused the boys with boiling water. When this didn't work, he also allowed this friend to drop a red-hot coal into William's hand. He had hoped to "exorcize his devils." The boy never awakened from his trance, but he bore a scar on his palm for the rest of his life.

Occasionally, the spirits that surrounded the young men tried to defend them, appearing in front of their father and scaring him away from the house. Eventually, the fear and frustration became more than he could stand. Wanting the boys out of his house – but realizing their money-making potential – he sold the boys to a traveling showman. Spiritualism was now at the height of its popularity and audiences eagerly packed theaters, beer halls, and sideshow tents to witness the exhibitions put on by the brothers. But unlike the Davenports or the Fox sisters, the Eddy brothers were the property of their manager. They had no say in when or where they performed – or what was done to them during the shows. The next 14 years of their lives turned into a hellish period of abuse, violence, and sadism.

As part of the exhibition, their manager would bind and gag the boys and then challenge audience members to try and awaken them from their trance states. The abuse they suffered at the hands of random audience members made the beatings from their father seem kind in comparison. The Eddys were locked in small wooden boxes to see if they could escape and hot wax was poured into their mouths to see if they could produce "spirit voices" when their tongues were too burned to talk. They were poked, prodded, pinched, slapped, and punched, leaving them scarred and damaged for the rest of their lives. On several occasions, they were even stoned and shot at by angry mobs. William Eddy had the bullet scars on his body to prove it. Infuriated mobs attacked them and their promoters for every reason imaginable – except for the justifiable one of preventing further abuse of two children. Some of the protestors were religious fanatics, convinced the Eddys were in a league with the Devil, while others were skeptics who felt cheated out of their money because the manifestation had been fake. They barely escaped from Danvers, Massachusetts with their lives. In Cleveland, an angry mob seized William and only a last-minute rescue prevented him from the pain of hot tar and feathers. In larger cities, like New York and Philadelphia, they were safer from violence, but were still subjected to threats and indignities.

William and Horatio Eddy

And these were two children.

But the Eddy brothers gave performances that were so sensational and so profitable that the abuse continued until the death of their father in 1860. Only then did their tours and their suffering finally come to an end. They returned home to their mother and a sister, Mary, and another sister, Delia, who later married and moved out of state. When Julia passed away 13 years later, William, Horatio, and Mary took over the farm. Julia had allegedly foretold the time and circumstances of her death. The spirits told the three remaining children that William was to become one of the most powerful mediums of the age and instructed them to build a "circle room" for séances. The farmhouse was opened as a modest inn and by 1874, the family's spirit manifestations were known throughout the United States. Soon, their reputation would spread across the ocean and beyond.

The Eddys were no ordinary tavern-keepers, though. By then, the two brothers were understandably embittered men, hostile and suspicious after a lifetime of abuse, and trusting only one another. Colonel Olcott later described them as two men who could easily make "newcomers feel ill at ease and unwelcome."

This might have been the reason why the Eddys were so disliked in their own community and why the local press scathingly attacked them in print. The *Rutland Herald* continued to denounce the family even after two New York dailies published extensive accounts attesting to the authenticity of the phenomena on the farm. The attacks even found their way into subsequent histories of Rutland County, where Chittenden was located. In the 1880s, local gazetteers reported, "their spiritual trickery has long since been exposed" but never published a single detail of the exposure. No matter how many people signed affidavits attesting to having seen spirits, skeptics maintained that delusions combined with an elaborate hoax explained the whole thing.

But those who came from outside the region went away from the farm stunned and shaken. As unsociable as the Eddys were, they rarely had a vacancy in their inn. Spiritualists from all over America and Europe flocked to Chittenden to take part in séances that were held every night except Sunday. The Eddys charged $10 per week at the inn, which was high for the time, but not exorbitant. Overflow visitors found other lodging nearby, which should have lessened the hostility of the locals toward the Eddys, but failed to do so. Perhaps they imagined the profits being made by the Eddys were so much greater than their own that they had become jealous of the family. The Eddys did make money from their enterprise, but the costs they incurred housing and feeding a seemingly endless stream of tourists likely subtracted quite a lot from their balance.

Colonel Olcott obtained a room for Kappes and himself on the second floor. Like all the visitors, he had access to the entire house. Apparently, all but the most gullible guests used this freedom to search the premises – hopefully or fearfully, depending on their beliefs – for evidence of theatrical props and assorted items that might aid in tricking those who came to witness the séances. Where did the Eddys hide the mirrors, wires, costumes, and sheets? Olcott scoured the house from cellar to attic, but was unsuccessful in finding anything that revealed the happenings he had read about as a hoax.

On the first day at the farm, Olcott was a witness to an outdoor séance. In the bright moonlight of a warm summer evening, a group of 10 participants traveled down a path into a deep ravine. They assembled in front of a natural cave, formed by two large stones that had collapsed atop one another, forming a wide archway. Olcott later learned that it had been dubbed "Honto's Cave," in honor of the Native American spirit that often appeared there. Olcott used a few moments to suspiciously investigate the cave and was satisfied that there was only one entrance and no exit that could be found behind the rocks. He determined that there was no way that anyone could slip in or out of the cave and not be seen. The entrance was in full view of the audience.

Horatio Eddy acted as the medium for the séance. He sat on a camp stool under the arch, draped in a makeshift spirit cabinet that had been formed by shawls and branches cut from small trees. With Horatio inside of the cabinet, a gigantic man, dressed in Native American costume, emerged from the darkness of the cave. Horatio addressed the spirit and at the same time, an audience member cried out and pointed up toward the top of the cave. Standing, silhouetted against the moon, was the form of another Indian. To the right side of the cave, a spectral female had materialized on a ledge.

Altogether, 10 such figures appeared during the course of the séance. The last spirit, William White, the late editor of a Spiritualist newspaper, emerged from within Horatio's cabinet. He was dressed in a black suit with a white shirt and was said to have been recognizable to one of the guests who read the newspaper and recognized his picture from its pages. All of the figures, including White, vanished at the same time. A few moments later, Horatio left the cabinet and signaled that the séance was over.

After the bizarre event had ended, Olcott and Kappes carefully searched the cave and the surrounding area for any clues that might have been left behind by hoaxers. They searched for any sign of conspirators, costumes, and pored over the soft dirt, looking for footprints.

They found nothing to indicate that anyone other than Horatio Eddy had been near the cave – no one who was alive anyway.

Olcott was intrigued, but not convinced, by the séance. He was sure that he would be able to more easily detect fraud within the controlled setting of the Eddy house. This was where the next séance was scheduled to take place. He and Kappes had thoroughly examined the large circle room, which was located on the second floor of the house. They drew maps, charts, and diagrams. They took numerous measurements, sure they would find false panels, secrets doors, hidden passages, or open spaces between walls that didn't match the exterior design of the house. But they found nothing out of the ordinary.

Olcott wouldn't give up. He convinced the newspaper to hire workmen to come and examine the place. Using carpenters and engineers as consultants, another thorough search was conducted. The experts found nothing. After this, Olcott and Kappes were finally convinced that the walls and floors were as solid as they seemed.

This made what Olcott saw the during the nights that followed even stranger.

Each séance was basically the same. On six nights each week, visitors would assemble on wooden benches in the upstairs séance room. A platform that had been assembled there was illuminated by a single kerosene lamp, further dimmed by being recessed in a barrel. William acted as the primary medium. He climbed onto the platform and entered a small cabinet. Moments later, soft voices began to whisper, as if in the distance. Sometimes they would be singing, accompanied by eerie music. Musical instruments that had been placed in the room came to life. Strings were plucked, tambourines were shaken, and they often soared above the heads of audience members. Disembodied hands appeared and they touched the spectators. Odd lights appeared and unexplained sounds filled the room.

And then things really got strange. The first spirit form emerged from the cabinet, then another. They walked out one at a time, or in groups, numbering as many as 20 or more in a single evening. Some appeared completely solid, very visible, while others were semi-transparent and ethereal. The appearance of them awed the frightened spectators. They ranged in size from over six-feet-tall to very short – and it should be noted that William was only five-feet, nine-inches tall – and usually appeared to be Native Americans or elderly Yankees. Oddly, though, there are also scores of reports of spirits from other races and in traditional African, Asian, and Russian costumes, as well as others. The weird figures not only appeared, they also performed, sang, and chatted with the audience like a spectral lounge show. They brought their own musical instruments, clothing, hats, and scarves.

Olcott was stymied. Where had the figures come from? He had examined the cabinet and platform and found no trap doors, nor hidden passages. There was no room inside of the cramped cabinet for anyone other than the medium. Olcott was familiar with the workings of stage magicians and fraudulent mediums, but could find none of their tricks present at the Eddy house.

Nearly every kind of supernatural phenomena imaginable reportedly occurred at the Eddy house: rappings, moving objects, spirit painting, automatic writing, prophecy, speaking in tongues, visions, unseen voices, levitation, apports, and more. Olcott noted

(Above) The seance room inside of the house.

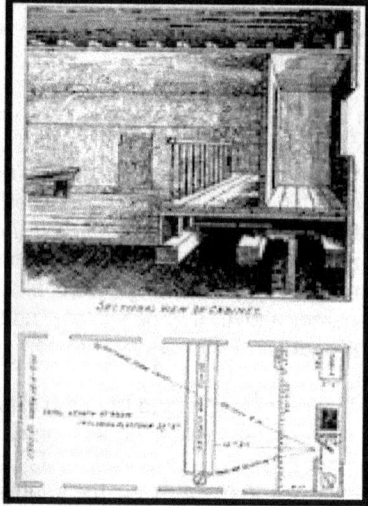

Drawings by Olcott of cross-sections of the spirit cabinet. According to his account, he was unable to find any fraud to explain the bizarre manifestations.

(Right) The interior of the spirit cabinet, a solid room with no exits or trap doors.

the appearance of at least 400 different full-bodied manifestations during his various visits to the Eddy farm. He concluded that if the séances had been a theatrical stage show, it would have required an entire company of actors and more than a dozen trunks filled with costumes. And yes, his inspection of the premises revealed no place to hide either actors or props. The idea that the Eddys had hired an itinerant acting troupe was further dispelled by the convincing manner of the spirits. One woman spoke to the spirit of what she said was her dead husband in Russian and the spirit replied perfectly. A number of other languages were also heard. It was impossible that the Eddys had faked this – the two men could barely read or write and spoke in such poor English that guests could scarcely make out what they were saying.

In addition, such an elaborate show would have cost a fortune to produce each night. The Eddys would have had to have paid the actors, invested in costumes, and then hired someone to manage the special effects involved for the manifestations. The

Eddys, however, barely had any money to their name. Most of the séance visitors that arrived did not pay. A fee was only collected from those who rented a room and the $10 per week made from the rooms would not have financed the nightly performances. In Olcott's mind, fraud was physically and financially impossible.

Olcott was now beginning to believe that the dead were returning at the Eddy farm. He witnessed departed friends and relatives who returned to see visitors in the audience, leading to tearful reunions, as well as seemingly foreign apparitions, with no connection to anyone in Vermont, who seemed as baffled by their appearance as the people in the séance room were. Another newspaper, the *New York Sun*, sent a correspondent to Chittenden and he corroborated much of Olcott's account. Meanwhile the fascination with the Eddys was spreading. And while Olcott's interpretation of the manifestations at the Eddy farm essentially supported the contention that mediums could assist the dead in reconstructing themselves, other experts were lining up on both sides of the debate. Two men with clearly antagonistic views found themselves drawn in mid-October 1874 to what locals called the Eddy's "ghost shop."

Dr. George Miller Beard was a Yale graduate and had studied at the New York College for Physicians and Surgeons. After his service during the Civil War, he established a practice in New York that specialized in treating people with nervous diseases. He was one of the first medical men to experiment with electricity as a stimulant and in 1874, he began a study of Spiritualism, convinced that it was based on either trickery or delusion.

Beard arrived in Chittenden on October 12, 1874, and wearing a disguise to make himself look disheveled and poor, gained admittance to the circle room with an electrical device. His object was to apply a strong electrical current to one of the "spirits" that emerged from the cabinet. He didn't mention until later that if the "spirits" had been living people, as part of a hoax, the jolt that he would've given them could have killed them. Beard was discovered before he could carry out his experiment, which he explained to Olcott could have great scientific importance. He admitted then that "no human being could take the shock without a violent muscular contraction." Or worse.

The Eddys became suspicious of Beard and would not allow him to conduct the experiment himself. He and Olcott trained one of the regular séance attendees, Ed Pritchard, to use the device. After two electrodes were grasped by Honto, the Native American spirit, for which the nearby cave was named, Pritchard released the charge. The spirit held on for several minutes, but nothing happened.

Olcott took this as more proof of the Eddys' authenticity. Beard was perplexed but he discounted the test in an interview with the *Sun*, saying, "It was of no service. I could not see how it was applied. Powerful current when applied may be very painful. Applied in another way, it may not be felt." In other words, he lied about his own test. He had been standing nearby when it took place and had watched the figure as it held the electrodes in its hands.

Beard went on to say that he was sure that the rest of the manifestations were caused by the mediums in various disguises, accomplished through use of their "flexible and limber" bodies. They could get away with this trickery because most of their visitors were "weak-brained, simple-souled, amiable and sincere Spiritualists, the riff-raff of modern society." Keep in mind, this was a man who was a leading expert in the treatment of people with mental illness in the nineteenth century. It's not surprising that there would be no major accomplishments in the field for another decade or so.

Colonel Olcott was angered by Beard's interview. For one thing, he was far from a "weak-brained, simple-souled man" and could hardly be called "riff-raff." He noted that Beard failed to indicate how the uneducated Eddys could speak several languages or how they could have been speaking in and out of the spirit cabinet with a room full of witnesses, "simple-minded" as they might be. He also demanded that Beard find one person who could authoritatively speak against the mediums, when Olcott was unable to do so.

Beard attended one séance at the farm, while Olcott remained on the property for more than 10 weeks. It was surely a test of his endurance. He left disliking the food, the weather, and the Eddy brothers, but he was convinced of the fact that the two men could contact the dead.

The experience at the Eddy farm in Chittenden was surely a turning point in Olcott's life, not only because of his exposure to the manifestations of the Eddy brothers, but also because of a chance meeting that occurred there with someone with whom he would spend the remainder of his days.

On the sunny morning of October 14, 1874, Olcott stepped out onto the Eddy porch to smoke and met one of the most flamboyant of the many international visitors to the farm: a strange, heavyset Russian woman named Helena Petrovna Blavatsky. Madame Blavatsky had not yet reached the height of her fame at this point but already commanded great respect in occult circles. She was a theatrical woman with a powerful personality and a flair for the dramatic and made an impression at the Eddy farm by smoking cigars and appearing in a variety of veils and flowing dresses.

Many of the visitors in 1874 were already aware of Madame Blavatsky. She had been born in Russia in 1831 to German parents with excellent social credentials. She married young but later abandoned her husband to explore both the physical and spiritual worlds. She visited an odd assortment of places such as Canada, Mexico, Texas, and India and made a first attempt to enter the forbidden country of Tibet. A short time later, she vanished. For a decade between 1848 and 1858, Madame Blavatsky was not heard from and she would often refer to that period as her "veiled years." Her cloudy allusions to this time period were always vague and always intriguing. She may – or may not – have spent seven years at a mountain retreat in Tibet, but she truly did learn much of Indian mysticism and acquired more than a dabbler's knowledge of the Jewish Kabbalah. From this learning, she would later piece together the novel religion of Theosophy, a curious mixture of many faiths and philosophies.

Madame Blavatsky returned to the world scene in 1858. At home in Russia, she began offering Spiritualist séances, mixed with overtones of the East. She came to America and soon established herself as one of the best-known practicing mediums and occult teachers in the country. This is the reason why she made such a dramatic appearance when she came to Chittenden in 1874. She not only attended séances at the farm but also volunteered to play appropriate music on the pedal organ that the brothers had recently acquired for the séance room. The Eddys were quick to latch onto her services. Everyone expected something marvelous to happen --- and they were not disappointed.

The group gathered that night in the séance room as Madame Blavatsky played the organ. William sat entranced in his cabinet and suddenly, the curtains swept aside and a curious figure walked out. He was a tall, swarthy man who was costumed in velvet, decorated with gold braid, bedecked with tassels, and wearing high, leather boots. The man bowed, made gracious gestures of welcome and then walked toward the observers with his hand pressed to his heart in greeting. Then, apparently from nowhere, a lance appeared in his empty hand. It was nearly 10-feet-long and decorated with what were said to be ostrich plumes. The man stomped across the platform, returned to its center, gave a military salute and then began to melt into some sort of mist. The mist or smoke apparently emanated from the man and he blended into the cloud and then disappeared.

Olcott and Madame Blavatsky

The crowd roared with both bewilderment and approval but Madame Blavatsky regarded it all with calmness. She was, after all, accustomed to oddities and was somewhat of a puzzle herself.

Madame Blavatsky did not remain in Chittenden for long. In three years, she was to publish her acclaimed *Isis Unveiled*, the classic textbook of Theosophy that would attract more than 100,000 followers around the world. Always drawn to India, she went to Madras in 1879, where she established the world headquarters of the Theosophical Society. She performed so many alleged miracles in India that an investigation was warranted by the Society for Psychical Research in 1884. The miracles collapsed under scrutiny but her disciples rationalized that a few outward, even though questionable, wonders are necessary to draw the masses to the true inner faith. The anniversary of her death in 1891 is still remembered today and referred to as "White Lotus Day."

Colonel Olcott departed soon after Madame Blavatsky. Not only did he chronicle his time at the Eddy farm for the newspaper, but he also wrote a massive book about them called *People from Other Worlds*. The book, over 500 pages long, is full of precise drawings of the apparitions, the grounds, the house, and even detailed plans of its construction, proving that no hidden passages existed. He also recorded over 400 different supernatural beings and collected hundreds of affidavits and scores of eyewitness testimony to the amazing events. He reproduced dozens of statements from respected tradesmen and carpenters who had examined the house for trickery. A modern reader would have to look very hard to discover anything that Olcott did not investigate.

In spite of his careful attention to detail and impeccable credentials, many read this story today and are first inclined to dismiss the events as fanciful tales from another time. But can we really do that? The reputation of Colonel Olcott prohibits us from dismissing the story out of hand. His extensive documentation, along with his investigative skills, suggests that the events were not part of a hoax. Olcott remained skeptical and analytical throughout his 10-week stay at the farm, and yet he came away convinced that the Eddys had the power to contact, and communicate with, the dead.

Colonel Olcott left Vermont as a believer. The once skeptical military investigator was convinced that the dead could – and did – communicate with the living.

In fact, he was so convinced of the reality of the spirit world that he left his career and his wife and devoted the rest of his wife to the study of the occult and the arcane. His soon very intense friendship with Madame Blavatsky led him to rent an eight-room apartment for himself and his friend to serve as a headquarters for the burgeoning Theosophical movement. It became a cramped cabinet of curiosities where, amid stuffed baboons, Japanese cabinets, jungle paintings, mechanical birds, and occult trinkets, New York's spiritually adventurous – ranging from inventor Thomas Edison to Major General Abner Doubleday – gathered to discuss, argue over, and marvel at strange and mysterious ideas.

To Olcott's family and friends, the whole arrangement would have been bizarre enough if his new roommate was merely one of the many mediums that he had taken to writing about. But this was odder still. His companion – with whom he grew passionately close but never shared a bed – was an overweight, unattractive, myth-weaving high priestess of the occult. Together, they wrote books, traveled the world, and launched the Theosophical Society. After a few years, they left America and moved to India, where they endeared themselves to the countless Hindu worshippers. Olcott spoke in temples and open squares in India and Sri Lanka, where he urged young people and their families not to relinquish their traditions and to argue against colonialist missionaries. He lobbied the English authorities to permit a national celebration of Buddha's birthday, during which worshippers rallied around an international Buddhist flag that Alcott helped design. He raised money for schools and educational programs and wrote a book about Buddhism that is still read in Sri Lankan classrooms today. Within 20 years of Olcott's first visit, the number of Buddhist schools in the island national grew from four to more than 200.

Had any of his old friends in the military or the law inquired as to what had become of Henry Olcott, they might have chuckled over the thought of the retired investigator with an eye for fraud now traveling through the Orient with a Russian magician – just as they would have laughed about his embrace of the Eddys' manifestations. But that would be far too shallow a reading of Olcott's character. After his awakening at the Eddy farm – and his introduction to Madame Blavatsky – Olcott understood himself to be on the mission of a lifetime. It was mission that touched Hindu and Buddhist cultures so deeply that Olcott may be the single most significant Western figure in the modern religious history of the East. Decades after his arrival there, the Buddhist nation of

Ceylon enshrined his image on a postage stamp and marked his death with a national holiday.

And it started with a séance on a ramshackle farm in Vermont.

Over time, the manifestations at the Eddy farm began to wane. The two brothers and their sister, Mary, went their separate ways. Bickering and fighting had driven them apart. They began turning away the Spiritualist boarders and, except for a rare séance, lived off the farm and their savings. The glen at "Honto's Cave" became overgrown and the unhappy Eddys were more or less ignored by their neighbors. Horatio moved out and bought a house across the road, where he took up light gardening, occasional séances, and doing magic tricks for local children. Mary moved to the nearby village of East Pittsford, where she became a full-time professional medium – although not a successful one. Reports of fraud were common. William dropped out of public life altogether and lived as a bitter recluse on the family farm.

The first of the Eddy's to die was Horatio on September 8, 1922. William lived for another 10 years. He never married and refused to ever participate in a séance again. He died on October 25, 1932, at the age of 99. If either of the men had any secrets about the weird events at their home, they took the secrets with them to the grave.

So, what really happened on the Eddy farm in Chittenden, Vermont?

In 1969, writer John Mason reported that almost no one living in the area of Chittenden was familiar with the Eddy brothers' strange story. A few local residents recalled stories told by their parents that led them to believe the whole thing had been a hoax, a fraud. And perhaps they were right --- for just about everything about the story of the Eddy brothers seems to be worthy of serious questions. Too many of the events and details are reminiscent of well-known deceptions and the work of tricksters, who, unlike the Eddy brothers, were unmasked as frauds.

But if the Eddy brothers were fakes, how did they do what they did? It would have taken trunk after trunk of costumes to stage the long-running "spirit carnival" in the second floor séance room. Hundreds of colorfully garbed characters appeared at different times, with elaborate headdresses, fancy props, uniforms, and plumed spears. Where were such things manufactured? How were they paid for? Where were they stored? There was no rapid transportation in those days, no nearby theatrical warehouses, and no place to hide the things once they were delivered. The dimensions of the spirit cabinet were limited and it was impossible that anyone other than William Eddy and perhaps one other small person could have been concealed inside of it. So, where did all of the mysterious figures come from? There were no uses of clever light projection or mirrors, smoke machines, or easily detectable wires. No matter which way we turn, we are confronted with the choice between the impossible and the preposterous.

Whatever the reader chooses to believe, it cannot be denied that something amazing and mysterious occurred in Chittenden, Vermont, and on the farm of the Eddy brothers, although what this may have been -- we may never know for sure.

6. THE WOMEN BEHIND THE CURTAIN
SEX, SEANCES AND THE SUPERNATURAL

Although most readers cannot – thankfully – comprehend such things today, there was a time in American history when women were considered second-class citizens, or worse. Unable to vote, unable to practice medicine or law, unable to easily obtain a divorce, even in the direst circumstances, women were treated in a fashion that did not even approach "unequal" – it was far below that.

In many ways, it was Spiritualism that began to change those things.

By the middle nineteenth century, men had been running things in America for so long that no one could remember life being any other way. American society was all neatly structured – men went to work; they were the breadwinners, the leaders and the decision-makers; they made and enforced all the laws. They could mistreat and abuse their wives in any way that they wanted, and many did. It was not illegal, and often not even frowned upon, for a man to beat his wife and children. Women were meant to remain at home, obedient and duty-bound to tend to the household and raise the children. If a woman chose or was forced to work, it was generally in the poorest-paying occupations. With the exception of teachers, headmistresses, midwives, and a handful of writers and poets, there were few opportunities for women. If they needed employment to support themselves and family members, it was for wages that were well below what men earned, and in a job such as servant, domestic, mill worker, seamstress, or laundress. As America became more industrialized, many young women worked 16 hours a day in factories for pathetically little money and under terrible conditions. Prostitution was common in every city, large and small. When families moved west, wives also performed heavy and tiring farm labor.

The legal rights of women were severely limited, if they existed at all. Once they married, rich or poor, women essentially became the property of their husbands. Their most important function was providing children. It was not unusual for desperately poor girls and young women who became pregnant to abandon or murder their babies. There were no social service programs, as we know them today, and there was little help offered to women and girls who were living in wretched poverty.

When a woman married, she had no property rights and if she worked, her salary went to her husband. By law, she could not withhold sex from her husband, no matter what the circumstances were. Seeking a divorce meant disgrace and forfeiting the custody of her children. Women could not serve on juries or give testimony in court. Universities, medical, and law schools barred their admission. The right to vote was still many years away.

And while this may have been the normal state of affairs in this county, not everyone was content with this restrictive social structure. Many women chafed at the inequality and the inherent unfairness of the system. They were depressed, angry, and frustrated by its constraints and inequities. Some became physically and emotionally ill. Yet by mid-century, little progress had been made to improve the status of American women.

Then, in 1848, two important and separate events occurred in Western New York that would ultimately bring about a drastic change in the social landscape of the country. In late March of that year, the Fox sisters reported spirit rappings in their Hydesville home and the Spiritualist movement was born. Across the country, interest in communicating with the dead became so popular, so quickly, that many were caught off guard. Mediums and séances seemed to emerge virtually overnight in nearly every town and city in the country. The movement attracted several million adherents in a short amount of time, from the most humble home to the White House.

The other important event was the emergence of a movement supporting women's rights. Not far from Rochester, New York, where Kate and Margaret Fox moved during the summer of 1848 and took along their astonishing spirit raps, a landmark gathering occurred in the village of Seneca Falls. It was a conference about women's rights and it had been organized by two women dubbed as "firebrands," a moniker that was either positive or negative, depending on which side of the fence you were on. Elizabeth Cady Stanton and Lucretia Mott were great leaders – or outrageous agitators, some would say. They had organized the Seneca Falls Convention to deliberate women's equality and press for "social, civil and religious rights."

Stanton, a native of upstate New York and a soon-to-be Spiritualist, had heard the Fox sisters' spirit raps. Mott was a Quaker from Philadelphia. There were far fewer members of her faith in Western New York, but all of them were deeply committed to social causes and were considered among the "liberal religions," which also included Unitarians and Universalists. For example, in Rochester, the Quaker community numbered less than 600, but all of them were involved in the abolitionist movement and actively assisted slaves who escaped from the South on the Underground Railroad. Many Quakers also became deeply involved in both the Spiritualist movement and the cause for women's rights.

Spiritualists, by their own definition, opposed Christian orthodoxy and churches that preached centuries-old dogma. Spiritualism's emphasis was on personal responsibility and the right of the individual to find God and salvation in his or her own way. Therefore, it was not surprising that Spiritualism embraced the women's movement, as well as later reform efforts for temperance, prisons, and labor. Spiritualists represented rebellion against death and rebellion against authority. They saw the need for women to move beyond their traditional roles. In fact, many consider Spiritualism to be a major – if not *the* major – vehicle for the spread of women's rights in mid-nineteenth century America.

Women could not be ordained as clergy in Christian churches. In fact, many churches banned them from even publicly addressing congregations. The ban stemmed from a biblical prohibition against women "preaching in public," first stated by St. Paul in the New Testament. In contrast, within the Spiritualist movement, males and females had equal standing. What's more, many women mediums became very well-known. As those who often brought messages from the dead, women assumed leadership roles. In contrast, Americans who maintained traditional beliefs were appalled by both Spiritualists and feminists. Although there were many male mediums who became popular during the nineteenth century, the popular perception held that mediumship was the domain of women. In such a way, Spiritualism and women's rights became forever intertwined.

While most men ignored or scoffed at foolish talk about women assuming positions of power, influence, and authority through hard work or schooling, by mid-century there was an angry undercurrent that grew into the women's rights movement, stirred by strong and determined leaders like Susan B. Anthony, Elizabeth Cady Stanton, and several others. Men reacted by defending the status quo – women were the "fairer sex" and at the same time were considered fragile beings that needed to be protected and sheltered.

Spiritualism's contribution to the emancipation of women was significant. The Fox sisters and their spirit rappings came along at just the right time and they tore apart the males-only mentality that was taken for granted in American society. Despite the fact that there were a number of male mediums, once the Spiritualist movement became so readily identified with women and girls, it was a perception that remained intact for generations, well into the twentieth century. For many women, Spiritualism opened a door to career opportunities that were virtually unprecedented.

The world of spirits had literally placed women at the head of the séance table.

The reception that women mediums received, however, was mixed at first. Primarily, the chief opposition came from religion, not science, at least in the beginning. The noted jurist Oliver Wendell Holmes called the Fox sisters the "Nemesis of the pulpit." The press was largely antagonistic toward Spiritualism and many newspapers took note of the connection between mediumship and femininity. A newspaper article in 1850 even labeled some male mediums as "addled-headed feminine men." Eventually, when studies were conducted, it was found that by the end of the nineteenth century, as many as eighty percent of mediums were women.

By the days when the Spiritualist movement began its rise, Americans had progressed quite some distance in their religious beliefs from the time when women associated with the supernatural were tried and hanged as witches. Spiritualists tried hard to distance themselves from the occult with its stereotypes of witches and evil spells and by the middle 1800s, regarded their principles as a "scientific religion." But there were still many fundamentalist preachers who attempted to convince Christians that Spiritualism was the "work of the Devil," and some went even farther, branding mediums as the "witches" they tried so hard to avoid. Most Americans had moved beyond the fire and brimstone doctrines of the early nineteenth century, especially in the North, so such preaching by evangelical ministers found a limited audience. The Catholic Church decided not to take any chances with Spiritualism and simply forbade Catholics from consulting mediums or attending séances altogether.

Spiritualism had become a force to be reckoned with and was a concern to many established Christian denominations. It also posed a threat of a social and political nature. The movement was upsetting the very foundation of church and society. Spiritualism's close ties to the new women's rights crusade created a two-fold problem. Both radical movements had the potential to weaken Christian conformity while, at the same time, challenge the traditional role of women. Spiritualists were strong advocates for a women's right to vote as a means of "political empowerment."

Who exactly were the mediums, those women behind the curtain in the Spiritualist séance rooms, who traveled around the country to speak to the dead – and why had they chosen to do so?

For one thing, mediumship was a career that afforded women a degree of independence during a time when such a thing was rare. It also gave women a measure of attention and importance that few other occupations offered in the nineteenth century. Curiously, few women saw mediumship as a way of earning a large amount of money. Actually, for most male and female mediums who charged for séances, the compensation was a modest one. If asked, most replied that they felt a "calling" to bring communications from the spirit world. For many, that may well have been true, for few of them ever achieved wealth. Some claimed that they had not even wanted to demonstrate their abilities in public, but the spirits insisted that they do so.

The fact that some requested a fee for séances became controversial. There were many critics who lashed out that mediums who had been given a "spiritual gift" had no right to accept money. After all, they had not attended school or had any formal training. Spiritualists countered that mediums had expenses, as did everyone, and, therefore, had every right to a fee. As far as not requiring an education to conduct séances, mediums reminded critics that they provided a skill and ability that few had. Asking to be paid for providing a service that helped many people – especially the bereaved – was not unreasonable.

That raised another question from skeptics: If a medium charged a price for attending a séance, was the client certain that he or she had chosen a genuine medium? Fraud was rampant in the movement, even in the early years, and there was a question as to how many people had paid for bogus séances. For legitimate mediums, this was a serious concern and they understood the difficult task of building a reputation for honesty if they wanted people to pay, especially when there was competition from many charlatans.

Some did not request to be paid at all. Nettie Colburn Maynard, who was the favorite medium of Mary Todd Lincoln, who helped President Abraham Lincoln and his wife cope with the death of their son, Willie, never charged for sittings. She had to earn a living working in a government office by day, while conducting séances at the White House and private homes in the city in the evening. It was Nettie who allegedly invoked the spirit of Daniel Webster when President Lincoln was in doubt over signing the Emancipation Proclamation.

The most famous medium of the nineteenth century, Daniel Dunglas Home, did not receive money for his many séances. However, he made it a lifelong practice to accept "gifts," some of them very expensive, from clients, most of whom were wealthy.

The Fox sisters, on the other hand, nearly always asked for a fee when they held séances or put on public demonstrations. Kate and Margaret both died in poverty, though, exploited by their older sister, Leah, who enjoyed a comfortable living as a manager and a medium.

The woman medium earned between $400 and $600 each year, a modest sum even in the economy of the mid-nineteenth century. However, most of the women who became professional mediums were from poor backgrounds and it's doubtful that they could have earned more than that in another line of work. No one has a precise figure as to how many female mediums there were in America at that time, but to say that there were several thousand would not be an exaggeration.

Spiritualist publications, like *Banner of Light* and others, advertised mediums and the fees that they charged. A private sitting in a medium's home, for instance, was usually $1. If the medium came to the client's home, they usually charged up to $5. The same periodicals often printed letters from mediums who complained about poor compensation and the difficulty of the work. For the most part, though, they maintained their commitment to Spiritualism.

Most female mediums felt positive about what they were doing, but it was not an opinion shared by everyone. Skeptics and critics found nothing commendable about the so-called "feminine" personality required to be a medium. The stereotype of nineteenth century womanhood was that she was more spiritual, sensitive, and passive than a man, but in truth, the typical female medium fit this description perfectly. To the critics at the time, female mediums "represented above all else the corruption of femininity," because they were daring to speak up, speak out, and venture outside of the home. Mediums who earned their own way didn't require a man to take care of them, a fact that most men of the era despised. For this reason, both friends and foes of Spiritualism agreed that women had the characteristics that best qualified them to be mediums.

Many agreed that a woman's enhanced sensitivity and spirituality, as well as her intuitive nature, passivity, and tendency toward "nervousness" were all qualities that a good medium required. She was believed to be more virtuous than men, and more willing to sacrifice herself for others, even if it meant suffering, bearing pain, or foregoing her own happiness. In fact, these were the same qualities that women were thought to employ as a wife and mother. Stereotypical masculine traits such as strength, willpower, and logical thinking were supposedly not seen in mediums, at least according to the Victorian view. A man with an aggressive, intense, or forceful personality – all considered authentic male characteristics – would not make a good medium.

If you wanted a real expert and "scientific" opinion about these qualities, phrenologists who had studied such matters supported the idea that females were better suited as mediums than men. Phrenology was the study of the shape and size of the cranium as a supposed indication of character and mental abilities. It was later discredited as a science, but was taken seriously at the time. Experts stated that the shape and size of a woman's cranium indicated the necessary character and mental faculties for this type of work.

Although Victorian era generalizations and sensibilities may seem silly to modern readers, they were accepted by nearly all women and men in their day. But women mediums applied a positive spin to the labels that were assigned to them by critics. Yes, many women acknowledged, they were willing to "sacrifice for the spiritual benefit of others," but female mediums saw their "sacrifice" as an indication of how important their work really was.

Women who were Spiritualist mediums not only attained a certain distinction, they also achieved entry into the male-controlled world of the time. Where else in nineteenth-century America could a young woman, like Nettie Colburn Maynard or Kate Fox, dare to offer advice to the President of the United States? Was there any other place but a séance where a woman could express her opinions to men, including some of the most important figures in the country in the fields of business, law, literature, science and politics – all of which were closed to women? These men actually listened to what they were told, a rarity in an era when a woman's voice was largely ignored. Female mediums suddenly had the freedom to say things in public that would be unthinkable in any other situation. Spiritualist séances and lectures were among the very few venues where women even had a chance to speak in public. Even better, a medium could claim immunity from anything disagreeable that she might say, stating that she'd merely been given the message to speak by the spirits while in a trance. Therefore, if a male sitter was not pleased, it was not the medium's fault. She was a passive conduit who merely repeated what the spirits passed along to her. A man couldn't blame the medium.

She did not control the spirits – the spirits controlled her.

DEFYING THE TRADITIONS OF THE DAY

While many women mediums conducted séances in private homes or settings, some women broke another social barrier by appearing in public before audiences who paid to see her. These mediums – "trance speakers" – often became very well known. During the Victorian era, women were seriously discouraged from public speaking because it was thought to be inappropriate. But trance speakers defied that prohibition. They earned a slightly better income than those who gave private séances, and trance speaking fascinated audiences. Typically, there was a $1 fee per person. However, when mediums traveled, they were responsible for their own expenses, which diminished their income. Traveling was not easy or comfortable during the nineteenth century, especially for women, so those who toured as trance speakers required stamina, in addition to the energy they needed for their demonstrations. It was not a glamorous life. Audience size and reaction varied from town to town. Meanwhile, wherever female mediums went, fundamentalist ministers attacked them for doing the work of the Devil, while secular critics branded the whole business as fraud.

Two of the best-known trance speakers of the era were Emma Hardinge and Cora Richmond.

Cora was described as America's "most famous Spiritualist speaker." If the story of her birth is true, she was destined to a life dedicated to "psychical awareness." She had been born with a "veil," or membrane, over her face, which was an omen believed to foreshadow her life's work. Her family embraced Spiritualism and when she was 11, she was permitted to live in a Spiritualist community called Hopedale, founded by a Universalist minister named Adin Ballou, who, while now forgotten, was one of Spiritualism's earliest advocates.

Cora Richmond

By the age of 16, she had become a popular public speaker and traveled around the country giving inspirational lectures while in a trance. The subjects she spoke about were often chosen at random by scientists and she addressed each one with remarkable eloquence. It was assumed that she and other trance speakers would not know the subjects they spoke about without help from the spirits. She lived in Baltimore for many years and then moved to England in 1873. There, Cora gave an astounding 3,000 trance lectures, winning great acclaim.

When she returned to America, she settled in Chicago and became one of Spiritualism's most important leaders. In 1892, she conducted funeral services for the Lincolns' former medium, Nettie Colburn Maynard. A year later, she helped found the National Spiritualist Association of Churches, which is still in existence today. Cora continued her trance speaking, and those who heard her stated that she offered fascinating revelations about the spirit world. She claimed that the federal government's Joint Congressional Committee on Reconstruction requested her advice from the spirit world for questions facing the country after the Civil War. She was also a highly-regarded healer, and unlike many other female mediums, she maintained control of all of the money she earned.

Emma Hardinge

Emma Hardinge was born in London's East End in 1823. By age 11, she was working as a music teacher and her theatrical talents brought her to America in 1856. While in the country, she met a medium named Ada Hoyt and this experience resulted in her conversion to Spiritualism. In a short time, she was fostering her own psychic powers. Emma demonstrated her abilities – which included mediumship, automatic writing, prophecy, and psychometry – before the Society for the Diffusion of

Spiritual Knowledge, the first Spiritualist organization in America, founded in New York in 1854.

A public presentation technique that was often used by Spiritualist speakers was to select a committee from the audience and have its members ask the medium to speak spontaneously on a subject selected by the committee. Harding was considered adept in these situations. In one well-documented case, she provided remarkably accurate details about a steamer that sank at sea. The information, which she logically could not have obtained any other way but psychically, allegedly came to her from the spirit of a crew member who had drowned in the disaster.

Emma's greatest success was as a very effective spokesperson for Spiritualism. She spoke passionately for, and about, the movement, and traveled widely to promote it. She was also a successful editor and author on the subject. Emma wrote that "the spirits claimed their method of communion was organized by scientific minds in the spirit spheres" and that the spirits "referred to the Fox house at Hydesville as one peculiarly suited to their purpose from the fact that it being charged with the aura requisite to make a battery for the working of the telegraph, also to the Fox family as being similarly endowed." The suggestion that spirit communication was somehow related to, or caused by electricity, remained a common theory among nineteenth century Spiritualists.

In 1875, Emma became one of the founders of the Theosophical Society in New York (along with Henry Olcott and Helena Blavatsky) and her influence on Spiritualism was considered so important that after her death in 1899, an institute and library were named for her in England. Throughout her career, Emma earned a better living than most mediums, while her husband successfully managed her business affairs.

Emma was lucky when it came to her money, as were others. Trance medium Samantha Mettler used her income to help support her family when her husband's business fell into bankruptcy. But others were badly exploited, often taken advantage of by fathers and husbands. When that occurred, there was little if any sympathy from the community.

Occasionally, female mediums earned the attention of a wealthy patron who provided her with a respectable income. During the nineteenth century, there were a number of successful and affluent men who could afford a medium exclusively to hold their own private séances. Cornelius J. Vanderbilt, Henry Seybert, David Underhill, and Horace Day were among the rich and powerful who employed their own mediums this way. Even a woman who was a fraud might find herself lucky enough to cash in. In New York during the 1880s, such a thing happened for an infamous and spurious medium named Madame Debar, when a wealthy attorney provided her with an elegant home, the *New York Times* reported.

Another understandable lure for women who became mediums was for the attention they received. Whether it was criticism or praise, it was a way to gain notoriety that no other occupation provided. For a young woman who'd had an unhappy or lonely childhood, as many did, mediumship became an escape, and at the same time, it attracted public notice. For some, any attention was better than none at all.

It was not unusual to find children working as professional mediums. It was a fact that audiences liked attractive young female mediums and before Spiritualism became all the rage, it was extremely rare to see a girl, or even a woman, speak on stage.

Children were considered less likely to engage in "trickery or deception than an adult" the Spiritualist newspaper *Banner of Light* noted in what was a typical nineteenth-century way of thinking. What could be more innocent than the young Fox sisters taking the stage and demonstrating how the spirits made themselves known through them? Many "child mediums" traveled the country in the 1850s, when trance speaking reached its peak of popularity. If something that a child medium said seemed dishonest, as with adults, there was always an available excuse – blame it on the spirits who controlled her.

Elizabeth Doten was one of the best-known female trance speakers of her day. "Woman does not need to cultivate her intellect in order to perceive spiritual truths," she once stated. She was immensely popular for offering inspirational advice and wisdom that she said came from spirits and she often gave public recitals of improvised poetry from the dead. Doten once claimed that she'd received spirit communications from Edgar Allan Poe. While in a trance, she composed a poem that was said to be remarkably similar to Poe's style and use of language. In 1885, when she was in her mid-fifties, she ceased mediumship and lectures, saying that she could no longer discern between messages that were from her mind and those that came to her from the spirit world.

Laura de Force Gordon was both a trance speaker and suffragist. She had a gift for speaking spontaneously on any subject that was asked by audience members, even in specific areas of science that she knew nothing about in her waking state. A native of Pennsylvania, she built her career in the Mid-Atlantic States and in New England, before moving with her husband to California, where she continued public speaking, although more about suffrage than the spirit world.

There were many "lady trance mediums" who achieved fame in the nineteenth century. And none of them could have been as "frail and passive" as their male critics claimed. If we consider the thousands of miles they traveled on poorly paved and rutted roads, in every kind of weather, by horse, wagon, carriage, coach, boat, and train, then they must have been truly hale and hearty adventurers, equal to any man of the day. Among the best-known were Elizabeth Lowe Watson, Cora Richmond, Emma Hardinge, Elizabeth Doten, Emily Beebe, Emma Jay, Sarah Horton, and Melvina Townsend – names that are now lost to history.

Other names, though, have endured. Some of them remain known today for the mediumistic marvels that have become part of their legacy, while others have a more notorious claim to fame.

THE INVALID MEDIUM

It was common during the nineteenth century for mediums – both male and female – to discover their abilities as children. Others who began their careers later in life had struggled with bad relationships with men, abusive husbands, abandonment, and illness. Spiritualism, quite literally, gave them the strength to survive and to do something extraordinary with their lives.

Achsa Sprague was a medium whose talents awakened in 1853, when she was 25. By then, she had been an invalid for the past five years, stricken with a painful and debilitating disease that affected her joints and left her bedridden. A schoolteacher by the age of 12, she was now permanently confined to her home in Plymouth Notch, Vermont, with no hope of recovery. The pretty young woman with dark hair and intense eyes, faced a bleak future. She had been a brilliant girl, with a sharp mind and quick wit, and now she was completely dependent on her mother. She missed her students, her life, and her independence. Traditional medical treatments, such as were available at the time, had failed her and now Achsa began searching for other methods of healing.

When Spiritualism began sweeping across the county, she was open-minded to its possibilities. She discovered that she had found the ability to communicate with spirits and after several months, began to heal herself. By late in 1853, Achsa had received sufficient help from the spirit world through her self-taught mediumship that she actually began to recover from her long, disabling illness. In her diary and journal, Achsa wrote that her life had changed from invalid to trance speaker. She always credited her spirit guides for her healing.

Achsa Sprague

The diary still exists today and shows the way that her life transformed. In 1849, she had written: "Once more I am unable to walk or do anything else... miserable in both mind and body. I have looked with gloomy eyes into the dark and mysterious future... I am slowly but surely giving up. What hope is there for me but in death? And what will death bring?"

After her miraculous healing in 1854, her tone changed dramatically: "I had a beautiful walk last evening by moonlight."

Whether her illness had made her more susceptible to becoming a medium is open to debate; but many mediums claimed they'd been seriously ill prior to the development of their abilities. There has long been speculation that head injuries, fevers, and serious trauma, preceded the appearance of psychic powers, and therefore, there might be a connection between certain afflictions and emerging psychic ability.

Because of the inadequacy of medical science in the nineteenth century, many diseases were unknown or not yet identified, so we cannot be certain what condition Achsa suffered from before her mysterious healing. However, the symptoms described by her at the time suggest that she may have had a form of tuberculosis, rheumatoid arthritis, or something like lupus, which typically attacks young women, but was too poorly understood to diagnose or treat in that era. No matter what she had, though, the fact was that she was somehow healed – presumably by the spirits – and how that occurred remains a mystery.

After she was healed and regained her strength, Achsa left her home in Vermont and became a deeply dedicated trance speaker, traveling the country and speaking about her experiences. She embraced mediumship as a religious calling and, because of her dedication, the beautiful young woman rejected all suitors and marriage proposals. An unusually independent woman for that era, Achsa became very popular, earned a reputation for her sincerity, and was one of the most demanded female speakers in the entire country. She constantly had requests for speaking engagements, more than she could physically keep up with, and her personal story of Spiritualism inspired all who attended her lectures.

Of course, no matter how well thought of she was in the Spiritualist community, she still faced the same scorn from critics and skeptics that other independent women – especially mediums – were forced to endure. It speaks volumes about Achsa's character that she refused to let harsh words and scathing editorials sway her from what she considered her mission. Her journal, which is still held at the Vermont Historical Society – offers a rare glimpse into the hopes and fears of one of the most inspiring trance speakers of the period.

Sadly, Achsa Sprague died in 1862 at the age of only 34. Her time on earth had been brief and had been filled with pain and hardship, but according to Achsa, she had risen above it all with help from the spirit world.

THE WOMAN WHO BROUGHT SPIRITUALISM TO ENGLAND

There were several Spiritualists who traveled to England almost as soon as the Fox sisters spearheaded the movement, but credit as the first of them to gain celebrity and attract attention was Maria Hayden, the wife of Boston journalist W.R. Hayden, who edited the *Boston Atlas* and a monthly newsletter called *The Star-Spangled Banner*. Like many other Spiritualists of the time, they were ardent abolitionists and were among the first to hold meetings and arrange séances that could deliver messages from beyond the veil.

In 1851, Maria and her husband invited Daniel Dunglas Home to conduct a séance at their house in Connecticut. He was only about 18 at the time, but impressed them immensely. Hayden wrote a glowing review about the séance in his newspaper, which certainly enhanced Home's reputation. Whether Maria was aware of her own abilities at that time remains unclear, but soon after, she began to be known as a practicing medium who specialized in the rapping method that had been pioneered by the Fox sisters and other early Spiritualists.

In 1852, Maria took her act on the road, so to speak, and sailed to England in the company of a man named Stone, a rather forgotten figure who lectured about "electro-biology," one of the many names for hypnosis at the time.

It is uncertain how old Maria was at the time she went to England, but she was described as young and vivacious, well-educated, and well-mannered. Everyone who met her was charmed by her and quite impressed with her mediumistic skills. The newspapers had done a good job advertising for her before she ever arrived, so her reputation spread before she could even put on an exhibition. Once she had settled, she was sought out and put to the test.

The first séance that she conducted took place at a home in Cavendish Square. It was attended by a small, select group of writers and poets, including the publisher Robert Chambers and the novelist Catherine Crowe, who would go on to write a book about the supernatural called *The Night Side of Nature, or Ghosts and Ghost-Seers.* The book became a bestseller of the era and examined ghosts, apparitions, poltergeists, telepathy, and psychic phenomena. Maria impressed the people present so greatly that the night led to a slew of new invitations to perform. It took two years for Robert Chambers to be convinced of her abilities, but once he was, he stood behind her wholeheartedly.

Maria's method involved the standard production of raps as replies to questions, which was still new at the time and like nothing that had yet been seen in England. Many people thought her method and answers were wonderful, but some questioned the fact that she could only give coherent answers if she was looking at the alphabet. Robert Chambers later attested that he had seen her give unaccountably accurate answers even with the alphabet behind her back.

For the next several months, she gave séances that were well-attended and which only garnered positive reviews. As the newness wore off, however, the skeptics began writing scathing pieces about her in many of the popular periodicals of the day. Despite the negativity, Maria maintained a positive reputation and was instrumental in converting many in England to the Spiritualist movement. Her husband lent his hand to the cause by producing a magazine called *The Spirit World* in 1853. It was the first Spiritualist magazine in Britain, but it was short-lived. The Haydens returned to America later that same year.

Her departure was never explained, but it apparently had something to do with the spirit world – or perhaps her lack of communications from those dwelling in it. Soon after returning to the United States, Maria began studying medicine and eventually became a doctor with a successful practice.

She never performed a séance for the public again.

THE STORY OF PATIENCE WORTH

It's difficult to say exactly where the story of Pearl Curran and Patience Worth fits into the history of women and the supernatural. The strange events in the case began in 1913, years after the golden era of Spiritualism, but at a time when interest in the movement was still alive and well. For decades, ordinary people had been entertained by "home circles," those small gatherings of friends and family members who tipped tables, listened for raps, and believed they might be talking to ghosts. Talking boards – or Ouija boards, the most popular brand – were also very popular. According to those who used them, the boards allowed ordinary people to communicate with the spirits. Questions were asked aloud and then the spirits would make a wooden pointer (planchette) on the board move about under the light touch of the sitters. The ghosts would then spell out messages to the people present.

Controversy has raged since the inception of talking boards as to whether or not these messages are real spirit communications, clever hoaxes, or simply hidden thoughts that are dredged up from the unconscious minds of the sitters. Such boards are still in use today and are as much of an enigma now as they were at the turn of the last century.

Which is, perhaps, why what happened to an ordinary St. Louis housewife in 1913 remains such a mystery after all of these years.

Pearl Curran had no interest in the occult prior to 1913. She was born Pearl Leonore Pollard in Mound City, Illinois, in February 1883. Her father was a railroad worker and sometimes newspaperman. She grew up in Texas, playing outdoors and exploring the countryside. Her parents, George and Mary, were easy-going and never really demanded much from Pearl, which probably made her an indifferent student. She left school after the eighth grade and began to study music in Chicago, where her uncle lived. She also played the piano at her uncle's storefront Spiritualist church, where he was a medium. But Pearl and her parents were not Spiritualists and, in fact, had no interest in the movement at all. Pearl had attended Sunday school as a child but few of the teachings ever stuck with her. She did not attend church as an adult and never read the Bible.

Pearl Curran

In fact, she rarely read much of anything at all. She had enjoyed popular children's books of the day, like *Black Beauty* and *Little Women*, and was always entertained by fairy tales, but, probably thanks to her lack of education, she had little interest in reading or writing. Her only creative outlets were playing piano and dreaming of perhaps someday acting on stage, but she gave up that idea at age 24 when she married John Curran, a widower with a teenage daughter.

Her marriage was as uneventful as her childhood had been. The Currans were not rich, but they made a comfortable living. Pearl had a maid to take care of the household chores and she and her husband enjoyed dining at restaurants and going to the theater. They were a social couple and enjoyed getting together with friends and playing cards with neighbors in the evening. The Currans seldom read anything, outside of the daily newspaper and some of the periodicals of the day, and never really had an opportunity to associate with well-educated writers or poets. They were happy, though, and content in their ordinary middle-class apartment on Kingsbury Avenue with their close friends and acquaintances.

They could have never imagined the changes that were coming to their lives.

In the afternoons, Pearl would often visit with her friend, Emily Grant Hutchings. Emily was a Spiritualist and a well-known writer. Her poetry and fiction appeared in many magazines, including *Atlantic Monthly* and *Cosmopolitan*. She was also a regular feature writer for the *Sunday-Globe Democrat*. During the St. Louis World's Fair, she was on the staff of the general press bureau, writing an article a day for every day for 24 weeks, which were printed all over the world.

Emily and her newspaperman husband, Charles Edwin Hutchings, were on cordial terms with the author Mark Twain. She later wrote a novel and several short stories that she claimed were dictated to her by Twain after his death, using a Ouija board with the help of a St. Louis medium with the wonderful name of Lola Viola Hays. That was in 1917, after Emily and Pearl had fallen out. They were still good friends on the hot evening of July 8, 1913, when Mrs. Hutchings brought a Ouija board to Pearl's apartment. It's very likely that Pearl had seen a talking board before, and perhaps even experimented with one, while at her Spiritualist uncle's house. She later claimed that she had, but that she didn't find it particularly interesting. In fact, she believed that using a Ouija board was a boring and silly pastime. Before July 8, she had never seen the pointer spell out anything but gibberish.

But this afternoon was different. Pearl and Emily placed their hands on the planchette and Pearl's mother sat nearby with a pad and pencil, ready to transcribe any messages that "came through." To the ladies' surprise, the message that was spelled out made perfect sense. "Many moons ago I lived. Again I come. Patience Worth is my name," it spelled out.

The three women were startled. They certainly knew no one by that name. Who was Patience Worth? Was she a real person? Pearl was the most skeptical of the three; she doubted that the dead could make contact with the living by way of a wooden board. However, at her friend's urging, she asked the sender of the message to tell them something about herself. Replies to her queries began to come through the message board and were recorded by Pearl's mother.

According to the spirit who called herself Patience Worth, she had lived in Dorsetshire, England, in either 1649 or 1694 (the pointer gave them both dates), but even that information was difficult to obtain. Patience spoke in an archaic fashion, using words like "thee" and "thou" and sometimes refused to answer their questions directly. When Mrs. Hutchings pushed for more information, the spirit first replied by saying "About me ye would know much. Yesterday is dead. Let thy mind rest as to the past." Eventually, though, the ladies would learn that Patience claimed to have been an unmarried woman who had emigrated to America, where she was murdered by Indians on Nantucket island.

The initial contact with Patience Worth came through the Ouija board when Pearl and Emily controlled it. But it was soon evident that Pearl was mainly responsible for the contact, for no matter who sat with her, the messages from Patience would come. The messages continued to be very strange. The "spirit" seemed to have an extensive knowledge of not only seventeenth century vernacular but of clothing, mechanical items,

THE Genius OF THE OUIJA BOARD

musical instruments, and household articles of the period. Patience didn't seem to think much of Pearl's housekeeping, informing her through the board: "A good wife keepeth the floor well sanded and rushes in plenty to burn. The pewter should reflect the fire's bright glow. But in thy day housewifery is a sorry trade."

Pearl was fascinated with the messages that they were receiving and began devoting more and more time to the Ouija board. Eventually, though, the messages began coming so fast that no one could transcribe them. Pearl suddenly realized that she didn't need the board anymore. The sentences were forming in her mind at the same time they were being spelled out on the board. She began to "dictate" the messages from Patience to anyone who would write them down. She first employed a secretary, but later, Pearl recorded the words herself, using first a pencil and then a typewriter.

For the next 25 years, Patience Worth dictated hundreds of thousands of words through Pearl Curran. Her works were vast and consisted of not only her personal messages, but creative writings that included nearly 5,000 poems, a play, many short works and several novels that were published to critical acclaim.

Shortly after Patience made her presence known, the Curran home began to overflow with friends, neighbors, and curiosity-seekers. When word reached the press, Casper Yost, the Sunday editor of the *St. Louis Post-Dispatch*, began publishing articles about Pearl Curran and the mysterious spirit who seemed to be dictating to her. In 1915, he even published a book called *Patience Worth, A Psychic Mystery* and the housewife from St. Louis became a national celebrity.

People came from all over and the Currans, always gracious and unpretentious, welcomed visitors who wanted to witness the automatic writing sessions when Pearl received information from Patience Worth. Authorities in the field of psychic investigation came, as well as people from all over the country who had begun to read and admire the writings attributed to Patience. The Currans never charged any admission and all the writing sessions were conducted with openness and candor. There were no spooky séances, darkened rooms, or candles. John Curran and his friends would be in the next room, smoking cigars, and playing pinochle. Patience Worth Curran, the baby girl the Currans adopted in 1916, would be playing with her toys and food would be laid out on a table, buffet-style, for guests to help themselves. Pearl would usually just sit in a brightly-lit room with her notebook or typewriter and when the messages came to her, she began to write.

In addition to the stories and novels, Patience produced thousands of poems through Pearl Curran. One of her unusual abilities was to write poems that would suit any topic suggested by the company present. On January 12, 1926, at Straus's Studio in St. Louis, during a meeting of the Current Topics Club, suggestions were made by some of the members and Patience composed two poems called "Lavender and Lace" and "Gibraltar." Each poem was presented with no noticeable delay. Neither had ever been produced before. The famous poet, Edgar Lee Masters, was asked if anyone could actually write poetry that way, i.e. instantly and in response to random topics suggested by a group. He replied, "There is only one answer to that... it simply can't be done!"

Not surprisingly, many questioned the reality of the spectral Patience Worth. Critics simply refused to believe that the whole thing was not an elaborate hoax. And Patience did not offer much help in trying to get people to believe in her. Witnesses worked hard to get her to offer some details about her past but she seemed to think her origins were unimportant; however, she did mention landmarks and scenery around her former home in England. The newspaperman Casper Yost, who was one of the spirit's greatest defenders, took a trip abroad during the height of the phenomenon and when he reached Patience's alleged home in Dorset, he did find the cliffs, old buildings, a monastery, and scenery just as Patience had described. This was interesting, but it was hardly proof.

Perhaps the most convincing evidence that Patience Worth was not the conscious or unconscious creation of Pearl Curran was the material that she dictated for her books and stories. Patience seemed to be able to pass between old English dialects at will or could write in a semblance of modern English, as she did with most of her poetry.

The Story of Telka was one of her novels and it is a poetic drama of medieval life in rural England, written mostly in Anglo-Saxon words. It was composed during a series of sittings and as with other Patience Worth dictations, there were no revisions and no breaks where sentences left off and began again. The only comparable work to this novel is the Wickcliffe's Bible of the fourteenth Century, which is also composed of almost pure Anglo-Saxon. However, the language in The *Story of Telka* is different in that there are few words in the novel that modern readers cannot understand. It was as if the writer wanted to create something that seemed old but could still be comprehended by twentieth century readers. Many argued that it would be impossible for a person living in turn-of-the-century St. Louis to create such a dramatic work and then limit the vocabulary to easily understood words in an ancient form of their own language. It simply could not be done, they believed.

And this was far from Patience's only book. *The Sorry Tale* was a lengthy novel about one of the thieves who was crucified with Jesus. It brought to life the Jews, Romans, Greeks, and Arabs of the period. The book was also filled with an accurate knowledge of the political, social, and religious conditions of the time. Critics hailed it as a masterpiece. It had been started on July 14, 1915, and two or three evenings a week were given over to the story until it was completed. The tale proceeded as fast as John Curran could take it down in abbreviated longhand and continued each night for as long as Pearl was physically able to receive it.

Professor W.T. Allison of the English Department of the University of Manitoba stated that, "No book outside of the Bible gives such an intimate picture of the earthly life of Jesus and no book has ever thrown such a clear light upon the manner of life of Jews and Romans in the Palestine of the day of our Lord."

At the same time that *The Sorry Tale* was being produced, *The Merry Tale* was started as a relief from the sadness of the previous book. For a time, work was done on both novels during a single evening.

When the first words of the next book, *Hope Trueblood*, appeared, the sitters gathered at the Curran home were astonished. For the first time since Patience Worth's arrival, four years before, the material was in plain English. Her previous stories had dealt with ancient Rome, Palestine, and Medieval England. This book told the story of a young girl's effort to find her family in Victorian England. When the book appeared in England, no clues were given as to its mysterious origins and reviewers accepted it as the work of a new and promising author. One critic stated that "the story is marked by strong individuality, and we should look with interest for further products of this author's pen."

While critics were impressed with the works she produced, those who witnessed Pearl taking dictation from the spirit were even more astounded. For instance, *The Story of Telka*, which came in at over 70,000 words, was written over several sessions, but was completed in just 35 hours. This type of speed was fairly typical. Once, in a single evening, 32 poems were delivered, along with several short stories. On some evenings, Pearl dictated portions of four novels, always resuming the work on each one at the same place she left off. Pearl took down all of the words, usually in the presence of a number of witnesses, and never made any revisions.

Those who came to investigate the strange events often made requests of Patience to test her. She never hesitated to respond to questions or tasks they put to her. When asked to compose a poem on a certain subject, she would deliver the stanzas so quickly that they had to be taken down in shorthand. Weeks later, when asked to reproduce the poem, she could do so without any changes or errors. One night, author and psychic investigator Walter Franklin Prince, who was a regular visitor to the Curran house, posed an unusual task for Patience. Could she deliver a poem about the "folly of being an atheist" while simultaneously producing a dialogue that might take place between a wench and a jester at a medieval fair? He asked that she alternate the dialogue every two or three lines. Not only could Patience accomplish this, she did it so quickly that dictation was given to Pearl within eight seconds after the request was made. When she finished, Pearl stated that she felt as if her head had been placed in a steel vise.

It should come as no surprise to learn that Pearl Curran's life was permanently changed by the arrival of Patience Worth. While the alliance was undoubtedly a wondrous affair, as Pearl often stated, it also demanded a lot from her, both physically and mentally. She never allowed herself to become obsessed with Patience, though, and the Currans never attempted to exploit the "partnership" for material gain. Pearl continued, with the help of her maid, to do all her own shopping, cooking, and housework and she continued to visit with friends as she had always done. Two or three nights each week were set aside for writing sessions and Patience always dictated to Pearl no matter how many people were in the house. She only stopped when frightened by loud or sudden noises or when Pearl halted to converse with the guests.

Pearl explained that as the words flowed into her head, she would feel a pressure and then scenes and images would appear to her. She would see the details of each scene. If two characters were walking along a road, she would see the roadway, the grass on either side of it, and perhaps the landscape in the distance. If they spoke a foreign language, she would hear them speaking but above them, she would hear the voice of Patience as she interpreted the speech and indicated what part of the dialogue she wanted in the story. She would sometimes even see herself in the scenes, standing as an onlooker or moving between the characters. The experience was so sharp and so vivid that she became familiar with things that she could have never known about from living in St. Louis. These items included lamps, jugs and cooking utensils used long ago in distant countries, types of clothing and jewelry worn by people in other times, and the sounds and smells of places that she had never even heard of before.

On one occasion, Pearl was shown a small yellow bird sitting on a hedge. Patience wished to include it in a poem, but Pearl had no idea what kind of bird it was. Finally, Patience became frustrated and said, "He who knoweth the hedgerows knoweth the yellow-hammer." Pearl and her husband later consulted an old encyclopedia and saw that the yellow bird in her vision was not the type of northern flicker called a yellowhammer that is known in America, but a kind seen only in England.

In spite of the visions and odd experiences, Pearl never went into a trance during the writing sessions, as a Spiritualist medium would have done. She understood the writing as it came and yet while calling out the words to the stenographer, she would smoke cigarettes, drink coffee and eat. She seemed always to be aware of her surroundings, no matter what else might be going on with her.

As time passed, Pearl was not completely satisfied with the literary reputation that was being achieved by Patience Worth. She became determined to take up writing herself, even though she had never written anything before and never had the urge to do so. Unfortunately, though, her writings reflected her lack of education and talent.

She wound up selling two of her stories to the *Saturday Evening Post*, but likely more for her fame as a conduit for Patience than for her own literary ability.

Patience was tolerant but condescending of her host's abilities, which was likely what created a sort of love-hate relationship between them. Patience was often irritated with Pearl, but never failed to show her kindness. She simply seemed to think that her human counterpart was slightly stupid and that only by perseverance was she able to make herself understood, especially when Pearl failed to grasp the spellings and meanings of certain words. But they plodded on together, continuing to amass a great body of work until about 1922.

It was in that year that the connection between the two of them began to deteriorate, possibly due to changes in Pearl's life and the fact that she had become pregnant for the first time at age 39, giving birth to a daughter six months after her husband died. After her husband and then her mother died, the contact between Patience and Pearl came less and less often and eventually it died away.

By that time, public interest in the mystery had also faded, especially since no solution had ever been offered as to how Pearl had accomplished such remarkable feats. The Jazz Age had taken over America and suddenly Pearl Curran and her Puritan ghost seemed stodgy and old-fashioned. After the publication of several books and hundreds of poems, interest in Patience Worth vanished and cynicism replaced it. Debunkers accused Pearl of hiding her literary talent in order to exploit it in such a bizarre way and become famous. However, exhaustive studies have shown this to be highly unlikely, if not impossible. Scholars have analyzed Patience's works and have found them accurate in historical detail and written in such a way that only someone with an intimate knowledge of the time could have created them.

Pearl Curran died of pneumonia in California on December 4, 1937. The *St. Louis Globe-Democrat* headlined her obituary with the words: "Patience Worth is Dead." And whatever the secret of the mysterious "ghost writer," it went to the grave with her.

What really happened to Pearl Curran? Did an entity speak to Pearl from beyond the grave? Or could the writings have simply come from her unconscious mind?

While there were several women with the name Patience Worth listed on passenger logs of ships sailing from England to America in the seventeenth century, there is no evidence that any of them were the Patience Worth who made contact with Pearl Curran. Yet experts who studied Pearl Curran doubted that she could have produced the works attributed to the ghost on her own. She was a woman of limited education with no knowledge of the language used or the history and subject matter that was written about by the alleged Patience Worth. Pearl simply could not have created such works of literary quality on her own.

But could the writings have come from her unconscious mind? Was Patience Worth a secondary personality of Pearl Curran? This too seems unlikely because on the rare occasions when secondary (or split) personalities have been documented, they have always been shown to supplant the main personality for a time. This was not true in Pearl's case. Her own personality co-existed with that of Patience Worth, and Pearl was well aware of this fact.

So, what did happen at the Curran home in 1913? Was it a true case of afterlife communication, or the greatest hoax ever perpetrated on both the literary and Spiritualist communities? It's unlikely that we will ever know for sure, but in the absence of any other explanation, this one must be filed under "unexplained."

OUT OF THE DARKNESS

There were few things that captured the attention of the nineteenth century public like Spiritualism did. Spiritualism moved women into the spotlight of public attention in a way that nothing had ever been able to do before and perhaps for this reason, as the movement changed and adapted through the decades, it became more galvanizing, more controversial – and definitely more fascinated with sex.

In hindsight, such a development was completely understandable. There were a number of things that were largely seen as taboo during this era – communication with spirits, women's rights, and sex. We have already demonstrated the links between the emancipation of women and the Spiritualist movement, and it's easy to understand why more openness about sex soon followed.

Needless to say, this led to controversy, both in the bedroom and out of it. There were plenty of marital problems in the nineteenth century, just the same as things are today. However, because a divorced woman was often stigmatized, and her options to leave her husband were few, there was less divorce, but many unhappy marriages, as well as outrageous amounts of wife and child abuse, alcoholic husbands, and many who deserted their families. In fact, many women who became mediums understood these problems in others, because many – although not all -- had come from similar backgrounds.

In cases where mediums learned that their female clients had serious marital problems, or were in danger because of physical or sexual abuse, and with no laws to protect them, the spirits often advised that "wives divorce their husbands." Outraged critics charged that female mediums were encouraging "immoral behavior," but, of course, the mediums could always say the spirits were to blame. For Spiritualists, divorce seemed a reasonable response to misery and abuse. For the more conservative, divorce for a woman was not considered an option, and Spiritualist advice to the contrary posed a grave threat to family stability. The critics stated that women mediums were nonconformists, and symbolized defiance of nineteenth century values.

And in many cases, they were a threat – but for good reason. This was a period of history when women were considered the "weaker sex" and were treated as second-class citizens. Within the Spiritualist community, though, women were leaders and spokespersons, which they could not be in everyday life. There were many double standards for women at the time, especially when it came to sex. Female trance speakers often traveled alone, and there's no question that some of them found themselves in circumstances that permitted promiscuity. Even during séances, some women mediums had the opportunity to do things under the cover of darkness that they never would have done in polite society. Séances were held that involved scantily-clad "apparitions" and mediums were quick to disrobe to prove that they had secreted no ghostly props under their clothing. Spirit summonings were conducted in lingerie, filmy shifts, and, in some cases, nothing at all.

Critics were outraged. This was activity that defied the rigid Victorian standards. The strict morality of the nineteenth century did not encourage sexual relations – except for procreation by married couples. Public discussions of sex were taboo and, most of the time, the subject was avoided in private, too. Of course, many mediums and Spiritualists ignored propriety, just as many non-Spiritualists did, but this issue provided enemies of Spiritualism and women's rights with another line of attack.

Conservatives particularly accused Spiritualists of supporting "free love," which, in those days, meant "promiscuity and infidelity." Because of this, Spiritualists posed a threat to the "sacred institution" of marriage and shocked religious opponents. Actually, most Spiritualists were not in favor of free love, but the two became connected in the public mind. This connection was formed because it was said that many women Spiritualists criticized "marriage as the root of women's oppression," wrote Ann Braude.

Spiritualists did not oppose marriage. What they vehemently criticized was the unfairness of marriage and the laws that deprived women of equal rights, kept them subservient, and often amounted to their subjugation by men. Further, Spiritualists argued, women were frequently forced to marry because of a lack of economic opportunities, and then have children, whether they wanted to or not. The answer was not to abolish marriage, but to improve the laws that governed it. All of this is largely a general rule today, but it was a groundbreaking attitude in the nineteenth century and was harshly criticized by a wide-reaching section of society.

As the years passed, Spiritualism became more steeped in controversy and in no instance was this more true than in the story of the first woman – a spirit medium – who ran for President.

" MRS. SATAN" FOR AMERICA

In 1872, American history changed forever when a woman named Victoria Woodhull became the first woman to try and become President of the United States. She had an uphill battle ahead of her. As a woman, she wasn't even allowed to vote. If elected, she would have been too young at the age of 34 to serve, but it didn't matter because she only received a handful of votes. Even her running mate, Frederick Douglass, voted for President Ulysses S. Grant. On Election Day, she was in jail for slandering the most famous minister in the country.

When Hillary Clinton was nominated as the Democratic Party's choice for the presidency in 2016, Victoria Woodhull, a largely forgotten novelty in the historical record, was suddenly in the spotlight for the first time in more than a century and a half. She began to be lauded for her trailblazing advocacy of woman's rights – including the movement for "free love" and divorce – and her work in the suffrage movement of the day. But what most people neglect to mention is that Victoria Woodhull didn't achieve her greatest notoriety as a presidential nominee, but rather as a Spiritualist medium who started the first female brokerage firm on Wall Street by charging some of the nation's wealthiest men to contact the dead.

When someone once asked shipping magnate, financier, and railroad tycoon Cornelius Vanderbilt for financial advice, he replied, "Do as I do, consult the spirits!" His conduit between this world and the next was Victoria Woodhull.

Born Victoria Clafflin in Homer, Ohio, in September 1838, her childhood was a nightmare. Her mother was an eccentric who had "memorized the Bible

Victoria Woodhull

backward and forward." Her father was a con artist who abused his family and was one described by a neighbor as a "one-eyed, one-man crime spree." He fled town after allegedly burning down his own mill for the insurance money and stealing petty cash from the post office. Locals took up a collection so that his family could follow after him. Victoria was the seventh of ten children, four of whom did not live to adulthood. She had only a few years of formal education before being put to work in her father's traveling medicine show. She and her younger sister, Tennessee, gave séances, performed as fortune tellers, and sold fake elixirs to the gullible.

At age 15, she was married for the first time to a drunken, philandering physician named Canning Woodhull. They had two children together, but divorced in 1864. She later married two more times.

In 1868, Victoria and Tennessee moved to New York City, where business and industry were growing rapidly in the years after the Civil War. Millionaires were being made in the shipping, construction, and railroad businesses, and through a series of fortunate coincidences that put the sisters in the right place at the right time, they met tycoon Cornelius Vanderbilt. He was the richest man in America, had an eye for beautiful women, and was obsessed with contacting his late mother. Victoria soon became his personal spirit medium.

Within two years, using the stock advice that was gleaned from the "spirits" during her séances with Vanderbilt, Victoria and Tennessee became known as the "lady brokers." Vanderbilt helped them to establish a stock brokerage office, the first of its kind for women of that era. The sisters did very well financially and realized a sizable profit.

With some of their earnings, they established a weekly newspaper that was designed to cast attention on topics that were of interest to feminists of the time, such as equal rights and suffrage. In 1871, Victoria and her political positions had become so well-known that she appeared before the House Judiciary Committee to speak on behalf of women's rights. In doing so, she became the first women to ever testify before a congressional committee.

But her stance on women's rights was not what earned her the nickname of "Mrs. Satan." That came about because of her support of another controversial topic of the time: free love. She believed in the right of a woman "to love who I want for as long as I want," then to divorce. Under the law, she said, marriage for women was slavery. By the age of 31, she was a millionaire, but when she walked into Delmonico's restaurant without a male escort, she was refused a seat. She tried to vote in 1871, claiming that the 14th Amendment guaranteed women that right. As she had told the congressional committee, "we don't need the right to vote, we have it."

But it was in 1872, that Victoria Woodhull truly earned her place in American history when she ran for president. It was a daring move that caught the attention of the press, politicians, and the public. It was the first time that a woman – and a Spiritualist – sought the highest office in the land. She won the nomination of the Equal Rights Party. The former slave and abolitionist Frederick Douglass was named as her running mate, but if he knew it, he never acknowledged the nomination and campaigned for President Grant.

Even though Victoria could have never been elected, none of that mattered. Her goal was to call attention to women's rights issues – and to herself. Few regarded Victoria's candidacy seriously; but the press was more than happy to write about her efforts because it sold newspapers. During her run, she did gain support from a few women's rights groups and from some Spiritualists, but her radical position toward free love alienated most of those who would have helped her. Conservative newspapers and religious organizations began accusing every one of America's four million (or more) Spiritualists of supporting free love and while it was a false charge, it inflamed passions.

Things turned ugly during her campaign. Reverend Henry Ward Beecher, brother of Uncle Tom's Cabin author Harriet Beecher Stowe, had attacked Victoria's notion of free love from his Brooklyn pulpit. Shortly before the election, Victoria's newspaper printed a story that revealed that Beecher was having an adulterous affair with a parishioner, Mrs. Elizabeth Tilton. The result of the allegations was a full-blown scandal and an embarrassing trial for Beecher on adultery charges.

The newspaper story may have been accurate, but under a federal law against mailing "obscene" material, Victoria was arrested and jailed, where she spent Election Day. By the way, the winner of the 1872 election was Ulysses S. Grant, who went on to a second term in office.

In the wake of the scandal, her arrest, and the election, Victoria was called a "vile jailbird" by Harriet Beecher Stowe and an "impudent witch." Others called her much worse. She was later cleared at trial but the events ruined her health, her finances, and her reputation. In 1877, she moved to England, where she married a banker, still supported liberal causes, and lived comfortably until her death in 1927.

She seemed destined for historical oblivion. The Spiritualists wanted nothing to do with her because they believed that she had used the movement to simply further her radical women's rights agenda. Following the Civil War, when so many people were seeking mediums to contact their loved ones, Victoria Woodhull had soured the movement's reputation. The bereaved were more concerned with speaking with their loved ones than with listening to speeches about social injustice.

Victoria's radical position on free love had caused rifts within the women's rights movement, as well. Even bold feminist leaders like Susan B. Anthony, who had once welcomed Victoria, later distanced herself. When Anthony and Elizabeth Cady Stanton wrote a six-volume history of the suffrage movement, Victoria's contributions were reduced to one brief mention.

She would likely have been forgotten altogether -- along with her presidential candidacy -- if not for another, far different woman who made history in 2016.

SEX IN THE SEANCE ROOM

Spiritualism changed after the Civil War, which brought staggering death tolls – and a staggering number of people who wanted to reach those who had died in the conflict. By the 1870s, mediums had become so prevalent that they were forced to step up their showmanship to retain their audiences. Many spectacular displays were reported that seemed to have more to do with the theatrical than the spiritual. Flying objects, birds, musical instruments, glowing spirit hands, table tipping, and spirit materializations all became séance staples. As the dazzling and dramatic became such an important part of séances, Spiritualism's credibility became increasingly challenged. The press and the clergy were as hostile as ever and some scientists had joined the skeptics in their efforts to debunk the entire movement. With the exposure of many physical mediums as frauds, and their array of effects shown to be tricks, Spiritualism was barraged with criticism.

Start mixing in a little sex and things got even worse.

Spiritualism was born in an era of scientific and literary achievement, but many people turned to a belief in the spirit world as an antidote to the scholarly agnosticism that could be found in the daily newspapers and on the lips of scientists and writers. It was also an escape from the restrictions of society. Many faithful Spiritualists used the séance chamber as a way to express their need to explore new things, to seek out ideas that were seen as beyond the norm, and also as a way to express sexual needs, wants, and desires. When interacting with the spirits was not titillating enough, mixing in a little eroticism guaranteed that the evening would become more exciting. For this reason, we can never underestimate the role that sex played in the Spiritualist movement.

By the later years of the nineteenth century, Spiritualism had become engorged with sex, although this was largely unknown by the public. Unless someone was an actual participant in a séance, or part of an experiment to test the skills of a medium, they were unlikely to read about what was taking place in the séance room. Sex was simply not something that was discussed in public, let alone in newspapers and scientific journals.

In reading the reports of the era, though, it's clear that there existed a strong and scientific connection between mediumship and sex, although it went carefully unmentioned. Dr. W.J. Crawford, a lecturer in mechanical engineering at the Municipal Technical Institute at Belfast, Ireland, carried out a long series of experiments that he devised for the purpose of finding out what part of medium Kathleen Goligher's body

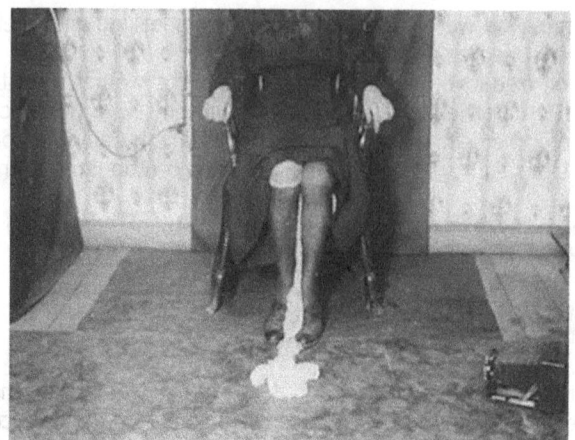

"Ectoplasm" appears from a medium's vagina during a seance

produced the mysterious psychic substance known as ectoplasm. The experiments were based on his findings that a type of powder would stick to the ectoplasm and that by placing the powder on the medium's shoes and around her legs, the track of the ectoplasm could be revealed. Careful as he was in his choice of words — speaking about the "top of the stockings" and "inside the legs of the knickers to the joint of the legs" or the ectoplasm returning "by way of the trunk" — it was clear that he was referring to the ectoplasm coming from the medium's vagina, even if he didn't come right out and say it.

For plainer language, there is Baron Schrenck-Notzing's account of the mediumship of Willie Schneider: "With the increase of phenomena, the bodily movements became stronger, the clonic shakings more powerful, cramp-like, the pulse flew up and the respiration grew labored. Perspiration stood on the forehead of the medium. The whole process is very much like a birth process. Biologically, the erotic activity is unmistakable."

Another report about Schneider came from Dr. W. Osborne: "Finally, I could not fail to observe that all of the phenomena produced by an effort on the part of the medium (who perspires very strongly during the demonstration), point to happenings which hang together with the sexual sphere of the medium. It is difficult to make accurate observations in this respect, but the whole corporeal attitude of the medium during and before the phenomenon, the cramp-like increase of the totality of body energies, the rhythm of his movements, his great general excitement which strives to reach a high point after the achievement of which the phenomena begin and the medium is visibly exhausted and satisfied, speak for the idea that these things somehow hang together with his sex."

General Joseph Peter of Munich also wrote about Willie Schneider: "The medium, as the phenomena was about to happen, was often in fear and excitement. Willie pressed himself trembling to me and groaned in anxiety. From time to time, however, it seemed he was possessed by erotic feelings; he stroked the hands of his controls with his cheek and began to bite me on the arm. 'Mina' [his female controlling spirit] would only desist after very emphatic requests."

There was a lot of heavy breathing going on in the séance room. Willie Schneider, Mina Crandon, and Eusapia Palladino (more about all of them later) were known to have experienced sexual thrills while "entranced." Although the word "orgasm" was not mentioned by researchers, they did use "voluptuous," "sensual," and "climax," if they were feeling unusually daring. It was rumored that the distinguished scientist Sir William Crookes was infatuated with his young medium, Florence Cook, and was caught flitting around the séance room in her underthings by Sir George Sitwell. Mediums like Victoria Woodhull advocated "free love" and were not above using their charms to fascinate clients like Cornelius Vanderbilt. And the list went on.

There is no question that the séance room could be a fevered place. Mediums were often strip-searched and tied to chairs. Fraudulent ones stripped off their clothes to impersonate spirits. Spirits fondled legs, patted thighs, and kissed sitters in the dark. In comparison to the everyday segregation of sexes at that time, séances could be a thrilling experience.

Famous Italian medium Eusapia Palladino, was one of the most sexual Spiritualists of the early 1900s. She claimed that after excessive mediumistic practice, she would bleed more freely during menstruation. Her trance states were also very peculiar, especially to some of the strait-laced observers of the time. Enrico Morselli wrote: "The passing into a more advanced state of trance is truly indicated by sighs, yawns, sobs, of alternating redness and pallor of the face, perspiration on the forehead, light transparency of the palms of the hands, the alteration of voice and the quick changes of facial expression. Eusapia then progresses through a diversity of emotional states and now she is prey to a species of concentrated rage which she expresses with quick movements, with imperious commands, with sarcastic phrases directed at her critics, with smiles and loud laughter which is something diabolical. Then she passes into a state of decided voluptuous ecstasy, throwing about both her arms, squeezing us with her tensed thighs and trembling feet, resting her head and abandoning her whole body on my or Barzini's shoulders while we fearlessly resist this innocent attack against our masculine emotions."

Simply put, sex could not be disassociated from Spiritualism because mediums were human beings. They either had a normal, if somewhat impaired, sex life, or they had none, in which case something abnormal was likely to happen. If the energies bound up within the body cannot be released in a physical way, then it would certainly be expended in some other manner. In mediumship, sexual energies may have furnished fuel for the many physical, and perhaps mental, manifestations that occurred during séances.

In other cases, the things that happened were just plain weird – and far too shocking for some of the strait-laced investigators of the time.

SEX AND THE SPIRIT MEDIUM

Toward the end of the nineteenth century, the rise of Spiritualist organizations caused a relative decline in the sort of mediumship practiced by some of the early members of the movement, who were often exposed as frauds. New, organized groups began taking steps to examine the claims of their own members and they did so with such thoroughness that mediums – both good and bad -- began to act with caution. Exuberant exhibitions with trumpets, rope tricks, and whirling ghosts began to quietly fade away. This is not to say that physical mediumship began to disappear from the scene, but in the 1880s, the emphasis began to shift away from tipping tables and tooting horns to a more serious attempt to examine those proofs of spirit existence in the form of messages and information. Commercial mediumship suffered for a time, but people began to speak about the legitimacy of the movement for the first time in, well, ever.

And then along came Eusapia Palladino. This Italian peasant woman became almost single-handedly responsible for restoring the prestige of physical mediumship and went on to become perhaps the most famous – and controversial -- medium of the period. If respected spirit mediums had truly begun to acquire an air of respectability, it only took Eusapia Palladino to upset the wagon and get critics in an uproar again.

Eusapia Palladino

Eusapia Palladino was born near Bari in southern Italy in 1854. Her mother died shortly after she was born and her father was murdered in 1866, leaving Eusapia an orphan at the age of 12. Even then, it was later reported, she had already experienced many strange and supernatural events, such as rapping sounds on the furniture, eerie whispers, and unseen hands that would rip the blankets from her bed at night.

Friends and relatives sent Eusapia to Naples, where it was hoped that she would find a position as a nursemaid. Things did not go well. The family that hired her was disturbed by the fact that the eerie events occurred around the young woman and were bothered by the fact that Eusapia refused to conform to life in the city. She had a stubborn streak that ran through her character, which often showed itself in her refusal to take a bath, comb her hair, or learn to read. She was soon dismissed from her position.

She took shelter with some family friends who dabbled in Spiritualism. Eusapia attended a séance one night and almost as soon as she sat down at the table, it tilted and then rose completely into the air. She began to act as a medium to reportedly avoid being sent to a convent, although she claimed that she was afraid of her powers and avoided using them. The family with whom she was living asked Eusapia to stay on with them, and continue holding séances, but with her typical stubbornness, moved out and began to work as a laundress. She later married a merchant named Raphael Delgaiz and worked in his shop for a time before starting to offer séances on a professional basis.

In 1872, a wealthy and influential Spiritualist couple named Damiani sought Eusapia out. They had heard good things about the séances that she had been conducting and wanted to introduce her into society. Unfortunately, the coarse and rude young woman was no more interested in education and social polish than she had been years before and her introduction was a disaster. The Damianis' efforts to develop and study Eusapia's powers proved thankless and she lapsed back into a life of ordinary mediumship, virtually unknown outside of a small circle in Naples.

In this way, Eusapia would have lived out her entire life, if she had not come to the attention of Ercole Chiaia, a doctor and dabbler in the occult, who sought her out in 1886. Acting almost like a manager, Chiaia took upon himself to publish an open letter to the famed Italian psychiatrist and criminologist Cesare Lombroso. In the letter, which he wrote as if describing a patient, Chiaia gave a summary of Eusapia's mediumistic abilities and urgently requested Lombroso's help in determining whether she possessed some sort of new physical force. The letter turned out to be a stroke of genius for Eusapia's career. Even though Lombroso ignored the letter (at that time), her livelihood saw an immediate boost.

In the letter, Dr. Chiaia wrote:

She is 30 years old and very ignorant; her appearance is neither fascinating nor endowed with the power which modern criminologists call irresistible; but when she wishes, be it day or night, she can divert a curious group for an hour or so with the most surprising phenomena. Either bound to a seat or firmly held by the hands of the curious, she attracts to her the articles of furniture which surround her, lifts them up, holds them suspended in the air like Mahomet's coffin, and makes them come down again with undulatory movements, as if they were obeying her will. She increases their height or lessens it according to her pleasure. She raps or taps upon the walls, the ceiling, the floor, with fine rhythm and cadence. In response to the requests of the spectators something like flashes of electricity shoots forth from her body, and envelops her or enwraps the spectators of their marvelous scenes. She draws upon cards that you hold out, everything that you want --- figures, signatures, numbers, sentences, by just stretching out her hand toward the indicated place...

This woman rises in the air, no matter what hands tie her down. She seems to lie upon empty air, as on a couch, contrary to all the laws of gravity; she plays on musical instruments --- organs, bells, tambourines --- as if they had been touched by her hands or moved by the breath of invisible gnomes. This woman at times can increase her stature by more than four inches.

She is like an India rubber doll, like an automaton of a new kind; she takes strange forms. How many legs and arms has she? We do not know. While her limbs are being held by incredulous spectators, we see other limbs coming into view, without her knowing where they come from. Her shoes are too small to fit these witch-feet of hers, and this particular circumstance gives rise to the intervention of a mysterious power.

The letter, which would lead to Eusapia Palladino's introduction to the public spotlight, described happenings that were allegedly typical of her career so far. Most of the incidents in the letter were common to séances performed by physical mediums, but others were much rarer – and harder to explain. What, for example, was to be made of the phantom feet and limbs that appeared, were studied, and could not be debunked? Nearly the entire history of Palladino's next 30 years was devoted to accounts of the committees and investigators who sought to answer these, and other, mysteries about her.

The first major researcher to seek out Eusapia was Cesare Lombroso, the same man who had ignored the letter from Dr. Chiaia for nearly two years. He came to Naples in 1890 and arranged to hold several private séances with Eusapia at his hotel. Most of these initial sessions were below the level of Eusapia's usual impressiveness, with one exception. At the close of one séance, the lights had been turned up and the observers were discussing their impressions while Eusapia was still tied to a chair, about 18 inches in front of the curtain that formed her spirit cabinet. Suddenly, sounds were heard from the alcove behind her, the curtain began to swing and billow forward, and then a small table emerged from behind it and began to slide across the floor towards the medium. Lombroso and his associates hurried into the cabinet, convinced that a confederate must be hiding inside, but it was empty, save for a few musical instruments. The observers were stumped and Lombroso dismissed any previous doubts that he had about Eusapia's abilities. He had no explanation for what he had seen.

Lombroso published a report of his findings and it was greeted with both shock and surprise. Lombroso had an excellent reputation as a psychiatrist who often helped the police with difficult cases – sort of a nineteenth century "profiler" – and if he could be so readily convinced of Palladino's paranormal talents, then there must be something truly amazing about this woman. Other investigators began contacting the medium and in October 1892, Eusapia was asked to sit for a scientific committee in Milan. Among its five members were Lombroso himself and Professor Charles Richet, a noted student of psychic phenomena and a winner of the Nobel Prize in physiology and medicine in 1913. His interest in the paranormal was ignited by Eusapia and he went on to publish several books about psychic phenomena and investigate other mediums during his career.

The séances that were held for the Milan committee were the first of which there were relatively reliable records concerning the manifestations of Palladino. They are also the first to not only make note of unexplained occurrences, but also of something else that would shadow the career of the medium: Eusapia cheated.

There was no question whatsoever, even among her most ardent supporters, that she took advantage of every lapse in attention or muscular relaxation on the part of those who were supposed to "control" her movements, so that she could produce touches, raps, or movements of objects by erroneous methods. Sometimes her tricks were clumsy and obvious and at other times, subtle and clever, but it could not be denied that she cheated. It seemed to make no difference to her that she might be exposed in these activities -- as she repeatedly was. Given the slightest opportunity, Eusapia cheated.

One of her most common ruses was to convince the two people assigned to hold her arms that each had continued to keep contact with a separate limb, when actually, one of them had transferred his hand to her other arm. This was possible because Eusapia constantly moved about while in her trances, thrashing restlessly back and forth. As she rocked back and forth, tossed her head, and waved her arms about, it took great skill on the part of the handlers to be sure they were not both controlling the same hand. This was especially true as the handlers were usually allowed only to follow the medium's hands by touch but not to restrain her movements in any way. Because of all the excitement, it was also nearly impossible to decide whether or not Eusapia's hands were where they were supposed to be.

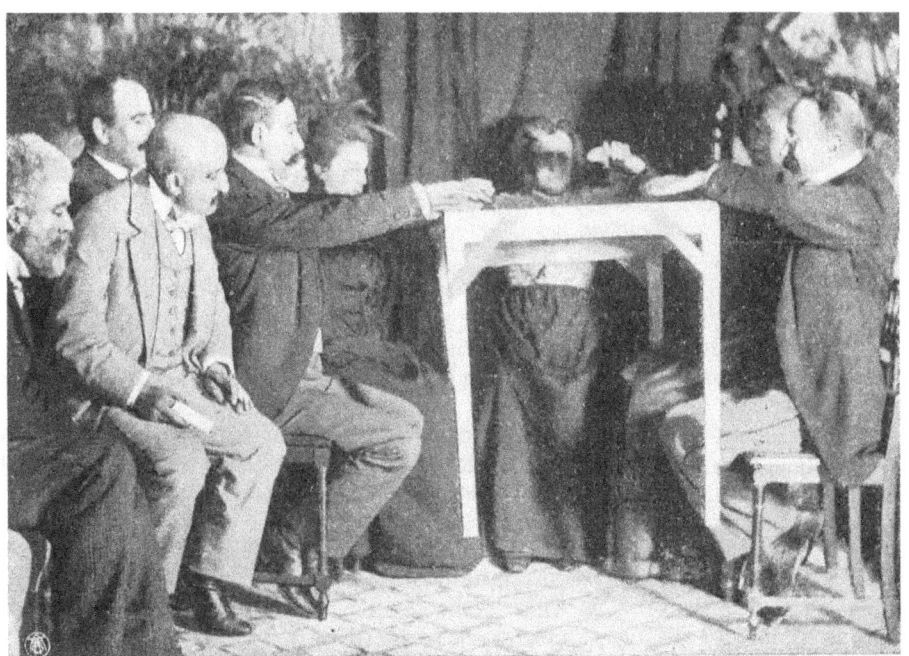

A photograph from one of Eusapia Palladino's many seances

But yet, Eusapia was a complete enigma – she cheated, but not always. The eyewitness reports made it clear that she would cheat whenever she could, but there were also manifestations that occurred that could not be explained. During the sessions, which were held by a dim red light, members could see and feel what were apparently a number of spectral hands that groped outward from behind the cabinet curtain while the medium remained plainly visible in front of them. Chairs moved, tables lifted, objects took flight. All of this occurred while Palladino was under close observation. The lights were on, there were no confederates in the room, no one imagined anything – paranormal events occurred. There was no explanation for them. Even given the fact that Eusapia was not above faking certain effects, was it possible for anyone -- let alone a semiliterate peasant woman with no knowledge of applied mechanics -- to bring about such happenings through trickery? That is the exasperating problem that haunted the scientific minds of the time and still haunts us about Eusapia Palladino today.

Eusapia continued to baffle scientists and investigators. She performed for Russian zoologist N.P. Wagner in Naples in January 1893 and then did so again later in Rome. She sat for Polish psychologist Julian Ochorowicz in Warsaw at the end of the year and at the beginning of 1894. During every session, the results were mixed. Some of the effects that occurred were plainly the result of cheating. Some of them could have been produced by cheating, although witnesses were prepared to state that no cheating had taken place. And some of the effects were judged to be inexplicable in terms of any of the methods of deception that Eusapia had so far been known to use ---- and possibly inexplicable in any way whatsoever.

A more revealing series of séances was held in 1894 at the home of Professor Charles Richet in France. Almost every member of this group of sitters was major name in the fledgling field of psychical research. In addition to Richet himself, the earlier mentioned Dr. Julian Ochorowicz, and the German researcher Baron von Schrenck-Notzing, there were also four highly-influential English investigators -- Sir Oliver Lodge, Professor and Mrs. Henry Sidgwick, and Frederick William Henry Myers, all of whom had been founders of the Society for Psychical Research (SPR) in 1882, which will be discussed in the next chapter.

The entire group was very aware of the medium's tendency to cheat and the need for suspicious watchfulness. In spite of this, they observed the cabinet curtain billowing when there was no breeze, they experienced repeated "spirit touches" at times when all were certain that Eusapia could not have been responsible, and saw and heard objects being moved around the séance chamber. One of these items was a large piece of fruit -- a melon that weighed more than 15 pounds. It somehow moved from a chair behind the medium to the top of the séance table. Even if Eusapia had managed to get a hand (or foot) free on this occasion, it's difficult to guess how she could have grasped an object as smooth as a melon, somehow moved it from a chair behind her to a table, and managed to do it before the eyes of a group of trained observers. It seems impossible and because of this, alternate theories emerged to explain the incident. Some suggested that the observers had simply hallucinated the "magic melon." Others claimed that one or more of the committee members had been in league with the medium, which seems even more unlikely given the reputations of those present.

So, how did this bizarre event occur? No one knew then and no one knows now. It was after this incident that investigators came to realize that there was a need for the more extensive use of recording devices and photographs during investigations. That way, the control of the medium and the occurrence of the phenomena would not be subject to errors in human perception. Unfortunately, even after this important series of séances, such improved methods of investigation were not used with Palladino until a later period, and even then, were not as thoroughly applied as they should have been.

After the sittings in France, the next important sessions with Eusapia took place in England and were generally regarded as a disaster. Of the four English participants in the investigations of Professor Richet, only Sir Oliver Lodge had found himself completely satisfied that Eusapia's phenomena were in part paranormal. The others, Myers and the Sidgwicks, wanted further trials before they could reach firm opinions. They invited Palladino to sit for them at Myers's home in Cambridge, where she went in the late summer of 1895.

Unfortunately, no detailed record of the Cambridge séances was ever published by the SPR and so we have no way of knowing what led to the conclusions reached by those involved. We only know that in October 1895, Professor Sidgwick announced at the society's general meeting that nothing had been witnessed at Cambridge that could not be put down to trickery. He then went on to withdraw what limited support that he had for Palladino, based on the French sittings, and to state that he had come to believe that all her manifestations were fraudulent. Myers joined Sidgwick in rejecting the

Cambridge séances, although he did choose to reserve judgment on what he had seen in France, which he claimed was more impressive.

No one knows for sure what occurred in Cambridge that summer, but it was clear there were things about Palladino that would have likely offended the Sidgwicks and their friends, regardless of the quality of her mediumship. In fact, had it not been for her inexplicable abilities, it is highly unlikely that these cultivated English people would have ever associated with a person like Eusapia. Regardless of her reputation as a medium, she did not fit into the mold of other important mediums at the time. She had none of the social graces or charm so many mediums possessed and certainly none of the sober, upright character of the upper crust character of the SPR members and their friends. Instead, she was almost everything that her Cambridge hosts were not: poorly educated, coarse, emotional, loud, and quite uninhibited about her interest in the opposite sex.

Eusapia Palladino was crude and the complete opposite of the repressed Victorians who had invited her to England. She tended to wake from her trances hot, sweaty, and sexually aroused. On many occasions, she tried climbing onto the laps of male sitters at her séances. She was not shy in making in clear that she was looking for intercourse, or that she wanted it immediately. Despite her weight and unattractive appearance, she had no shortage of men who were happy to volunteer – all for the good of the spirit world, of course.

Needless to say, Eusapia's overtly sexual behavior was considered quite unacceptable in Victorian England. The Cambridge investigators tried to make Eusapia as comfortable as possible, however, but only under their own terms. They wanted her to be in a receptive state for her séances, but there was a limit to their generosity. Professor Myers' wife took her shopping, allowed Eusapia to cook Italian meals in her kitchen, and listened to her incessant chatter, even though Mrs. Myers spoke only a few words of Italian and had no idea what Eusapia was talking about. The Myers's young son, Leo, was recruited to play croquet with her on the lawn, but the boy complained that she cheated during every game.

Eusapia was unhappy during her stay in England. She hated the climate in Cambridge, the cool summer weather, the polite conversation, and cultured people. She fell into an ill-tempered sulk that carried over into the sittings. She became indifferent about the entire situation, refused to be tied in place, sometimes wouldn't allow her feet to be held, and performed poorly. Because of this, little happened. Tables tipped a time or two, but that was about all. It's not surprising that Sidgwick and Myers had enough of the troublesome medium and withdrew their support of her after that summer.

A denunciation by the SPR should have damaged Palladino's career but as it turned out, her work was far from over. She left England and returned to Italy, where she had always felt most comfortable. She presided over numerous séances in private homes and the sitters were apparently satisfied, for she continued to be in great demand. It was not until November 1898 that Eusapia consented to be examined by another scientific committee. This time the investigation was held in Paris and the organizer was Camille Flammarion, an eminent astronomer and a student of the paranormal. One of his chief assistants was Professor Richet.

The Paris séances produced several manifestations that were familiar --- and some that were decidedly strange. During one session, Eusapia was seated at one end of a table, and controlled in the usual way, when the sitters were stunned by the sight of a series of semi-transparent female half-figures that seemed to glide out of her body and down the length of the table.

Richet apparently felt the Paris séances were so interesting that they ought to be extended, and when the sittings sponsored by Flammarion had ended --- and Flammarion himself had declared that he was satisfied that trickery could not account for what had occurred --- Eusapia consented to continue the sittings. Richet quickly organized a new series of séances and invited Frederick Myers to attend as a private individual and not as a representative of the SPR. According to their individual accounts, these further sittings were truly remarkable. But as with the Cambridge séances, it is unfortunate --- and more than a little mystifying -- that no official records exist to tell us why they were so exciting.

Whatever occurred, it led the formerly skeptical and hostile Myers to declare at the general meetings of the SPR for December 1899 that he was now convinced of Palladino's gifts. He had just witnessed, he told the group, phenomena "far more striking" than the séances that he had attended with Eusapia in 1894. However, neither Myers not Richet ever published any notes on these sittings, though in the case of Myers, the continuing negative attitude of his friends in the SPR was likely responsible for this.

The only surviving account comes to us from the unofficial notes of Professor T. Flournoy of the Faculty of Sciences at the University of Geneva, who was also present at the séances. Flournoy was an experienced observer of the Spiritualist movement but does not go into enough detail about what he saw to permit any sort of strict analysis. Regardless, there is no reason to doubt his overall description of the conditions of the séances. It's interesting to note that this time Eusapia not only agreed to produce her phenomena in a light that, while dim, was more than sufficient for her movements to be seen by the sitters, but she also allowed her wrists and legs to be firmly held rather than just followed about.

Under these conditions, which were more satisfactory for scientific observation than the medium usually allowed, the manifestations that took place were familiar, but could hardly be dismissed when so many were at a loss to explain them. The curtains of the spirit cabinet blew about, as if in a strong breeze, although the closed séance room was still and quiet. A zither that lay on the floor of the cabinet, well out of the medium's reach, began to play and at first repeated a single note over and over again, and then began to thump up and down on the floor. Finally, the instrument was seen leaving the cabinet and landing on the table in front of the sitters. During these and other happenings, the witnesses felt themselves pushed, pinched, patted, and even struck by what they described as a "large hand." Everyone agreed that Eusapia's hands were not only tightly held, but were clearly visible at all times.

Word spread about this new round of séances and Eusapia's fame increased once again. Judging from the fact that she had allowed the test conditions in Paris to be much stricter than normal, she must have seen these sittings as a way to recover ground that she had lost when the SPR withdrew its support of her. If this was her plan, then she succeeded. Even in England, the Cambridge disaster was all but forgotten and it seemed that every scientist in Europe was anxious to have a séance with Eusapia Palladino.

The next investigations were carried out in Genoa in 1901, under the sponsorship of a society called the Minerva Scientific Circle. This time, careful records were kept and published, but the manifestations were far below the level usually carried out by Palladino. It should be noted that Professor Enrico Morselli, the group's leading investigator, though fully aware of Eusapia's continued cheating, calculated that at least 75 percent of what occurred during the sittings was genuinely paranormal.

Over the course of the next few years, Eusapia sat for one committee after another, but time was wearing on her and she was growing old. Her strong face had begun to sag and lines etched her features. Sometimes, she was unable to perform and sometimes she found herself so exhausted after a séance that she was barely able to walk. The feeling of constantly being put to the test was starting to irritate her and it manifested itself as contempt for her sitters. She was tired, but she could not stop. The séance room was her workplace and she had no other way to make a living.

She was studied by Professor Bottazzi of the Physiological Institute of the University of Naples in 1907 and by Jules Courtier of the Paris General Psychological Institute at intervals from 1905 to 1908. In every session, the same problems occurred again and again. Eusapia made all the rules as to what kind of control of her movements would be allowed. Any attempt to overstep these rules resulted in an absence of any phenomena. On the other hand, the kind of control that she permitted remained far from foolproof. She was not only adept at the substitution of hands trick that she had been using for years, but she could also sometimes slip a foot out of a shoe in such a way that the handler never realized the shoe was empty. One stray hand or foot could do a lot of damage when it came to the reliability of the séance.

The one innovation implemented by Courtier was the fairly extensive use of recording devices during the séance. Measurements were taken of the temperature, humidity, barometric pressure, and electrical conditions in the room. Courtier also measured Palladino's pulse and respiration rate and the decrease in weight of various objects that levitated in the séance room. Nothing astonishing was shown by these tests but they did serve to provide evidence that, at least on this occasion, the phenomena was real and was not merely caused by hallucinations on the part of the witnesses. While much more progressive than any other investigative methods used up to that time, the sensors still didn't reveal anything about what caused the manifestations, whether it was Eusapia or some "unknown physical force."

In 1908, Eusapia performed in Naples for a three-man committee that was likely the most formidable that she had ever encountered. One of the men was Hereward Carrington, an American researcher who, though only 27 at the time, had been engaged in exposing fraudulent mediums for eight years and had written a book on their methods called *The Physical Phenomena of Spiritualism*. Carrington had persuaded the SPR -- despite their continued misgivings about Palladino – to allow the group's secretary, Everard Feilding, to accompany him to the séances. Feilding had little experience in the séance room, but he was skeptical of the paranormal. The third member of the committee was William Wortley Baggally, who had been investigating the paranormal for more than 30 years. He stated that he doubted that he had ever actually met a genuine medium and was an accomplished amateur magician who amused his friends and colleagues by duplicating the tricks of fraudulent Spiritualists.

The men were not presupposed to believe in spirit communication and Eusapia faced an uphill battle to convince them she was genuine. They planned to document everything to the letter. The séance records were taken by a shorthand stenographer and appeared in detail in Feilding's later book, *Sittings with Eusapia Palladino & Other Studies*. The records gave a minute-by-minute account of the researchers, extensive descriptions of the séance room and its furnishings, diagrams and measurements, and even careful notes on any changes in lighting. The phenomenon witnessed were not only noted but were classified and discussed in separate sections, but ample space was given for each investigator to note any disagreements that he might have and to state his own conclusions.

Throughout the sessions, the investigators reported movements and levitations of the séance table, movements of the cabinet curtains, bulging of the medium's dress, raps and bangs on the table, noises inside the cabinet, the plucking of a guitar, movements of a small table from the cabinet onto the séance table, movement and levitation of the small table outside the curtain, transportation of other objects from the cabinet, touches by unseen fingers and hands, appearances of hands from behind the curtain, appearances of heads and objects that looked like heads from the curtain, mysterious lights, sensation of a cold breeze issuing from a scar on the medium's brow, and the untying of knots. In short, it was an amazing night – which made the skeptical investigators all the more perplexed. They were baffled. They could find no easy explanation for what they had witnessed. In their notes, they wrote:

It was only through constant repetition of the same phenomenon, in a good light and at moments when its occurrence was expected, and after finding that none of the precautions we took had any influence on impeding it, that we gradually reached the conviction that some force was in play which was beyond the reach of ordinary control, and beyond the skill of the most skillful conjurer.

The investigators offered only two explanations. One, that they were under some sort of hallucinatory trance that had been caused by Palladino, or two, that there was some sort of unknown, unascertained force at work. The men reluctantly adopted the latter explanation. They wrote:

We are of the opinion that we have witnessed in the presence of Eusapia Palladino the action of some telekinetic force, the nature and origin of which we cannot attempt to specify, through which, without the introduction of accomplices, apparatus, or mere manual dexterity, she is able to produce movements of, and percussive and other sounds in, objects at a distance from her and unconnected with her in any apparent physical manner, and also to produce matter, or the appearance of matter, without any determinable source of supply.

The report turned out to be a tremendous victory of Eusapia. In light of the newly gathered evidence, the SPR specifically withdrew its ban on Palladino and reasserted her place among mediums meriting serious investigation, in spite of her continued cheating. Most investigators, familiar with the medium and her trickery, felt that she was psychologically unable to discontinue it. Easily identified, they chose to ignore it because she also produced genuine phenomena at the same time.

One can hope that Eusapia enjoyed this small moment of glory, for it would be her last. By this time, her health was bad and her séances were suffering because of it. Hereward Carrington was anxious to have her visit the United States so that his American colleagues might have the opportunity to witness her performances. Despite her failing health, she journeyed to America in 1909 and stayed for almost six months – the most disastrous period of her career.

In her younger days, Eusapia would have loved the raw vibrancy and excitement of America. She would have seen it as a challenge, but by 1909, she was aging, tired, in poor health, and used to being taken seriously. However, the American press did not treat her as a visiting celebrity or even a scientific enigma. Instead, they saw her as a carnival sideshow and treated her more as an oddity than as a person who had stumped scientists in the major cities of Europe. She received many requests to perform but most of them came from music hall managers rather than from scientific committees. The prevailing attitude, from both the public and other mediums, seemed to be one of suspicion and hostility. Eusapia was very unhappy and soon became angry and difficult to work with. As proven at Cambridge, when Eusapia was unhappy, her séances suffered.

At first, she managed to get through them without much in the way of trickery. She performed 31 séances in America and Hereward Carrington oversaw 27 of them to prevent her from cheating. When she was under his controlled system, her physical mediumship continued to be impressive. But Carrington could not be present for her last four séances and that's when things went badly. Eusapia was sick, tired, and underestimated American audiences, who she felt were inexperienced. She did what she always did when phenomena was slow in developing – she cheated.

Unfortunately, two private detectives were in the audience one night and she was quickly exposed. Her acts of fraud received major press attention and irrevocably damaged her reputation in America. On May 10, 1910, a *New York Times* story appeared that stated, "In the séances held in this city recently, this greatest spiritualistic imposter in history was unmasked."

Her supporters rallied to her defense, but it did little good in America. In Europe, Eusapia continued to be regarded as a genuine wonder. As she had grown older, her powers had weakened, but it was generally regarded that she possessed genuine psychokinetic abilities. In time, the research into such abilities moved from the séance room to the laboratory. If she'd been tested properly, under strictly controlled conditions, in a laboratory setting, might scientists have gained more knowledge about psychokinesis and the paranormal?

But Eusapia Palladino didn't live to see those changes come about. When she left America, she went into retirement. There would be no further chances for science to explore the mysteries of this medium. She was an old, ailing woman now and she vanished into history. By the time she died on May 16, 1918, she was one of the most studied mediums in history, but she left an exasperating legacy behind. It's doubtful that the questions raised by her mediumship will ever really be answered.

7. SCIENCE AND THE SUPERNATURAL
THE BEGINNINGS OF THE PARANORMAL INVESTIGATION FIELD

Although it's already been established, it doesn't hurt to reiterate the fact that, if not for Spiritualism, the study of the paranormal would not exist. There would be no ghost hunting teams in matching black t-shirts, no silly reality shows, and on a more serious note, no paranormal investigation field of any kind. It was because of the claims of the Spiritualists, about their contact with the dead, that a need for the scientific investigation of such claims would come about.

Spiritualism not only created celebrities of the mediums who profited from it, but it also made legends of the men who came along to question their claims. They were men like Houdini and Harry Price, who were hated by the Spiritualists for their debunking of the fraudulent mediums. These men did not investigate the Spiritualists because of their lack of belief in the possibility of ghosts, but because of the need to question the evidence that was being presented. The scientific investigations of those men, as well as the scores who came before them, would set the standard for ghost hunters to come and would establish the need to question the evidence of ghosts, ruling out all of the possible explanations for the activity before accepting the idea that the phenomena could be real.

Spiritualism was unfortunately riddled with cases of deliberate fraud. It was easy to fool the thousands of people who were looking for a miracle, and many of the mediums and practitioners began lining their pockets with the money they had swindled from their victims. This is not to say that all the Spiritualists were dishonest. Many of them were good and kind people who truly believed in the honesty of their faith. And, of course, there were also those whose abilities remain unexplained today.

Spiritualism was born with good intentions, but no matter how honest some of the early followers of the movement may have been, they soon fell under the scrutiny of investigators. Some of them were simply intrigued by the reports of strange happenings at séances and wanted to take a closer look, while others who were baffled and perplexed by the movement that was taking America by storm, defensively lashed out at what they did not understand. These learned men could not explain mediumship and other psychical phenomena within the limits of their expertise and so it was easier to debunk and dismiss the whole movement rather than wrestle with what it was and how it worked.

Scientists were in a fragile place when Spiritualism was born. By the 1850s, science had managed to challenge the hold that religion maintained in American Society and had started to offer a new version of truth for people to examine. The days of miracles were over, they stated, and the world should be examined under the harsh light of reality. And then Spiritualism came along. It offered "proof" of life after death, of spirits, and of communication with loved ones who had passed away. The American public was fascinated by it and science began to be ignored, so the scientist establishment fought back. Resentful over the fact that it had managed to loosen the hold that religion had on society, only to lose its footing to Spiritualism, the debunking of mediums began to be encouraged. Editorials and printed articles professed a blatant disregard for anything that hinted at the supernatural. If it could not be explained, it did not exist.

And after all of these years, not much has changed. The relationship between science and the supernatural remains as tenuous now as it was in the nineteenth century. Those courageous and open-minded individuals who dared go beyond the acceptable limits of debunking, to examine or test psychical claims often paid a heavy price when colleagues scorned them and called their reputations into question.

From practically the first reports of spirit rappings in New York in 1848, the people who openly doubted the Fox sisters' claims of communication from the spirit world included those who had a skeptical, or so-called rational, view about the supernatural. Most men of science were hopeful that anything to do with the supernatural had been banished to the darkest corner of human experience to be forever forgotten.

But those who assumed that "ghost stories" would go away could not have been more wrong. Once millions of Americans became fascinated by Spiritualism, it was folly to think that they were not thinking about what awaited them after death. In addition, ordinary people did not really care about what scientist's thought, or what they did not believe in. Scientists would often claim they were acting on the public's behalf – protecting them from the dishonesty of spirit mediums. Grief-stricken people, though, were more concerned about hearing from a departed loved one than they were about psychological or scientific explanation about how what they believed in could not be true. Many of them insisted that such questions were not the responsibility of scientists anyway. They should be relegated to the domain of religious beliefs and faith, not to science, an "orderly branch of knowledge involving systemized observations and experimentation." Psychic happenings were elusive, and the question of testing for an invisible spirit world seemed to be impossible to most people.

When the Fox sisters initially claimed to experience their spirit raps, few were even sure what to call the strange occurrences. Were they occult? Psychical? Demonic? Magnetic? If the field of science wasn't even certain what to call the unseen phenomena, where and how would it begin to test its existence? At the time, there was no generally accepted definition of the inexplicable field that came to be known as "paranormal."

The spirit world rarely cooperated with those investigating it. It did not conform to any established scientific protocols. When many mediums were exposed as frauds and charlatans, it become a convenient excuse for skeptics and establishment scientists to discredit all of them. But what if there was no evidence of trickery? What was to be done with evidence of genuine psychic phenomena and authentic mediums? How could they be explained? Too often, doubting scientists found the easiest way was to conclude that all psychic events were fraudulent. It was a lazy and insincere approach. The press was also quick to jump on any allegation of fraud, but was rarely moved to say that a medium, which had never been shown to be fraudulent, might be genuine.

In fairness, scientists, doctors, and psychologists of the nineteenth century have very little knowledge, equipment, or experience with which to test the paranormal, even if they had wanted to do so. In fact, the irony was that Spiritualism played an important, although unwitting, role in the development of American psychology. Prior to the concepts of Sigmund Freud, Spiritualism was already paving the way for theories about the conscious and subconscious mind.

But neurology, psychiatry, chemistry, physics, and other disciplines that would later factor into the study of the paranormal by scientific means, were not well understood in that era. For example, theories to explain mediumship ranged from claiming it was blatant fraud, to involuntary muscle action, to physical disease, to insanity. Some believed that mediums experienced hallucinations or delusions that were due to "excessive excitement of the nervous system." In this way, "hysteria" could be used as an explanation for psychical experiences. Spiritualists often contended that contact with the spirit world was something electromagnetic. Electricity was the wonder of the nineteenth century because it was clearly present, could be proven, and had been tested. In addition, the electric telegraph connected the United States from New York to California, so the analogy that defined mediumship as the "spiritual telegraph" was quickly adopted.

When finally, in the 1850s, the movement officially became known as "Spiritualism," few scientists showed any interest at first. The cynical ones dismissed it as "humbug" and it would take a few years before any of them would take the time to attend séances and begin to examine the reports of strange happenings.

Eliab W. Capron was a reporter and zealot devoted to social causes who lived in Auburn, New York, not far from where Kate and Margaret Fox went to live after causing the initial commotion in Hydesville. Capron sought out the sisters to witness the spirit raps and to write about them.

Although not a scientist, he performed one of the first experiments with the girls. It was a simple test of his own design. Capron placed several small shells in his clenched fist and held them out of sight behind his back. Then he asked for the spirits to make the same number of raps as the number of shells that he was holding. The spirit raps answered correctly.

Next, Capron picked up another handful of shells, but this time, he avoided counting them. He had no idea how many he held. He asked the spirits to produce the number of raps equal to the number of small shells that he held and, again, the spirit raps produced an accurate reply. That presumably ruled out telepathy on the part of the Fox sisters. In 1855, Capron wrote one of the first important books about the new movement, *Modern Spiritualism*, and based on his experiences, he continued to support Spiritualism and the Fox sisters.

But, of course, not everyone agreed with Capron that the spirit raps might be genuine. In February 1851, for the first time, the public heard the theory that the raps were produced by the Fox sisters "snapping their knee joints." The idea was published in the *Buffalo Commercial Advertiser* by three medical professors from the University of Buffalo – Doctors Austin Flint, Charles A. Lee, and C.B. Coventry – after visiting with the two girls. Not long after was the additional supposition that Margaret and Kate had also cracked their toe joint to create spirit noises. The Buffalo professors found their ideas to be rather unpopular. In fact, a growing number of Americans either ignored or criticized the doctors, mocking their theory of "toe-ology." Skeptics, however, were quick to embrace their idea and ran with it.

A second investigation seemed to support the doctors' conclusion – but all was not what it seemed this time around. In April 1851, Mrs. Norman Culver, an in-law of the girls' brother, David, published an alleged "confession" that was supposed to have come from Kate. Mrs. Culver had sworn that she would get to the bottom of the spirit raps controversy, with no intention of taking a neutral stance. She made it clear that she wanted to smear the sisters and the growing Spiritualist movement.

But Mrs. Culver tripped herself up with the story that she attributed to Kate Fox. According to her allegations, when another committee tested the sisters in Rochester, they held Margaret's ankles so that she couldn't move her legs or toes. But the raps were still heard because they were faked by the Fox family's Dutch servant girl, who was hiding in the cellar, creating the knockings when she heard those upstairs asking questions of the spirits. But Culver had not bothered to check her facts before announcing this "confession." For one thing, the Rochester investigations were held either in committee members' homes or in a public space. Neither Kate nor Margaret had any servants, Dutch or otherwise. Finally, Margaret was the only one who was tested. Kate was not there – she was living in Auburn at the time – so she could not have been an accomplice to fraud or even witnessed the events.

Mrs. Culver also claimed that Kate admitted to "other tricks" the girls used, including learning to read facial and body language of spirit circle attendees for clues, and distracting witnesses to make them think the raps were coming from other places in the room.

It turned out that Culver had not acted alone in her campaign to discredit the Fox sisters. She had been talked into making her statements by one of Kate and Margaret's most hostile detractors, C. Chauncey Burr, a lawyer, Universalist minister, mesmerist, and self-proclaimed opponent of Spiritualism. Another enemy of the sisters was a mesmerist and phrenologist named Stanley Grimes, who had hypnotized Andrew Jackson Davis before the young man gained fame as a medium and seer. Grimes accused the girls of every imaginable trick and deception he could conjure up, including mechanical devices, ventriloquism, and collusion with witnesses.

And such things were bound to happen. As the girls became more famous, the number of opponents and critics increased in proportion to how well-known they became. The revelations by Mrs. Culver – even though they were blatantly untrue – resulted in many in the press dubbing the Fox sisters, the "Rochester Imposters." The only newspaper that came to their defense was the *New York Tribune* because editor Horace Greeley remained one of their great supporters.

After the attack by Mrs. Culver, Eliab Capron responded to every one of her accusations. But that would not be the last word. Skeptics found out that some of the testing that had been done with Margaret had been conducted at the home of Isaac and Amy Post, who had befriended the girls. The Posts had a servant girl who was fascinated by spirit communications – and she was Dutch. But even if the things Mrs. Culver alleged were true, it did not explain how the spirit raps responded to the questioner's thoughts, knew the number of shells that Capron held in his hands, or provided sitters with information that could have been known by the sisters.

Investigations into the reality of the Fox sisters' séances were numerous. Test after test was applied. The debunkers faced two problems, to explain how the rappings were produced, and the intelligence that was answering the questions, which in many cases were mentally asked. The second problem was never tackled, but the first often was and with great enthusiasm.

As the Fox sisters became more famous and the fascination with Spiritualism continued to grow, not only were the straight-out detractors trying to sink the movement, but, as if in direct response to the debunkers, there began a genuine effort among scientists, as well as by interested amateurs, to investigate the phenomena surrounding the paranormal events of Spiritualism. A need to try and apply the laws of science to the reported activity began to arise.

During those early years of the movement, scientists who wanted to investigate the claims of mediums often functioned independently. There was little coordination among those interested in paranormal research and there would not be a permanent American organization dedicated to psychical research until 1885, and that was three years after the British created the Society for Psychical Research (SPR). The British were first, ahead of the Americans, in their examination of mediumship and other paranormal phenomena, including survival after death, crisis apparitions, hauntings, clairvoyance, telepathy, premonitions, and telekinetic events.

In the middle nineteenth century, interest in Spiritualism by traditional American science was erratic and haphazard. Perhaps most scientists did not consider the subject worthy of serious attention. In those relatively rare cases when a scientist came forward to examine a paranormal claim, he was expected to debunk and dismiss it. William B. Carpenter, a noted British physiologist of the period, was disgusted by the fascination with Spiritualism in America and Britain. He called it an "epidemic delusion," similar to the witchcraft hysteria that had ravaged both continents in past centuries. Some early physicians believed mediumship and a propensity toward psychic experiences was an illness that required treatment and needed to be treated.

One of the first American scientists with the courage to support Spiritualism was Robert Hare, a respected chemistry professor at the University of Pennsylvania. His position on the paranormal made him an exception among his colleagues – but that was not how his story began. In 1853, Hare was one of the first scientists to attack the credibility of Spiritualism. He initially wrote about the movement as a way to try and "stem the tide of popular madness, which, in defiance of reason and science, was fast setting in favor of the gross delusion called Spiritualism."

Hare was 72-years-old when he undertook his studies of Spiritualism and expected to discredit it scientifically. He created his own testing devices, including one that was designed to measure minute changes in the weight of a glass of water in a metal cage. Could a medium influence the balance of the glass without touching it? Hare's first test subject was a medium named Henry Gordon, and to the professor's surprise, his device found substantial changes in the water's weight. Eminent British scientist Sir William Crookes (more about him soon) later tested famed medium D.D. Home using similar methods.

Another instrument was a wheel with the alphabet printed on it that spelled out messages. The disc was placed so that it could be seen by the medium. Hare discovered that Gordon could, using some unknown method, spell out messages that had a specific meaning for the people witnessing the test.

Hare's original purpose was to show that Spiritualism was a fraud, but instead, he concluded that there was "some rational being" of an unknown nature that caused spirit communications. Hare said that he had taken "the greatest possible precaution and precision," but had arrived at a very different explanation than the one that he initially believed. He had shown that a "power and intelligence other than that of those present was at work." No longer a critic, he instead became a proponent of Spiritualism. His colleagues in the scientific community roundly criticized him and some of the verbal attacks were quite vicious. At Harvard University, the reaction to Hare's findings was equally hostile. The faculty passed a formal motion condemning Hare's "insane adherence to a giant humbug." In 1854, the American Association for the Advancement of Science refused to even listen when Hare attempted to speak to its members about Spiritualism. He was literally shouted down. He responded to the animosity by resigning from the association.

But Hare courageously refused to give up. He believed there was good reason to continue his investigations and he experimented with several other mediums, including one named A.D. Ruggles who, in a trance state, spoke several foreign languages he did not know in his normal state. Hare again examined Henry Gordon when the latter demonstrated levitation in 1852, becoming one of the first mediums to exhibit this ability. Hare concluded that Gordon's powers were evidence of an inexplicable psychic force.

He continued his work until his death in 1858, at age 77. His skeptical colleagues decided that an explanation for his interest in Spiritualism was a simple one: he had gone senile.

At the same time that Spiritualism was starting to grow in the 1850s, new advances were also being made in the fields of science and technology. To some it seemed that science and Spiritualism could not be further apart, each functioning in an entirely separate world. But this was not really the case – they had to meet at some point.

During the middle nineteenth century, there was no force in nature that was more intriguing to the general public than electricity. The marvel of electricity, truly coming into its own with the successful introduction of the telegraph in 1844, just four years before the events in Hydesville, joined science and Spiritualism in the minds of those who believed that spirit contact was of an electric nature. Many considered Spiritualism to be a "scientific religion," and the comparison to electricity was obvious in the popular term of "spiritual telegraph," a reference to how mediums got in touch with the other side. In addition, both spirit contact and electricity were invisible forms of energy.

There were many theories that circulated that linked spirits and electricity. One theory was that souls vibrated with a mysterious electrical charge that could be detected by mediums. Others believed the opposite was true – that mediums acted as a signal to spirits, which is why they chose to make contact with them. Of course, there were many who feared that electricity might run wildly amok. This meant that the mediums might be taken over or inhabited by negative spirits that they could not control. No one truly understood how electricity worked. It might be just as dangerous as it was beneficial.

Michael Faraday

In 1853, Michael Faraday, one of England's most respected scientists, turned his attention to Spiritualism. Faraday was both a physicist and chemist who became widely known for his experiments with electromagnetism and for inventing the first electric generator in 1831. He was deeply religious and had no personal desire to become a Spiritualist. His interest in the movement was generated by annoyance that psychical researchers were not testing Spiritualist claims with what he considered was the correct scientific approach. So, Faraday began his own series of experiments. In the early 1850s, that meant looking into spirit raps and table tipping, the most popular scientific manifestations of the time.

After Faraday observed many demonstrations of table tipping, he drew his conclusion about what was causing the events to occur. His theory was that the unconscious expectations of the sitters were creating a muscle pressure that was causing the tables to move. Faraday designed an apparatus to measure even the tiniest movement of the séance table. He found that those motions were sufficient to make a small, lightweight table seem to move on its own. Skeptics often point to the same theory to explain why the planchette on a talking board moves from letter to letter. Of course, most Spiritualists disagreed with Faraday's theory, maintaining that people's hands attracted "spirit energy" and the messages came from discarnate beings.

Faraday's conclusion may be an explanation for a limited number of psychical occurrences, especially telekinetic activity. But it left many unanswered questions about Spiritualism, including how mediums were able to give accurate messages, and did not explain other phenomena, like spirit materializations, clairvoyance, telepathy, and hauntings. And perhaps he knew it. When Faraday had the opportunity to test D.D. Home, the noted scientist refused, so he never got Home into his laboratory. There's a very good chance that Faraday knew that Home might exhibit powers that he would not able to so easily explain.

There is no story in the history of American Spiritualism that is as weird as Spiritualist John Murray Spear's collision with science in the 1850s – and that's saying a lot. Spear was well-known in Boston as a Universalist minister and social reformer, especially for his efforts to improve prisons. In 1851, he became interested in Spiritualism and became one of the hundreds of thousands who converted to the movement. He wasted no time in developing his own psychic abilities.

Three years later, he announced that a group of spirits calling themselves the "Association of Electricizers" told him to build what they called a "New Motor" that would be a source of inexhaustible and "self-generated" power, utilizing the "magnetic life" found in nature. The machine would behave as a "living organism," almost like a human body. In other words, it was a "spirit designed perpetual motion machine."

John Murray Spear

Following instructions received from the spirit world, Spear and his followers constructed the strange apparatus near Lynn, Massachusetts. It was made of copper and zinc, and cost about $2,000 to build. Spear genuinely believed there was evidence of life in the mechanics of the device, a sort of "God machine."

Such news did not sit well with many people, who read about the machine in the wide press coverage that was given to Spear and his followers. Some compared it to Frankenstein's monster – the creature from the 1818 novel that was given life, but had no soul. The story had raised concerns about the ethics of science and technology, and what its limits should be, and now people were worried about the same thing in regards to Spear's device.

But the public never needed to worry. Spear's contraption didn't work. He blamed it on the vague messages from the spirit world and refused to give up on it. The machine was moved from Lynn to Randolph, New York, a location with a higher elevation so that the device would better function. One night, however, a mob of angry and frightened locals destroyed it, contending that its creation was "blasphemous." After this, Spear wisely abandoned his plans, but he remained a polarizing figure in the movement for decades. In later years, he was complimented for his sincerity, patience, and unswerving belief in the spiritual origin of the mission he undertook.

Interestingly, in the years since Spear attempted to produce his new source of power, others have also sought a new "motor force in nature." The best known were Nikola Tesla – who was regarded as a genius -- and Wilhelm Reich, whose controversial theory of "orgone energy" puts him squarely in the same camp as Spear. "Orgone" was described as a "universal life force," a massless, omnipresent substance that Reich believed could be gathered using a mechanical device. Like John Murray Spear, he was wrong.

Despite the interest shown in Spiritualism by some members of mainstream science, true scientific investigation of the paranormal remained a scattered effort in America until late in the nineteenth century. It was as if researchers were waiting to see if the movement hung around that long so they could determine it worthy of study. They found out that it was just as baffling as it was when it first arrived on the scene and debate continued whether everything from spirit raps to physical phenomena – flying trumpets, ectoplasm, materializing spirits – were even possible.

There also remained a valid concern about exactly what instruments could investigate something as unstructured as spirit phenomena. What could be built? And what would it measure? There were legitimate questions asked about the possibility of clairvoyance, premonitions, and telepathy. Were they psychical or supernatural in nature? Were they caused by an energy that was not yet discovered? Or did they originate from discarnate entities? Such questions only annoyed the Spiritualists, for it called into question their strong belief that all psychic experiences were attributed to the spirit world.

The issue of testing was critical. Scientists were adamant about the fact that, in order for psychical energy to be proven, it had to be measured under strict conditions. In an era that was fascinated by electricity, modern machinery, and theories about invisible energy, a form of measurement was essential. It was no surprise that legitimate scientists wanted to measure the abilities of Spiritualists in a way that guaranteed a non-biased result. And it wasn't as if professional mediums objected to being tested. In fact, many in the movement actually urged scientists to examine psychical phenomena. However, the nineteenth and early twentieth centuries were a time when there were few organized academic studies of the paranormal, and the handful of university-backed investigations always came to the same conclusion: there was no scientific evidence of psychical phenomena. And even though there was no conclusive scientific evidence that paranormal events were not real, the prevailing rationalist opinion was that you had to prove it to be so, before it could be accepted as so.

Many cynics suggested that professors had made up their minds to oppose the paranormal before they examined it, regardless of what was presented. This certainly seemed to be the case. It seemed the answers were already in before the questions were ever asked. Didn't this make the resulting tests to be completely biased? Whatever the explanation, the paranormal was rarely welcome in the hallowed halls of American academia in those days.

THE SCIENTIST AND THE MEDIUM

There were some academics, however, who pushed for investigating the spirit world. Among them was the famed British physicist Sir William Crookes, who was one of the first scientists in England or American to advocate the scientific investigation of psychical phenomena. Although his investigations would take him dangerously close to scandal, his research began with the best of intentions.

His interest in Spiritualism was spurred by the death of his younger brother in 1867. After he consulted with several mediums, Crookes decided that he would personally investigate Spiritualism. His decision was greeted with wide approval. The popular press felt sure that Crookes would soon show that Spiritualist claims were nothing more than ridiculous humbug. Crookes appeared to share that view. When he announced that he was going to begin his investigations, he stated that he had no preconceived notions on the subject and then added, "The increased employment of scientific methods will produce a race of observers who will drive the worthless residuum of Spiritualism hence into the unknown limbo of magic and necromancy." This statement was taken as a disclaimer of belief in Spiritualism, but if Crookes' private beliefs had been better known, his words would have been more clearly interpreted to mean that he intended only to disprove the "worthless residuum" who were frauds. In diary entries that were written just months before his investigations began, he noted that he was already a firm believer in the possibility of an "unknown power."

Crookes was born in London in 1832 and was largely self-taught, with no regular schooling, until he enrolled in the Royal College of Chemistry at age 16. He graduated in 1854 and took a position as the superintendent of the meteorological department at Radcliffe Observatory, Oxford. A year later, he took a teaching position as a professor of chemistry at Chester Training College, but resigned after one year because he was not given a laboratory in which he could do research. Although he tried to find another teaching position, he was never successful and most of his later work was done in a laboratory at his home. In 1856, Crookes married Ellen Humphrey, with whom he had eight children, and from his home, he began writing and editing for scientific journals like the *Chemical News*. He also helped to found the *Quarterly Journal of Science* in 1864. In 1861, Crookes achieved the first of his scientific discoveries: the element thallium and the correct measurement of its atomic weight. This got him elected a Fellow of the Royal Society at age 31.

Then, in 1867, came a turning point in Crookes' life with the death of his youngest brother, Phillip. The two men had been very close and Crookes was distraught over his brother's death and, like others of the time who suffered a great loss, he turned to Spiritualism for answers. At the urging of his friend and fellow scientist, Cromwell Varney, Crookes and his wife attended several séances to attempt contact with Phillip. Although the details of these sessions are unknown, Crookes believed they were successful. One of his first séances was with the famous medium D.D. Home, where Crookes was amazed to see phenomena that he never dreamed possible before. The scientist was not content to simply observe Home's manifestations, he also attempted to re-create them in the laboratory and, according to his records, this was successful.

Crookes applied strict scientific controls during his research with Home and the meticulous testing failed to find any evidence of fraud. He believed that Home possessed a "psychic force" which emanated from his body, and he wrote a paper on the subject, believing it to be of scientific importance. Not surprisingly, the paper was first rejected and then met with scorn and derision when it was finally published. His critics, mainly other scientists, lashed out and stated that the phenomena Crookes reported could not have occurred, that it was simply impossible. "I never said that it was possible," Crookes replied. "I only said that it was true."

Although the scientific community frequently criticized him, Crookes continued his investigations into the spirit world, testing mediums and publishing material on the science of the afterlife. Crookes last series of sittings were experiments conducted with a medium of rather dubious reputation named Anna Eva Fay. After this, he turned away from psychic research for a time and returned to his scientific pursuits.

In 1875, Crookes earned the Royal Medal for his work and one year later invented the radiometer, a device which demonstrated the effects of radiation on objects in a vacuum, and a special device called the "Crookes Tube" that went along with it. This invention would lead to the discovery of cathode rays, X-rays, and the electron.

Crookes went on to serve on scientific committees, earned prestigious awards for his discoveries, and invented an instrument that would be used to study subatomic particles, and yet he never wavered in his belief in Spiritualism. In 1916, after the death of his wife, Crookes attempted to communicate with her and was unsuccessful, but after a visit to a spirit photographer, he obtained what he believed to be photographic proof that her presence was still with him. Sadly, this plate, under modern study, appears to have been double-exposed – an obvious fake.

Crookes died in April 1919, never questioning that fact that the spirit world was genuine and that there were things his beloved science would never truly be able to explain.

In addition to his work with D.D. Home, there was one medium with whom Crookes was most closely linked: the controversial Florence Cook. It would be his work with this young woman, barely out of her teens, that would not only overshadow much of the important work that Crookes did in the world of psychical research, but would lead to an alleged sex scandal that would forever taint his reputation.

During the 1870s, Florence Cook was one of the Spiritualist movement's most famous mediums. She was known for her ability to produce full-form spirit manifestations in a well-lighted room. Her ability came from her work with a spirit cabinet, the addition to séance rooms in America and England that was first introduced by the Davenport brothers. As more spectacular effects became necessary to keep public interest after the Civil War years, dramatic spirit forms began making their appearance at séances. But the phenomenon only seemed to occur when a closed cabinet was involved. Obviously, skeptics and critics pointed out that observers had no way of knowing what kind of trickery was taking place within the cabinet, but the mediums had a clever defense: they insisted that it was only possible to manifest the dramatic effects in this way because "spirit energy" had to build up in an enclosure, acting like a sort-of battery. Once that energy was concentrated, it could be converted into a visible spirit entity. Sitters were always cautioned never to touch the medium or the materialized spirit. Apparently, it was dangerous because it

Florence Cook

could cause the ectoplasm that the spirit was composed of to suddenly be absorbed back into the medium's body.

Full materializations were a specialty of Florence Cook. Her best-known materialization was that of her spirit guide, Katie King. Katie already had a long history before being forever connected to the persona of Florence Cook. She first appeared during the initial Spiritualism craze of the 1850s and graced the séances of many famous mediums. Like her spectral father, John King, "Katie" was not her real name. In life, she was said to have been Annie Owen Morgan, the daughter of the pirate Henry Morgan, who had been knighted and appointed governor of Jamaica. He preferred to be known as "John King" in the afterlife, though, and his daughter adopted his name. In life, Annie Morgan had been a self-professed liar and cheat, as well as a thief and an adulteress -- and all this before she died in her twenties. Her new mission, in death, was to prove to the world the truth of Spiritualism and, of course, to prove the talents of a few mediums in particular. One of these was Florence Cook.

Florence (or Florrie, as her mother called her) was born in London's crowded, impoverished East End in 1856 and as a child claimed she could hear the voices of angels. Her mother would later state that the girl had always been aware of the presence of spirits, but her psychic gifts only began to manifest at age 15, when she levitated a piece of furniture during a table-tilting session with friends. She was still an adolescent when she began conducting séances in her home, where she became known for being able to manifest "spirit faces." To create a cabinet of the kind mediums used, Florence would sit inside a large cupboard in her family's breakfast room. A hole had been cut high up on the door and it was here where the faces would appear.

Florence would climb into the cabinet and would allow herself to be bound to a chair with ropes about her neck, waist, and wrists. The door would be closed and the sitters would sing a hymn to create the proper mood. The cabinet door would be opened to show that Florence was still tied to the chair, and then closed again. A few moments later, the faces would appear in the opening. When they finally vanished, the doors would again be opened and Florence would be revealed, still tied to her chair and apparently exhausted from allowing the spirits to use her energy to appear. A few people noticed that the faces, which were draped with a thin white cloth, looked an awful lot like Florence. They suggested that the girl simply slipped her ropes, stood on the chair to stick her face through the hole, then tied herself back up again. Nevertheless, the audience loved her performances and she soon gained a following. Many were impressed by the fact that she never charged a fee for her séances. A number of sitters apparently came merely because she was an exceptionally attractive young lady.

With that in mind, it's no surprise that the pretty young girl quickly became famous. In addition to her looks, her séances had other appeals as well, including the fact that the spirits had a habit of tossing her into the air and -- on at least one occasion -- ripping her clothing off. While Florence basked in the newfound attention, some of her friends, and her employer, were becoming unsettled by her new gifts. Miss Eliza Cliff for one, in whose school Florence worked as an assistant teacher, was reluctantly forced to discontinue her employment. The girls in the school were unsettled by the strange happenings that seemed to occur around Miss Cook and their parents were afraid that the young ladies might become affected themselves. She was quite fond of Florrie, she said, but was "compelled to part with her."

It was in 1872 that Florence first manifested the spirit of Katie King. During a regular séance, a white face appeared in the darkness outside the curtains of Florrie's cabinet. The floating mask was announced to be the face of Katie King, who was already a spirit to be reckoned with in America. But the Katie that appeared for Florence was not the mysterious and ethereal figure of Spiritualist writings --- she was a proof of the resurrection of the dead, a spirit made flesh, and a young woman who could walk among and talk with the sitters. Her new body was almost indistinguishable from that of a living girl. She was a beautiful young lady in fact -- and unfortunately -- very closely resembled Florence Cook.

All, of course, noticed the difference in attire from Florence's long, dark, full dress with sizable sleeves, to that of Katie, who emerged from the spirit cabinet in which Florence was bound, out of sight of the sitters. She looked quite a lot like Florence, except that Katie had a quantity of white cloth draped over her head. She was young, pretty, dressed in a white gown, barefoot, and in short sleeves, a rather revealing costume for the Victorian era, and not at all the way that Florence dressed.

The spirit manifested by Florence Cook, known as "Katie King." Despite the many similarities between the young woman and the ghost, believers insisted that they were not the same entity.

Florence always entered her spirit cabinet when she wanted to go into a trance. As long as 30 minutes might pass before the curtains parted and Katie emerged, leaving Florence unconscious in the cabinet. Occasionally, when Katie was present, Florence could be heard sobbing and moaning inside the cabinet, as if the manifestation were draining her energy. At first, Katie simply smiled and nodded to the audience, but later, she began to walk among them, offering her (strangely solid) hand and talking to them. She was fond of touching the sitters and allowing them to carefully touch her, as well. After Katie returned to the cabinet, Florence would be found, still tied up and seemingly exhausted.

Spiritualists considered Katie's materializations a marvelous phenomenon. Skeptics were sure the manifestations were just a thinly disguised Florence Cook. But many wondered how Florence, who was tied up in the cabinet, could release herself from her bindings to become Katie, and then tie herself up again as she had been before. One observer, a British minister, after witnessing one of Florence's séances, remarked,

"Spiritual or material, it was clever." In other words, even if you did not believe that Katie was a spirit taking physical form, it made for an entertaining evening. Florence and Katie were soon famous on both sides of the Atlantic.

As noted, it was believed that spirit forms, like Katie, were made up of that mysterious substance called ectoplasm. It was believed that interfering with ectoplasm – or with the entranced body of a medium – could be dangerous to the medium's health. If this was true, then Florence had a very close call one night.

On the night of December 9, 1873, one of the sitters at a Cook séance was a man named William Volckman. Although an invited guest, he apparently became quite agitated by the "obvious similarities" between the medium and the spirit. In a fit of anger, he jumped up and grabbed Katie by the wrist, announcing loudly that she was Florence in disguise. For a spirit, Katie put up quite a fight and managed to succeed in leaving several bloody scratches on the man's nose. Katie was finally rescued by Edward Elgie Corner, Florence's fiancée. He was assisted by the Earl and Countess of Caithness and by barrister Henry Dunphy. They were friends of the Cook family and aware of the inherent danger to a medium that was caused by interfering with an apparition. They seized Volckman and a scuffle ensued, allowing Katie to make her escape. According to Dunphy, she disappeared, dissolving from the feet upward. Volckman was determined to follow up on his assault, though, and he rushed to the cabinet. He threw open the curtain and there was no sign of Katie, but he did find Florence with her clothing in disarray. She was, however, still tied up.

Was this a case of a skeptical investigator gone berserk, or something else? It is significant that shortly after this incident, Volckman married another famous London medium named Agnes Nichol Guppy, a portly widow who was very jealous of Florence and her fame. The incident with Volckman did not immediately harm Florence's career as a medium, but it did shake the faith of some. She suffered a slight reversal of fortune for a time and began looking for a new angle to pursue to garner some much-needed favorable publicity.

Around this same time, medium D.D. Home was undergoing testing by Sir William Crookes. Florence quickly got in touch with Crookes and offered to add her own contribution to psychical research. Crookes was delighted to investigate the now-famous partnership between Florence and Katie and happily agreed to a series of private séances. Shortly after, what many consider to be the most problematical investigations of the Spiritualist era began.

Once the investigations started, Crookes invited Florence, and occasionally her mother and sister, to stay with him at his home on Mornington Road in northwest London. Crookes knew that most Spiritualists had a distrust of scientists and he hoped to rectify this by inviting the young woman into his home and befriending her. Mrs. Crookes was in the house, but was not much in evidence, as she was expecting their tenth child at the time and was usually confined to her room.

The first time that Crookes had experienced Katie had been when Florence had initially approached him about the investigations. He had visited the Cook home and took part in a séance. He was well aware of the fact that many skeptics believed that Florence and her spirit guide, Katie, were one in the same person, but Crookes took note that while watching the materialized Katie, he distinctly heard "a sobbing, moaning sound from behind the curtain where the young woman was supposed to be sitting." Crookes may have been impressed by this, but Florence's critics were not.

In March 1874, Crookes obtained what he felt was "absolute proof" that Florence and Katie were two separate entities. During a séance, Katie had walked among the sitters for a time and then retreated behind the curtain where Florence had been bound to a chair. In a minute, she reappeared and asked Crookes to accompany her behind the curtain. According to his account, he found the unconscious form of Florence Cook, still bound with sealed tape. Katie had vanished, leaving Florence behind. He wrote: "I found Miss Cook had partially slipped off the sofa, and her head hanging in a very awkward position. I lifted her onto the sofa and in so doing, had satisfactory evidence, in spite of the darkness, that Miss Cook was not attired in 'Katie' costume but had on her ordinary black velvet dress, and was in deep trance." Crookes' account stated that he checked three different times to be sure that the woman on the floor, illuminated by a dim gas light, was actually Florence and he was convinced that she and Katie were separate individuals.

However, Crookes had still not seen them together. This opportunity came on March 29, he said, when Katie invited him into the cabinet after he had turned out the gaslight in the room. He carried with him a phosphorus light, which cast only a very dim glow. However, Crookes claimed to be able to see adequately. He wrote:

I went cautiously into the room, it being dark, and felt about for Miss Cook. I found her crouching on the floor. Kneeling down, I let air enter the phosphorus lamp, and by its light I saw the young lady dressed in black velvet, as she had been in the early part of the evening. And to all appearances perfectly senseless; she did not move when I took her hand and held the light quite close to her face, but continued quietly breathing. Raising the lamp, I looked around and saw Katie standing close behind Miss Cook. She was robed in flowing white drapery as we had seen her previously in the séance. Holding one of Miss Cook's hands in mine, and still kneeling, I passed the lamp up and down so as to illuminate Katie's whole figure, and satisfy myself thoroughly that I was really looking at the veritable Katie... and not the phantasm of a disordered brain. Three separate times did I turn the lamp to Katie and examine her with steadfast scrutiny until I had no doubt whatever of her objective reality. At last Miss Cook moved slightly, and Katie instantly motioned me to go away. I went to another part of the cabinet and then ceased to see Katie, but did not leave the room till Miss Cook woke up, and two of the visitors came in with a light.

Was this proof that Katie really was a ghost?

Perhaps --- but not all the sitters at her séances were completely convinced. Many of them insisted on extreme measures to prevent Florence from practicing trickery. Customarily, before the séance would begin, Florence would be bound with a cord or sealed with tape. Each time, the bindings were found to still be intact at the end of the evening. And although the indignities that were later inflicted on mediums, like filling their mouth with fruit juice to prevent ventriloquism and checking all of their orifices for secreted ectoplasm, were never pressed onto Florence, her hair was nailed to the floor on at least one occasion. Believe it or not, Katie still appeared.

After Crookes began regularly testing Florence, he produced several dozen photographs of Katie King and was allowed to test her appearances with Florence in plain sight. During the test, Florence reclined on a sofa behind a curtain and wrapped a shawl about her face. Soon, Katie appeared in front of the curtain. Crookes checked to be sure that Cook was still lying on the sofa and he saw that she was --- although incredibly, he never moved the shawl to be sure that it was really her.

In all, Crookes created 55 photographs of Florence and Katie, but only a handful of them remain today. The rest were destroyed, along with the negatives, shortly before his death in 1919. Crookes used five cameras, two of them stereoscopic, operating simultaneously during the sessions. Many of the photos were both poorly shot and questionable in authenticity and while many of them purported to show both Katie and Florence at the same time, they offered little proof that they were two separate beings. In one, Katie is seen standing in the background while Florence is slumped over a chair, apparently in a trance. Unfortunately, though, an "ectoplasmic shroud" hides Katie's face.

One of the few photographs taken that purportedly showed Florence and Katie at the same time, even though "Katie's" face is covered, concealing her identity. Needless to say, skeptics were not convinced.

One of Crookes's assistants was a man named Edward Cox. He was one of Britain's best-known psychical researchers at the time, as well as a practicing attorney. He had helped with the testing of Daniel Home, and was supportive after he had witnessed his levitations and other psychical abilities. Cox had a sharp eye for details and was well-acquainted with the trickery that some mediums engaged in. In addition, he was skeptical about the existence of spirit phenomena even though he believed in the possibility that some inexplicable "forces" existed – forces that had "both power and intelligence, but imperceptible to our senses."

Cox's opinion of Florence Cook was largely negative, and his notes implied that he felt she was a fraud. To prove it, he devised a very simple test that would conclusively prove if Florence and Katie were the same person, or if they were two separate beings – one human, and one a ghost. Cox suggested that a dab of indelible India ink be placed on Florence's forehead. Then if the alleged spirit, Katie, emerged from the cabinet with ink on her forehead, then she was obviously Florence, pretending to be the ghost.

But strangely, Crookes never followed Cox's suggestion, and the simple ink test was never done.

Crookes didn't seem to need proof of Florence's integrity. He often defended her to critics. He stated that Florence agreed to every test that he put her though, without hesitation, and that he had never seen the slightest inclination that she was trying to deceive him. Crookes wrote, "Indeed, I do not believe that she could carry on a deception if she were to try and if she did she would be certainly found out very quickly, for such a line of action is altogether foreign to her nature."

In 1874, Crookes stated that he had proof that Florence was not posing as Katie. He and a man who was Florence's benefactor were permitted entry into the spirit cabinet, where they saw and touched two separate beings. For Crookes, that put to rest the accusation that Florence was pretending to be Katie.

But not everyone was convinced. Critics stated that Katie looked so much like Florence because that's who she was. It was not simply good enough to cite Crookes's integrity and his stature as a scientist to convince someone of the authenticity of the séances. Edward Cox knew that both Florence and Katie were "solid flesh." Both breathed, and even showed beads of perspiration. He thought it was highly improbable that a spirit entity would manifest such clearly human functions. He expressed his doubts in a letter to D.D. Home: "I am satisfied that a large amount of fraud has been and is still being practiced."

Was it possible that Florence employed a double to pretend to be Katie King? Many historians – and every skeptic, of course – have reached that conclusion. It's not as outrageous as it might sound. During the investigations, a young medium named Mary Showers stayed at the Crookes' residence while Florence was there. She performed a sort-of "double act" with Florence. The two of them went into trances together and would create two manifestations – one of Katie and one of "Florence Maple," a ghost who bore more than a passing resemblance to Mary. Would it not have been possible for Mary, or even Florence's sister, to have stepped into the spirit cabinet and pretended to be an unconscious Florence, slumped over with her face covered, while Florence walked around as Katie? Or couldn't Mary, who was only in her teens in the middle 1870s, have posed as Katie, which might explain why some thought Katie appeared to be younger than Florence?

If Florence was posing as Katie, could there have been more to it than simple fraud? It's been suggested that perhaps Florence truly believed that she was manifesting a spirit, but had actually created a split personality – Katie King. Florence was an upstanding and proper young Victorian woman, but Katie flirted and teased, wandering about the darkened séance room and sitting on the laps of the men who were present. She touched them and allowed herself to be touched. On at least one occasion, she stepped out of her robes, revealing that she was naked underneath. "Now you can see that I am a woman," she said. Could Katie have been a way for a repressed young woman to act out her innermost desires? And if so, was it a conscious impersonation, or was she truly convinced that the manifestation of "Katie" was real?

If this was a hoax, then the most puzzling question in all of this was how Sir William Crookes, an eminent scientist, inventor of the radiometer, and discoverer of the element thallium, could be so easily duped by a fraud? And if he knew it was all a hoax, would he have been willing to risk his well-earned reputation to engage in a Spiritualist fraud by insisting that Katie King was a materialized spirit? It seems unlikely that he would have gone along with it, just as it seems unlikely that he was so easily fooled.

So, what is the answer?

Many years later, a British researcher claimed that there was substantial documentation that Crookes and Florence were having an affair, right under the nose of the scientist's wife. That would explain Crooke's willingness to either believe in the existence of Katie King, or colluded with her to manufacture fraudulent results in the tests. At the time the two of them met, Crookes was in his early 40's and married with a large family; Florence was 18. His infatuation with the pretty young woman, it was said, clouded his judgement and objectivity. By stating that Florence was genuine assured him easy access to her affections. Having a scientist of Crookes's reputation declare her legitimate served Florence well, even if it meant a sexual relationship with him. In short, the two of them may have been using each other. Of course, there is no hard evidence of this, but it would be naïve not to at least consider the possibility of it.

There is one other possibility to explain the manifestations – that they were real. Florence may have been a genuine medium, Katie King may have been an actual spirit, and Crookes's investigations were not as flawed as they appeared to be. Although Crookes behaved strangely for a man with a scientist's regard for detail --- such as omitting names and addresses of witnesses from his record --- this may have been in regard for Florrie's strict rules of secrecy.

Why even consider this idea, when so much of the evidence points to the contrary?

There are some very strange eyewitness reports that have survived from the séances. According to novelist Florence Marryat, Katie resembled Florence in some ways, but was remarkably different in others. She stated that Katie was taller and heavier than Florence and that Katie had reddish hair, while Florence's hair was dark and almost black. Crookes had also noted a number of differences between the two young women. Katie was taller, heavier, and broader in the face, had a fairer complexion and longer fingers. Florence had pierced ears, Katie did not. On one occasion, Florence had a large blister on her neck but when Katie appeared, her neck was as fair and smooth. During one séance, Katie was breathing (although again, why does a ghost breathe?), while Florence was being treated by a doctor for a severe cough.

Unbelievably, though, Crookes's skills at scientific analysis failed him once again. Just like when he failed to check under the shawl to make sure the unconscious woman was actually Florence, he took no comparison photographs to show the pierced and unpierced ears, the shape of their faces, or the length of their fingers. Or if he did, he left no record of them. This seems amazing in that Crookes was investigating a phenomenon that could theoretically change the way the world believed.

But not everyone was so careless. Cromwell Varley, the famous electrician who worked on the Atlantic cable, believed that he had proof that Katie and Florence were not the same person. Varley, an ardent Spiritualist, designed a test to prove that Florence was still in the cabinet while Katie walked about the séance room. Florence was placed in an electrical circuit with wires connected to coins that were placed on her arms so that a small current was running through her body. A large galvanometer --- an instrument that detects and measures small electrical currents --- was placed 10 feet away from the cabinet. It was placed on a mantelpiece in full view of the sitters so that the flow of electricity could be monitored. If the medium broke the circuit in order to leave the cabinet dressed as Katie, the galvanometer would register wild fluctuations. Katie appeared as usual and there was no change in the current. Crookes asked Katie to plunge her hands into a chemical solution that would cause a change in the current flow if Florence had managed to dress as Katie and still get out of the cabinet. Again, the galvanometer showed no fluctuation in the current.

Did this prove that Katie and Florence were not the same person? Perhaps, but it still didn't prove that Katie King was a spirit. It's still very possible that she could have been Florence's sister or her friend, Mary Showers. There are just too many unanswered questions about the entire affair to know anything for sure.

Critics believe that by May 1874, Florence was becoming worried about the attention that her appearances as Katie King were receiving. Fearing exposure, she suddenly and unexpectedly announced that Katie's visits to "dear Florrie" were over. Her time had come to an end. Crookes later wrote of a scene that he witnessed when Florence and Katie said their final goodbyes. According to his account, Katie made one last appearance in the séance room and then walked over to where Florence was lying on the floor. She touched the medium on the shoulder and implored her to wake up, explaining that she had to leave. They talked for a few moments until "Miss Cook's tears prevented her from speaking." Crookes was asked to come over and hold Florence in his arms, as she was falling to the floor and sobbing hysterically, and when he looked around, the white-robed figure of Katie was gone.

With Katie now gone, there was no point in Florence staying on for further investigations. In fact, she told Crookes for the first time, she had been married about two months before to Edward Corner. Crookes soon returned to his work as a physicist. He was supportive of future psychical investigations, but he was never directly involved with them again. Some believe that Crookes's abandonment of the field was due to the fact that he was aware of Florence's hoax, or was heartbroken when she left him. But, of course, those suppositions are based on the idea that they actually had an affair, of which no evidence exists.

After Katie departed, Florence went into retirement for six years, but then returned to the Spiritualist scene manifesting a new spirit, this one named Marie. This new spirit partner managed to provide even more entertainment that Katie had, singing and dancing for the sitters at her séances, and providing contact with the spirit world.

But there was something about "Marie" that was beginning to bother people. At a séance in 1880, Sir George Sitwell noticed that Marie's spirit robes covered corset stays, so he reached out and grabbed hold of her. He held on tightly to her and when he pulled aside Florence's curtain, he found that the medium's chair was empty. He was not surprised to discover that he was holding onto Florence, clad only in her underwear.

After that, Florence would only perform if someone were tied up in the cabinet with her. On at least one occasion, Florence Marryat participated and she later testified that during Marie's appearance, she was firmly tied to Florence in the cabinet. This wasn't enough to keep her audience, though, and Florence vanished into relative obscurity as a housewife in Monmouthshire. She gave her last séance in 1899 and passed away at age 48 in 1904, a footnote in Spiritualist history and one that left many questions behind.

THE FIRST "GHOST HUNTERS"

Between 1876 and 1900, the world saw scores of amazing discoveries and inventions – the telephone, electric lights, the science of fingerprinting, the Kodak "box camera," medical improvements, automobiles, motion pictures, wireless telegraphs, the discovery of radioactivity, airships, and more. But not everyone was happy with the advance of technology. By 1893, when Tesla's alternating current turned Chicago's World Columbian Exposition into a city of lights, most people who had grown up after the Civil War had started to think that the new technology of the approaching twentieth century was more exciting than the Spiritualism that had come of age in the 1800s.

At the same time, however, thanks to many poets and writers, more Americans began to explore alternative thinking and mysticism as a path to a spiritual truth. Writers like Walt Whitman encouraged readers to contemplate Eastern beliefs, and America's sense of religious curiosity began to threaten the more conservative Christian denominations, which were already battling Charles Darwin's highly contentious and controversial theory of evolution. Even though every important scientist in the country had embraced his explanation for the origin of the species, it was a direct contradiction to Christianity's certitude in the literal world of the Bible that God had created the universe in six days.

Spiritualism experienced a renewed interest during the 1880s, but a decade later and through the early twentieth century, the movement was clearly on the decline in America. It remained of greater interest in England, especially after World War I brought a desperate need for comfort for the hundreds of thousands who lost sons, husbands, and loved ones in the fighting.

By the turn of the century, it had become clear that people had tired of fraudulent mediums. Americans were living longer and had healthier lives, so there was less thought about imminent death. However, in the increasingly mechanized society, many felt that psychic phenomena needed to be explained scientifically and rationally. It seemed obvious to many that strange things took place and now such things needed to be explained. Spiritualism had tried to define itself as a "scientific religion," but that was difficult to establish. On the other hand, by seeking the protection of "religion," Spiritualists also hoped to avoid efforts by law enforcement to crack down on so-called "fortune tellers." The movement had proven to be incapable of cracking down on the frauds in its midst.

What seemed to be needed was not a police investigation but rather a serious, scientific investigation of Spiritualism and other psychical claims, carried out by an organization of objective researchers who were dedicated to seeking the truth –

whatever that might be. The Spiritualist movement had always lacked a cohesiveness and a single authoritative voice to represent it. This was the reason why its ranks were so riddled with fraud and why its many claims had remained unproven for decades.

In 1882, psychical research took a giant leap forward from séance room to scientific setting when a group of insightful British men – most of them educated at Cambridge University – formed a new association for investigating the paranormal and named it the Society for Psychical Research, or SPR, as it came to be called. It made its purpose very clear from the start: "To examine without prejudice or prepossession and in a scientific spirit those faculties of man, real or supposed, which appear to be inexplicable on any generally recognized hypothesis."

Why what can only be called as a landmark moment in supernatural history occurred first in England and not in America remains a bit of a mystery. It's thought that perhaps since Britain was a much older and longer established society that it was "better organized" in the nineteenth century. It had its own thriving Spiritualist movement, with many mediums and dozens of publications. America was larger, much more diverse, spreading to the west, and the people had a streak of independence that the Europeans thought of as "unruly." Many British scientists and thinkers, whether opponents or supporters of Spiritualism, seemed less intimidated about delving head-long into the field than their American counterparts. Or perhaps, as some Yanks have suggested, the Brits just thought they were smarter.

Regardless of why it happened, the first investigation society formed itself in Great Britain. Events were set into motion one day toward the end of 1881, when a respected physicist from Dublin, Professor William Barrett, was invited to the London home of journalist and Spiritualist Edmond Dawson Rogers. The two men were engaged in a lively discussion about Spiritualism when Rogers suggested that a society be formed with the goal of encouraging the greatest scientists in England to investigate psychical phenomena. Barrett, who'd long had an interest in mesmerism and Spiritualism, embraced the idea. He knew there had been earlier attempts to create such organizations in England and America, but all were short-lived. Barrett was determined to make sure this one worked, which would require the right people to be involved.

Barrett took the idea to his friend Frederick W.H. Myers, and then to Edmund Gurney, but neither man was optimistic about the success of such a society. Myers was a professor at Cambridge with a curiosity about what evidence existed for a spirit world. Gurney was a scholar with an interest in telepathy and hypnotism. However, they agreed that if Professor Henry Sidgwick would serve as the group's president, they'd lend their support to the effort. Sidgwick, a well-respected philosopher at Cambridge with a reputation for being highly skeptical and critical, agreed to the job.

On February 20, 1882, the Society for Psychical Research was formed with Sidgwick at the helm. Including the president, a 19-member council was named: 13 of them were Spiritualists, six, including Sidgwick, were not. One Spiritualist chosen was an author, Mrs. George Boole. Several months later, unhappy that she was the only woman who had been appointed to the council, she resigned. It would be nearly 20 more years before another woman – Sidgwick's wife – was appointed. This seems ironic considering the fact that woman had long dominated the Spiritualist movement.

Henry Sidgwick, the first President of the Society for Psychical Research

The group was successful from the start, perhaps because of the ages of the founding officers and members. Most were in their twenties and thirties at the time – the oldest was Sidgwick at 43. Despite its scientific goals, the SPR was not founded by only scholars and scientists. The group was composed of a variety of occupations, including a schoolteacher, accountant, businessman, lawyer, and hotel owner. All of them had been brought up in religious homes. They did their best to maintain high standards of scholarship in their journal, and the members took their investigations and research very seriously.

Sidgwick divided the SPR members into committees, each to investigate a particular phenomenon, including telepathy, hauntings, physical mediumship, spontaneous experiences, and mesmerism. Each committee was charged with issuing reports of their findings. Sidgwick also named those he considered best qualified to examine specific topics: Barrett researched dowsing; Gurney studied phantasms of the living; Mrs. Sidgwick was responsible for a study of apparitions; and Richard Hodgson, trained in law and with a fierce dedication to exposing frauds, investigated Theosophy. Other SPR members delved into deathbed visions, clairvoyance, and the statistical probabilities of chance.

The SPR looked closely to a phenomenon that was known as the "crisis apparition," in which an individual witnesses an apparition of someone they knew at the same time that person, although far away, has suffered a crisis, such as injury, serious illness, or death. The SPR received a surprisingly large number of responses from people who had experienced crisis apparitions, and the researchers attempted to confirm and authenticate thousands of such incidents – a nearly impossible task. When the SPR publicized its findings in 1886, it likely disappointed many Spiritualists, for the conclusion was that crisis apparitions were not spirits, but rather hallucinations projected by telepathy from the individual in crisis to the relative or loved one who sees or hears the "apparition."

An original SPR member who was not a Spiritualist, Edmund Gurney, wrote a highly-regarded book on the subject called *Phantasms of the Living*. He collaborated with F.W.H. Myers and Frank Podmore, a skeptic who considered most phenomena fraudulent. The book was over 1,300 pages long and details the first-hand accounts that had been collected by the SPR. The book remains a valid tool today – although some dispute the idea that crisis apparitions are hallucinations, and instead suggest they are the spirit of a person in crisis. Whatever the explanation, they still occur and science is no closer to explaining them today than it was in 1886.

The SPR investigators and their respective committees worked so hard that, within just a few years after the society's foundation, they were already producing over 500 pages of research each year – an incredible amount of research. During this time, the society earned a reputation for being notoriously tough in its investigations. One of the first things to be examined was Madame Blavatsky's Theosophical movement and her physical phenomena, which had impressed many. She even went as far as to call them "miracles." An investigation led by Richard Hodgson resulted in a scathing SPR report that unequivocally called her a fraud, and seriously damaged the reputation and credibility of Theosophy in England and America. The Hodgson report was later criticized for being too hasty in its conclusions but, by then, the damage was done.

Hodgson was also a part of the SPR investigations into the medium Eusapia Palladino that were described in an earlier chapter. Hodgson passed away before Palladino embarked on her disastrous American tour, but he was involved in the tests conducted by the SPR of another famed physical medium, William Eglinton. The society became interested in the medium after hearing the widely-spread reports of the phenomena that occurred during his séances, including apports that "appear from nowhere," phantoms, and that he "levitated to the ceiling." Eglinton was best-known for his slate writing skills, which he began demonstrating in 1884. He once gave a séance attended by British Prime Minster William Gladstone, who was so impressed that he joined the SPR. The well-known English naturalist Alfred Russell Wallace, who had helped Darwin devise his theory of evolution, was also convinced that Eglinton was genuine.

The SPR gathered many accounts from people who had attended Eglinton's séances and, despite the number of awestruck accounts, the investigators knew that slate writing was open to trickery. It was Richard Hodgson who spoiled the medium's game. He watched Eglinton carefully and concluded that there was fraud afoot. Eglinton, he said, employed "distraction," among other deceptions. On that basis, the SPR declared that Eglinton's manifestations were nothing more than "clever conjuring." Others were less skeptical and spoke on Eglinton's behalf. The SPR had angered the Spiritualist community once again. Eglinton responded by publishing dozens of testimonials in the Spiritualist publication, *Light*. After thousands of sittings – and only a handful of accusations of fraud – Eglinton gave up mediumship and became a successful journalist.

Over the course of the next couple of decades, the society managed to weather both scandal and embarrassment, as mediums they endorsed were found to be fraudulent; Frederick Myers got involved in a sex scandal with a female psychic investigator who turned out to be a fraud; Edmund Gurney was found dead under strange circumstances; and in 1888, the founders of the Spiritualist movement, the Fox Sisters themselves, publicly confessed to being fakes. Even though the credibility of this confession was in question, it was still used by other scientists to make the SPR members look like fools. By the early 1900s, the reputation of the society was rather tarnished, but nevertheless, still intact. The society's work continues today.

"ONE WHITE CROW"
THE SEARCH FOR SPIRITS IN AMERICA

In 1885, three years after the founding of the SPR, William Barrett encouraged the founding of a similar society across the Atlantic and the American Society for Psychical Research (ASPR) was founded in Boston by several scientifically-minded researchers.

The society soon gained the support and interest of famed philosopher and psychologist William James. His investigation of the medium Leonora Piper – and his conclusions – make up one of the most important incidents in America's paranormal history.

James, one of the most respected scientists in nineteenth century America, was a man of intellect and integrity and was unafraid to wade into the turbulent waters of psychical research. He had already earned a reputation as one of the most influential thinkers in the country, a seminal figure in philosophy, and a pioneer in the psychology field when he began making a name for himself in the study of the paranormal.

William James

Born in New York City in 1843, James came from an unusual family that encouraged intellectual curiosity. His father read Swedenborg, and one of his four siblings, Henry, became a popular novelist. By the time that William was three-years-old, he had already traveled to Europe, and eventually learned to speak several languages. He was a brilliant young man, accomplished in both philosophy and psychology, and also earned a degree from Harvard Medical School. He joined the faculty there before he turned 30, and taught there for many years.

James was first drawn to the paranormal as a young man. Early in his career, he went through a period of depression following the death of a close friend, and during this time, encountered what he believed was a hallucination of a former patient in the asylum where he had treated him. And that wasn't all. Soon after, James learned of a New Hampshire woman's dream vision that proved so accurate that she was able to locate the body of a drowned child. James wrote, "After this, the universe changed for me altogether."

Once his interest in psychical research began, he became one of its outstanding voices. One of his goals was to reunite science and religion by extending science so that it embraced the relationship between "mind, body, and spirit." This concept, abandoned as medicine became increasingly specialized in the twentieth century, returned as the holistic health movement of recent decades. James also regarded traditional, Bible-based religious beliefs to be "absurd," but recognized the useful role that they played in people's lives. He believed that the core of genuine spirituality was an inner, mystical experience, one of the basic tenets of the more recent "New Age" movement. James's philosophy about religious dogma being not necessarily the same as spirituality is an outlook embraced today by millions of Americans, proving that William James was a man ahead of his time.

James's search for a personal spiritual perspective began his interest in psychic phenomena, but it would be his careful investigation of trance medium Leonora Piper that would convince him once and for all that paranormal abilities were real.

Leonora Simonds Piper was born in Nashua, New Hampshire, in June 1859, and the first inkling of what awaited her in the future occurred when she was only eight-years-old and was playing in the garden one day. She felt a sharp pain in her right ear and then a whispered voice that said: "Aunt Sara, not dead, but with you still." Terrified, she ran into the house and told her mother. It later turned out that Aunt Sara had died at that very moment.

In 1881, Leonora married a shop assistant named William Piper of Boston, with whom she had two daughters, Alta and Minerva. According to Alta, who later wrote an extensive biography about her mother in 1929, Leonora's mediumship began in earnest in 1884 after Piper's father-in-law took her for a medical consultation with J.R. Cook, a blind clairvoyant who had a reputation for psychic cures.

Leonora Piper

Piper lost consciousness at Cook's touch and entered a trance of her own. Later, she attended a home circle sitting with him and again entered a trance. This time, she produced a message for one of the other sitters, a well-known local judge who stated that the contact she made with his dead son included the most accurate message he had received in almost 30 years of his interest in Spiritualism. This incident made her popular throughout the city, and many clamored for readings with her. Leonora was both disarmed and disturbed by the unexpected attention, but she reluctantly began agreeing to a limited number of sittings in her home. This was how she came to the attention of William James.

One of the sittings was for James's mother-in-law, who had heard about Leonora through friends. She made an appointment with her out of curiosity. After her sitting, she returned to the James' home very excited and told the James that, while in a trace, Leonora had told her facts about relatives, living and dead, that she could not have possibly have known about in any normal way. James laughed at her credulity and called her a "victim" of a medium's trickery. He gave her an explanation as to how mediums accomplished their fraud, but his mother-in-law refused to consider this and returned for another séance the following week. This time, she convinced her daughter to accompany her. Both women were now impressed with the medium and returned to Cambridge to tell James all about her. Again, the professor tried to discourage them but they would have nothing to do with it. Instead, they insisted that James visit the medium himself and, irritated that they would not accept his logical explanations for the alleged spirit messages, he agreed.

When James arrived at the Pipers' home, he was surprised to note the complete absence of Spiritualist props --- no cabinet, no red lights, circles of chairs, trumpets, or bells. The sitters, of which there were two or three others present, merely sat wherever they liked in Leonora's modest but comfortable parlor. Leonora herself also surprised the professor. She was quiet and shy and there was nothing flamboyant about her, as he had observed with so many other mediums. She politely warned her guests that there would be nothing sensational about the séance and that she did not manifest spirits or cause things to fly about. She would simply go into a trance and one of her "spirit controls" would then take over. She had no control over whether messages would be given, or not.

James was greatly surprised and impressed by her abilities. Leonora summoned up the names of his wife's father, and even that of a child that he and his wife had lost the previous year. He gave her no information to work with and, in fact, was purposely quiet throughout the séance so that she would have nothing with which to guess facts from. He later wrote: "My impression after this first visit was that Mrs. Piper was either possessed of supernormal powers or knew the members of my wife's family by sight and had by some lucky coincidence become acquainted with such a multitude of their domestic circumstances as to produce the startling impression which she did. My later knowledge of her sittings and personal acquaintance with her has led me to absolutely reject the latter explanation, and to believe that she has supernormal powers."

James arranged more sittings and asked if she would be amenable to stringent testing. At that time, he was forming the ASPR and was searching for worthwhile subjects to study. She agreed and James undertook a lengthy investigation of Leonora's séances that lasted 18 months, during which time he supervised nearly every aspect of her readings – his purpose being to eliminate any possibility of collusion or fraud on her part. His observations convinced him that Leonora had no advance knowledge of her subjects for whom the readings were highly accurate, and her only help seemed to come from her spirit guides, one of whom was named "Dr. Phinuit." James's tests were also able to rule out mind reading on Leonora's part. She was psychically strongest on the first names of subjects, personalities, and health problems of both sitters and the dead.

Unlike so many other mediums of the era, Leonora did not engage in theatrical displays of flying objects, ectoplasm, knockings, rappings, table tilting, spirit manifestations, or the other assorted theatrics that became so popular after the Civil War. On rare occasions, she inexplicably produced the sweet smell of flowers, but otherwise, she was strictly a mental medium who produced eerily accurate messages from the spirits to their friends and families.

James was stumped and made appointments for 25 of his friends to visit her as well, thus starting research that would continue for the remainder of Piper's career. At that same time, the professor was involved in the starting of the ASPR and was searching for worthwhile subjects to study. He secured the right from Piper to manage her sittings. He continued sending test subjects to her for the next two years, and then turned over the investigation to Richard Hodgson from London, who had been sent to America to take over as the Research Officer for the ASPR.

James was certain that Leonora Piper possessed genuine psychic ability, and although he could not determine the source, he remained doubtful about the spirits as an explanation. He questioned whether some other form of psychic phenomenon was responsible. He was firmly convinced that she had abilities that were beyond the ordinary, however, and as he famously wrote: "To upset the conclusion that all crows are black, there is no need to seek demonstration that no crows are black; it is sufficient to produce one white crow; a single one is sufficient. My white crow is Mrs. Piper."

William James's study of Leonora Piper came to an end because of work obligations, but he did not believe that the study of her should be at an end. He contacted SPR members in England about her and Richard Hodgson – the hardest-working man in the paranormal business – came to the United States, took up residence in Boston, and continued the testing of Mrs. Piper. The SPR arranged for Leonora to be paid an annual stipend so that her tests would give the SPR unprecedented and exclusive access to her as a medium.

Like James, Hodgson began his work with Leonora assuming her to be a fraud. His research in England had unmasked several fraudulent mediums and had given him a working knowledge of conjuring. He knew what to look for in a hoax and expected to find the similar qualities in Leonora Piper. He made appointments for 50 sitters with her, keeping their identities secret from the medium, and kept detailed records of the séances. He even hired private detectives to follow her about and to make sure that she was not compiling information about possible sitters. Although she never behaved in any suspicious manner, Leonora continued to produce eerily accurate information about people she had never met and about whom she knew nothing.

After a sufficient number of tests had been conducted, James wrote up Hodgson's conclusions, and neither man believed Leonora had resorted to fraud or trickery, especially considering the "close observations as to most of the conditions of her life." James noted in 1898 that he would be willing to wager money that Mrs. Piper was honest.

Even after the report was published, Hodgson was not yet finished with Leonora. He had an idea that would impose even stricter controls on her: he would take her to England. Once there, she would be in an unfamiliar country and among people she did not know. Mrs. Piper agreed and traveled to England in November 1889. She resided at the home of F.W.H. Myers in Cambridge, and it was more than just hospitality that prompted the invitation – as his guest, Myers could observe all of Leonora's comings and goings. He chose sitters for her séances at random, and their identities were unknown to her. She was in England from November 1889 to February 1890 and gave 88 sittings. She was carefully supervised the entire time. She was watched everywhere she went, as was anyone she spoke to, and anything she read was cautiously censored. While most would have felt confined by such scrutiny, Leonora remained remarkably patient and cooperative. She even consented to having her mail opened and read by SPR investigators.

The records of the SPR show that some of the séances were nothing short of remarkable. As mentioned earlier, one of Leonora's primary spirit controls was "Dr. Phinuit" (pronounced "Finney") who was supposedly a French doctor, but who seemed to know nothing about medicine and could not speak French. He was never able to give an account of his earthly life either, and this led many researchers to theorize that Phinuit was really a secondary personality of Leonora, a manifestation of her tremendous psychic ability. Phinuit may not have been what he claimed to be, but through him, Leonora possessed information she logically should not have had.

At one séance on December 24, 1889, Leonora was sitting with Sir Oliver Lodge, Alfred Lodge, and a Mr. and Mrs. Thompson, a couple that Myers had chosen at random. Sir Oliver was a prominent member of the SPR and Alfred was his son. Dr. Phinuit suddenly spoke up through Leonora and asked the sitters: "Do you know Richard, Rich, Mr. Rich?"

Mrs. Thompson replied, "Not well. I knew a Dr. Rich."

Mrs. Piper responded: "That's him. He's passed out. He sends kindest regards to his father."

There was no further mention of Dr. Rich during the séance and in fact, no mention of him at all during the next 40 sittings that Mrs. Piper took part in. It would not be until the 83rd séance, when Mr. and Mrs. Thompson were again present, that Dr. Rich was mentioned again. In fact, on this occasion, his spirit asked to speak through Leonora Piper. Through Leonora, Dr. Phinuit suddenly said: "Here's Dr. Rich!"

Piper: "It is very kind of this gentleman (meaning Dr. Phinuit) to let me speak to you. Mr. Thompson, I want you to give a message to my father."

Thompson: "I will give it."

Piper: "Thank you a thousand times; it is very good of you. You see, I passed out rather suddenly. Father was very much troubled about it, and he is troubled yet. He hasn't got over it. Tell him that I am alive --- that I send my love to him. Where are my glasses?

(The medium passes her hands over her eyes)

Piper: "I used to wear glasses. I think he has them and some of my books. There was a little black case I had --- I think he has that too. I don't want that lost. Sometimes he is bothered by a dizzy feeling in his head-- nervous about it --- but it is of no consequence."

Thompson: "What does your father do?"

(The medium took up a card and appeared to write on it and then pretended to put a stamp on the corner)

Piper: "He attends to this sort of thing. Mr. Thompson, if you will give this message, I will help you in many ways. I can, and I will."

As it turned out, the senior Mr. Rich was the head of the Liverpool Post Office. Sir Oliver Lodge investigated the facts provided by the sitting and discovered that Dr. Rich had worn glasses but this was something unknown to Mrs. Piper. Dr. Rich had been a stranger to her and to Lodge. The Thompsons barely knew the man and did not know his father at all. They learned that Mr. Rich had been very distressed about his son's death and had been suffering from some dizzy spells, just as the spirit had stated. Lodge and Thompson did give the man the message that allegedly came from his son and he considered it both extraordinary and inexplicable.

After being tested in England – and likely feeling like a laboratory rat who had successfully navigated a maze – to astounding results, Leonora returned to America and resumed her work with Richard Hodgson. For the investigator, this situation was nothing like what he had gone through with Eusapia Palladino or others – Leonora Piper was not a medium for whom excuses had to be made. She was the SPR's grand prize, a woman with genuine abilities whom the researchers were about to observe and test exclusively, and perhaps even obsessively.

Just about anyone who studied Leonora came away with the same conclusion: she had some kind of "supernormal" power or ability, but, of course, there was a lot of disagreement about what exactly it was. The so-called "spirit theory" was disagreeable to the scientific men, who opted instead for the possibility of telepathy, clairvoyance, hallucinations, some unknown energy – anything but ghosts. Hodgson was firmly in agreement with these men of science. He did not believe that the dead could communicate with the living – until something extraordinary happened that changed his mind.

Richard Hodgson

Hodgson, a very private man, rarely spoke of his personal life with Leonora Piper, despite the fact that he had spent countless hours with her observing her sittings and they had developed a cordial relationship. One day when he was the subject of a reading, Leonora told Hodgson that the spirit of a young woman was communicating a message she wanted him to know. The spirit identified herself to Leonora, then told the medium that she had recently passed away. Hodgson was stunned – he immediately knew who Leonora was talking about.

Years earlier, when he had been a young man in Australia, Hodgson fell in love with a girl that he very much wanted to marry. However, her parents refused to allow it because of the differences in the couple's religions. Hodgson was heartbroken, moved to England, but never married. He never saw or spoke again to the young woman that he'd lost. But she reached out to him after her death and communicated with him through Leonora Piper. Hodgson was both shaken and moved by the message, but he had no way to confirm or deny it – he did not know what had happened to her when he left Australia. But one thing that he did know was that Leonora's communication was not based on telepathy, and further, Leonora could not have known about this personal and painful part of his life long ago.

Hodgson soon sent word to Australia and contacted old friends who would know of his beloved's fate. It was exactly as Leonora said: the woman had died just a short time before. Apparently, she had never stopped think of him and after death, had contacted him the only way that she could. Hodgson was saddened by this turn of events, but he couldn't help but marvel at Leonora's gift.

This incident had a profound effect on Hodgson, who had always rejected the "spirit hypothesis" to explain mediumship. In 1897, he wrote in the *SPR Journal* that he now had no doubt that he had experienced genuine spirit communication. This was quite a statement from the no-nonsense investigator who had spent most of his career exposing one fraud after another. After 15 years of investigating Leonora Piper, he finally – reluctantly – accepted that the dead had communicated through her. He issued a second statement on the matter and planned a third report, but died suddenly of heart failure at the age of 50 in 1905. At the time, Hodgson was the secretary for the ASPR and an important part of the organization. His death left a daunting vacancy to be filled.

Interestingly, there is a little more to the Hodgson story. After his untimely death, his spirit allegedly communicated messages to several people, including an SPR colleague, James Hyslop, and a British medium named Mrs. Holland.

Hodgson left an indelible mark on the paranormal field. His many years of study and testing of Leonora Piper were of great value to the scientific research of the paranormal, and he also trained Columbia University philosophy professor James Hyslop to become one of the best psychical researchers in American history. Even before his death, Hodgson had tasked Hyslop with continuing the investigation of Leonora's ability. Like his friend, Hyslop was quite skeptical of mediumship before he met Leonora in 1888. He employed every caution possible when testing her and required at least a dozen sittings with Leonora to become convinced that he was witnessing genuine mediumship. Her sessions with him changed his mind after he received messages from his late father, brother, and several uncles.

Leonora Piper had no idea how difficult Hyslop had been to convince – he was a man whose life was overshadowed by the finality of death.

James Hyslop was born in August 1854 in Xenia, Ohio. His early life was marked by tragedy. When James was born, he had a twin sister, who died a short time later. Another sister, a few years older, died when he was still a young child. When Hyslop was 10, two younger siblings died from scarlet fever. It was an era when nearly all families were scarred by the tragic loss of children, but the Hyslop family seemed unluckier than most.

The string of deaths had a profound effect on Hyslop, whose family was devout Presbyterians. Perhaps hoping to find answers in religion, the young man chose the ministry as a career. His parents were pleased, but while attending the College of Wooster, from which he graduated with a Bachelor of Arts degree in 1877, he had a crisis of faith that changed his mind completely about religion. He decided to embrace materialist philosophy instead and, in 1879, traveled to the University of Leipzig to study under Wilhelm Wundt, the founder of the first formal psychology laboratory. He later received a doctorate in psychology from John Hopkins University in 1887, taught briefly at Bucknell University, and then joined the staff at Columbia, teaching logic and ethics. In 1891, he married Mary Fry Hall, an American woman that he met in Germany.

Although he had no interest in the paranormal before 1886, an article that he ran across about telepathy captured Hyslop's attention. The article told of a young boy who reportedly saw an apparition of his father and a team of horses going over a bank into a stream some 25 miles away. Hyslop suspected the story was "some illusion of memory or error in judgment as to the facts," and not any sort of psychical event, and wrote to the author of the article. The reply he received was not easy to dismiss and he became intrigued.

After hearing a lecture by Richard Hodgson, Hyslop became interested in psychical research and joined the ASPR. He was soon assisting with investigations, and while aware of the implications of psychical research for philosophy, he had no room for consideration toward life after death. His mind was changed by Leonora Piper, though, and soon began to believe that he was communicating with the dead.

Unfortunately, tragedy returned to Hyslop's life. His wife, Mary, passed away suddenly in 1900, leaving him to raise three small children on his own. To make matters worse, he suffered a nervous breakdown the following year, and in 1902, on the advice of his doctor, resigned from his position at Columbia. Friends felt that he would never completely recover from his shock and loss, but Hyslop proved them wrong. Within a year, he was back to his former self and devoted more of his time to psychical research.

James Hyslop

Richard Hodgson died in 1905, the same year that Hyslop published his first book, *Science and a Future Life.* The passing of the dynamic Hodgson left a terrible void in the ASPR, and a year later, the organization disbanded. But Hyslop reactivated it in 1907 and became the ASPR's principal researcher and a strong advocate of "survival of death." He worked with a number of different mediums, as well as strange cases.

One such case involved what Hyslop came to believe was a spirit possession. It involved a woman named Etta de Camp, an editor and proofreader for *Broadway* magazine, who had never written anything other than letters before 1908. After reading about spirit communications received through automatic writing, though, she decided to give it a try. She reported a tingling feeling, like a mild electric shock, after within a few days, began turning out copious amounts of writing. Unnerved by the writing, she tried to stop, but when she did, she had terrible headaches and experienced sharp pains in her ears. When she stopped resisting, the writing seemed to pour out of her. At first, none of the writing made much sense and so she complained to the spirits that if they could not write well, then they needed to bring her someone who could. From that point on, the writings became more coherent and included a pronouncement that Etta would soon be visited by a writer who wanted someone to finish the stories that he had left incomplete when he died.

Soon after, Etta's hand scrawled that the spirit of Frank R. Stockton had arrived and wished to communicate through her. She told Hyslop that she felt a sensation of intense pain but when Stockton took control of her hand, the pain went away. Stockton had been popular during the late nineteenth century as a whimsical writer of stories that were mostly for children, but with a humorous, cynical, and often bizarre bent. His most famous story, "The Lady or the Tiger," is still popular today.

Allegedly under the control of Stockton's spirit, Etta began to write short stories in the late author's style. She showed them to her employer, George Duysters, who introduced the young woman to James Hyslop. Duysters gathered the material that Etta had written – as a conduit for Stockton's spirit -- and took them to Stockton's former editor at *Harper's Magazine*, who found them to be the late author's exact style.

Etta continued to write Stockton's stories, although Hyslop lost contact with her between 1910 and 1912, while he investigated other matters. By 1912, Etta was close to a nervous breakdown, so Hyslop agreed to participate in a series of sittings with her. During these sittings, he became convinced that Stockton truly was in possession of Etta's body when she wrote out his stories.

Etta later wrote of her experiences in *The Return of Frank Stockton* in 1913, a fascinating book regardless of the reader's beliefs, and included transcriptions of all the stories that she received through automatic writing. After the initial publicity, Etta married and settled down to a private life. She never heard from Stockton again. Perhaps he finally finished the stories that he still had left to write?

Two of Hyslop's most famous cases could not have been accomplished without the participation of a medium named Minnie Meserve Soule, who he began working with after taking over the leadership of the ASPR in 1907.

Minnie was born in Boston in 1867 and her mother died when she was only four years old. Her father remarried and she lived with him and her stepmother until she was 16, when she left to go to New Hampshire and live with her mother's family. In New Hampshire, she completed her education and began teaching. She later moved to Somerville, Massachusetts, where she taught until she met Charles Soule and married him in 1897.

Minnie's psychic experiences dated back many years. They first came as precognitive dreams, which foretold events that might be as far as five years in the future. However, it was not until after she was married that her mediumistic skills began to manifest. At first, she heard the names of people in her head, as well as descriptions of them, even though she had never met them. After that, she began to receive automatic writings, often from people who had died years before. One message, which was written in a fine hand that was not Minnie's own, was signed in her mother's name. She showed the letter to her father, who then brought her a letter her mother had written to him while she was alive. The handwriting was so similar that it was impossible to distinguish between the real signature and the one that had come from Minnie's writing.

Minnie was controlled by several Native American spirit guides, a popular sort of "psychic persona" during this period in Spiritualist history. The early 1900s was a time of great "romance" for many people in regards to the Native Americans. By this time, the Indian populace had been largely wiped out or moved to reservations in the West. This "lost" quality seemed to make them more appealing in social circles and combined with the popularity of Theodore Roosevelt, who had a great respect for the Indians, a

Native American motif became all the rage. One of Minnie's guides, "White Cloud," prescribed herbal remedies for illnesses and cured so many of her friends and sitters that Minnie kept a stock of herbs on hand to fill his prescriptions. Another, "Sunbeam," a young woman in life, gave spoken messages, sometimes purportedly in the Choctaw language. A Massachusetts college professor once wrote down these words phonetically, using the English equivalents, and during his vacation the following summer, went to a Choctaw reservation to confirm them. He found that all the phrases were accurate. Unfortunately, no record of this compelling evidence seems to have survived.

In the early days of her mediumship, Minnie was completely conscious of the communications that were made through her. She became so exhausted from this, however, that she asked her spirit guides for help and they started causing her to black out during their communications. From that point on, her séances were conducted in a full trance. Tests would later show that she remembered absolutely nothing that occurred while she was in the midst of a trance.

In 1907, Minnie began working with James Hyslop and the ASPR and they continued a productive relationship for many years. Their work together, and the quality of her communications, placed Minnie in the company of such eminent mediums as Leonora Piper and Eileen Garrett, although Minnie is not so well remembered today. It was their friendship that likely caused Minnie to receive communications from Hyslop after his death in 1920. The communications were said to be filled with evidence of actual spirit contact. These reports have never been published but they remain in the ASPR archives.

During her work with Hyslop, there were two cases that stood out above all others and truly gained Minnie the reputation that she earned as one of America's great mediums. The first was the Thompson-Gifford Case, which James Hyslop believed proved the reality of spirit obsession.

Frederic Thompson, a metalworker and sometimes artist, first visited Hyslop in 1907. Thompson claimed that he was under the influence of the late R. Swain Gifford, a well-known landscape artist of the late 1800s, and that he was experiencing strange urges to paint trees and coastlines that he had never seen before. Although Thompson had met Gifford one summer in Massachusetts, and had contacted him once to ask for a recommendation to the Tiffany Glass Company, the two men were barely acquaintances and certainly not close friends. Thompson had moved to New York in 1900, where he was employed doing metal and jewelry work, and was not aware of it when Gifford died in January 1905.

By the late summer and fall of 1905, Thompson was experiencing overwhelming urges to paint. He didn't understand the urges, he was not a painter, but he began to see images in his mind and felt compelled to paint them. Recognizing some of the images that he saw as scenes from the area around New Bedford, Massachusetts, where he had met the artist, he began to jokingly refer to the alter ego that seized him as "Mr. Gifford." Thompson's wife, Carrie, later confirmed this fact to Hyslop.

In late January 1906, Thompson saw an advertisement for an exhibition of works by the "late R. Swain Gifford" and for the first time, realized that Gifford was dead. He went to see the exhibition and became fascinated by the similarities between Gifford's paintings and his own recent works. One day, he claimed to hear a voice in his head speak: "You see what I have done. Go on with the work." Moments later, he fell to the floor unconscious.

Thompson went on with the paintings, even as his personal life and his finances fell victim to his compulsions. He believed that he was going insane --- two doctors had diagnosed him as paranoid --- and he finally went to see Hyslop after hearing about his work in psychical research. Hyslop was intrigued, although he first felt that Thompson was likely suffering from a personality disintegration. But he also believed that if there was any truth to Thompson's claims, that consulting a medium might shed light on the situation.

On January 18, 1907, Hyslop and Thompson met with a medium named Margaret Gaule. She almost immediately sensed the presence of an artist, even though Hyslop had given her no information about Thompson, and even introduced him to her as "Mr. Smith." Gaule described landscape scenes, trees and water, in almost the same way that Thompson had described them to Hyslop a few days earlier.

On March 16, Hyslop took Thompson to Boston to meet with Minnie Soule. Her spirit guide "Sunbeam" gave her information about Gifford's personal habits, even his clothing, furniture, and rugs --- all of which was later confirmed by Gifford's widow --- and vividly described a scene of gnarled trees overlooking water. This was a scene that had haunted Thompson for days and one that he found impossible to get out of this head. These communications convinced Thompson that he was not losing his mind and so he left for the New England coast to search for the places that he was seeing in his mind.

Throughout the summer and fall of 1907, Thompson traveled to all the places that Gifford had loved in life. He soon began to recognize locations that he had been compelled to paint and he also heard music and heard the voice that had earlier spoken to him. On one of the trees that Thompson found, he discovered that Gifford had carved his initials, "R.S.G. 1902."

By early 1908, Thompson was painting large canvases and selling them. Prominent art critics who saw his exhibitions stated that they bore an uncanny resemblance to the works of R. Swain Gifford. Hyslop still had suspicions that Thompson was merely acting on his desire to be a painter and that his association with Gifford had influenced him more than he thought.

To prove whether Thompson was obsessed with the spirit of Gifford or had simply incorporated the memory of Gifford into his work, Hyslop decided to try and establish contact with the dead artist. He and Minnie Soule began meeting with Thompson on a regular basis. During a séance that took place on June 4, 1908, Soule appeared to be receiving communications from Gifford and she began to realize that the self-involved artist was elated over his power to return and to finish his work by influencing Thompson. Later séances revealed hundreds of evidential communications about colors, scenes, and locations that indicated Gifford's control over Thompson. A later séance would also finally reveal the artist's identity when he caused the medium to scrawl "R.S.G." during an automatic writing session.

Hyslop firmly believed that he had found a true case of spirit obsession in the Thompson-Gifford Case. Later investigations, some alleging fraud or some sort of telepathy, were never able to refute Hyslop's conclusions.

After the last series of séances, Gifford's spirit never bothered Thompson again. Thompson left his metalworking career and became a full-time painter, joining the prestigious Salmagundi Club for professional painters in 1912. He worked in New York for several years and then moved to Martha's Vineyard, just off Gifford's beloved Massachusetts coastline. Thompson continued to paint and sculpt, showing his work in various exhibitions and making a good living, through the 1920s. He vanished from history and is believed to have died in 1927.

The other famous case involving James Hyslop and Minnie Soule was the very strange Doris Fischer Case. It was the last major case that Hyslop was involved with and he later came to believe that one of the possessing spirits in this case affected his health in such a way that he suffered a stroke in 1919.

The story of "Doris Fischer," whose real name was Brittia L. Fritschle, was first reported by fellow ASPR investigator Walter Franklin Prince. Doris had suffered an extreme traumatic incident when she was a child. Her abusive and alcoholic father had treated her horribly and she began exhibiting multiple personalities at the age of three in 1892. She also displayed acute psychic tendencies and was able to foresee her mother's unexpected illness and death. Doris was forced to continue living with her father and she began to retreat more and more into the personalities of "sick Doris" and the malevolent "Margaret." Walter Prince and his wife eventually adopted Doris and named her Theodosia. Prince was familiar with the newly recognized syndrome of multiple personalities and he and his wife helped Doris to regain some normalcy in her life.

Hyslop first became involved in Doris' case in 1914. For a number of years, he had theorized that some psychotic states were caused, or at least aggravated by, spirit influences. He had seen how psychic "cures" could affect patients and had come to believe that spirit communication was just as beneficial to some patients as psychological therapy was. With that in mind, Hyslop took Doris to sit with Minnie Soule, who he hoped could find and eliminate the possessive spirits who were harming the girl's state of mind.

During the séances, Minnie communicated lengthy messages for Doris from her mother. The medium also heard from a spirit that called itself "Count Cagliostro," a demonic and sexual presence that terrified the young woman and made Hyslop uncomfortable, as well. He encouraged the spirit to leave the séances and Doris.

Minnie also heard from the spirit of Richard Hodgson, the former leading member of the ASPR, who confirmed Hyslop's suspicions of spirit influence and promised to help all that he could. Finally, Minnie also received messages from a young Native American spirit who called herself "Minnehaha," or "Laughing Water." Hyslop was skeptical of such a spirit, since Minnehaha was the heroine of Longfellow's famous poem "Hiawatha" but he went along with it since he was impressed with "Minnehaha's" knowledge of Doris's issues and her claim that she had accidentally caused some of the girl's problems.

During the séances, Hyslop came to believe that one of Doris' personalities, Margaret, was not an offshoot of Doris' mind but an actual possessing spirit. Hyslop asked why the spirits were hurting Doris and was told by Minnie's spirit guides that they were evil influences. They also told Hyslop that Doris's case was no different from hundreds of other instances of insanity and multiple personality that could be easily cured by psychic exorcism. By 1915, Hyslop was convinced that Doris was possessed and he wrote about the case in his 1918 book, *Life After Death*.

Hyslop came to believe that "Count Cagliostro" was the leader of the spirits possessing Doris, and he exorcised him from her body. The other spirits were helpless without him and Hyslop quit the case in hopes that Doris had been cured. Unfortunately, Hyslop was wrong and to make matters worse, it's possible that the spirit was responsible for Hyslop's health issues that began the following year – or so Hyslop believed.

Doris moved back in with the Princes and resumed a normal life for a while. She never really recovered from her experiences, though, and died in a mental hospital a few years later, still dealing with her psychic disturbances and various personalities.

The Doris Fischer case became the last major investigation for James Hyslop. He believed that his health was irreparably damaged by his involvement in the Fischer case. He suffered a stroke in late 1919 and six months later, he was dead.

Meanwhile, Leonora Piper was still very involved with ASPR investigations. By 1906, several of the original members of the SPR had died, including Hodgson, Edmund Gurney, and Frederick W.H. Myers. There were a number of "cross correspondence" experiments conducted to determine if these three men could – or would – communicate from the afterlife. The results seemed to indicate that several of the mediums who participated in the tests, including Leonora, each received part of a spirit message from them that had to be deciphered and pieced together to form a complete communication. Although the conclusion seemed to suggest the accuracy of the communications were beyond mere chance, some researchers were not convinced.

In 1906, a year after Hodgson's death, Leonora made another trip to England to continue the testing and she took part in the complex network of medium communications that were dubbed the cross correspondences. She returned to America in 1908, but her sittings were badly managed for a time. The psychologists G. Stanley Hall and Amy Tanner were allowed to experiment with her until 1909, and while Tanner later wrote a book about the research called *Studies in Spiritualism*, the sittings were unorganized and often questionable. Sittings were largely devoted to personal matters, sitters were left unsupervised, and séances were only sporadically documented. Leonora was also subjected to very harsh treatment, evidently in order to test the depths of her trance. Testing mediums in painful ways – which often meant intimate searches and near torture – was nothing new to psychical researchers, but Leonora had never been subjected to extreme treatment before. Her daughter Alta later stated that after one test that was done to make sure that she was truly in a trance state, Leonora suffered a "badly blistered and swollen tongue, which caused Piper considerable pain and inconvenience for several days."

The shock to Leonora's system was so great that her abilities were suspended for more than a year. They did not return until 1911. There was no physical reason for her powers to vanish, but it's been suggested that she suffered from an unconscious fear of entering a trance because she was afraid of what might happen to her when she was unconscious.

Her abilities restored, Leonora returned to England in 1915. There, in a trance state, she predicted that Sir Oliver Lodge's son, Raymond, would die. Her prediction proved to be accurate.

Lodge was one of the core members of the SPR and had experienced earlier sittings with Leonora, starting in 1889, but the message he received from her in 1915 changed his life.

Sir Oliver Lodge (right) and his son, Raymond, who was killed during World War I. The esteemed scientist's book about his communications with his dead son became a sensation.

Born in 1851 in Penkhull, Staffordshire, England, Lodge was the son of a successful businessman. As a boy, Lodge was sent away to boarding school, but unhappy there, he was brought home at 14 to help with his father's business. For the next seven years, he traveled as an agent for his father. When he was 16, Lodge visited an aunt in London, where he attended some university classes in physics. This sparked his interest in the subject and in 1872, he entered a full course at the Royal College of Sciences. In 1874, he enrolled in University College, London, where he received his degree in 1875 and a doctorate in 1877. After that, he was appointed assistant professor of physics at University College. He married Mary Marshall that same year and together they had 12 children, six sons and six daughters.

Throughout his career, Lodge was responsible for many advances in the study of physics. He conducted early research in electricity, worked on a radio before Marconi, and even invented the spark plug. Albert Einstein, who used some of Lodge's research when he created his theory of relativity, credited him for his pioneering work. He was also a leader in the field of psychical research in the late nineteenth and early twentieth centuries.

In 1889, he had first worked with Leonora Piper and was impressed with messages that the medium delivered from his late aunt. During séances in Liverpool, Leonora told Lodge of long-dead relatives about whom he knew nothing --- information that was later verified.

In September 1915, Leonora delivered a message to Lodge that was said to have come from his friend Frederick Myers, who had died in 1901. In the message, which was mysterious at the time, Myers told Lodge that he would be near his friend "to ease the blow which was coming." A few days later, the message became clear, as Lodge learned that his son, Raymond, had been killed in a battle in France.

After Raymond's death, Lodge visited several mediums, in addition to Leonora Piper, including England's well-regarded Gladys Osborne Leonard, and became convinced that he had made genuine spirit contact with his son. At one séance. Lady Mary, Lodge's wife, was told that Raymond had appeared in a photograph with his walking stick. Through another medium came a more detailed description of the photo, including that someone was leaning on Raymond's shoulder in the picture. The Lodges had no such photograph and dismissed the messages as meaningless. Shortly after, a friend (who knew nothing of the séances) mailed them a photograph --- which matched the photo from Raymond's communications exactly. Lodge would go on to describe these events, and the séances that followed, in his book *Raymond: A Life*, which was published in 1916. The book created a sensation, earning praise from the Spiritualist community and, predictably, scorn from the scientific establishment.

Lodge died in August 1940, leaving behind a sealed envelope, the contents of which he was to try and communicate to SPR members after his death. To this date though, no satisfactory messages regarding its contents have ever been received.

Leonora Piper continued to be tested by investigators until her retirement in 1927. By then, she was in her late sixties. She died on July 3, 1950, and has since come to be regarded as a medium of the first rank. She gave much of her life in the service of science and, as a result, many who had previously doubted the possibility of survival after death became convinced of its reality. There is no question that her contributions to psychical research were enormous. The large number of documented eyewitness accounts, evidence from the many tests Leonora had undergone, and published reports by researchers and scientists provided an unequaled amount of material about the history of mediumship.

There seems to be little doubt that she was, in the words of William James, the "white crow" that proved that not all crows are black.

THE NEW CENTURY OF PSYCHICAL RESEARCH

The founding of the SPR forever changed the nature of psychical research. It was the start of it becoming a science, with disciplined experimental methods and standardized methods of description, all established by some of the finest minds of the day.

The SPR was lucky in that it thrived, in part due to the donations of its upper crust members, who could afford the time that was needed for lengthy investigations, the travel, and the freedom to not hold down a daily job. The SPR's American counterpart was not as fortunate. The early history of the ASPR was a more turbulent one. Given the controversial nature of psychical research, financial and scientific support was lacking in the United States. The ASPR could not sustain itself as an independent entity, so much of the research that was done had to be carried out by British members, like Richard Hodgson. He worked tirelessly until his death in 1905. Without him, the society disbanded the next year. After its dissolution, James Hyslop revived the group and absorbed it into his own organization, the American Institute for Scientific Research.

Following Hyslop's death in 1920, the ASPR was once again an independent entity. Dr. Walter Franklin Prince conducted most of the research but he also became embroiled in controversy. The problems involved a Boston medium named Mina Crandon, who was known professionally as "Margery." (More about this in a later chapter). The ASPR's board believed her to be genuine, but Prince was certain she was a fraud. There had even been favorable articles written about her in *Scientific American*, and when the magazine's assistant editor was named to a research position in the ASPR, Prince was outraged. He resigned from the ASPR and, along with several other equally disgruntled members, formed the Boston Society for Psychical Research.

The two groups remained estranged until 1941, when the internal dissension was resolved. George Hyslop, whose father had been one of group's early pioneers, became the new president, and he went to work raising the society's research standards, which had fallen off during the organization's troubled decades.

Dr. Gardner Murphy led the ASPR for the next 20 years. During his tenure, the nature of science had changed and grown immeasurably and Gardner pressed for parapsychologists to engage in more laboratory research, as Dr. J.B. Rhine had done at Duke University in the 1930s (more about that later in this chapter). In 1962, Dr. Karlis Osis joined the ASPR as its research director, and remained with the society until his death in 1997. He had worked with Dr. Rhine at Duke and was especially interested in extra-sensory perception (ESP), psychokinesis (PK), and deathbed visions. Dr. Gertrude Schmeidler, a psychologist and professor, was long associated with the ASPR's ESP testing and helped to mold the society into the modern version of itself.

Like its British counterpart, the ASPR continues its research today. In recent years, it has merged psychical research with other scientific disciplines, an approach that will potentially lead to a greater understanding of parapsychology and its effect on human nature.

THE "GHOST BARON"

While the two great research groups in Britain and America were testing mediums, investigating "cross correspondences," and doing psychical research with Leonora Piper, Gladys Leonard, and other mediums, additional groundbreaking work was being done in Europe that would have an effect on America and paranormal research to come.

One of the most famed psychical researchers of the early twentieth century – although seldom mentioned today – was the German psychotherapist Baron Albert von Schrenck-Notzing. He became famous for his experiments and extensive studies of physical mediumship and his work earned him the nickname of *Gespensterbaron* or the "Ghost Baron."

Schrenck-Notzing was born in May 1862 in Oldenburg, Germany. He came from a noble family that could traces its roots back to the fifteenth century and included many

Baron Albert von Schrenck-Notzing

civil and military men employed by the grand dukes of Hanover and Oldenburg, which gave him his hereditary title. As part of his education, he studied treatments of nervous disorders with his fellow student Sigmund Freud and received his medical degree in 1888 for a study of the therapeutic use of hypnosis in a Munich hospital.

Schrenck-Notzing devoted himself full-time to his medical practice and established himself as one of the foremost authorities of the day on hypnosis, sexuality, and criminal pathology. His studies of hypnotism introduced him to psychical research, an interest that was strengthened by his friendship with French physiologist Charles Richet, who he had met at a conference in Paris in 1889. The baron translated Richet's reports on his telepathy experiments into German in 1891, which increased his interest in paranormal activities. The following year, he married Gabrielle Siegle, who came from a wealthy industrial family, and became financially independent. Soon after, he gave up his medical career and devoted all of his time to psychical research.

Schrenck-Notzing started working in the field by devising a series of telepathy experiments, based on what Richet had done. The direction of his research changed completely, though, after Richet invited him to take part in a series of séances with medium Eusapia Palladino in 1894. The baron became fascinated with physical mediumship and began traveling through Europe, working with different mediums. He was often impressed with what he experienced, although he also managed to expose a number of the mediums as frauds. This seemed to show that Schrenck-Notzing was anything but gullible, but so many questions have been created by his investigations into a medium named Marthe Beraud -- who became known as "Eva C." -- that some members of the psychical research community agreed with his former medical colleagues when they suggested that the baron had lost his mind.

Schrenck-Notzing began investigating Marthe Beraud in 1909, but she had started her career several years earlier and had, in fact, been investigated by Charles Richet at that time. Unlike many other mediums of the time, Beraud did not produce raps or tilt tables. While she was in her trance, she exuded ectoplasm that would shape itself into various forms, including faces and entire spirit forms.

Marthe's career began in 1902 and for the next two years, she was the frequent guest of her fiancé's parents, General and Mrs. Noel, at Villa Carmen, their home in Algiers. The Noels had formed a spirit circle with a group of their friends and often held séances in their home with a medium and seamstress named Vincente Garcia. Vincente managed to materialize a turbaned figure that described himself as a "priest of ancient Hindustan" and gave his name as "Bien-Boa." Like far too many other full-form apparitions of the time, he walked around the séance room, talked with the sitters, and even drank lemonade.

In 1904, Marthe's fiancé was killed in the Congo, and whether it was the shock of his death or something else, Marthe began to take part in the séances. She soon displayed a remarkable talent. She quickly replaced Vincente as the regular medium, although – rather strangely – "Bien-Boa" stuck around and was later joined by his spirit sister, "Beroglia." Concerning the antics of this spectral pair, a former president of the SPR commented in 1961: "The souls of the departed may conceivably inhabit forms resembling Bien-Boa; if so, we must endure the prospect with fortitude." In other words, he was not impressed. Incredibly, though, the Noels and their spirit circle were delighted by the manifestations and received the performances with enthusiasm.

Word of the new medium reached Paris and gained the attention of Charles Richet, who had also investigated Eusapia Palladino. Richet went to Algiers to observe Marthe's séances and surprised just about everyone by declaring himself favorably impressed by what he had seen. As time would pass, many would question what Richet could possibly have seen in Marthe Beraud, especially after the difficult conditions that he had imposed on Palladino. The reason for his belief in Marthe is of great interest. It was, in his own words: "The absolute honorableness, irreproachable and certain, of Marthe B., fiancée of Maurice Noel, son of the general." Unfortunately, this type of conviction, based on the reputation of people and not their actions, would often taint Spiritualism. It led to the downfall of many serious investigators, who, because of their respect for the people involved or their own personal sense of honor, failed to expose what should have been obvious fraud.

Richet's opinion was even more incredible when we consider that, according to testimony at the time, Marthe was not even serious about her deception at first. She regarded the whole thing as a grand joke and even admitted it to some of her friends, although never to Richet or to the Noels. In 1904, an attorney named Marsault, who attended a séance at Villa Carmen, claimed that the young medium confessed that she faked the phenomena for fun. She hinted to Marsault that the mysterious "Bien-Boa" just might be the Noels' coachman dressed up in white muslin and smuggled into the house with the help of other servants. The whole thing was a game until Richet showed up from Paris and the game became very real. One has to wonder if Marthe then wished that she had never started her performances --- or did she only regret the admissions of fraud that she made to her friends?

Not long after Richet wrote glowing reviews of Marthe's séances, she vanished from the Spiritualist scene. Several years passed and the location changed from Algiers to the city of Paris in 1909. A series of dramatic séances had been announced at the home of Juliette Bisson, performed by a new medium named Eva C., which is understood to be a pseudonym for a woman named Eva Carriere. The phenomena reported at Eva's sittings included striking materializations, although not of full forms, but of incomplete manifestations of ectoplasm. The séances were witnessed by Charles Richet, who wrote of them: "A kind of liquid or pasty jelly emerges from the mouth or breast, which organizes itself by degrees, acquiring the shape of a face or a limb... I have seen this paste spread on my knee, and slowly take form so as to show the rudiment of the radius, the cubitus or the metacarpal bone."

Eva C., as it turned out, was Marthe Beraud. The young woman, deprived of the security that had been taken from her by her wealthy fiancée's death, saw a chance for her to make a profitable living for herself as a medium. Through her earlier mediumship, she had acquired friends, supporters, attention, and even an adoptive mother in Juliette Bisson, who allowed the young woman to live with her. Through Bisson, Eva came to the attention of Baron von Schrenck-Notzing, who began to investigate the medium.

He would later write a book about her called *Phenomena of Materialization*, which was published in both German and English. It is a highly detailed and exhaustive examination of Eva C., and in the book, Schrenck-Notzing never reveals the fact that Eva C. was also Marthe Beraud. It is believed that he concealed her identity because he was afraid of the allegations of fraud that were made against her in Algiers. Was he concerned about the medium's privacy or concerned about his own work being discredited?

Whatever the answer, Schrenck-Notzing's findings concerning Eva C. sounded impressive on the surface. The séances, which were held over a period of four years, were never held in the darkness, but under a red light. The séance cabinet, which was a curtained off corner of the room, was always searched. In spite of the fact that Eva was stripped naked in front of witnesses and then clothed in a close-fitting garment from neck to feet, she continually produced mysterious-looking ectoplasm that gave the impression of faces, limbs, and unidentifiable living shapes.

Despite all of the precautions, critics suggested that Eva was somehow able to secrete these shapes somewhere on her person. The investigators searched her mouth, vagina, and rectum, but nothing was found. Another theory was that she was able to swallow the props and then regurgitate them. She was given an emetic that caused her to vomit but nothing out of the ordinary was found. Her supporters suggested that even if she had been able to smuggle props into the séance room, the conditions would have made it impossible for her to use them.

Regardless, it's obvious from the photographs that were taken during the séances that she somehow managed to get phony props into the séance cabinet.

As the séances took place, Schrenck-Notzing employed a battery of eight cameras, two of them stereoscopic, and about 225 photographs were taken during various stages of the phenomena. The cameras were arranged to take pictures simultaneously in order to record phenomena at a number of vantage points (including above and behind the curtain), not usually accessible to the investigators.

The photographs of Eva C. are indeed remarkable --- but not because they show genuine ectoplasm. What they show, in almost every case, are "materialized" faces that appear completely flat and often with creases as if they had been folded. Later, after the publication of Schrenck-Notzing's book, which featured the less-than-mysterious images, several of the "spirit faces" were found to be those of perfectly real, living people whose pictures had appeared in the Paris newspaper, *Le Miroir*. One photo, taken from above the cabinet, captured the production of "ectoplasm" that had writing on it that appeared to be a newspaper headline or advertisement. The manifestations were obviously fraudulent and somehow, Eva – or some confederate in the audience – had smuggled in the "ectoplasmic images," despite an alleged complete search of the medium.

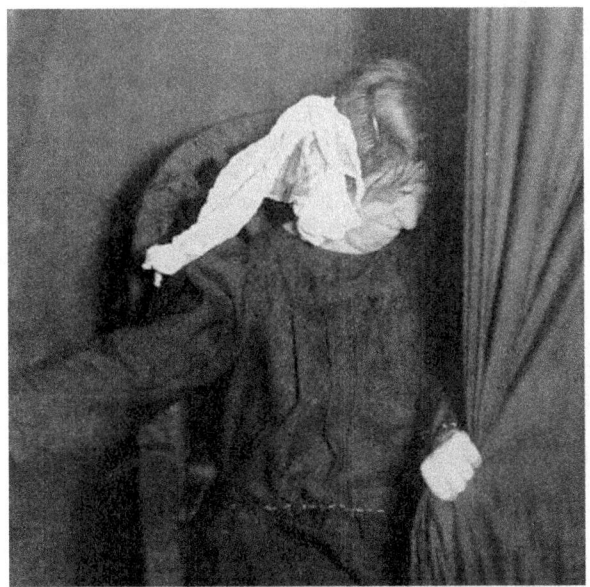 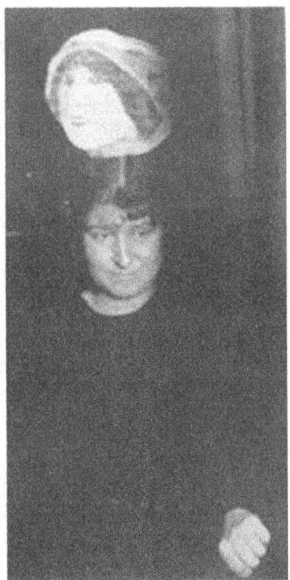

Two photographs of Eva C., "manifesting ectoplasm" with faces that were later determined to have been cut out of a magazine

How was the fraud accomplished? Skeptics didn't care. All that mattered was that the hoax was exposed. Those in the Spiritualist community – who had a lot to lose by the promotion of fraudulent mediums – wanted to know how such blatant trickery was carried out. Most of the blame was directed not towards Schrenck-Notzing, but towards Juliette Bisson, Eva's greatest supporter. Many believed that she had assisted with the fraud in order to dupe the baron and gain additional publicity for the medium. These allegations were never proven, however, and Bisson would later publish her own book about Eva.

Despite his book, Schrenck-Notzing was never really damaged by the "mediumship" of Eva C. He was openly critical of the ectoplasm that was produced and offered many examples of newspaper clippings that matched the "spirit faces" that appeared during the séances. Even so, his research was unpopular with both the public and the scientific community when it came to Eva C.

As for Eva herself, she unbelievably continued her career as a medium. After 1914, when German researchers were no longer able to come to Paris, Gustave Geley, the director of the Institut Metaphysique in Paris, continued the investigations of Eva C. Once again, the world of science declared that Eva's manifestations were genuine, but in this case, we have something of a mystery on our hands. When Dr. Geley was killed in an accident in 1924, his successors found some peculiar papers in his files. No one knows just what these papers may have been, since permission to publish them was refused by the Institut Metaphysique. Some of those involved with the investigations believe that the items in question may have been photographs that proved Eva C. was a fraud. If true, then Geley must have known that Eva was a fake and for some reason, suppressed the information. However, no accounting of this information has ever been made public and Geley's supporters maintain that the accusations are baseless.

In 1920, Eva interrupted her testing with Geley to travel to London for sittings with the SPR. Dr. Eric Dingwall and Dr. V.J. Wooley were the society's chief investigators during 40 sessions that were held in London. Their results were disappointing in that the phenomena was either weak or nonexistent, although the researchers did manage to collect a small amount of "ectoplasm." When it was analyzed, it was found to be chewed-up paper.

They had too little information to make any conclusions about Eva C. The phenomena had been too scanty to justify any definitive judgment, they stated. Their report read: "If we had not been acquainted with the work of previous investigators we might have felt inclined to draw a negative conclusion from our own observations." Many feel that perhaps the SPR committee should have trusted its instincts. The case of Eva C. is a startling example of the cumulative effect of Richet's belief that the future daughter-in-law of a general is above suspicion.

Although not discredited by these events either, Eva must have felt that her time was running out. A series of séances held at the Paris Sorbonne in 1922 were also worthless and her career ended a short time later when she was married. The medium known as Eva C. was finally retired, bringing an end to one of the most regrettable series of incidents in Spiritualist history.

Baron von Schrenck-Notzing was undaunted by his research with Marthe Beraud, a.k.a. Eva C. When a retired naval officer, who had read *The Phenomena of Materialization*, wrote to tell the baron about two brothers who were physical mediums, he immediately made arrangements to have sittings with them. Schrenck-Notzing took up a regular study of Willi Schneider in 1919 and his brother Rudi in 1925. These two young men were eventually studied by not only the baron, but by some of the most important psychical investigators of the day, using some of the most sophisticated instruments then available.

The Schneiders were born in the small Austrian city of Braunau (also the birthplace of Adolph Hitler) to Josef and Elise Schneider. Their father was a printer and he and his wife had 12 children altogether, nine boys and three girls, but only six boys survived: Karl, Hans, Fritz, Willi, Franz, and Rudi. Rudi, the youngest, was born in July 1908. His parents were disappointed that he was a boy and went so far as to dress him in girl's clothing, curled his hair and even called him "Rudoline" for a time. He managed to sort out his identity for himself and became interested in sports, cars, and airplanes, preoccupations he shared with his brother Willi, who was five years older.

There are different versions as to how the Schneiders mediumistic activities began. The most widely told version is that in the spring of 1919, military officers stationed at Braunau began buying large quantities of paper from the print shop located below the Schneider's apartment. The family discovered that the officers were holding séances to combat their boredom and were using the paper for automatic writing.

Mrs. Schneider and some of her friends began experimenting with their own séances, but had little success. One afternoon, some of the Schneider boys decided to try also but nothing occurred until Willi arrived and took a turn with the pen and paper. Almost as soon as he touched it, the pen began to scrawl out messages that allegedly came from a spirit named "Olga," who would continue to act as Willi's guide in the days to come.

Willi Schneider

Soon, it was not only automatic writing that Willi was able to manifest. The table tilted and rocked and objects around the room began to move. At one early séance, the tablecloth was slowly raised off the table, even though no one was touching it at the time. The spirit of Olga continued to come through Willi and on another occasion, she instructed the family to cover a kitchen stool with a large cloth and to place objects, including handkerchiefs and a basin of water, next to it. Willi sat near the stool and, a few moments later, strange things started to happen. The water splashed out of the bowl, the sound of hands clapping was heard, and the objects placed near the stool started to move. Throughout the activity, Willi seemed unconcerned about the weirdness going on around and actually seemed to enjoy the confusion.

As the séances continued, the family, who were devout Catholics, asked the spirit if there was anything they could do to help her in some way. She told them that she wished to have some masses said for the repose of her soul. The masses were said and the séances continued. Olga, grateful for their help, promised that in return for their kindness, she would make their name famous throughout the world. It was a promise that she kept -- the events that started with Olga's arrival signaled the beginning of paranormal manifestations that would puzzle scientists and ordinary citizens around the world.

One of these ordinary citizens was a retired naval officer named Captain Josef Kogelink, a man not predisposed to believe in the supernatural and rather inclined to dismiss it as antiquated rubbish. However, his first encounter with the mediumship of Willi Schneider would change his mind. According to Kogelink, in those early days before Willi became internationally known, his ability to produce unexplained phenomena was at its height. He stated: "Not even the slightest attempt was made by him to support the supernormal phenomena through normal means. He never fell into a trance. He himself watched the manifestations with as much interest as any other person present."

Kogelink described how, on one occasion, the cloth that had been draped over a stool lifted and a small hand emerged from under it. He wrote: "I quickly and firmly grasped it and was just about to draw out from under the table what I thought must be there ---- when I found my closed fist was empty and a heavy blow was dealt against it."

Kogelink returned again and again to the Schneider home and regularly witnessed Willi's powers. He became increasingly convinced that he was observing genuine psychical phenomena. These happenings, he wrote, were quite splendid: "A zither was put on the floor, close to the tablecloth, and out from under the table there came a small hand with four fingers stroking the strings and trying to play. The hand was very well visible, looked like that of a baby and was very well developed in every detail as far as the wrist, above which it passed off into a thin... glimmering ray which disappeared behind the tablecloth... A large brush was put before the tablecloth. The hand grasped it and began to energetically brush the floor in front of and behind the cloth..."

As time progressed, the activity continued to change. In the beginning, Willi's spirit guide, Olga, had written out her wishes and instructions while Willi was fully awake. After a time, however, he began to fall into a trance and she started to speak through him with an unfamiliar, hoarse whisper. Also, at this stage, another phenomenon began to occur: Willi began producing ectoplasm. Captain Kogelink described it as being a cobweb-like substance. It first wrapped around the medium's face and then started materializing on one shoulder and then the other. The substance always disappeared without a trace. One day, Olga invited Captain Kogelink to take a closer look at it and from a distance of about 10 inches, he claimed to see a faint, undulating, glowing fog being emitted from Willi's head. It eventually settled into his hair and rested there like a hat, before being sucked back into his body through his nose.

Not surprisingly, Willi's activities began to draw local, national, and then international attention. Captain Kogelink contacted Baron von Schrenck-Notzing, certain that he would be interested in Willi and the phenomena that he was producing. Schrenck-Notzing began his investigations of Willi later in the same year that the phenomena began, 1919, but his most serious work began in 1921, after the boy had finished high school. Willi moved to Munich for a year and placed himself in Schrenck-Notzing's charge. Between December 1921 and July 1922, he had 124 séances with Willi and published his findings in 1924. During this time, he invited 27 university professors and 29 investigators, scientists, and interested parties to participate in the experiments. The phenomena that had been reported in the Schneider home continued to occur in the laboratory.

Schrenck-Notzing was an experienced investigator by the time that he began his experiments with Willi Schneider. He knew how to limit and detect trickery. The séance room was carefully searched in advance and kept locked during the sessions. Willi was strip-searched and required to wear special tights, covered with luminous buttons that would make any movements visible in the dark. The room was lighted with a red light bulb that was placed on the center of the table in the circle of sitters. The participants in the séance joined hands and those closest to Willi held onto his arms and legs. The objects that he was to manipulate were placed on the lighted table and were enclosed in a wire cage.

Under these specific conditions, Schrenck-Notzing and the other sitters heard rapping sounds, felt cold breezes, saw the items on the table levitate, and witnessed various materializations. These materializations started out as rather shapeless blobs but soon began to resemble arms and legs and saw the return of the mysterious hand described earlier by Captain Kogelink.

Among those who attended séances in 1922 were famed researchers Harry Price and Eric Dingwall. It was apparently with some amusement that Schrenck-Notzing allowed the two Englishmen to search the séance chamber for trap doors and false walls. Both men were familiar with conjuring techniques and the work of fraudulent mediums, so the fact that they satisfied themselves that intruders could only get in through the front door, which was locked and sealed during the duration of the séance, gave even more credibility to the activity that followed. During the séances, Willi produced a number of extraordinary manifestations, including the levitation of a table that rose with such force that Dingwall was unable to hold it down. After the series of tests, Dingwall thought the evidence strong enough to state that the phenomena did seem to be the work of unexplained "supernormal agencies." At that point, he felt he could "scarcely entertain with patience" the idea that all involved were engaged in a hoax. Both Dingwall and Price signed statements to say that they had witnessed genuine phenomena.

Dingwall's conviction did not last, though. He had a reputation as an inveterate skeptic about psychical phenomena, and later, he suggested that Schrenck-Notzing must have somehow been responsible for what they had witnessed. It's difficult to see how the baron could have managed such a feat, but this would not be the only time that Schrenck-Notzing would be stung by criticism from other researchers.

Eric Dingwall

Despite the amazing manifestations that he had created, Willi began to grow bored with being a medium. What he really wanted to be was a dentist. As he concentrated on his apprenticeship, his psychic skills began to weaken. He left Schrenck-Notzing's home and moved to Vienna, where he lived with a Dr. Holub, who ran a sanatorium. Late in 1924, after Holub's death, he traveled to London by invitation from the SPR, who wanted to arrange a series of sittings. The results were disappointing and even after he returned to Braunau and continued his work with Schrenck-Notzing, it was obvious that his powers were nearly gone. He gave up offering regular séances and died in 1971.

Before Willi's decline started in earnest, his spirit guide, Olga, made a strange pronouncement one night. In her hoarse, hurried whisper, she stated that she wanted to contact Rudi Schneider, Willi's younger brother, because he was, in fact, an even more powerful medium than Willi was. Their parents objected. Rudi was only 11 years old at the time, could not stay up late, and had been frightened during some of Willi's early séances in the Schneider home. Olga was adamant, though, stating, "He will come!"

And Rudi did. Even as the Schneiders were arguing with Olga, the door opened and Rudi walked into the room. He was in a trance, looking as if he were sleepwalking with his eyes closed and arms outstretched, and he joined the circle of sitters. The moment he sat down at the table, phenomena began to occur in the room.

Rudi, in his trance, began to speak as Olga. Willi, meanwhile, appeared to take on a new spirit guide. She announced herself as "Mina" and she spoke in a voice that was quite distinct from the one that he had previously used. Olga would never return to speak though Willi again. His younger brother Rudi now became the focus of the spirit's attention.

Rudi Schneider with investigator Harry Price

Baron von Schrenck-Notzing took an interest in Rudi and experiments were started almost at once. At first, they were held in Braunau, but later, the boy was taken to the baron's laboratory in Munich. The powers that Rudi had seemed to be equal to, or perhaps even greater, than those his brother once manifested.

From the start, the boy's father, Josef Schneider, decided to keep a record of Rudi's séances and he quickly learned what was needed in the way of documentation and evidence. His experiences with Willi helped to convince him of the need to keep a detailed accounting of every event that occurred. Each time there was a sitting, he entered the names of those present, the date, and the place in his record book. Then he, or someone that he appointed to do so, gave an account of what happened at the séance.

The two thick books that he compiled made for fascinating reading for later researchers. They were always described as Schneider's *geisterbucher* --- or "ghost books". He refused to be parted from them in his lifetime. The faded books can still be read today and contain notes from 269 separate séances. They not only provide credible evidence for the authenticity of Rudi's powers, but on one occasion, were even a help to Rudi when he was accused of fraud.

Two Viennese professors, Stefan Meyer and Karl Przibram, who had attended a séance with Rudi, later claimed that the controller had been influencing the sitting. Josef Schneider was able to defend his son by producing the page on which the professors had endorsed the séance record, one of them adding for good measure the words "the control was perfect." After that, they were obligated to retract the claim that they had caught Rudi cheating and instead had to state that they found no "natural" way to explain what they had witnessed.

But as time would pass, other events would come about that would cause some to question whether or not these men may have been correct when they thought that Rudi was faking some of the phenomena that occurred.

Rudi's mediumship began to be widely publicized following a visit by Harry Price in the spring of 1926. Price, being a master publicist for his work and investigations (as will be seen in a later chapter), brought a reporter from the *London Daily News* with him to Schrenck-Notzing's laboratory. As so often happened with Willi in the past, there were mysterious sounds, cold breezes, objects that moved, and phantom limbs that materialized from nowhere. The reporter was greatly impressed and wrote a series of articles about what he had seen. But more controversy over Rudi was soon to follow.

It erupted after the publication of an article in the paranormal journal *Psyche*, which floated a hypothesis of fraud that involved a confederate of Rudi's sneaking into the séance room unobserved. The article was written by an American journalist named W.J. Vinton, who had attended 10 of Rudi's séances in the company of Eric Dingwall. Vinton's hypothesis (which was obviously encouraged by Dingwall) was supported by J. Malcolm Bird of the ASPR. Bird attended only one séance, during which he was supposed to be guarding the door. Another skeptic was Walter Franklin Prince, who attended 10 séances, during which only some curtains moved. Having only this to judge by, he concluded that this could have been contrived.

Schrenck-Notzing was outraged by Vinton's (and by extension, Dingwall's) suggestions. He rightfully believed that the criticisms implied the inadequacy of his experimental methods, so the baron arranged for a series of sittings to be conducted under a newly devised system that was made up of electrical and tactile controls. The experiments were planned for 1929, but unfortunately, Schrenck-Notzing died on February 12, 1929, following an operation for acute appendicitis.

The psychical research world was stunned by the baron's untimely death, but Harry Price, who had always respected Schrenck-Notzing, implemented his planned electrical controls and invited Rudi to the National Laboratory for Psychical Research in London. Two series of experiments were conducted there in 1929 and 1930. Price extended Schrenck-Notzing's plans to include the entire circle of sitters. The hands and feet of the medium and all the sitters were joined together in a single electrical circuit, so that it would be impossible for any of them to have helped out the phenomena without everyone present knowing about it.

The experiments were extremely successful and all of the familiar Schneider family effects were present. There were icy breezes, temperature drops, curtains that moved, the levitation of the table, and even the materializations of arms and hands. Price, always quick to capitalize on the publicity that he gained, offered a £1,000 award to any magician who could duplicate what Rudi had done under the same controlled conditions. No one took him up on his offer.

Eugene Osty at the Institut Metaphysique in Paris arranged the next major series of experiments for Rudi in October and November 1930. These experiments used an infrared beam that crossed the room between Rudi and a table on which were placed objects for him to move. At first, the beam was connected to a number of cameras, which went off automatically when the beam was broken. This occurred a number of times, but during each incident, Rudi was always slumped over in his chair, seemingly deep in a trance. The cameras were then replaced by a bell, which would sometimes ring for 30 seconds or longer. Later experiments, designed to measure the deflection of the beam, found that it was never absorbed as completely as it would have been if broken by a material object. Whatever was crossing the infrared beam, causing the cameras to fire and the bells to ring, and at the same time moving the objects on the table, was only partially solid.

In the spring of 1932, Rudi returned to Harry Price's lab. He was now 28 years old and distracted by his fiancée, Mitzi Mangl, who he insisted on bringing with him. Out of 27 séances, little or nothing occurred during 18 of them. At the remaining nine, though, weak versions of the usual phenomena took place under the same conditions as before. Rudi's powers seemed to be waning, but they were still strong enough to confirm the earlier findings.

A series of sittings arranged by Sir Charles Hope were even weaker in terms of observable phenomena, but once again, the infrared apparatus noted the weird breaking of the beam. During 27 sittings, there was a record of 84 objects that moved and no fewer than 275 partial breaks in the infrared beam. It was hoped that the breaks could be captured on an infrared photographic plate that was devised by physicist John William Strutt (Lord Rayleigh), but this was unsuccessful, possibly for technical reasons. Further experiments with modifications to the photographs probably would have been carried out, but Harry Price managed to disrupt the proceedings with some startling information that would make Hope's reports completely pointless.

According to Price, he had photographic evidence that Rudi had managed to free one of his arms and move a handkerchief during his sittings at the National Institute for Psychical Research in March 1932. The allegation rocked the paranormal community, as did the photograph when it was released. It had been taken during a séance and showed Rudi reaching for a table. The camera had been triggered by movement from the medium. The resulting image was grainy and shadowed, but it managed to destroy Rudi's reputation and embarrass investigators, including Harry Price, who had declared him to be genuine. Those who claimed that Price was simply a publicity-seeking fraud, who wanted to keep Sir Charles Hope's findings from overshadowing his own, were hard-pressed to explain why he would have made himself look so ridiculous in this matter.

No one can explain, if Rudi had been a fraud all along, how he had managed to produce such incredible phenomena under the stringent conditions employed by Schrenck-Notzing, Harry Price, Sir Charles Hope, Eugene Osty, and others. It's possible that his powers were fading and to make up for the fact, Rudi had resorted to trickery to enhance the weak phenomena that was still occurring.

We will never know for sure, but we do know that Rudi gave up mediumship soon after the exposure, married his fiancée, and became a very successful automobile mechanic. He died in Austria in 1957.

SCIENCE AND THE UNSEEN

By the middle of the 1920s, Spiritualism began its inevitable decline. America had other distractions. The Great War was now a thing of the past. The Spanish Flu Epidemic that had claimed so many lives was now a fading memory. People were living longer and were in better health. Death was no longer on the average American's doorstep. People were now dying in hospitals, not in homes. Undertakers no longer made house calls. The dead were now taken to the mortuary and funerals were held at the funeral parlor. Even the parlor had been renamed; it was now the living room.

As Spiritualism began to wither away, organized scientific interest in the paranormal also slowed, until very little research was being conducted. Frustration and disappointment discouraged many scientists from further testing. Following the deaths of most of the original SPR and ASPR founders who had dedicated themselves to psychical research, the next generation of their members were hampered by the extensive revelations of fraud that had plagued the Spiritualist movement for years.

There were several reasons for the "death" of Spiritualism. It was forced from America's center stage in the first quarter of the twentieth century by the development of new measurements of the unseen worlds in the realms of psychology and physics, soft science and hard science. By the late 1920s, the world of the unseen – inhabited by spirits and invisible beings – had become the subject of real scientific scrutiny. We could see neither the atom nor the subconscious, but both medical and physical science had shown them to exist. They had been discovered and proven by science in a way that the paranormal had never been. Science had decided that – in the words of fictional detective Sherlock Holmes – "The world is big enough for us. No ghost need apply."

Spiritualism never returned to the fever pitch that followed the Hydesville rappings. Its golden age had lasted more than a century-and-a-half and there had been nearly 11 million Spiritualists in America, according to some estimates. Physical mediums and séances gave way to low-key, less-flamboyant practitioners, the best of whom used their gifts to communicate with the deceased and bring messages of hope and comfort to the living.

It was the abilities of the psychics and mediums who weathered the near demise of the Spiritualist movement who captured the attention of the last remaining scientists with an interest in the unknown. One of them was Joseph Banks Rhine, a young psychology instructor who joined the faculty of Duke University in Durham, North Carolina, in 1927. He would not oversee the destruction of paranormal studies. In fact, he elevated it by finally placing it in the kind of scientifically controlled and academic setting that so many before him had longed to see. Through his long and distinguished career, J.B. Rhine moved psychical research in the twentieth century to a place where both defenders and detractors agreed that he became of the most important figures in American parapsychology.

Rhine was born in the small western Pennsylvania town of Waterloo in 1895. By 1925, he had graduated from college and earned a Ph.D. in biology. Five years later, he married his childhood sweetheart, Louise Weckesser, who shared his life and work, becoming a highly-regarded parapsychologist herself. Early in their careers, the Rhines

J.B. and Louisa Rhine in the 1960s

agreed that they had little interest in teaching biology. Instead, they dedicated themselves to researching psychical phenomena.

Rhine's initial interest in the paranormal had come about in 1922, when he attended a lecture about Spiritualism by author Sir Arthur Conan Doyle. He was further intrigued when he participated in psychical research experiments conducted at Harvard University by Dr. Walter Franklin Prince, who had been president of the ASPR. While in Boston, the Rhines attended a séance with the well-known medium Mina Crandon (a.k.a. Margery) but left dissatisfied, convinced she was a fraud. Doyle, an ardent Spiritualist, disagreed when the Rhines – and everyone else, as we'll see in a later chapter – spoke out against Margery. Rhine was also unhappy with the ASPR for supporting her as a genuine medium. He came to the conclusion that "experimental science" was the best way for psychical research to advance, and he named the new field of study "parapsychology."

In 1926, an opportunity arose for the Rhines to study under Dr. William McDougall, who would become the chairman of the psychology department at Duke University. They leapt at the chance, resigned their teaching positions, sold all of their furniture, and moved to Boston, where McDougall was then teaching. At first, Rhine attempted to study mediumship, but soon found it as frustrating as other scientists before him. What he wanted was proof -- verifiable, scientific, replicable proof. But so had all of the other investigators who preceded him. What Rhine did have, though, was sheer force of character. Passionate about his research, led by his understanding of scientific method, and supported by his wife and partner who believed in his work just as strongly as he did, Rhine was ideally suited to drag psychic phenomenon away from ectoplasm and tipping tables and into the world of the scientific laboratory.

In 1927, Rhine's mentor, Dr. McDougall, moved to Duke University; the Rhines soon followed. Rhine taught psychology as an instructor, but the bulk of he and Louise's time in the first few months was devoted to analyzing the records of a man named John Thomas, who had compiled 750 pages of notes on conversations he had with his late wife through spirit mediums. Rhine was convinced that the mediums referred to information about Thomas and his wife that they could not have known by conventional

Testing with Zener cards in the Rhine laboratory

means. But, he noted, this did not mean that the information was actually coming from the dead woman – it could have easily have been coming from Thomas's mind.

To Rhine, this seemed to be a much more plausible area of research – the ability of the human mind to obtain information outside of the limiting principles of time, space, and physics. He was convinced that such abilities existed and he termed them "extra-sensory perception."

Rhine abandoned the search for proof of survival after death and instead began to focus on ESP. His first tests for telepathy were informal. He used a numbered card or a normal playing card to see whether his subjects – ordinary people, usually students, and not mediums or people who had a reputation for being psychic – could guess a card without seeing it. What he found, however, was that people tended to have favorite cards, and would suggest those rather than try to really guess what card was being displayed. Rhine wanted an entirely new set of cards, with images that had no previous associations in the minds of his subjects. For this, he turned to a colleague in the psychology department, Dr. Karl Zener.

Zener, whose usual work specialized in conditional responses (think Pavlov's dog), selected five simple symbols for the deck he created for Rhine – star, square, circle, cross, and three wavy lines – because people didn't seem to have specific feelings for or against any of them. The deck came with five sets of five symbols, meaning that the chances of guessing the first card correctly was one in five, but the chances of making 10 or more correct guesses in a run of 25 cards was at least one in 20.

The tests were fun and popular with Duke students, so the Rhines had no shortage of subjects. In 1931 alone, they conducted 10,000 ESP tests with 63 students, many of them scored better than chance. Some scored so well above chance that they were statistically significant, like Duke divinity graduate student Hubert Pearce, who once made 25 consecutive correct identifications, a full run of the Zener deck.

In 1934, Rhine published "Extra-Sensory Perception," considered by many psychic researchers to be a milestone work in the history of the paranormal. While most parapsychologists reacted positively and realized Rhine's work was significant, skeptics, of course, criticized Rhine's test conditions because there was likely no amount of evidence that would change the minds of those with a single purpose of debunking the paranormal. They criticized his methods of compiling statistics, or just flatly stated that his work had no value. There were also those who questioned whether subjects might have been able to read through the backs of the cards, and thus see the shapes on them. This was one of the most ridiculous of the accusations since Rhine had taken every possible precaution to prevent such "sensory clues." Rhine was a trained scientist – he was not testing subjects off the street in his basement. He ignored the detractors and continued the experiments.

The popular reaction to Rhine's work was largely uncritical and approving. By the mid-1930s, even as the country remained in the grips of the Great Depression, the media took note of Rhine's tests, and soon there were stories in some of America's most popular magazines, like *Reader's Digest, Harper's, Time,* and many others. In 1935, Rhine's work saw a massive boost when a wealthy patron gave him and his lab $10,000 a year for two years, with the possibility of extending that to $10,000 a year for five years if all went well. With the money, Rhine set up his own lab, still under the Duke auspices, but separate from the psychology department. Thanks to the donor, the lab was the most well-funded at the university.

Meanwhile, the general public's appetite for ESP research was seemingly limitless. By 1937, you could buy Zener cards from the local newsstand for 10-cents a pack. Rhine's book *New Frontiers of the Mind* was chosen as a Book of the Month Club selection, ESP experiments became the subject of radio shows, and everyone wanted to talk about telepathy. Rhine's reputation as the country's preeminent parapsychologist meant that people who'd had weird, inexplicable experiences or felt that they had abilities that others did not, thought of him as their champion—a scientist who actually believed in what others canned the impossible.

But there was a downside. As Rhine became better-known and accepted by the public, criticism of him and his wife increased. Some of it was particularly hostile, and most of that came from fellow psychologists. The public's embrace of parapsychology did not make it acceptable to most other scientists. Despite the initial promise of the lab, and the hundreds of thousands of trials that the Rhines believed established the validity of ESP, parapsychology still had the taint of occult. Zener, who spent the rest of his career at Duke as a perceptual psychologist, and later chair of the department, asked that the cards no longer be called "Zener cards," because he no longer wanted to be associated with Rhine's ESP research. McDougall, Rhine's champion and mentor, and William Preston Few, the Duke president who agreed to Rhine's lab, had both died. Rhine had few defenders and overall, most psychologists of the era remained antagonistic toward Rhine and the paranormal in general. The reason wasn't very complicated: most of them were concerned with stubbornly protecting their own theories and careers. If Rhine was correct about ESP and could prove it genuine, traditional assumptions about the limits and capabilities of the human mind would have to be reconsidered. It was easier to dismiss Rhine than to face the new threat of paranormal theories.

Of course, not everyone was, or has been, so short-sighted about Rhines' work. At least one well-regarded psychologist, Gardner Murphy, was on Rhine's side. He had also had his share of battles and was willing to defend Rhine's research. Together, Murphy and the Rhines were forceful and articulate, and presented a good argument for the worthiness of parapsychology. Later, Murphy became the president of the ASPR and the Rhines became role models for others in the scientific and academic communities who dared to examine ESP and other psychical phenomena.

The Rhines continued their work through the 1930s, and resumed it after World War II with more students at the Duke Parapsychology Laboratory. As time passed, though, the connection between the lab and the university began to fall apart. Even though the Parapsychology Lab was funded from outside sources (including the Office of Naval Research, the Army, and the Rockefeller Foundation), its lack of support within the university put it in jeopardy. In 1948, the Lab became a non-teaching independent unit within the university, losing its access to graduate students and further distancing itself from the school.

When Rhine retired in 1965, the lab closed. He founded a nonprofit research center, the Foundation for Research on the Nature of Man, to continue the research, and continued to be involved in ESP research until his death in 1980. The Rhine Research Center still exists today, but perhaps its greatest legacy was the other organizations that formed in its wake, including the Parapsychological Foundation in New York in 1951, the Parapsychological Association in 1957. The Psychical Research Foundation was founded in 1960, in Durham, North Carolina, and began specializing in poltergeist cases and out-of-body experiences. As interest in the paranormal grew, it branched out into past lives research, dream telepathy, psychic healing, near-death experiences, remote viewing, and more.

What remains clear after all of these years is that J.B. Rhine was a pioneer in psychical research. He was truly the first to find the middle ground between science and the paranormal, where real research could take place.

Today, it seems remarkable that Rhine was able to establish a paranormal research center at all. To say that paranormal research is still on the fringes of the established scientific community is a massive understatement. The National Science Foundation, in its surveys on the public perception of science, refers to ESP and the study of psychic abilities as "pseudoscience." The official case for the existence of "real" ESP is considered tenuous because attempts to replicate studies that seem to prove such abilities exist have not been consistently successful – largely because no academics are willing to put in the kind of time that J.B. Rhine and others did. They dismiss it all as "junk science," and not worthy of bothering with.

Will this mindset ever change? No one can say. For now, the puzzling word of scientific research remains somewhere between science and spirituality and we remain uncertain if it belongs with either, or both.

One thing that we do know is that by the 1930s, when J.B. Rhine began delving into the psychic side of the paranormal, the Spiritualist movement had breathed its last dying gasp.

As most scientists abandoned their research into Spiritualism, mediums, and ghosts, though, there were others who were waiting in the wings to take up the quest for answers. Science had grown bored with chasing spooks. The many technical advances in the scientific field drew their attention away from things that had turned out to be impossible to prove.

But this did not mean that the mystery was solved.

The search for answers fell into the hands of the amateurs, the conjurers, and the skeptics, who hammered the Spiritualist movement so hard that they made sure that it could never truly be revived again.

8. "GAMBOLS WITH GHOSTS"
THE DEATH KNELL OF THE SPIRITUALIST MOVEMENT

"All professional mediums cheat."

That was a statement that expressed the thoughts of Camille Flammarion, the famous French psychical researcher. However, like so many other investigators of the day, he was also convinced after nearly 60 years of studying paranormal phenomena, that many of the mediums that he encountered were genuine. And he was not the only one to think so. Hereward Carrington wrote: "Many genuine mediums will frequently resort to fraud when their powers fail them, or when phenomena are not readily forthcoming." He said that medium Eusapia Palladino, whom he considered to possess authentic powers of the highest order, "would constantly trick whenever the occasion for her to do so was presented."

Spiritualists learned to live with a certain amount of fraud as, one after another, even the most respected mediums were caught impersonating spirits or attempting to trick the sitters at their performances. Like some of the investigators, Spiritualist leaders believed that a single case of fraud was not enough to completely dismiss the work of an otherwise gifted medium. This permissive attitude toward occasional fraud explains why, even after an exposure, most mediums were able to continue filling their séance rooms. Combined with the need for the public to believe in something extraordinary, the Spiritualist movement thrived for decades.

And that was precisely how an unorganized band of amateurs, conjurers, and magicians – most of whom were more interested in self-promotion than in the public good – managed to wreak such havoc on the entire movement that Spiritualism finally died an ugly death in the late 1920s, never to return as it once was.

From the beginning, investigators of the paranormal were an overconfident lot. Debate raged as to whether a competent scientist could ever be fooled by a fraudulent medium.

They could be.

One of the first to debate the subject was Sir William Crookes, who presented a paper on the subject to the British Association for the Advancement of Science in 1876. Crookes was sure that the controls he applied when testing mediums made fraud impossible. Of course, we have already discussed the testing of Florence Cook in the eminent scientist's laboratory, and so, if the reader is skeptical of Crookes' methods, you have every right to be. Sir William Barrett certainly was. He argued that a skilled conjurer or magician could be equipped with devices and, under whatever conditions were imposed, re-create whatever effect the mediums could produce.

Although controls in the early days of psychical research were rather slack by modern standards, a great number of mediums were exposed as frauds. In 1876 -- the same year that Crookes and Barrett debated the subject -- three mediums who had large followings were caught red-handed as frauds.

Francis Ward Monck, a minister turned medium, was challenged by a magician who insisted on searching the medium during a séance in Huddersfield, England. Monck ran into a room, locked himself in, and managed to escape through a window. Later, a pair of stuffed gloves -- which had posed as mysterious "spirit hands" -- was found among his belongings. Monck was arrested and placed on trial for fraud. Dr. Alfred Russell Wallace, who had investigated many mediums, appeared as one of the defense witnesses. He claimed that he had seen Monck manifest a "spirit woman" without trickery, but his testimony had little effect after Sir William Barrett took the stand. Barrett claimed that he had once caught Monck simulating a partially materialized spirit with a piece of white muslin cloth on a wire frame. Monck was found guilty of fraud and sentenced to three months in prison.

Dr. Henry Slade, an American medium known for spirit writing on slate blackboards, visited Britain that same year. Professor Ray Lankester was determined to expose Slade as a fraud. Together with another investigator, he visited Slade and observed his techniques. During a second séance, Lankester suddenly seized the small blackboard before the "spirit writing" was to take place. He found that a message had already been written on it. Lankester then wrote a scathing letter about Slade in the *Times* on September 16, and then sued him for obtaining money under false pretenses. The case was heard on October 1. Once again, Dr. Alfred Russell Wallace appeared for the defense. Despite his support, Slade was found guilty and sentenced to three months in prison at hard labor. The sentence was later thrown out under appeal and Slade quickly left England before Lankester could come after him again. When he returned to the country two years later, he used the false name of "Dr. Wilson."

William Eglinton was the third popular medium to be exposed in 1876. The accounts of his séances are some of the most dramatic that have been recorded and include many materializations that took place outdoors and in broad daylight. Thomas Colley, the Archdeacon of Natal in Southern Africa and the Rector of Stockton in England, finally exposed Eglinton. Archdeacon Colley was an eager psychical researcher and he cut off pieces of the white robe and beard of a spirit that Eglinton allegedly manifested. Later investigation showed that the items that he snipped off exactly matched some muslin and a false beard that was found in the medium's suitcase. His exposure of Eglinton did not make Colley discredit all mediums. He was a firm believer in the genuineness of other mediums, including Francis Ward Monck, and had once offered a large sum of money to a magician to try and duplicate Monck's materializations with trickery. The magician attempted to manifest a spirit, but failed.

This reinforces the strangeness of mediumship -- that although three well-known mediums like Monck, Slade, and Eglinton were exposed in fraud, many reputable scientists and psychical investigators had no doubts that all three men were also capable of extraordinary paranormal feats that did not require trickery.

But as scientists lost interest in mediums and séances, others stepped in to expose scores of Spiritualists as frauds. A perfect example of this occurred in the 1940s when a military officer exposed the fraud of a medium named Helen Duncan, who he believed was preying on the widows of men killed in the war.

Helen Duncan was born in Scotland in 1898, married at the age of 20, and began to develop psychic talents that were much in demand by the 1930s and 1940s. She traveled the country during this period and held séances in private homes and Spiritualist churches. She convinced thousands of people that the dead could return in various forms but most often, through ectoplasm, that slimy, white substance said to be manifested by spirits. In reality, Helen's "ectoplasm" was found to be nothing more than a mixture of paper, cloth, egg white, and surgical gauze. She regurgitated the substances on demand. Any lingering doubts about this were dispelled by the medium's husband, who gave an interview late in life that admitted he had seen his wife swallowing various things before her séances.

In addition to her ectoplasmic forms, Duncan also worked with spirit guides. One in particular was a child named "Peggy," who played an important role during the séances. However, in 1933, at a sitting in Edinburgh, a policewoman grabbed at "Peggy" as she passed by her and discovered that the ghostly girl was actually a torn piece of white underwear. Duncan was arrested, charged with fraud and fined £10. Less than two months later, she was back at work.

Undaunted by her exposure, Duncan proceeded to give a series of test sittings for the National Laboratory of Psychical Research, under the direction of its founder, Harry Price (who we will read much more about later in the book). Photographs taken during her sessions revealed that the "ectoplasm" she produced was a length of cheesecloth whose bound edges, texture, and creases were clearly visible.

None of her exposures made any difference to Helen's public. Outside of the laboratories, her fame continued to grow and sitters continued to insist that they recognized departed friends and loved ones in the ectoplasmic faces that she materialized. During World War II, her mediumistic powers were much in demand by relatives of those who had died in the service. She held many séances in Portsmouth, Hampshire, the home port of the Royal Navy, and one of these, held on January 19, 1944, was raided by the police. A plainclothes policeman who was present blew a whistle to give a signal and other officers burst in. A grab was made for the ectoplasm issuing from the medium and the séance was abruptly brought to an end. Although nothing incriminating was found, Duncan, along with three others who arranged the séance,

Helen Duncan

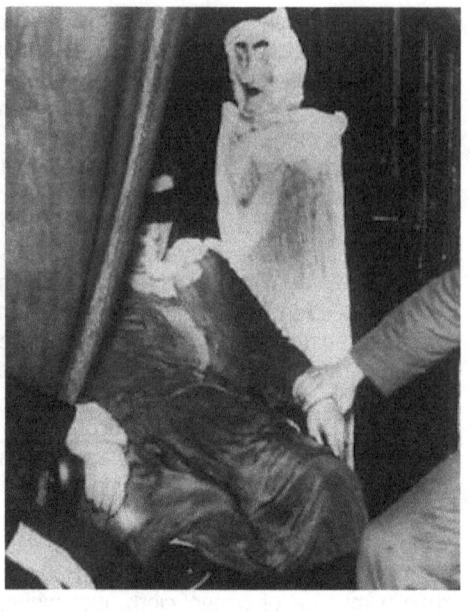

(Right) One of the less than authentic "manifestations" from one of her seances.

Ernest and Elizabeth Homer and Francis Brown, was taken to the Portsmouth magistrate's court and arraigned on charges of conspiracy.

At the preliminary hearing, the court was told how Lieutenant R.H. Worth of the Royal Navy had attended one of Duncan's séances and suspected fraud. He bought two tickets for 25 shillings each for the night of January 19, and took a policeman named Cross with him. Cross grabbed the "ectoplasm" that floated past him (which he believed was a piece of white sheet, although no sheet was found when the séance was raided) but he was unable to hang onto it. After the hearing, bail was refused and Duncan was remanded to Holloway Prison in London for four days before the case was resumed in Portsmouth.

The prosecution seemed to be unsure of what to charge the medium with. At her first appearance at Portsmouth, she was charged under the Vagrancy Act of 1824, but the charge was then amended to one of conspiracy. When the case was eventually transferred to the central criminal courts, the Witchcraft Act of 1735 was cited. Under this ancient act, the defendant was accused of pretending "to exercise or use a kind of conjuration that, through the agency of Helen Duncan, spirits of deceased persons should appear to be present." Other charges were brought under the Larceny Act (which was more accurate) and she was accused of taking money "by falsely pretending to be in a position to bring about appearances of the spirits of deceased person."

Spiritualists were dismayed by the use of the outdated witchcraft laws, largely because her supporters believed that her powers were genuine. The prosecution, however, clearly believed that Duncan was a fraud, which was why they charged her with larceny. The inclusion of witchcraft in the charges against Duncan managed to bring a lot of publicity to her trial, which took place in late winter of 1944 and lasted for seven days. Numerous witnesses testified to events they had seen at Duncan's séances. One of them, Kathleen McNeill, claimed that she had attended a séance where her sister had appeared. This sister had died just a few hours before, after an operation, and news of her death could not have been known to Duncan at the time. At another séance, McNeill claimed that her father strode out of the spirit cabinet, looking just as he had when he was alive.

Two journalists, H. Swaffer and J.W. Herries, were also called by the defense. The flamboyant Swaffer told the court that not only was ectoplasm real; it could not have been regurgitated by the medium. That was ridiculous, he stated. Herries claimed that he had seen Sir Arthur Conan Doyle materialize at one of Duncan's séances. He noted the author's rounded features and mustache and recognized his voice, he said.

The prosecution had to make little effort to convince the jury that Duncan was a fraud. They made liberal use of photographs taken at Duncan's séances showing blatantly fake "ectoplasm" emerging from the medium's mouth and nose. One particular favorite was a photo of the spirit child "Peggy" slithering out of Duncan's nostrils. In the photo, the "ectoplasm" boasted a face that was obviously that of a child's doll.

Prosecuting counsel John Maude produced a long piece of butter muslin and referred to the report by Harry Price, who stated that he believed Duncan swallowed the material and then vomited it back up. The jury seemed convinced that she was a fraud. At the start of the trial, the defense offered the jury an actual demonstration of Duncan's mediumship, but the judge declined the offer and stated that perhaps Mrs. Duncan should testify as a witness instead. The defense replied, however, that Helen could not testify, as she was in a trance during the séances and unable to discuss what transpired. On the final day, the judge changed his mind and asked the jury if they wanted to see Helen Duncan perform. After a couple of minutes of discussion, they declined the offer.

It took just 25 minutes for the jury to return their verdict: they found the defendant guilty of conspiracy to disregard the Witchcraft Act. They were discharged from giving verdicts on the other counts. The judge deferred pronouncing sentence until after the weekend but when the court did reconvene, he stated that the verdict had not been concerned with whether "genuine manifestations of the kind are possible... this court has nothing to do with such abstract questions. The jury has found this to be a case of plain dishonesty." He sentenced Duncan to serve nine months in prison and the medium was led away moaning and crying.

Helen Duncan served her sentence at Holloway Prison. The Spiritualist movement, shocked by the verdict, called for a change in the law to prevent such prosecutions in the future. They felt that Duncan had been unfairly treated, but they did cool their enthusiasm for her after the trial. Public perception was that a fraud had been exposed and officials in the movement decided to put some distance between themselves and the medium.

When she was released from prison on September 22, 1945, Duncan announced that she was retiring from séances, but thanks to the large number of faithful followers that she still had, she soon changed her mind. She continued to offer private séances for years afterward.

In 1951, the Witchcraft Act of 1735 was repealed and replaced with the Fraudulent Mediums Act. Helen Duncan's trial had certainly prompted this change in the law but hopes from the Spiritualists that they would no longer be subjected to police harassment were short-lived. In November 1956, police raided a séance taking place in Nottingham. They grabbed the medium, searched her, and photographed her. They shouted that they were looking for beards, a mask and a shroud but found nothing.

The medium conducting the séance was Helen Duncan.

Duncan almost immediately became ill after the raid, possibly from shock, and died five weeks later. The doctors listed the cause of death as diabetes and heart failure, but a certain segment of the Spiritualist community thought otherwise. Some complained of "police brutality" and even "murder," mostly because the medium had been interrupted during a trance, which all agreed could be extremely dangerous. Even today, Helen Duncan is still seen by some as a "martyr" to the cause of Spiritualism, a victim of the world's intolerance.

To most though, she is seen as just another fraudulent medium that, unlike most in the same circumstances, actually got her day in court. Those who point to the egg white and muslin "ectoplasm," the phony photographs, and the torn underwear "spirit guides" would say that in this case, justice prevailed.

But most of the exposures of mediums that occurred in the early twentieth century were not the work of concerned members of the general public or police officers – exposing Spiritualist fraud became a staple of magic acts all over America.

From the earliest days of Spiritualism, there had been a running battle between mediums and magicians. In 1853, just five years after the Fox Sisters gained fame in Hydesville, a magician named J.H. Anderson of New York issued the first challenge. He offered a monetary award to "any poverty-stricken medium" who could produce raps in the public hall where he gave his regular performances. The Fox Sisters were among those who accepted Anderson's challenge, but Anderson backed out and, amid catcalls and hisses from the audience, refused to allow the mediums on the stage.

One of the greatest of the early rivalries between mediums and magicians involved the Davenport brothers. As described earlier in the book, Ira and William Davenport were professional mediums who were the first to popularize the spirit cabinet in their performances. Although the phenomena they produced was typical of the Spiritualist séances of the day, the Davenports were ambiguous about their powers. They never presented themselves as Spiritualists, but on the other hand, insisted the manifestations they created were genuine. While in England, they became the subject of controversy. They held séances every night for more than two months in a hall in London. Various committees studied these demonstrations without finding any evidence of fraud but, regardless, there was widespread public opposition and even hostility. Earlier in the book, we discussed the Davenports' confrontation with John Nevil Maskelyne, one of Britain's most famous stage magicians, who was convinced that he had caught the brothers cheating at the Cheltenham Town Hall. He was so sure that he could recreate their "tricks" that he rented a theater in which to do so and spent years offering "spirit shows" that duplicated the tricks of mediums.

One of the first books ever written about debunking the methods of fraudulent mediums was published by a magician named David P. Abbott. It was called *Behind the Scenes with Mediums* and did a thorough job of revealing conjuring techniques that were used to produce "ghostly" effects. Abbott, who was a magician and a member of the ASPR, based his book on personal observations of scores of phony mediums. In one chapter, he described the seemingly astonishing performance of a woman who gave séances in a theater. She asked her audience to write down questions for her, sign their names on the paper, and then keep the papers in her possession. Then, from the stage, she would answer the questions. The effect was startling but Abbott revealed how easy it was to do with the aid of accomplices. Because many of the members of the audience did not have paper with them, assistants handed out pads of paper for their use. These pads were scored into sections so that each person could tear off the square on which he had written his question, keep the paper, and then pass the pad on to someone else who needed it. The tablets, however, were specially prepared with a developing wax so that the writing would leave an impression behind that could be read later.

Assistants collected the pads and then seemed to place them in front of the medium on the stage. What they actually did, though, was switch the pads, giving her blank ones and smuggled the used ones under the stage. These were quickly developed and then handed to a confederate with a radio transmitter. The medium had a small receiver tucked behind her ear, and hidden by her hair, which was connected to a carefully concealed wire that ran down to copper plates in her shoes. When she stepped on two nails hammered into the stage floor, she completed the radio circuit and heard her accomplice read the questions. In addition, other assistants in the theater picked out people who wrote questions on their own paper, and read their questions while collecting the pads throughout the audience. As soon as they could, they wrote down the questions they had spotted and sent them below stage to be read along with the others. Most people came away from this performance believing they had witnessed something paranormal.

A similar trick was also used, often to the amazement of audiences. Theater attendees were invited to write questions on pieces of paper, addressing their questions to dead friends, relatives, and loved ones. They were also asked to sign their names. Each question was then sealed in an envelope and given to a medium. The medium would then hold up the envelope, read the message without ever opening it, and pass along an answer from the spirit world. This was one of the simplest frauds to carry out. All that it required was an assistant to pretend that the first envelope belonged to him. The medium would hold up the envelope, make up a fake message that was inside and the assistant would claim the message was his. The medium would then open the envelope to "prove" that she was correct about what message was inside. What she was actually doing was opening the next envelope, which belonged to an audience member, and memorizing the message. She would then ask the question and answer it ---- supposedly never looking inside. Then, she would open the next audience member's envelope and pretend it contained the message he had just read. And so on, and so on, staying one step ahead of the audience as she psychically "peered" into the envelopes and "heard" messages from the other side.

Almost 50 years after Abbott wrote about this "question and answer" trick, a British medium made a small fortune by using very similar methods but with equipment that was more sophisticated. William Roy has been described as one of the most audacious fake mediums of the modern times. Before his exposure in 1955, he was one of the most popular mediums in England --- only to be denounced by the Spiritualist publication, *Two Worlds*.

According to accounts, much of Roy's success came from duping sitters using a microphone-relaying technique that demonstrated "direct voice" communications from the spirits in full light, an achievement that was beyond the abilities of his rivals. To do this, he ran a wire under the carpet from the microphone and amplifier to two brass tacks, the heads of which protruded above the carpet. He adapted a hearing aid as a miniature loudspeaker and attached it to the cuff of his sleeve, running wires to it up his sleeve, inside of his jacket and down his trouser leg to his shoes. There, they connected to the soles with two metal plates, one on each shoe, so that when he stood on the tacks, the circuit was completed and an assistant could produce voices through the miniature loudspeaker. The voices would then come from Roy's wrist, far enough away from his mouth to avert suspicion.

Roy, whose real name was William George Holroyd Plowright, was paid quite well by a British tabloid, the *Sunday Pictorial*, for a five-installment confession in 1958. He shamelessly posed for photographs with his "spirit voice" apparatus, which eventually found its way to the Metropolitan Police Detective Training School. He also boasted of the way that he had gained his wealth by taking advantage of grief-stricken people, researching their histories and lives. He examined voter's lists, visited the National Registry office to look over birth, marriage, and death records, and used newspapers to scan obituaries and the details of wills. He kept all this information in a card file index and traded information back and forth with other fake mediums. "We phony mediums traded information --- like swapping stamps," he admitted.

When sitters arrived for one of Roy's séances, they were asked to leave their coats and handbags in a waiting room. Roy listened to their conversation by way of a concealed microphone before they entered the séance room. Meanwhile, an assistant searched their bags and coat pockets for further clues in letters, tickets, and receipts --- any information that Roy could use to confirm his "psychic" powers. His séances were high-tech for the time, using the latest special effects to create spirit voices, music and mysterious lights. Masks and cheesecloth were also used by Roy to create "materializations."

Spiritualists knew that Roy was a fraud as early as 1951 but agreed not to reveal it in return for his promise to stop conducting séances and leave the country. Roy did so for a time, but then came back to England and started back to his old tricks. After *Two Worlds* exposed him as a fraud in 1955, he sued them for libel, and with the case in the court system, the newspaper was prevented from saying anything else. When Roy abandoned the lawsuit in 1958, he agreed to pay court costs to the magazine editor, and immediately after, *Two Worlds* released all its evidence concerning his fraud. At first, Roy continued to deny the charges and then when the *Sunday Pictorial* offered him a large sum of money, he cheerfully confessed. By the time the story was published, Roy had left the country once again.

In the tabloid article, he ended the story with this statement: "Even after this confession, I know I could fill séance rooms again with people who find it a comfort to believe I am genuine."

In 1968, he was given the chance to see if this was true --- it was. A medium using the name Bill Silver was discovered to be William Roy. Once again, it was a Spiritualist newspaper, *Psychic News*, which exposed him. The story revealed that some of the sitters even knew the medium's real identity as William Roy, but were still convinced by his phenomena, which included voiced communications from beings who lived on Venus. The sitters included a Catholic Bishop and some of the members of the Beatles. When challenged by the newspaper, Roy had the nerve to claim that his earlier confession had been a "pack of lies" and that he had always been genuine.

REVEALING THE IMPOSSIBLE

"Is Spiritualism a fraud? Are the spirit-rappings and the spirit-forms of the séance, the prophecies of the palmist and the clairvoyant, the visions of the trance mediums, genuine evidence of a spirit-world, or are they mere catchpenny tricks, engineered by charlatans to charm money from the pockets of the credulous?"
Pearson's Magazine, March 1910

It would continue to be magicians, though, who would do the greatest damage to the Spiritualist movement. From the early days, they were adept at recreating the "miraculous" phenomena of the mediums. On stage, they duplicated and then exposed their effects. The methods practiced by the mediums were simple, the conjurers claimed, and were merely stage illusions just like the ones being created before audiences in vaudeville theaters across the country. "If I can only get your attention intently," one magician claimed, "an elephant could pass behind me and you would not see it."

One of the most flamboyant of the early twentieth century debunkers was William S. Marriott, who wrote a series of articles about fraudulent mediums for *Pearson's Magazine*, starting in 1910. Unfortunately, little is known about Marriott's early years, how he got started in the magic field, or what led him to pursue the truth behind Spiritualist mediums. What we do know is that he was described as a likable man with "a pair of well-waxed mustaches" and that he was a professional magician who performed under the name of Dr. Wilmar. At some point, in the early 1900s, he became interested in exposing the hoaxes that were being carried out by fraudulent mediums. He took up this task before any other magicians, including those who became famous for it by the 1920s.

One of Marriott's first, and most valuable, exposures came when he located and publicized a copy of a catalog called "Gambols with Ghosts: Mind Reading, Spiritualistic Effects, Mental and Psychical Phenomena and Horoscopy." It was a secret catalog that was being circulated among mediums and was filled with tricks, apparatus, and paraphernalia that could be used to dupe the public. The catalog was issued in 1901 by Ralph E. Sylvestre of Chicago and was designed for private circulation among mediums,

William S. Marriott with some of the "ghosts" that he purchased from a catalog for fraudulent mediums

on the understanding that it would be returned to Sylvestre when tricks had been selected from it. It was never meant to be seen by the general public.

The catalog had an introduction that read: "Our experience during the past 30 years in supplying mediums and others with the peculiar effects in this line enable us to place before you only those which are practical and of use, nothing that you have to experiment with. We wish you to thoroughly appreciate that, while we do not, for obvious reasons, mention the names of our clients and their work (they being kept in strict confidence, the same as a physician treats his patients), we can furnish you with the explanation and, where necessary, the material for the production of any known public 'tests' or 'phenomena' not mentioned in this, our latest list. You are aware that our effects are being used by nearly all prominent mediums of the entire world."

This notorious catalog included equipment for slate-writing, stuffed ghosts, self-playing guitars, self-rapping tables, materializations, and a "Complete Spiritualistic Séance." Marriott obtained many of these illusions from the catalog and had himself photographed posing with them.

Marriott had become disenchanted with the deceptions being carried out by dishonest mediums. Spiritualism was riddled with cases of outright fraud. Many deceptive mediums would do whatever they could to bilk unsuspecting clients and sitters out of money to "contact their deceased loved ones." And while not every medium was dishonest, there were enough of them to color the entire movement -- and to give Spiritualism a bad name.

One of the most thrilling aspects of any séance was the materialization of the spirits. Some mediums, like Florence Cook, built an entire career on such materializations. Because the appearance of the spirits was so important to a good séance, fraudulent mediums would do just about anything to cause it to happen -- from smoke to mirrors to even more dishonest shenanigans.

As the heyday of the Spiritualist movement began to wind down, the fraudulent mediums became more and more sloppy with their tricks and manipulations. Gone were the days of elaborate stage shows. They had been replaced by cheap displays and shoddy hoaxes. A case that illustrates this point was reported in newspapers in 1906. As it turned out, two ardent and legitimate Spiritualists were responsible for exposing the fraud.

These men went to an apartment where a séance was to be conducted and became suspicious of the chair and the cabinet used by the medium. They managed to examine the chair and found a secret compartment in the rear, and a keyhole, which was carefully concealed beneath the upholstered material that covered the rest of the chair. The investigators then had a key made, which would open the lock, and found another secret compartment that was 15 inches deep.

At the next séance, the men noticed that the back of the chair seemed to be stuffed much better than the rest of it and suspected that "ghostly" materials had been placed there before the sitters arrived. During the séance that followed, the men were not surprised to see that all manner of "ghosts" materialized, and when it was over, they exposed the medium as a fraud. They opened the secret compartment on the chair with their own key and began removing the items contained inside. They found a collapsible dummy head made of pink material, a flesh colored mask, six pieces of china silk that comprised about 13 yards of material, two pieces of black cloth, three beards and two wigs of various color and length, a telescoping rod from which drapery could be hung to represent a second ghost, a small flashlight with four yards of wire and a switch, which would be useful to make "spirit lights," and various other contraptions.

Exposures like this one prompted Marriott to begin his own investigations and he soon made a name for himself --- and many enemies among the frauds of the Spiritualist movement.

In 1909, *Pearson's Magazine* approached Marriott and asked him to conduct, on the magazine's behalf, a series of investigations of spirit mediums. The results were published afterward in four issues of the magazine. In the first installment, he delved into Spiritualist séances and wrote of several hilarious incidents that occurred. At one séance, the medium entered the spirit cabinet as the lights were being turned out and after a time, the curtain parted and a stately form emerged from the cabinet. The "spirit" was partially luminous and carried a shimmering globe in his hand, which he held near his face to make it more visible. The figure graciously inclined his head, gestured as if to bless the sitters, and then retired back into the cabinet. Marriott wrote more of what happened next:

This should have closed the séance. Tonight, an unrehearsed effect was in store for the believers. As the form entered the cabinet, he sat down on what he thought was the settee. It happened to be my knees. I had quickly slipped into the curtained enclosure and was sitting, waiting for him to come back. As my arms went around him, he gave a yell followed by language which I will not repeat. My friend had the light up in a moment. And there for the faithful was the edifying sight of the medium, clothed in flimsy white draperies, struggling in the arms of myself!

Marriott's reputation as an investigator was widely known. He was a friend of investigator Harry Price and through him, acquainted with Everard Feilding, who was intensely interested in psychical phenomena. Feilding frequently held séances at his home with notable mediums and Marriott was often called in to "vet" the phenomena --- often with amusing results.

On one occasion, Feilding invited a German apport medium to London. The medium specialized in causing fish, flesh, and fowl to appear in the séance room and often worked in semi-darkness. Feilding invited him to dinner one night and it was arranged that a séance would be held after the meal, to which Marriott was also invited. The medium arrived very early, but so did Marriott. Both had the run of the home for a considerable time before dinner was ready to be served.

Shortly before the meal was announced, the medium was placed in another part of the house while Feilding and Marriott thoroughly examined the dining room. They made a curious --- although not completely unexpected --- discovery. Carefully hidden in the folds and frame of a silk lampshade that was suspended above the table, they found a dozen large boiled prawns. A slight jerk of the shade caused the prawns to fall onto the table. The men replaced them in their original positions after they had made a few "adjustments" to them.

After dinner, the table was cleared, and as dessert and coffee were being served, a discussion took place about the séance that was to follow. It was agreed that the sitting should be held around the dining room table -- an arrangement the medium heartily endorsed. Most of the lights were put out and the séance began. In a few minutes, the medium was in a deep trance, which was marked by his rapid breathing and waving arms. Suddenly, a shower of something fell onto the guests. All the lights were turned on and it was discovered that a "miraculous" fall of prawns had taken place. They had seemingly fallen from nowhere. But what astonished everyone even more was that each of the prawns had a red band of silk tied in a bow around it!

One can only wonder what the medium was thinking when this occurred but Marriott had a good laugh at himself. The magician had come to the house with a reel of red silk, hoping to make good use of it, but he had not anticipated prawns. He later presented one of them – a red silk bow, not a prawn -- to Harry Price for his museum of such objects.

Perhaps the most famous and controversial case that Marriott involved himself in – and some say under dubious circumstances --- was the case of the Bangs sisters, who were able to create "spirit paintings" with psychical powers. The case was originally investigated by David P. Abbott, who was mentioned earlier in the chapter as the author of *Behind the Scenes with the Mediums*.

After the release of his book, Abbott received many letters about fraudulent mediums that his readers hoped that he would investigate. Several of those letters told of a Chicago duo known the Bangs sisters, two women who commanded top dollar for their supposed materializations of portraits of loved ones, painted by the spirits.

Lizzie and May Bangs intrigued Abbott. On one hand, he wanted to help those who had fallen victim to them by exposing the secret of their spirit portraits, but on the other, he was just as fascinated with uncovering the method behind what seemed to be an almost perfect magic effect --- the miraculous materialization of paintings in full view. Visual tricks were neatly done using covers, curtains, and cabinets but a gradual, unconcealed appearance was almost unheard of.

As the manifestation was carried out, the Bangs sisters began by sealing a photo of the client's loved one between two slates, then sending the customer away to come back the next day. When they returned, he was sent to an upstairs room in the sisters' home and was seated facing a window. The sisters displayed two large canvasses, stretched onto wooden frames, placed them face-to-face, and positioned them vertically in front of the window. The bottom edges of the frames rested on a table just under the window sill, with sunlight from the window glowing through the pale fabric of the canvasses. To block any stray light, the mediums draped curtains on the sides and tops of the frames. May and Lizzie then sat down on each side of the window, each with a hand on one side of the canvasses.

After a dramatic wait of about 30 minutes or so, the sitter began to see patches of dark stain and color gradually appear between the canvas, which was translucent from the window light. The shapes gradually became sharper and brighter until they formed a fully defined portrait of the sitter's dead loved one. The mediums then separated the canvasses and displayed the result of their powers: an impressive painting for which the client would pay a hefty fee to the Bangs sisters.

David Abbott

The Bangs manifestation seemed like a miracle --- but it wasn't.

It was a trick, but a very clever one. When magicians first heard of the effect, they doubted it could be real. Once David Abbott unraveled the secret, though, it began appearing at magic shows across the country. Inventive conjurer P.T. Selbit toured Europe and America with just the "spirit paintings" as a stand-alone act. A number of competing shows followed, put on by magicians as famous as Howard Thurston, and it never failed to astonish those who witnessed the effect.

But who were the Bangs sisters and how did they manage to create one of the most amazing effects in the history of fraudulent Spiritualism?

The Bangs family moved to Chicago from Atchison, Kansas, in 1861. Edward Bangs, the father of the two future mediums, was a tinsmith and stove repairman, and his wife, Meroe, was a spirit medium, who recruited her two young daughters into helping with her séances. The oldest daughter, Elizabeth Snow Bangs (Lizzie), was born in 1860 and Mary, known as May, was born a few years later, in Chicago. The family also had two sons, W.B. and Edward.

By 1872, Lizzie and May were stealing the limelight during the Bangs family séances. They produced a wide variety of Spiritualistic effects, including slate writing and the movement of tables and furniture. The girls were often bound and placed in a spirit cabinet and sitters were stunned when music played and hands waved about from

The Bangs sisters — Lizzie and May

an opening in the door. At the conclusion of many of the séances, May was able to manifest a "spirit kitten," a hairless feline that was supposedly born in the next world.

A reporter named Steven Sanborn Jones wrote about the girls in an article called "An Evening with the Bangs Children" in 1872 and he, like so many other trusting Spiritualists of the time, felt the girls could not be part of any trickery: "It must be remembered that these mediums are young children. There is not a particle of deception in their nature. Their hearts are free from guile, and in all their actions, they exhibit the innocence of their nature. No one would accuse them of deception."

By 1888, the Bangs sisters had become prominent Chicago mediums, performing lucrative cabinet séances, still assisted by their mother. Most considered their home the leading Spiritualist establishment in the city, and it was not uncommon for there to be long lines of people crowding into their parlor in hopes of a sitting. One of their clients was Henry Jestram, a wealthy Chicago photographer. Shortly after he became a regular member of their séance circle and spent a large part of his fortune paying huge fees to the sisters, he went insane and was committed to an asylum. The publicity surrounding his breakdown -- some rumors blamed the sisters -- was not good for the Bangs and likely led to their first arrest on April 2, 1888.

Two plainclothes detectives attended a Bangs séance and witnessed a procession of spirit entities emerging from the cabinet. When a ghostly Russian princess, clad in a regal gown, made her appearance, the detectives seized her. The "princess" resisted furiously, throwing wild punches at the officers. One of the detectives loudly announced: "I have a warrant for you, May Bangs!" At that point, the ghost's mask fell off and the medium was revealed behind it. The sisters, along with some of the sitters at the séance, put up such a struggle that the detectives had to draw their guns so they could clear the room. A subsequent search of the premises revealed a case filled with white muslin shrouds, wigs, disguises, and theatrical make-up. The sisters, along with the case, were loaded into a patrol wagon, taken to the police station, and locked up.

Sadly, though, shortly after her arrest for obtaining money under false pretenses, Lizzie Bangs' seven-year-old daughter died. Newspapers reported that during the child's funeral, her mother went into a trance and delivered a bizarre speech that blamed the little girl's death on the "persecution that I have received."

By this time, Chicago newspapers were referring to the pair as "the notorious Bangs Sisters" and editors had a field day with the sisters' romantic dramas. Lizzie was married and divorced once. May had been married four times. In November 1890, May received a divorce from her second husband, wealthy chemical manufacturer Henry H. Graham. Their brief, drama-filled relationship had started during an 1887 séance in which May told the newly widowed Graham that his late wife had contacted her and said that he should marry the medium, adding that his dead infant had sent a message too: "Dear papa, I would like this lady for my new mama."

In 1907, May married again, this time to Jacob Lesher, a leather manufacturer. The medium allegedly proposed to him three times before he was finally convinced of the match by messages May received from Lesher's dead mother. One message told him that he would "feel 25 years younger and never again be sick" if he married the medium. Within two years, Lesher was bankrupt. The *Chicago Tribune* reported: "Business tips from the spirit world are blamed for the failure of Jacob H. Lesher, formerly rated a millionaire, and the husband of May Bangs, a 'spirit painter.'"

Despite exposures and negative publicity, eager customers continued to come to the Bangs' séances and they remained as popular as ever. True believers saw their harassment by the newspapers and the authorities as what Lizzie had claimed at her daughter's funeral -- "persecution."

In 1891, a bill was passed in the Illinois Senate prohibiting anyone from "impersonating the spirits of the dead, commonly known as spirit-medium séances, on penalty of fine and imprisonment." At least one Chicago Spiritualist blamed the Bangs sisters for this new law. In a *Tribune* story, he stated that although "they were gifted with unearthly powers, their greed for gold had led them to abuse it." A short time later, a Chicago grand jury attempted to indict the sisters, but failed due to technicalities.

In 1893, the sisters took a new approach and began to produce "spirit typewriting" during sittings with G.W.N. Yost, the inventor of the typewriter. The spirits began pecking out messages from celebrities that ranged from Moses to assassinated U.S. President James Garfield.

In 1894, they managed their most bizarre stunt yet. The sisters traveled to Massachusetts and again made headlines by conducting a weird wedding in which they married a wealthy woman to the departed spirit of her dead fiancé.

Between 1895 and 1899, the Bangs continued to host twice-weekly séances for their Chicago customers on Sunday and Wednesday nights. One of the continued highlights of each sitting was a slate-writing exhibition that occurred, when the spirits would mysteriously leave behind messages from the other side.

In 1900, British psychical investigator Reverend Stanley L. Krebs scheduled a sitting with the sisters, secretly intent on discovering their method of slate writing. He wrote about his visit in an extraordinary exposé that was published by the SPR in 1901.

The sisters had asked Krebs to bring with him a sealed envelope containing a letter that he had written to a deceased friend, along with blank paper for a reply. He had brought along what they had asked him to bring, but he brought something else too --- a small mirror – which the mediums would not have approved of. He positioned the mirror in his lap once he was seated at the séance table. This gave him an excellent view of anything that might be occurring under the table.

Lizzie placed Krebs' envelope between two slates and tied them together with twine. But when she briefly turned her back, Krebs quickly examined the slates and found that the medium had slipped a small wedge between them, which opened a slight gap. Moments later, Lizzie turned back and Krebs, with help from his mirror, saw her pick up the slates and let his envelope drop down into her lap. As Lizzie tried to distract Krebs by making guesses about his dead friend's name, he saw her bend down and place the letter onto a small, dark colored tray that was attached to a long handle. The tray was then drawn backward, under the medium's chair, and then beneath the door located behind Lizzie. Krebs later surmised that May was on the other side of the door, unsealing the envelope and reading the letter. About 10 minutes later, Krebs saw the tray slide back into the room from under the door. Under the pretense of shifting positions in her chair, Lizzie bent down, snagged a piece of paper, placed it on her lap, and then quickly read it. She soon began reciting names that she was suddenly receiving from the spirit world. Obviously, all of it was information from Krebs' letter, which had been written down by May.

After several more minutes, he spied movement in his mirror and saw his envelope being secretly slipped back into the room. The medium continued trying to distract Krebs with her trance recitations as she smoothly snapped up the envelope and slipped it into the space that she had created between the two slates. She removed the small wedge as she did so. Then, with a dramatic flourish, she allowed Krebs to untie the slates, open his re-sealed letter, and read the spirit messages on the paper --- which had been written by May Bangs, who was very much among the living.

Krebs concluded his SPR article: "After the whole affair was over, I arose and thanked Miss Bangs for the most interesting exhibition she had given me, whereupon she kindly offered still more, namely, to take me into her sister's house and show me the 'spirit portraits' there."

Unfortunately, the investigator did not accept Lizzie Bangs' offer, which caused the spirit paintings to remain a mystery for a few more years.

The "spirit paintings" brought the Bangs sisters more fame --- and more income --- than any of their earlier specialties, like slate writing. Spirit photographs had been popular for many years already and many mediums made a good living selling these usually quite dubious prints. As the Bangs sister soon discovered, though, they could make a fortune by giving the sitter a truly large and magnificent display of artwork that he could display in his home as a treasured keepsake of his "otherworldly" experience.

The sisters told their customers that the spirits, using some sort of mysterious process they called "precipitation," created the paintings.

Despite the notoriety of the Bangs sisters' paintings, they were not the first to allegedly put spectral artists to work. In the 1870s, a Scottish medium named David Duguid made spirit paintings appear at his séances. However, after a long career of nearly 2,000 séances, Duguid was caught perpetrating fraud in Manchester, England. His spirit oil paintings appeared on little cards that sitters brought with them to the séance. In 1905, he was caught bringing ready-made paintings to the séance room, which he attempted to exchange for the blank cards the audience had provided. When he was searched, the original cards were found hidden in his trousers.

Around 1888, another medium --- who was frequently jailed for fraud --- known as Ann O'Delia Dis Debar (among other pseudonyms and spellings) made headlines when she was tried and imprisoned for swindling wealthy attorney Luther Marsh. Ann sold Marsh dozens of paintings that had been supposedly created by the spirits of prominent artists, including Rembrandt. Her methods were nothing like those of the Bangs' gradual appearances, though. In one account, she and an accomplice switched a blank canvas for a painting as she led her sitter out of the room. Another visitor said that he witnessed the switch by accident while looking in a mirror in the séance room.

The Bangs sisters began producing their spirit paintings as early as 1894. At that time, however, they were not yet using their astounding, rear-lighting technique. Instead, they sealed the empty canvas in a box and when it was opened a few days later, a painting had appeared on the canvas. In the sitter's absence, of course, the mediums just opened the box, switched the canvases, and closed the box back up again.

Around 1898, another pair of mediums, known as the Campbell brothers --- actually not brothers but friends, Allan Campbell and Charles Shourds --- made paintings that were created in a style close to the backlighting method later used by Lizzie and May. The Campbells stood a large canvas on a table in front of a window in a dimly lighted room, while the medium and sitter waited at a nearby table. A silken curtain was drawn in front of the canvas and was parted periodically to allow glimpses of the gradual materialization of the painting. This presentation sounds so remarkably close to what was done by the Bangs sisters that it seems likely that the sisters learned of the medium's method and adapted it for their own séances.

Whatever the origin of their spirit paintings technique, the canvasses helped to increase both their business and their notoriety. The paintings began to sell to their customers for anywhere between $15 and $150. One of their more prominent customers was Reverend Dr. Isaac K. Funk, of the dictionary publisher, Funk & Wagnall. Dr. Funk reportedly paid $1,500 to the sisters for several paintings. His experience was described for the *Tribune*: "There he sat before a bare canvas in a darkened room...On one side was Mary Bangs and on the other, Elizabeth. Softly they communed with the spirits of 'departed artists' until one consented to paint the picture, through the mediums, for the wealthy publisher. Slowly, a beautifully tinted portrait of a deceased relative of the minister was thrown upon the canvas."

A group called the Chicago Spiritualist League complained that the sisters were harming the reputation of believers who followed Spiritualism as a religion. At one meeting, newspapers reported that the leader was asked whether the Bangs' spirit paintings were frauds. He replied: "Most emphatically, yes. There is no such thing as a 'spirit painting.' These paintings are the work of human hands. Do you suppose a spirit is going to return to this earth to paint pictures for the pecuniary gain of some medium?"

Despite frequent complaints and a general unhappiness about the work of the Bangs sisters, they managed to escape any serious brushes with the law. In a newspaper interview, the Illinois States Attorney said that the sisters could be prosecuted for fraud, but they never were. There was only one minor arrest in 1908 when May was charged with violating the city's fortune-telling law. She was released after paying a $25 fine.

The success of the Bangs sisters provoked many explanations as to how the paintings were created --- aside from being the actual work of ghosts. The suggestions were always based on speculation, though, since it seemed no investigator was willing to pay the hefty fee to actually witness the painting process in person.

One local printer proposed that the blank canvas was switched under one of the sister's skirts for a prepared painting. It was then wrapped in several layers of tissue that could be progressively removed to make the portrait seem to gradually appear.

Another theory stated that the paintings were actually enlargements of the sitter's photograph that had been airbrushed over by an artist. The sitter had to bring along a photograph of the relative they wished to have painted, this theory proposed. The photo was smuggled out of the room and the séance was continued the next day, giving the sisters time to take the photograph to the artist so a larger version on canvas could be prepared. As a result, the portraits invariably mirrored whatever image the sitter brought along. If for some reason the sitter had no photograph, the mediums used a stock portrait that matched the basic age and gender of the loved one. Any inaccuracies were dismissed with the excuse that the image showed how the relative now looked in the spirit world. While this was certainly plausible, this theory did not explain how the portraits gradually appeared almost before the eyes of the surprised clients.

A Kansas City minister named A.T. Osborn publicly announced that an explanation for the Bangs' portraits had come to him in a dream. He claimed: "They made a magic-lantern slide. The portrait was thrown on a blank canvas by means of a stereopticon. A dissolving-view device caused the picture to fade from the blank. The painted enlargement was slipped on the trick table and a cover whisked off the moment the magic lantern view vanished." The Bangs sisters, of course, knew the method was wrong and they promptly telegraphed the minister and offered him $1,000 if he could correctly demonstrate the secret of the paintings. When Osborn accepted, they sent another telegram demanding that the minister wager $1,000 in return. He balked at the demand, saying: "Whoever heard of a minister with $1,000?"

The Bangs sisters continued to offer their séances and spirit paintings to wealthy patrons and customers. Occasionally, they even took their show on the road, visiting Spiritualist camps like Lily Dale, New York, where they materialized a sample portrait on stage to promote private sittings after their show. The controlled conditions of their Chicago home, however, proved to be elusive onstage. In a 1910 demonstration in Kansas City, newspapers reported: "Something was the matter with the lights in the building, which prevented this part of the performance." At another program, the lamp used to illuminate the canvases set fire to the sisters' equipment.

The mediums, mercifully, took less time onstage to make paintings appear than they did at home, where the process could take at least an hour. During a 1909 appearance at Camp Chesterfield, they required only eight minutes to materialize one of their portraits.

The continued popularity of the Bangs sisters' spirit paintings perplexed psychical investigators and magicians alike. Newspapers and magazines offered rewards to readers who could duplicate their methods and, while many theories surfaced, none were accurate.

David P. Abbott pondered the secret of the paintings in correspondence with *Open Court* magazine readers and the letters were later collected in his book, *Behind the Scenes with the Mediums*. To explain the paintings, Abbott knew that he needed to solve several major puzzles. How did the mediums obtain a photograph of the sitter's loved one? (Abbott had apparently not seen the article written by Krebs for the SPR, which explained how the Bangs managed to get a photo, or in that case an envelope, out of the séance room). How did they make the image gradually appear on the canvas? How was the blank canvas switched for the finished portrait? And finally, how did all of this occur in the simple setting of a small room on the second floor of a house in Chicago?

In his first attempts to resolve these questions, Abbott proposed a variety of improbable and complicated methods – none of which explained the Bangs' simple procedure. He suggested everything from hidden assistants snapping secret photographs with telescopic lenses, concealed slide projectors, and mechanical switching tables. He discussed the problem with his publisher, Paul Carus, as well as many other friends and colleagues. He also exchanged letters with Dr. Isaac Funk, who had paid dearly for several Bangs portraits. In April 1907, Funk offered to pay for a Bangs sisters séance if Abbott could make the trip to Chicago. Dr. Funk had apparently started to have some misgivings about the legitimacy of the mediums and he wished for someone to investigate their methods, even though he did not want his name to be associated with the investigation. Unfortunately, Abbott was forced to turn down Funk's offer. The time and expense of the trip, as well as the editing on his book and operation of his business, prevented him from making the trip. However, he did urge Dr. Funk to take a magician with him on his next trip.

Dr. Funk eventually sent Abbott's friend, Hereward Carrington, to visit the Bangs sisters. Carrington, a prolific writer, magician, and psychical investigator, had a long history of detecting fraudulent mediums. However, when he arrived at their Chicago home, the sisters refused to demonstrate their paintings for Carrington. They knew his reputation and likely feared exposure. The investigation was back at square one.

Meanwhile, a man named Phillip H. Meyers, who invented the original "Talking Teakettle" and made props for Spiritualists, announced in the *Chicago Tribune* that he had the secret of the Bangs sisters' paintings --- but would only reveal it for a price. In 1908, through an intermediary, Abbott contacted Meyers and had his friend Ralph W. Read try to negotiate a price. Meyers' price turned out to be too high for the two men but he did sell them what he said was the secret of the Bangs' slate writing. To Abbott's disappointment, it was just a common technique that Abbott already knew and not even the same one that Krebs had discovered several years before.

At that point, Abbott decided to save himself any future monetary losses and instead, experiment on his own. This frugal move soon led Abbott to his long sought after secret.

On February 18, 1909, Abbott excitedly wrote to Paul Carus: "I really believe I have solved this secret by reason alone." His joy was premature. His incorrect solution seemed to have been a mechanism that would wind up layers of silk covering the painting, gradually allowing more and more light to penetrate the canvases, as if the painting was gradually developing. But this mistake did lead Abbott to the correct answer a short time later.

On February 22, he wrote to Carus:

I built a quarter-sized model of a screen. I designed one that would roll up or unreel the silk rapidly or slowly. It was but 1/8-inch thick. I made three frames and tacked canvas on them. One was a picture, size 9 x 14 inches. I placed a table and the canvases in position, lowered the blinds, and pinned on the side blinds as per directions.

Now, all of this brought about an unexpected result. First, I arrived at the conclusion that no screen is used in actual practice; and second, I made the discovery of a new principle, which surely is the correct one. It is so absurdly simple that at first sight, one would give it little credence, but after two hours of actual experiment, I cannot help but believe it is the right thing.

Simplicity is really in its favor. Mediums seldom use much paraphernalia, as they must always be prepared to "make a quick getaway." So, whatever is used, we must expect it to be something simple. In fact, the simple things have always produced the greatest effects.

Now, what I discovered is this: If two canvases be faced together and in position, and if there be upon the rear canvas a portrait in transparent colors (pastel, crayon, airbrush work, etc.), this — to be plainly visible — must be in actual contact with the surface of the front canvas. At a distance of 1/8-inch, the outlines begin to be indefinite — not sharp; at a quarter of inch, much more so, while at a half-inch the image is very confused in appearance and looks like a view from a lantern out of focus, a cloud of color, etc. At a distance of one inch, the image appears to be some confused shadows, and at two inches' distance, all trace of the portrait has disappeared.

Now it is only necessary for the rear canvas to be slowly moved toward (or from) the front canvas to cause the picture to materialize or to fade out precisely as described. The motion must be slow and uniform, and is very difficult to control by hand....

I can best compare the effect produced to what one witnesses when viewing a lantern slide wholly out of focus, and then see it slowly brought into focus. First, there is not even a shadow; finally, some indistinct shadows appear; these soon seem to be an indistinct cloud consisting of some colors mingled together. These gradually change into the image but with quite indistinct outlines, which become more and more sharp until the picture appears quite plain and sharply defined, yet it shows a slight smoky effect caused by looking at it through a canvas and viewing it by transmitted light.

All of this corresponds exactly with the descriptions I have received of the effect. It would appear just like a lantern image, only it would not be this, and the picture would really be in the window as is claimed.

Carus wanted to publish Abbot's explanation in *Open Court* magazine, but Abbott refused. Before this was done, he wanted to understand the Bang's entire method. Despite discovering simple ways to produce paintings, he continued to look into more complicated ideas that would explain the remaining details of the sisters' technique. He suggested that the blank canvas was initially switched for a painted one using a dumbwaiter-type device that was secreted in the walls of their home, with an assistant below exchanging the paintings. To explain the final alterations --- which the Bangs sisters created through suggestion or by adding changes in the sitter's absence --- Abbott envisioned a complex system of colored patches, controlled by threads, or areas on the canvas that could be developed using chemicals.

Paul Carus became almost as obsessed with finding out the answer to the mystery as Abbott was. In one 1909 letter, the distinguished publisher even went as far as to suggest that Abbot arrange a séance with the sisters and then have accomplices break into the house, ransack the place, and make off with the appliances of the spirit painting act. We'll never know if he was serious about this or not, but luckily, Abbott decided not to heed this piece of questionable advice.

At this point, William S. Marriott entered the scene. By this time, the magician had become quite well known for his Spiritualist exposures but, as some would say, he still had to make a living. When he contacted David Abbott in August 1909 to inquire about the secret of the Bangs sisters' paintings (by this time, word had leaked out that Abbott had solved the mystery), he did not do so solely for the cause of furthering paranormal investigation.

Marriott sent a letter to Omaha, Nebraska, where Abbott was living, and asked him if it was true that he had solved the case. Abbott replied that not only had he duplicated the marvel, but he had also managed to add several touches that would make the feat effective onstage. He innocently described the routine to Marriott in detail, explaining how the diffusion of light from the painting that had been slipped into place would cause a new painting to appear on the blank canvas as it was slowly moved forward.

Marriott was thrilled with the information and he not only built the necessary equipment that he needed but he went on tour, presenting the appearance of the "spirit paintings" as a vaudeville show.

As the fame of Marriott's paintings spread, the magician became acquainted with one of the Bangs sisters' most devoted clients, the decorated British Vice-Admiral W. Usborne Moore. In 1909, Moore had traveled to Chicago, had visited the mediums, and purchased several portraits from them. Moore was a true believer and he discounted any reasonable explanations for the Bangs' phenomena. Although Marriott showed him Abbott's methods for materializing the paintings, Moore continued to maintain that the sisters would never rely on such trickery and that the conditions at their home were not suitable for the sort of stage performances that Marriott did.

Moore had recently read Hereward Carrington's exposé of the sisters in the *Annals of Psychical Science* and denounced him in an issue of the Spiritualist magazine, *The Light* in 1911. Carrington (with whom Abbott had also shared the secret of the paintings) responded in a later issue of the Spiritualist journal. He wrote: "...Mr. David P. Abbott and myself worked together over this problem; but I was forced to stop at the time, owing to press of other matters, and Mr. Abbott continued his experiments alone. I think I am safe in saying that he has now succeeded in duplicating the Bangs sisters' portraits exactly — and by trickery."

Admiral Moore responded in *The Light*, stating that while the Abbott-Marriott trick was well known in England, and that it surpassed in skill every conjuring trick he had ever witnessed, he still did not believe it was the secret behind the authentic paintings created by the Bangs sisters. Once again, he fell back on the standard reply of many Spiritualists when the phenomena they believed in could be duplicated by natural means ---- just because it could be duplicated did not mean the original phenomena was not genuine.

In 1911, magician P.T. Selbit began a national tour with the "spirit paintings," having purchased a license from William T. Marriott to do so. Abbott came backstage to see him at the Orpheum Theatre in Omaha and showed Selbit copies of his correspondence with Marriott. By then, Selbit had paid more than $10,000 in royalties to Marriott, who still claimed to be the "originator" of the act.

A few years later, Abbott completed a long essay about the spirit portraits for the April 1913 issue of *Open Court* magazine. That same year, Paul Carus released the article as a separate booklet called *The Spirit Portrait Mystery: Its Final Solution*.

This was not the end of the spirit paintings, but it did mark the end of the Bangs sisters' career.

Selbit's tour allowed many magicians the chance to see the painting effect, and because the secret was not terribly difficult to realize, a number of performers began to present their own versions. Vaudeville magician William J. Nixon performed his spirit paintings in his stage shows. An Australian painter named Henry Clive, who later became a renowned illustrator, toured with his version in the 1920s.

Abbott's hard work soon became common knowledge, and Nixon published the technique in a 1916 booklet. Will Goldston exposed the technique in his *Annual of Magic 1915-1916*. The magician Alexander included the effect in his book *The Life and Mysteries of the Celebrated Dr. Q* in 1921, and by the 1930s, Thayer's Magic Company was selling a ready-made version in their catalogs. The technique is rarely seen today though, since, like many magic effects, spirit paintings can be all too easily dismissed as the result of electronics.

By the time that *Open Court* magazine published Abbott's article, the mediums had largely faded from sight. Census records from 1920 show that May Bangs was still living in Chicago, but no mention can be found of Lizzie. She is believed to have died in 1922 but no records have been found of her death, or of the death of her sister. Whatever became of the two women after the demise of their careers as mediums is unknown.

The undoing of the Bangs sisters came at the hands of David Abbot, and by extension, William S. Marriott and even P.T. Selbit – not scientists or psychical investigators, but magicians. Once "spirit paintings" began appearing on the vaudeville stage, it became impossible for any medium to convince a séance attendee that the paintings came from the hands of the spirits, and not their own.

The exposure of the Bangs sisters' paintings by a group of magicians was just one of many of the debunkings that took place in this period. As science lost interest in chasing mediums, the magicians – usually working in their own self-interest – took up the cause. Magicians like Marriott were followed by some of the great names in American magic, who all offered the exposure of Spiritualistic frauds in their stage shows. Men like Harry Kellar, Howard Thurston, and Joseph Dunninger – the "Kings of American Magic" – all performed what were often referred to as "spook shows" during their performances.

Vaudeville shows during the first two decades of the twentieth century often devoted at least one portion of the show to a magician who duplicated the effects that could be found in the séance rooms of the era. After the tables tipped, the ghosts flew, and the magician escaped from what seemed to be an impossible binding of ropes, he would then explain how the tricks took place so that the audience would understand how fraudulent mediums preyed on the public. These crusading magicians were so dedicated to Spiritualism's destruction that they turned the magic world on its ear. Never before had a magician revealed how his tricks were accomplished, but now he was doing so in the "interest of the public good." The conjurers were criticized, but the complaints were dismissed. They weren't offering the secrets of *real* magicians; they were the tricks of phony mediums, fooling people and telling them that spirits were real.

Ghosts weren't real, were they?

To the chagrin of many of these stage performers – feeling the same irritation felt by scientists in decades past – the public refused to stop believing in spooks. The magicians and the amateur investigators were doing everything in their power to banish Spiritualism to the shadows where it belonged, but it refused to die – not yet, anyway. In the wake of the Great War, scores of people sought contact with their lost husbands, sons, brothers, and loved ones. Spiritualism should have been long gone, but tragedy had brought it back to thrive for a few more years. New technology and inventions should have made people lose interest in talking with the dead. Why speak to ghosts when you can turn on the radio and listen to music, entertainment, and news? Science had turned its back on Spiritualism, preferring to test for ESP than to investigate mediums who communed with the dead. The stage magicians were fervently proving to their audiences that mediums were simply clever conjurers and that nothing they saw in the séance room was real – so, why wouldn't they listen?

Spiritualism just refused to die. It had been kicked, beaten, trampled, and burned, but it still managed to entangle hundreds of thousands of people every year in the early 1920s. What would it take to finally destroy the movement for good?

As it turned out, it took one man.

He was no ordinary man and, in fact, didn't have a particular hatred for Spiritualism itself. He had always believed in the possibility of communicating with the dead, but when he tried to put that belief into action and contact the spirit of his beloved mother, he found one fraud after another. And he went looking for revenge. He didn't want to just destroy the mediums that he believed were taking advantage of the gullible and heartbroken, he wanted to destroy Spiritualism altogether and, as we will soon see, he would do anything to make that happen.

The story of that man is one of struggle, grief, a destroyed friendship, and the desperate need to humiliate one of the most famous mediums in America. It is also the story of a man that became a hero to millions of people, risked everything to succeed, and literally turned himself into a household name.

That name was Houdini.

9. AMONG THE SPIRITS

HOUDINI, CONAN DOYLE AND THE BATTLE THAT KILLED SPIRITUALISM

If there was any single event that finally put Spiritualism into the grave, it was the public feud that raged between two of the world's most famous men of mystery – Harry Houdini, the celebrated illusionist and escape artist, and Sir Arthur Conan Doyle, author and creator of Sherlock Holmes, history's greatest fictional detective. The two men were among the world's greatest celebrities in the early twentieth century. Both were acclaimed in their individual fields, had accomplished much both professionally and personally, and had – as it turned out – vastly different opinions on the reality of Spiritualism.

While the two men would eventually become bitter toward one another, their antagonisms never dissolved into hatred. They were friends and were men to whom friendship meant everything. They were always an unusual pair, even when it came to their physical appearances. Doyle was a large man, tall, robust, with a thick mustache. He liked and trusted people and was outgoing and gregarious by nature. Houdini was small, wiry, physically strong with intense eyes and dark, wavy hair. He was a tireless performer, always in the spotlight, excitable and filled with energy. They first met in London in 1920, when Houdini was on tour. The two men were both filled with opinions and unwilling to compromise their beliefs, and yet, an unlikely friendship was born and grew into a deep affection.

The affection died when they finally collided over Spiritualism, but the friendship remained. Houdini emerged from the melee as the first important psychical debunker in American history, and Doyle remained one of Spiritualism's greatest defenders. Their battle intensified, finally reaching its peak during the affair of Mina "Margery" Crandon, the most famous medium of the 1920s. The words exchanged, verbally and in print, between the two men could never be taken back. Their relationship was destroyed and Spiritualism itself became collateral damage.

Harry Houdini

Harry Houdini was born in Budapest, Hungary, on March 24, 1874, but grew up as Erich Weiss in the small Wisconsin town of Appleton, where his father served as a rabbi. Legend has it that young Erich was apprenticed to a locksmith, where he learned to assemble and take apart locks with his eyes closed. If this part of his life story is true, it was a skill that served him well later in life. What we know for certain is that Erich gained two lifelong preoccupations as a boy: a love of magic and a devotion to his mother. Erich left home at 12 and moved to New York, where he got a job in a necktie factory. Soon, though, he was performing as a magician in the beer halls and theaters. He gave himself the name "Houdini," after the famed nineteenth century illusionist, Robert Houdin. He traveled and performed with one of his most applauded illusions being one he called "Metamorphosis." This involved an assistant being placed into a locked box, who then switched places with the magicians within seconds after a curtain was lowered. Houdini's brother, Theo, could make the switch very quickly, but Houdini soon met someone who was faster.

Houdini met Wilhelmina Beatrice Rahner while he was performing at Coney Island. He was 20 when he impulsively married the tiny brunette singer, who weighed only 94 pounds. From then on, Bess, as he called her, became his stage partner and constant companion. Bess's widowed Catholic mother was furious about the marriage, but Harry's mother, Cecilia, welcomed the newlyweds into her home.

Appearing in vaudeville theaters across the country, Houdini's career took off when he began devising clever – and dangerous – escape acts. They earned him wide publicity, for it seemed that no restraints could hold him. He freed himself from shackles, ropes, jail cells, chained boxes, and more. He constantly punished his body, pushing himself to his physical limits, especially in the famed Chinese Water Torture tank, and when he dangled from skyscrapers and bridges, while in a straitjacket, as the crowds below watched him twist and turn himself free. He became famous all over the world. The newspapers and silent films of the era loved him, and Houdini embraced the attention. He toured tirelessly and his reputation grew until he was the most famous escape artist and illusionist in the history of the world.

The event that most affected Houdini's life was the death of his mother in 1913. Houdini would say later that her death had been "a shock from which I do not think recovery is possible." He was touring in Europe when she died. One morning after a particularly rousing performance the night before, Harry was being interviewed by a group of newspapermen when a telegram arrived for him. Houdini ripped open the envelope and discovered that his beloved mother had died. He fell unconscious to the floor. A physician was called in and examined the stricken magician. He prescribed immediate hospitalization, but when Houdini objected, he insisted on a long period of rest. Houdini canceled the rest of his European bookings and returned to New York.

He was desperate to see his mother one last time before she was buried, so he wired Theo and asked him to delay the funeral until he could get there. He booked immediate passage on a ship, and when he arrived in New York, he went straight to his mother's home. He passed the day by her side. At some point, late in the night, he stopped the grandfather clock that Cecilia always wound while he was away. Houdini later said that he felt that his life had stopped, too.

After the funeral, Harry visited the cemetery daily. Some times in the dark hours of the night, Bess would hear him call his mother's name. During the day, he read and re-read the letters that Cecilia had written to him over the years. Later, he had them translated into English so that he could read them more effortlessly. It was the only way that he had to keep a little part of her alive.

Cecilia's death was the greatest blow that Harry ever suffered. With the trauma of her death, and the void it left in his life, Houdini was so grief-stricken that he was almost inconsolable. Whenever he was in New York, he spent hours at her gravesite. He was observed many times lying face down on her grave, holding long conversations with her. He soon became fixated by a search for a way to communicate with her.

And like so many others did when faced with a death they could not endure, Houdini turned to Spiritualism.

For years, he earnestly searched for a genuine medium to contact his mother, but became increasingly frustrated after repeated attempts to receive an accurate message. He found frauds everywhere – mediums trying to pass off cheap magic tricks as the work of the spirits. He knew he could duplicate their methods on stage and it was not long before his efforts to reach his mother became secondary to his need to expose the frauds. He quickly became very bitter and willing to believe that all the mediums were fakes. He began investigating their methods and claims and later became a self-appointed crusader against them.

While touring in England, Houdini visited more than 100 mediums with devastating results. He was appalled by the cold-hearted nature of professional mediums who took advantage of grief-stricken mothers and widows who flocked to séances in the hope that they might talk with their lost sons and husbands. He attended as many as two séances each day. He always maintained to his critics that he had an open mind – he believed in the possibility of communicating with the dead, he said – but found no evidence to suggest that Spiritualism was anything other than self-deception or purposeful trickery. Houdini wrote, "The more I investigate, the less I can make myself believe."

It was while Houdini was in England in 1920 that he met Sir Arthur Conan Doyle, one of the world's most beloved writers and, by that time, one of Spiritualism's greatest supporters.

Conan Doyle was born in Edinburgh, Scotland, on May 22, 1859, to an Irish Catholic family. He received a Jesuit education and graduated from Edinburgh University with a medical degree. He was eager to start a medical practice after graduation and had also developed a love for writing. He hoped to supplement his practice by selling short stories

Sir Arthur Conan Doyle

to the magazines of the day, but while in school, he recognized the importance of working first and writing later. He wrote and sold a short story or two and then, as a third-year student, he signed on as a ship's surgeon for a whaler that was making a seven-month voyage to the Arctic. Conan Doyle got along well with the ship's crew. He was by now a massive and strong young man, an all-around sportsman, and a man of incredible strength. His boxing skills also served him well and he won a bout with the ship's steward on the first night out of port. The trip to the Arctic so fulfilled his taste for action and adventure that he signed on to another ship the following year. This time, he was a ship's surgeon on a voyage taking cargo and crew down the west coast of Africa. This adventure was far less enjoyable and he became extremely ill, likely with malaria. When he returned home, he opened a medical practice in the small village of Southsea.

Bored by the long gaps between patients, he returned to writing. The first of his Sherlock Holmes stories, *A Study in Scarlet*, was published in 1887, and Doyle modeled the detective after Dr. Joseph Bell, a respected Scottish surgeon and one of his favorite professors at university. He had always been intrigued by Bell's use of deductive reasoning to diagnose patients. Sherlock Holmes used that same reasoning to solve complex crimes, eliminating the impossible until whatever remained was the answer. He was meticulous in his investigations, displayed keen powers of observation, and often bewildered his devoted companion, an everyman named Dr. John Watson. The stories became enormously popular and Holmes and Watson soon overshadowed their creator.

Conan Doyle always considered Holmes to be his secondary work, inferior to the historical fiction that he wrote, but millions of readers disagreed. There was such an outpouring of grief and anger after Conan Doyle killed off Holmes that he was forced to bring him back to life for a novel, *The Hound of the Baskervilles*, and dozens of additional stories.

During Conan Doyle's years of success, he married twice, buried one wife after her death from tuberculosis, traveled to South Africa during the Boer War, introduced skis to Switzerland, became an early automobile enthusiast, was the first to suggest life jackets for soldiers on troop ships, served as a newspaper correspondent during World War I, and continued writing short stories and novels. He enjoyed wealth and great fame, so what could have made him give all of that up to devote his life to Spiritualism?

Conan Doyle's interest in Spiritualism began when he was still an almost penniless young doctor living in Southsea. It was during a time when science was just starting to question the idea that another world might exist beyond our own and Doyle became caught up on the study, as well as in the burgeoning Spiritualist movement. He avidly followed the research that was being done by Sir William Crookes and Alfred Russel

Wallace and even attended several séances. He kept detailed notes of what occurred there. Early in his research, he began to consider the idea that a great amount of the phenomena that he witnessed was genuine and that the knocks, raps, horn-blowing and messages from the dead were worthy of at least a cautious optimism.

Eventually, he was no longer wary of the movement – he jumped in with both feet. There has been much debate as to what finally immersed Conan Doyle completely into the Spiritualist movement. Most believe that it was because of the grief that he suffered in the wake of the Great War. First, his wife's brother and Doyle's friend, Malcolm Leckie, had been killed, along with two nephews and several other friends and relatives. And then Kingsley, the only son of his first marriage, and his beloved brother Innes, both died within a few weeks of one another. Kingsley had been badly wounded on the Somme and had died of pneumonia in October 1918. Not long after, Innes, now a Brigadier General, also came down with pneumonia and died. Conan Doyle said and wrote very little of these deaths, but they were devastating to him and were likely the greatest grief he had ever suffered.

Soon after Kingsley's death, he was convinced that he heard the voice of his son during a séance with a Welsh medium. On the other hand, two years later, he would also be convinced that he embraced the materialized spirit of his mother with the help of two American mediums, William and Eva Thompson. Within days, these mediums were exposed as frauds and were arrested at another séance by police officers that found wigs, costumes, and fluorescent makeup among their belongings. In spite of this, Conan Doyle was not swayed from his newfound beliefs.

Before that incident, a short time after the death of Malcolm Leckie, a sick friend of Lady Jean Doyle came to stay at the Conan Doyle home. Her name was Lily Lauder-Symonds and she had a reputation for being a gifted medium. While she was there, she offered to conduct a séance for the family and delivered a message from Lady Jean's brother, Malcolm, with whom Conan Doyle had shared a close friendship. Years before, the two men had shared a private joke about a guinea coin that Leckie had given to Conan Doyle as his first "fee" when he became an Army doctor. Doyle had cherished the small token and wore it on his watch chain. The message that Conan Doyle was given by Lauder-Symonds concerned the guinea, an item that most people, including the medium, knew nothing about. This was likely the incident that finally convinced Sir Arthur of the legitimacy of Spiritualism. Shortly after, he embraced the movement, although he did not go public with his beliefs right away due to his involvement with British war efforts.

Soon after the war's end, he announced his conversion to the public in the Spiritualist magazine, *The Light*. While Spiritualists around the world applauded his valiant efforts, his critics were instantly unkind. None of them could understand how the creator of the logical detective, Sherlock Holmes, could be so gullible about the so-called "wonders" of Spiritualism. But Conan Doyle's convictions came from his supreme self-confidence, and whether the public shared his beliefs of not, he never doubted that he had found the true path. Conan Doyle plunged into Spiritualism with the considerable vigor that he showed to everything else. No matter what was thrown at him, he could not be shaken in his beliefs. He was firmly convinced that life continued after death and that contact with the spirit world was entirely possible.

Doyle began lecturing for the Spiritualist cause in October 1917, appearing in Bradford and London. In the years that followed, he visited almost every town in England, finding what he described as critical, but attentive audiences. It's possible -- and more than likely -- that most people came to hear the creator of Sherlock Holmes rather than because of their interest in the spirit world, but if this was the case, he didn't care. After storming through London, Doyle and his family also visited Australia and the United States, all on behalf of Spiritualism. He lectured all over Europe and in South Africa, Kenya, and Rhodesia. In 1926, he published a spiritual adventure story called "The Land of the Mist," which featured the popular Professor Challenger character from his earlier book, *The Lost World*. He also wrote a large, two-volume set called *The History of Spiritualism* and throughout the 1920s, spent a £250,000 advancing the Spiritualist cause.

During this same time period, Lady Jean began to develop the skills of a medium, which was in sharp contrast to her earlier feelings about the movement. She had disapproved of her husband's interest in the occult and disliked his concerns with Spiritualism, which she called "uncanny and dangerous." However, her brother Malcolm's death during the war changed her feelings, and in 1921, she was suddenly given what her husband called the "gift of inspired writing." She soon began to receive messages from the other side and the loved ones they had lost soon began to make regular appearances at the Doyle's home circle.

In his books, writings and personal appearances, Doyle recounted dozens of bizarre and seemingly unexplained occurrences, but whether they were the product of the supernatural or his own willingness to believe, is unknown. He often claimed to touch phantom hands, to see objects move about, to witness the wondrous works of talented mediums, and to possess notebooks filled with information that had been given to his wife from spirits --- information that Doyle believed was "utterly beyond her ken." He also came face to face with at least one ghost and investigated a haunted house in Dorset. He chronicled this adventure in his book *On the Edge of the Unknown*, which makes compelling reading whether you believe in the mysteries of Spiritualism or not. Strangely, the house burned down after Doyle's investigation and a child's body was found buried in the garden. After the body was found, the haunting ceased and Doyle came to believe that the child's spirit may have been responsible for it since nothing out of the ordinary ever occurred at the site after the blaze.

Conan Doyle also collected a huge number of spirit photographs, most of which he believed to be genuine, including one of a ghostly woman that was taken at a haunted inn in Norwich. In 1922, he penned a book on the subject called *The Case for Spirit Photography*. Unfortunately, the vast majority of the photos that Conan Doyle championed appear blatantly fake today, the obvious results of fraud and double exposure.

Conan Doyle and Houdini first met in 1920, during the magician's tour of England. The two of them became good friends, despite their opposing views on the supernatural. Houdini was delighted to learn that there was at least one intelligent person who believed in Spiritualism and found that man in his friend Conan Doyle. The author was convinced of the value of the movement to the world and had given up most of his

Haunted Friendship: Sir Arthur Conan Doyle and Harry Houdini

lucrative writing career to lecture about Spiritualism. He also found that Houdini's knowledge of the spirit world was as vast as his own, although their attitudes differed.

Doyle agreed with some of Houdini's methods in exposing fraudulent mediums because he believed that their existence damaged the legitimacy of the movement. Lacking his new friend's magical training, though, he was less able to see how fraud was accomplished. Houdini worked to try and show the secrets practiced by the fraudulent mediums to Doyle, but the author merely insisted that the mediums he knew were good and honest people who would never try and trick or cheat their followers. Besides that, Doyle stated, just because the feats of the spirits could be duplicated did not mean that they were not real. Just because Houdini could prove that fraud was possible was not enough to convince Doyle that it actually occurred.

Conan Doyle, always the optimist, felt that with time and patience, Houdini would see the light and come around to share his views on the spirit world. There is a long-held assumption that Houdini did not believe in the afterlife, or the ability to communicate with the dead. Skeptics are proud to claim him as one of their own and boast that he believed every medium was a fraud. That simply is not true. Houdini made it clear in his 1924 book, *A Magician Among the Spirits*, that he started his quest for spirit contact because he believed it to be possible. It was only after repeated disappointment with inept or fraudulent mediums that he turned so ferociously against them. If he had heard what he believed was a genuine message from his late mother, his attitude toward the question of spirit communication might have been entirely different. Instead, the last years of his life were spent in a wild public rant against all mediums that brought his friendship with Conan Doyle to a crashing end.

SEANCE ON AN ATLANTIC CITY AFTERNOON

The beginning of the end was in June 1922.

Conan Doyle and his family came to America for a speaking tour about Spiritualism, which got off to a rocky start after a press conference in New York that was harshly criticized in the *New York Times*. He didn't let this bother him, though. He caught up with old friends and then gave his first lecture at Carnegie Hall in the middle of a heat wave that turned the theater into an oven. The crowd listened attentively as he spoke for more than an hour about the mysteries of the spirit world.

Conan Doyle offered seven lectures in New York, all of which were well received. He spoke of his own experiences with mediums and at séances and showed lantern slides of spirit photographs, mediums exuding ectoplasm, and more. Some of the happenings at the lectures were on the unsettling side, however. Women fainted when the strange, spectral faces glowed on the screen, accompanied by the eerie strains of music from a Victrola. Others called out, begging for word from their dead loved ones. Every new slide brought a chorus of screams, moans, and fainting spells. Disturbed people wandered up and down the aisles, some sobbing uncontrollably. When each lecture ended, Doyle's dressing room was packed with well-wishers.

It must have made for a weird and chilling series of talks -- and things were going to get worse. Newspaper reports of Doyle's New York lectures caused an extraordinary rush of suicides by people who wanted to see the "next world" immediately. Several of them made front page news. One woman, Maude Fancher, heard Doyle giving a speech on the radio and then murdered her son and consumed the contents of a bottle of Lysol cleaner. Before she swallowed the poison, which took a week to kill her, she wrote a letter to Conan Doyle and told him that Spiritualism inspired her to the act. Then, she left a detailed letter for her husband explaining that she wanted her baby nestled in her arms when she was placed in the tomb.

A Brooklyn potter, Frank Alexi, stabbed his wife in the head with an ice pick, claiming that he had seen an evil spirit sitting there that had followed him home from Carnegie Hall. A young man killed himself and his roommate because, he explained, "there were no gas bills in the afterlife."

Conan Doyle, when confronted with these and several other peculiar incidents, stated without hesitation that they were the result of "a misunderstanding of what Spiritualism is meant to be."

This bit of bad press must have encouraged Doyle to get away from the thick of things and meet with several mediums of whom he had heard about. He attended a few séances, including one in which a "spirit" continually referred to him as "Sir Sherlock Holmes." At another, an apparition appeared from a spirit cabinet with the face of Doyle's late mother. When he grasped the spirit to embrace her, he was stunned to find the muscular shoulders of a man beneath the "spirit robes." Rather than expose the medium on the spot, Doyle waited to do it privately. Before he could do so, though, the medium was caught in a hoax. When Doyle was accused of aiding the medium in his fraud, he related the story of the séance --- but no one would believe him and he was savaged in the press.

With all of this going on, a meeting with his friend Houdini must have seemed a welcome respite. The two dined together and then returned to the magician's New York apartment. There, he tried to explain to Doyle how the glove-like paraffin casts, supposedly of "spirit hands," were created. A rubber glove would be filled with air, the wrist packed with wood, and then it would be dipped in paraffin wax. If fingerprints were needed, the first step would be to get a mold of a hand in dental wax or plaster; an impression would be made of the palm side of the hand, then of the back, and the two sides would be fitted together. Next, the entire hand would be duplicated in rubber and the fingerprints preserved. Once it was dipped in the paraffin, the process was complete. Doyle refused to accept this as the only explanation for the otherworldly hands that appeared at séances -- maintaining that just because it could be duplicated by ordinary means did not mean that it was not created by extraordinary means in the first place.

Needing a break from his hectic, and sometimes controversial, schedule in New York, Doyle took his family to Atlantic City. He sent a message to Houdini and suggested that he come down for a short vacation. Houdini enthusiastically accepted, and soon Doyle was floating in the hotel swimming pool and admiring the length of time that the magician could remain under water, holding his breath. While Lady Jean and the children played with a beach ball, Doyle and Houdini sat in deck chairs, looking out over the ocean and discussing aspects of Spiritualism. As Conan Doyle described the work done by a Mrs. Deane in London, Houdini maintained a stoic silence, knowing that Mrs. Deane had been caught substituting a photographic plate from her purse for one exposed at a séance. And the discussion went on.... Houdini offered comments and careful observations, but he had no intention of upsetting his friend and ruining their peaceful and enjoyable holiday.

On Sunday, Bess Houdini joined the happy group. Sir Arthur was excited to see her, as was her husband, who had been enjoying the time spent playing with the Doyle children. He had been entertaining them with small magic tricks and delighted in their laughter. He eagerly spent a few moments alone with Bess, though, and the couple was sitting on the beach one afternoon when a young lifeguard's son came running along to tell them that Lady Jean wanted to give Houdini a private séance in her suite. Houdini, who was impressed with Lady Jean's obvious sincerity and decency, was thrilled. Perhaps he could at last obtain proof of survival after death, and when Conan Doyle later told him that Lady Jean would try and get a message to the magician from his adored mother, he was beside himself.

Houdini went up to the suite with Doyle and Lady Jean greeted him there with great affection. She sat down at a large table, where a pile of paper and a pencil lay ready. Doyle sat next to his wife and Houdini sat on the opposite side of the table. Conan Doyle then offered a solemn prayer and asked his wife if she was ready. Her hand struck the table three times (a Spiritualistic code for "yes") and then she sank into a deep trance.

Houdini wrote later: "I had made up my mind that I would be as religious as it was in my power to be and not at any time did I scoff during the ceremony. I excluded all earthly thoughts and gave my whole soul to the séance. I was willing to believe, even wanted to believe. It was weird to me and with a beating heart I waited, hoping that I might feel once more the presence of my beloved mother..."

Lady Jean began to breathe deeply and her eyes fluttered. Her hand, as though moving on its own, dashed with amazing speed across sheets of paper. Conan Doyle handed them one by one over to the magician. Houdini turned pale and began to tremble. The message began: "Oh my darling, thank God, thank God, at last I'm through. I've tried, oh so often -- now I am happy. Why, of course, I want to talk to my boy -- my own beloved boy -- friends, thank you, with all my heart for this." The message continued with an expression of joy about Mrs. Weiss' new life and the beauty of the next world. She concluded with "I wanted, oh so much -- now I can rest in peace." Doyle then asked Houdini if he wanted to ask his mother a question for "her reply will prove that she is at your side."

Houdini looked extremely upset and could not speak. Conan Doyle suggested a question. "Can my mother read my mind?" Houdini silently nodded his agreement and Lady Jean's hand began to move again. "I always wanted to read my beloved son's mind," the message continued, "there is so much that I want to say to him." The message then went on for several hundred words, mostly expressing joy at communicating with her son and her appreciation of the Doyles.

At the end of the séance, Houdini sank back in his chair, utterly drained and exhausted. Then, unseen by Doyle and Lady Jean, Houdini scribbled with a fragment of pencil a small note on the first sheet of paper. "Message written by Lady Doyle claiming the spirit of my dear Mother had control of her hand --- my sainted mother could not write English and spoke broken English." A moment later, he picked up a sheet of paper and boldly wrote on it a single word "Powell." He looked at Conan Doyle and his eyes issued a challenge to the other man. He had been thinking of his friend Powell, a fellow magician --- if his mother had been reading his mind, wouldn't she have known this?

But Doyle misunderstood the message completely and he stood up from his chair in shock. A good friend of Doyle's, Ellis Powell, editor of the *London Financial News*, had died just three days earlier. He was convinced that Houdini was trying to say that Powell was in the room. Houdini didn't have the heart to disillusion them on the spot but a few days later, he sent Doyle a letter to let him know that he was thinking of his magician friend and that he was not trying to tell him that a spectral presence was in the room.

Houdini left the hotel and returned to New York to wrestle with his conscience. Should he disclose the truth --- that his mother had not come through, that the day of the séance had been her birthday and there was no reference made to it, that he felt no presence in the room, no smell of her favorite perfume --- and that when the message ended, he felt as alone and lost as he had when she died? If he were to reveal this, the Doyles would be hurt and perhaps even ruined. On the other hand, if he kept quiet, he would be allowing the Spiritualists a false victory. Out of decency, he decided to withhold any statements about the séance until after the Doyles left America.

The Doyles never expected the blow that awaited them. They remained friendly with Houdini, dining, and attending the theater with him. He came to the docks to see them off when they departed by sea on June 24. For some reason, Houdini held back on speaking out about the Doyles until December 19, 1922. At that time, he issued a release that stated there was not the slightest evidence that his mother had "come through" Lady Jean. His mother could not read or write and could barely speak English and, in addition to that, Lady Jean had started her automatic writing by scrawling a cross on the top of the paper. His mother had been Jewish and would have never have done this.

Conan Doyle protested Houdini's claims, stating that language and earthly dates meant nothing to the spirits, but Houdini was not convinced. He did not think that the Doyles had deliberately tried to deceive him but had deceived themselves by their own gullibility. As for the Doyles, they weathered Houdini's criticisms, although his statement damaged their once friendly relationship. Doyle tried to remain loyal to the magician and convinced himself that Houdini was too nervous about the encounter with his mother's spirit to admit that it was genuine. They also claimed in some reports that another message had also come through that day --- claiming that Houdini would die soon --- and this was the reason he denied the authenticity of the communication.

For a short time after this, the two men tried to pretend that their friendship had not been ruined but it was too late to salvage it, for the hurt was too deep on both sides. To the Doyles, Houdini was willfully blind and appallingly ungrateful, but to Houdini, the Doyles had made a terrible mockery of the deep feelings that he had for his mother. Both men were too stubborn to be swayed to the other's way of thinking, and while they would meet again, there was no escaping the damage that had been done.

THE *SCIENTIFIC AMERICAN* PRIZE

In 1923, Houdini joined a committee that was put together by *Scientific American* magazine, which offered a reward for any medium that could prove their psychical gifts were genuine. The initial prize for an authentic exhibition was $2,500. There was also a secondary prize for anyone who could produce a genuine spirit photograph. The committee consisted of Dr. William McDougall, professor of psychology at Harvard; Dr. Daniel Fisk Comstock, from the Massachusetts Institute of Technology; Dr. Walter Franklin Prince, research officer for the American Society for Psychical Research; Hereward Carrington, prolific writer on the occult; and Houdini.

The committee had been Houdini's idea. He had been approached by the magazine to write a series of articles on Spiritualism but, because of his vaudeville commitments, could not accept the offer. He suggested instead the formation of an investigative committee on which he would serve for no fee -- if he were granted the right to select or reject its other members. Houdini did not exercise his power of approval to limit committee membership to people he knew would agree with him. The committee would eventually have several members with whom Houdini could not get along. Even the original membership was problematic. Houdini's opinion of Carrington, for example, was that the writer was an opportunist who professed to believe in Spiritualism because it was a good way to sell his books on the occult.

Before Houdini left on a cross-country vaudeville tour, he promised to cancel his bookings whenever he was called for an investigation. In Denver, Colorado, Houdini crossed paths with his estranged friend, Sir Arthur Conan Doyle. During Doyle's previous lecture tour of America, Houdini, with difficulty, had avoided a public controversy with his friend. Now, as newspaper headlines spoke of Sir Arthur's "spirit truths," counter-arguments from Houdini began making the wire services. In Denver, the Doyles and their children were Houdini's guests at the Orpheum Theater. Harry sent a box of candy to their young daughter and a bouquet of violets for Lady Jean. In his dressing room after the show, Houdini and Sir Arthur were again at odds over whether or not spirit photographs could be produced by trickery. The next day, Doyle insisted that a couple called the Zancigs were genuine mediums. Harry knew otherwise. In 1906, the Zancigs had been with him on the road. Julius Zancig was a member of the Society of American Magicians and Houdini once bought an act from him, complete with all the silent and spoken cues. He added it to the collection and sometimes pulled it out when he wanted a convincing "mind-reading" act. The Zancigs were no more psychics, Houdini stated, than he was.

On May 9, 1923, the *Denver Express* newspaper ran a story:

DOYLE IN DENVER DEFIES HOUDINI AND OFFERS TO BRING DEAD BACK AGAIN

Sir Arthur Conan Doyle, here to preach the gospel of Spiritism, is going to back his psychic forces with $5,000 against the skepticism of Harry Houdini, the magician, who recently asserted that all séance manifestations were fakes. The famous writer so asserted on his arrival from Colorado Springs late yesterday when informed Houdini was also in Denver.

"Houdini and I have discussed Spiritism before," said Sir Arthur. "I have invited him to attend a sitting with me, each of us backing our beliefs with $5,000. I have even offered to bring my dead mother before him in physical form and to talk to her. But we have never got together on it."

The Doyles met Harry and Bess that evening in the lobby of the Brown Palace Hotel. Sir Arthur was apologetic, explaining to Harry that the newspaper had put words in his mouth. Houdini was very understanding. He had not seen the article, but he knew that reporters sometimes misquoted the people they interviewed. He was sorry to have to miss Doyle's lecture at the Ogden Theater because of his own performance at the Ogden Theater that night, but Bess was going to accept the Doyles' invitation to attend the talk and she would tell Harry all about it later.

On Doyle's recommendation, Houdini and his assistant, Jim Collins, went to see Alexander Martin, a Denver photographer whose pictures of the living also showed the faces of the dead. Martin posed Houdini in a straight-backed chair with Collins standing behind him. When the plate was developed, the print showed four ghostly faces in the background -- two bearded men, an Indian, and a shrouded woman. The next day, Harry returned for another sitting and this time, he posed alone. Five "spirit extras" appeared on the print -- four bearded men and one who wore a mustache. Three of the "spirits" wore glasses. Houdini almost burst out laughing when he saw that the man with the mustache was the late Theodore Roosevelt.

Houdini may have been amused, but he was not impressed. He believed that Martin was using a double-exposure technique. Before his arrival, he surmised that Martin had snipped the heads from other photographs, put them on a black background, and exposed the plate, masking the area in the center. With this prepared plate, ghostly extras would "materialize" when Martin photographed his subject. Houdini later created his own spirit photographs in New York. In one of them, he clasped his own spirit self in his arms and in another, Abraham Lincoln appeared with him.

Meanwhile, there was no rush of applicants for the *Scientific American* prizes. It was easy for a photographer to produce mysterious photos on his own plates, in his own studio, or for a medium to conjure up phenomena when surrounded by hymn-singing believers. Why would they risk their reputations being tested by observers who were well-versed in psychology, physics, and trickery?

A few mediums did come forward. One of them, George Valiantine, was more daring that his fellow Spiritualists. He had given two séances for *Scientific American* while Houdini was on the road. The first had been unimpressive. During the second, a trumpet had floated in the dark, lifted by a spirit Indian -- according to the medium, at least. The trumpet tapped various sitters, whacked a spectator's head, and then crashed to the floor just as Fred Keating, a young magician friend of Hereward Carrington, tried to grab it.

Houdini attended the third séance, and this time, the investigators brought their own tricks with them. Unknown to the medium, men in an adjoining chamber were following his movements with light signals, a dictaphone, and a stopwatch. Valiantine's chair had been wired. Whenever he left his seat, a light flashed in the control room and a note was made of the time. By comparing the times that Valiantine got out of his chair and the times when phenomena was recorded in the séance room, it was obvious that the medium, not the spirits, had been raising a ruckus in the dark. The *New York Times* quoted Houdini when the medium was exposed.

J. Malcolm Bird, an associate editor of *Scientific American* and the secretary for the investigative committee, was annoyed by the newspaper story. The *Times* reporter should not have written the story until he, Bird, had printed an article in *Scientific American*. He resented being scooped. When the *Times* followed up with an interview with Houdini, Bird was enraged. The medium-trapping system had been devised before Houdini, who was busy with his vaudeville tour, came on the scene. Yet to the public, it appeared that the magician had exposed Valiantine. Bird disliked Houdini immensely. This would be the first time the two men clashed, but would not be the last.

In California, Conan Doyle was upset by another newspaper story. Quotes from Houdini in the *Oakland Tribune* were "full of errors." He had to "utterly contradict" them. Perhaps Sir Arthur had forgotten he had been misquoted in Denver. Harry replied that he had given the Oakland reporter material for a single article, which had been expanded into a series. He couldn't help the fact that his statements had been misconstrued. The friendship between the two men had reached a point that it was almost beyond repair.

Houdini spent more time attacking fraudulent mediums than arranging spectacular escapes during his fall vaudeville tour. In late September, he spoke to a psychology class at the University of Illinois on "The Psychology of Audiences" and "The Negative Side of Spiritualism." The latter topic took up most of the class time. In October, he gave an illustrated lecture on mediums and their methods at Marquette University in Milwaukee.

Meanwhile, medium Nino Pecoraro applied for the *Scientific American* prize money while Houdini was still on the road with his lecture tour. Conan Doyle, during his first American lecture tour, had attended a séance held by Pecoraro and had been tremendously impressed by him. He noted that the medium, while bound with wire, caused a bell to ring, a tambourine to spin in the air, and a toy piano to play. Hereward Carrington, a committee member, had arranged the séance for Doyle. There was reason to think that the committee might give Pecoraro a comparatively sympathetic hearing.

Doubtlessly believing that Pecoraro would have too easy a time of it, *Scientific American* publisher Orson Munn urgently requested Houdini, then playing in Little Rock, Arkansas, to return to New York and attend a test séance. Fellow committeemen planned to tie the Italian medium with a single long rope and Houdini laughed. Even amateur escapologists could free their hands when trussed up in such a manner, he told them. Houdini slashed the rope into short lengths and secured the medium himself. After that, the medium produced no manifestations.

Houdini returned to his theater tour in the Midwest. He spoke at several more colleges, which became rehearsals for a lecture tour that was booked for him around the country. His anti-Spiritualism campaign had been only for his spare time during his Orpheum tour. Now he was free -- at least for 20 one-night shows -- to devote his full energy to counteracting the propaganda that was being spread by people like Sir Arthur Conan Doyle.

Houdini's lectures were a huge success, even though most people who attended the shows came more to see him perform than to hear about his exposures of the Spiritualists. He found that he had to mix entertainment with his message to appeal to the crowds. To say that a medium employed a trick spirit slate was not enough. He had to show how the slate was used. The actual demonstration drove his point home and delighted the audiences at the same time.

The publication of Houdini's book *A Magician Among the Spirits* in 1924 brought violent attacks from believers, cheers from the skeptics, and the inevitable end of his friendship with Sir Arthur. He wrote that he treasured Doyle as a friend. Sir Arthur was a "brilliant man", he had a "great mind" -- except where Spiritualism was concerned. Houdini respected Doyle's beliefs and was convinced that he was sincere, but the eminent author refused to accept the fact that many of the mediums he endorsed were frauds. Houdini listed instance after instance of mediums that Sir Arthur trusted even though others had found them to be frauds. He quoted the written message that Lady Doyle claimed had come from his mother in Atlantic City --- then revealed why it could not have been from her spirit.

Doyle was angered and saddened by the book. He had been fascinated with Houdini the man, but when his friend attempted to destroy his beliefs and held him up to ridicule, any further friendship between them was impossible.

Houdini and Conan Doyle never spoke to one another again – but their battle was not yet over.

THE MEDIUM AND THE MAGICIAN

Houdini was back on tour when he received news that the investigative panel had deadlocked over a medium named Mina Crandon, who used the stage name of "Margery." They stated that they believed Crandon to be genuine and were prepared to give her the $2,500 award. J. Malcolm Bird was a supporter of Crandon and was eager to give her the magazine's endorsement. He allowed word of the panel's favorable findings to reach the press. "Boston Medium Baffles Experts," one headline announced. "Houdini the Magician Stumped," cried another. Houdini, who had not even been present during Crandon's séances, much less stumped by them, was stunned to think the magazine would even consider approving a medium that he had never seen. Publisher Orson Munn called him in for a consultation and he publicly told *Scientific American* that he would forfeit $1,000 of his own money if he failed to expose Margery as a fraud.

When it was discovered that Houdini was now going to be involved in the investigations of Margery, Sir Arthur Conan Doyle, an avid supporter of the medium, was outraged. He called it a "capital error" placing such an enemy of Spiritualism into the investigation. He wrote: "The Commission is, in my opinion, a farce." Mina Crandon, however, seemed to welcome the opportunity to test her mettle against Houdini. The prize money meant nothing to this wealthy woman but the opportunity to win the approval of such a prestigious committee --- at the expense of the mighty Houdini --- proved too great a temptation for her to resist.

Houdini traveled with Orson Munn by train to Boston, and on the way, he reviewed the findings of his colleagues on the investigative panel. To his way of thinking, the investigation had been badly handled from the start. Margery did not perform under the test conditions that had been agreed upon for all mediums. She was allowed to hold her test séances at her home in Boston, which opened things up widely for the possibilities of fraud. Most of the committee members had availed themselves of the Crandons' generous hospitality during the proceedings, staying in their home, eating their food, and enjoying their company. Houdini believed that this had badly compromised their objectivity and later, it was learned that accepting food and a bed from the Crandons were the least of the problems. One investigator had actually borrowed money from Margery's husband, while another hoped to win his backing for a research foundation. Worse yet, the "distinguished" panel was not unaware of Margery's physical attractions. Years later, at least one committee member would tell of his amorous encounters with the celebrated medium. Whether truth or fantasy is unknown, but regardless, he was smitten with the woman.

Mina Crandon created a firestorm of controversy in the early 1920s but in truth, she was a rather unlikely medium.

Mina Stinson had been born in Ontario in 1888, the daughter of a farmer. She moved to Boston when she was 16 so that she could play the piano, coronet, and cello in local bands and orchestras. After working as a secretary, an actress, and an

Mina Stinson, who would become known as the medium "Margery."

ambulance driver, she married a grocer named Earl P. Rand, with whom she had a son. They remained happily married until a medical operation introduced her to Le Roi Goddard Crandon, a prominent surgeon and a former instructor at the Harvard Medical School. She divorced Rand in 1918 and married Crandon a short time later.

Mina had no psychic experiences early in her life and in fact, had no interest in the spirit world at all until her husband became interested in séances in the early 1920s. One evening in May 1923, Dr. Crandon invited several friends over for a "home circle" meeting. The group gathered around a small table and soon had it tilting in response to the sitter's questions. Crandon suggested that they each remove their hands form the table, one at a time, to see which individual was responsible for the paranormal activity. One by one, each of them took their hands away but the table only stopped rocking when the last of the sitters lifted her hands. Dr. Crandon had solved the mystery --- the medium was his own wife.

At first, the idea of being a medium seemed like a lark to Mina. Throughout the summer of 1923, the Crandons held one séance after another at their home. Each time, Mina seemed to exhibit some new ability. It seemed that Dr. Crandon only had to read about some new spirit manifestation before his wife could duplicate it.

Within a month of her first official séance, Dr. Crandon announced a plan to place his wife under hypnosis so that they could try and make contact with the psychic control who would serve as her spirit guide. At first, Mina resisted this idea, claiming that she didn't want to miss any of the "fun" while she was under hypnosis. Eventually, though, she gave in to her husband's wishes and soon, a male voice made itself heard to the Crandon home circle.

The voice belonged to Mina's brother, Walter Stinson, who had been crushed to death in a railroad accident in 1911. From this point on, Walter's spirit was a regular presence in the

Crandon séance room. He proved to have a strong personality, a quick wit, and was given to using rough language. Many visitors to the séance room became convinced of what they heard simply because they could not imagine that such coarse and vulgar language would come from the mouth of the pretty doctor's wife. Many observers noted that Walter's voice did not seem to come from Mina at all. The sound seemed to emanate from another part of the room and would continue even when Mina was in a trance or had a mouth filled with water. The effect seemed so remarkable that one skeptic, searching for a plausible explanation for what he had experienced, wondered if perhaps Mina was able to speak through her ears. The ghostly "Walter," along with his sister, began to find fame all over the world.

But Mina hardly needed Walter's help to become a popular medium – especially among her male sitters. Mina resembled nothing so much as a light-hearted flapper. Even Houdini conceded that she was an exceedingly attractive woman, and one psychic researcher warned his colleagues to "avoid falling in love with the medium." She usually greeted her sitters wearing nothing but a flimsy dressing gown, bedroom slippers, and silk stockings. This attire, leaving almost nothing to the imagination, was intended to rule out the possibility of trickery or concealment, but it also tended to distract male visitors. Mina's slender figure, fashionably bobbed hair, and light blue eyes made her, in the words of one admirer, "too attractive for her own good." To make matters more titillating, it was rumored that it was not uncommon for her to hold sessions in the nude and, according to some, she was especially adept at manifesting ectoplasm from her vagina.

Dr. Crandon believed that his lovely wife was a "remarkable psychic instrument" and her took her abroad to build up a consensus of favorable opinion from European experts. One of these was Sir Arthur Conan Doyle, who declared her to be a "very powerful medium" and said, "the validity of her gifts was beyond all question." J. Malcolm Bird, from *Scientific American*, shared Doyle's opinion and wrote a series of articles extolling her virtues. It was Bird who gave her the name "Margery," in an effort to protect the Crandons privacy. Under this stage name, her fame steadily grew.

By bringing Margery to the attention of *Scientific American*, Conan Doyle had inadvertently started the most controversial portion of her career. With the urging of Bird, the panel had deadlocked about the authenticity of the phenomena that occurred in her presence. None of the more skeptical members of the committee would commit to anything without Houdini's opinion, which was why Orson Munn brought him back into the investigation. Not everyone was happy about this. J. Malcolm Bird who (unbelievably, given his opinions about Margery to start with) had been assigned to observe, organize, and record the investigations with Margery. Bird wanted Houdini disqualified from the panel and for this reason, started the investigations without him.

Houdini quickly traveled to Boston, though, anxious to see the medium for himself.

On July 23, Houdini called at the Crandon house, which was located at No. 10 Lime Street. He wanted to see Margery perform under the same circumstances that his colleagues had experienced. The medium, meanwhile, relished the idea of converting the notorious debunker to her cause. Some observers saw the séance as an acid test --- not just of Margery's authenticity, but of Spiritualism itself. The movement was experiencing its last gasp, as far as the public was concerned, but the arrival of a new medium – proved authentic by a committee of skeptical observers – might be enough to start a revival.

Houdini and Munn booked rooms at the Copley Plaza Hotel, ignoring the offer that the Crandons had made for the two men to join the other members of the committee at their home. They did accept a dinner invitation from the Crandons, however, and found Dr. Crandon to be a gracious host and a fascinating conversationalist. Margery, as they had heard, was a beautiful woman -- attractive, sensuous, and confident.

It was so hot that evening that the men -- Crandon, Houdini, Munn, Bird, and R.W. Conant, who worked in the committeeman Comstock's laboratory -- removed their coats in the upstairs séance room. Bird confessed to Houdini that the room itself had never been thoroughly examined. Harry immediately went to work to remedy this sloppy oversight. There was no door to be locked between the room and the hallway leading to the stairs. He inspected the séance props -- a megaphone, a three-sided cabinet, a phonograph, which usually played Margery's favorite song "Souvenir," and a bell box. The 14-inch-long wooden box contained batteries and a bell. A slight tap on a lever on the top would complete an electrical circuit and the bell would ring.

Margery and the four men sat in chairs forming a circle. She asked them all to link hands with one another. The medium was between Houdini and her husband in the circle. Bird sat outside of the circle, his right hand clasped around the linked hands of Margery and the doctor. Margery's right foot was pressed against her husband's left and her left foot was pressed against Houdini's right. These body contacts were meant to prove that the medium's hands and feet were "under control" when the manifestations began.

Houdini watched and observed as a spirit bell rang, a voice called out to him in the darkness, and a megaphone crashed to the floor at his feet. If these manifestations impressed him, he gave no sign of it. When the lights came back on, Houdini politely thanked his hosts and left. On the drive back to the hotel, he finally spoke to Munn about what he was feeling. "I've got her," he said. "All fraud, every bit of it. One more sitting and I will be ready to expose everything."

Houdini was impressed by what he had seen at the Crandon home and very impressed with the famous Margery --- though not by her supernatural powers, he quickly assured Orson Munn. At his hotel that night, he explained how and why his conclusions about Margery differed from those of some members of the panel. One feat that had puzzled the panel was the ringing of a "spirit bell box." Although sitters on either side of her held Margery's hands, and her feet were in contact with theirs, the bell box rang many times during the séance, a happening that she attributed to Walter.

Usually, the bell box sat on the floor between Margery's legs, but Houdini had insisted that it be placed on the floor at his own feet. Regardless, the bell rang repeatedly anyway. Houdini had a ready answer for this: "I had rolled my right trouser leg up above my knee. All that day, I had word a silk rubber bandage around that leg, just below the knee. By night, the part of the leg below the bandage had become swollen and painfully tender, thus giving me a much keener sense of feeling and making it easier to notice the slightest sliding of Mrs. Crandon's ankle or flexing of her muscles... I could distinctly feel her ankle slowly and spasmodically sliding as it pressed against mine while she gained space to raise her foot off the floor and touch the top of the box." In other words, Margery's foot, and not a spirit, had been responsible for the ringing of the bell.

Another of the evening's mysteries had involved a megaphone that, according to the spectral voice of Walter, had levitated in the air above the sitters' heads. Walter commanded that Houdini tell him where to throw the object and the magician instructed him to throw it in his direction. Moments later, the megaphone crashed to the floor in front of him. Houdini had an explanation for this, too. Earlier in the evening, when one of Margery's hands was free, she had snatched up the megaphone and had placed it on her head like a dunce cap. In the total darkness of the séance room, no one could have seen her do this. She later made the megaphone fly across the room by simply snapping her head forward. Houdini said: "This is the slickest ruse that I have ever seen."

The next day, Houdini and Munn returned to Lime Street. In the séance room, alone with the publisher, he demonstrated that his explanations were practical.

After his first séance, Houdini refused to speak publicly about Margery. He did not reveal his opinions over what had occurred that night. Instead, he asked that more stringent tests be performed. It was rumored that Margery had somehow outwitted Houdini -- and rumors also flew that perhaps her powers were genuine after all. Houdini ignored the rumors. He was convinced that he knew the truth about the medium.

That night, the tests were resumed in Dr. Comstock's apartment at the Charlesgate Hotel. His secretary, Gladys Wood, searched Margery before the séance and made a statement: "She removed most of her clothes and I examined her and them carefully. She wore a loose green linen dress into the séance room and I examined this carefully before she put it on. She also removed her shoes, and I examined her feet and shoes carefully. She then put her shoes on again. She also took down her hair, which I searched."

Dr. Comstock sat outside the circle recording his observations with a dictaphone. The events began at 8:45 p.m. Walter's voice called for a card table to be substituted for the heavy table around which the circle had been formed. The card table was put into place with the bell box on top of it. Background music was supplied by a phonograph and Dr. Comstock noted when it was started and stopped. The first manifestation in the darkened room was the movement of the threefold screen that had been set up behind Margery. At the end of the séance, it was found closed and flat, but still standing upright.

The card table eerily tipped in the dark and fell toward Houdini, but it never fell completely over. At 9:45 p.m., it finally lurched over sideways, spilling the bell box to the floor. At 10:07, the bell box was put, at Walter's suggestion, between Houdini's feet. At 10:12, the bell rang shrilly three times. Walter shouted for Munn to straighten up. The publisher admitted that he had been bending over. Walter instructed Munn to tell the bell how many times it should ring and it chimed five times at his suggestion. Walter bid the sitters "good night" and the séance was abruptly over.

Dr. Comstock, Houdini, Munn, and Bird went to another room to discuss the events that had occurred. Houdini said that he had released his grip on Munn's hand in the dark and had reached under the table when it was tilting. He felt Margery's hand underneath the table, lifting it. He had quickly pulled his hand away and reached for Munn's ear in the dark. He leaned over and whispered, "Shall I denounce and expose her now?" The publisher whispered back that he should wait.

Houdini, who had rolled up his trouser leg again, revealed that Margery's stocking had caught on the garter of his right stocking. When she complained that the buckle was hurting her, he had unfastened it. After that, he could feel her leg moving as it extended toward the bell box. He was all for calling the newspapers immediately and exposing Margery as a fraud. The other men voted him down.

Munn and Houdini took the night train to New York. Bird stayed on as the Crandons' guest. During the trip, Munn told Harry that the September issue of the magazine had already gone to press, carrying an article by Bird praising Margery's mediumship. Houdini advised him to stop the presses. When the public learned that Margery was a fraud, the article would be embarrassing to the prestigious magazine. At first, Munn objected to the cost of remaking the issue, but he finally agreed to do it and the Bird article was removed.

Houdini was not the only member of the committee bothered by Bird's actions and writings. Dr. Walter Franklin Prince was also disturbed by Bird's early articles in *Scientific American*, lauding Margery's gifts. He and Houdini were even more annoyed by his statements to the press. Bird was not a committee member, he was an employee of the magazine. Both men believed that the committee should be independent of the publication. They met with Munn and voiced their complaints.

If, Munn said, Margery was using trickery, as Houdini claimed, the committee had to prove this to the public. Houdini was given the assignment of constructing a device that would prevent the medium from using her head, hand, and foot in the manner that he described.

Houdini made plans for additional séances. To assure proper control at future sittings, he designed a special "fraud preventer" cabinet, a crate with a slanted top that had openings at the top and sides for the medium's head and arms. Once inside, Margery's movements --- and her chances for deception --- would be severely limited. Reluctantly, Margery agreed to the séance from inside of the cabinet, but not before Houdini and Dr. Crandon exchanged such harsh words that they nearly came to blows. Dr. Crandon had earlier boasted to Sir Arthur Conan Doyle that he was willing to "crucify" any investigators who doubted his wife. Houdini was, not surprisingly, on the top of his list.

J. Malcolm Bird offered to take Houdini's "fraud preventer" to Boston on his car, but Houdini, trusting no one, replied that he would transport it himself. He and Collins, his assistant, lugged it to Dr. Comstock's apartment early on the morning of August 25, 1924. It was an odd-shaped box that might have been a storage crate for an old-style slanted top desk. There was ample room inside for the medium to sit comfortably on a chair. Semicircular holes were cut out of the hinged front and top panel so that when the cabinet was closed, a hole was created to circle the occupant's neck. Her hands were extended through holes in the cabinet sides so that committeemen could "control" them. Provision was also made for panels of wood to be nailed over the side openings should the committee wish to test her with her hands inside of the box.

After the Crandons inspected the box, they withdrew and held a hasty conference. When they returned, the doctor insisted that Margery be allowed to have a tryout in the device with her friends before she submitted to the committee's test. Reluctantly, the committee agreed.

The first séance with the cabinet was held behind closed doors as the investigators waited in another room. In 30 minutes, Dr. Crandon ushered his friends out and the committee into the room. Bird, who was not present at the séance, wrote one version of what happened. Houdini, who was actually present, offered another. Both agreed that the sloped front of the box broke open in the dark. Dr. Crandon stated that Walter was responsible. Houdini said that Margery forced it open with her shoulders as it had only been held in place by two narrow strips of brass. With the front open, Margery could have leaned forward and reached the bell box, which was on a table in front of her, with her head.

Houdini demonstrating the fraud prevention box that he created for the séances with Margery.

The argument between Houdini and the Crandons became so heated that Walter's voice called out for peace and quiet. Margery's friends rushed into the room to replace the investigators and "psychic harmony" was temporarily restored. When the committee members were invited to return, Walter demanded to know how much Houdini was being paid to stop the phenomena in the séance room. Houdini replied that he was actually losing money since he had to pass up a theater date in Buffalo to come to Boston for the séance. The séance then continued, but no manifestations were produced.

Eventually, Walter told Dr. Comstock to take the bell box under a light and examine it. Walter exclaimed that Houdini had done something to the bell so that it would not ring. An examination of the bell revealed that a piece of rubber had been wedged against the clapper so that it would not ring. Outraged, Dr. Crandon accused the magician of trying to sabotage the proceedings, a charge that Houdini repeatedly denied.

The committee members were angry. Even if he had not placed the rubber in the bell box, they stated that Houdini had not managed to build a "fraud proof box" as he claimed he would do. Harry replied that he hadn't expected Margery to break out of it. He vowed that he would have the box in proper condition for the séance the next night.

As for the rubber wedge -- Margery or her friends must have put it there to try and discredit him.

For the second séance, the box was heavily reinforced. Four staples, hasps, and padlocks had been added. Unexpectedly, J. Malcolm Bird showed up for the session. Munn had told him to stay away from the hotel and Bird wanted to know why. Houdini and Dr. Prince were more than happy to enlighten him -- Bird had given the Crandons information about the committee's findings in July and had also released unauthorized statements to the press. Before he was escorted from the hotel suite, he was allowed to formally resign as secretary for the committee.

Once again, Bird and Houdini told different stories about what occurred at the August 26 séance. Bird, who still believed in the authenticity of Margery's mediumship, but who was not present, said Houdini was satisfied by a search conducted by a woman of Margery's body and clothing. Houdini, on the other hand, wrote that he had objected to the superficial examination that was carried out. But Dr. Crandon would not permit a physician to be called for a more thorough search of his wife's anatomy.

The record of the séance was lacking in some important details. Apparently, a pillow was placed under Margery's feet in the box, but it was not known who suggested this be done or who actually put the pillow there.

Houdini held Margery's left hand as it was extended from the box. On the other side, Dr. Prince took her right hand. This was an important change, as prior to this, Dr. Crandon had always controlled his wife's right hand. Harry repeatedly cautioned Dr. Prince not to release Margery's hand, not even for a moment.

Margery asked why he made such an issue of this. Harry replied, "I'll tell you, in case you have smuggled anything into the cabinet box you cannot conceal it as both your hands are secured and as far as they are concerned, you are helpless."

"Do you want to search me?" Margery asked.

"No, never mind, let it go," he replied. "I am not a physician."

Walter's voice sounded in the room. "Houdini, you are clever indeed, but it won't work."

Walter claimed that there was a collapsible carpenter's ruler under the pillow on which Margery rested her feet. While Houdini had not been in the room just prior to the sitting, Walter said that his assistant had been there, insinuating that Houdini arranged to have it hidden there. His voice became loud and abusive, "Houdini, you god damned bastard, get the hell out of here and never come back! If you don't, I will!"

The box was unlocked and a new carpenter's ruler, which was two-foot long and folded into six-inch sections, was found tucked under the pillow. Dr. Comstock suggested that it had been left there when the box was being repaired. Orson Mull brought Collins into the room to be questioned. Collins said that his ruler was still in his pocket and he pulled it out to show them. Houdini dictated a statement to the stenographer who was present: "I wish it recorded that I demanded Collins to take a sacred oath on the life of his mother that he did not put the ruler in the box and knew positively nothing about it. I also pledge my sacred word of honor as a man that the first I knew of the ruler in the box was when I was informed so by Walter."

In Houdini's opinion, the folding rule had been planted in the box in order to make him look bad. He swore that he had not placed it there and the Crandons made the same claims. They blamed Houdini for the ruler and he blamed them. He resented anyone that would take their word --- and especially the word of Walter, the spirit guide --- over his.

No one knows how the ruler ended up in the box. In his biography of Houdini, author William Lindsay Gresham quoted Collins as admitting, years later, that he had hidden the ruler in the box on Houdini's instructions. The source of the story, although not given by Gresham, was Fred Keating, a magician who had been a guest of the Crandons in the house on Lime Street at the time Hereward Carrington was investigating the medium. Keating, however, was biased against Houdini. Several days before Gresham interviewed him, Keating had seen an unpublished manuscript in which Houdini, while praising Keating as a magician, commented in unflattering terms about Keating's skills as a psychical investigator. Author Milbourne Christopher believed that the story of Collins' so-called confession was sheer fiction.

Unfortunately, the investigators did not thoroughly rule out all possibilities of fraud. If the ruler had been taken to a laboratory for analysis, fingerprints might have been found to show who had last handled it. The *Scientific American* committee, however, was not that scientific.

On the day of the third and final August séance, Munn, Prince, Houdini, and the Crandons had dinner together. Houdini later wrote that Margery said she had heard he planned to denounce her from the stage of Keith's Theater. If he did, she said, her friends would give him a thrashing. She didn't wish her son to read someday that his mother was a fraud.

Houdini, who usually had a soft spot for mothers, was unmoved by her words. "Then don't be a fraud," he told her.

Dr. Comstock brought a medium-control device of his own that night. It was a shallow wooden box into which Margery and an investigator, sitting face-to-face, put their feet. A board was locked in place over their knees. The sides of the box were open, except at the bottom and top so the restraint wouldn't interfere with a "psychic structure." When the medium's hands were held, and the bell box was on the floor by the new restraint, she was under excellent control.

According to Houdini's account, while the committee waited for the bell to ring and other manifestations to occur, Dr. Crandon turned to him and spoke, "Some day, Houdini, you will see the light, and if it were to occur this evening, I would gladly give $10,000 to charity."

Harry replied, "It may happen, but I doubt it."

The doctor repeated. "If you were converted this evening I would willingly give $10,000 to charity."

Dr. Comstock's fraud control was effective. When Margery's hands were held by someone other than her husband and while her hands and feet were immobilized, no spirit phenomena was produced. Nothing occurred that night.

Houdini had not been converted and Dr. Crandon still had his $10,000.

The aftermath of the Margery séances was troubling for everyone involved. There were many, including some of the committee, who believed that Houdini had been the one who was caught cheating this time. He was widely discredited for it, leading some to doubt the integrity of some of his earlier investigations. In any case, *Scientific American* finally declined to grant the prize to Margery, in large part because of Houdini's accusations. The confrontational magician had quarreled, often violently, with every member of the committee. J. Malcolm Bird, whom Houdini suspected of active collusion with the Crandons, was angry with the magician and he continued to insist Harry should have been disqualified at the very beginning.

Houdini further outraged Bird, the Crandons, and their supporters when he published a small book called *Houdini Exposes the Tricks Used by the Boston Medium Margery*. He was adamant about the fact that Margery was doing nothing more than using clever tricks as "proof" of the spirit world. In his final verdict on the medium, he wrote: "My decision is, that everything which took place at the séances which I attended was a deliberate and conscious fraud."

From the other side, Walter chimed in his final words about Houdini. He ended them with a prediction: Houdini would be dead within a year, he said. Houdini managed to defy this prophecy, but not by much. He died in 1926, and in an interview with the press, Margery had only good things to say about the magician, praising him for his virile personality and great determination.

Despite Houdini's exposures, Margery emerged from the debacle relatively unscathed. She continued her séances, and by the end of 1924, she had begun to produce even greater manifestations, including "spirit arms" that rang the bell box and caused things to fly about in the séance room.

In 1925, J. Malcolm Bird published a book that supported Margery and as the research officer of the American Society for Psychical Research, he was able to sway many other ASPR members to her side. They became her greatest supporters and devoted hundreds of pages in the ASPR journal to her séances.

Eric J. Dingwall, an officer of the Society for Psychical Research in England, read of his American colleagues' support, and decided to investigate the medium for himself. He wanted to see the ectoplasm that Margery was manifesting and Dr. Crandon allowed him to view them by the light of a red lamp, which Crandon flashed on and off to reveal quick glances at the phenomenon. Too much light, Dr. Crandon said, would have an inhibiting effect on the ectoplasm. Dingwall wrote to a friend: "The materialized hands are connected by an umbilical cord to the medium. They seize upon objects and displace them. Later, when he was permitted to grasp one of the "ghost hands," he described it as feeling like "a piece of cold raw beef or possibly a piece of soft, wet rubber."

Halfway through his investigations, though, Dingwall began having doubts. Dr. Crandon's red lamp never allowed him to see the ectoplasm actually emanating from Margery's body. He had only seen it after the fact. Odder still, many of the photographs revealed that many of the emanations seemed to be hanging from slender, almost invisible threads. Others who looked at the photos said that the "hands" looked suspiciously like animal lung tissue, a substance that Dr. Crandon could have obtained through his work at Boston hospitals. Dingwall's final report on the case was inconclusive.

As usual, Margery was unconcerned. Sitters continued to file into the séance room at the Crandons' Lime Street home. One investigation after another raised allegations of fraud, but no one was ever able to make the accusations stick. Even J.B. Rhine, who would later become one of the leaders of American paranormal research, was intrigued by Margery, but was unimpressed with what he saw. As always, though, Conan Doyle defended the medium and when Rhine published an unflattering account of his experiences with Margery, Doyle bought space in several Boston newspapers to run a reply. The black-bordered message read simply: "J.B. Rhine is an ass."

In 1928, Margery began to develop a highly unusual manifestation that made her even more widely known in the remaining Spiritualist circles. On the table in front of her during a séance would be placed two dishes, one containing hot water and the other cold. In the first dish was a piece of dental wax. When the wax was softened, it was claimed that her spirit guide, Walter, would make an impression of his thumb on it. Then, the thumbprint was put into cold water to harden. The prints appeared mysteriously on the same night that Margery obtained the wax from her dentist. A so-called fingerprint expert that was called in by the Crandons stated that the thumbprint matched one that was taken from an old razor that once belonged to Walter Stinson.

Margery had confounded the skeptics and believers were enthralled by this new manifestation. It was almost as if the spirit was leaving a calling card, even better. The excitement soon came to a crashing end, however.

Psychic researcher E.E. Dudley set out to compare Walter's wax print with those who were regulars at the Crandon séances and made a surprising discovery -- Walter's thumbprint was identical in every way to that of Margery's dentist, Dr. Caldwell. Someone had apparently used a sample thumbprint that Dr. Caldwell made for Margery to create a metal die-stamp that was suitable for making impressions in wax.

This was the end of the ruse. Many of Margery's most devoted followers drifted away. J. Malcolm Bird, once her staunchest defender, admitted that, at times, he had been guilty of elaborations and half-truths about Margery's so-called "wonders." Even Conan Doyle was strangely quiet. The scientific community let it be known that Margery's séances were no longer of interest.

The last days of Spiritualism were finally over.

Margery's decline was quick and tragic. After the death of Dr. Crandon in 1939, Mina grew depressed and turned to alcohol for consolation. She began to look older than her years, gained weight, and watched as her beauty faded away. She continued to hold séances, managing to find a few people who still believed in her, and during one sitting, she grew so distraught that she climbed to the roof of her home and threatened to throw herself off. She died at the age of 54 in 1941.

Many researchers today believe that some elements of the paranormal were present in Crandon's séances, but just what was genuine and what was not remain unknown. Crandon and her husband were known for baiting investigators and trying to fool them if possible. The Crandons simply never seemed to care who believed them and who did not. Just what secrets did Mina Crandon hold? We'll never know – she took them with her to her grave.

"DEATH! DEATH FOR HOUDINI!"

Houdini quickly recovered from the accusations that were thrown his way after the Scientific American investigations. Throughout the rest of 1924, he embarked on another nationwide lecture tour, blasting the fraudulent mediums that he was trying to drive out of business. The tour took him to small towns where he had never played before and to big cities where he was a vaudeville favorite. His contract paid him $1,500 per week, plus transportation, although in the larger cities he received fifty percent of the net receipts. Houdini was definitely making more money debunking phony Spiritualists than the disreputable mediums were bilking from their clients.

He traveled the country and his anger towards Spiritualism seemed never-ending. It had become a personal vendetta, and it did not seem to matter how he caught mediums cheating, as long as he won, and could proclaim all of Spiritualism was trickery and a swindle, and those who believed in it, "poor misguided souls."

Houdini's incessant hounding of mediums even took him to the nation's capital on the morning of February 26, 1926. He testified before a House of Representatives committee in support of bill H.R. 8989, which would ban fortune-telling in the District of Columbia. This bill, and two similar ones, introduced in the Senate, had the magician's complete approval.

Houdini contended that Washington, D.C. was a haven for a countless number of fraudulent mediums, many of whom were giving séances for very influential people, including senators, congressmen, and high level officials. What if spirit communications were influencing the decisions of men in the government? Despite the fact that this had been going on since the Fox sisters, Houdini raised an alarm.

First Lady Florence Harding visited mediums during her husband's scandalous 1921-1923 presidency. Houdini claimed that he'd heard "on good authority" there had been séances in the White House. Equally appalling to the magician were "persistent" rumors that First Lady Grace Coolidge also consulted mediums in the White House. Houdini feigned great anger about the situation, claiming that it meant that Spiritualism was guiding the American government. He demanded a ban on mediums, psychics, and other occult practitioners, and asked President Coolidge to order an investigation into how such people had infiltrated the government. But the president never replied to Houdini's demand for a law banning all mediums.

Houdini refused to surrender to Spiritualists and their allies in Congress. He convinced a New York congressmen to introduce legislation that would prohibit fortune-telling in the District of Columbia. The proposed law called for a $250 fine, six months in jail, or both for anyone convicted of passing themselves off as a "professional medium offering services to the public."

The Spiritualists, their associations, and publications were as vehemently against the bill, and two similar ones, as Houdini was in favor of it. The room where the Subcommittee on Judiciary of the Committee on the District of Columbia held their public hearing was jammed. Among the spectators were Spiritualists, as well as palm readers, crystal gazers, and clairvoyants.

Houdini addressed the committee: "Please understand that, emphatically, I am not attacking a religion. I respect every genuine believer in Spiritualism or any other religion. But this thing they call Spiritualism, wherein a medium intercommunicates with the dead, is a fraud from start to finish. There are only two kinds of medium, those who are mental degenerates and who ought to be under observation, and those who are deliberate cheats and frauds. I would not believe a fraudulent medium under oath; perjury means nothing to them. How can you call it a religion when you get men and women in a room together and they feel each other's hands and bodies? The inspirational mediums are not quite as bad as that. But they guess and by 'fishing' methods and by reading obituary notices get the neurotics to believe that they heard voices and see forms. In thirty-five years, I have never seen one genuine medium."

Washington abounded with fortune-tellers, lucky charm sellers, card readers, and mediums of every kind, Houdini claimed. For $25, anyone could buy a clairvoyant license, then point to it and say: "If I were not genuine, I could not get a license."

Houdini repeated his offer of $10,000 for proof of mediumship. He took a telegram from his pocket, crumpled it and threw it on the table. He dramatically looked back at the audience. "Read that, you clairvoyant mediums, and show me up. Tell me the contents of that telegram." The Spiritualists remained silent.

Representative Frank Reid, a Republican from Illinois, broke in: "I will tell you what it says -- please send more money."

Houdini replied: "You can make your own deductions. You are not a clairvoyant."

"Oh yes, I am," Reid quipped, setting off a round of laughter.

Houdini smiled and crumpled up another telegram and tossed it on the table. "All right, if you're a clairvoyant, tell me what this wire is."

"It is asking if it didn't come," Reid said.

Houdini shook his head. "No, sir. Everyone guesses at it."

Although these statements came from the official proceedings of the committee, newspapers gave varying accounts of what occurred that day. Different statements were given as to what Representative Reid said and some even claimed that he jumped out of his seat saying, "That's an invitation to you to appear before the committee this morning -- I win the $10,000!"

The *New York Morning Telegraph* account included an incident that was not mentioned anywhere else. When Houdini called on any of the mediums in the room to tell him the name his mother called him before he was born, a palmist, standing just outside the door, remarked, "She probably called him an incipient damn fool."

The hearing was adjourned until May 18. When the session resumed, Houdini returned to Washington to be the star witness for those who supported the bill. For three days, he attacked the mediums and they lashed back at him when they took the stand. Harry showed how he could produce a "spirit" voice form a trumpet without moving his lips and cause a message to appear on a pair of blank slates. When the Spiritualists called him "vile" and "crazy," he asked Bess to come forward.

Harry said to her, "I want the chairman to see you... On June 22, 1926, we celebrate our thirty-second anniversary. There are no medals and no ribbons on me, but when a girl will stick to a man for thirty-two years as she did, and when she will starve with me and work with me through thick and thin, it is a pretty good recommendation. Outside of my great mother, Mrs. Houdini has been my greatest friend. Have I ever shown traces of being crazy, unless it was about you?"

"No", Bess quietly replied.

"Am I brutal to you or vile?"

"No."

"Am I a good boy?"

"Yes."

"Thank you, Mrs. Houdini."

The hearings ended on May 21. Despite Houdini's testimony, and best efforts, no bill to ban fortune-telling was ever passed.

In October 1926, Houdini began a week-long engagement in Providence, Rhode Island. When his beloved Bess awoke sick and feverish one morning, Harry, who never consulted a doctor himself unless Bess cried and threatened to leave him, had a physician at her bedside within the hour. The doctor pronounced ptomaine poisoning as the source of her illness and Houdini put in a hurried call to New York to summon a nurse to come and travel with her. On Friday evening, Bess' temperature rose and Houdini sat with her throughout the night.

On Saturday morning, the fever finally broke. Harry managed a few hours of restless sleep between the matinee show and the evening performance. After the last show, Harry saw Bess, her nurse, and his troupe off for Albany at the railroad station, then boarded the last train for New York. He dozed occasionally in his seat, but the stops and starts of the train in various stations kept him awake for most of the journey.

Harry had a meeting with his friend, Bernard Ernst, when he arrived back in the city but the family maid told him that Ernst had not yet returned from a trip, but was expected anytime. Houdini was welcome wait, and so he dozed on a couch in the living room until Ernst arrived.

A few hours later, Houdini called Albany. The nurse reported that his wife's condition had not changed. He met with Frank Ducrot, owner of Houdini's favorite magic shop, because he needed several pieces of apparatus for his show. He telephoned Albany again but the nurse advised him not to worry. She planned to stay with Bess through the night.

Houdini took the early morning train to Albany, again staying awake most of the trip. Bess was better when he arrived at the hotel, but was still not well enough to leave her bed. He managed a brief nap before the opening night performance on October 11. During the show, a chain slipped during Houdini's famous Chinese Water Torture Cell escape and he fractured his ankle. A doctor in the audience advised him to end the show and go to the hospital, but he refused. In fact, he finished the entire performance painfully hopping on one foot. Afterwards, he stopped at Memorial Hospital in Albany for treatment and x-rays. He was ordered to stay off his feet for at least one week, but he continued his shows anyway.

The newspapers predicted that Harry's injury would keep him off the stage for some time, but the reporters underestimated his stamina and drive. It would take more than a broken bone to stop a Houdini tour. He fashioned a leg support for himself and went on to Schenectady and Montreal.

On October 18, he opened at the Princess Theatre and a doctor examined his ankle. He told him the same thing that the earlier doctor had -- stay off it for a week and the bone would knit. Houdini continued to lecture and perform, although he did remain seated during his lectures. After one lecture at McGill University, students and faculty members surged forward to meet him. One young man showed Houdini a sketch he had made while Harry had been talking. The magician pronounced it as an excellent likeness. He autographed the picture and invited the artist to make a close-up portrait later in the week backstage at the theater.

On the afternoon of Friday, October 22, the McGill University artist, Samuel J. Smiley, and Jack Price, a fellow student and friend, met Houdini in the theater lobby around 11:00 a.m. There was a crowd at the ticket window and Houdini arrived with Bess, the nurse, and a secretary. The nurse suggested that they have lunch and Houdini agreed that it was time to eat. He made a hot dog appear from the hat of a startled female bystander, and then escorted the students to his dressing room. He hung up his hat and overcoat, took off his jacket, rolled up his sleeves, removed his tie, opened his shirt collar, and leaned back on the couch to look through a pile of letters on his dressing room table. He was talking about his career as Smiley began to draw some lines for the portrait.

He was hard at work on the drawing when a third student, J. Gordon Whitehead, came in and began talking to the magician. Houdini was very courteous to the young men, but was also occupied with his mail. He wasn't paying close attention when Whitehead asked if it was true that Houdini could withstand powerful blows to the stomach. He absently replied that he could, as long as he had time to brace himself in anticipation of the punch. The boy, thinking that Houdini had given permission for just such a demonstration, suddenly leaned forward and struck him four times in the abdomen with a clenched fist. When Houdini looked startled, the boy quickly backed away, explaining in a panic that he thought that Houdini had given him permission to hit him. Smiley and Price thought Whitehead had gone mad and grabbed for the boy to pull him away. Houdini stopped them with a pained wave. Whitehead felt terrible seeing the performer so clearly in pain, but the magician soon recovered enough to reassure the young man that he was fine, and soon went onstage for his show.

Throughout the evening, Houdini was seen wincing in pain and late that night, he admitting to crippling pains that continued to get worse. He was unable to sleep when he returned to his hotel room and Bess, believing that he had a stomach cramp or a strained muscle, massaged him in an effort to make him more comfortable.

His performances over the next two days consisted of hours of agony, save for brief intermissions when he fell into a restless sleep. After his final Saturday show, he finally told his wife about what had happened in the dressing room. By then, it was too late to get a doctor. An assistant wired the show's advance man in Detroit and told him to have a physician ready that could see Houdini when they arrived. The train arrived late and Houdini went straight to the Garrick Theater, rather than to the Statler Hotel, where Dr. Leo Dretzka was waiting in the lobby. When the doctor finally got to the theater, he found Houdini busy helping his assistants with props for the evening show. There was no cot in the dressing room where Dr. Dretzka could examine the magician, so Houdini stretched out on the floor. He was diagnosed as having acute appendicitis.

He had a fever of 102 degrees but refused to go to the hospital for the emergency surgery that he needed. He was scheduled to perform at a sold-out show that night and was determined to be there. The theater manager had already told him that the house was full. Houdini replied: "They're here to see me. I won't disappoint them."

By the time that he took the stage, his fever had gone up to 104. He was tired, feverish, and tormented by abdominal pains, plus he was hobbling on the broken ankle from two weeks earlier. He somehow managed to perform the entire show, although his terrified assistants were continually forced to complete some motion that Houdini couldn't manage. Spectators reported that he often missed his cues and that he seemed to hurry the show along. Between every act, he was taken to his dressing room and ice packs were used to try and cool his fever. Toward the end of the evening, he began doing what he called "little magic" with silks and coins, card sleights, and accepting questions and challenges from the audience. He remained on the stage throughout the evening but just before the third act, he turned to his chief assistant and said "Drop the curtain, Collins, I can't go any further." When the curtain closed, he literally collapsed where he had been standing. Houdini was helped back to his dressing room and he changed his clothes but still refused to go back to the hospital.

He went to his hotel, still convinced that his pain and illness would subside. It was not until the early morning hours, when Bess threw a tantrum, that the hotel physician was summoned. He in turn contacted a surgeon and Houdini was rushed to the hospital, of course, against his will. An operation was performed immediately but the surgeons agreed that there was little hope for him to pull through. His appendix had ruptured and despite the efforts of medical experts, it was suggested that Bess contact family members.

Despite the seriousness of his condition, Houdini managed to hang on until the early afternoon of October 31. Finally, he turned to Bess and his brother, Theo, who he affectionately called "Dash," and spoke quietly to them: "Dash, I'm getting tired and I can't fight anymore. I guess this thing is going to get me."

A moment later, Houdini stepped through the curtain between this world and the next.

Of course, that is far from the end of the story.

Many mysteries still surround the death of Houdini, although many of these mysteries have come about thanks to the fact that there are at least seven different versions of how his death occurred. They include him dying in the arms of Bess in Boston and Chicago, dying while hanging suspended upside-down in a glass tank, dying while performing at the bottom of a river, dying while trapped in a locked casket, and others. Houdini died of a ruptured appendix. However, it's likely that the appendix did not rupture when the young man punched him in the abdomen in his dressing room. This could have caused the actual rupture, but Houdini was probably suffering from appendicitis before the incident. Regardless, legend has turned the infamous punch into the generally accepted cause of death.

Soon, more mysteries began to rack up – some were fiction, some were fact, others were outright lies, and some were just downright weird. Almost immediately, reports came pouring in from clairvoyants who claimed to have predicted Houdini's death, and to have witnessed signs and omens of it. A Mr. Gysel stated that at 10:58 on the evening of October 24, a photograph of Houdini that he had framed and hung on the wall suddenly "fell to the ground, breaking the glass. I now know that Houdini will die," he allegedly said.

Gysel's prediction came as no surprise to Houdini's Spiritualist adversaries, who had been predicting his death for years. Sooner or later, they were bound to be correct. In 1924, Margery's spirit guide, Walter, had given him "a year or less," predicting "death! Death for Houdini!" And he was not the only one. Earlier in 1926, Houdini's estranged friend, Sir Arthur Conan Doyle, was attending a séance in England when a disturbing message came through: "Houdini is doomed, doomed, doomed!" And on October 13, a medium named Mrs. Wood wrote a letter to the novelist Fulton Oursler that read: "Three years ago, the spirit of Dr. Hyslop said 'the waters are black for Houdini' and he foretold disaster would claim him while performing before an audience in a theatre. Dr. Hyslop now says the injury is more serious than has been reported and that Houdini's days as a magician are over."

According to some accounts, Houdini himself had premonitions of the coming events. Among his clippings was one from 1919 recording the collapse, onstage in Detroit, of a comedian named Sidney Drew. The performer had taken ill in St. Louis, but had continued to play, against all advice, until in Detroit, when he could simply go no further. Those who discovered this clipping among Houdini's belongings must have found the death of the comedian to be eerily similar to that of Houdini. Why the magician would have saved it is unknown.

His friend, fellow magician Joseph Dunninger, also had an eerie story to recall after Houdini's death. He said that on one early morning in October 1926, Houdini called him in New York and asked him to bring his car to Houdini's home on West 113th Street, because he had to move some things. When the car was loaded, he asked Dunninger to drive through the park.

Dunninger said that as they got to the exit on Central Park West, around 72nd Street, Houdini grabbed him by the arm and urged him to go back to his house. Puzzled, Dunninger asked him if he had forgot something. "Don't ask questions, Joe," Houdini replied, "just turn around and go back."

Dunninger drove back to the house and when they arrived, Houdini climbed out of the car and stood looking at the house in the rain. He stayed that way, water dripping down his face and soaking his clothing, for a few minutes and then he got back into the auto without saying a word. Dunninger drove off and when the two men again approached the western exit of the park, he glanced over and saw that Houdini's shoulders had started to shake. He was crying. His friend asked him what was wrong and Houdini gave a rather cryptic answer: "I've seen my house for the last time, Joe. I'll never see my house again."

"And as far as I know," Dunninger later wrote. "He never did."

THE HOUDINI SEANCES

Houdini publicly stated: "I am willing to be convinced. My mind is open, but the proof must be such as to leave no vestige of doubt that what is claimed to be done is accomplished only through or by supernatural power."

To prove that he did have an open mind, the magician made a pact with several of his friends that if he should die, he would make contact, if at all possible, from the other side. He devised a secret code with the one person that he trusted most, his wife Bess, so that if a message should arrive from the beyond, that she would be able to determine that it was really from Houdini. Some have suggested that Houdini came up with the idea of the "death pact" because he was already receiving some foreboding of his death (which was just three years away) but this is not the case. He merely wanted to demonstrate that he believed in the possibility of the other side.

Early in Houdini's career, he and Bess had performed an act in which he played the part of a medium and created fake séances on stage. In the act, they used a code that contained both alphabetical and numerical symbols. Before his death, Houdini used that code to create a secret message with Bess that he promised to communicate with her after his death – if spirit communication was possible. After all, Houdini was a master of impossible escapes – if anyone could escape death, it would be Houdini.

Not long after Houdini died, the famous "Houdini Séances" began. While Bess planned to honor her husband's requests about attempting contact with him after death, this may not have been what prompted her to seek the secret code that he promised to try and send her from beyond the grave. Bess wasn't trying to simply honor Harry's wishes, she was lost without him. She desperately needed to hear from him because she had no idea what to do with her life without Harry's guidance. They had been together since Bess was a young woman and she had been living inside of his closed world, filling the role as his wife and assistant for decades. She had been his partner in a very real sense and he always stated that Bess was his "beloved wife... and the only one who had ever helped me in my work." Although their life had not been perfect, it had never been dull and as huge as Houdini's ego had been, he never made it a secret that he depended on her totally. With her beloved husband gone, Bess was drifting, depressed, and empty.

But her life moved shakily on. While she was not rich, Houdini had left a trust fund for her and substantial amounts of life insurance had been carried on him. She had to pay heavy inheritance taxes, but she had more than enough to live comfortably for the rest of her life. She sold their house on West 113th Street, moved to Payson Avenue in another part of the city, and became lost in alcohol and misery. She tried opening a tea room and thought of taking a vaudeville act on the road, but none of these projects really got off the ground. She soon began to spend her time attempting to contact her husband. Every Sunday at the hour of his death, she would shut herself in a room with his photograph and wait for a sign. She spread the word that she was waiting for a secret message from her husband, and word spread far and wide that Bess had offered $10,000 to any medium who could deliver a true message from Houdini.

Almost weekly, a new medium came forward, claiming to have broken the code. By the late 1920s, interest in Spiritualism had died, but there was still interest in spirit communication by the public. Ouija boards were still selling as a novelty and there were still a few mediums to be found. Those who wrote or contacted Bess with what seemed to be nothing more than guesses about the Houdini code were turned away, until 1928, when Bess heard an announcement by a medium named Arthur Ford that consisted of a single word that came, not from Houdini, but from his mother, Cecilia Weiss. The word was "forgive."

Bess soon made a startling announcement of her own – Ford's message was the first that she had received which "had any appearance of the truth."

What made this message special? "Forgive" was the one word that Houdini had always hoped to hear from his mother in the séance room. It had to do with an incident that happened many years before. When his brother Nat's wife, Sadie, had abandoned him to marry another brother, Leopold, Houdini had been shocked and angry. The once close-knit harmony of the Weiss family had been destroyed. Harry could not bring himself to forgive his brother unless his mother told him to. She died before he could discuss the family crisis with her. This was the one reason that he had searched so tirelessly for a genuine medium and was so infuriated when he found nothing but frauds.

Was Arthur Ford a genuine medium? Or was he simply another fraud?

Arthur Ford was born in Florida in 1896, raised in a religious family, and ordained as a minister. While serving in Europe during World War I, he began experiencing psychic visions and voices. As a deadly influenza epidemic swept through Camp Sheridan, Illinois, he dreamed the next day's death list. Then voices began to whisper the names of soldiers who were soon killed in action. Ford's first clairvoyant experience was a waking vision of his brother, George, accompanied by an ominous feeling. He later learned that George had become seriously ill with influenza that same day and died soon after.

Ford returned to Transylvania College in Lexington, Kentucky, after the war and resumed his studies. He graduated with a mediocre record, but in 1922, was ordained as a minster of the Disciples of Christ Church in Barbourville, Kentucky. He also married Sallie Stewart, but their marriage only lasted five years.

Popular in the pulpit, leading to a great deal of attention, Ford soon grew restless with standard religion. He continued to experience psychic visions and left the church to travel on the lecture circuit,

Arthur Ford

speaking about Spiritualism. He moved to New York, where he trained himself to enter trances, speak to the dead, and allow the dead to speak through him in return.

In 1924, Ford announced that a spirit named "Fletcher" would now serve as his control. Fletcher had been a French-Canadian boyhood friend of Ford's and had been killed during the war. Fletcher was actually his middle name and he used that, the spirit said, so as not to embarrass his Catholic family.

To communicate with Fletcher, Ford wrapped a black, silk handkerchief around his eyes to shut out the light and then breathed deeply until falling into the trance that would allow Fletcher to come through. He said that he was never aware of Fletcher using his vocal chords to speak and never remembered anything that occurred while he was in a trance. With Fletcher's help, Ford's psychic ability grew more impressive. Although critics often accused him of trickery, Ford often astounded audiences and took advantage of the waning days of Spiritualism to make contacts all over the world.

In the late 1920s, he founded the First Spiritualist Church of New York, the first of several such organizations that he would create and lead, and traveled to England, where he met important Spiritualists like Sir Arthur Conan Doyle, who was very impressed with the young man.

In 1930, Ford suffered a traumatic auto accident. He was driving through North Carolina with his sister and another woman as passengers, when a truck went out of control and hit their car broadside. The two women were killed and Ford suffered serious internal injuries, a broken jaw, and crushed ribs. His doctor, who was interested in psychical phenomena, discovered that Ford had out-of-body experiences while on morphine. To experiment, the doctor gave him more and more morphine until he was addicted. His struggle to overcome the addiction caused him to suffer from insomnia. To combat the lack of sleep, he drank, and over the next decade, became a serious alcoholic.

Ford was at the height of his career in the late 1930s, hiding his personal problems from the public and most of his friends. Professionally, he rarely socialized with other psychics and openly denounced fraud. He was accused of trickery himself and while he always denied it, after his death, his private papers revealed that he cheated from time to time by researching the backgrounds of famous people who came to his sittings. He had an almost photographic memory and kept voluminous files of newspaper clippings and notes, which provided material for his readings.

In 1938, Ford was married a second time to Valerie McKeown, an English widow that he met on tour. They moved to Hollywood and were happy for a time, but Ford's alcoholism was a serious toll. He missed lectures, suffered blackouts, and appeared drunk in public. His abilities left him – and so did his wife – and Fletcher disappeared. His health deteriorated and he was plagued by recurring illnesses and depression. By 1949, he was hospitalized with a complete physical breakdown. Alcoholics Anonymous helped Ford get his life back on track. Except for an occasional wild bender, he managed to control his drinking, but never gave it up. He ate badly, followed fad diets that endangered his health, suffered heart attacks, comas, and diabetes but still managed to resume his work as a psychic when Fletcher returned in 1950.

In 1956, he helped found the Spiritual Frontiers Fellowship, an organization dedicated to awakening man to his spiritual nature. He was 71 when he conducted a famous televised séance in Toronto, Canada, for Bishop James Pike. Pike's young son had committed suicide in 1966, and the distraught bishop was anxious to make contact with him. At first, Ford was opposed to the televised séance and said afterward that if he had any idea of the publicity it would generate, he would have turned it down. But friends convinced him to proceed and the show was taped in Toronto in September 1967. Although Ford provided information that Bishop Pike considered evidential, the séance was – and still is – widely debated.

Ford spent his final years in Miami and died of cardiac arrest on January 4, 1971. Needless to say, mediums around the world claimed to hear from him a short time later.

In 1928, though, Ford was still a young man and had not yet achieved the notoriety that soon awaited him. Early that year, he delivered his first message to Bess Houdini, which had allegedly come from her husband's mother. The one-word message managed to get Ford plastered across the front pages of newspapers across America. Bess was cautiously optimistic that the message was genuine, or so the newspapers claimed. In November, another message came to Ford, this time, he said, from Houdini himself. In a trance, the medium relayed an entire coded message: "Rosabelle, answer, tell, pray, answer, look, tell, answer, answer, tell."

After this information was relayed to Bess, she invited Ford to her home and he asked her if the words were correct. She said they were and Ford asked her to remove her wedding ring and tell everyone present what "Rosabelle" meant. This was the word that made the message authentic, a secret known only to Bess and Harry themselves. It was the title of a song that had been popular at Coney Island when they first met. The rest of the message was a series of code words that spelled out the word "believe." The code was one that the Houdinis had used during the "mind-reading act" they perfected in their early days of performing.

For all intents and purposes, this made the message genuine. This was the final clue that Houdini had promised to relay from the next world. Arthur Ford had done it! He had become the first medium to pass on a message from Houdini from the other side. A splashy story appeared in the newspaper, touting Arthur Ford as the man who broke the Houdini code – but, almost as soon as it appeared, the controversy began.

Accusations of fraud began to be leveled against Ford. Bess had apparently deemed the message authentic at first, but friends quickly urged her to retract her support. In truth, though, Bess only ever went halfway in her endorsement of Ford. She wrote a brief letter:

Regardless of any statement made to the contrary, I wish to declare that the message, in its entirety and in the agreed upon sequence, given to me by Arthur Ford is the correct message prearranged between Mr. Houdini and myself.

Beatrice Houdini

It is interesting to note that this statement merely specifies that the message is correct. It does not state that Bess believed it was obtained by psychic means. But perhaps she did at the time, who knows? Friends were soon to convince her otherwise.

The charge against Ford was led by Houdini's friend, Joseph Dunninger, who stated that he was quite willing to believe that Ford delivered the correct code and message to Bess – because it was in common use by sideshow performers and had even appeared in a biography written about Houdini two years before he died. Ford was skewered by the press, skeptics, and Houdini's fellow magicians. On their advice, Bess withdrew the offer of $10,000.

And they may have been right. Although it would not be discovered until after he died, more than four decades after the alleged Houdini message, Arthur Ford collected extensive files on many of the people that he did readings for, offering them seemingly random information about their lives to make his séances seem authentic. In those days before the internet, he must have been quite a researcher, so he easily could have found the information about the "mind-reading act code" and used it to try and pull one over on Bess.

But, here's the weird thing: Dunninger and various skeptics were able to claim that Ford tricked Bess with the code, but they never explained how he had managed to come up with his original message – the one he said was from Harry's mother, and the one that got Bess's attention in the first place. There was nothing in a Houdini biography about the word "forgive" – the word that Houdini had been hoping to hear from Cecilia when he first began trying to make contact with her spirit. The family disagreement between Houdini and his brothers was not publicly known. It was a private side to his life that he had not shared. So, how had Ford known about it? Was it a lucky guess, or did the medium really make contact with the other side?

Arthur Ford certainly maintained that he had, going to his grave with the firm belief that he had actually received a message from Houdini. In 1928, Ford was a respected member of the psychic community. He had also recently distinguished himself by challenging the magician Howard Thurston to a debate at Carnegie Hall, which Ford won. Thurston, who had been carrying on Houdini's tradition of exposing fraudulent mediums, was stymied by being unable to explain some of the effects that Ford produced. After he came forward with the code, he claimed that jealous colleagues turned on him and joined in with the newsmen and skeptics as they accused him of fraud.

What's the truth of Arthur Ford and the Houdini code? Reality or fraud? It's possible that it was a little of both. It's true that Ford could have easily found out about the code since it had been around for years before Houdini and Bess ever used it. It was also easy to discover the "Rosabelle" story, especially for a savvy researcher like Ford, which he was discovered to be after his death. But I'm not willing to simply write off the "forgive" message that he initially obtained. For that one, I don't think the answer is quite so simple.

Strangely, this would not be the last mystery that surrounded Houdini's alleged afterlife.

Bess Houdini continued to hold séances in hopes of communicating with her late husband, but as the years went by, she began to lose hope that she would ever hear from him. The last "official" Houdini séance was held on Halloween night of 1936, 10 years after Houdini had died. A group of friends, fellow magicians, occultists, scientists,

Bess Houdini and Eddy Saint at the last official Houdini Seance

and Bess Houdini herself gathered in Hollywood, on the roof of the Knickerbocker Hotel. Eddy Saint, a former carnival and vaudeville showman who had also worked as a magician, had arranged the gathering. He had been recommended to Bess a few years before in New York to act as her manager, although concerned friends had actually hired him to watch over her and to protect her from being taken advantage of. A genuine affection developed between them and eventually they began sharing a bungalow together in Hollywood, a place where Bess had enjoyed living during her husband's brief movie career.

Coverage for the "Final Houdini Séance" was provided by radio and it was broadcast all over the world. Eddy Saint took charge of the proceedings and started things off with the playing of "Pomp and Circumstance," a tune that had been used by Houdini to start his act in later years. He noted for radio audiences: "Every facility has been provided tonight that might aid in opening the pathway to the spirit world. Here in the inner circle reposes a medium's trumpet, a pair of slates with chalk, a writing tablet and pencil, a small bell, and in the center, reposes a huge pair of silver handcuffs on a silk cushion."

Saint continued coverage of the event, finally crying out to make contact with the late magician: "Houdini! Are you here? Are you here, Houdini? Please manifest yourself in any way possible… We have waited, Houdini, oh so long! Never have you been able to present the evidence you promised. And now, this, the night of nights… the world is listening, Harry... Levitate the table! Move it! Lift the table! Move it or rap it! Spell out a code, Harry... please! Ring a bell! Let its tinkle be heard around the world!"

Saint and the rest of Bess's inner circle attempted to contact the elusive magician for over an hour before finally giving up. Saint finally turned to Bess: "Mrs. Houdini, the zero hour has passed. The ten years are up. Have you reached a decision?"

The mournful voice of Bess Houdini then echoed through radio receivers around the world. "Yes, Houdini did not come through," she replied. "My last hope is gone. I do not believe that Houdini can come back to me --- or to anyone. The Houdini shrine has burned for ten years. I now, reverently... turn out the light. It is finished. Good night, Harry!"

The séance came to an end, but at the moment it did, a tremendously violent thunderstorm broke out, drenching the séance participants and terrifying them with a terrific display of lightning and thunder. They would later learn that this mysterious storm did not occur anywhere else in Hollywood --- only above the Knickerbocker Hotel. Some speculated that perhaps Houdini did come through after all, as the flamboyant performer just might have made his presence known by the spectacular effects of the thunderstorm.

With the passing of Houdini in 1926 and Conan Doyle just four years later, the feud between them came to an end. The harsh stories, cutting words, and angry arguments had been fodder for newspaper writers for years and had turned both of the legendary men into bickering children. Their opposing views on Spiritualism managed to tear the movement to shreds, and while remnants of it remained in the public eye for years to come, the soul of Spiritualism had been destroyed. Mediums, fearing the cynical and glaring light of the new era, steered clear of the séance room and turned to psychic predictions and newspaper horoscopes.

To this day, the legend of Houdini still survives, as does the literary legend of Conan Doyle and his timeless detective, but organized Spiritualism is gone. In America, it faded away in the 1930s, and yet, the basis of the two men's argument – the truth behind claims of the paranormal – still lingers on.

The mystery continues and it is no closer to being solved.

10. THE ORIGINAL "MODERN GHOST HUNTER"
HARRY PRICE AND THE SEARCH FOR HAUNTED HOUSES

Although the investigation of psychical events dates back at least to the first public exhibitions by the Fox sisters (and probably even earlier), the first psychical research society was not organized until 1882, when the SPR began in England. Other organizations followed, testing mediums and attending séances, trying to discover if the paranormal events that were allegedly occurring were real. As science lost interest in chasing spooks, magicians and amateur investigations took up the cause, intent more on debunking fraudulent mediums than with delving into the authenticity of incidents connected with the next world. In time, as the mediums changed their methods, even those investigations died out. Science had turned to investigating the mysteries of the human mind – ESP, telekinesis, and clairvoyance – and ghosts would have likely been relegated to the dusty back rooms of haunted history if not for the men and women who began seeking spirits in the 1920s and 1930s.

The new investigations didn't focus on mediums and Spiritualism – they were strictly looking for ghosts.

It wasn't until this new era that psychical research truly began to delve into hauntings and what caused them to occur. Almost all psychical research had initially questioned whether the effects that occurred during séances could be linked to the dead. Were spirits returning to communicate with the living? Did the dead speak through mediums? These questions were an important part of the research, but as time passed, the research began to deal more strongly with the paranormal effects created by the medium. Whether those effects were linked to the spirit world became of secondary concern. The new research was different. It wasn't as concerned with the dead who

Ghost Hunter Harry Price

were returning, but with the dead that were still here. In other words, are ghosts real? And do they haunt the places that were linked to them in life?

Although there were a number of researchers who became active during this era, the chapter that follows focuses on one man in particular – the man I consider to be the "original modern ghost hunter." His influence on the paranormal field of the early twentieth century is beyond measure and that influence continues today. Most present-day ghost hunters – ignorant of the history of the field – emulate Harry Price with every investigation they conduct and, sadly, few of them have any idea they are doing it.

But it's Price's influence on the paranormal field that earns him a place in a book about the birth of the spirit world in American history. The work that he accomplished during his lifetime may never have crossed the Atlantic, but his legacy is one that effects the paranormal field in this country, as well as his own.

Harry Price, although disliked and distrusted by many, remains one of the most important figures in the formative years of ghost research. He had a highly charismatic personality and his energy, enthusiasm, and passion for the paranormal made him the first "celebrity ghost hunter." He was instrumental in making ghost research accessible to the general public, realizing that only by making the research entertaining could he attract the attention of the masses. And there is no question that Price loved attention. Mixed throughout his legitimate research were the bizarre attempts that he made to investigate a talking mongoose and a spell that would turn a goat into a man. With every step of the way, he had newspapers, radio newscasters, and reporters following his every move.

His flamboyant showmanship, his larger-than-life personality, and his refusal to go along with those who wanted to keep the paranormal confined to a laboratory made Price many enemies in the psychical research field. Much of that resentment came from the fact that Price had no real scientific training, but was still so skillful at what he did. He was a deft magician and an expert at detecting fraud, so he was never taken in by the many phony mediums that plagued paranormal research when he was first starting out. His success became a point of contention for those who considered themselves established paranormal research.

His work was groundbreaking, no matter what other investigators and mainstream scientists thought of him. His investigation at the house known as Borley Rectory became the first documented attempts to track down evidence of a haunting at a single location. He created the ghost hunter's "tool kit" and also developed the first how-to guide for investigating a haunted house.

I cannot stress enough how important Harry Price is to the history of paranormal research. He first emerged as an investigator during the volatile era when investigators were still trying to validate the claims that were made by mediums during the waning days of the Spiritualist movement. Price, with his headstrong sense of right and wrong and his need for attention, quickly made a name for himself. But he also started making enemies too – the kind that would wait until after his death to try and smear his research, his reputation, and everything that he had accomplished. I have never made it a secret that I have great admiration for Harry Price and his work and continue to defend his place in history, despite his occasional missteps and the hoopla that often surrounded everything he did. Was he perfect? Far from it, but I'll let the pages that follow present the evidence of his worthiness as a pioneer in the field and allow you to judge the merit of my argument for yourself.

Harry Price was born on January 17, 1881, in London, the son of a grocer and traveling salesman. He was educated in New Cross, first at Waller Road Infant's School and then at Haberdashers' Aske's Hatcham Boy's School. At 15, he founded the Carlton Dramatic Society and wrote a number of plays. He had an avid interest in coin collecting and wrote several articles for the *Askean*, the school's magazine.

One of the plays that Price wrote for the dramatic society was about an early experience that he had with a poltergeist, which took place at a manor house in Shropshire. He was 15 at the time and he and a friend obtained permission to stay in what was regarded locally as a haunted house. Rumors had spread about the strange activity. A retired canon from the Church of England had moved into the old manor house with his wife and, within weeks, curious events began to take place. Initially, they happened only in the farm buildings – doors unlocked, animals were let out of their pens, tools vanished, rocks fell on the roof of the woodshed – but suddenly those events stopped and happenings began occurring inside of the house.

The ancient manor house had been restored several times and was described as a comfortable place. The first sign that something odd was taking place was when the canon and his wife began hearing the sounds of children's feet running back and forth on the gallery at the top of the wide staircase that led up from the large entry hall. The noises were heard at night and shortly after, the maids began complaining that pots and pans in the kitchen were being disturbed. Items leapt from shelves, vanished, and banged about, upsetting the entire household. The canon, already not in the best of health, began to suffer sleepless nights because of the activity. Things soon got worse. The children's footsteps were replaced by the steady thump of a man's heavy boots and they marched through the house all night long. The canon finally left the house on holiday, hoping to get some peace and quiet.

Around the time of his departure, Price was on his way back to school and stopped in the village to visit friends. They told him about the rumors of strange goings-on at the manor house and his interest was piqued. The household had temporarily vacated the manor, leaving it in the care of a worker and his wife. Somehow, Price and a friend managed to persuade the caretaker's wife to let them chase the ghost.

Price was taking his Lancaster stand camera with him to school and on the day of their adventure, he rode a bicycle into town and purchased some magnesium powder for its flash, along with a bell switch, a roll of wire, two batteries, and some sulphuric acid. He assembled the batteries and switch and prepared the flash powder, intent on photographing whatever was plaguing the house. To make sure the powder flashed when he needed it to do so, he mixed gunpowder from several shotgun cartridges into the magnesium powder. He used the wire to hook up an electrical circuit that would ignite the powder. With all of these items – plus matches, a candle, lantern, piece of chalk, ball of string, photographic plates, and food – Price and his friend said goodbye to their companions and made their way across the fields to the manor house. They arrived just as it was getting dark.

They searched the entire house when they arrived – basement to attic – and then closed and locked every window. They locked the doors of all of the rooms and removed the keys. The doors leading into the house were all locked, barred, and bolted, and chairs were placed in front of them. The house was empty and there was no way to get inside. The two young men locked themselves into a small parlor and, in the lantern light, waited impatiently for something to happen.

The boys were getting tired, but when Price's friend said that he heard a noise upstairs around 11:30 p.m., they were instantly alert. A few minutes later, a thudding sound occurred and they were convinced it was someone walking around. That sound was followed by what seemed to be someone stumbling over a chair. They quickly realized they were not in the house alone.

Just before midnight, they heard the sounds again – heavy boots stomping around the room upstairs. They left the room and crossed the upstairs gallery, waited for a moment at the top of the steps, and then began to descend. The boys counted the steps – there were 15 in all – and then they paused, as if wondering which way to go next. They weren't in suspense for long. They started back up the stairs, each step plainly heard. When they reached the top, they stopped. There was no more sound.

Price and his friend waited, ears pressed to the door, for a few minutes and then decided to investigate. As Price reached for the door handle, they heard the footsteps start to descend the wooden stairs again, clomping, one after another. They counted the steps as they came closer and closer, listened as they paused for another moment in the hall, and then started back up the stairs again.

The boys had gathered their courage and decided to see who – or what – was on the staircase. Price grabbed his camera and opened the door. His friend followed with the lantern. The footsteps had gotten as high as the fifth stair and when the parlor door creaked open, they abruptly stopped.

Price wrote many years later: "Realizing that the ghost was as frightened of meeting us as we were of seeing it (although that is what we had come for), we thought we would again examine the stairs and the upper part of the house. This we did very thoroughly, but found nothing disturbed. I think we were disappointed at not seeing anything we could photograph, so decided to make an attempt at a flashlight picture if the poltergeist would descend the stairs again."

Using a small household ladder, Price set up a stand for his camera. He placed it about 12 feet from the bottom of the staircase. On top of the ladder, he heaped a pile of his powder mixture and wired it up with the battery. The wire ran from the staircase and into the parlor, where he hooked up the switch. He would fire the camera from that spot. Price focused the camera on the stairs, inserted a plate, uncapped the lens, and then hurried back into the parlor with his friend. They locked the parlor door – just in case, I suppose. The boys lay down on the carpet near the door and, with trigger in hand, continued their vigil.

Nearly an hour passed before they heard anything. It started again in the room above them and then followed the same routine of walking to the staircase, pausing, and then walking down. When the footsteps reached the bottom, they stopped and Price tried to visualize where the footsteps halted. Minutes passed and then the steps began their return journey up the stairs. With their hearts racing, the boys counted the steps and at the seventh, Price pushed the button on the switch and the flash powder exploded in the hall outside. The light was so bright that even the parlor was illuminated by the glare from under the door.

At the same moment that the flash went off, the footsteps on the stairs faltered and stumbled, a sound that the boys could plainly hear. It was followed by what sounded like someone falling down.

"It was difficult to say who was the more startled," Price later recalled, "the poltergeist or myself, and for some moments, we did nothing."

After the young men got over their astonishment, they opened the door and found the hallway filled with a white smoke that was so dense they could hardly breathe. They retrieved the camera and fled the house. After the plate was developed, they found that the photograph that they attempted to take of the ghost was nothing more than a washed-out, over-exposed negative.

But Price would never forget the time that he and his friend frightened a ghost.

BECOMING ENGLAND'S FAVORITE GHOST HUNTER

After graduating from school, Price worked several jobs, including as a journalist and paper salesman. He developed a lifelong interest in magic and conjuring and his expertise in sleight-of-hand and magic tricks helped him immensely in what would become his all-consuming passion: the investigation of paranormal phenomena. In 1908, Price met and married a wealthy heiress, Constance Mary Knight. With his fortunes secured, he began his pursuit of the unknown.

By the time that Price joined the Society for Psychical Research in 1920, he had already begun his career as Britain's most famous ghost investigator. He had spent many hours at alleged haunted houses and in the investigation of Spiritualist mediums. He was also an expert magician and soon made a name for himself within the SPR for using his magic skills to debunk fraudulent psychics, then in keeping with what was the main thrust of the current SPR investigations. Unlike most magicians of the era, though, Price endorsed some mediums that he believed were genuine.

Price's first major success in psychical research came in 1922 when he exposed the 'spirit' photographer William Hope, who was making a fortune taking portraits of people that always seemed to include the sitter's dead relatives. Price investigated and soon published his findings. He claimed that Hope used pre-exposed plates in his camera, which he learned by secretly switching the plates the photographer was using with plates of his own. In the same year, he traveled to Germany with fellow investigator Eric Dingwall and investigated Willi Schneider at the home of Baron Albert von Schrenck-Notzing in Munich. In 1923, Price exposed the medium Jan Guzyk, who was, according to Price, "clever, especially with his feet, which were almost as useful to him as his hands in producing phenomena."

Price wrote that the photographs depicting the ectoplasm of the medium Eva C., taken with Schrenck-Notzing, looked artificial and two-dimensional. He was convinced they were cardboard and newspaper portraits and bemoaned the lack of scientific controls during her séances. Price was right. When investigated, it was discovered that most of the "ectoplasm" she produced was simply chewed paper. Price also investigated Maria Silbert and caught her using her feet and toes to move objects in the séance room. He exposed the "direct voice" mediumship of George Valiantine in London. In a séance, Valiantine claimed to have contacted the "spirit" of the composer Luigi Arditi, speaking in Italian. Price wrote down every word that was attributed to Arditi's ghost and they were found to be word-for-word matches from a common an Italian phrase-book.

He also invented devices that could be used for the testing of mediums. One such device was a voice control recorder that he used to expose medium Frederick Tansley Munnings, who claimed to produce the independent "spirit" voices of Julius Caesar, the infamous murderer Dr. Hawley Harvey Crippen, and King Henry VIII. Price was able to prove that all of the voices were those of Munnings. In 1928, Munnings admitted fraud and sold his confessions to a newspaper.

It was only chance that led Price into another aspect of his career. One afternoon, while taking the train from London to his country home near Pulborough, Price met a young woman named Stella Cranshaw. The two happened to strike up a conversation about psychic anomalies, during which Stella, who was a hospital nurse, told the investigator that she had been experiencing strange phenomena for years. She said that rapping noises, cold chills, and household objects inexplicably taking flight had been bothering her for some time. Price, excited at the prospect of a new test subject, told her that he was a psychic investigator and asked if she would submit to being tested as a medium. Stella agreed and a series of séances were scheduled at the London Spiritualist Alliance. Stella was given a modest payment for her time since she was required to take off work in the afternoons to come to the sittings.

The first séance brought some surprises, namely that Stella, who had never considered herself a medium, had a spirit control who came through to the sitters. The spirit guide, "Palma," communicated by rapping and would follow requests made to it, like moving a heavy oak table in various directions around the room. At the same séance, thermometers recorded rapid temperature drops. These swift changes would become a staple of Stella's séances.

Price brought several newly-created devices into the séance room in an effort to study the phenomena scientifically. One of the regular sitters built a special double table with the inner portion of it being a wire cage where items that were to be manipulated could be placed. The first time that it was used, several musical instruments were placed inside and a rattle was somehow thrown out of the closed cage. Price designed new equipment of his own to test the young woman's abilities. One of them was the "telekinetoscope," a clever device that used a telegraph key that when depressed would cause a red light to turn on. A glass dome then covered the key so that only psychic powers could operate it. During the séances, the red light often turned on, even though the switch could not be manipulated by hand.

Unsuspecting medium Stella Cranshaw

During the sittings, always conducted in front of witnesses, Stella managed to produce all sorts of strange physical phenomena. During one séance, for example, she managed to levitate a table so high that the sitters had to rise out of their chairs to keep their hands upon it. Suddenly, three of the table legs broke away and the table itself folded and collapsed. Needless to say, this ended the sitting.

The first series of séances ran for 11 sittings and was finally stopped by Stella, who was exhausted by the weekly trials. She often grew very tired during the séances; her pulse would race and the sudden drops in temperature caused her to shake uncontrollably. She saw a doctor about her exhaustion and he recommended that she rest. Her exhaustion and her frequent absences from work caused her to lose her job at the hospital where she was employed.

Price also suffered because of the séances with Stella. He was widely criticized by fellow magicians, and even some psychical investigators, for taking Stella seriously. The SPR was uncomfortable with Price's affiliation with the London Spiritualist Alliance, feeling that it was too closely aligned with the Spiritualist community, even though an SPR officer had attended Stella's sittings. They convinced Price that any further séances should be held at the SPR headquarters. SPR officers were also unhappy that Price had been paying Stella for the tests, even though he specially stated that it was only because she was missing work – and then lost her job – because of the experiments.

Price managed, with some difficulty, to convince Stella to continue with the séances. She had found a secretarial job with a manufacturing company and was reluctant to jeopardize her new employment. Finally, she agreed to two more séances in late 1923. After this, she immediately ended her association with him. Their relationship, which had been warm, now turned chilly, for reasons that are not altogether clear. Stella publicly pleaded fatigue but different reasons are suggested in a letter that she wrote to him in 1926. By this time, whatever had occurred was forgotten and Stella began working with Price again after an absence of three years. In her letter, she apologized and stated that she had "badly misjudged" him in 1923.

The 1926 sittings were held at Price's National Laboratory for Psychical Research, which was then newly established at the London Spiritualist Alliance. The phenomena that manifested around Stella was similar to what it had been, although it was weaker than it been a few years before. She offered 14 séances before bringing things to an end in August. She returned to work with Price again in 1927, so that he could study the anomalous temperature drops and participated in a series of 9 final sittings with him in 1928, shortly before she was married.

Stella married Leslie Deacon in August 1928 and she brought her career as a medium to an end. She never worked professionally and all her sittings were conducted with Harry Price. What became of her later in life is unknown, but she is believed to have lived into her 60's, spending the remainder of her life in London.

In the end, Stella's career as a medium turned out to be short-lived but the careful research earned her great respect in psychical circles. Harry Price's handling of the investigation earned him prestige and respectability as well.

After the end of the sessions with Stella, Price began searching for further mediums to investigate. He traveled to Munich for a series of sittings with Willi Schneider at the laboratory of Baron Albert von Schreck-Notzing, the flamboyant investigator. Price was so impressed with what he saw during the séances that he invited Willi to his own laboratories in 1929. He was also inspired with the publicity-seeking methods of von Schreck-Notzing, too, and decided to emulate him in his own career.

Price continued to test – and in many cases, expose – mediums, trying to measure aspects of each séance in a scientific manner. He managed to record strange temperature drops and other phenomena that finally convinced him of the reality of the paranormal. From this point on, he devoted more of his time to pursuing genuine phenomena rather than debunking mediums, which did not sit well with the SPR. Price had already been in a number of disputes with the SPR and the relationship became so strained that Price decided to form the National Laboratory for Psychical Research in 1923. It would take another three years to get it up and running, but it so angered leaders at the SPR that they returned Price's donation of a massive book collection. To make matters worse, after Price's death, it would be three members of the SPR who would attempt to unfairly discredit him.

Most of the members of the SPR treated Price with something verging on contempt. In those days, the main officers of the society were made up of the British upper class and most were related to one another by marriage. Price was most definitely not of their class and breeding -- his father was salesman for a paper manufacturer -- and this in itself seemed to make his research suspect in many of their eyes. He was simply, in the words of one of the members of the society's governing council, "not a gentleman." He was also looked down upon for the fact that he was not as well educated as other members and had no formal scientific training.

Price had little use for class envy and made a formal offer to the University of London to equip and endow a Department of Psychical Research, and to loan the equipment of the National Laboratory and its library. The University of London Board of Studies in Psychology responded positively to this proposal. In 1934, the National Laboratory of Psychical Research, which held Price's collection, was reconstituted as the University of London Council for Psychical Investigation with C. E. M. Joad as chairman and with Price as Honorary Secretary and editor, although it was not an official body of the University. His collection of books, papers, and materials were donated to the University by his widow in 1976 and they remain on display there today.

Meanwhile, in 1927, Price joined the Ghost Club, a sort of rival organization of the SPR, and remained a member until it (temporarily) closed in 1936. It would be Price who re-established the Ghost Club in 1938, with himself as chairman, modernizing it, removing the connections to Spiritualism, and turning it into a group of mostly open-minded skeptics who gathered to discuss and investigate the paranormal. He was the first to admit women into the club.

While the various dramas were playing out on the organizational stage, Price was still investigating the cases that came along, from mediums to general strangeness. In 1926, he learned of a Romanian peasant girl named Eleonora Zugan, who was apparently experiencing violent poltergeist phenomena, including flying objects, slapping, biting and pinching. The girl had been rescued from an insane asylum by a psychic investigator that Price had met in Vienna. Price returned to London, with the girl, and began a series of laboratory tests that were only partially successful. Testimony and reports from the tests claimed that "stigmata" appeared on the girl's body under conditions that precluded the possibility of the girl producing them by natural means. It was also stated that she could move objects with her mind, although no cause could be discovered for her abilities outside of the fact that she had been severely abused as a young child. Eleonora's abilities ceased abruptly at the age of 14 when she entered puberty.

In 1929, Rudi Schneider, whose abilities were said to surpass those of his brother, traveled to England to be tested by Price. The investigator was still adding new scientific technology to his array of gadgets and one device wired the hands and feet of Rudi, and everyone else seated around the séance table, to a display board. A light would signal if anyone moved enough to break the electrical circuit. Despite these controls, Rudi was said to have produced an array of effects, including ectoplasmic masses, rappings, and table levitations. Lord Charles Hope, a leading SPR investigator, was astounded, as was Price himself. At the end of the sessions, Price declared that the phenomena produced by Rudi was "absolutely genuine" and "not the slightest suspicious action was witnessed by any controller or sitter."

In the spring of 1932, Price began testing Rudi again. In these sessions, he planned to photograph Rudi's manifestations as further evidence of his psychic abilities. Although Price obtained some favorable results, the sittings were not as successful as before. Rudi's talents seemed to have diminished. In the Fall, Lord Charles Hope conducted more tests of the young man and while he too noticed a decline in his abilities, still maintained that his powers were genuine. And then, as Hope was preparing his report,

Price rocked the paranormal community with the announcement that Rudi was a fraud. As evidence, he produced a photograph that was taken during a séance and which showed Rudi reaching for a table. The grainy image managed to destroy Rudi's reputation and embarrass the investigators who had declared him to be genuine, including Harry Price himself. Those who claimed that Price was simply a publicity-seeker were hard-pressed to explain why he would have damaged his own reputation in this way.

Price tested one more medium in 1933. Frank Decker, believed to be gifted with various paranormal abilities, was investigated at the National Laboratory of Psychical Research. Under Price's strict scientific controls, Decker failed to produce any phenomena at all. By this time, there were few credible mediums left to test and Price began turning his attention away from testing mediums and toward investigating bizarre phenomena and haunted houses. In 1936, he took part in a live radio broadcast for the BBC from a supposedly haunted manor house in Kent. This show cemented his place as a groundbreaker in paranormal popular culture.

But not all of Price's publicity stunts went as well, or were nearly as successful. One case took him to Mount Brocken in Germany. He went there with C.E.M. Joad and members of the National Laboratory to conduct a "black magic" experiment involving the transformation of a goat into a young man. The transformation was supposed to occur after an invocation performed by a young maiden – film actress Gloria Gordon – and while it produced a great deal of publicity, no magical transformation took place. Price became the subject of ridicule, but he always claimed that he carried out the experiment "if only to prove the fallacy of transcendental magic."

One of Price's strangest vases was that of Gef, the Talking Mongoose of Cashen's Gap. The case began in 1931 with a disembodied voice plaguing the Irving family, who lived at Cashen's Gap, an isolated spot on the Isle of Man. The voice claimed that it belonged to a mongoose, a weasel-like creature. It told the Irvings that it ate rabbits, and it spoke in various languages, imitated other animals, and even recited nursery rhymes.

Price investigated the case in the company of R.S. Lambert, then editor of a popular radio show called *The Listener*, but the animal refused to manifest until after they had left. Lambert, who investigated other supernatural cases with Price, almost lost his job over the Cashen's Gap affair. The publicity around the case caught the attention of his employers at the BBC and one of his supervisors concluded that Lambert's interest in the supernatural reflected poorly on the broadcaster's competence. Lambert sued him for defamation of character and kept his job.

Price and Lambert eventually published a book about the affair – *The Haunting of Cashen's Gap (1936)* – and in it, they avoided saying that they believed the story, but reported it as though with an open mind. Hair from the alleged mongoose was sent to Julian Huxley, who sent it to naturalist F. Martin Duncan, who identified it as dog hair. Price suspected that it belonged to the Irvings' sheepdog, Mona. Price also asked Reginal Pocock of the Natural History Museum to examine pawprints allegedly made by Gef, as well as impressions of supposed tooth marks. Pocock could not match them to any known animal, though he conceded that they might have been "conceivably made by a dog." He did state that none of the tooth impressions or tracks had been made by a mongoose.

However, the Irvings were firmly convinced that something strange was happening in their home. When Price visited the Irving home, he noted double walls of wooden paneling covering the interior rooms of their old stone farmhouse. There was considerable space between the stone and wood walls that could "make the whole house one great speaking-tube, with walls like sounding boards." By speaking into one of the many openings in the panels, it was possible to convey a "phantom" voice to anywhere in the house.

Price and Lambert left Cashen's Gap less than enthusiastic about the case, but it was later investigated by Nandor Fodor, a pioneer in the field of poltergeist phenomena connected to human subjects. Intrigued by the accounts, he traveled to Cashen's Gap and interviewed many witnesses to the events, even many who were hostile to the haunting. He couldn't shake their testimony – they were convinced that what happened was real. Although he jokingly suggested that it might have been caused by a mongoose who learned to talk, he believed that the events many have been caused unknowingly by Voirey Irving, the 13-year-old girl who lived in the house with her family. She was closely associated with the "talking mongoose" manifestations and might have been producing them in a way in which she was not aware.

The case remains unsolved, although I think we can safely rule out the idea that the culprit was an actual talking animal.

The year 1929 marked a turning point in Price's career, although the case in which he first became involved with that summer would not be made public for several years in the future. The house that was at the heart of the case, a deteriorating old place in Essex called Borley Rectory, would take over Price's life and, more than anything else that he did, make him both famous and infamous.

Price's interactions with Borley Rectory brought him a windfall of new publicity in newspapers and on the radio. He also wrote two books about the house -- *The Most Haunted House in England (1940)* and *The End of Borley Rectory (1946)*. Both books became very popular and entrenched Price solidly in the popular culture of the paranormal field.

Despite what his critics said about him, there was no question that Price was the most famous ghost hunter in England -- and perhaps in the world after *LIFE* magazine ran a piece about Borley Rectory in the 1940s. Publicity aside, though, his books about the house set the standard for psychical investigations and marked the first time that the general public was exposed to detailed accounts of paranormal research. Even today, Price's books about Borley Rectory make for compelling reading and it's easy to understand why they turned into the bestsellers of the day.

"THE MOST HAUNTED HOUSE IN ENGLAND"

Perhaps the most famous haunted house in history – certainly in England – was Borley Rectory in Essex. It was Harry Price who put the place on the map and the last

Borley Rectory – "The Most Haunted House in England"

10 years or more of his life were dominated by the long, complex, frustrating, and undoubtedly rewarding investigation of the house and its haunted history. None of his previous cases ever involved as many people, aroused as much interested, generated as much publicity, or caused him as many problems as the crumbling old rectory did. His two books about the house captured the imagination of the public. At the time of his death, he was starting work on a third book about Borley and even today, interest remains in the place dubbed "the Most Haunted House in England."

In recent times, much of the interest in the case has been negative. Critics and attention-seekers have maintained the whole thing was a hoax – a publicity stunt created by Price. One journalist accused him – after he was dead, of course, and unable to defend himself – of deliberately lying about the phenomena and producing the activity in the house with a "pocketful of pebbles and bricks." This obviously ignored the fact that literally dozens of people experienced activity in the house and swore to what they had seen, heard, felt, and experienced. Unlike the journalists, skeptics, and critics, they were present when the activity occurred. They experienced while living, sleeping, eating, and maintaining watch at the rectory. They assured the doubters that the house was truly as haunted as Harry Price claimed.

There is a reason that Borley Rectory has maintained its fearsome reputation over the last eight decades – it has done so because dozens of people stated without question that it was haunted. Strange things were happening in Essex and Harry Price and his ghost hunting recruits were right in the thick of it. However, the story of the rectory began long before Price – or the ghosts --- took up residence there.

The tiny parish of Borley is located in a quiet, sparsely populated county near the eastern coast of England, not far from Essex's border with Suffolk. Harry Price began the chronicle of the lonely place in 1362, when Edward III bestowed the Manor of Borley upon the Benedictine monks. But that early history of the future rectory was so shrouded in mystery that all that was known for certain is that the manor was in the possession of the powerful Waldegrave family for at least 300 years. Between 1862 and 1892, the Reverend H.D.E. Bull, a Waldegrave descendant, was the rector of Borley. A year after his appointment, he built Borley Rectory. Despite local warnings, he had built the house on a site believed by locals to be haunted. His son, the Rev. H.F. Bull, succeeded his as rector and remained in the position until his death in 1927. The rectory was then vacant for over a year, until October 1928, when the Rev. Guy Eric Smith was appointed to the role. However, he quit the rectory just one year after moving in, plagued by both the ghosts and the house's deteriorating state.

There had been strange happenings reported in and around the rectory for many years before the residency of the Rev. Smith, but all concerned had kept them quiet. In 1886, a Mrs. E. Byford quit her position as a nanny at the rectory because of "ghostly footsteps." More than 14 years later, two daughters of Henry Bull first spotted what would become the famous "phantom nun" on the rectory's front lawn. The sighting occurred in the middle of the afternoon and would coincide with other strange happenings that were reported by the family, including phantom rappings, unexplained footsteps, and more. The young women were repeatedly unnerved by these events, but Reverend Bull seemed to regard them as "splendid entertainment." He and his son, Harry, even constructed a summer house on the property where they would enjoy after-dinner cigars and watch for the phantom nun to stroll across the lawn, her head bowed in sorrow. The sightings were said to be so frequent that the men were rarely disappointed.

Rev. Harry Bull often discussed the spirits with his friend J. Hartley, who later supplied information to Harry Price. In 1922, Bull told Hartley that in his opinion, "The only way for a spirit, if ignored, to get into touch with a living person, was by means of a manifestation causing some violent physical reaction, such as the breaking of glass or the shattering of other and similar material elements." Bull told Hartley that after his death, if he were discontented, he would adopt this method of communicating with the inhabitants of the Rectory.

The members of the Bull family were not the only ones to see the ghostly nun on the grounds or outside the gates of the rectory. Fred Cartwright, a local carpenter, told Harry Price that he saw her four times in two weeks. Prior to 1939, there had been 14 legitimate sightings of the nun and three of those people had also seen a spectral coach, and horses "with glittering harness," sweep across the grounds. Two others had claimed to see an apparition of a headless man on the property.

In June 1929, two years after the death of Harry Bull and nine months after Rev. Smith came to the rectory, a story about ghostly occurrences at Borley appeared in a newspaper. The next day, Harry Price received a telephone call from a London editor and was asked to investigate. He was told about various types of phenomena that had been reported there and given a lengthy laundry list of weird happenings – phantom footsteps, whispers, the headless man, a girl in white, the spectral coach, the ghost of Henry Bull, and, of course, the phantom nun.

Price was told that local legend claimed that a monastery had once been located on the site and that a thirteenth-century monk and a beautiful young nun were killed while trying to elope from the place. The monk was hanged and his would-be bride was bricked up alive within the walls of her convent. Price scoffed at the idea of such a romantic tale, but was intrigued by the many stories associated with the house.

Price was accompanied on his first visit to Borley by V.C. Wall, a well-known journalist, and Miss Lucie Kaye, his long-time – and likely long-suffering -- secretary. Together, they listened to the experiences of Rev. Smith and even observed some minor examples of poltergeist phenomenon for themselves. Price also conducted a long interview with Miss Mary Pearson, the rectory's maid, who had seen the ghostly coach and horses twice and was firmly convinced the house was genuinely haunted. Later that night, the group held a séance in the "Blue Room" of the house, where many of the manifestations had allegedly occurred, and they were purported to make contact with Harry Bull. Whether they did or not, they were startled when a piece of soap jumped up off the floor with no assistance. The following day, Price conducted more interviews and spoke with Rev. Bull's daughters and the Coopers, a man and wife who had lived in a cottage on the rectory grounds. They had moved out in 1920, blaming uncomfortable feelings caused by the ghosts.

The events that occurred, and the witness interviews that were documented, were enough to convince Price that something supernatural was going on at the house. That early summer afternoon kicked off Price's more than decade-and-a-half long obsession with Borley Rectory. He became fascinated with the house and it came to represent the most exciting and baffling puzzle of his career.

Price's second visit to Borley came two weeks after the first. This time, he documented the appearance of a religious medal and some other items that seemed to show there was a Catholic element to the haunting. There were also several times when bells rang throughout the house, although the bell wires -- once used to summon the servants -- had been cut many years before. The constant ringing was a source of great annoyance for Rev. Smith and his wife and this, along with other unnerving manifestations, convinced the couple to abandon the house on July 14, 1929.

Over the course of the next 14 months, the rectory remained empty and yet the happenings reportedly continued. According to local accounts, a window on the house was opened from the inside, even though the rectory was deserted and the doors were securely locked. The main staircase was found covered with lumps of stone and small pieces of glass were said to have been scattered about. Locals who lived nearby reported seeing "lights" in the house and hearing what were described as "horrible sounds" around the time of the full moon.

Even though Rev. Smith and his wife moved out of the house because of the ghosts, things had really been rather peaceful up until that point. All of that would change, though, in October 1930, when the Reverend Lionel Foyster and his wife, Marianne, replaced Smith. The Foysters' time in the house would see a marked increase in paranormal activity. People were locked out of rooms, household items vanished, windows were broken, furniture was moved, odd sounds were heard, and much more. However, the worst of the incidents seemed to involve Mrs. Foyster, who was thrown from her bed at night, slapped by invisible hands, forced to dodge heavy objects which flew at her day and night, and was once almost suffocated with a mattress.

The activity during this period was more varied and far more violent than before. Rev. Foyster kept a diary and later compiled a manuscript that was never published called "Fifteen Months in a Haunted House." Harry Price would later use large excerpts from the manuscript in his books about Borley. There is no question that Rev. Foyster, Marianne, their adopted daughter, and later, a young boy who stayed with them as a guest, went through some strange and sometimes terrifying experiences. The manifestations reached their peak when a series of scrawled messages began appearing on the walls inside the house, written by an unknown hand. They seemed to be pleading with Mrs. Foyster, using phrases like "Marianne, please help get" and "Marianne light mass prayers."

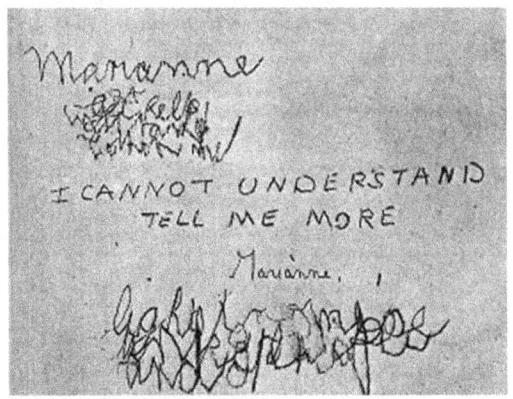

The mysterious writings that appeared on the wall at Borley Rectory.

Things got so bad by May 1931 that the Foysters left the rectory so that they could get a few days of peace and quiet. In June, Dom Richard Whitehouse, a friend of the Foysters, began an investigation. He found things inexplicably scattered all over the unoccupied house, but never saw any of the activity occur. When the family returned, the violent manifestations began again – usually directed toward Marianne. One night, she was hurled from her bed three times.

In September 1931, Price learned of the new and more violent manifestations. A short time later, he and some of his friends paid a visit to the rectory and met the Foysters. While looking around the house, Price and a few others experienced locking and unlocking doors and witnessed a bottle fly across the room. Because nearly all the poltergeist-like activity occurred when Mrs. Foyster was present, Price was inclined to attribute it to her unknowing manipulations. He also considered the idea that some of it might be trickery. Based on earlier accounts, however, he did believe that past residents had seen the ghostly nun and had experienced things that could not be explained. He had also witnessed strange events for himself, when Marianne Foyster was not present. Price knew the rectory did not fit into any preconceived notions of a "haunted house," which was one of the reasons the case was so intriguing.

Even though some of the current activity could be caused by a human element in the house – either psychically or through trickery – Price accepted that there were actual spirits present, as well. He believed that one of the spirits had found the rector's wife to be sympathetic to its plight. This was the only explanation he could find for the mysterious messages. He believed the writings had come from another young woman, one who seemed to be from her references, a Catholic. These clues would later fit well into Price's theory that the Borley mystery was a terrible tale of murder and betrayal, in which the central character was a young nun, although not the one of legend.

A short time after Price's visit, Mrs. Foyster, Dom Richard Whitehouse, and the Foysters' maid, Katie, were seated in the kitchen with all the doors and windows closed, when bottles began to appear, seemingly from nowhere, only to shatter on the floor. At the same time, the bells in the house suddenly began ringing.

The months that followed brought more ringing bells and door locking but after a séance was held, things quieted down considerably. The bells still rang occasionally and items flew about, but there was what was described as a "different atmosphere" after the sittings. The remainder of 1934 was quiet but in 1935, the manifestations returned and became more violent. Things frequently vanished and were broken and by October, the Foysters had reached the limits of their endurance. They decided to leave the house and the church decided to sell the place, as they now believed that it was unfit for any parson to live in it.

The church offered the house to Harry Price – for about one sixth of its value – but after some hesitation, he decided not to buy the place. Instead, he signed a lease to rent it for a year. Price planned to conduct an extended, around the clock investigation of the house, using scores of volunteer investigators to track and document anything out of the ordinary that occurred there. As it turned out, the investigation was never that organized. Even so, in spite of often poor record-keeping and periods when the house was unoccupied, the year-long investigation remains a landmark in the annals of the paranormal.

Price's first step was to run an advertisement in the personal column of the *Times* on May 25, 1937, looking for open-minded researchers to literally "camp out" at the rectory. They were to record any phenomena that took place in their presence. The advertisement read:

HAUNTED HOUSE: Responsible persons of leisure and intelligence, intrepid, critical, and unbiased, are invited to join rota of observers in a year's night and day investigation of alleged haunted house in Home counties. Printed Instructions supplied. Scientific training or ability to operate simple instruments an advantage. House situated in lonely hamlet, so own car is essential. Write Box H.989, The Times, E.C.4

Price was deluged with potential applicants, most of whom were unsuitable. After choosing more than 40 people, he then printed the first-ever handbook on how to conduct a paranormal investigation. It became known as the "Blue Book." A copy was given to each investigator and it explained what to do when investigating the house, along with what equipment they would need. As part of the investigation, he coined the idea of a "ghost hunter's kit, which included tape measurers to check the thickness of walls and to search for hidden chambers, still cameras for indoor and outdoor photography, a remote-control motion picture camera, finger-printing kit, various powders to use for checking for footprints, and even portable telephones for contact between investigators.

During the investigations, the researchers were allowed wide latitude when it came to searching for facts. Some of them employed their own equipment, others kept precise journals, and others turned to séances, which would prove interesting over the period of 1937 to 1938. The greatest aid to Price in the investigations was Mr. S. H. Glanville. He and his family took a special interest in Borley and spent countless hours there. It was Glanville who compiled with great zeal the famous "Locked Box," which contained a detailed record of the Borley story from its beginning to the night of a fire that occurred in 1939. Some of the material was eventually published in Price's books and Glanville was put in charge of the investigations when Price was not present.

The observers that Price recruited came from all different professions, outlooks, and interests, but all of them contributed to the pile of data that began to accumulate. Many of them spent nights in the empty rectory, where one room had been set up to serve as a "base" and where various instruments had been installed. Some of them came alone and others came in groups, skeptics, believers, and debunkers alike. A good many of them neither saw nor heard anything, but quite a few of them had strange experiences. These experiences were wildly varied from footsteps to moving objects, to strange sounds, or eerie lights. Many of them witnessed full apparitions – rarely seen by just one person at a time – and the majority of those sightings were of the phantom nun.

The corps of observers established that Borley Rectory was the center of some intense paranormal disturbances. The number and variety of the disturbances provided an answer to the claims that Harry Price staged the haunting of the rectory for publicity or other purposes. Price did not witness the vast majority of the observations, accounts, and reports. He was not even present most of the time. Instead, the reports came from independent observers who often had no idea that others were experiencing the same events at other times.

There were two important developments during Price's tenancy of the house. One was the observation of the "wall writings." The frantic cries for help were often hard to decipher and had first started to appear during the Foysters' occupancy of the rectory. Most of them were addressed to "Marianne" and some have suggested that Mrs. Foyster herself had written them, although none could provide a motive for such a pointless hoax. However, the scrawls – written in the same hand -- continued to appear on the walls long after Mrs. Foyster had left the Rectory. Price believed that they provided vital clues to the mystery behind the haunting. The observers who noted the new messages marked and dated all of them so that there would be no mistake as to which dated from the Foyster' occupancy and which had appeared later.

The other important development of 1937 – 1938 was the series of séances that was held by Mr. Glanville, his family, and several friends. During a sitting with a planchette (a device used for automatic writing), an alleged spirit named "Marie Lairre" related that she had been a nun in France but had left her convent to marry Henry Waldegrave, a member of a wealthy family whose manor home once stood on the site of Borley Rectory. While living at the manor, her husband had strangled her and had buried her remains in the cellar. The story went well with the most interesting of the

Borley phenomena, namely the reported phantom nun and the written messages. Price theorized that the former nun had been buried in unconsecrated ground and was now doomed to haunt the property seeking rest.

In March of 1938, five months after Marie's first appearance, another spirit, which called itself "Sunex Amures," promised that the rectory would burn down that night and that the proof of the nun's murder would be found in the ruins. Borley Rectory did not burn that night, but exactly 11 months later, on February 27, 1939, a new owner, Captain W.H. Gregson, was unpacking books in the library when an oil lamp overturned and started a fire. The blaze quickly spread and the rectory was gutted. It was said that the fire started at the exact same point that the spirit had predicted and that "strange figures were seen walking in the flames."

The building itself was finally demolished in 1944, but the story was far from over.

The publication of Price's first book on Borley, *The Most Haunted House in England*, brought Price a deluge of letters. The wall-writings, the planchette messages, and the various reports from the observers led to arguments, new theories, and new facts. Price was able to point out the parallels and similarities in a dozen other hauntings.

The rectory was now in ruins, but this did not keep the curious away. Throughout the years of World War II, visitors often explored the rubble and occasionally spent the night in the eerie remains of the building. In 1941, H.F. Russell, a businessman, paid a visit to the Borley grounds with two of his Royal Air Force officer sons. While there, he claimed that he was seized by an invisible presence and dashed to the ground. Two years later, some Polish officers spent the night in the ruins and claimed to see and hear several chilling sounds and sights. In particular, they saw a shadow on the part of the lawn dubbed the "Nun's Walk" and a man's figure in one of the burned-out rooms. While there, the Polish officers rebuilt the floor in the Blue Room and erected chairs and a table where séances could continue to be held.

Other visitors included a commission from Cambridge University, which was formed by A.J.B. Robertson of St. Johns College. He would go on to contribute a long essay to Price's second book on Borley. Robertson and his colleagues were interested in the inexplicable "cold patches" in the house. They investigated the house from 1939 until the demolition of the rectory in 1944. The report that Robertson wrote at the end of the investigation was cautious, but stated: "There appears, in fact, to be something at the rectory which cannot all be explained away. It must be remembered that the investigations described here form only part of a much wider survey which has brought to light very many mysterious phenomena."

Rev. W.J. Phythian-Adams, Canon of Carlisle, conducted some of the most fascinating investigations at the rectory. After reading Price's book, studying plans of the house, looking at photographs of the wall writings, and doing a detailed analysis of Borley's history, Canon Phythian-Adams prepared a detailed and convincing account of events leading up to the haunting. He used the data connected to the Waldegrave family, as well as statements from a medium that Price had contacted to use psychometric powers on an apport that had been found by an observer in the Borley sewing room, to create his report. He combined all the pieces of the Borley story into a tangible story. He collated the wall writings with the séance messages and extracted the symbolic and literal meanings of the information that had been gathered. There had been many other attempts at interpreting the messages, especially the wall writings, and all had concentrated on the desperate attempts the nun had made to try and get the living to do something for her. But no one else tried to do what Canon Phythian-Adams had achieved – creating a consecutive narrative that sounded convincing.

There would be those who would say that his story (recounted earlier in the story of "Marie Lairre") was nothing more than clever guesswork, but Canon Phythian-Adams told Harry Price to dig for the nun's remains and he told him exactly where to dig. In August 1943, in the company of Rev. A.C. Henning; Dr. Eric H. Bailey, Senior Assistant Pathologist of the Ashford County Hospital; Roland F. Bailey, his brother; Flying Officer A. A. Creamer; Captain W.H. Gregson and his two nieces, Georgina Dawson and Mrs. Alex English, Price began his excavations in the cellars of the ruined rectory.

On the exact spot where Canon Phythian-Adams indicated (having never visited the site), they found a large antique brass preserving pan, a silver cream jug, and a jawbone with five teeth on it. Dr. Bailey declared it to be a left mandible, probably from a woman. They also found part of a skull. The next day, they also found two religious medals, one of which was made of poor quality gold. Price took the bone fragments from Borley to the studios of A. C. Cooper, Ltd., well-known art photographers, who would then document the finds. At the studio, another strange act in the Borley haunting was played out.

While setting up the skull to have it photographed, it slipped from two sets of hands and broke into four pieces. Moments later, an expensive oil painting fell off its easel with no explanation and crashed to the floor. A clock that had not worked in more than 10 years suddenly started ticking again, functioning for just 20 minutes before stopping again, this time for good. Five months later, the Cooper studios were destroyed by an air raid. Coincidence? Perhaps, but based on all the other strange happenings connected to Borley, it was worthy of mention.

In May 1945, a Christian burial was provided for the bones that were found. This seemed to provide the ghost with the rest she had long sought and a service was later conducted by the Rev. Henning in the small village of Liston, less than two miles from the rectory.

The nun was never seen at the house again, but weird events continued to occur. They were frequent enough that Price made plans for a third book about the site, although it was never completed. As his research progressed, Price lined up 50 new witnesses to more recent phenomena, including Rev. Henning, officials from the BBC, local residents, and strangers. It seemed that after the ruins of Borley were demolished, the ghosts moved to Borley Church, where a great many manifestations began to occur in the vestry and throughout the building. Many reliable people heard the organ being played when the church doors were locked and no one could possibly enter. Rev. Henning, then rector of the church, was one of the witnesses and he contributed his accounts to Price for the third book.

But Harry would never write that third volume on the history of Borley Rectory. He died from a heart attack in his home in Pullborough on March 29, 1948. And almost as soon as he was in his grave, the attacks on his labors and volumes of research began. The attacks came from within the SPR, the organization that Price had battled with long before he became involved with Borley Rectory. On October 9, 1931, a past president of the SPR, William Henry Salter, had visited Borley in an attempt to persuade Rev. Foyster to sever his links with Price and work with the SPR instead. When Foyster refused, SPR members began their attempts to discredit him through what psychical researcher John L. Randall called "dirty tricks," but the most egregious betrayals of Price would come after his death.

In 1948, almost immediately after he died, Eric Dingwall, Kathleen M. Goldney, and Trevor H. Hall, three members of the SPR – two of whom had once been among Price's most loyal associates – began a smear campaign that targeted Price and his work at Borley Rectory. They published their attacks in a 1956 book, *The Haunting of Borley Rectory*, and claimed that Price had fraudulently produced the phenomena at the house. Although none of them were present, or took part in the investigations at the house, they stated that the phenomena was either faked or due to natural causes such as rats or due to strange acoustics caused by the odd shape of the house. It was also alleged that Marianne Foyster was actively engaged in fraudulently creating haunted phenomena. Price, it was said, "salted the mine" and faked several happenings while he was at the rectory. The SPR version of the events provided fuel for the debunkers and several have added their own unsubstantiated theories about methods Price used to fake the haunting.

But there was a backlash to the criticisms. SPR researcher Robert Hastings came to Price's defense, as did other members of the organization in the years to come. Price's literary executor Paul Tabori, eminent researcher and author Peter Underwood, and author Ivan Banks have all published books that have defended Price against accusations of fraud.

To this day, the debate still rages in England about the validity of the country's "most haunted" house. And perhaps that's the reason that the story of Borley Rectory has never really died – and Harry Price remains such a fascinating and controversial figure. No matter what disparaging things have been written about him, there is no question that he earned his place in the history of paranormal popular culture. He was a pioneer and a new brand of "ghost hunter," much different from the scientists, debunkers, and Spiritualists who thrived in the past.

He was the first modern ghost hunter and would set the stage for those who followed in his wake.

11. PARANORMAL PRELUDE
PROPHETS, PAST LIVES AND PARANOIA

After the death of Houdini, there was a handful of other magicians and conjurers who carried on the traditions of exposing mediums and creating their own stage shows based on manifestations that occurred in séances. Performers like Houdini's friend Joseph Dunninger delved into the spirit world and put together "mind reading acts" based on what psychics claimed to be able to do for years. These performers put together weekly programs in vaudeville houses and wowed audiences with levitating tables and floating ghosts, preferring to offer spooky thrills instead of supernatural debunking.

By the 1930s, a new form of popular entertainment was starting to emerge in the movie houses of the day. These midnight "spook shows" consisted of a variety of routines that focused on ghosts, offering modern audiences a new look at old stunts like spirit cabinets, slate writing, levitations, and the "dark séance." Everything old had now become new again – and it was meant to be scary. Performers with stage names like El-Wyn, Greystoke, Rajah Raboid, and Francisco traveled the country, packing theaters, and terrifying a generation of young people at midnight shows into the 1950s.

But, like the heyday of Spiritualism, the golden days of spook shows were numbered. By the early 1950s, audiences had become tired of ghosts and spooks and wanted more from the shows. After World War II, Americans knew about horror first-hand. They had seen the survivors of the Nazi concentration camps and atomic bombs were much more frightening than anything magicians could conjure up on stage. Many shows began adding more horrific elements to the program, like skeletons and monsters, but they managed only to last until the early popularity of television and then "spook shows' – like Spiritualism – died out for good.

Ghost hunting in America, it seemed, had died along with Spiritualism. Ghosts could still be found in the occasional film, or read about in a book or article from England, but Americans with an interest in the paranormal were largely left with stories of psychics, the groundbreaking work done by J.B. and Louisa Rhine, and regional folk stories that often appeared in the back pages of newspapers. There wasn't a lot of room for ghosts in America's popular culture during the years of the Great Depression and World War II.

But there was still room for the paranormal.

It was in the 1920s that a man often referred to as "the greatest mystic who ever lived in America" rose to fame and the articles and books written about his eerie trances catapulted him to fame across the country. His name was Edgar Cayce and he had an influence so vast that the record of his thousands of readings completely altered the American vocabulary, making words like *reincarnation, clairvoyance, meditation, channeling* and *past lives* into household words. The cures that he prescribed to his ailing "patients" – herbs, whole foods, and mind-body therapies – laid a foundation for the alternative medicine treatments that swept the country long after his death. This strange figure, perhaps more than any other, exposed the country to the mystical side of the paranormal.

"THE SLEEPING PROPHET"

Edgar Cayce was born on March 18, 1877, in the small Western Kentucky town of Beverly. It was the kind of town that didn't see its first paved roads until 1932 and tobacco was the major crop. Nearly everyone owned farmland, worked on it, or knew or was related to someone who did. The Civil War was only a dozen years in the past when Cayce was born and the line between whites and blacks was a sharply divided one. Although Cayce's childhood was sometimes rough – his father was a drinker and could sometimes be abusive – but overall, the family had a very close bond. Outside of home, school, and church, there was little to do in town. Even visiting the larger, nearby community of Hopkinsville required a buggy ride of more than 12 miles.

In this small corner of the world, Cayce grew up a sensitive, awkward boy. Tall and thin for his age, he spent most of his time playing and wandering in the woods and fields alone. Adults found him to be distant and distracted – and a teller of strange stories. He often told of visitations from fairy-like "friends" and communications from dead relatives. At nine, when most boys were fishing and playing baseball, Cayce became fascinated by scriptures and begged his father to buy a Bible for their home. He began reading through the entire book every year. Friends, family members, and townsfolk didn't know what to make of the odd boy.

One night, at age 13, the boy who spoke to invisible friends, knelt by his bed and prayed for the ability to help others. Just before falling asleep, he later recalled, a glorious light filled his bedroom and the figure of a woman appeared at the foot of his bed, telling him: "Thy prayers are heard. You will have your wish. Remain faithful. Be true to yourself. Help the sick, the afflicted."

Cayce first discovered his ability to do trance readings in 1901 when, ill with chronic laryngitis, he entered a hypnotic trance and diagnosed his own sickness. In the years ahead, he worked on the fringes of accepted medicine – with hypnotists and homeopaths – going into trances and prescribing folk cures, natural remedies, and more conventional treatments for hundreds of people. Over and over again, stories and accounts claimed that his readings and remedies worked. Newspapers and medical investigators started paying attention and, in what became Cayce's first appearance on the national stage, *The New York Times* ran a long article about him on October 9, 1910. The headline read "Illiterate Man Becomes a Doctor when Hypnotized."

Cayce wasn't illiterate, but he didn't have much of an education. He never made it past the eighth grade, and although he taught Sunday School at his Disciples of Christ church, he'd never read much of anything except for the Bible. He'd also never been far from home. In the early 1920s, he spent a few years wildcatting in the Texas oil fields, where he tried and failed to raise money for a hospital based on his clairvoyant cures, but he mostly stayed close to the region where he grew up. He was an ordinary man who, like the historical prophets of the Bible, was plucked from his normal life to embark on a mission that he never sought out on his own. Years later, in the 1960s and 1970s, when an era of spirituality and occultism exploded in America, Cayce became a prophet for those times, pointing the way to what became known as the New Age.

Edgar Cayce

Figures of that time would look back to 1923 as the starting point for America's New Age. That autumn, Cayce was in Selma, Alabama. After his failed ventures in Texas, Cayce resettled there with his family to resume his second career as a commercial photographer and to enroll his 16-year-old son, Hugh Lynn, in high school. Cayce's readings had reportedly cured Hugh Lynn of blindness at age six, after a flash powder accident, and the young man was devoted to his father's mission. Cayce's wife, Gertrude, was less enthusiastic. She had suffered during her husband's absences while dealing with a new baby son, Edgar Evans, and just wanted her family to have a normal life.

In September, a wealthy printer from Dayton, Ohio, named Arthur Lammers met Cayce at his photography studio. Lammers had first heard about the psychic during his oil-prospecting days and wanted to see him for himself. Lammers was a hard-driving businessman, but also an avid seeker in Theosophy, ancient religions, and the occult. He and his wife maintained a Victorian mansion in Dayton that was filled with occult books and relics from all over the world. He wanted Cayce to use his powers for more than medical diagnosis – he wanted to learn the secrets of the ages. What happens after death? Is there a soul? Moreover, Lammers wanted to understand the mysteries of the pyramids, astrology, alchemy, reincarnation, and the wisdoms of ancient Greece and Egypt. He believed that Cayce was the man to unlock these secrets for him.

Cayce was hesitant. He had been willing to put up with the whispers of his churchgoing friends and neighbors regarding his trance readings, but astrology and other occult topics felt vaguely sinful to him. But while a humble man on the surface, Cayce still had ambitions. After years of struggling to put food on the table and to provide for his family, Cayce was enticed by the new sense of mission – and with the promise of putting a little money in his pocket. Lammers urged him to move to Dayton, assuring Cayce that he and his wife and children would be well cared for there.

Cayce traveled to Dayton with Lammers and soon uprooted Gertrude and Edgar Evans to join him in a small apartment that Lammers had rented for them. Hugh Lynn stayed with friends in Selma to finish out the school term. Cayce also brought along to Dayton an attractive, 18-year-old stenographer named Gladys Davis, whom he had recently hired to transcribe his readings. Gertrude might have been upset at the younger woman living with the family, but Gladys's devotion seemed limited to Cayce's readings alone, which she spent the rest of her life organizing. Even so, Dayton meant another period of uncertainty for Gertrude. There is little record of the loneliness she must have felt or her difficulty in making new friends. Cayce seemed oblivious to this. For he and Lammers, the move marked the start of an extraordinary journey.

Cayce and Lammers began their explorations at a downtown hotel on October 11, 1923. In the presence of several guests, Lammers arranged for Cayce to go into a trance and give him an astrological reading. Whatever the waking Cayce might have felt about occult subjects vanished while he was in a trance state. He expounded deeply on astrological questions, affirming astrology's basic values, even as he alluded to misconceptions about the way it was used in the West. Near the end of the reading, Cayce casually mentioned that this was Lammers's "third appearance on this earthly plane. He was once a monk." There was stunned silence in the room. Cayce had offered an unmistakable reference to reincarnation, which was exactly what Lammers was looking for.

The men continued their readings over the next month, probing deeper into various kinds of spirituality. From a trance state on October 18, Cayce introduced Lammers to what seemed to be an entire philosophy of life, dealing with reincarnation, man's role in the cosmic order, and the hidden purpose of existence – basically that the body was only a vehicle of the soul. The soul remained the same, passing through various physical forms but remaining the same person. Lammers believed this – reincarnation – was the golden key to life's mystery. He believed that the doctrine that had come from Cayce in the readings seemed to synchronize the wisdom traditions of the world – Eastern philosophies, Judaism, and Christianity. Lammers's enthusiasm aside, the religious ideas that came from Cayce's readings did articulate a compelling theology, marrying a Christian outlook with the cycles of karma and reincarnation that were central to Hindu and Buddhist ways of thought. If there was an inner, or occult, philosophy behind the world's historic faiths, Cayce had come as close as anyone to defining it.

The time in Dayton was a period when Cayce went beyond medical clairvoyance – though he never abandoned it as the main focus of his work – and became more and more involved in "past lives." The lives that became part of his readers were never ordinary. Subjects were often said to have been ancient princes or priestesses, inhabitants of lost civilizations, historic kings or famous warriors. Cayce said that he obtained the information about his subjects' past lives from cosmic records imprinted on the *akasha*, or universal ether. The "akashic records" were a concept derived from Hindu writings and they had been popularized by Madame Blavatsky in the nineteenth century. Cayce, with his Christian worldview, equated them with the Book of Life.

His readings favored historical settings and characters from places like Atlantis, Greece, Egypt, and the pre-Colombian empires of the Americas. Past lives were not without tragedy. While some of Cayce's subjects had been princes and princesses, conquerors, and priests, others had been victims of war, rape, and brutality – sufferings that, in Cayce's philosophy, explained the present-day problems in the lives of the subjects. Cayce's subjects often reported feeling relieved at being able to understand their current pathologies or obsessions as the result of tragedy or violence in a previous incarnation.

The Cayce family – in their twentieth century version – provided an example of this. Hugh Lynn Cayce later made the startling admission that throughout his teenage years, he experienced a profound sexual longing for his mother. It came to a head in 1923 when he traveled to Dayton to rejoin his family for a troubling holiday season. When his father came to pick him up at the train station, Hugh Lynn hugged him and felt the crinkle of paper – Edgar had stuffed his thin overcoat with newspaper to help protect him against the cold Ohio winter. Lammers, it seemed, had experienced several business setbacks that had left the Cayce family nearly destitute. While embroiled in out-of-town lawsuits, Lammers had not even bothered to send the Cayces a few dollars for groceries. For their Christmas dinner, the family shared a chicken so small it could be cupped in Hugh Lynn's hands. It was also during this visit that Hugh Lynn, who had always stood solidly behind his father, was told about Cayce's new psychical experiments into past lives. As a Christmas gift, his father had secretly done a reading for his son, discovering that High Lynn had once been a great ruler in Egypt.

At first, Hugh Lynn was stunned by this turn of events – from his father's poverty to his change in focus for his abilities – but the more he listened, he claimed that he began to understand his own inner conflicts, which included his agonizing attraction toward his mother and a jealousy and resentment he felt toward his father. Cayce told his son that Hugh Lynn had been an Egyptian monarch who coveted a beautiful dancer named Isis. But Isis was in love with a high priest, Ra Ta, with whom she had a daughter. Angry, the king exiled them both. The high priest, Cayce explained, was an earlier incarnation of himself, and the dancer Isis was a past life of his mother. Hugh Lynn had taken every measure to conceal his feelings, but he now understood them, thanks to the revealing reading offered by his father.

Even by Cayce standards, this was weird.

But whatever the source of Cayce's past-life plots, hundreds of people sought him out, and most of them stated that his readings provided them with a sense of context and meaning that helped them resolve feelings of anguish and helplessness in their lives. Poverty-stricken or not, his fame spread.

In 1925, a wealthy patron helped Cayce to escape from Dayton. He relocated to Virginia Beach, a community that had been suggested to him during a reading. Cayce enjoyed the beach, fishing, and ocean climate. In Virginia, he finally raised enough money to start the "Hospital of Enlightenment" that had never gotten off the ground in Texas. In 1929, Cayce and his supporters opened a 30-bed facility on a small hill overlooking the ocean. It provided a comfortable, cozy setting that looked more like a seaside inn than a hospital. Amid the sunshine, shuffleboard, and walks in the sand, the Cayce Hospital had a staff of doctors, nurses, osteopaths, and chiropractors. Patients could receive clairvoyant diagnoses and alternative therapies, such as massage and colonics, as well as X-rays and blood tests. Cayce delivered a metaphysical sermon on Sunday and personally prescribed meditation as a physical and emotional aid for the first time in American medical history.

It was the happiest period in Cayce's life, but it was not meant to last. The arrival of the Great Depression closed the hospital within two years. Attempts to open a metaphysical college, Atlantic University, met with similar results. Cayce became depressed and withdrew from most public life, finding solace in gardening, fishing, chopping wood, and reading his Bible. He was bitterly disappointed, but his clairvoyant readings continued. Each cost $20 and included a membership in his new organization, the Association for Research and Enlightenment (ARE). Records show that he sometimes reduced, or waived, fees altogether, particularly during the Depression, when he often gave readings for a dollar or two for an injured laborer, sick housewife, or parent of an injured child.

In the kind of medical encounter that happened often in Cayce's career, a respected New York publisher, William Sloane, had an unforgettable brush with the readings. In 1940, Sloane agreed to consider a manuscript about the "sleeping prophet" called *There is A River*, by Thomas Sugrue. It was a highly sympathetic biography by a journalist who had been Hugh Lynn's college roommate and who believed a Cayce reading saved his life. Sloane was initially wary but changed his mind when one of Cayce's clairvoyant diagnosis helped one of his own children. The child had been in terrible pain and the family had been to all of the doctors and dentists in the area. All of the tests had been negative, but the pain continued to worsen. He wrote to Cayce and told him that his child was in terrible pain, told him where he would be and when, and enclosed a check for $25. Cayce wrote back and told him there was an infection in the jaw behind a particular tooth. Sloane took the child to the dentist and told him to pull the tooth. The dentist refused, stating that his professional ethics prevented him for pulling a tooth with nothing wrong with it. Sloane eventually persuaded him to pull the tooth and, discovering the infection that Cayce had diagnosed, treated the problem and the pain went away. After that, Sloane immediately made plans to publish the book.

There is A River was published in 1942, less than three years before Cayce's death, and brought him the kind of national attention that his followers believed he deserved. The wave of attention that followed the glowing reviews of the book brought equal attention to astrology, karma, mind-body healing, and reincarnation. Such material began making inroads into mainstream publishing houses, including another title that began its publishing life with William Sloane and further established Cayce and his ideas.

That book was *The Search for Bridey Murphy*, which was published in 1956 by Morey Bernstein, an amateur hypnotist and scrap metal and heavy machinery dealer. Inspired by Cayce's career, he conducted a series of experiments with a Pueblo,

Colorado, housewife who, in a hypnotic trance, regressed in a past-life persona – an early nineteenth century Irish country girl named Bridey Murphy. While in a trance, the women spoke in an Irish brogue – she had never been out of Colorado – and provided comprehensive details about her life in Ireland, a place the housewife knew nothing about. The book became sensationally popular and even inspired a feature film that was rushed into production the following year.

Suddenly, reincarnation – the ancient Hindu concept that Americans hadn't really heard of before World War II – was the latest craze. People began hosting "Come as you Were" parties and books on occultism, hypnosis, and reincarnation became mainstream hits. But not everyone was amused. Medical authorities had long been seeking a proper place for hypnosis, which had made considerable strides since the days of Andrew Jackson Davis and the mesmerists of the middle nineteenth century. Just before the publication of *The Search for Bridey Murphy*, the British Medical Society had cautiously affirmed the medical benefits of hypnosis, but condemned its use for probing psychical powers. This set off a tug-of-war between medical authorities, like the American Medical Association, which saw hypnosis as little more than a way to "allay anxiety in relation to dental work," and others who believed it held potential for the exploration of clairvoyance or higher forms of perception. Philosophers and scientists like William James wanted to strip away the carnival atmosphere of hypnosis without dismissing reasonable inquiries into the potential of the human mind.

Within the work of Edgar Cayce, there existed something far more than fodder for reincarnation parties, paperback books, and hobbyist hypnotists. Cayce's work went often unappreciated in his lifetime. The "self-realization" themes of many of his trance readings were a major part of the alternative spiritual movements of later decades. He would reach his highest level of fame in the 1960s and 1970s, where the unusual depth of the backwoods philosopher, who never finished grade school, was called "illiterate" in the press, read little beyond the scriptures, and taught at religiously conservative Sunday Schools, would finally be appreciated.

There is nothing in Cayce's background that would suggest an ability to communicate with the kind of insight and depth that he did. Leaving aside whatever debate may be had about the question of his psychic abilities, or even whether such things exist, Cayce appeared to tap into something that was knowing, kind, and capable of touching the souls of his fellow humans – and it all seemed to come from somewhere else, somewhere other than the obvious experiences of his life.

"Knowledge not lived is sin," Cayce wrote just a few months before his death in January 1945. In both word and action, Cayce embodied this principle. Inner teachings, he believed, should be methods of service to others. Cayce understood the ancient belief that stated that saving a single life is the same as saving the world and he truly believed that he was a "channel" – as he put it – for good into the world. The "sleeping prophet" of the New Age that was to come, brought hope and dignity into the lives of people for whom conventional ideas had failed.

Whether you believe in Cayce's trance readings, past lives, or prophecies, there is no denying that he did manage to save more than a single life during his time on earth, and so, perhaps in a way, he managed to save us all. Regardless, his work ushered in a New Age that would help to find a place in the American psyche for the paranormal.

IT MUST BE *FATE*

As the 1950s brought us the age of rocket ships and space flight, Americans became less interested in psychical worlds than in those that lay out beyond the stars. For those with an interest in the unexplained, though, space brought even more mysteries – as well as possibly unknown intelligences as fantastic as anything that could be conjured up in a séance room.

Intriguing possibilities emerged during the final days of World War II, when Allied fighter pilots – men with character and clear thinking that no one could question – brought home strange reports of flying objects they called "foo fighters." The objects were silver spheres that appeared from nowhere and flew alongside the pilots' planes. The disks had no obvious means of propulsion but seemed to be controlled by someone intelligent. Many believed the ships were some sort of secret weapon, but scientists were baffled.

Soon, others were seeing similar objects in the sky. Starting in 1947, Americans – notably a Washington state pilot named Kenneth Arnold – began to report a spate of "flying saucer" sightings. The flying objects appeared over Los Angeles, Washington, D.C., and, most famously, near Roswell, New Mexico. The U.S. military took the matter seriously enough to launch official investigations and a new term entered American popular culture: *Unidentified Flying Objects*, or UFO's for short. But the military investigations, rather than reaching a conclusive explanation or even framing a meaningful question, became a mish-mash of contradictory statements, half-truths, cover-ups, and plenty of material for conspiracy theorists.

For readers of the pulp fiction magazines of the day, a similarly compelling but more sinister story was unfolding. In the 1940s, scores of readers were kept enthralled by reports of "inner earth" and its horrifying inhabitants. Stories of a "hollow earth" had a long history and the legend resurfaced in a series of "true" stories that began being published in January 1944 in the pulp *Amazing Stories*. Richard Shaver, a Pennsylvania writer, artist, factory worker, and sometime mental patient, began writing accounts of an underground race that was set on destroying humanity. Shaver knew, he claimed, because he had been among them, deep inside of the earth. The tales were published, embellished, and defended by the magazine's energetic editor, Ray Palmer, which gave them an air of credibility. Readers were thrilled with the stories and some even wrote in to report their own encounters with evil figures who lived in the caverns under the earth.

Amazing Stories editor, Ray Palmer

The science-fiction fan base of the magazine revolted against the stories. They wanted tales of rocket ships, laser guns, and alien-pounding heroes, not "strange but true" paranormal dramas. One group passed a resolution condemning Shaver's "inner-earth" talks as a danger to readers' mental health. In 1948, Ziff-Davis, the corporate owner of the magazine, got tired of the complaints and banned the "Shaver Mystery," as it had come to be known, from its pages.

Palmer, angry and disappointed, resigned in protest. Part true-believer but mostly opportunist, Palmer took a stand to continue with the Shaver narrative and a range of other occult tales in a series of poorly edited, digest-sized magazines like *Mystic* and *Search*. But they never really got off the ground. The sloppily-written articles actually made the bizarre and the unknown seem boring. The only redeeming quality of them was Palmer himself. He wrote in *Mystic* in 1953: "When you read this story, you will tell yourself that it is fiction; the editors assure you that it is. But what if it isn't?" Who can argue with that kind of logic?

Palmer's magazines refused to pay for content, believing that, since it wanted to present the truth, that the trust could not be bought. However, it could certainly be sold. Some of his magazines' liveliest content came from the bazaar of advertising featured in each one. It offered occult schools that taught Rosicrucian, Mayan, and Yogi mysteries and ads for talking boards, magic crystals, and Tarot cards. There was even a UFO-celebrity endorsement for dandruff shampoo from flying saucer witness Kenneth Arnold. It was a masculine brand of shampoo, "Because Ken's no sissy, and he doesn't put perfume on his hair."

Mystic and its spin-offs faded into obscurity and, by the 1960s, were gone. The sole occult digest to survive the Palmer era was a magazine that he co-founded and then quickly left in the hands of his partner, Curtis Fuller: *Fate*, a monthly that continues to this day. Fuller, along with his wife, Mary, expanded the magazine's focus and increased readership to well over 100,000 subscribers. With its "true reports" on the occult and the unexplained – and a standard of writing that aimed a little higher than what appeared in Palmer's journals – it ignited a new interest in the paranormal in America.

Promoted as "the world's leading magazine of the paranormal," it began publishing articles, opinions, and personal experiences relating to UFOs, psychic abilities, cryptozoology, alternative medicine, yoga, divination methods, predictive dreams, reincarnation, mental telepathy, archaeology, warnings of death, and well, things that were pretty strange. Some of the articles in the early years dealt with alternate theories about the Mound Builders; the "10 Lost Tribes" in America; Thomas Edison and the "little people"; Druids in Chicago; the healthy advantages to eating dirt; how to see human auras; sacred hula dancing; how to be a mind reader; psychic dogs; how nude monks were really the abominable snowmen of the Himalayas; the upcoming colonization of Venus; a severed head that spoke; Lyndon Johnson's call for a "UFO alert"; telepathy with rattlesnakes; and a lot of articles about Voodoo, snake-handling and speaking in tongues, Edgar Cayce, Aztecs, Mayans, Hindus, Mormons, and the "love orgies of Baal."

But one of the most popular parts of the magazine was the ghost stories – articles, stories, first-hand accounts, haunted houses, poltergeists, and more. When the magazine first began publishing in 1948, ghosts were an integral part of its format. *Fate* managed to spark not only a new interest in the paranormal in America, it also reintroduced us to the accounts of ghosts and hauntings that had been gathering dust for years.

As the 1950s dawned, ghosts were popular again. There was a revived interest in not only hauntings, but in Spiritualism, as well. Articles appeared in *Fate* about Arthur Ford and the "Houdini Code," about Mina "Margery" Crandon, arguing both for and against her abilities. Spiritualist communities like Camp Chesterfield in Indiana began to see a growing number of people who were interested in the other side. There was not the kind of mania that had surrounded Spiritualism in the nineteenth century – or even after World War I – but people were talking about ghosts again and interest was on the rise.

PROMINENT AMERICAN GHOSTS

"One spring morning several years ago, I started out from North Cliff Farm in Virginia on an adventure that had long been prodding my mind. I planned to spend the better part of a year motoring the length and breadth of the country, painting a series of canvases. I wished to document the American scene, emphasizing particularly the architecture of the various regions. I was told hundreds of ghost stories, tales of endless variety, some not suitable for brush or pen, and as the weeks passed I realized I was becoming intimately acquainted with an American tradition of folklore of tremendous vitality and importance. And so in this book, in word and picture, I present a kind of panorama of the disparate personalities whose perturbed shades still bulk large in ghostly legends of the American scene."

Those words were written by James Reynolds in 1954 as a prologue to his book, *Ghosts in American Houses*, a travel guide to haunted places around the country. He later followed that up with a similar book about Ireland. *Ghosts in American Houses* is certainly not one of the best ghost books ever written, nor is it an enduring classic, but the fact that it sold as well as it did in the 1950s was evidence about the way that ghosts had emerged once again in America's paranormal pop culture.

There were other books that also appeared during that era, like *The Men Who Wouldn't Stay Dead* by Ida Clyde Clark, *Things that Go Bump in the Night* by Louis Jones, and books by Nandor Fodor, like *Haunted People*, which, in the 1950s, began exploring the idea that not all poltergeist outbreaks could be explained as ghosts.

One of the best-selling titles of the era was Susy Smith's *Prominent American Ghosts,* which was published in 1967 after a lengthy excursion that the author made around the country in a search for haunted places. Smith wrote 30 books in her lifetime, and while many of them were about other aspects of the paranormal, she made her mark on the ghost community with her famous title. She was also a fascinating personality who delved into spirit communications and even offered a reward to anyone who could discover her version of Houdini's famous "code" after her death.

Susy was born Ethel Elizabeth Smith in June 1911 in Washington, D.C. She was the only child of an Army officer and his wife and traveled widely, spending more than 10 years of her early life in San Antonio, Texas. As a result, Susy majored in journalism at the University of Texas and later attended Hunter College in New York. She was married for just over two years in her 20's. On the rebound from a broken love affair – she found out her fiancée was married to another woman – she met M.L. Smith and married him two years later. The marriage was never happy and fell apart after Susy became seriously ill from blood poisoning. The infection gravely affected her left hip and an operation left her with a left leg two inches shorter than the right, and a lifetime of chronic pain and discomfort.

Susy had started her career as a journalist, working for several newspapers, but she always had an interest in the paranormal and spent a lot of her time chasing down stories of haunted houses, reincarnation, witchcraft, and psychic animals. In 1955, her research became serious after an experience with a Ouija board in Salt Lake City convinced her that the dead were trying to speak to her. She began researching after-death communications and paranormal phenomena and after sensing her dead mother's presence, began to try and make contact with her. In 1956, while using a talking board, Susy received a message that told her to "get a pencil" and to "go into a trance." She followed the instructions and, using automatic writing, began receiving messages from her mother.

Against her mother's advice, she also began communicating with a spirit who said his name was "Harvey." He proved to be troublesome, angry, and once materialized with an old man's face in Susy's bathroom mirror. She quickly broke off all contact with him.

Another spirit that she made contacted with – and remained in communication with for many years – was a man who called himself "James Anderson." He had been introduced to Susy by her mother. James gave Susy a great deal of material and served as a companion to her. A medium once told Susy that James was in fact William James, the late philosopher and paranormal researcher, and when asked, the spirit confirmed this was true. Susy later wrote a book about her experiences with James in 1974. Later in life, though, she often questioned the source of her material, wondering if she had conjured it up from her own subconscious. It seems possible, especially considering that the book contained a large amount of personal material, including details about the author's two suicide attempts.

The "unbearable anguish" that Susy had suffered from after broken love affairs, physical pain, and emotional issues led to her attempted suicides. She had gone to her doctor to get pain pills, intending to overdose, but he gave her a liquid medication instead. Susy proceeded with her plan and wrote out a farewell letter, but choked on the medicine. The second attempt occurred in 1963. She was in Europe when she broke her foot and was forced to convalesce in an Italian hospital. Confined to her bed, she focused on her misery, on a failed love affair, and on the "miserable uselessness" of her life. She made plans to kill herself, but backed out at the last minute.

It turned out to be paranormal research that literally saved Susy's life. She submitted to tests for evidence of survival communication and received training for analysis of psychic experiences at the Parapsychology Laboratory at Duke University, which was run by J.B. and Louisa Rhine. She also received a grant from the Parapsychology Foundation to condense Frederic W.H. Myers' two-volume work, *Human Personality and Its Survival of Death* into a single volume and then received another grant to write a book about medium Gladys Leonard.

It was in the 1960s that Susy undertook her trip around the United States to write *Prominent American Ghosts*, her most popular work and a paranormal classic.

In 1971, she moved from Cuernavaca, Mexico, to Tucson, Arizona, where she founded the Survival Research Foundation. In 1997, the Susy Smith Project in the Human Energy Systems Laboratory at the University of Arizona was created by Dr. Gary E. Schwartz and Dr. Linda G.S. Russek to continue her research. Russek, who called Susy the "matriarch of survival research," persuaded her to write her 30th book in 2000, *The Afterlife Codes*, a recounting of the highlights of her life's research of survival after death.

By this time, Susy was in her eighties and was mostly housebound due the crippling effects of her earlier illness. She died on February 11, 2001. She had no survivors.

However, as with many other researchers of the paranormal, death was not the end of Susy's story. In the fashion of Houdini, Susy created a phrase as an afterlife code by which she would attempt to prove her survival after death. The code, known only to her, was kept in a fraud-proof computer. The code was a phrase that had been combined with the alphabet by a computer, so that a jumbled sequence of letters was produced. Only the computer could decode it to check for a match. As a control, two telepathy codes were also placed on the computer, known only to Dr. Schwartz, Dr. Rusek, and Susy Smith. The telepathy codes tested whether a living person picked up the codes mentally rather than from the secret code Susy tried to send from the afterlife.

Before she died, Susy set up a $10,000 fund for any living person who managed to discover her code. Anyone who believed that they had received a message from Susy could test the accuracy of their code at a website that had been set up for the purpose. The code remained unbroken for years, and eventually the project was discontinued, leaving lingering questions about afterlife communication in its wake.

It was also during this period that a man who would become one of the most famous names in modern ghost hunting came to prominence. His name was Hans Holzer and his books, television appearances, and investigations would earn him a generation of fans. Unlike today's paranormal shows that permeate the cable arena like a plague of locusts, Holzer was one of the only voices for the supernatural during the era. A frequent guest on late night talk shows, he was also a consultant to Leonard Nimoy's *In Search Of*, and appeared on the groundbreaking show several times. Among Holzer's fans were Elvis Presley and Dan Akroyd, who has admitted, "I became obsessed by Hans Holzer, the greatest ghost hunter ever. That's when the idea of my film *Ghost Busters* was born." Holzer was the first paranormal researcher to become widely-known in America, and while he has been erroneously credited with coining the phrase "ghost hunter" (sorry, Harry Price did that in 1936), there is no denying the impact that he had on the paranormal pop culture landscape of the mid-twentieth century.

Hans Holzer

Holzer was born in 1920 in Vienna, Austria. His interest in the supernatural was sparked at a young age by ghost stories that were told to him by his uncle. At the University of Vienna, he studied ancient history and archaeology, but with World War II eminent, his family fled to the United States in 1938. Holzer settled in New York City, where he remained for the rest of his life. He enrolled at Columbia University, where he studied Japanese and at the London College of Applied Science, he earned a master's degree in comparative religion, followed by a Ph.D. with a specialty in parapsychology. His career was varied enough to include a teaching position at the New York Institute of Technology, an annual lecture schedule, television and feature film production, numerous appearances on radio and television, and the publication of 138 books during his lifetime.

His first book, *Ghost Hunter*, was published in 1963 and became a bestseller. Calling himself a "scientific investigator of the paranormal," Holzer believed that ghosts did not know they were dead. "A ghost is only a fellow human being in trouble," he said. He considered intelligent spirits to be "stay behinds," lingering after death and remnants of a still-active intelligence. He was convinced that ghosts relived their final moments of life over and over again, like a needle stuck in the grooves of a vinyl record. Holzer was determined to help these unfortunates realize that they were indeed dead, allowing them to depart their captivity on earth. He believed that many hauntings were simply imprints or recordings left behind, and not the presence of stuck souls.

These were groundbreaking ideas at the time and helped to make Holzer the go-to expert for television and radio shows. Unlike many paranormal investigators, Holzer did not shy away from mediums and sensitives. He never had much use for equipment –

carrying only a camera and a reel-to-reel tape recorder during his investigations – and preferred to check out alleged haunts with well-known trance mediums like Ethel Johnson-Meyers, Sybil Leek, and Marisa Anderson. He traveled all over the country, and throughout the world, searching for evidence of ghosts.

He didn't always find such evidence. Thanks to his reliance on "reputable mediums," many of Holzer's investigations turned up "evidence" that simply didn't fit the facts. For example, in his book *America's Haunted Houses*, Holzer wrote about Ringwood Manor in New Jersey, an important historic site. An earlier house had been built on the property in 1762 and was eventually acquired by Robert Erskine, a member of the Continental Army and surveyor general to George Washington. Erskine had provided Washington with the maps needs to help win the Revolutionary War. His grave is located on a small cemetery on the property. In 1807, Martin Ryerson tore down the original house and erected a portion of the current structure. In 1854, the property was purchased by New York mayor Abram Hewitt, who converted it into the present-day mansion. It remained in the Hewitt family until 1936, when the estate was bequeathed to New Jersey. Holzer investigated Ringwood Manor with medium Ethel Johnson-Meyers, and she supposedly made contact with the spirits of two former servants. One was said to be responsible for the ghostly footsteps heard in the house and the other complained bitterly about his mistress, Mrs. Erskine, who he claimed often abused him. Holzer stated in the book that Mrs. Erskine was unhappy with the presence of the ghost hunters in her home and repeatedly told them to leave.

The curator of Ringwood Manor at the time, Elbertus Prol, was annoyed with Holzer's account. Aside from the fact that Prol had never encountered anything ghostly at the house, he stated that there was no evidence that Mrs. Erskine ever mistreated her servants. He also adds that the house as it exists today was never seen by Mrs. Erskine. The original house on the property had been torn down and the new house was not even close to the site of the old one. That means that when Holzer wrote, "The center of the haunting seems to be what was once Mrs. Erskine's bedroom," the whole story falls apart. Holzer obviously based his findings on the history that was given to him by the medium – and this was not the only time that such methods got him into trouble.

Holzer's most infamous investigation became the so-called "Amityville Horror" case, which will be discussed in-depth in a later chapter. In January 1977, Holzer, with Ethel Johnson-Meyers in tow, visited the house at 112 Ocean Avenue in Amityville, New York. The owners – as most readers know the basics of the story – claimed that the house was haunted and were driven from the house in terror by demonic happenings. A year before they had moved in, a young man named Ronald DeFeo, Jr. had murdered his entire family in the house. During Holzer's investigation, Ethel Johnson-Meyers claimed that the house had been built on a Native American burial ground and that the angry spirit of a Shinnecock Indian chief named "Rolling Thunder" had possessed DeFeo and made him kill his family. The claims that the house was built on sacred Indian land was hotly denied by the Amityville Historical Society and it was the Montaukett Indians, and not the Shinnecocks, who had been the original settlers in the area. Of course, that was only a very small part of the problems with the Amityville case, as we will later see.

Holzer, however, ignored the history and went on to write *Murder in Amityville*, which became the basis for the not-so-classic film *Amityville II: The Possession* in 1982.

Holzer married once and had two daughters. He divorced after the birth of his second daughter and passed away in 2009. The prolific author left an indelible mark on the paranormal field, his career only marred by the often inaccurate information given to him by the "psychics" that he chose to work with. There is no question that he was one of the most authentic personalities and well-intentioned ghost hunters to emerge from the early days of the modern era. His legacy should be remembered today as one of the researchers who moved the paranormal away from the shadows of the séance room and into the bright lights of the public arena.

And there was one other event that took place during this era, in 1952. A Connecticut couple named Ed and Lorraine Warren founded the New England Society for Psychic Research, which would become one of the first actual ghost hunting groups in modern history.

We will take a much closer look at the Warrens and their work in a later chapter.

12. THE DEVIL RIDES OUT

THE RISE OF THE OCCULT IN 1960S AND 1970S AMERICA

The 1960s opened American society to a new range of movements and innovations, from eastern philosophies like Transcendental Meditation and Zen Buddhism, to Native American Shamanism, and the witchcraft resurgence that came from England. Largely the work of writer Gerald Gardner, the revival, or reinvention, of witchcraft emerged in England a short time after World War II. Only in 1951 did Britain lift its last law against witches. The Witchcraft Act, dating to the mid-sixteenth century, was finally repealed, thanks to the efforts of British Spiritualists who occasionally found themselves harassed by its restrictions. Without fear of any legal reprisals, Gardner brought witchcraft to a new generation of followers.

Gardner, who had spent most of his life as an adventurous customs agent in Borneo, British Malaysia, Singapore, and other far-off trading posts of the British Empire, retired on the southern English coast in the 1930s. He used his retirement to study folklore and tribal rites that he had encountered in the Far East. He also delved into the research of anthropologist Margaret A. Murray, who suggested that an ancient "witch cult" had survived through the centuries in England and Western Europe. An American folklorist named Charles G. Leland had promoted a similar idea in the early 1900s, linking folk magic and nature cults as the "old religion." Gardner later claimed that he was initiated into one of these covens during World War II and they secretly met in the forest to cast binding spells against Hitler and the Nazis.

In 1954, Gardner published a book that would become a bestseller in both England and America, a slender volume called *Witchcraft Today*. It laid out the surviving beliefs and seasonal rituals of the nature-based cults that he claimed still existed. Gardner called their members "Wica," an Old English term for "wise" or "clever folk." In America, this new faith became known as Wicca. Gardner's new and old theology was borrowed, invented, half dreamed up and half grounded in a wide mixture of folklore and traditional practices. It was, above all, a new religion that met the needs of the times. Wicca was based in nature, sexually free, and female-affirming. By the late 1960s, its message of a do-it-yourself spirituality was embraced by hundreds of thousands of young people. Wicca – or paganism – became one of America's fastest-growing religious movements, even gaining recognition as an official religion in the United States military. It's still widely in practice today, gaining new followers every year.

"DO WHAT THOU WILT"

But not everything to do with witchcraft in the 1960s was immersed in nature and the old religion. It was during this period that a darker element began to seep into the popular culture. In England, the so-called "King of the Witches," Alex Sanders told an array of wild stories to the press about his initiation into witchcraft as a child in the 1930s and about meeting infamous magician Aleister Crowley. He also invited reporters to attend black masses, where the participants – mostly young women – were always naked. Sanders was an unrepentant narcissist, with a larger-than-life ego and an insatiable need for attention. When the press pestered him for salacious accounts of nude rituals and magical spells, he willingly obliged. And the more media attention he got, the more followers he attracted. By 1965, he claimed 1,623 initiates in 100 covens. A romanticized biography and a film about his largely fictional exploits led to greater publicity, guest appearances on talk-shows, and public speaking engagements. All of this was to the chagrin of other witches, who saw Sanders as exploiting their faith and dragging it through the gutter of the sensational press.

While Sanders was quite the attraction in England, America had its own black magic ringmaster in the 1960s. His name was Anton Szandor LaVey and he founded the Church of Satan in 1966 and grabbed national headlines. His image as a charming Mephistopheles lured in fans and followers, including many who moved in Hollywood circles. He was a showman, con artist, and the face of a new America movement.

LaVey -- whose real name was Howard Stanton Levey – was born in Chicago in April 1930. His family relocated to San Francisco and he spent most of his early life in California. He learned about witchcraft, spirits, and the occult from his grandmother and developed a deep interest in dark literature and in the pulp horror fiction of the era. He also developed musical skills and was especially adept at the organ and the calliope. LaVey dropped out of high school and began working in circuses and carnivals, first as a roustabout and later as a musician. He played the calliope for the "grind shows" on Saturday nights, and played the organ on Sunday mornings for the tent revivals. He later noted seeing many of the same men attending both the strip shows on Saturday night and the church services on Sunday mornings, which reinforced his cynical view of religion. When the carnival season ended, LaVey began earning a living playing the organ in Los Angeles bars, nightclubs, and burlesque theaters.

Moving back to San Francisco, LaVey worked as a police photographer for a time. A short time later, he met and married Carole Lansing, who bore him his first daughter, Karla Maritza, in 1952. They divorced in 1960 after LaVey began seeing Diane Hegarty. They never married, but she was his companion for many years, and bore his second

Anton LaVey publicity photo

daughter, Zeena Galatea LaVey in 1964. LaVey's final companion was Blanche Barton, who gave him his only son, Satan Xerxes Carnacki LaVey, in 1993.

During the 1950s, LaVey dabbled as a psychical investigator, looking into what his friends on the police force cheerfully referred to as "nut calls." LaVey soon became known as a San Francisco celebrity. Thanks to his paranormal research and his live performances as an organist, he attracted many California notables to his parties. Guests included Michael Harner, Chester A. Arthur III, Forrest J. Ackerman, Fritz Leiber, Dr. Cecil E. Nixon, and Kenneth Anger. He began presenting lectures on the occult to what he called his "Magic Circle," which was made up of friends who shared his interests. It was a member of the circle who suggested, perhaps jokingly, that he could start his own religion based on the ideas that he was coming up with.

LaVey took this suggestion seriously, and on April 30, 1966, Walpurgis Night, he launched his new religion. He shaved his head, declared the founding of the Church of Satan, and proclaimed 1966 as "the Year One," Anno Satanas - the first year of the Age of Satan. He exhibited a flair for self-promotion that would have impressed P.T. Barnum. In the years that followed, Satan rewarded him well. He acquired numerous properties, a fleet of classic cars, and even a yacht. In the interviews, articles, and books that followed, it became obvious that LaVey had put together a mish-mash of ideologies, ritual practices, and beliefs. His church did not literally worship Satan, but a personification of man's carnal nature. The motto was stolen from Aleister Crowley – "Do What Thou Wilt" – and as long as no one got hurt, all was well. Essentially, the Church of Satan was more about the publicity that it generated than about any kind of black magic or devil worship – but boy, the rituals and trappings of it all sure looked scary in the photographs that began showing up in national magazines and on television.

Media attention followed the founding of the Church of Satan, leading to coverage in newspapers all over the country and the cover of *Look* magazine. The *Los Angeles Times* and the *San Francisco Chronicle* were among those that dubbed him the "Black Pope." LaVey performed satanic weddings, satanic baptisms (including one for his daughter Zeena), and satanic funerals. He released a record album entitled *The Satanic Mass*. He appeared on talk shows with Joe Pyne, Phil Donahue, and Johnny Carson, and in feature-length documentaries. Since its founding, LaVey's Church of Satan has attracted scores of followers who shared a jaded view of organized religion, including celebrities like Jayne Mansfield, Sammy Davis, Jr., Marilyn Manson, director Robert Fuest, ufologist Jacques Vallee, author Aime Michel and many others.

But not all of the publicity was good.

One of the converts to LaVey's Church of Satan was Jayne Mansfield, one of America's top pinup girls. On June 29, 1967, she died a horrible and violent death along a lonely roadway near Biloxi, Mississippi. Her death had a sobering effect on the Hollywood film community and strange repercussions in the occult community of the time, as well. Jayne's death was said to have been caused by a curse gone awry. Jayne was involved in a violent relationship with an abusive boyfriend named Sam Brody and she asked LaVey for help. Allegedly, LaVey cursed the man and told Jayne to stay away from him if she didn't want to become collateral damage from the curse. She didn't follow his advice and was killed, along with Brody, in the terrible crash.

The publicity that followed Jayne Mansfield's death attracted what LaVey felt were the "wrong sort of people" to the church. These were the people that even LaVey feared – the sick, the mentally ill, and the ones mad enough to believe that they could commit crimes and have the protection of the Devil himself. LaVey saw himself as a shameless schemer and manipulator, which he believed the Devil would also be. His "black masses" were more for entertainment than devil worship. It was pure theater for the curious, who were treated to the sight of a naked girl tied down on an altar while people in black robes chanted and sang.

Devout Christians and moralists were outraged by LaVey's shameless self-promotion and the inflammatory nature of his widely-publicized beliefs, but the truth of the matter was that they needed a "devil" like him to complain about. They needed LaVey to be a real "evil" or their crusade against him would lose its meaning. LaVey might have been Satan's best promoter, but he made a valid point when he wrote, "Satan has been the best friend the Church has ever had. He's kept them in business all these years."

The Christians lost their adversary on October 29, 1997, when LaVey died at St. Mary's Hospital in San Francisco of pulmonary edema. For reasons open to speculation, the time and date of his passing were listed incorrectly on his death certificate, stating that he died on Halloween. LaVey's funeral was a secret, by-invitation-only satanic service held in Colma, California. His body was cremated, with his ashes eventually divided among his heirs.

LaVey had played a very important part in ushering in a new era in America's paranormal pop culture. The years that followed saw a rise in books, magazines, and films that dealt with the occult, witchcraft, and, of course, the Devil himself.

In 1968, Roman Polanski's film, *Rosemary's Baby*, was released. The film starred Mia Farrow as Rosemary Woodhouse, a young mother-to-be who grows increasingly suspicious that her overfriendly elderly neighbors (played by Sidney Blackmer and an Oscar-winning Ruth Gordon) and self-involved husband (John Cassavetes) are hatching a devilish plot against her and her baby. The film was scary and very entertaining and spawned decades of occult films in the years ahead. However, it has rarely been outdone for its sheer psychological terror. The next year, ironically, director Polanski's wife, the beautiful actress Sharon Tate, was one of the victims murdered by the followers of Charles Manson, who had connections to various Satanic cults in California.

The Devil seemed to be alive and well in American popular culture, but at that time, few were paying attention to the ancient belief in possession and exorcism. Catholics and fundamentalist Christians believed that the Devil or demonic entities could enter and take control of a person's body and mind, but most Americans gave the concept little thought. Most dismissed it as a superstition of times long past.

Then, in 1973, *The Exorcist* hit movie theaters all over the country. The film was about an ordinary 12-year-old girl who becomes possessed by a demon. It was both riveting and terrifying, chillingly enhanced by makeup and special effects that included the possessed girl's head spinning around, her vomiting green bile, and levitating over her bed. All the while, an old priest and a young priest try desperately to cast out the hostile demon from the tortured girl, played by actress Linda Blair. The deep and scratchy voice of the demon that spoke through the possessed girl added another layer of terror for audiences. Stories circulated about people fainting in the theater, moviegoers fleeing into the street, and vomiting in the aisles.

Suddenly, possession and exorcism were all the rage. Movie audiences and readers demanded more about the subject. The number of Americans who thought that demons were in their homes, possessing their children, multiplied, as did the call for exorcists. To add to everyone's fear was the reminder that *The Exorcist*, based on a book by William Peter Blatty, was inspired by a true story that occurred in 1949.

At the time, Blatty was a student at Georgetown when he read a newspaper story about a Maryland boy who had been possessed and underwent an exorcism in St. Louis. According to the article, the child and his family had been plagued by a series of bizarre and terrifying events. Objects and furniture in the boy's room flew about; inexplicable sounds shook the house; sounds of scratching were heard inside the walls. The covers and blankets were ripped from the bed and the bed itself actually moved around the room. Tortured by the chaos, the family could find no peace. They turned to doctors, who admitted the boy to the hospital for a battery of tests, but they could find nothing physically or mentally wrong with him. The family then contacted their Lutheran minister – who eventually told his story to the newspaper – and after witnessing the strange phenomena that surrounded the boy, suggested they contact the Catholic Church, who had experience with "this sort of thing."

Meanwhile, the frightening events continued to occur in the home and were getting worse. Letters and words – a priest later described them as "brandings" – appeared on the boy's skin and directed the family to St. Louis, where relatives lived. Jesuit priests were sent to observe the boy and the mysterious phenomena and permission was given for an exorcism. The rituals began at the relative's home, were moved to a church rectory, and finally to an Alexian Brothers hospital on the south side of the city. The exorcism went on for weeks before the boy was finally free of whatever had possessed him.

The story fascinated Blatty, who had once considered becoming a priest. If the story was true, the concept of demonic possession and exorcism still had meaning in the modern world. More than 20 years later, Blatty, by then a Hollywood writer, researched Catholic demonology, and sat down to wrote a novel about the exorcism, moving the location, changing the boy into a young girl, and setting the story in the present day.

With help from a friend who was a priest, Blatty managed to get his hands on a copy of a "diary" that had been kept by one of the priests involved in the exorcism. In the pages were troubling entries about furniture that shook and crashed, a bed that levitated off the floor, unexplained noises, cold spots, and more. Blatty's novel made the strange events even more terrifying and the film version went even further in exaggerating the possessions.

There is no question that *The Exorcist* --- the end result of a true story that actually took place and one I have recounted in my book, *The Devil Came to St. Louis* – had a tremendous effect on paranormal popular culture in America. Unlike the Spiritualist mediums, the ghost hunters, and the clairvoyants of the past, *The Exorcist* never claimed to be anything but a novel. Yes, it was based on a real story, but it was the fictional version of the events that inspired the flood of books, cases, and documentaries that followed – all of which claimed to be true.

The Exorcist was a defining moment for the 1970s and the paranormal. The preceding decade had seen a rise in interest in the occult, witchcraft, and the Devil, but after the release of Blatty's book, and the film that followed, audiences demanded more. The fact that *The Exorcist* was based on real events meant that there must be other stories out there which were also true.

And if there weren't, well, then someone would make them up. But, we're getting ahead of the story…

Suffice it to say, popular culture demanded more of the Devil's work, more demons, more exorcisms, more of the sinister side of the paranormal. *The Exorcist* would color almost everything to do with the paranormal for the rest of the decade and into the 1980s.

PARANORMAL IN PAPERBACK

The 1960s and 1970s saw a new trend in paranormal pop culture – paperback books. For the first time, readers across America had access to cheap, easy-to-read books about everything from ghosts to Bigfoot, sea monsters, phantom ships, UFOs, and the Bermuda Triangle (another big topic of the 1970s that we'll steer clear of in this book).

Paperback books had been around since the nineteenth century, but it was not until World War II that Pocket Books began catering to soldiers, offering a small book that would fit right into the back pocket of a man's trousers. Other companies entered the paperback publishing field after Pocket Books' inception, including Ace, Dell, Bantam, Avon, and other smaller publishers. At first, paperbacks consisted entirely of reprints, but in 1950, Fawcett Publications' Gold Medal Books began publishing original works in paperback. Sales soared and genre categories began to emerge as more publishers began printing their own cheap, readily available, easily carried books. Revolving metal racks, designed to display a wide variety of paperbacks in a small space, found their way into drug stores, dime stores, supermarkets, gas stations, and just about anyplace where people might be looking for a way to fill a few hours of free time.

And with the rise of paranormal paperbacks, we once again saw the resurgence of ghosts. Amidst all the clutter of monsters, demons, and witches, we had dozens and dozens of books about hauntings. Over the years, I have picked up hundreds of dog-eared, well-read, worn down paperback books on ghosts and the supernatural, managing to amass a pretty good, albeit a rather lurid, collection. *Fate* magazine got into the act, reprinting hundreds of ghost stories from back issues into paperback collections, along with dozens of editors who specialized in the strange and the macabre.

The paperback writer who probably made the greatest impact on me when I was growing up was Richard Winer, who wrote three books on ghosts and a fourth on ghost ships, along with several books about the Bermuda Triangle. Winer's biography stated that he had attended the University of Minnesota and had spent most of his life as a journalist and photographer. He had also been a "professional sailor, treasure hunter, yachtsman, hobo, and soldier of fortune." How much of this was true didn't matter much to me at age 11, but later in life, I would find that many of the ghost stories that Winer included in his books were either embellished, or wildly inaccurate. The important thing to me, though, was that Winer – along with two-time co-author Nancy Osborn – traveled the entire country, visiting places, and collecting stories from spots that were believed to be haunted. I still have the worn-out copy of his book *Haunted Houses* that I took with me to New Orleans for my very first visit, and suffice it to say, if not for the paperbacks of the 1970s, you likely wouldn't be holding this book in your hands today.

The occult boom in the 1970s ushered in a new wave of ghostly tales for American audiences. Many of the accounts that made it into print during that decade had occurred in the past, but were books that had been unable to find an audience before the paranormal became popular again. Others emerged in the wake of the country's greatest paranormal pop culture event, which occurred in the late 1970s and have a chapter all its own.

SPINDRIFT

One of those stories had its start back in 1957, but the deadly events that occurred wouldn't play themselves out for some time, culminating in the death of an author and the horrific murder of a child. It was in 1957 that actress Jan Bryant Bartell moved into a large old mansion at 14 West 10th Street, just off Fifth Avenue, in New York. Just weeks after moving in, she claimed to feel a "monstrous moving shadow that loomed up behind" her. She turned and saw nothing there, but couldn't shake the feeling that she was not alone, and maybe never would be, in the already aging house with fretted balustrades and Civil War-era glass in the windows.

The incident left Jan shaken, but it wouldn't be the last one to occur in what turned out to be a seven-year period of psychological, and sometimes physical, torment that Jan suffered at what she believed were the hands of the house's former occupants, reaching out from beyond the grave. The place would come to be known by the nickname, "The House of Death."

Some say there is a curse that touches the people who live in the house. Jan Bartell died under mysterious circumstances just weeks after finishing a book about her experiences there. Most notoriously, No. 14 was the site of a grisly murder in 1987, when former criminal defense attorney Joe Steinberg beat a six-year-old girl to death. But that was just part of the house's history...

The classic brownstone was built sometime in the 1850s, just before the Civil War, when the area around Washington Square was booming. It was originally one house, but is now split up into ten different apartments. Legend states that the house has witnessed 22 deaths, which would not be that unusual for a house of its age, except that some of those who died within its walls never left. The most famous former resident was Mark Twain, who lived in the house for a year in 1900. Though he died in Connecticut, he has been seen in the house. But not all the ghosts are that of a kindly old writer, however. Residents have reported encounters with the dead so chilling they have fled the place, never to return.

The most detailed account of haunted life in the building comes from Jan Bartell's memoir, *Spindrift: Spray from a Psychic Sea*, which was written in 1973, just before she died.

The "House of Death" that was featured in the book Spindrift

On the first day that Jan and her husband, Fred, moved into the top floor that was once the servant's quarters, she felt the strange chill of the house closing in around her. But, due to a housing shortage at the time, she had no choice but to stick it out.

The strange occurrences started small – footsteps following her up the stairs, a brush across the back of her neck, a pungent rotting smell that would come and go. Then, things got darker. Shadows moved across rooms and there was a mysterious chair that Jan's dog would bark and growl at, as if it saw something she could not. Then a phantom, shriveled grape appeared on a clean dinner plate, even though the couple hadn't bought grapes in months. She found furniture inexplicably moved from its usual place. The sound of crashing glass followed her around the house. The bizarre rotting smell was joined by another – a fragrant perfume that wafted through rooms and then faded away. One day, the vision of a man appeared and Jan reached out to touch it. She claimed that the figure was made up of a cloudy film that froze her fingers at the tips. The man vanished, leaving behind a cloying and sickly sweet smell that also disappeared a few moments later.

Jan and Fred decided to fight back. They called in a paranormal researcher and a medium to see if they could help. Immediately, the medium felt a presence – or perhaps three of them: a young girl with curly hair, an aborted child, and a small gray cat. In a trance, the medium was possessed by the spirit of a young woman who was born in 1848. She blamed Abraham Lincoln for killing her husband by making him fight in the Civil War. She was angry and filled with resentment toward those who had "invaded" her home. When the researcher ordered her to leave the Bartells in peace, the spirit refused.

After that, Jan and Fred no longer felt safe. They moved away shortly after the séance, although Jan was unable to shake the feeling that the house had poisoned her in some way. She died mysteriously, just after finishing her account of life at No. 14, or at least that's the dramatic ending to her story. After the Bartells left Greenwich Village, they moved to suburban New Rochelle and bought a home. Jan died on June 18, 1973 – either from a heart attack or, as some believe, by suicide. She had suffered bouts of depression throughout her life and it's thought her time at No. 14 may have pushed her over the edge.

We may never know what happened to Jan Bartell, but beyond the events of *Spindrift*, the house's story wasn't over. More than 15 years after Jan died, a much more shocking series of tragic events occurred in the "House of Death." Joel Steinberg, a wealthy attorney, and his girlfriend, Hedda Nussbaum, an editor of children's books at Random House, moved into the house. They were a well-liked, professional couple and told friends and neighbors they had adopted two children, Lisa, 6, and Mitchell, 18 months old. But in 1987, their happy façade fell apart, revealing a drug-fueled house of horror and abuse.

After freebasing cocaine all evening, Steinberg beat Lisa, leaving her broken and bruised on the bathroom floor. He then went out to meet friends, leaving Nussbaum alone with the children. However, she was too terrified of Steinberg's wrath to help Lisa in the next room. Steinberg returned home late that night and he and Nussbaum freebased more cocaine until around 4:00 a.m. Lisa was still lying on the bathroom floor. It wasn't until 6:30 a.m. that Nussbaum finally summoned the courage to call the police. When they arrived, they found the second-floor apartment in eerie disarray. Nussbaum answered the door with her face bruised, battered, and bleeding. She wandered the apartment, hiding behind doors, while medics attended to Lisa. Mitchell, soaked in urine and covered in filth, was found tied to a playpen with a rope around his waist. Lisa died three days later in the hospital.

As it turned out, residents of the building had reported Steinberg before, on suspicions of abusing Nussbaum and Lisa. There was no follow-up to the reports and the abuse continued. Steinberg was eventually convicted of first-degree manslaughter and served 16 years in prison. The investigation revealed that he had never legally adopted either of the children.

Since Steinberg's horrific crime, the house has been relatively quiet. It seems that the kind of horror that occurred there has even made menacing spirits seem tame in comparison.

NIGHT STALKS THE MANSION

Published in 1978, in the wake of *The Amityville Horror* (although this one is a bit more believable) was a book called *Night Stalks the Mansion* by Constance Westbie and Harold Cameron. Actually set in the late 1940s, it didn't gain any traction as a book until the paranormal resurgence of the 1970s. A year after its hardcover release, it became a paperback bestseller and introduced a generation of ghost enthusiasts to the eerie adventures of Harold Cameron and his family after they moved into an old house near Philadelphia. The house – although never named in the book was the Heilbron Mansion in Delaware County, Pennsylvania. It burned down in 1987.

Written as a first-person account by Harold Cameron, it tells the two-year saga of Cameron, his wife, and five children, who, after his job transferred him to Philadelphia, were living in a cramped hotel room, trying to find a house in a crowded market after World War II. Finding little available for a large family, Harold saw an advertisement for a fully-furnished,

Heilbron Mansion before it was destroyed by fire in 1987.

17-room mansion, available to rent for a low price. He went to look at the house and it fascinated him, even after having an eerie experience when he arrived. After discussing it with his wife, they decided to sign a binding two-year lease. The great deal on the house quickly turned out to be too good to be true and the lease turned out to be iron-clad. No matter what, the Camerons weren't getting out of it.

Almost immediately after moving in, they all began hearing footsteps in the house – the sound of what seemed to be a woman in slippers – and heavy boots on the gravel outside. There was, of course, no one living who was present at the time. Strange noises, smells, and the feeling of being watched intensified the longer the family remained in the house. Visitors to the house – including a young woman who worked at Cameron's ad agency and thought a haunted house seemed like fun -- also witnessed these strange occurrences. Friends, relatives, and even the hired staff fled the house, disturbed by what they experienced.

Unable to break their lease, the Camerons resolved to learn to live with their ghostly inhabitants, and even come to think of them almost fondly. The two presences in the house were later revealed to be a distinguished lady who frequented the home's library, but whose footsteps could be heard leaving that room and ascending the stairs to the third floor. The second ghost was of a male, whose footsteps were heard walking along the gravel drive. Over the course of their stay in the home, the pieces fall into place about who these ghostly visitors may be. An elderly man, once a slave who worked the original mansion, filled in the missing pieces, but paid a dear price for it.

The Camerons moved out of the house after their lease came to an end and Harold Cameron eventually became a minister and decided to write the story of their time in the mansion. The book reads almost like a detective novel, as Cameron tried to track down clues about the house's history. Unlike many other books of the time, the events described come across as very believable and while time has revealed that not all of the history Cameron related in the 1940s about the house was accurate, the reader is convinced that the family experienced something otherworldly in the old house.

It's a moving story, well-written, and delightfully creepy and I highly recommend it. I first picked it up in my early 'teens – right after it appeared in paperback – and I have always had a soft spot for this book. A signed copy of it has a place of honor in my collection.

GHOSTS OF FLIGHT 401

Although John Fuller's book was written about this chilling story about three years after it happened – followed by a television movie, as well – Eastern Airlines Flight 401 crashed northwest of Miami on December 29, 1972. The flight has since become one of the most famous aircraft flights in the annals of the supernatural. It was a haunting that affected dozens of airplanes as the ghosts of the fatal flight became attached to the salvaged parts that were taken from the downed plane.

It was an ordinary flight on a cold winter's night until the crew noticed a problem with the landing gear. An indicator light was out and they were unable to manually check to see if the gear had deployed. The airplane crashed northwest of Miami, into the heart of the Everglades, a vast swamp region of water, sawgrass, marshland and alligators. The plane was traveling at 227 miles an hour when it hit the ground. The left wingtip hit first, then the left engine and the left landing gear. Together, they slashed three long trails through the heavy sawgrass. Each trail was five feet wide and more than 100 feet long.

When the main part of the fuselage hit the ground, it continued to move through the grass and water, coming apart as it went. It hit once, lifted into the air and then slammed back down again with a hard, grinding sound. About halfway along its path, the nose of the plane spun clockwise and careened around until it was sliding backwards. As the plane was skidding through the swamp, a fireball rushed through the cabin, from front to rear. Passengers felt a blast of cold air and then a wet wave of fuel as the plane broke apart. The huge white fuselage crumpled and tore into five large sections and countless smaller pieces. From the first impact to the point that it came to a shuddering halt, the plane traveled more than one-third of a mile.

Passengers drowned in the murky water. Others were thrown from the plane, suffering broken bones, paralyzing injuries and death. When rescue workers arrived on the scene, survivors were taken to two hospitals around Miami that were closest to the crash site. Only 32 of those on board managed to survive the crash.

A long investigation into the crash stated that it was caused by pilot error, specifically, "the failure of the flight crew to monitor the flight instruments during the final four minutes of flight, and to detect an unexpected descent soon enough to prevent impact with the ground. Preoccupation with a malfunction of the nose landing gear position indicating system distracted the crew's attention from the instruments and allowed the descent to go unnoticed." In the tragic ending, 103 people died – all because of two burned-out light bulbs that would have cost $12 to replace. And ironically, the plane's landing gear was found to be in the down and locked position after all, which meant that the disaster should have never happened at all.

Captain Bob Loft and flight engineer Dan Repo were among the people who lost their lives when Flight 401 crashed into the Everglades on that December night in 1972. Initially, both men were among the survivors but Loft succumbed to his wounds about an hour after the crash, before rescuers could get him to the hospital. Repo, critically injured, was reportedly angry when he was pulled from the wreckage. He survived about 30 hours before he also died.

Both of the men would be found to be at fault by the NTSB investigation, although most of the blame fell on Loft's shoulders. They were accused of being preoccupied with finding a source for the indicator light problem and ignoring the fact that the plane was steadily losing altitude. When they discovered what was wrong it was too late – a fact that apparently haunted both men after their deaths for their ghosts soon began to be encountered aboard other Eastern Airlines jets.

Apparently, to save costs, Eastern ordered the salvageable parts of the aircraft to be removed and incorporated into other Eastern planes. Soon after, reports of the ghosts of Repo, Loft and even some unidentified flight attendants were encountered on various Eastern flights. For the next year or so, they were most often seen on Eastern's aircraft Number 318, or on other planes, all of which contained salvaged parts from Flight 401. Eastern crew members and passengers saw the ghosts or heard them speak on the plane's intercom systems or received verbal messages and warnings from them. Witnesses also experienced cold sensations and invisible presences, aircraft power turning on by its own volition and a tool inexplicably appearing in a mechanics hand when no one was in the area.

Substantiation of the sightings was difficult, however. Eyewitness reports made to Eastern's management were met with skepticism and a fear of further damaging the airline's reputation and causing a further loss of business. The crash had done enough damage and for the public to hear that the ghosts of some of the lost plane's crew were visiting other flights could make for a public relations disaster. For the most part, eyewitness crew members were told that perhaps seeing a psychiatrist would be in order – which most took as a precursor to being fired. After that, most were reluctant to talk to anyone investigating the hauntings and the sightings that did occur were often covered up. Log sheets that contained the sighting reports, as well as the names of witnesses, mysteriously disappeared from the planes on which they occurred. Normally, a logbook would contain entries for several months, but these pages vanished. To this day, many hotly deny the stories of the ghosts from Flight 401, despite the scores of credible witnesses that eventually came forward.

Of course, denying the existence of the ghosts did not stop them from being seen. The eyewitness reports continued and were so widely circulated throughout the aviation community that Eastern finally removed the salvaged parts associated with Flight 401. Many believe the reports were so numerous because the ghosts allegedly visited different planes at various times of the day and night, thereby exposing themselves to a wide range of people. In addition, Repo and Loft were often recognized by people who had once worked with them. Both men, especially Loft, had been with Eastern for many years and had worked with hundreds of different crew members.

Repo was seen more often that Loft and was often spotted in aircraft Number 318's galley, where flight attendants claimed to see his face reflected in the door to an oven. The attendants also reported that the galley felt unusually cold and clammy, or that there was the strong presence of someone in the room with them. During one incident, Repo's ghost allegedly repaired an oven that had an overloaded circuit. It wasn't until another engineer came to fix the oven, and told a flight attendant that he was the only engineer on the plane, that she realized something was strange. She looked up Repo's photograph and realized that he was the man who had first come to make the repairs.

But Repo's ghost seemed to be especially concerned about the safety and operation of the plane. When his ghost appeared, he often made suggestions or gave warnings to crew members who only realized that he was an apparition after he had vanished. Repo's ghost was seen on the flight deck, either sitting at the engineer's instrument panel or with just his face reflected in it. During one visit, a flight engineer was making a pre-flight inspection when he recognized Repo's ghost. Before vanishing, the spirit told the engineer that he had already made the inspection.

Repo's ghost once warned a flight engineer that there would be an electrical failure on the plane and a check revealed that there was a faulty circuit. Another time, his ghost warned an attendant about a fire on the plane and on still another occasion, the phantom pointed out a problem in the plane's hydraulic system. Repo's ghost even told a captain that there would never be another crash on an L-1011, because "we will not let it happen."

On several occasions, Captain Loft's ghost was seen sitting in the plane's first class section. During one incident, a flight attendant asked the uniformed man why his name was not on the passenger list. When he did not respond, she called her supervisor over, along with a flight captain. It was the captain who recognized Loft sitting in the seat and moments later, the ghost disappeared. Loft's ghost also appeared in the crew compartment and it was suspected that his voice was heard during one flight, warning passengers about seat belts and smoking rules. No one else claimed to have made the announcements.

Eventually, once the parts from Flight 401 were removed from the various planes, the hauntings came to an end. Eastern Airlines ceased operations in January 1991, leaving behind a mystery of what actually happened on the planes that were said to have been visited by ghosts.

THE ENTITY

Published in 1978, Frank De Felitta's book, *The Entity*, was said to be a novelized account of a true haunting – novelized because "no one would believe that it was true." The book caused a sensation and when the movie version of it, starring Barbara Hershey, came out in 1982, ghost enthusiasts went looking for the real story, which had started for researchers Barry Taff and Kerry Gaynor from the Department of Parapsychology at UCLA on August 22, 1974. That was the date the two men first visited the Culver City, California, home of Doris Blither. A short time earlier, she had heard Taff and Gaynor discussing the paranormal in a local bookstore and had approached them about her haunted house. The two men agreed to meet with her at her home, not realizing at the time how terrifying and baffling the case would turn out to be.

Doris lived in the small home with her six-year-old daughter and three sons. The house was filthy and they were living in squalor. The terrible living conditions – the house had been twice condemned by the city -- and the tumultuous relationship between Doris and her sons gave the investigators serious reservations. It was later discovered that Doris had suffered abuse from her parents and from several men in her past.

There was an obvious tension between the three boys and their mother and Taff and Gaynor feared that their resentment of Doris might be causing the negative feelings in the house. Doris told them that she was being repeatedly attacked and raped by the spirits that were present. Taff and Gaynor spent many hours documenting the reported events and speaking to witnesses who had seen apparitions in the house. In spite of this, they became concerned that Doris was either crazy or making things up. They did not plan to pursue the case at all.

However, a few days later, Doris called and informed them that five individuals outside of her family had now seen the apparitions. So Taff and Gaynor decided to return to the house with cameras and tape recorders. They immediately noticed something odd when they entered Doris' bedroom. Even though it was a hot, August night and the windows were closed, the temperature was unusually low when compared to the rest of the house. The cold spots faded in and out irregularly, sometimes completely disappearing.

The house where the real "Entity" case took place. It was not in such good condition in 1974.

One of the unexplained photos that investigators took inside of the house.

They could find no source for the cold areas. Soon, other manifestations began to be present in the house.

The first of many inexplicable happenings occurred while Gaynor was talking to Doris' oldest son in the kitchen. He was standing a short distance from a lower kitchen cabinet when the cabinet door suddenly swung open and a pan jumped out of it, landing about three feet away.

After examining the cabinet, Taff and Gaynor went into the bedroom again with Doris and her friend, Candy, who had joined them for the evening and who purported to be psychic. Taff took a photograph of the bedroom with a Polaroid SX-70 camera and it came out perfectly. After they were in the room for about 15 minutes, Candy shouted that she sensed something in the corner. Taff ran back into the room with the camera and immediately aimed and fired it at the corner.

The photograph that resulted was bleached completely white, as if it had been exposed to some sort of intense energy or radiation. The same thing happened a few minutes later when Candy again directed their attention to the corner. The next photo still bleached out, but not as badly as the first time. Puzzled, Taff took another photo (thinking that something might be wrong with the camera) but this time in the living room. This photo came out fine, as did subsequent photos taken by Kerry Gaynor in the bedroom. The only difference was that these photos were not taken while Candy "sensed" something else in the room with them.

Candy again warned about the presence of an entity in the room, this time standing directly in front of her. Taff fired the Polaroid in her direction and he obtained an odd photo of Candy. Her face was completely bleached out, yet her dress and the room behind and around her was completely clear and distinct. Another photo, this time taken by Kerry Gaynor under the same conditions, again captured Candy with bleaching all around her face, even though the rest of the photograph was again very clear.

At this point, they became convinced that something out of the ordinary was occurring in the house.

Over the course of the next 10 weeks, a team from UCLA was almost always present in the house. They returned many times for investigations, bringing dozens of eyewitnesses, researchers and photographers with them. Initially, most of the researchers were skeptical of the events reported by Taff and Gaynor, but soon, more of them began to share their belief of the happenings after witnessing them for themselves.

One night, what can only be described as a "light show" took place in the house in front of 20 startled onlookers. Most of the photos that were taken of them, though, were disappointing. The light was so bright that most of them came out overexposed. One of the witnesses present that night was Frank De Felitta, the author who would go on to write the book based on the case. De Felitta would later vividly recall the light as it moved into the center of the room and the shouts from those present. He said that Doris started screaming as the light moved toward her, cursing and daring the entity to show itself, instead of just a light. At that point, it started to appear and witnesses would later claim to see a part of an arm, a neck, and what looked like a bald head. Everyone present saw the same thing at the same time, ruling out any individual's hallucinations.

Over the next few weeks, the activity continued, but the intensity that was experienced by the witnesses started to decrease. Doris, however, claimed that the rapes continued and displayed bruises and scratched on her thighs as evidence.

Eventually, the family moved out of the Culver City house and the phenomenon at the house stopped. Future residents never reported anything out of the ordinary and it has since been restored and in good condition.

Doris fled Culver City for Carson, California, then moved to San Bernardino, to Texas, and then back to San Bernardino again. According to her claims, the spirits followed her and her family to every place they moved to. Over time, she became more unstable and she later reported that she had become pregnant by the ghost. A medical test revealed her physical symptoms to be the result of a hysterical pregnancy. After that, Doris dropped out of sight and has not been heard from since the 1990s. Her children have never come forward to speak about the case.

What really happened in that Culver City house? No one can say. According to science, there was *something* occurring in that house. Instruments, Geiger counters, and photographs documented it. People who were present saw that *something* with their own eyes. But whether it was caused by the supernatural, or the troubled machinations of Doris's mind, remains a mystery.

As I am sure most readers have realized by now, a very important story of the 1970s has remained absent thus far – the so-called "Amityville Horror." This is a story that is so complicated, so strange, and so convoluted that I felt that the story of the Lutz family – as well as Ed and Lorraine Warren, who profited from the story more than anyone – deserved a chapter all its own.

13. "AMERICA'S GHOST HUNTERS"
GHOSTS AND GULLIBILITY IN THE AMITYVILLE ERA

I was barely a teenager when the sensational book by Jay Anson, *The Amityville Horror*, was unleashed on the American public. I will never forget snatching up a copy of the book from the revolving metal rack at the local grocery store, reading it, and then reading it again. I was utterly fascinated. The cover of the book assured me that it was A TRUE STORY, which made it one of the most terrifying things that I had ever read – and this from a kid who was reading Stephen King novels and *The Exorcist* long before I probably should have been. Could things like those described in the book really happen? Could ghosts destroy a family the way that evil spirits did George and Kathy Lutz? Could a ghost force someone to kill, as demonic entities allegedly caused Ronald DeFeo to murder his entire family?

And scariest of all – could I, along with the rest of America it seemed, be duped into believing that the events in the book actually happened? The answer to that question is YES. *The Amityville Horror* became one of the best-selling books of the 1970s, turned an ordinary family into celebrities, inspired a bad film and a lot of worse sequels, and had a lot of people believing that demons and ghost pigs were out to get anyone who lived in the house. And who knows? Maybe it would be your house next!

The problem with the whole story is that it simply wasn't true. The whole story was – as one of the principals later admitted – made up over a few bottles of wine. But why? Why go to all the trouble? That's a complicated question with several different answers, but the main thing to remember is that this was a story that, for a variety of reasons, simply spun out of control. Once it started, no one knew how to stop it. Some regretted it, some tried to hide their involvement, some hoped it would go away, and others built their entire reputations from it, refusing to back down in the face of all evidence to the contrary.

The Amityville Horror became a runaway train and it either ran you down and left you bloody on the tracks, or you hung on for dear life and just kept spinning the story to wherever the train would take you. In this chapter, we'll look at what happened, how the story began, what led to the popularity of it, and how so many people were fooled by it all. It's a story of heartbreak, gullibility, greed, attention-seeking, and regret, but to really understand it, we must start the story in November 1974, when the truly tragic events in the timeline took place.

THE REAL HORROR IN AMITYVILLE

The story begins, not with the unlucky Lutz family, but with a dark night in November 1974, when Ronald "Butch" DeFeo murdered his entire family in what would become the most infamous house in America.

The house at 112 Ocean Avenue in the upscale Long Island community of Amityville was home to the DeFeo family in 1974. On the surface, the DeFeos seemed to be a happy, All-American family. Ronald, Sr. had been born and raised in Brooklyn and ran a successful Buick dealership that he had taken over from his father-in-law. In 1965, he had moved his family – wife, Louise, sons, Ronald, Jr., who was known as "Butch", Mark and John, and daughters, Dawn and Allison – to Amityville and into the sprawling Dutch Colonial, waterfront house with the distinctive quarter-moon windows.

"High Hopes" – the DeFeo house in Amityville, New York

It was perfect for the family, with two stories, an attic, and a boathouse on the river. When the family moved in, they erected a signpost in the front yard that read "High Hopes," a physical reminder of what the house meant to them.

To friends and neighbors, the DeFeos looked like a happy family, but appearances were deceiving. Ronald, Sr. was an angry man, given to bouts of anger and violence. He and Louise often fought, and he was a threatening figure to his children, as the oldest child, Butch often bore the brunt of his father's ill temper. He was an overweight, sullen boy who was often picked on in school. His father harassed him to stand up for himself – but never at home. Ronald, Sr. had no patience for backtalk or disobedience. But as Butch got older, he was no longer tolerant of his father's abuse. Their shouting matches turned physical and Ronald, even with his own anger issues, began to realize this his son's temper and violent behavior were not normal. Louise sent him to see a psychiatrist, but it did little good. Butch insisted there was nothing wrong with him and he refused to open up to the counselor.

Ronald "Butch" DeFeo, Jr. (lower right) with his brothers and sisters

Feeling out of alternatives, the DeFeos began placating Butch by giving him whatever he wanted. When he needed money, he only had to ask. When he was 14, his father gave him a $14,000 speedboat to cruise the Great South Bay. By age 17, he had been kicked out of the parochial school that they had enrolled him in because of his drug use. His behavior was more erratic than ever and his outbursts more volatile. Altercations with this father became more frequent, and more dangerous.

One night, when Butch was 18, a fight started between Ronald and Louise and to settle the matter, Butch grabbed a 12-gauge shotgun from his room, loaded a shell into the chamber, and went downstairs. Without hesitation, he put the muzzle in his father's face and pulled the trigger. Mysteriously, it did not fire. Ronald froze in place and watched in stunned silence as his son lowered the gun and walked out of the room. He was unaffected by the fact that he had nearly killed his father in cold blood. The incident was over, but Butch's reaction was a foreshadowing of things to come.

In the fall of 1974, things got worse between Butch and his father. Butch had been given a weekly allowance for "working" at the Buick dealership for his father and was spending it all on drugs and alcohol. One night in early November, a manager entrusted him to take the cash deposits from the dealership to the night drop box at the bank. Butch soon returned, claiming that he had been robbed at gunpoint on the way to the bank – the deposit was gone. Ronald, Sr. exploded into a rage when he heard Butch's story, berating Butch and the manager who had entrusted him with the money in the first place. The police were called and when they arrived, they wanted to speak with Butch. Instead of continuing to claim that he had been robbed, Butch became tense and antagonistic with them. When he realized they thought he was lying, he turned violent, cursed at the officers, and slammed several dents into the hood of one of the cars in the dealership's showroom to emphasize his rage. The police backed off for a moment, but Ronald, Sr. had come to his own conclusions about the reason for his son's behavior – he knew he'd stolen the money.

On the Friday before the murders, the police asked Butch to look at some mugshots and see if he might be able to identify the thief who allegedly robbed him. He initially agreed to do it, but backed out at the last minute, afraid to go to the police station.

When his father heard that he didn't go, he confronted Butch and demanded to know why he wouldn't cooperate with detectives. The confrontation grew heated and Butch ran to his car and drove away.

The night of Wednesday, November 14, was a cold one in Amityville. The streets were quiet and so was the house at 112 Ocean Avenue. Everyone in the house was asleep, with the exception of Butch, who was brooding in his room in the attic. The more he worked things over in his mind, the more determined he was to solve his problems once and for all. He paced back and forth for hours, and then finally, took a .35-caliber Marlin rifle from a storage space where he kept several weapons, and started, silently and with purpose, toward his parent's bedroom. He opened the door, walked in, raised the rifle to his shoulder and, without any hesitation, fired at his father. The first shot ripped into Ronald's back, to the left of his spine. A second shot punched through his back and struck his heart.

Next to Ronald, Louise had awakened but before she had time to do anything more than clutch the crucifix that she wore on a gold chair around her neck, Butch had turned the gun on her. He shot her twice, shattering bones in her rib cage and collapsing her right lung. He turned away from her as she died in a spreading pool of blood on the bed.

Despite the sound of four rifle shots, no one in the house was awakened. Butch left his parents' room and walked down the hall to the bedroom that was shared by his brothers, John, 9, and Marc, 12. He entered the room and shot each of them one time as they lay sleeping. Marc died instantly, but John, whose spinal cord was severed by the bullet, bled to death. The additional shots had failed to awaken his sisters. He continued down the hall to Allison's second-floor bedroom. As Butch walked into the room, Allison, 13, stirred and looked up just as he pointed the rifle at her face and pulled the trigger. His youngest sister was killed instantly. Butch then walked upstairs to the third floor and entered the attic bedroom where his 18-year-old sister, Dawn, a secretarial school student, was still sleeping. Butch killed her, too.

It was now just after 3:00 a.m. In less than 15 minutes, Butch DeFeo had brutally murdered his entire family in cold blood. Butch stripped off his clothing, which had been spattered with blood, showered, shaved, and dressed in his customary jeans and work boots. He found a pillowcase and stuffed it with his bloody clothes, a bloody towel, eight shell casings that he had carefully collected from the rooms where his family lay dead, a rifle case, a pistol holder, one full box of .35-caliber Marlin ammunition, and one empty box. He took all of it out to his car, along with the murder weapon, which he tossed in the water at the foot of Ocean Avenue. Fearing that the items in the pillowcase might float, he drove into Brooklyn and dropped the pillowcase, with its gruesome contents, into a storm drain. After that, he had breakfast at a nearby diner and then reported to work at the Buick dealership as if nothing out of the ordinary had happened.

When his father didn't show up to work, Butch called home several times, feigning concern. He finally left work around noon, after first calling his girlfriend, Sherry Klein, to tell her that he was coming over. On his way, he ran into his friend, Bobby Kelske, and stopped to talk. After that, Butch went to Sherry's house, where he told her that he had tried to call home several times but had never gotten an answer. He tried again in her presence. Still, no answer. Puzzled, but seemingly not overly concerned, he met up with Bobby Kelske at a local bar while Sherry went shopping. At the bar, he told anyone who would listen that he had been calling home all day, looking for his father, but no one answered his calls. He planned to drive over and check on them. Butch returned a few minutes later in a panic, pleading for help – someone had shot his family.

A group of patrons from the bar hurried over to the Ocean Avenue house, but Bobby Kelske was the only one who went inside. He went upstairs to the master bedroom and found Ronald and Louise on the blood-soaked bed. When he left the house, he found Butch beside himself with grief. The police were called and Officer Kenneth Geguski was the first to arrive on the scene less than 10 minutes later. Butch was now sobbing uncontrollably on the front lawn with a group of men from the bar gathered around him. The officer went inside and then called headquarters from the kitchen. Butch had followed him inside and as he listened to Geguski's call about his murdered parents and brothers, he told the officer that he also had two sisters. Geguski put the receiver down and hurried back upstairs. By this time another village patrolman had arrived, Officer Edwin Tyndall. The two of them found Dawn and Allison. There was too much blood for them to even guess what kind of gun had killed the DeFeos.

By 7:00 p.m., the neighborhood was buzzing about the events at "High Hopes." The house was filled with police detectives and crime scene personnel, while neighbors and curiosity-seekers gathered on the front lawn. Suffolk County detective Gaspar Randazzo was the first to question Butch, the massacre's sole survivor. Butch claimed that the family might have been killed by a notorious mafia hitman who had long had a grudge against his family. Detective Gerard Gozaloff joined in the questioning and suggested that if the murders were indeed linked to organized crime, that Butch might still be a target. Any further questioning should take place at police headquarters. It was there that they were joined by a third detective, Joseph Napolitano.

At the station, Butch gave the police his written statement. He claimed to have been home the night before, and said he stayed up until 2:00 a.m. watching a World War II thriller on television. At 4:00 a.m., he reported hearing the toilet flush in the bathroom that his brothers and youngest sister shared. Since he couldn't go back to sleep, he decided to head to work early. He described the rest of his day, leaving work early, visiting with Sherry and Bobby, drinking at the bar, and trying to reach his family by telephone.

After Butch gave his statement, the detectives continued to question him about his family, and about his suggestion that a hitman, Louis Falini, might be the killer. Butch explained that Falini had lived with them for a time, and that he had helped Butch and his father carve out a hiding space in the master bedroom closet where Ronald, Sr., kept a stash of gems and cash. The argument with Falini had stemmed from an incident where Falini criticized some work Butch had done at the auto dealership. Around 3:00 a.m., the detectives had finished with their questions and Butch went to sleep on a cot that had been set up in a file room. He gave every appearance of being a cooperative witness, and so far, detectives had no reason to consider him a suspect.

But that changed as soon as they began examining the evidence. When cleaning up the scene, Butch had been careless enough to leave boxes of .35-caliber Marlin ammunition in his room – the caliber and type of ammunition that matched the bullets recovered at the scene. Subsequent questioning of Bobby Kelske led to the discovery

 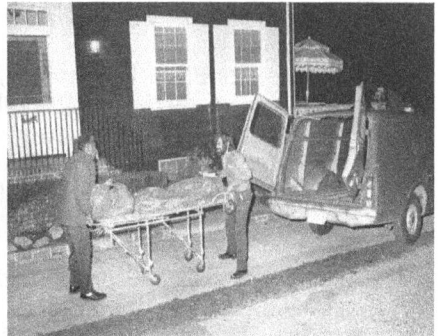

(Left) The crime scene at the DeFeo house attracted scores of onlookers and curiosity-seekers. (Right) The bodies of the DeFeo family being removed from the house.

that Butch was a "gun fanatic," and that he was suspected of staging a recent robbery of receipts from the family Buick dealership.

Detectives realized that Butch had possibly been playing them and might be a suspect in the murders. At the very least, he likely knew more about the killings than he had told them so far. At 8:45 a.m., Detective George Harrison shook Butch awake. He sat up with a groan and as he rubbed his face, he asked if detectives had found the killer yet. Harrison told him that he didn't have any news about the supposed hitman. Instead, he read Butch his Miranda rights. Butch protested that he had been cooperative and even waived his right to a lawyer, seemingly to prove that he was an innocent victim with nothing to hide.

By this time, Gozaloff and Napolitano were exhausted. Two other officers, Lieutenant Robert Dunn and Detective Dennis Rafferty, took over the interrogation. Rafferty read Butch his rights again, and proceeded to question him about the prior two days. Rafferty focused on the time of the murders. Butch had written in his statement that he was up as early as 4:00 a.m., and that he heard his brother in the bathroom at that time. Rafferty continued to press Butch until he got him to reconsider his earlier claims of when the crime took place. Butch stated that it had been after he left for work, but new information narrowed the time down to between 2:00 and 4:00 a.m. There was no way that Butch could have heard a toilet flush when he said that he did.

As the questions continued, Butch's story fell apart. The detectives hammered at the discrepancies in Butch's version of events and what the evidence said actually happened. Once the time of the murders was established, they were able to put Butch at the scene. At first, Butch tried desperately to make the best out of a deteriorating situation, trying to make the detectives believe that while he had indeed been present in the home during the murders, but had been hiding in fear of being discovered and killed. He insisted that he had only been in each bedroom after the murders had taken place. Rafferty then told him about the ammunition that had been found in his room. Even more desperate, Butch continued to lie. His new version of events had him being awakened at 3:30 a.m. to see Louis Falini with a gun to his head. He had forced Butch to accompany him as he went from room to room, methodically killing each member of the DeFeo family.

The police let Butch keep talking, and he eventually implicated himself as he described how he gathered and then discarded evidence from the crime scene. They kept him talking, shouting more questions at him and then finally one of them asked him if it had really happened the way Butch claimed.

"No," Butch finally confessed. "It all started so fast. Once I started, I just couldn't stop."

The trial of Ronald DeFeo, Jr., for the murder of his family, began on October 14, 1975, nearly a year after the murders took place. The prosecution of DeFeo was the responsibility of Gerald Sullivan, an assistant district attorney of Suffolk County. Despite Butch's confession, despite the fact that he had been able to lead investigators to the exact spot where he had disposed of the evidence, and despite the fact that Butch's rifle was positively identified as the murder weapon, Sullivan took no chances in his approach to prosecuting the case. He had extensively questioned Butch before the trial started and knew he was a pathological liar.

Butch was represented by well-known New York defense attorney William Weber, who had already tried to get the case thrown out by saying that Butch did not have a lawyer when he confessed. Weber also planned to use Butch's pattern of behavior to show that he was insane. But Sullivan knew that Butch DeFeo was not crazy. He was a violent, cold-blooded killer. His opening statement said as much and asked the jury to consider all of the facts and to not provide Butch with an excuse for his actions.

Butch's mental state was the thing on which his acquittal or conviction would rest. Weber was pushing the idea that Butch had been legally insane at the time of the murders. Sullivan argued that this was not the case, presenting a full portrait of a man who was capable of murdering six defenseless members of his own family. He called a number of witnesses, including police officers and detectives who worked the case, as well as relatives and friends of Butch. He used their testimony to build his case, but no witness was as damning to Butch as Butch himself.

When Butch took the stand, he was well-coached to offer bizarre answers, even once claiming that he had murdered his family in self-defense – they were going to kill him if he didn't kill them first. Sullivan wanted to make sure that the jury didn't get the impression that Butch was a deranged lunatic so he frequently interrupted his weird diatribes about his family and how he "became God" when he picked up the rifle. He ridiculed Butch for claiming he did not recognize his mother's photograph and he noted the inconsistencies between what Butch was saying now and the story he gave police on the night of the murders. Sullivan knew that Butch wouldn't give him many straight answers, but he thought that if he could get him angry enough, he would reveal the twisted sense of pleasure he'd gotten from killing his entire family. Sullivan made Butch so angry that he actually threatened the prosecutor's life.

The case for both sides depended on Butch's mental condition and each retained the services of a highly reputable psychiatrist. Dr. Stephen Schwartz appeared for the defense. He was experienced in the criminal field, had interviewed scores of defendants, and testified in hundreds of court cases. He would later gain widespread notoriety as the psychiatrist who found David Berkowitz to be criminally insane in the wake of the "Son of Sam" murders.

Sullivan knew that what he did at this point in the trial was crucial to his case. He had his own expert witness, but he knew that he had to keep the trial on track. As he later wrote about the case: "The jurors had been learning about DeFeo and his murders for almost two months. They had listened to his lies and vituperation for days. Dr. Schwartz had only talked to him for hours. I would show that the psychiatrist didn't know the real Butch DeFeo."

Sullivan's break came while Weber was questioning his own expert witness. In a move that could only be interpreted as overconfidence in Schwartz's ability on the stand, Weber only asked a few preliminary questions and then allowed Schwartz to lecture on psychosis, disassociation, and criminal insanity. Sullivan noticed several key points that Weber didn't challenge and he focused on those. He opened his line of questioning by referring to Schwartz's prior experience as an expert witness, attempting to rattle him by demonstrating how much research he had done into Schwartz's background. He then moved to the DeFeo case and began questioning Schwartz about why Butch would have removed evidence from the scene if he was insane. Why bother with it?

Schwartz offered several opinions but Sullivan continued to press him. Hotly, Schwartz finally retorted that he was "not hiding this crime from anybody by picking up the shell. The bodies are there. The bullets are in the people."

"Everything that he could get that would connect him with the crime, he removed from the house, didn't he?" pressed Sullivan.

"What you are talking about is trivia compared to the six bodies," Schwartz responded flatly.

His indifferent response angered the prosecutor. "Trivia that he removed the evidence out of that house that would connect him to the crime, trivia that has nothing to do with whether he thought that the crime was wrong?" responded Sullivan.

Sullivan next took aim at Schwartz's actual diagnosis of Butch as a neurotic.

"So, it's your testimony, as I understand it, Dr. Schwartz, that the fact that it wasn't too bright to throw everything in that sewer drain all together in one location is significant of the fact that it was neurotic that he did this?" Schwartz responded that this was the case, noting that Butch appeared to be acting without any clear purpose in mind, someone distracted by paranoid, neurotic delusions. This would become Schwartz's greatest mistake in his testimony.

"Did he tell you about not wanting to leave clues for the police?" asked Sullivan.

"I asked him about the casings, and he said he didn't want to leave the police any clues as to what kind of gun it had been. He was not a friend of the cops, and he didn't want to help them."

Schwartz had now just contradicted himself. Sullivan knew it and it's likely that the psychiatrist knew it, as well. The district attorney almost laughed. "Okay, now you know why he removed the casings, don't you?" he asked derisively.

Dr. Harold Zolan testified for the prosecution. Sullivan devised an elaborate question-and-answer exchange with Zolan, making every deliberate effort to give the jury access to Zolan's thought process, so that they might come to understand how Zolan had reached his assessment. He wanted them to reach the same assessment for themselves. Unlike Schwartz, Zolan attributed Butch's behavior to him having an antisocial personality, a form of personality disorder he distinguished from any kind of mental illness. Essentially, those with such a personality disorder are fully aware of their actions and are fully able to comprehend the difference between right and wrong, but are motivated by an imperious, self-centered attitude. When finished, Sullivan was confident that between his methodical questioning and Zolan's well-thought-out responses, the jury finally had the clinical evidence they needed to find Butch guilty of murder.

On Wednesday, November 19, 1975, the judge sent the jury into deliberations. Despite Sullivan's painstaking efforts, the prosecutor knew that a guilty verdict was not a sure bet. He was rewarded for his skepticism when the jury's first vote came back 10-2, with two holdouts who were still uncertain about Butch's mental state at the time of the murders. After reviewing transcripts of DeFeo's testimony, however, the vote came back at a unanimous 12-0.

On Friday, November 21, 1975, Ronald DeFeo, Jr., was found guilty of six counts of second-degree murder. Two weeks later, he was sentenced to 25 years to life in prison on all six counts. He remains incarcerated with the New York State Department of Corrections today.

But this was not quite the end of Butch DeFeo's story – and it was just the start of the story of 112 Ocean Avenue in Amityville.

THE LUTZ FAMILY MOVES IN

The tragic murders in Amityville made grim local news, but few people outside of New York heard about the house where they occurred until nearly a year and a half after the massacre took place. That publicity came for much different reasons.

The next chapter in the story began on December 18, 1975, when George and Kathy Lutz bought the house on Ocean Avenue for $80,000 (which translates to over $372,000 in today's dollars). Just a week before Christmas, they moved into their "dream home" with Kathy's three children from a previous marriage. Of course, according to later accounts, their dream home turned into a nightmare.

Almost from the moment that they moved into the house, the Lutz family insisted that they noticed an unearthly presence in the place. They heard mysterious noises they could not account for. Locked windows and doors inexplicably opened and closed. George Lutz, a sturdy former Marine, claimed to be plagued by the sound of a phantom brass band that marched back and forth through the first floor of the house. After a Catholic priest came to the house, agreeing to attempt an exorcism, an eerie disembodied voice told him to "get out."

After the aborted exorcism, the events intensified. The thumping and scratching sounds grew worse, a devilish creature was seen outside of the windows at night, and green slime oozed out of the walls and ceilings. The family was terrified by ghostly apparitions of hooded figures, plagued by clouds of flies that seemed to come from nowhere, cold chills, moving objects, and sickly odors. Their telephone service was repeatedly disconnected, although repairmen could not understand how or why.

Kathy reported that she was often beaten and scratched by unseen hands and that, one night, was levitated into the air above the bed. She was also unnerved by the repeated contact between her daughter and a ghostly devil pig named "Jodie."

Meanwhile, George was going through his own ordeal. He woke every morning around the same time that the DeFeo murders had taken place. He believed that his personality was being affected by an "evil spirit" in the house, turning him into a surly, angry, and abusive man.

The haunting eventually became too much for them to endure. They held out for 28 days before they fled the house, leaving all of their furniture and many of their possessions behind. The demonic spirits, they said, had driven them from their home.

And after that, things got really scary.

George and Kathy Lutz

In February 1976, George Lutz started making calls about his haunted house in Amityville. He contacted several paranormal investigators in the New York area, including Dr. Stephen Kaplan, who was then executive director of the Parapsychology Institute of America. Lutz asked Kaplan if there was a fee to have someone from the Institute come and investigate his house for paranormal activity. Kaplan said there was no fee involved, but that the findings would be publicized. If the house was haunted, the family was liable to get some publicity. But if it wasn't haunted – or worse yet, some kind of hoax was going on – people would know about that, too. Lutz agreed, but a few days later, George called and canceled the investigation, stating that he and his wife didn't want any publicity.

Kaplan wasn't surprised; he received calls like that all the time. He had mostly forgotten about the call, which was why he was so stunned a short time later when he turned on the television and saw New York's Channel 5 news team doing a live feed from Amityville. Accompanying the news crew were two other people who had received a call from George Lutz – Ed and Lorraine Warren, America's most famous demonologists. The news crew filmed a dramatic séance in the house that night as the Warrens assured the audience that the house was haunted.

It was that night when the Amityville story began gaining speed – it would be a little while later before it went completely off the rails. When it did, there was no question that the Warrens were the ones behind the controls.

THE DEMONOLOGIST AND THE MEDIUM

For those only slightly familiar with the Warrens, I'll urge you not to confuse them with the characters of "Ed and Lorraine Warren" that are featured in the popular *Conjuring* films. Real life is a much different story. Lorraine Warren is said to be a clairvoyant and trance medium with an uncanny ability to contact the next world. Her late husband, Ed, was an expert on hauntings – most of which seemed to involve demons – as well as exorcism. Starting in the 1950s, they came to be recognized authorities when it came to ghosts and haunted houses. In 1976, they were at the height of their popularity and so their stamp of approval on the Amityville house caught the attention of the country.

Ed and Lorraine Warren

Ed and Lorraine Warren were both born in Bridgeport, Connecticut – Ed in 1926 and Lorraine a year later – but did not meet until they were teenagers. Ed's father was a state trooper and devout Catholic and enrolled Ed in parochial school. The Warren family lived in a large, older home that was rented out by an elderly woman with a mean disposition. Ed was five-years-old when she passed away and he always told the story of seeing his first apparition when she showed up in his bedroom closet a few days after she died. His father always told Ed that there must be some logical explanation for the paranormal experiences he had, but his father never came up with one. Ed was often so terrified by the ghost in his closet that he refused to stay home alone. And she was not the only ghost he saw, Ed claimed. Another spirit that frequently visited was his late aunt, who had been a nun. During her visitations, she allegedly told Ed that he would someday consult with priests, but would not become one, which Ed used as his reasoning for his life as a self-proclaimed demonologist. The Warrens moved out of the old house when Ed was 12. By then, he had gotten used to the strange happenings in the place and, in fact, used his exposure to the supernatural as fuel for his future research into the paranormal.

Just three blocks from the Warren home lived Lorraine Rita Moran, daughter of an affluent Irish family. Lorraine attended Laurelton Hall, a Catholic girl's school in nearby Milford, and it was while at school that she learned her gift for clairvoyance at age 12. On Arbor Day that year, the nuns organized a tree-planting for the students and as soon as her sapling was placed in the ground, Lorraine began staring at the sky, seeing the tree as it would look when it was full-grown. The nuns considered her psychic ability to be sinful and sent her off for a weekend retreat of prayer.

When Ed was 16, he was working at the Colonial Theater in Bridgeport and met Lorraine. The following year, on September 7, 1943, his 17th birthday, he enlisted in the U.S. Navy. He spent the war as an armed guard aboard a Merchant Marine ship. He and Lorraine married on May 22, 1945. They were both 18. Their only child, Judy, was born just six months before Ed left the Navy. After the war, Ed attended Perry Art School, which was affiliated with Yale, but left to travel around New England, painting and looking for haunted houses.

Ed's favorite pastime was to hear stories about local haunted houses and then make a little money by painting the house and selling the painting to the house's owners. Even more, he loved to be invited inside and allowed to take a look around. Eventually, his experiences with ghosts led the Warrens away from a career as itinerant artists to full-time work as paranormal consultants. Frightened home owners confided in the Warrens about their experiences and the Warrens soon found themselves giving advice to not only the owners of the homes, but to interested strangers, as well. Finding that the negative energy associated with teenagers and young adults attracted spirit activity – or so they claimed – the Warrens began giving lectures at colleges to encourage their listeners against unwittingly inviting trouble into their lives. It was a sort of "Scared Straight" program for the paranormal.

Like the Warrens themselves, "Annabelle" is much different than the version that movie audiences have seen.

The Warrens amassed a large archive of detailed interviews and reports from haunted families, as well as from other investigators, along with photographs, audio and video recordings of paranormal activity, and even founded an Occult museum of haunted objects, dolls, and other items.

Perhaps the most famous object in their museum was a doll referred to as "Annabelle." There is scant information about the haunting connected to the doll – other than that provided by the Warrens – but the Raggedy Ann doll was allegedly given to a nursing student by her mother in 1970. When the doll began exhibiting strange behavior, a medium revealed that it was possessed by a dead woman named "Annabelle Higgins." The student and her roommate felt sorry for the spirit and granted Annabelle permission to reside in the doll. However, when frightening events continued to occur, they contacted the Warrens, who declared that Annabelle Higgins was not a spirit at all, she was a demon. Ed, who had been referring to himself as a "demonologist" by that time, even though he had no education or training in the subject, took the doll back to the museum to put it on display for safe-keeping. It was placed in a glass cabinet with a cross over its head with a sign that warned, "Positively Do Not Open." Before his death in 2006, Ed apparently warned visitors that the last man to mock Annabelle ending up dying in a motorcycle crash. Whether this was truth or fiction is unknown since no names or evidence to back up this claim was ever offered. It's a spooky story, but there's nothing to back up the tale, which oddly, is strikingly similar to a 1963 episode of the *Twilight Zone* television show in which a woman named Annabelle gives her daughter a doll that comes to life and terrorizes the family.

Regardless, the Warrens investigated all over America and overseas. After being invited to a place, they arranged a visit as soon as possible. Once at the site, they usually split up, with Ed conducting interviews of the witnesses and Lorraine walking through the house to see if she could discern any spirit activity. Lorraine could usually detect a presence almost immediately and would be able to tell if they were earthbound, human spirits or if they were demonic. Earthbound spirits, she maintained, usually remained at a place because of a sudden, violent, or tragic death and often didn't realize that they needed to move on to the other side. But a demonic presence was an entirely different matter. These inhuman spirits attempted to overpower their victims through physical, mental, and emotional abuse. The Warrens always stressed that God did not let evil visit humans, but that humans must in some way invite malevolence into their lives by using a Ouija board, or by experimenting with witchcraft and the occult. Once allowed inside, demons took control in three stages: infestation, oppression, and possession. In severe circumstances, the final outcome could be death.

During the infestation stage, the Warrens claimed that the demon's goal was to create chaos and fear through strange happenings – footsteps, whispers, inexplicable sounds, moving objects, and so on – and would inspire fear by knocking on doors three or six times, mocking the Holy Trinity. Too often, they said, the work of a demon could be dismissed as pranks or overactive imaginations, but make no mistake, the diabolical was art work.

Once fear has taken hold, the oppression stage begins, when the demon dominates the victim's will. According to the Warrens, this meant an increase in demonic manifestations in the house, like screams, heavy breathing, footsteps, hellish moans, inhuman voices coming from the television, smells of sulfur and rotting flesh, movement of large objects, and the materialization of a dark form that the Warrens believed personified evil. The victim would start to believe that he or she was insane and would have dramatic personality changes and mood swings.

Finally, if there had been no intervention for the victim, then they would be possessed by an inhuman evil. This usually meant that the demon would speak through the victim, foul odors and fluids would emanate from the body, and would no longer resemble themselves. But if the afflicted could get help – whether from the local clergy, or particularly from the Warrens – then hope existed that the demonic presence could be expelled through exorcism. The Warrens stated that the expulsion of the demon had to be a religious process and had to be performed by a priest who had been named as an exorcist by the church. As a demonologist, Ed could identify the problem and offer prayer and support, he said, but could not perform the actual exorcism.

Keep in mind that much of the Warrens' expertise came from a mingling of Catholic doctrine with theories that appear to be created wholesale from their own beliefs. For instance, Ed came up with the idea of the "psychic hours" that run from 9:00 p.m. to 6:00 a.m., with the most vicious hauntings occurring at 3:00 a.m. Why? Because this is an insult to the Holy Trinity. Needless to say, no evidence exists to say this is the truth, except for claims that can be traced back to the Warrens.

Over the course of their careers, the Warrens estimated that they investigated over 8,000 cases. To understand what occurred at Amityville in 1976 in regards to Ed and Lorraine, we should probably take a look at a few of their most famous – and infamous – cases.

"The Conjuring" Case

In the winter of 1970, Roger and Carolyn Perron and their five children moved into an old home in the quiet countryside outside of Harrisville, Rhode Island. The home, known as the Old Arnold Estate, allegedly became a nightmare for the new occupants.

Even though the entire family was terrorized by supernatural happenings, Carolyn seemed to receive the worst of it. She described one of the earliest incidents in a newspaper interview, stating that she awoke from

The Perron family in 1970

sleep to see a woman in a gray dress, her head hanging to one side, moaning, "Get out. Get out. I'll drive you out with death and gloom." The family described strange sounds, missing objects, footsteps, and eerie happenings in the night. Carolyn was subjected to the greatest terrors of the haunting when she was assailed by the spirit of the woman she had seen.

The spirit was that of Bathsheba Thayer, who had been born in 1812 and lived nearby with her husband, Judson Sherman. Bathsheba gave birth to four children, three of whom died very young. Rumors spread that Bathsheba had actually sacrificed her children to the devil in the process of casting black magic spells. The story had an impact on the Perrons, who became convinced that Bathsheba haunted their home. At first, the ghost tried to get Carolyn to leave by pinching and slapping her, but the torture soon got worse. It began to burn her and it stabbed her with what Carolyn said felt like a needle. When the family still didn't leave the house, the spirit took possession of Carolyn.

Enter the Warrens.

As soon as they arrived at the Perron home, Lorraine sensed the darkness that emanated from Carolyn. In an attempt to free the family from the haunting, the Warrens set about spiritually cleansing the house.

The frightening events inspired the 2013 film, *The Conjuring*, and introduced film-goers to the characters of "Ed and Lorraine Warren," played by Patrick Wilson and Vera Farmiga. Lorraine served as a consultant for the film, which pays particular attention to Carolyn's possession and the cleansing conducted by the Warrens. In reality, though, the Warrens did not solve the Perron family's problems. In fact, their actions seemed to further aggravate whatever forces were at work. The Perron family remained stuck with the house for years due to financial constraints and were unable to sell it until 1980. After that, the Perrons fled to Georgia – and their paranormal problems followed. Andrea Perron, the oldest of the children, has since written a three-volume series about the family's troubles.

While certain events depicted in the film were exaggerated for the purpose of entertainment, Lorraine Warren has insisted that it was mostly accurate to real-life events. The problem is that other sources have insisted otherwise – and have quite a bit of evidence to back up their claims.

There seems to be little argument about the fact that the house was haunted, although later events that were documented don't come close to being as extreme as those alleged by the Perrons, but the problems arise when history tries to tell us *why* it was haunted.

In 2014, I was contacted – along with a lot of other researchers – by Norma Sutcliffe, the current owner of the home where the Perrons once lived. She had delved into the history of the house and, without much effort, discovered a lot of factual errors in what had been presented as the truth by the film. Sutcliffe, along with journalist Kent Spottswood, discovered that, among other things, the "witch" featured in the story, Bathsheba Thayer Sherman, was never considered a witch by local residents and that all of the devil worship, infant sacrifices, and general witchery was pure fabrication. Whether the Perrons were simply told the story and took it to heart is unknown, but there was no truth to it, which debunks the entire basis of the haunting. Norma Sutcliffe has since sued Warner Brothers, which distributed the film, due to an influx of trespassers and harassment following the film's release.

The Perrons – along with the Warrens, of course – have always maintained the veracity of their claims, and perhaps they truly encountered something unexplainable that terrified them. It should be clear, however, that at least some of the backstory surrounding the haunting is the stuff of fiction.

A "Haunting in Connecticut"

The story of the Snedeker family has long been one of the most controversial of the Warrens' cases. The film version – which even Lorraine Warren admits was "embarrassing" – greatly exaggerated even the claims of the family who experienced the haunting. Unfortunately, even those claims have come into question after the assertions that were made by the author who was hired by the Warrens to write a book about the case.

In real-life, the story involved the Snedeker family who, in 1986, purchased a home for a great price and for its convenient location to a hospital where their son was receiving treatment for cancer. Of course, the great deal on the house comes with a price – it was once a funeral home where the morticians were rumored to have been caught having sex with the corpses. This naturally meant the place was haunted and the family began experiencing strange sounds, demonic entities, and, of course, a possession. More or less, it's the same thing that the Perrons went through years earlier in another house with what turned out to be a questionable history.

Most of the questions about the legitimacy of the story began almost as soon as the book about the case was published. The book, *In a Dark Place: The Story of a True Haunting*, was credited as having been written by Ed and Lorraine Warren, Carmen Reed, Al Snedeker, and Ray Garton. The latter was a horror novelist who was hired by the Warrens to help shape the Snedeker's narrative. In an interview with *Horror Bound* magazine, Garton said he "interviewed all the family members about their experiences, and soon realized that there was a problem: "I found that the accounts of the individual Snedekers didn't quite mesh. They couldn't keep their stories straight. I went to Ed [Warren] with this problem. 'Oh, they're crazy,' he said, 'You've got some of the story - just use what works and make the rest up... Just make it up and make it scary.'"

Oh, boy….

And the hits just kept on coming. Carmen Reed, formerly Carmen Snedeker, claimed that she had no idea that the house had ever been a funeral home. She said that she'd not been in the basement due to renovation materials blocking the stairway, and only found the embalming equipment after they moved in. However, the former owner of the house, said that he was aware of it. The site had been the location of Hallahan's Funeral Home in Southington, Connecticut, for decades and the family had been informed of it prior to the purchase.

In 2009, neighbors of the Snedeker family (as well as Ray Garton) attributed most of the paranormal happenings to the family's serious drug and alcohol abuse. In addition, the current owner of the house, Susan Trotta-Smith, states that the house is not haunted now and never was. In an interview, she stated firmly, "We've lived in the house for 10 years. Our house is wonderful. The stories are all ludicrous."

The "Devil Made Me Do It"

On February 16, 1981, Arne Cheyenne Johnson, a 19-year-old from Brookfield, Connecticut, stabbed his landlord, Alan Bono, multiple times with a pocketknife. Bono died a few hours later in the hospital and Johnson was picked up by the police two miles from the murder scene. Eight months later, Johnson appeared in court with a plan to enter a plea of not guilty, due to demonic possession.

It all started on July 3, 1980. Johnson's fiancée, Debbie Glatzel, had a little brother named David, age 11. One night, he woke up screaming, claiming that he had been visited by a "man with big black eyes, a thin face with animal features, jagged teeth, pointed ears, horns, and hooves" – in other words, the Devil, or at least someone who looked an awful lot like him. David was, everyone agreed, not the kind of kid who liked scary movies, or who was likely to make things up, and he was visibly shaken by this experience. He became withdrawn and quiet. Debbie asked Arne Johnson if he would stay with her family for a while and see if it would help David get out of his depression.

Arne, of course, agreed but things didn't get better. David reported more nightmares about the terrifying man, who promised to take his soul. Odd scratches and bruises began to appear on the boy and all the injuries seemed to happen while he was asleep. Odd sounds, which Arne couldn't explain, were heard in the attic. Worst of all, David began to claim that he was now seeing the "beast man" while he was awake.

Rather than seeking psychiatric help, the family first brought over a priest to bless the house. This didn't help. In fact, it made things worse. The sounds in the attic got louder, David's visions increased, and he began to hiss at his family and speak with multiple voices. He started to quote from *Paradise Lost*, a book that most 11-year-olds aren't exactly familiar with. During the night, someone had to stay up and watch David, who woke every 30 minutes, sometimes having seizures.

Since the priest hadn't helped the problem, guess who they called next? Ed and Lorraine Warren began making regular visits to the Glatzel home, bringing more priests with them, and performing "three lesser exorcisms." Ed Warren commented that he and Lorraine knew "there were 43 demons in the boy." While the priests involved denied any exorcisms had actually transpired in the Glatzel home, David began to show signs of improvement, especially after the boy was placed into counseling and moved to "a private school for disturbed children."

But Arne Johnson was not so lucky. Apparently, a few of the demons exorcised from David entered his body. He started making the same kind of growls and hisses that David had made, as well as slipping into "trances" off and on for a period of months before killing Alan Bono with a five-inch pocket knife, stabbing the man over and over as Debbie watched.

Martin Minella, Arne's lawyer, was the one who came up with the idea of the "Devil Made Me Do It" pleas. He found two cases in England where demonic possession was used as a plea, although neither of those cases went to trial. He figured that it was worth a shot in America.

It didn't work. Judge Robert Callahan refused to accept the plea since there was no evidence to show that Johnson was possessed. Johnson eventually went to prison for his crime. He had been found guilty of first-degree manslaughter and received a 10- to 20-year sentence, although he only served five. Arne and Debbie married after he was released.

In 1983, a book called *The Devil in Connecticut* by Gerald Brittle was released about the case. In 2006, the book was reprinted and became the subject of a bitter lawsuit. The Glatzel family sued the publisher and the author, saying that it violated their right to privacy, was libelous, and that it intentionally caused emotional distress to the family. David and his brother, Carl, claimed that the possession story was a hoax created by the Warrens so that they could exploit David's mental illness. Both Lorraine Warren and Gerald Brittle denied David and Carl's claims, but the lawsuit was settled out of court in February 16, 2012 --- exactly 31 years to the day of the death of Alan Bono.

Something tells me that this one probably won't be made into a movie in the *Conjuring* series.

"The Haunted"

Another of the infamous cases connected to the Warrens – or as some would claim, blown out of proportion by the Warrens – was the story of the Smurl family, who from 1974 to 1987, claimed to be at the mercy of demonic spirits.

After flooding forced them to move out of their home in Wilkes-Barre, Pennsylvania, Janet and Jack Smurl, along with their two young daughters and Jack's parents, moved into a duplex a short distance away in West Pittson. The place was a bit of a fixer-upper and they put a lot of work into repainting and repairing the place. It was during this time that the strange events began to take place.

The Smurl family during the publicity surrounding their haunted house.

At first, the happenings were benign. Tools went missing and then reappeared and old wall stains seeped through fresh coats of paint. Then, kitchen appliances caught on fire, even though they were unplugged and terrible smells overwhelmed the house, then dissipated a few minutes later.

But the Smurls didn't let the small problems get to them. Jack was promoted at his job and he began coaching his daughter's softball team. Janet became pregnant with twin girls and helped to organize an anti-drunk driving group at the local high school. The girls were doing well with their schoolwork and Jack's parents were happy. But soon, their luck started to change.

They got into financial trouble after Mary, Jack's mother, suffered a heart attack. The ghostly happenings in the house intensified. Mary and Janet both claimed to hear disembodied voices that sounded exactly like the other – Janet thought she heard Mary calling her name, while Mary thought she heard Janet and Jack in the middle of a terrible, abusive argument. Strange black masses formed and floated through the house. Janet said that she was visited in her bed at night by a malevolent force that molested her in her sleep. Jack claimed that, while lying next to Janet in bed, he heard a young woman whispering and saw a shadowy figure move along Janet's leg.

Things got worse. A light fixture fell from the ceiling, injuring one of the daughters. The family dog was flung against a wall. Janet said she was picked up by an invisible presence, which dangled her six feet in the air, and then threw her across the room. Jack said that a female spirit entered the living room and raped him while a baseball game was playing on the television. Allegedly, neighbors heard the sounds of screams coming from the house while the Smurls were away.

Terrified, the Smurls called the Warrens. While in the house, Ed claimed that he saw "a dripping message on a mirror that told him to 'Get out.'" After inspecting the place, Lorraine concluded that the Smurls shared their home with four spirits: a harmless elderly women, a young and possibly violent girl, a man who had died in the house, and – naturally – a demon that used the other three spirits to destroy the family.

Group prayer sessions and exorcisms were conducted, and yet the attacks continued. So, the Smurls went public with their story in hopes that someone might hear about their plight and know how to help. But the family was soon tormented by something that may have been worse than a demon – the press.

Oddballs camped out in front of their house. Cameras flashed all night long and reporters shouted questions each time they got a glimpse of the Smurl family. Cars filled with curiosity-seekers cruised by the house all night, hoping to get a glimpse of the ghosts. The Smurl family was at the center of a media circus.

Representatives from the Roman Catholic Church in nearby Scranton were uncertain as to what might be causing the activity. Multiple priests visited the Smurls to bless their home and reported "nothing unusual" seemed to be going on. There was, the Church stated, no "harmful activity" taking place. In 1986, a local priest actually moved into the house, hoping to witness the demonic forces first-hand. Nothing happened. After two nights without issue, he moved out.

In 1987, unable to deal with the spirits any longer – or unable to deal with the public scrutiny, you can take your pick – the Smurls moved out of the duplex. Allegedly, supernatural happenings followed them to their new home, until a church-sanctioned exorcism cleansed the place in 1989.

Despite the skepticism expressed about the case by church officials, the press, and the public, the Smurls' story was turned into a book titled *The Haunted* with Ed and Lorraine's name emblazoned on the cover right next to the name of the author, journalist Robert Curran – even though their involvement in the case did nothing to assist the Smurls with their reported problems.

But why let the truth get in the way of a good story?

Subsequent owners of the duplex say that nothing unusual has ever happened in their home.

If the reader has started to notice a pattern with these stories, that was the intention. The cases that were handled by the Warrens almost always had several things in common: traumatized family, a "rescue" that didn't really do a lot to help, followed by a book or some sort of publicity that benefited the Warrens. In each case, almost no documentation of anything – history in the case or the hauntings – existed, outside of what the Warrens did, said, or claimed. In every case, the book labeled the contents as a "true story," but as one reviewer best put it when writing about their book *Werewolf: A True Story of a Demonic Possession*: "Please note the Warrens' assurance that this is a 'carefully documented' case – they forgot to include the documentation, though."

By the way, I won't bother to try and debunk that case here because it really debunks itself: man gets violent with the police, blames a werewolf demon, gets an exorcism, man is cured.

Sigh.

The Lawsuit

As most readers likely agree, legal problems can be even scarier than ghosts and demons. As has been noted, *The Conjuring* case was turned into a Warner Brothers film in 2013 and made a lot of money for the studio. Critically acclaimed, it first introduced the characters of "Ed and Lorraine" and spawned follow-up films like *The Conjuring 2*, *Annabelle*, and more sequels to follow. However, in 2016, author Gerald Brittle – author of the 1983 book *The Devil in Connecticut*, which ran into legal problems with the Glatzel family – sued Warner Brothers for copyright infringement.

According to *The Hollywood Reporter*, Brittle claimed that he had exclusive rights to make derivative works based on the cases discussed in his book. The lawsuit maintained that Brittle had an exclusive contract with the Warrens that dated back to 1978, before his even wrote his book. There was a "no competing" work provision that, according to him, was still in effect. Because of this, he claimed that Warner Brothers, New Line Pictures, and even director James Wan were not supposed to make *The Conjuring*, or any of its subsequent sequels or spin-offs.

In the lawsuit, it stated that Lorraine Warren gave the studio and production company the right to use the "Warren case files," which the movies were based on, even though, years earlier, she had granted exclusive rights to the files to Brittle. It also expressed disbelief that Warner Brothers, which had a large number of lawyers who specialized in intellectual property rights deals, would not have found Brittle's book or the deals related to it. Brittle maintained that New Line explicitly told the screenwriters not to read *The Demonologist*, presumably because the studio knew that it did not have rights to the book.

The bad news for New Line is that many of those involved with the film *did* admit to reading the book and publicly announced it. Two years before the film hit theaters, James Wan wrote, "I watch/read a lot of scary stories. But, 'The Demonologist,' true life account of Ed & Lorraine Warren, is the scariest book I've read." Actress Vera Farmiga, who played Lorraine Warren in the film, said, "My research relied heavily on 'The Demonologist.' It scared the daylights out of me. Profoundly."

Prior to the release of *The Conjuring 2* in 2016, Warner Brothers was sent a cease and desist letter, which was ignored. Their claim was that the movies are based on "historical facts" and actual events that occurred in the lives of Ed and Lorraine Warren. And there is where things get sticky.

According to Brittle, the Warrens actually lied quite a lot about what happened in their stories. He said that he believed the couple at the time he wrote the book, but later believed he was "duped." And he was not the first writer to claim the Warrens extravagantly embellished their stories. Ray Garton, the horror writer who penned *In a Dark Place* about the so-called "Haunting in Connecticut," admits that, after finding a lot of credibility problems with the Snedeker story, Ed Warren told him, "They're crazy. All the people who come to us are crazy, that's why they come to us. Just use what you can and make the rest up. You write scary books, right? Well, make it up and make it scary. That's why we hired you."

Garton added: "To the best of my knowledge, the Catholic church has absolutely nothing to do with the Warrens in any official way and there are questions about the legitimacy of the priests who work with them. Since writing the book, I've learned a lot that leaves no doubt in my mind about the fraudulence of the Warrens and the Snedekers -- not that I had much doubt, anyway. I've talked to other writers who've been hired to write books for the Warrens -- always horror writers, like myself -- and their experiences with the Warrens have been almost identical to my own."

And there lies the heart of the legal issue. If the Warrens' "case files" are actually "historical fact," then Brittle has no case. True events in history are not protected by copyright laws. However, if the stories were made up – in whole or in part – and that's what went into Brittle's book, then *The Demonologist* is essentially a work of fiction. If a judge decides that the book is fictional, then Warner Brothers may have a big problem on its hands.

At the time of this writing, the lawsuit is still pending, and I have no prediction as to the outcome.

Besides their demon rescue work, lectures, and tours to promote the 10 books that were written based on their experiences, the Warrens also founded the New England Society for Psychic Research in 1952.

In March 2001, Ed Warren collapsed from heart problems after a trip to Japan. He was hospitalized for a year and was in a coma for several months. He spent the next four years being cared for by Lorraine, who was by his side when he passed away on August 23, 2006. Lorraine is semi-retired now, still making occasional public appearances but staying away from the kind of investigations that she did when Ed was alive.

There is no question that the Warrens enjoyed a long and well-publicized career. If for no other reason, they deserve credit as two of the best-known ghost hunters of the modern era. Like Hans Holzer, they were already dealing with hauntings when there was no one else around as competition. Every first-hand account of contact with Ed and Lorraine portrayed them as kind, well-meaning people, who truly believed in what they were doing.

Were they, as Harry Houdini stated about his friend Sir Arthur Conan Doyle, genuine and well-intentioned people who had been deceived by their own gullibility? Perhaps, or perhaps not. The only ones who can say for sure are the Warrens themselves, and no matter how I may feel personally about the authenticity and outcome of many of their cases, I think it's obvious that they loved one another without question.

And that, if nothing else, makes their legacy as one of the most famous couples in paranormal popular culture continue to live on.

THE "AMITYVILLE HORRIBLES"

Before the news broadcast, the Warrens had borrowed a key from George Lutz – who allegedly refused to go back inside – so that they could visit the house. According to Ed and Lorraine, most of the Lutzs' belongings were still in the house; there was even food in the refrigerator. It was obvious, they said, that the family had left in a hurry. The Warrens brought two other psychics to the house and all agreed there was an "unearthly presence" in the place. Ed also claimed that he experienced heart palpitations that he blamed on the "occult forces" in the house. The psychics had a slightly different variation of the story that Ethel Johnson-Meyers – the medium brought to the house by Hans Holzer – had spun. They claimed that not only did the ghosts of angry Shinnecock Indians haunt the property, but so did a number of "inhuman spirits," i.e. Ed and Lorraine's standard "demons." They claimed that the Shinnecock Indians had used that parcel of land as a place where sick and insane members of the tribe were isolated until they died. It had not been a burial ground because the Indians had believed the land was "infested with demons."

They also suggested that an Indian spirit had possessed Butch DeFeo and caused him to murder his family – an addition that would become important to the story that would follow.

Around this time, the Lutzs claimed that they were contacted by Butch's attorney, William Weber, who, in turn, claimed that they contacted him first. Whatever happened, the Lutzs and Weber met to discuss some of the aspects of the case. According to psychics, the Lutzs had a very haunted house on their hands and Weber had a client who was facing a long prison sentence. At that time, Weber stated that he was weighing book offers about the DeFeo murders and the rumors that were spreading about the house in Amityville factored into an idea that he had about getting his client a new trial. For several hours, they discussed ideas, but the Lutzs decided not to work with Weber – a decision that they would later regret after a lawsuit that he filed against him.

George and Kathy moved to San Diego, California, and made a deal with author Jay Anson. Together, they wrote what would become the best-selling book, *The Amityville Horror*, which was published in 1977. Anson never visited the house, but based the book on 45 hours of taped interviews that George and Kathy provided him with. The book was adapted to film in 1979, followed by a number of bad sequels. Not surprisingly, the Warrens were hired by producer Dino de Laurentis to serve as consultants for the picture, which is likely how the events in the film became even more outrageous than what was in the book. The Warrens also made the rounds of all the television talk shows of the time, discussing the horrifying events in Amityville.

As the movie became successful, even more books were sold. *The Amityville Horror* was in theaters, bookstores, magazines, on television, and soon was known around the world. People were so shocked by it because the sensation story was absolutely true – it said so right on the cover of the book.

But, as we all know, when something seems too good to be true, it often is.

It took a couple of years, but the story began to fall apart. It was certainly possible that a house that had experienced such a terrible history could certainly be haunted. It's possible that the murders did, in fact, cause a haunting to occur at 112 Ocean Avenue – at least for a while – but it would soon become obvious that nothing had occurred like the events that were recounted in the book.

As mentioned earlier in the book, one of the first things that didn't ring true was the tall tale of the property itself. The mediums claimed that the house was built on Shinnecock Indian tribal grounds, but that story was refuted by both Native Americans and the Amityville Historical Society, who stated that there was no evidence of burial grounds, or anything else, on the property. Besides that, the Montaukett Indians, not the Shinnecock, had been the original inhabitants of the area.

But that was nothing compared to the revelations that were still to come.

In 1979, Butch DeFeo's attorney, William Weber, confessed to his part in the Amityville Horror story on a radio show hosted by author Joel Martin, a colleague of Stephen Kaplan, who had received one of George Lutz's first telephone calls about the house. Weber admitted that he and Lutz had concocted the story of the haunting over a few bottles of wine. Weber had hoped to get a new trial for Butch, using what Weber called the "Devil Made Me Do it" defense. If he could make it look like Butch believed he was possessed, he could potentially re-introduce an insanity defense. If the DeFeo house was accepted by the public as "haunted," then it would make it much easier to sell the defense to the public. According to Weber's account, George Lutz merely wanted to get out from under a mortgage that he couldn't afford. His business was in trouble and a lucrative book deal just might save his company.

The Lutzs ended up filing a lawsuit against Weber and Paul Hoffman, a writer working on a story about the hoax. They also sued Bernard Burton and Frederick Mars, two clairvoyants who had been to the house, as well as *Good Housekeeping, New York Sunday News*, and the Hearst Corporation. They sought $5.4 million in damages for invasion of privacy, misappropriation of name for trade purposes, and mental distress. Weber countersued for $2 million, alleging fraud and breach of contract. He maintained that the Lutzs had promised that sum from the proceeds of the book. The case went to trial in New York in 1979 and the judge dismissed the Lutzs' lawsuit, saying that from testimony, "It appears to me that, to a large extent, the book is a work of fiction, relying in large part upon the suggestions of Mr. Weber."

Things got even uglier as the story was slowly picked apart.

The so-called "Red Room" in the basement – a secret room where the book alleged that occult ceremonies took place – was actually an area that was used for toy storage by the DeFeo children and the only "secret" about it was that it contained a pipe well that gave access to the house's water pipes if they needed to be repaired.

No evidence was ever found of a "demonic face" in the bricks of the fireplace, and in the late 1970s, the original front door of the house – blown off its hinges in the book – was still in place and intact. In fact, the extensive damage to doors and windows that was recounted in the book never happened at all. All the old hardware – hinges, locks, and doorknobs – was still in place and there had been no disturbances to the paint or the varnish.

In addition, a local newspaper columnist who was suspicious about the story, discovered that a few days after "fleeing for their lives from the house, never to return," the Lutzs came back to hold a garage sale. He also discovered that during their "28-day nightmare" they never once called the police for assistance, which would almost definitely have occurred under the circumstances.

And he wasn't finished. On the day that the Lutzs claimed to find "cloven hoof prints" in their yard, there was no snow on the ground in Amityville. He also learned that the role of the priest – called Father Mancuso in the book, but actually Father Ralph J. Peccaro – was greatly exaggerated. In the book, the priest is terrorized by a demon while trying to bless the house. He is then stalked by the spirit back to the rectory, where he is afflicted with boils, bleeding palms, and a fever. In the movie version, he is attacked by swarms of flies. In real life, however, the priest never even set foot in the house. The Lutzs had talked to him over the telephone. He was never affected by the "demons," but he was irritated with the story. Father Peccaro later filed suit against the Lutzs and their publisher for invasion of privacy and the distortion of his involvement in the case. A settlement was reached with him out-of-court.

Jim and Barbara Cromarty, who later moved into the house, maintained that the place was not haunted. Because of the problems that they experienced with curiosity-seekers, they sued the hardcover and paperback publishers of *The Amityville Horror*, as well as Jay Anson and George and Kathy Lutz. They stated that the entire case had been a hoax from the beginning and it had "blighted their lives." The suit was later settled with them out-of-court for an undisclosed amount.

Subsequent owners – who removed the familiar half-moon windows on the front of the house and even changed the street address – have continued to have problems with tourists and what the locals call the "Amityville Horribles" but have never – not even once – had a problem with ghosts or demons.

So, what happened after it was learned that the "Amityville Horror" was really the "Amityville Hoax?"

Well, not much. The early 1980s revelation that the Amityville story was a fraud didn't get much airtime. The real story was not as interesting to the media, so the general public didn't hear as much about it. Besides that, the Warrens and their supporters were still claiming that the story was true. Ed and Lorraine had become so entrenched in the validity of the story that they couldn't backtrack on their claims. They were simply in too deep and all they could do was to keep going. In spite of confessions and evidence to the contrary, Ed continued to claim that the story was true until the day he died. Lorraine still maintains it today, which was why a reference to Amityville was included in the film, *The Conjuring 2* – a movie about a case that the Warrens weren't even involved with, the Enfield Poltergeist, which is featured in the next chapter.

Kathy Lutz died of emphysema in 2004 and George died two years later. Unlike William Weber, he continued to claim that *most* of the story was true, although he conceded that some of the details had been exaggerated by Jay Anson, or invented by the media. They had certainly been invented by *someone* – the media just ran with it.

During interviews, George sometimes said that he was unable to describe the phenomena that he witnessed in the house, but there had been demons in the house – he knew them by name. When asked to name them, he refused, claiming that they would appear if he mentioned their names out loud. When asked where he got this idea, he said that he read it in a book, although he couldn't remember the name of it. Perhaps he was supplied with that information by a "demonologist" that he met somewhere?

Those who claim that the Amityville story was true – and yes, believe it or not, there are still people out there who believe it – often point to the fact that George and Kathy Lutz took lie detector tests and passed, supporting their claims of a demonic infestation in the house. However, there is a reason that polygraph tests are not admissible in court. They are easy to pass, especially when you have convinced yourself that the story you are telling is the truth.

And there may have been elements of the truth to the story.

Toward the end, George did backtrack a little when he described the events that occurred in the house. His updated accounts of cold spots, smells, and a slamming door or two were a far cry from the allegedly "true" events that were recounted for the book. He stopped claiming to "flee" from the house, saying instead that the family had moved out because the place was so oppressive that he fell into a deep depression that changed his personality. A haunting? Perhaps – but it wasn't even close to the story that had been peddled to the public.

Sadly, to this day, a large percentage of the general public – force-fed the story since the 1970s – still believe *The Amityville Horror* is true. The truth was never as exciting or glamorous as the original story and so, far too few people ever bothered to listen or to research it on their own. As time has passed, more stories have appeared about the true facts of the case, but many people who see it on a list of haunted houses, or in a movie, or on a television show, never bother to wonder if the facts in the case really add up.

Trust me, they don't.

The Amityville Horror was the perfect blend of fact and fiction that came along at just the right time in American paranormal popular culture history and managed to terrify everyone who picked up the book. But it was a story – a good story, but a story nonetheless.

The real "horror" of it is how long it had managed to endure as the truth.

14. THINGS THAT GO BUMP IN THE NIGHT
POLTERGEISTS OF THE 1970S AND 1980S

Starting in the 1950s, stories of poltergeists wreaking havoc in American homes began filling the pages of magazines like *Fate*. Clipped from newspapers, paranormal investigators were able to fill scrapbooks of stories of slamming doors, smashing objects, flying rocks, and more – havoc wreaking by invisible forces that could not be explained.

Was it ghosts that were causing this destructive behavior? Not necessarily. In days gone by, paranormal researchers were convinced that spirits were to blame for the violent behavior that occurred in what were thought to be haunted houses and dubbed such spirits "poltergeists," a German word that meant "noisy ghosts." But by the 1950s, thinking had changed on the subject. Science had invaded the paranormal world, shifting gears to ESP testing and logical explanations for things that had been frightening people for generations. Thanks to researcher like Nandor Fodor, Raymond Bayless, and others, researchers began taking another look at the now widely-reported accounts of destructive "spirits" and were beginning to feel that while rambunctious spirits might be the culprits in some cases, many hauntings had a force behind them that, while not supernatural, was just as mysterious.

In this kind of poltergeist case, a variety of different phenomena could occur -- knocking and tapping noises, sounds with no visible cause, disturbance of stationary objects like household items and furniture, doors slamming, lights turning on and off, fires breaking out and much, much more. In these cases, though, the source of the problem was not the dead – it was the living. Researchers theorized that the cause of the activity was a person living in the household, dubbed the "human agent." The agent was usually an adolescent – more often a girl than a boy – and usually one that is emotionally troubled. It was believed that she could unconsciously manipulate items in the house using psychokinesis (PK), the power to move things by energy generated in the brain. This kinetic type of energy was unexplained, but even some mainstream scientists began exploring the idea that it does exist.

It was unknown why such energy seemed to appear in some young women around the age of puberty, but researchers began documenting a large number of cases. It seemed that when the activity began to manifest, the girl was usually in the midst of some sort of emotional or sexual turmoil. The presence of the energy was almost always an unconscious one, and it was rare when agents actually realized they were the source of the destruction around them. They had no idea they were the reason that objects in the home became displaced and were usually under the impression that a ghost – or some other kind of supernatural entity – was present instead. The bursts of PK activity would come and go and most poltergeist cases peaked early and then slowly faded away.

Researchers also found that while most cases manifested around young women, it was possible for puberty-age boys – and even older adults – to possess this same kind of ability. As with the young women, the vast majority had no idea that they were causing the activity and were surprised to find there was even a possibility that strange things were happening because of them.

In the late 1970s and early 1980s, there were two cases that made headlines and made an impact on the paranormal popular culture of the era. One of them took place in England, so it wouldn't normally be covered in a book about American hauntings, but the case was so sensational that it was widely covered in the states, as well. In addition, it was one of the stories that really inspired this book – in a roundabout way.

In the summer of 2016, the film, *The Conjuring 2* was released in theaters and featured the characters of "Ed and Lorraine Warren" traveling to England to involve themselves in the famous Enfield Haunting case, which, of course, involved a demon. In reality, the Warrens had nothing to do with the case and there were certainly no demons connected to it. What actually happened is that they invited themselves to visit the beleaguered family in hopes of getting some of the media attention that was taking place, stayed for about an afternoon, and left. They were not present during any of the reported activity that took place in the home.

I was so irritated after seeing the film – mostly because I felt like the Warrens were stealing attention from the real investigators of the case, including Guy Lyon Playfair, who wrote an excellent book on the haunting called *This House is Haunted* – that I became determined to write a book that detailed the history of ghost hunting and paranormal popular culture because I feared that new arrivals to this wacky field were unaware of its past. And so, if you're reading this book, that is the reason for it.

The other case is a homegrown American poltergeist case. It was one that got a lot of attention in newspapers, magazines, and on television when I was in high school and was making headlines – oddly – about the same time that *Ghostbusters* was hitting theaters, kicking off another upsurge in interest about the paranormal. Sadly, though, there was nothing funny about the Columbus poltergeist case. It ended with angry accusations of fraud, ruined lives, and sent a troubled young woman to prison.

THE ENFIELD POLTERGEIST

Between 1977 and 1979, the story of what was happening in a small rented house in Enfield, North London, shocked the people of England and, eventually, in America. Those who followed the galvanizing events were spellbound and they baffled police officers, psychics, paranormal experts, and skeptical reporters alike. The case involved levitation, furniture flying through the air, moving objects, cold breezes, physical assaults, water appearing on the floor, and even items bursting into flame. A policewoman even signed an affidavit that she had seen a chair move by itself. She was just one of more than 30 witnesses to the strange events, which unfolded for more than a year behind the door of an ordinary-looking house, on a suburban street of identical houses, and left those involved permanently scarred.

Not surprisingly, many questioned if it was all a hoax – but no explanation other than the paranormal has ever been convincingly put forward.

Most of the activity in the Enfield case was directed at Janet (center), who was 11 at the time it all began.

The events began on the evening of August 30, 1977, in the home of Peggy Hodgson and her four children – Margaret, 13; Janet, 11; Johnny, 10; and Billy, 7. Peggy was anxious to get the children to bed and heard Janet complaining upstairs that her and her brother's beds were shaking. Peggy ordered them to bed and thought no more of it until the following evening, when something more disturbing occurred.

Peggy heard excited laughter coming from upstairs and she went to tell the children to settle down. When she went into the room, the children told her that they heard noises coming from the floor. Janet said that it sounded like a chair moving, so Peggy took the only chair out of the room and moved it downstairs. Hoping this would settle them down, she began getting ready for bed. Then, she heard the same shuffling sound that Janet had mentioned. She hurried to the children's room and found them asleep. Then, she heard four distinct knocks from the wall. She turned on the light and saw nothing out of the ordinary – until a heavy chest of drawers slid out away from the wall. She pushed it back, but found that it was being propelled toward the door by an invisible force.

Shaken by the incident, Peggy woke up the children, got them dressed, and they went next door to the home of their neighbors, Vic and Peggy Nottingham. Vic, a burly construction worker, went to investigate. He also heard the noises – knocking sounds in the bedroom, in the walls, and the ceiling. "I was beginning to get a bit frightened," he later confessed.

Unsure of what else to do, the Hodgsons called the police, who were equally mystified. WPC Carolyn Heeps, who responded to the call at the affected home, saw a chair move. "A large armchair moved, unassisted, four feet across the floor." She inspected the chair for hidden wires, but could find no explanation for what she had seen. Eventually, the officers left, telling the family that the incidents were not a police matter since they couldn't find anyone who was breaking the law.

The next day brought more strange happenings, so the Hodgsons and their neighbors called the press. The *Daily Mirror* sent a photographer and reporter to look into things and they stayed for several hours. *Daily Mirror* photographer Graham Morris said, "It was chaos, things started flying around, people were screaming." Some of the events were captured on film, and the images were disturbing. One photo showed Janet apparently being thrown across the room. In others, her face was contorted in pain. The BBC also visited the house, but the crew found the metal components in their recording equipment had been twisted, and the recordings erased.

The press got the attention of the SPR, England's first paranormal research society. It sent investigators Maurice Grosse and Guy Lyon Playfair, a poltergeist expert who subsequently wrote a book about the affair. Grosse later said, "As soon as I got there, I realized that the case was real because the family was in a bad state. Everybody was in chaos."

The investigators were soon in the middle of the apparent psychic activity and witnessed levitating furniture, chairs spun around and flung across the room, and the family hurled from their beds at night. In an interview, Maurice Grosse recalled, "When I first got there, nothing happened for a while. Then I experienced Lego pieces flying across the room, and marbles, and the extraordinary thing was, when you picked them up they were hot."

On the night of September 8, Grosse and three reporters were keeping watch when they heard a crash in Janet's bedroom. The discovered that her bedside chair had been thrown several feet across the room. Janet was asleep at the time and no one had seen the chair move. However, it happened again an hour later, and this time one of the photographers captured the incident on film. Shortly after this, Grosse was joined by Playfair and the two men spent the next year studying the case.

While the two men maintained the veracity of the haunting, they also found reason to doubt some of the claims. Along with two skeptical SPR investigators, they tried to debunk many of the events. Some dismissed the entire case as a hoax, while one SPR member described it as "overrated," stating that several incidents had been staged. Grosse and Playfair agreed about some of the phenomena. At one point, they caught Janet and Margaret bending some spoons and once saw Janet toss an iron bar across the room. Years later, Janet admitted, "Oh yeah, once or twice (we faked phenomena), just to see if Mr. Grosse and Mr. Playfair would catch us. They always did."

Whether real or faked, the events were apparently chilling to witness. Aside from banging on the walls, things flying about, and furniture moving on its own, Janet was said to have levitated off her bed, and to have spoken in a voice purportedly belonging to a man named Bill Wilkins, who had died in the house before the Hodgsons moved in. The male-sounding voice came out of Janet's mouth. It said: "Just before I died, I went blind, and then I had an 'emorrhage and I fell asleep and I died in the chair in the corner downstairs." The voice was recorded by Maurice Grosse, and bizarrely, the son of Bill Wilkins later confirmed the events described were accurate.

Was there actually a ghost haunting the house? Or had Janet – or even Peggy – tapped into something in the energy of the house? The case had much in common with other poltergeist incidents, including the involvement of two young girls around the age of puberty. There was a lot of tension in the house. Peggy had never resolved her feelings about her divorce from the children's father and was under a lot of pressure as a single mother. The family was stuck in a terrible situation. Janet and Margaret were teased and boys shouted things at her brothers. Janet had a short stay at the Maudsley Psychiatric Hospital in London.

The famous photograph that allegedly shows Janet being thrown into the air by poltergeist forces. Critics claimed the photo simply captured her in flight after jumping off the bed.

She later admitted, "I was bullied at school. They called me 'Ghost Girl.' I'd dread going home. The front door would be open, there'd be people in and out, you didn't know what to expect and I used to worry a lot about Mum. She had a nervous breakdown, in the end."

In the end, it was a priest's visit to the house that brought an end to the worst of it. Tensions were eased and things began "quieting down" in the fall of 1978. The family later maintained that the occurrences did not stop entirely and Peggy continued to report noises in the house.

Not long after the press attention died away, Janet's younger brother, Johnny, died of cancer. He was just 14 years old. Janet's mother developed breast cancer and died in 2003. Janet had left home long before that, moving out at age 16, and marrying young.

To this day, she rejects any suggestion that the whole story was faked in pursuit of fame or money. In an interview, she stated, "I don't care whether people believe me or not, I went through this, and it was true."

But, of course, not everyone was convinced. Janet's "disembodied voice" was always one of the most criticized part of the case. In one interview for BBC Scotland, Janet was observed to gain attention by waving her hand, and then putting her hand in front of her mouth while she claimed the voice was heard. Maurice Grosse made tape recordings of Janet and believed there was no trickery involved. However, stage magicians who specialized in ventriloquism dismissed the recordings as nothing "beyond the capabilities of an imaginative child." According to Janet in later interviews, tests were performed with her mouth filled with water – and the voices were still heard. But if any record of those tests survive, they are not readily accessible.

Skeptics have picked apart the tape recordings, the photographs, and everything else about the case – including the credulity of the investigators – but have failed to explain the eyewitness accounts of others who observed the incidents occur, including neighbors and police officers.

It's very possible that many – perhaps even most – of the incidents that occurred around the girls, from the levitations to flying objects, were faked. I agree that the photo of Janet "levitating" in her room looks a lot like her merely jumping off the bed, but what about the people who swore to the fact that they heard the knocking sounds, or the police officer who witnessed the moving chair?

It's very possible that for much of this case, the people involved saw what they expected to see. They believed that a poltergeist outbreak was occurring and so they attributed everything that was happening to the paranormal. I think that it's more likely that there was indeed some legitimate activity occurring – caused by stress, tension, and energy in the house – but the media attention paid to the case, as well as the attentions of the investigators, convinced Janet and Margaret to keep things going long after the genuine energy in the house had faded. This is something that commonly occurs in many poltergeist cases, making them so elusive and difficult to investigate. Far too often, things happen that cannot be explained, followed by other events that occur which are easily explained, often leading to the entire case being dismissed as fraud.

Was it a hoax? Was there real poltergeist activity occurring in the house? I'm afraid that remains a mystery, as the arguments both for and against the authenticity of the case seem to have equal merit.

THE COLUMBUS POLTERGEIST

The tragic story of Tina Resch is one of the most intriguing and controversial cases in the modern annals of the paranormal. In 1984, a young girl in Columbus, Ohio, began apparently manifesting psychokinetic activity in her parents' home. Thanks to a hasty photograph of a telephone that seemingly took flight under its own power, the case captured the attention of the American public, believers, and skeptics alike, and it went on to become one of the most famous paranormal happenings of the late twentieth century – and a horrific portrait of a young woman's shattered life.

In March 1984, John and Joan Resch lived in a house on Blue Ash Road in Columbus with their son, John, their adopted daughter, Tina, and four foster children. That same month, Tina, 14, became the center of a series of strange and frightening events. It was an ordinary Saturday morning that suddenly became unusual when all of the lights in the house went out. John and Joan assumed that some kind of power surge had occurred and they telephoned the local utility company. It was suggested that they call an electrician, and a contractor named Bruce Claggett came to the house. He assumed, as the Reschs did, that there was a problem with a circuit breaker. He soon learned differently. Once he got the lights on again, they refused to turn off. He even taped the light switches in the off position, but they turned right back on again. Closet lights that operated with a pull string would be turned out, but seconds later the bulbs flared back to life. Claggett finally gave up, unable to explain what was going on.

By that evening, things had gotten stranger. Lamps, a set of brass candlesticks, and clocks had flown through the air. Wine glasses had shattered. The shower turned on by itself. Eggs had lifted up out of a carton on the kitchen counter and smashed against the ceiling. Silverware, after rattling in the drawer, had jumped across the room. A wall picture that refused to stop rattling, was finally placed behind the couch to silence it, and yet it slid back out again three different times.

Over the weekend, a pattern began to develop. The focus of the weird activity was Tina, who had been struck by many of the flying objects. Wherever she was, bizarre things happened. A chair tumbled across the floor in her direction and was only stopped from hitting her because it became wedged in a doorway. Neighbors and family members saw Tina hit by flying objects, which came from opposite sides of the room from where she was standing.

Around midnight on Saturday, the Reschs finally called the police. Officers came to the house, but there was nothing they could do. The only break from the strange events came on Sunday when Tina left the house to go to church, and then in the afternoon when she went out to visit a friend.

By Monday morning, the house was a wreck. Nothing seemed to stop the incidents, which had now been witnessed by police officers, reporters, church officials, and neighbors. Desperate for help, the family turned to the media for an explanation. When reporters from the *Columbus Dispatch* arrived, they saw the happenings for themselves. One of the reporters, Mike Harden, knew of a scientist named William G. Roll, who had worked on similar cases. He suggested to Joan Resch that she contact Roll and see if he could help.

Dr. Roll arrived in Columbus on March 11. As the project director of the Psychical Research Foundation in Chapel Hill, North Carolina, he had long been considered the country's leading expert on poltergeist phenomena. Roll was born in Bremen, Germany, in 1926, where his father was the American vice-counsel. He graduated from the University of California at Berkeley in 1949, where he studied philosophy and psychology, the closest fields he could find to psychical research. In 1950, he went to England to study at Oxford, and with the support of the Society for Psychical Research, and famous psychic Eileen Garrett, he set up a small research laboratory, where he worked from 1952 to 1957.

While at Oxford, Roll got in touch with J.B. Rhine at Duke University in North Carolina. In 1957, Rhine invited Roll to come to Duke and a year later, he was sent, along with fellow parapsychologist J.G. Pratt, to investigate a poltergeist that was plaguing a house in Seaford, Long Island. Their report concluded that the disturbances were most likely the result of unconscious manipulations by a young boy in the family. Roll and Pratt coined the term "recurrent spontaneous psychokinesis" (RSPK) to explain these types of cases. It is in general use today as another name for poltergeist activity.

Dr. William Roll

By the time he came to Columbus, Roll had investigated well over 100 cases of poltergeists, both modern and historical. From his reports and personal observations, Roll determined that there were patterns of RSPK effects in the reported "haunted" locations. These inexplicable, spontaneous physical effects repeatedly occurred when a particular person was present. He believed that the activities were expressions of unconscious PK carried out by the individual acting as the agent.

Roll's past research certainly made him qualified to study the events in Columbus, but even so, he had little idea of what to expect from the case. He had come at the invitation of Joan Resch, after seeing the case widely reported in the newspapers. He and an assistant ended up spending a week in the house, and while the poltergeist activity seemed to calm down just after the pair arrived, it made a noisy return by the end of the week.

The most impressive events occurred on March 15, when Roll observed a brief flurry of activity first-hand. The incidents that he witnessed took place when he and Tina were alone on the second floor of the house. As things began to happen, Roll stayed very close to her and left his tape recorder running so that he would have an accurate account of the events. A slamming sound came from the bathroom when a bar of soap was thrown from a dish on the sink. He and Tina walked into the bathroom and then emerged again. As they did so, a picture on the wall to their left suddenly fell to the floor. Roll had the girl under observation the entire time and saw no movement on her part. Tina became upset because the picture was one of her mother's favorites. Fortunately, it was not broken, but the nail had been ripped out of the wall. Roll offered to nail it back up again and was working on this when another incident occurred.

Roll later reported, "I was keeping Tina under close watch throughout this period, so when I hammered in the nail, she was standing right next to me and I was very aware of her exact position and what she was doing. Before I proceeded, I placed my tape recorder on the dresser, which was behind us and to our left. As I was hammering in the nail, we heard a sound like something falling to the floor. We turned around and my tape recorder was on the ground." The recorder had somehow managed to travel about nine feet, seemingly without assistance. Roll was sure that Tina had not touched it.

Roll had been tapping the nail back into the wall with a pair of pliers that he had found on the dresser. When he was finished, he had laid them down. During the few moments that his attention was focused on the traveling tape recorder, the pliers had also been flung from the top of the dresser and had landed about six feet away. Tina had been nowhere near them at the time.

As the case made national news, accusations of fraud were immediately made by debunkers, even though none of them had investigated the case. As a follow-up, three representatives of the Committee for the Scientific Investigation of Claims of the Paranormal (CSICOP) decided to travel to Columbus and showed up unannounced on March 13. One of the group members was the debunker and magician James Randi, who had already publicly attacked the case in the press. The CSICOP investigators became more skeptical when Joan Resch refused to allow Randi into the house. She had no objection to the other two investigators, both scientists, but would have nothing to do with Randi. Because of this, the entire CSICOP team decided to withdraw for reasons that remain unclear and began to issue negative statements about the case, even though they never entered the house.

One of the strangest twists in the saga of the Columbus poltergeist came about when *Columbus Dispatch* reporter Mike Harden returned to the house and brought along photographer Fred Shannon, a 30-year veteran of the *Dispatch*. The newsmen would make national news themselves with their involvement in the case and released a series of photographs that shocked the country.

Shannon received a call from Harden on March 5, 1984. Harden phoned him directly from the Resch home and asked him to come to the house immediately. Shannon packed up his gear, never realizing that he was about to embark on one of the most bizarre assignments in his career. Even Harden's words of warning over the telephone did not prepare him for what he was about to experience. His documentation of the events that he observed became compelling evidence about the reality of the case.

Mike Harden met him at the door. He was introduced to the Reschs and they began to explain to him about the strange happenings that had been taking place. The "force," as they were calling it, was hurling household objects all about the place and most of the disturbances seemed to be aimed at Tina. They began to show him around the house, starting in the dining room, where the chandelier had been damaged by flying wine glasses, as well as by other objects that had crashed into it. The force had almost destroyed the fragile long-stemmed wine glasses that the Reschs kept in the room. When Shannon arrived, only one glass remained on the portable bar in the corner.

After looking over the damage for a few minutes, John and Joan went into the adjoining kitchen, leaving the photographer alone in the dining room with Mike Harden and Tina. Moments later, they followed the girl's parents into the other room and, within seconds, they heard the sound of glass shattering in the dining room. Joan Resch groaned aloud, "Uh-oh, there goes the last wineglass." They raced back into the dining room and found the splintered remains of the glass in the opposite corner from where it had been. There had been no one in the room at the time the glass broke.

Perplexed, Shannon followed the rest of the group back into the kitchen a few minutes later and, to his surprise, found that the force again chose that moment to react. A tremendous clatter was heard in the dining room and when they returned, they found that six metal coasters -- which had also been sitting on the portable bar--- had sailed through the air in the same direction as the wineglass. They were now lying on the floor near the broken glass. Again, there was no one in the dining room.

When they returned to the kitchen, the Reschs began telling Harden and Shannon about all of the things that had happened in the room. For example, "all hell broke loose" whenever Tina opened the door to the refrigerator. Eggs flew out and splattered on the ceiling, jars overturned, and containers of leftovers burst open and expelled their contents onto the floor. On one occasion, a stick of butter erupted from the icebox and sailed across the room to become lodged between two cabinet doors. Instead of slowly sliding to the floor, though, the butter inexplicably began moving upwards toward the ceiling.

The Reschs took them into the living room. They recalled when a large, overstuffed chair chased Tina out of the room, cart-wheeling until it slammed into a wall and dislodged a picture. Shannon was intrigued by the story, so he decided to take a photo of the chair and the picture, the frame of which was still intact, although the glass was shattered. He asked Tina to pose next to the chair and to hold the picture so that he could see it through his camera lens. Just as he shot the photo and the flash went off, he heard a loud crash. Tina claimed that the picture had been knocked out of her hands. Skeptical, he assumed that she had just dropped it, but then he realized that Tina was still holding the corner of the frame in her hands, as if something had struck it hard enough to knock it away from her, leaving her holding the small, broken corner of frame.

Unnerved and upset, Tina sat down on a couch in the family room. As Shannon and Harden turned to go back into the kitchen, they heard a tremendous booming sound. Without thinking, Shannon immediately turned and snapped a photo. The developed image would later show Tina covering her head because the lamp on the stand next to her had crashed to the floor. Since his eyes were not on her at the time, Shannon was unable to say for sure whether or not Tina knocked over the lamp herself, but he was confident that she had not. He later said, "I had swung around so rapidly that I don't see how she would have had time to knock over the lamp and so completely cover her head. She was covering her head because she had been attacked by so many various objects. She was a badly frightened girl and her fear never left her all during the time these things were going on. At this point, I had been in the house for 15 minutes!"

Tina sat down on the arm of a chair across the room from the couch where she had been sitting. Shannon took up a position in the doorway near a love seat, with his back to the kitchen. Suddenly, the love seat that was next to him began to move towards Tina. It pivoted on one leg and shuffled toward her about 18 inches. The photographer was so startled that he didn't even take a photo of the shocked expression on the girl's face. He explained, "I knew the photo wouldn't mean much to someone who wasn't there, as I was, to see what had happened. Anybody who chose to think that way would say it was just a setup. So, I was looking for other things to happen. I didn't have long to wait."

Shannon and Harden decided to observe the girl more closely and took a seat on the couch, with Tina on the loveseat, facing them. On the floor in front of her was a colorful afghan, which Joan Resch had earlier explained had once risen off the floor and had covered Tina. Moments after the journalists sat down, this event was repeated and Shannon snapped a photo of the afghan draped over her body. He had no explanation for how it could have lifted from the floor and could find no method by which Tina could have accomplished this on her own.

Later, the three of them went into the kitchen and were talking with John and Joan, when they all heard a loud sound in the unoccupied family room. Shannon stated that it sounded, "like a cannon had gone off --- it had that much force." They went to investigate and learned that a heavy bronze candlestick -- which had been on the floor to the immediate left of the loveseat and near the back door -- had taken flight a short distance and had banged into the door. The door, which was made of metal, was hit with such force that it was dented in two spots. The Reschs had started placing heavy objects like the candlestick on the floor because it seemed that items left on walls and tables had a habit of flying in Tina's direction. Once, a wrought-iron clock had flown from the wall and had hit her in the back of the head, leaving a lump.

A few moments later, another bronze candlestick took flight from the other side of the loveseat, near the kitchen. Tina was sitting in a chair in the family room and Shannon and Harden were watching her from a couch across the room. No one was anywhere near the candlestick and yet somehow, it moved. Tina said that she had seen it happened and that it had "flown four or five feet into the kitchen before making a 90-degree turn and shooting down the hallway." She said that it had been turning end over end through the air. Shannon admitted that he had not seen the candlestick move, but he had certainly heard it. As it propelled itself, the object made a roaring sound, an incredible noise that he said sounded "something like a locomotive."

A moment later, the journalists jumped to their feet and hurried into the hallway after the candlestick. The first thing they saw was that the hanging overhead lamp was swinging wildly back and forth, as though just missed by the hurtling object.

Most of the other incidents that Harden and Shannon saw in the family room involved telephones, which were located on a stand next to the chair where Tina was sitting. Usually, two telephones were kept on the stand. The reason for this was that when the outbreak began, the house was plagued with all sorts of electrical problems, including malfunctions with the telephone in the family room. So, the Reschs bought a second, cheap phone and installed it next to the sturdier, original phone. Both sat on the stand next to the chair in the family room, but it was the second phone that was most affected by the "force" in the house.

According to Fred Shannon, he was present on seven different occasions when one or the other of the phones flew in Tina's direction. The first two times, they hit her on the left side and fell next to her on the couch. During the other incidents, the phones flew over Tina's lap in the direction of the loveseat. The events occurred unexpectedly, usually minutes apart, but happened in seconds. This made it nearly impossible for Shannon to get a photograph. At one point, he sat for more than 20 minutes with the camera up to his eye, waiting for something to happen, but nothing did. Each time that he would lower the camera so that he wasn't immediately ready to take a photo, the phone would go flying through the air.

That caused him to wonder if he was dealing with a blind force after all. Could it be aware of his presence? If this was true, he decided to devise a strategy. He brought the camera to his eye, his finger poised on the trigger, and waited, watching Tina for about five minutes. Then, without taking his eyes off her, he lowered the camera to the level of his waist, keeping it pointed in her direction, and his finger on the shutter. As he did this, he turned his head in the direction of the kitchen, where the Reschs were talking

The photograph of the flying telephone that was captured by veteran photographer Fred Shannon for the Columbus Dispatch

with some visitors. He waited patiently for something to happen, pretending that his attention was somewhere else.

A few seconds later, he saw a white blur out of the corner of his eye and by the time that he pressed the shutter of the camera, a phone had streaked through the air and had sailed all the way across the chair in which Tina was sitting. The resulting photo captured not only the flying telephone, but also the frightened expression on Tina's face as she jerked backwards to keep from being hit. In all, Shannon managed to get three different photos of the telephone in flight, but the first one was the one that got the most attention. The day after it appeared in the local newspaper, it was picked up by the Associated Press, and made front pages all over the country.

The photo was immediately attacked by the debunkers – who had been complaining about the case all along – but Shannon was adamant about what he had seen. He emphasized in writing: "I am damned sure that she did not throw those phones. From what Mike and I observed, I would say that she couldn't possibly have thrown them -- absolutely no way. We were sitting in a well-lighted room; we were looking right at her. When one of us was looking away for a moment, the other had his eyes on Tina all the time. And of course, there were some objects that took flight while she was nowhere near them --- the candlesticks, for example."

Shannon also witnessed an incident with the telephones that did not involve Tina. It occurred just a few minutes after he took the astounding photo of the phone in flight. A Franklin County Children Services caseworker and an associate arrived at the house on business involving the Reschs' foster children. The caseworker sat down on the loveseat. Shannon warned her not to sit there, as he knew that she would be in the direct path of the telephone. She didn't take him seriously and made several comments to assure him that she thought the whole thing was a joke, but she humored him anyway by moving to the other cushion on the loveseat. She stood up, shuffled sideways and sat back down again. Just as she was lowering herself to the seat, the phone shot through the air and landed hard on the cushion where she had been sitting. If she had not moved, the phone would have struck her in the chest. The incident startled her so much that she and her co-worker quickly finished their business and left.

A little while later, Harden, Shannon, and Tina were standing in the middle of the family room when a box of tissues -- which was also on the phone table -- suddenly leapt into the air. It zipped past Shannon's leg and landed on a small table next to the couch. When it hit the table, it did not skip or bounce even though it had been moving at tremendous speed. Instead, it stopped in place as if it had been caught by a magnet or glued into position.

This was the last activity that Shannon witnessed in the family room, but his experiences at the Resch house were not yet over. He decided to take some photos in the kitchen and hoped that if he got Tina to open the refrigerator door, something would fly out of it. The family had told him that this had been happening for days. The kitchen was already a mess from past incidents and the Reschs had been cleaning the room during most of the time that Shannon and Harden had been in the house.

Tina waited in the kitchen as he set up his camera in the corner, directly across the room from the refrigerator. Shannon ducked down – in case there was any flying food – and asked Tina to open the door. She did, but nothing happened. She did this three times but nothing stirred. Since nothing happened, she made a sandwich for herself while Shannon packed up. He had been in the house for four hours and still couldn't believe the bizarre things he had seen.

As soon as Harden's story of the baffling activity in the house – and Shannon's remarkable telephone photograph – appeared in the newspaper, critics of the paranormal immediately went on the attack. None of them had been inside of the house – most had never been to Columbus – but were convinced that the whole thing was a hoax. The debunkers managed to obtain the negatives of the photos that Fred Shannon had shot in the house. Because there were three photos of a phone in the air above Tina's lap -- not just the one that appeared in AP wire stories -- Shannon was accused of faking the photos and having Tina throw the phone so that he could photograph it. Although Shannon explained how he managed to capture three photos, he was dismissed as a fraud. This was done without investigation of the scene, assessment of the evidence, and with no regard to Shannon's 30-year career and outstanding reputation.

The critics dismissed the entire case based on the fact that Dr. Roll stated that he believed that Tina had faked some of the less impressive activity in the house. However, he did believe that genuine activity was taking place, even when conceding there was some limited fraud involved, as well. He noted, "It is certain that Tina threw a lamp down on one occasion, that's obvious. She told me that she did the same thing on two other occasions. So, there's no doubt there were some fraudulent occurrences."

Roll stated that it was not uncommon for victims of poltergeists to get into the act themselves as part of the mischief-making. His year of experience had made it possible to create a profile and pattern for poltergeist cases. Roll found that nearly every case had a child or teenager at the center of it that had a great deal of internal anger, caused by a stressful home situation, abuse, or mental disturbance. He believed that the PK activity was unconscious and unknown to the agent and served as a way of venting hostility without fear of punishment. Thanks to the mental and behavioral issues that plagued the agents, genuine phenomena and trickery went hand-in-hand. The activity was brought on by stress and instability, but once the incidents occurred, were recorded, and gained the attention of others in the household – and sometimes the authorities and the media – the agent started to receive the much-needed attention they desired. Once this occurred, the activity usually stopped. To continue the attention, agents often faked further phenomena. Once they were caught in the act of doing this, critics were able to claim that the entire case was a hoax and any evidence obtained in the early stages of the outbreak could be easily discredited. Because of problems like this, many genuine cases never received the public attention they probably deserved.

Dr. Roll felt that the minor fraudulent incidents did not discredit the Resch case. There were simply too many people who had witnessed the activity – including Roll himself – for it to have been a hoax. He stated, "I can only say that when I was present, I couldn't find any ordinary explanation for the incidents I witnessed. In my opinion, it is very unlikely that they were caused normally. And, of course, there are a number of witnesses we interviewed in Columbus who had seen things under conditions where no family members could have caused them."

After the initial outbreak had come to an end, Dr. Roll took Tina with him back to North Carolina. In late March, he and other scientists conducted computer-based ESP and PK tests on her. The results of the tests were in no way striking, leading most to believe that she did not possess any long-term psychic abilities. As in other poltergeist cases, the mysterious happenings seemed to be confined to a short period of time. And while there were some minor poltergeist incidents in Roll's home, and at the home of a counselor where Tina was staying, the researchers believed that her aggressive manipulations were short-lived.

What caused the manifestations? No one knows for sure and the story behind the Columbus poltergeist remains a mystery. Poltergeist cases in general tend to occur with disturbed children who are suppressing hostility and anger. The displacement of energy acts as a safety valve for the pent-up emotions. In Tina's case, there had been recent problems at home over the fact that Tina, against the wishes of John and Joan, had begun searching for her biological parents. Also, Tina's best friend of two years had ended their friendship just two days before the events began. To make matters worse, the Reschs had recently taken Tina out of school because she was having trouble getting along with other students. She was apparently unpopular with most of her classmates and was having difficulty with one of her teachers. Because of this, she was being tutored at home and was seemingly "cut off" from the outside world. All of this may have combined to create an outward transference of energy.

Eventually, the activity ended and after Tina's return from North Carolina, only a few minor incidents were reported in her home. Roll was never sure of the cause of the outbreak, but his studies pointed to the theory that poltergeist agents seemed to suffer from disturbances in the central nervous system. This may have been the case with Tina Resch, for even though the bizarre incidents ended in her home, her story was not quite over.

Many poltergeist agents have been documented to be in poor mental health, which deteriorated further in stressful situations. This might explain the findings of many standard psychologists and mental health professionals. They often discover that patients with unresolved emotional issues are associated with, or have lived in, houses where poltergeist activity has been reported. In addition, while studying the personalities of those thought to be poltergeist agents, psychologists have found anxiety issues, phobias, mania, obsessions, dissociative disorders, and even schizophrenia. In some cases, psychotherapy may eliminate the poltergeist phenomena but apparently, not in all of them.

Despite counseling, Tina Resch went from being an unhappy child to being a disturbed adult. She went from one disastrous situation to another, including two marriages, the first at age 16, and two divorces and then a sentence of life in prison for the felony murder and aggravated battery of her three-year-old daughter, which occurred when the child was being watched by Tina's boyfriend. She claimed to be innocent of the crime, and witnesses confirmed that she was not present when it was committed. There was no trial. Instead, Tina accepted a plea bargain of life imprisonment rather than face the possibility of a death penalty. She was sent to a Georgia prison in 1994 and remains there today.

It was a sad ending to a puzzling story that played out in the public spotlight – with terrible results.

AFTERWORD
THE END OF THE BOOK AS WE KNOW IT

There are no more chapters in this book. I can't end the history of America's fascination with paranormal popular culture because the story simply isn't complete. There are too many stories that are left to tell – some good, some bad, some downright awful.

Chronologically speaking, we really two have things to blame for the state of the paranormal field today, whether you consider it to be in a good place or a bad one – television and the internet. The television shows came first and by that, I don't mean the reality television shows that we all know today. Before any of those was *Sightings*, the documentary-style show that ran from 1992 to 1997. There would be others similar to it, but *Sightings* was really the first, even though real hauntings and psychic experiences often appeared in shows like *In Search Of...* and even *One Step Beyond* in the 1950s and 1960s.

But what really sparked the resurgence in paranormal interest that continues today was the debut of a little show on Fox called *The X-Files*. It wasn't because the show focused on ghosts – that was a rare thing in the series – but because it tapped into the paranormal psyche of America. It also highlighted an interest in aliens, conspiracies, and a rising distrust in large government. *The X-Files* created a ready-made audience for paranormal reality TV. When the show ended in 2002, reality TV as its own genre was about to redefine television. That was the same year that *Most Haunted* arrived in Britain.

But there were still several steps to make to get Americans used to reality television.

In 1989, the show *COPS* – which follows the men and women of law enforcement, as the opening voiceover went – premiered on Fox. It was the first actual reality show and remains the longest-running show of that type in history. *COPS* was a direct result of the 1988 Writer's Guild of America strike, which lasted for 22 weeks. Networks scrambled to come up with alternative programming that didn't need writers. The economic benefits and convenience of reality-type TV was first considered during this prolonged strike, although it was almost a decade before the genre was fully in place. The strike, as well as advances with home computers and video editing systems, made reality TV possible. Handheld cameras further solidified the possibility and by the late 1990s, the public was familiar with grainy and jerky footage from camcorders since just about every home in America had one.

The paranormal reality shows would not come along until a decade after *COPS* and they owed everything to another household item that increased in popularity during the 1990s – the computer. Before the mid-1990s, only a small percentage of American homes had a computer. Aside from doing paperwork or writing term papers, computers had little use for the majority of people – and then the internet came along. That previously unknown entity, used only by academics and the military, opened a whole new world for average people.

This book has been about how the paranormal has been affected by the popular culture of America and much of that has dealt with the technology of the time. Spiritualism and the print media came into their own at the same time. Public séances were highlighted by the growth of popular culture in the late nineteenth century. Radio broadcasts spread fear of the unknown, like with *War of the Worlds*, a show that aired on October 30, 1938. Hosted by Orson Welles, the reality format of the broadcast caused panic among those who thought it was covering an actual alien invasion. The internet was just about to bring about the most important technological advance in the modern era.

Much like it was in the early twentieth century, the paranormal had fallen under the purview of scientists by the late 1980s. There wasn't much that was being done by amateur researchers by that time, aside from a few scattered groups and individuals. By the early 1990s, though, academic support for the paranormal had waned. The Duke Parapsychology Lab was reshuffled. John F. Kennedy University had stopped offering Parapsychology degrees in 1987. But the decline in academic interest came at a time of increased developments in personal technology – in other words, average people could now afford technology that had once been only in the hands of colleges and government offices. Audio, video, and emerging digital photography made it easier to document all aspects of life – including the parts with spirits, haunted houses, and disembodied voices. When the internet began gaining in popularity, it suddenly made it easy to discover information, share photos and theories with others who were interested in ghosts, and start forming groups of people who could go out and look for haunted places. As Harry Price had done decades before by opening up the world of ghosts to the average person, the internet had made it possible for amateurs to get involved in paranormal investigation.

Compared to today, the internet seemed impossibly small back then. When I started my first website in 1996, there were only perhaps a couple of dozen websites about ghosts on the worldwide web. Of course, that quickly changed, but in those days, the few sites that were out there were pretty basic and looked pretty silly. The internet offered a refuge for ghost enthusiasts who were looking for those who shared their interests and, as with anything else, battle lines began to be quickly drawn.

For the most part, the biggest problems in those days started because of "orbs."

And it's easy to know who to blame for that. Also in 1996, Dr. Dave Oester started the International Ghost Society (IGS), one of the first online ghost hunting societies in history. There is no question that he was ahead of the curve and broke new ground by offering a website and charging membership fees. He hosted classes and offered certifications in paranormal investigation, but began one of the greatest controversies of the era with his introduction of the concept of "orbs."

In 1994, he was quoted in a newspaper article that went out over the AP wire claiming that ghosts were everywhere and were visible in the form of photographed balls of light. This assertion came at an opportune time. Digital cameras were first becoming available. With the low-end, low-resolution quality of the early models, more orbs that ever started to appear in photographs – frequently caused by the failure of all of the pixels to appear in the images. Other factors -- like dust, pollen, insects, moisture, and the list goes on – caused these white images to appear. Oester stated, without any evidence and as a definite fact, that "orbs" were the souls of departed people who now appeared as balls of energy.

His position excited a lot of people -- it was easy proof of a ghost that a new technology could capture. Nearly every enthusiast was familiar with the famous ghost photos of the past – the Brown Lady of Raynham Hall, the Tulip Staircase ghost, etc. – but photos like that were almost impossible to obtain. Those were rare, once-in-a-lifetime events that would probably require thousands of snapshots and thousands of rolls of expensive film to be lucky enough to achieve. With a digital camera, there was no film required. If you didn't get a ghost in your photo, you just deleted it and tried again. But the beauty of "orbs" was that they were everywhere – any photo taken in the dark, in a dusty, abandoned place, or in a graveyard with lots of pollen-covered weeds was likely to capture an "orb." It was proof that the place was haunted, right?

To a lot of people this was a revolutionary idea and suddenly, everyone was going crazy about "orbs." But that didn't last. To many of us, this idea was infuriating. A little research and experimentation quickly revealed the flaws in the theory that "orbs" were ghosts. In addition, a lot of us also balked at the use of digital cameras for many years because the technology had not been developed to the point that it could be used as evidence of *anything*, let alone ghosts. Dust and pollen were not ghosts and the vast library of IGS photos that claimed otherwise became an embarrassment. I was not the only one to publish articles about the problems with "orbs" and digital cameras on my website, but my pages got a lot of traffic. There were a lot of people who agreed with me, but boy, I can tell you that a lot of people didn't – and were very vocal about it. Overnight, the battle lines were established with online debates about the "orb" controversy. For the most part, the controversy had died out over the years, although sadly, there are still those out there talking about "orbs" who don't realize that the nonsense was debunked years ago, and abandoned in favor of more authentic evidence. In the late 1990s, though, there was a lot of malice and hate among paranormal internet users, but it served as a great example of how the internet and technology were transforming the definition of a paranormal community.

By 2000, the resurgence of interest in the paranormal that had been spawned by the internet and the production of shows like *Sightings, Strange Universe, Haunted History,* and *Unsolved Mysteries*, finally brought about the first wave of paranormal reality shows. The very first show in America came from an unlikely source – MTV.

In 1992, MTV introduced a groundbreaking endeavor in reality television called *The Real World,* a show about "seven strangers, picked to live in a house, to find out what happens when people stop being polite and start getting real." The concept provided a first-hand look at people's lives, albeit from the safe distance on the other side of the TV screen, and, most important, it claimed to be real. These are the same elements that make paranormal shows so appealing. There had been other reality-type shows in the past, going back as far as the classic *Candid Camera*, but *The Real World* started the kind of reality television that we know today – with a story, plot, and characters.

Eight years later, MTV, seeing the popularity of the paranormal in the country, decided to launch a reality show of a different kind on the network called *Fear*. It was a game show of sorts, and while it only lasted two years, paranormal reality TV would not be what it is today without it. The initial concept of the show was different than what made it on air. I was involved in the early planning stages of the program – I furnished all of the equipment seen in the first few episodes, and in one, you'll see a copy of my *Ghost Hunter's Guidebook* in the foreground of an interview – but the show quickly changed to be less about hunting ghosts and more about scaring people.

The idea behind it was to send a series of contestants into reputedly haunted locations alone. The contestant who managed to make it through the night won the game. Each contestant was given a series of tasks that initially involved ghost hunting, but eventually turned into just scary challenges to make people cry. However, *Fear* did introduce significant innovations for the genre. For the first time, contestants filmed themselves, and perhaps most importantly, did so using Sony Nightshot as a video technique. Before long, the murky greenish-gray image would be a staple for reality TV. The show was popular, but expensive to produce. Some of today's must-see locations were featured on *Fear*, like the West Virginia State Penitentiary and the Waverly Hills Sanatorium. *Fear* started a trend in reality TV, but it was canceled after two seasons due to the production costs of the show, despite its popularity.

Other shows followed, all tapping into the paranormal, but not quite bringing the audience into the mix the way that reality shows would soon do. Fox Network began offering *Scariest Places on Earth* and *Real Scary Stories* for kids. Each was a scripted show, hosted by Linda Blair from *The Exorcist* with voiceovers from *Poltergeist* actress, Zelda Rubinstein, that sometimes dabbled in investigations. In 2002, I took part in a show for TLC called *America's Ghost Hunters*, which was a pilot for a possible series. The show was filmed in several places around the country, including Eastern State Penitentiary in Philadelphia, and while it aired, the series never happened. The network didn't think that anyone wanted to see ghost hunters wandering around in the dark at haunted places. Oops...

Later that same year, in England, a new show was launched called *Most Haunted*. It enjoyed massively huge ratings in Britain and became very popular in American after it aired on the Travel Channel. The show featured a group of paranormal enthusiasts, such as actresses, psychics, and university-trained parapsychologists as they traveled around the country – and later the world – in search of ghosts. Ridiculed by many for its unbelievable theatrics and lack of any solid evidence, *Most Haunted*, still broke new ground in paranormal reality TV.

Paranormal programming was already popular in the United States, but it's likely that the success of *Most Haunted* got the attention of American production companies, who started looking for a way to develop an American version of the show. Soon after, the initial scramble began to find paranormal investigators to participate in reality television. Almost as soon as *Ghost Hunters* began to air in 2004, just about anyone with a website or ghost hunting group had been contacted by a producer about the possibility of doing a show. "We're shooting a pilot," soon became a common – and soon, very comical – refrain from just about every group of people wearing matching black t-shirts that were emblazoned with their paranormal team logo.

In 2004, the Sci-Fi Channel – which would later, inexplicably become Syfy – began airing episodes of a new show called *Ghost Hunters*, featuring two average guys, Jason Hawes and Grant Wilson, who searched for evidence of ghosts. Unlike *Most Haunted*, the investigators on *Ghost Hunters* carried out actual investigations, without the theatrics of the other show. In many cases, especially in the early seasons of the show, they were apt to explain to property owners why their location was *not* haunted. Ghosts weren't everywhere, not on this show at least. The show ran for 11 seasons, finally coming to an end in 2016. During the height of its popularity, Grant Wilson left and came back, featured a number of established investigators as guests, and spun off several other short-lived series, like *Ghost Hunters International* and *Ghost Hunter's Academy*.

As mentioned, the popularity of *Ghost Hunters* led to a glut of paranormal reality shows. Scores of them followed, like *Ghost Adventures, Paranormal State*, and many, many others – some that are so bad that I won't even bother to list them here out of embarrassment for those who were involved. New shows are still being created today, which is why I can't call this final section of the book an actual "chapter." In the first quarter of this new century, America's paranormal popular culture is fixated on reality TV and I'm sure that things will remain that way for many years to come. Perhaps someday, when this trend has faded – as we saw the demise of séances and Spiritualism – we'll look back on the quaintness of this current era with nostalgia and as another turning point in the history of the paranormal.

Well, I'm finally finished – for now.

Obviously – if you have read enough of the book to get to this point – you know paranormal research did not start with *Ghost Hunters* in 2004, despite the fact that a lot of people seem to think this was the case. If you know someone like that, please buy them a copy of this since they are one of the reasons that it was written in the first place.

At the time of this writing, America has been fascinated with the paranormal for more than 170 years. It's been that long since the Fox sisters first gained public attention with a series of rapping sounds in their little cottage in Hydesville, New York. As it swept the country, it became deeply engrained in the popular culture of America, and there it remains. It has endured the exposure of spirit mediums, debunking by skeptics, the embarrassment of Amityville, and it will endure the disastrous effects that so many of the current spate of reality shows continue to have on it.

Ghosts have always been with us, whether we talk about them or not, and will continue to be as America's interests take further turns in the future.

BIBLIOGRAPHY

Anson, Jay – *The Amityville Horror;* 1977
Aykroyd, Peter – *A History of Ghosts;* 2009
Birnes, William & Joel Martin – *The Haunting of America;* 2009
---------------------------------- - *The Haunting of 20th Century America;* 2011
Blum, Deborah – *Ghost Hunters;* 2006
Brandon, Ruth - *The Spiritualists;* 1983
Brittle, Gerald - *The Demonologist: The Extraordinary Career of Ed and Lorraine Warren;* 1980
---------------- - *The Devil in Connecticut;* 1983
Brown, Slater - *The Heyday of Spiritualism;* 1970
Buckley, Doris Heather - *Spirit Communication for the Millions;* 1967
Carrington, Hereward & Nando Fodor – *Haunted People;* 1951
Chambers, Paul - *Paranormal People;* 1998
Cheroux, Clement, Andreas Fisher and Peierre Apraxine, Denis Canguilhem, Sophie Schmit – *The Perfect Medium: Photography and the Occult;* 2004
Christopher, Milbourne & Maurine – *Illustrated History of Magic;* 1976
Citro, Josepah A. – *Passing Strange;* 1996
Clarke, Robert -- *Spirits & Spirit Worlds;* 1975
Coates, James - *Photographing the Invisible;* 1921
Crowe, Catherine - *The Night Side of Nature;* 1854
Doyle, Sir Arthur Conan – *Edge of the Unknown;* 1930
----------------------------- - *History of Spiritualism;* 1926
Evans, Henry Ridgely - *The Spirit World Unmasked;* 1902
Fate Magazine – Various Issues
Garton, Ray - *In A Dark Place: The Story of a True Haunting;* 1992
Guiley, Rosemary Ellen - *Encyclopedia of Ghosts and Spirits;* 2000
Haining, Peter - *Ghosts: The Illustrated History;* 1987
Hall, Trevor - *The Medium and the Scientist;* 1984
---------------- - *The Spiritualists;* 1962
Horowitz, Mitch – *Occult America;* 2009
Houdini, Harry - *A Magician Among the Spirits;* 1924
Jackson, Jr., Herbert G. - *The Spirit Rappers;* 1972
Jaher, David – *Witch of Lime Street;* 2015
Jolly, Martyn – *Faces of the Living Dead;* 2006
Keene, M. Lamar – *The Psychic Mafia;* 1976
Leonard, Maurice – *People from the Other Side;* 2008
Martin, Joel & William J. Birnes – *Haunting of the Presidents;* 2003
Maskelyne, John Nevil – *Modern Spiritualism;* 1876
Maxwell-Stuart, P.G. – *Ghosts;* 2006

McHargue, Georgess - *Facts, Frauds and Phantasms*; 1972
McRobbie, Linda Rodriquez - *How One Man Used a Deck of Cards to Make Parapsychology a Science*; Atlas Obscura, 2016
Melechi, Antonio – *Servants of the Supernatural;* 2008
Miller, R. DeWitt - *Forgotten Mysteries*; 1947
Moore, L. - *In Search of White Crows*; 1977
Mulholland, John - *Beware Familiar Spirits*; 1938
Nickell, Joe – *Entities;* 1995
-------------- - *Science of Ghosts*; 2012
Northrop, Suzane - *The Séance*; 1944
O'Donnell, Elliot - *The Menace of Spiritualism*; 1920
Orbis Publishing – *Life After Death*; 1997
Peach, Emily - *Things that go Bump in the Night*; 1991
Pearsall, Ronald - *The Table Rappers*; 1972
Permutt, Cyril - *Photographing the Spirit World*; 1983
Picknett, Lynn - *Flights of Fancy*; 1987
Playfair, Guy Lyon – *This House is Haunted;* 1980
Price, Harry - *Confessions of a Ghost Hunter*; 1936
---------------- - *End of Borley Rectory*; 1946
---------------- - *Haunting at Cashen's Gap*; 1936
---------------- - *Poltergeist over England*; 1945
---------------- - *Search for Truth*; 1942
---------------- - *The Most Haunted House in England*; 1940
Rawcliffe, D.H. - *The Psychology of the Occult*; 1952
Reader's Digest Books - *Into the Unknown*; 1981
Roll, William & Valerie Storey – *Unleashed;* 2004
Ruickbie, Dr. Leo – *Brief Guide to the Supernatural;* 2012
Smith, Susy – *Ghosts Around the House;* 1970
-------------- - *Prominent American Ghosts;* 1967
-------------- - *Susy Smith's Paranormal World;* 1971
Sayed, Deona Kelli – *Paranormal Obsession;* 2011
Sawyer, J.F. - *Deliver Us From Evil: Taken from the files of Ed and Lorraine Warren*; 1973
Somerlott, Robert - *Here, Mr. Splitfoot*; 1971
Souter, Dr. Keith – *Medical Meddlers, Mediums & Magicians;* 2012
Spencer, John & Tony Wells – *Ghostwatching;* 1994
Stashower, Daniel - *Teller of Tales: Life of Sir Arthur Conan Doyle*; 1999
Stein, Gordon - *The Sorcerer of Kings*; 1993
Steinour, Harold - *Exploring the Unseen World;* 1959
Tabori, Paul - *Harry Price: Biography of a Ghost Hunter*; 1950
Taylor, Troy – *Devil & All His Works;* 2013
---------------- - *Ghosts by Gaslight*; 2007
---------------- - *The Haunted President;* 2009
Thurston, Herbert – *Ghosts & Poltergeists;* 1953
Von Schrenck Notzing, Baron – *Phenomena of Materialization* (1923 English Edition)

Walker, Mark – *Ghost Masters*; 1991
Warren, Ed & Lorraine – *Ghost Hunters: True Stories From the World's Most Famous Demonologists*; 1989
--------------------------- - *Graveyard: True Hauntings from an Old New England Cemetery*; 1992
--------------------------- - *The Haunted*, with Robert Curran with Jack Smurl and Janet Smurl; 1988
--------------------------- - *Werewolf: A True Story of Demonic Possession*; 1991
Washington, Peter – *Madame Blavatsky's Baboon;* 1993
Weisberg, Barbara – *Talking to the Dead;* 2004
Westbie, Constance & Harold Cameron – *Night Stalks the Mansion;* 1978
Wilson, Ian – *In Search of Ghosts;* 1995
Wicker, Christine – *Lily Dale*; 2003

Personal Interviews and Correspondence

SPECIAL THANKS TO:

April Slaughter: Cover Design and Artwork
Lois Taylor: Editing and Proofreading
Lisa Taylor Horton (who also helped with editing this time) and Lux
Haven and Helyana Taylor
Orrin Taylor
Rene Kruse
Rachael Horath
Elyse and Thomas Reihner
Bethany Horath
Mary Delong
Rosemary Ellen Guiley
Loyd Auerbach
Dennis William Hauck
Richard Senate
Hans Holzer
Harry Price

And the Entire Crew of the American Hauntings Tours and American Hauntings Ink

ABOUT THE AUTHOR

Troy Taylor is the author of more than 120 books on ghosts, hauntings, true crime, the unexplained, and the supernatural in America. He is also the founder of American Hauntings Ink, which offers books, ghost tours, events and excursions across the country. He was born and raised in the Midwest and currently divides his time between Illinois and the far-flung reaches of America.

www.ingramcontent.com/pod-product-compliance
Lightning Source LLC
Chambersburg PA
CBHW070958160426
43193CB00012B/1822